Manufacturing

Second Edition

Manufacturing involves the conversion of materials into products; it is a value adding activity. Organizations engaged in manufacturing of products attempt to add value to materials and parts in the most efficient manner, using minimum amount of manpower, material, money, time and space. Proper selection of materials and processes is vital for reducing waste and improving conversion productivity.

The book aims to provide a descriptive introduction to conventional manufacturing processes that have been used and refined over the past several decades. It also covers recently developed manufacturing processes together with considerations in product design when these processes are to be employed. The text provides extensive coverage on the fundamental principles and operational details of manufacturing processes such as metal casting, forging and forming and welding. It covers advanced topics such as evaporative pattern casting, isothermal forging, powder metallurgy, laser beam welding and friction stir welding processes in detail. It also includes a chapter on plastics and processing of plastics. A salient feature of the book is extensive use of line diagrams and photographs for visualization and elucidation of concepts. Questions at the end of each chapter help readers ascertain their level of understanding.

Intended for use by undergraduate students of mechanical, production, and industrial engineering for a first course in manufacturing processes, the book will also be useful for engineers and technologists engaged in designing, planning and manufacturing. Shop floor personnel will find here a valuable reference on various manufacturing process alternatives, together with the advantages and limitations of each.

H. S. Shan is former Emeritus Fellow and Head, Department of Mechanical and Industrial Engineering, Indian Institute of Technology Roorkee. He has more than 38 years of teaching experience at undergraduate and graduate levels. Along with 175 research papers, he has published two books *Modern Machining Processes* (1980) and *Work Study and Ergonomics* (1992). His research interests lie in conventional and advanced micro machining processes, manufacturing system design and work system design.

Manufacturing Processes

Casting, Forming and Welding

Second Edition

H. S. Shan

CAMBRIDGE
UNIVERSITY PRESS

CAMBRIDGE
UNIVERSITY PRESS

University Printing House, Cambridge CB2 8BS, United Kingdom

One Liberty Plaza, 20th Floor, New York, NY 10006, USA

477 Williamstown Road, Port Melbourne, VIC 3207, Australia

4843/24, 2nd Floor, Ansari Road, Daryaganj, Delhi – 110002, India

79 Anson Road, #06–04/06, Singapore 079906

Cambridge University Press is part of the University of Cambridge.

It furthers the University's mission by disseminating knowledge in the pursuit of education, learning and research at the highest international levels of excellence.

www.cambridge.org
Information on this title: www.cambridge.org/9781316638583

© Cambridge University Press 2017

First published in 2013 by Pearson Education Inc.
Second Edition: 2017 by Cambridge University Press

Printed in India by Rajkamal Electric Press

A catalogue record for this publication is available from the British Library

ISBN 978-1-316-63858-3 Paperback

Additional resources for this publication at www.cambridge.org/9781316638583

To the Almighty and my parents.
Their blessings have made everything possible.

Contents

20.2   Destructive Testing Techniques   444

20.3   Non-destructive Testing Techniques   447

20.4   Defects in Welds   451

21   Plastics and Shaping of Plastics

21.1   Introduction   460

21.2   Classification of Plastics   463

21.3   Properties of Polymer Melts   464

21.4   Plastic Shaping Processes   466

21.5   Plastic Shaping Processes (For Thermoplastics)   466

   21.5.1   Extrusion   466

   21.5.2   Injection moulding   470

   21.5.3   Blow moulding   474

   21.5.4   Rotational moulding   476

   21.5.5   Calendering   478

   21.5.6   Thermoforming (Vacuum Forming)   479

   21.5.7   Slush moulding   480

21.6   Plastic Shaping Processes (For Thermosets)   480

   21.6.1   Compression moulding   480

   21.6.2   Transfer moulding   482

   21.6.3   Cold moulding   484

   21.6.4   Lamination   484

21.7   Welding of Plastics   485

   21.7.1   Hot-plate welding of plastics   486

   21.7.2   Hot gas welding of plastics   487

   21.7.3   Friction welding of plastics   487

21.8   Safety Precautions   489

21.9   Considerations when Designing Plastic Components   490

21.10 Stresses in Integrated Plastic Parts   492

21.11 Fibre-reinforced Plastic   493

21.12 Recent Trends in Plastic Technology   494

Bibliography   503

Index   505

Figures

Tables

Preface

Manufacturing is a *value adding* activity, in which materials are converted into products, thereby adding value to the original material. Therefore, the aim of an organization engaged in manufacturing is to add value in the most efficient manner, using the minimum amount of manpower, material, money, time and space. Proper selection of materials and processes is vital for minimizing waste and maximizing efficiency. The sequence and location of operations must be organized in such a manner that permits smooth and controlled flow of material through the various stages of manufacturing.

This book has been written from the material used by the author for teaching two undergraduate courses related to manufacturing processes over several years at the University of Roorkee/Indian Institute of Technology Roorkee. The book aims to provide a descriptive introduction to the large number of manufacturing processes currently available. The subject matter has been dealt with in simple language along with line diagrams. The book covers recently developed manufacturing processes in addition to traditional processes that have been used and refined over the past several decades. An important feature of the book is that a section on product design considerations has been given in many of the manufacturing process chapters.

The book is designed to cover metal casting processes, metal forming and shaping processes (including high energy rate forming processes and powder metallurgy) and metal joining processes. It also includes a chapter on plastics and processing of plastics. At the end of each chapter, problems have been given to test the students' grasp of the subject matter.

The text is intended for use by students of mechanical, production and industrial engineering for a first course or a two-course sequence in manufacturing at their first and second year in a four-year degree program. The book will also be found useful by engineers and technologists in other disciplines where they might be engaged in designing and manufacturing. Shop floor personnel can use the book as a valuable reference for gaining in-depth knowledge about various manufacturing process alternatives together with the advantages and limitations of each.

Sincere thanks are due to my son Karan Singh and my wife Harpreet Kaur for their patience and valuable support during the period the manuscript was being written. I would like to applaud their commendable efforts during typing, proofreading and editing when the manuscript was being given a final shape.

In spite of all the efforts some variants of manufacturing processes may not have been given adequate coverage. Readers' comments and suggestions in this regard will be welcome.

1

Introduction to Manufacturing Processes

LEARNING OBJECTIVES

After reading this chapter, you should be able to understand:

- The meaning of the term *manufacturing*.

- The various materials generally used for product manufacturing.

- The classification of different manufacturing processes.

- The factors that influence the selection of a particular manufacturing process for a given product.

- The use of break-even analysis for selecting a suitable manufacturing process.

The term *manufacture*, first coined during the 1560s, is derived from two Latin words *manus* (hand) and *factus* (make). Meaning 'made by hand', this term describes the fabrication methods that were used in earlier times. Today, most manufacturing operations are, however, accomplished by mechanized and automated equipment under human supervision. In simpler terms, manufacturing can be considered as the process of converting materials into products by combining one material with an other, or by changing their shape, properties and/or appearance with the application of physical and chemical processes.

Manufacturing has always been important to humans. From the technological point of view, manufacturing is significant as the principles of science are applied to create and provide all the necessary goods and products for society. From the point of view of economics also, manufacturing is vital since it adds value to materials by changing their size, shape and properties.

Manufacturing is basically concerned with the production of hardware, be it a small item such as a rivet, a nut or a bolt, or anything bigger, such as a car, an aeroplane or a ship. The key ingredients for a manufacturing process are listed in Figure 1.1. The number and variety of products that an industry produces have an important relation to the cost at which the

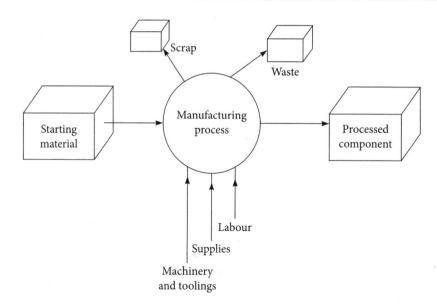

Figure 1.1   Basic model of a manufacturing process

products are offered to their users. In general, annual production quantities can be classified into three ranges: low (1 to 100 units), medium (100 to 10,000 units) and high (greater than 10,000 units). Here, product variety refers to the different product types or models produced in the plant. One type or model of a product varies from another if it has divergent features or different number of parts.

A manufacturing plant consists of a specific set of people, processes and systems that are capable of transforming a certain limited range of materials into products of higher value. The quantity and variety of products produced by a plant has an important influence on the way its people, facilities and procedures are organized. The capability of a manufacturing plant can be determined by: (i) its technological processing capability (which depends upon the available set of manufacturing processes, together with production and material handling equipment in the plant); and (ii) the production capacity (i.e., the maximum quantity that the plant can produce in a given time period under given operating conditions).

1.1 Materials in Manufacturing

Engineering materials can be classified into three categories, namely, metals, ceramics and polymers. This classification is based on the physical and mechanical properties of materials, which are different for each category. These differences further affect the manufacturing processes that can be used to create products from the said materials. Composites are simply non-homogeneous mixtures of the three basic categories of materials rather than a unique category, as can be seen in Figure 1.2.

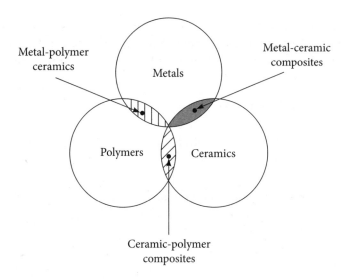

Figure 1.2 Venn diagram showing the three basic material types and their composites

Engineering metals are mostly alloys, which are composed of two or more elements, at least one of them being metallic. They can be classified into two basic groups: ferrous and non-ferrous. Ferrous metals contain iron; it is interesting to note that nearly 75% of the metal tonnage used in the world is of these metals. The most common ferrous metals used in engineering applications are steels (irons containing up to 2% carbon) and cast irons (irons containing from 2% to 4% carbon). All metallic elements and their alloys that are not iron based are referred to as non-ferrous metals. The most common non-ferrous metals used in engineering applications are aluminium, copper, nickel, magnesium, tin and titanium.

Ceramics are compounds containing metallic, semi-metallic and non-metallic elements. Typical non-metallic elements used in ceramics are carbon, oxygen and nitrogen. Based on the processing aspect, ceramics can be classified into two groups: (i) crystalline ceramics and (ii) glasses. Crystalline ceramics can be further grouped into two classes: traditional ceramics (e.g., clay or hydrous aluminium silicates) and modern ceramics (e.g., alumina, that is Al_2O_3). Glass ceramics are mostly composed of silica (SiO_2).

Polymers are compounds formed by repeating structural units called *mers*, the atoms of which share their electrons in order to form very large molecules. Polymers can be classified into three groups:

1. **Thermoplastic polymers** The molecular structure of thermoplastic polymers does not change when subjected to multiple heating and cooling cycles.

2. **Thermosetting polymers** The molecular structure of thermosetting polymers becomes rigid on processing and cannot be subjected to multiple heating and cooling cycles.

3. **Elastomers** These polymers are characterized by their significant elastic behaviour.

Composites consist of two or more homogeneous masses of material that are processed separately and then bonded together to achieve properties superior to those of the constituent materials. In most cases, the structure of composites consists of particles or fibres of one material bonded in another. The properties of composites depend on the constituent materials, their physical shapes and the manner in which they are bonded to form the composite.

1.2 Manufacturing Processes

Manufacturing processes are value-addition operations through which a material or a component can be transformed from one form into a better or more useful form. Manufacturing processes can be classified into two basic types, as shown in Figure 1.3.

1.   **Processing processes** These processes are performed in order to change the size, geometry or physical properties of a material or a component for the purpose of adding value to it.

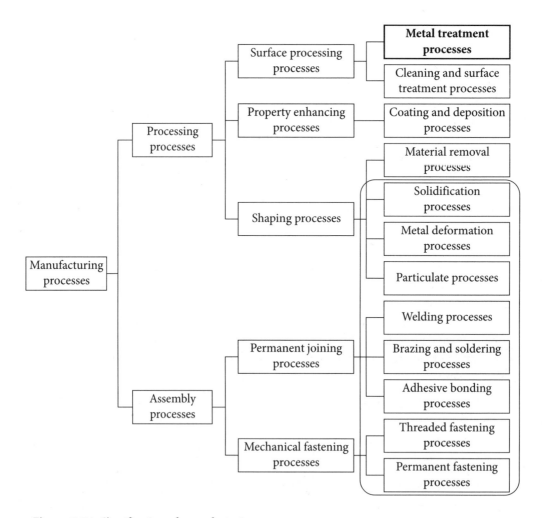

Figure 1.3   Classification of manufacturing processes

2. **Assembly processes** These processes are performed in order to join two or more components so as to create a new entity.

1.2.1 Processing processes

Processing processes can be further divided into three categories: (i) *shaping processes*, which are carried out to change the shape or geometry of the input work material; (ii) *property-enhancing processes*, which are carried out to improve the physical properties of the input work material with little or no change in shape of the component part; and (iii) *surface processing processes*, which are carried out to clean, treat, coat or deposit material on the exterior surface of the component part.

Shaping processes can be grouped into four categories (Figure 1.3).

1. **Material removal processes** All metal machining processes, both traditional and non-traditional, fall into this category. The starting material is a ductile or brittle, but solid metal. Either by applying force with the help of cutting tools or by any other means, material is removed from the starting component part in such a manner that what remains is the desired shaped part.

2. **Solidification processes** All metal-casting processes fall into this category. The starting material is heated to a molten state and then poured into a mould cavity of the desired shape where it is allowed to cool and solidify.

3. **Deformation processes** All metal-forming processes fall into this category. The starting material is a ductile solid metal. Forces that exceed the yield strength of the material are applied to displace and deform the material so as to obtain the final shape.

4. **Particulate processes** All powder metallurgy processes fall into this category. The starting material is in the powder state. Metal powders are compressed into the desired shape in a die and then sintered.

Surface-processing processes include all the operations carried out to remove dirt, oil and other contaminants from the workpiece surface to improve its properties. Processes that coat or deposit a thin film on the exterior surface of the workpiece are also included in this category of manufacturing processes.

Property-enhancing processes are carried out to improve the mechanical or physical properties of the work material. There is no intention of changing the shape or geometry but it might occur unintentionally. All heat treatment processes fall in this category.

Assembly process are carried out to join two or more metal pieces together. One type of joining processes makes a permanent joint while another type involves mechanical fastening, i.e., the parts may be dissembled and reassembled more than once without causing any serious damage to the component parts making up the assembly.

This classification of manufacturing processes is not mutually exclusive and, therefore, not a perfect one. For instance, some surface-processing operations may involve a little metal removal or small metal deformation.

The manufacturing processes encased by thick rectangle in Figure 1.3 will be covered in this book. A brief description of these manufacturing processes is given in the following sections.

1.2.2 Solidification processes

Also called casting processes, they are widely used to produce parts that generally require some follow-on processes, such as machining. A metal in the molten state is poured into a mould having the desired shaped cavity and allowed to solidify there. The metal, on solidification, retains the shape of the mould cavity, and is called a casting. The casting processes are of two basic types: the first one uses moulds of an expendable type (i.e., a new mould is required for each casting), and the second one uses moulds of a permanent type (i.e., the same mould can be used repeatedly). The major advantage of casting processes is that in a single step, it is possible to convert material in a crude form into a desired shaped part. Moreover, the excess or scrap metal can be easily recycled. Figure 1.4 exhibits a typical casting process.

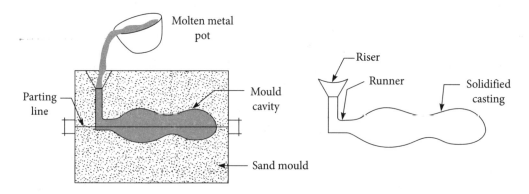

Figure 1.4   Schematic of metal solidification process

1.2.3 Deformation processes

Deformation processes typically utilize previously cast material. The material (in either cold or hot state) is plastically deformed with an externally applied force so as to produce the required shape. *Hot* and *cold* refer to the temperature of the material at the time it is being processed with respect to the temperature at which this material can recrystallize (i.e., grow a new grain structure). Material is not removed; it is only displaced and deformed to obtain the final shape. For a specific process, the form of material used may be the result of several previous operations. This category of processes includes all metal-working and metal-forming processes such as forging, drawing, bending, rolling and extrusion. It also includes sheet metal working processes, for example, bending, deep drawing, coining and embossing. Unconventional forming processes – high energy rate forming (HERF) and high velocity forming (HVF) processes – also belong to this category and are covered in Chapter 13. Figure 1.5 shows a schematic representation of some deformation processes.

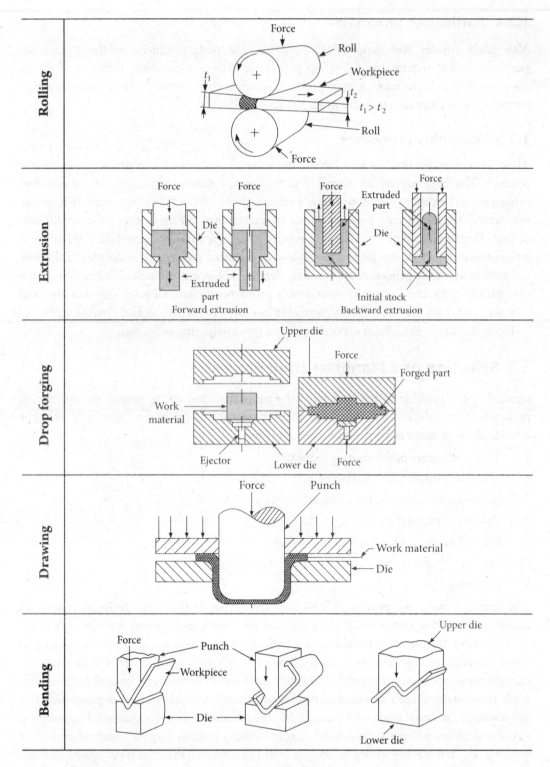

Figure 1.5 Schematic of some deformation processes

1.2.4 Particulate processes

Also called powder metallurgy (PM) processes, the parts produced by these processes generally do not require any follow-up processes, such as machining. Particles of metals are pressed in a die to make a 'soft' product, which is then sintered (i.e., heated to a high temperature in a furnace) in order to get the final product.

1.2.5 Assembly processes

These processes are used to join two or more metal components to produce the desired product. The large variety of assembly processes necessitates classifying them into two categories: (i) processes that produce permanent joints; and (ii) processes that create mechanical fastenings, i.e., produce joints by mechanical means without the application of heat. Depending upon the assembly process used, the joint produced may either be of a permanent nature or can be assembled and disassembled repeatedly. Examples of the first category of assembly processes are welding, brazing, soldering and adhesive bonding, while examples of the second category of assembly processes include all processes that are used to make joints with the help of rivets, threaded fasteners, press fittings and expansion fits.

Figure 1.6 shows the schematic of some basic types of joining processes.

1.3 Selection of a Manufacturing Process

Generally, it is possible to produce a part by more than one of the several manufacturing processes. The selection of the most suitable process is often not easy as it requires consideration of many factors such as the following:

1. Type and nature of the starting material
2. Size and geometrical shape of the part
3. Dimensional accuracy, tolerance and precision
4. Volume of production
5. Desired quality and properties of the part
6. Technical viability of the process and lead time
7. Economy

The material for a component is generally chosen from the view point of functional requirements of the component, although cost and processing factors are also given due consideration. Further, a standard material should be chosen for a component so as to avoid unnecessary high inventory costs. The type of component material influences the manufacturing process. For example, hard and brittle materials resist mechanical deformation, while these materials can be cast and machined through a number of other processes. The properties of a material may even be affected by the manufacturing process used. For instance, in order to obtain a better surface finish, a cold working process may be preferred over a hot working one, but it is important to keep in mind that when a material is processed through the former method, it can become more hard and brittle.

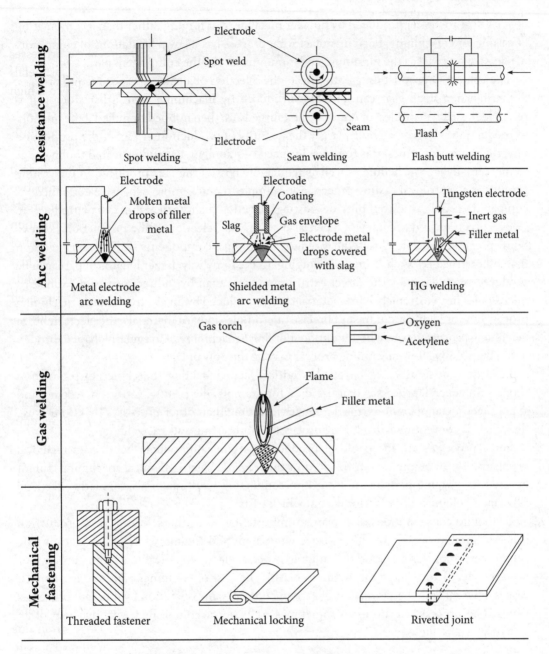

Figure 1.6 Schematic of some metal part assembly processes

Size, shape and shape complexity of a component have great bearing on the process selection. Flat components with thin cross-sections are difficult to cast; rather, such components can be better produced through rolling operation. Similarly, complex-shaped parts cannot be conveniently produced by mechanical working processes; rather for better results, these may be produced by casting and then machining. Accurate simple-shaped parts of small size are better produced by powder metallurgy or forging rather than a combination of casting and machining. Each manufacturing process has its own limitations of complexity of part shape as well as the maximum and minimum size of the component part.

The volume of production greatly affects the selection of a particular production process. For instance, a small gear can be either produced by machining from a bar stock if it is required in small quantities, or it may be first forged and then hobbed or milled if the quantity of production is large. Generally, larger the quantity of production or higher the production rate, the more economical it is to invest in special equipment and sophisticated tooling so as to meet the delivery schedule as well as reduce the cost of the part produced. A die casting process or a centrifugal casting process, for example, requires more expensive equipment as compared to sand casting but provides castings of better quality at a higher rate of production.

The precision and accuracy of a part also affects the selection of the production process. Some processes, such as closed die forging, can produce components with greater precision than other processes such as open die forging. In the same way, larger lengths of parts can be produced more easily by the direct extrusion process than by indirect extrusion. Similarly, micro-holes in an extremely hard material can be produced by an electrochemical machining process but for highly accurate and precise micro-holes in hard materials, the electron beam machining process may be a better option. For finish machining of irregularly shaped through holes, the abrasive flow machining process may be the only option.

Lead time in some cases becomes a critical factor affecting the choice of production process. In general, processes that use dies, for example, die casting, extrusion, forging, and some sheet metal operations, need a longer lead time than other processes that do not use dies, such as conventional machining processes, sand casting and arc welding.

Some processes are incapable of producing certain components because of technical problems. Many examples can be cited in this regard. Electrochemical machining cannot be used for shaping parts made from non-conducting work materials. Similarly, electrical resistance welding is not used for welding thick parts.

Economic considerations also play an important role in the selection of a production process. Some processes need expensive equipment and tooling while others do not. Die sinking operation can be done by a milling process, electrochemical machining process, or even the electric discharge machining process. The cost of equipment and tooling in each case is different and, therefore, cost of carrying out the same operation by different processes varies. The process selection can sometimes be better accomplished with the help of an analytical technique.

1.3.1 Analytical technique

From economic considerations, the selection of a manufacturing process from a set of processes can be made using an analytical technique, called break-even analysis (BA). The aim is to choose a manufacturing process that will produce the product of given specifications and of required quantity and quality at the lowest cost.

BA can be used if the cost and other data of all the feasible processes are known. Typically, it is essential to know the data regarding the following two types of costs.

Fixed costs (FC) Fixed costs are those that do not vary with the number of parts produced. These costs comprise investments made for the purchase of the equipment and tooling (jigs, fixtures, etc.) required for the process; supervisory and administrative office staff salaries; taxes; building depreciation; and so forth.

Variable costs (VC) Variable costs are those that typically change with the volume of production or the number of parts produced. The costs of direct material and direct labour, in addition to the costs of other items such as factory supplies (water, gas, electricity, consumables, etc.) add up to the total variable costs.

The total cost of manufacture of the required quantity (say n) of component parts is the sum of all the fixed costs and n times the variable costs (expressed in units of Rs per part).

$$TC = FC + n.VC$$

Graphically, the aforementioned relation can be represented as in Figure 1.7. If the fixed costs and variable costs of all the processes are known, it is possible to find the most economical process for a given volume of production.

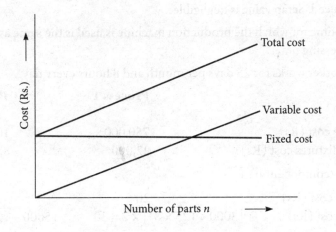

Figure 1.7 Total cost of manufacturing versus the number of parts produced

Example 1.1

A component part can be produced by Process 1 as well as by Process 2. Both involve the use of machinery, though of different types. The cost data for the two processes is given in the following table. If it is assumed that the component performance is not affected whether it is produced by Process 1 or Process 2, determine the following:

1. Which process should be employed if the number of parts required is 100,000?

2. What quantity of production will make both Process 1 and Process 2 equally economical?

	Process 1	Process 2
Machine cost (Rs)	1500,000	2000,000
Cost of jigs and fixtures (Rs)	22,000	8,000
Material cost per piece (Rs)	20	15
Processing time or standard time (hours)	2	1
Labour rate (Rs per month)	3,000	5,000
Machine power charges (Rs per hour)	10	10

State the assumptions made.

Solution

1. We can make the following assumptions:

   i.   The machines for Processes 1 and 2 will be discarded at 50% salvage value after the required number of parts has been produced.

   ii. Jigs and fixtures will be discarded after the required number of parts has been produced. Scrap value is negligible.

   iii. The time for which the production machine is used is the same as the processing time.

   iv. A worker works for 25 days per month and 8 hours every day.

	Process 1	Process 2
Fixed costs		
Machine cost (Rs)	750,000	1,000,000
Jigs and fixtures cost (Rs)	22,000	8,000
Variable costs/component part		
Material cost (Rs)	20	15
Labour cost (Rs)	$[3000 \div (25 \times 8)] \times 2 = 30$	$[5000 \div (25 \times 8)] = 25$
Power cost (Rs)	$10 \times 2 = 20$	$10 \times 1 = 10$

Total cost (Rs) of manufacture of 100,000 parts

$$\text{By Process } 1 = 772,000 + 100,000 \, (20 + 30 + 20)$$
$$= 7772,000$$
$$\text{By Process } 2 = 1008,000 + 100,000 \, (15 + 25 + 10)$$
$$= 6008,000$$

Therefore, from economic considerations, Process 2 is the preferred process.

2. Let n denote the quantity of production for which both Processes 1 and 2 will cost the same.

$$772,000 + 70\,n = 1008,000 + 50\,n$$

Or, $n = 11,800$

For a quantity of production less than 11,800, Process 1 will be economical, and for a quantity of production greater than 11,800, it will be economical to use Process 2.

Questions

1. Define manufacturing. Does manufacturing activity in a country affect the standard of living of people in that country? Explain briefly.

2. What are the various engineering materials used in product manufacturing? Which of these are most common and why?

3. Define polymers, composites and ceramics. Give some specific applications of each of these materials.

4. Differentiate between thermosetting and thermoplastic polymers. Give any five specific applications of each of the two types of polymers.

5. Discuss the factors that influence the selection of a particular manufacturing process for a given component. Explain how break-even analysis helps in the selection of the most economically viable manufacturing process.

Fill in the Blanks

1. Two important parameters of the product that directly control the cost of its manufacturing are _____ and _____.

2. In general, annual production quantity in the range 1 to 100 is classified as _____.

3. One type or model of a product varies from another if it has _____ or different _____.

4. On the basis of physical and mechanical properties, engineering materials can be classified into three categories, namely, _____ , _____ , and _____.

5. Engineering metals can be classified into two basic groups: _____ and _____.

6. The main element in ferrous metals is _____.

7. The most common ferrous metals used in engineering applications are _____ and _____.

8. From the processing aspect, ceramics can be classified into two groups: (i) _____ ceramics and (ii) _____.

9. Glass ceramics are mostly based on _____.

10. Polymers can be classified into three groups: _____ , _____ and _____.

11. The molecular structure of _____ polymers does not change when subjected to multiple heating and cooling cycles.

12. The molecular structure of _____ polymers becomes rigid on processing and cannot be subjected to multiple heating and cooling cycles.

13. Polymers known as _____ are characterized by their significant elastic behaviour.

14. _____ consist of two or more homogeneous masses of material that are processed separately and then bonded together to achieve properties superior to that of the constituent materials.

15. Manufacturing processes can be classified into two basic types: _____ and _____.

16. The process in which components are produced by first compressing the metal powder into the desired shape and then sintering it, is called _____.

17. Hot and cold working of metals refers to the temperature of the metal at the time it is being processed with respect to the temperature at which this metal can _____.

18. Flat components with thin cross-sections are difficult to cast; therefore, it is better that they are produced by _____ operation.

19. Accurate simple-shaped parts of small size are better produced by _____ process.

20. The category of assembly processes that are carried out with the help of rivets, threaded fasteners, press fitting and expansion fits is called _____.

Choose the Correct Answer

1. In manufacturing, what is added to the material?
   a. Heat
   b. Carbon
   c. Value
   d. Glue

2. The two Latin words from which the term *manufacture* is derived are
   a. *manu* and *facture*.
   b. *manus* and *factus*.
   c. *manus* and *fracture*.
   d. *mons* and *factu*.

3. In general, an annual production quantity of 100 to 10,000 is classified as what range of production?
   a. Low
   b. Medium
   c. Large
   d. Very large

4. The production capacity of a plant can be defined as
   a. the maximum quantity that it can produce in a given time period under given operating conditions.
   b. the minimum quantity that it can produce in a given time period under given operating conditions.
   c. the minimum quantity that it can produce in a given month.
   d. the average quantity that it can produce in any time period.

5. Engineering materials are classified into three categories, namely, metals, ceramics and

   a. non-metals.   c. compounds.

   b. non-ferrous metals.   d. polymers.

6. Titanium is

   a. ceramic.   c. composite.

   b. non-ferrous metal.   d. polymer.

7. Compounds containing metallic, semi-metallic and non-metallic elements are called

   a. ceramics.   c. composites.

   b. non-ferrous metals.   d. polymers.

8. Glass is a

   a. ceramic.   c. composite.

   b. non-ferrous metal.   d. polymer.

9. The manufacturing process in which molten metal is poured into a mould cavity of a desired shape and then allowed to cool and solidify, is known as

   a. forging.   c. prototyping.

   b. moulding.   d. casting.

10. The manufacturing process in which the starting material is in the powder state is known as

    a. powder forging.   c. powder metallurgy.

    b. powder moulding.   d. powder casting.

11. Manufacturing capability of a manufacturing plant can be estimated from

    a. the knowledge base of the technical people working in the plant.

    b. the number of components produced in the plant during the last year.

    c. the quantity and quality of raw materials being used by the plant.

    d. the production capacity of the plant together with its technological processing capability.

12. In general, if the annual production quantity of a plant is 1000 units, it is classified as

    a. low.   c. high.

    b. medium.   d. very high.

13. Engineering materials can be classified into categories as

    a. metals and ceramics.

    b. metals, polymers and ceramics.

    c. metals, non-metals, polymers and composites.

    d. polymers, ceramics and composites.

14. Engineering metals are mostly

    a. alloys, which are composed of two or more elements, at least one of which is metallic.

    b. pure metals.

    c.   ferrous metals.

    d.   non-ferrous metals.

15. Cast irons contain carbon in the range

    a.   0.1 to 1.0 %   c.   2.0 to 4.0 %

    b.   1.0 to 2.0 %   d.   2.0 to 8.0 %

16. Ceramics are compounds made of

    a.   metallic (or semi-metallic) and non-metallic elements.

    b.   non-metallic elements.

    c.   polymers.

    d.   crystalline elements.

17. Polymers whose molecular structure does not change when subjected to multiple heating
     and cooling cycles are called

    a.   thermoplastic polymers.   c.   elastomers.

    b.   thermosetting polymers.   d.   composites.

18. Composites are made up of two or more

    a.   homogeneous masses of material that are processed separately and then bonded
         together.

    b.   homogeneous masses of material that are processed and bonded together.

    c.   heterogenous masses of material that are processed separately and then bonded
         together.

    d.   heterogenous masses of material that are processed and bonded together.

19. Manufacturing processes which are carried out to change the shape or geometry of the work
     material can be classified into that of the following categories?

    a.   Material removal processes, solidification processes, deformation processes and
         particulate processes

    b.   Material removal processes, solidification processes, joining processes, deformation
         processes and particulate processes

    c.   Material removal processes, solidification processes, deformation processes and
         joining processes

    d.   Solidification processes, deformation processes, joining processes and particulate
         processes

20. The deformation processes are carried out typically on a material that has been

    a.   previously cast.

    b.   previously machined.

    c.   previously welded.

    d.   previously neither cast nor machined nor welded.

21. The component parts produced by particulate processing generally
    a. require follow-up processes, such as machining.
    b. do not require any follow-up processes, such as machining.
    c. have high elasticity and plasticity.
    d. have high hardness, brittleness and are non-permeable.

22. Break-even analysis can be used to determine the most economical production process
    a. if fixed and variable costs of all processes under consideration are known.
    b. if only fixed costs of all processes under consideration are known.
    c. if only variable costs of all processes under consideration are known.
    d. if fixed and variable costs of all processes under consideration together with volume of production are known.

23. Fixed costs of production are those
    a. that do not vary with the number of parts produced.
    b.   that do not vary with the time taken to produce the parts.
    c. that do not vary with the quantity and quality of machinery used for production.
    d. that do not vary with the location of plant where the parts are produced.

24. Variable costs of production are those
    a. that typically change with the cost of machinery used for production.
    b. that typically change with the location of plant where the parts are produced.
    c. that typically change with the volume of production.
    d. that typically change with the number of parts, which add up to make a product.

Answers

1. c.	2. b.	3. b.	4. a.	5. d.	6. b.	7. a.	8. a.	9. d.	10. c.
11. d.	12. b.	13. b.	14. a.	15. c.	16. a.	17. a.	18. a.	19. b.	20. a.
21. b.	22. d.	23. a.	24. c.						

2

Introduction to Metal Casting

LEARNING OBJECTIVES

After reading this chapter, you should be able to understand the following:

- The fundamentals of metal casting process and the circumstances when it is preferred over other manufacturing processes.

- The two basic types of metal casting processes – expendable mould casting processes and permanent mould casting processes.

- The requirements of a mould.

- The various casting terms.

2.1 Introduction

A component can be generally produced by several manufacturing processes, each offering its own advantages and limitations; the challenge lies in selecting the most economical and suitable process for a given component. Casting is one of the oldest and most popular methods of producing metallic products, whereby liquid metal is poured into a cavity known as the mould, and allowed to solidify and cool. The casting thus produced is almost an exact replica of the mould. This casting is cleaned and, if required, machined to the desired dimensions. Moulds are generally prepared in sand but can just as easily be made of metals or non-metals.

Advantages   Following are the advantages of the casting process.

1. Parts of any size – small, medium or large – can be cast. Parts weighing as small as a few grammes to as much as several thousand kilogrammes can be cast.

2. Parts having complicated or complex shapes can be produced. It is very easy to cast a part that has a heavy metal mass at specific area(s).

3. Parts can be produced in any quantity; the range can be from 1 to 1,000 or even more. Some casting methods are particularly suited to mass production.

4. Parts can be made of any metal that can be heated to a molten state. The casting process is particularly suitable for parts that need to be made from precious metals, since there is little or no loss of material. The process is equally suitable for producing parts from refractory materials or high strength materials.

5. Some casting processes are capable of producing parts in a net shape or a near-net shape requiring little or no further manufacturing operations to obtain the required geometry and dimensions of the parts.

6. Parts that require minimum directional properties of the metal can be produced by this process. Castings have better anisotropic qualities than forged or rolled parts.

7. The tools and equipment required for the casting process are simple and inexpensive.

Disadvantages The casting process may not be preferred for the following.
1. Parts that need to have high surface finish and dimensional accuracy.

2. Parts that have to be very thin or those that can be stamped out on a punch press.

3. Parts that have to be of porous-free structure such as pressure vessels.

4. Parts that need high tensile strength at all of its cross-sections such as crane hooks.

5. Parts that have to be made of highly reactive metals.

6. Parts that are thin and have deep cavities.

Applications Examples of cast products include automotive components like piston and piston rings, carburettors and engine blocks. Other applications of cast parts are for agricultural implements, pipes, wheels, gun barrels, large size machine beds, railway wheels and so on.

2.1.1 Economics

The cost of any component comprises the price of material, labour, tooling and equipment. In case of a casting, the various costs involved can be grouped under three heads: (i) pre-process, (ii) process and (iii) post-process. Pre-process costs include that of making moulds and dies requiring raw materials, equipment, time and effort. These costs vary from one casting process to another; for example, sand casting is relatively less costly than die casting, which requires both expensive materials and machining. Process costs include the cost of melting the metal and the cost of pouring molten metal into moulds or dies. The costs of furnace and other related machinery depend on the size, design sophistication and the level of automation. Post-process costs include the costs incurred in cleaning, inspecting and heat treating the castings. The amount of labour and skill requirement for cleaning and inspection processes can vary considerably depending on the casting process employed and the level of automation. Sand casting, for example, requires a substantial amount of labour because cleaning of sand casting is a time-consuming process but necessary. Inspection of sand casting requires skilled labour but is vital because of the relatively greater possibility of defects. On the other hand, a highly automated die casting process can maintain high production rate with only little labour requirement for cleaning and sampling inspection.

The economics of the casting process depend basically on the number of parts to be produced. For a small lot production of parts, the casting process is generally the only choice. However, for mass production of parts, the casting process may be chosen if the unit cost of production by casting is competitive when compared to other manufacturing processes.

2.1.2 Overview of metal casting technology

Metal casting, as a manufacturing process, is carried out in a foundry. A foundry is a factory equipped for carrying out various foundry operations such as making of mould, melting of metal, handling of molten metal, carrying out the casting process and cleaning of casting. The workers who perform the foundry operations are known as foundry men.

The metal casting process involves the following foundry operations:

1. **Mould making** A mould is a mass of material of specific size that contains a cavity whose geometry corresponds to the shape of the part to be cast. The actual shape and size of the cavity are almost the same as those of the desired casting. Moulds can be made from a variety of materials, including sand, plaster, ceramic and metal. The mould may be of open or closed type. Beside the cavity, a mould also contains a gating system that consists of passageways for permitting the molten metal to flow from outside the mould into the cavity.

2. **Metal melting** This is carried out in a furnace that heats and melts the necessary amount of metal.

3. **Metal pouring in mould** Molten metal is taken from the furnace in a ladle to the mould. Through the passage ways of the gating system, the molten metal is filled into the cavity of the mould and allowed to cool. Once the metal has solidified and the casting has cooled sufficiently, it is taken out from the mould.

4. **Cleaning and further processing of casting** Depending upon the need, the surface of the casting may be cleaned, excess metal trimmed from the casting and sent for heat treatment and/or machining.

2.2 Metal Casting Processes

Metal casting processes can be broadly classified according to the type of mould used. There are two types of moulds: expendable (i.e., single-use) and permanent (i.e., multiple-use) moulds. An expendable mould is destroyed in order to remove the casting from it, after the molten metal that was poured into it has solidified. Such moulds are made of sand, plaster and similar materials, whose form is maintained by using some kind of binder. Sand casting typically uses an expendable mould made of sand into which the molten metal is poured.

A permanent mould is one that can be used again and again to produce several castings. It can be made from a metal or a ceramic refractory material that can withstand the high temperature of the molten metal. In permanent mould casting, the mould is made of two or more parts so that it can be opened to permit removal of the casting. Die casting is the most familiar process in this category.

All expendable mould casting processes make use of patterns for creating cavities in moulds. While investment casting process and full-mould casting process use single-use patterns, other casting processes in this category use multiple-use patterns. Table 2.1 classifies casting processes based on the type of mould used.

Table 2.1 Casting process classification

Expendable mould casting	Permanent mould casting
Green sand	Permanent mould
Dry sand	Die
CO_2 sand	Gravity
Shell sand	Low pressure
Investment	High pressure
Full mould	Centrifugal
Plaster mould	Slush
Ceramic mould	Continuous

2.2.1 Choice of casting process

The following factors influence the choice of a particular casting process:

1. Number or volume of castings required
2. Complexity of shape, that is, external and internal shape, minimum wall thickness, and type, size and shape of core required
3. Surface finish, dimensional accuracy and tolerance desired
4. Size and weight of casting
5. Properties (tensile strength, rigidity, air or water tightness, etc.) required in the casting

Due to the large number of factors involved, it is generally difficult to choose which casting process will be the best for manufacturing a given part. However, the data given in Table 2.2 can serve as a guide.

Table 2.2 Comparison of different casting processes

S. No.	Casting process	Material choice	Part complexity	Minimum wall thickness	Surface finish (R$_a$ μm)	Precision and tolerance (mm/mm)	Mechanical properties	Remarks
1.	Sand casting	Wide	Considerable	3 mm	Not very good, 10–25	±0.6 to 0.3	Fair to high	No limit to part weight, size, shape
2.	Machine moulding	Wide	Considerable	3 mm	Good 10–20	±0.12	Fair to high	Useful for small parts
3.	Shell mould casting	Wide	Moderate	2 mm	Very good 1–5	±0.003 to 0.005	Good	Good dim. accuracy, small parts
4.	Plaster mould casting	Narrow Brass, Cu Bronze, Al	Considerable	1 mm	Excellent 1–5	±0.25 to 0.125	Good	Intricate shape parts
5.	Investment casting	Wide	Considerable	1 mm	Excellent 1–3	±0.125	Excellent	Intricate shape parts
6.	Centrifugal casting	Wide	Considerable	2 mm	Very good 2–10	±1.25	Excellent	Large cylindrical parts; high prod. rate
7.	Full mould casting	Wide	Considerable	2 mm	Good 5–20	±1.25	Good	Most metals can be cast; no limit to part complexity
8.	Die casting	Non-ferrous	High	0.5 mm	Excellent 1–2	±0.003 to 0.005	Excellent	High rate of production

2.2.2 Requirements of a mould

The requirements of a mould are as follows:

1. A mould must have the cavity of desired shape and size, taking into account contraction and other allowances (contraction allowance is typically 1% for cast iron, 1.25% for aluminium and 2% for steel).

2. A mould must be made of a material that can withstand the in flow and weight of molten metal before solidification (molten metal is just as heavy when in molten state as when in solid state).

3. A mould must be able to ensure the following:

    i. efficient feeding of liquid metal to all areas of the mould cavity before the metal starts to solidify;

    ii. easy escape of gases from the mould during and after pouring of liquid metal in the mould;

    iii. unrestricted solidification and contraction of the metal in the mould after it has been poured; and

    iv. easy removal of casting from the mould after cooling.

2.3 Expendable and Permanent Moulds

The choice whether to use expendable moulds (i.e., which can only be used once) or permanent moulds (i.e., which can be used repeatedly to make a large number of castings) depends upon the number of similar castings required, their size and shape, and the metal of the castings. In most instances, the choice is quite obvious. The thumb rule is to use a permanent mould when large quantities of small- to medium-sized castings of non-ferrous metals are needed; otherwise, one may use expendable moulds.

2.3.1 Expendable mould casting processes

Expendable mould casting processes can be grouped into two categories; the first category comprises those processes that employ multiple-use patterns; and the second category comprises those processes that employ single-use patterns.

1. Expendable mould casting processes that employ multiple-use patterns include the following:

    • Sand casting and its variants such as green-sand casting, skin-dried sand casting, dry-sand casting, sodium silicate bonded sand casting, and shell mould casting

    • Plaster mould casting

    • Ceramic mould casting

    • Vacuum mould casting

2. Expendable mould casting processes that employ single-use patterns include the following:

    • Investment casting

    • Full mould casting

2.3.2 Permanent mould casting processes

In all permanent mould casting processes, a re-usable mould called *die,* made of either some metal, alloy or graphite, is used. The mould segments are generally designed for rapid and accurate opening and closing. The mould is preheated and clamped shut, and the molten metal is poured in under gravity or external pressure. After solidification of the metal, the mould is opened and the solidified product is taken out. After a spray of lubricant on the mould faces, the mould is then re-closed. Since the heat from the previous cast is often sufficient to maintain mould temperature, molten metal can be poured for the next casting. The following processes fall under this category:

- Die casting
  - Gravity die casting
  - Low pressure die casting
  - High pressure die casting
- Centrifugal casting
- Semi-centrifugal casting
- Centrifuging
- Continuous casting
- Slush casting

2.4 Metal Casting Terminology

There are many terms used in metal casting technology, some of which have been used here and others that will be used in the subsequent chapters of this book. It is necessary to define these terms before going into the details of the different casting processes. Reference may be made to Figure 3.1.

Casting   The term is used to describe both the process and the product that is produced when molten metal is poured and allowed to solidify within a mould.

Pattern   It is an almost duplicate form of the final cast product to be produced. It is used to make the mould cavity.

Draft   It is the taper on the vertical faces of a pattern given to facilitate its withdrawal from the mould.

Flask   A flask or a moulding flask is an open box-like structure which holds the sand mould. A two-piece mould comprises two moulds contained independently in two flasks – the top one is called *cope,* and the lower one is referred to as *drag.* Similarly, a three-piece mould comprises a cope, a drag and an intermediate mould (called *cheek*).

Moulding Sand   It is a mixture of silica, clay and water in appropriate proportions. For making the mould, moulding sand is filled into the space around the pattern in the moulding flask.

Facing Sand   It is a carbonaceous material applied on the inner surface of the mould cavity in order to improve the surface finish of the casting.

Parting Line   It is the interface that separates the cope and the drag halves of a mould. The term is also used to denote the parting surface of two halves of a pattern or a core.

Pouring Basin It is a small funnel-shaped cavity at the top of the mould into which the molten metal is poured. Also called pouring cup, it is a part of the gating system.

Sprue It is the vertical passage through which the molten metal flows down from the pouring basin. This is also a part of the gating system.

Runner System It comprises horizontal channels that carry the molten metal from the bottom of the sprue to the mould cavity.

Gate It is the inlet for the flow of molten metal into the mould cavity.

Gating System It is the network of passageways through which molten metal flows to fill the mould cavity.

Riser It is the extra cavity created in the mould that is also filled with molten metal. The function of the riser is to act as a reservoir of molten metal for the supply of additional metal to the casting as it shrinks during solidification. Figure 3.15 shows two basic types of riser – a *blind riser* and an *open riser*.

Core This is an insert made from sand having the size and shape as that of the cavity desired in the casting. It is placed in the mould prior to pouring the molten metal.

Core Prints These are recesses in the mould, created for providing support to the core. The term *core prints* is also used to identify (i) the extra portions added to the pattern that make the recesses in the mould, and (ii) the extra portions of the core that fit into the recesses.

Core Box It is the mould or die used for producing cores.

Chaplets These are metal pieces placed in the mould cavity either for giving support to the core or to anchor the core in place. They are usually made of the same material as that of the casting since they have to finally fuse with the molten metal.

Chills These are metal pieces placed in the mould to increase the rate of solidification of molten metal in the regions where they are placed. They are usually made of the same material as the casting as they have to finally fuse with the molten metal.

Vents These are fine passageways created in the mould for the escape of air from the mould cavity when the molten metal flows in to fill the mould cavity. The vents permit the escape of gases that may be produced when the molten metal comes in contact with the sand and the core in the mould.

2.5 Safety in Foundries

Safety in foundry operations is as important as in any other manufacturing operations. The need for safety of human beings, materials and equipment arise in foundries due to the following:

1.   Particles of sand and other chemicals or compounds used in foundries harmful to human beings and foundry equipment

2. Glare, fumes and high heat from molten metal, as well as splashing of molten metal during transportation or pouring into moulds

3. Leakage of fuels from pipes going to furnaces and at control valves

4. Improper handling of hygroscopic fluxes that may absorb moisture and cause danger

5. Presence of moisture or water in moulds, crucibles and other locations where it may rapidly get converted into steam, and cause danger of explosion

6. Presence of cracks, wear and so on in crucibles, tools, and other equipment

It is essential that regular checks and inspection of tools and equipment are carried out to eliminate any hazardous situation. Calibration and maintenance of critical equipment like pyrometers should be undertaken on a regular basis. Arrangements for adequate ventilation should be made and use of personal safety equipment such as gloves, aprons, face shields and safety shoes should be made compulsory.

Questions

1. What are the various basic manufacturing processes? As an engineer, when would you prefer casting as a manufacturing process over other manufacturing processes?

2. For the production of 1000 pieces of a non-ferrous component, what could be the advantages if it is produced by casting as compared to forging?

3. Classify the casting processes.

4. What is a mould? What are the requirements of a good mould?

5. Describe some major advantages and limitations of the expendable mould casting processes.

6. Give some possible advantages and limitations to the use of multiple-use moulds.

7. Name any three common mould materials for permanent mould casting. What metals would you recommend to be cast by this process? Give reasons.

8. What factors affect the choice of a particular casting process? Discuss.

9. What characteristics of a product would prohibit you to recommend casting as the manufacturing process?

Fill in the Blanks

1. _____ are the passageways created in the mould for the escape of gases produced when molten metal is poured into the mould cavity.

2. Two major limitations of the casting process are that, generally, the cast products are _____ and _____.

3. A two-piece mould comprises two parts – the top one (called_____) and the lower one (called _____).

4. _____ are metal pieces that are placed in critical regions of the mould to increase the rate of solidification of molten metal in those regions.

5. _____ are recesses in the mould and _____ are metal pieces placed in the mould cavity, both for giving support to the core.

6. _____ is fine dry sand that is sprinkled upon the mating surfaces of a mould so as to facilitate their separation.

7. _____ is a vessel used to transport and pour out molten metal.

8. An insert introduced in a mould, which is made of sand having the size and shape as that of the cavity desired in the casting, is called _____ .

9. _____ is one of the expendable mould casting processes that employ multiple-use pattern.

Choose the Correct Answer

1. Casting process may be preferred over other manufacturing processes for the production of
    a. small size parts.
    c. small as well as medium size parts.
    b. medium size parts.
    d. small, medium, and large parts.

2. Casting process may be preferred over other manufacturing processes because cast parts have
    a. minimum directional properties of the metal.
    b. maximum directional properties of the metal.
    c. generally porous-free structure and therefore, pressure vessels are mostly made by the casting process.
    d. high tensile strength at all of the cross-sections.

3. The pre-process cost of cast products
    a. varies from one casting process to another.
    b. is almost constant, irrespective of what casting process is employed.
    c. includes the cost of melting and pouring of molten metal into moulds or dies.
    d. depends largely on the fluidity of the cast metal.

4. The amount of labour and their skill requirement for cleaning and inspection processes of cast products can vary considerably depending on the
    a. particular casting process only.
    b. level of automation only.
    c. particular casting process and the level of automation.
    d. metals used for the products.

5.   The economics of the casting process depends basically on the
  a.   number of parts to be produced.
  b.   surface finish of the parts to be produced.
  c.   method used for the inspection of parts.
  d.   metal composition of the parts to be produced.

6.   The moulds used in the casting process can be classified as
  a.   expendable or permanent.
  b.   expendable or expandable.
  c.   solid or semi-solid.
  d.   Green sand, Black sand, or Red sand moulds.

7.   All expendable mould casting processes use
  a.   die for making mould.
  b.   pattern for making mould.
  c.   plastic for making mould.
  d.   high pressure liquid metal for making casting.

8.   The choice of a particular casting method is influenced by
  a.   the percentage moisture in the moulding sand.
  b.   the availability of the pattern material.
  c.   desired surface finish, dimensional accuracy and tolerance.
  d.   cost of the component.

9.   Which one of the following is not a requirement of mould for the casting process?
  a.   A mould must be such that it ensures efficient feeding of liquid metal to all areas of the mould cavity before it starts to solidify.
  b.   A mould must have the desired shape and size taking into account contraction and other allowances.
  c.   A mould must be such that it ensures the use of a solid or unbreakable pattern.
  d.   A mould must be such that it ensures unrestricted solidification and contraction of the metal in the mould after it has been poured.

10.   The expendable mould casting processes can be grouped into two categories:
  a.   the processes that use wooden patterns and the processes that use patterns made of plastic or rubber.
  b.   the processes that employ multiple-use patterns and the processes that employ single-use patterns.
  c.   the processes that produce metal components and those that produce non-metal components.
  d.   the processes that produce simple-shaped components and the processes that produce complex-shaped components.

11. A sprue is
    a. the vertical passage through which the molten metal flows down from the pouring basin.
    b. the taper on a pattern given to facilitate its withdrawal from the mould.
    c. the inlet for the flow of molten metal into the mould cavity.
    d. an insert made from sand having the size and shape as that of the cavity desired in the casting.

12. Gate is
    a. the vertical passage through which the molten metal flows down from the pouring basin.
    b. the taper on a pattern given to facilitate its withdrawal from the mould.
    c. the inlet for the flow of molten metal into the mould cavity.
    d. an insert made from sand having the size and shape as that of the cavity desired in the casting.

13. Core is
    a. an almost duplicate form of the final cast product to be produced. It is used to make the mould.
    b. the taper on a pattern given to facilitate its withdrawal from the mould.
    c. the inlet for the flow of molten metal into the mould cavity.
    d. an insert made from sand having the size and shape as that of the cavity desired in the casting.

14. Core prints are the
    a. metal pieces placed in the mould cavity for giving support to the core or to anchor the core in place.
    b. recesses in the mould created for providing support to the core.
    c. colours used to identify different shapes of the core.
    d. metal pieces that are placed in the mould to increase the rate of solidification of molten metal in critical regions.

15. Core prints are used to
    a. manufacture or produce the core.
    b. facilitate easy removal of the core.
    c. support the core.
    d. give different shapes to the core.

16. Chaplets are
    a. metal pieces placed in the mould cavity for giving support to the core or to anchor the core in place.
    b. recesses in the mould created for providing support to the core.

   c.   horizontal channels that carry the molten metal from the bottom of the sprue to the mould cavity.

   d.   metal pieces that are placed in the mould to increase the rate of solidification of molten metal in critical regions.

Answers

1. d.	2. a.	3. a.	4. c.	5. a.	6. a.	7. b.	8. c.	9. c.	10. b.
11. a.	12. c.	13. d.	14. b.	15. c.	16. a.				

3

Expendable Mould Casting Processes

LEARNING OBJECTIVES

After reading this chapter, you should be able to understand the following:

- The fundamentals and the basic steps involved in producing a sand casting.
- The pattern and its requirements.
- The factors to be considered while selecting material for a pattern and the various pattern materials.
- The types of pattern and their specific applications.
- The necessity for giving allowances on pattern and the various pattern allowances.
- The elements of a mould and its requirements.
- The various materials used for making moulds.
- The elements of a sand mould and the types of sand used.
- The various types of sand moulds and methods for sand moulding.
- The core, its characteristics and types.
- The chaplets and the chills.
- The need for sand testing and various sand tests.
- The gating and risering system.
- Carbon dioxide moulding.
- Shell mould casting.
- Plaster mould casting.
- Ceramic mould casting.
- Investment casting.
- Evaporative pattern casting.

3.1 Introduction

The casting processes which use expendable moulds can be grouped into two categories:

1. Casting processes that employ multiple-use patterns: Under this category, the main casting processes are as follows:

    -   Sand mould casting and its variants like Green-sand mould casting, skin-dried sand mould casting, dry-sand mould casting, sodium silicate bonded sand mould casting and shell mould casting

    -   Plaster mould casting

    -   Ceramic mould casting

2. Casting processes that employ single-use patterns: Under this category, the main casting processes are as follows

    -   Investment casting

    -   Full-mould casting

3.2 Sand Mould Casting

Sand mould casting is also called *Green-sand mould casting* or simply *sand casting*. It involves the following steps:

-   Prepare a pattern that has almost the same size as that of the desired casting. The difference between the pattern size and the casting size is on account of the pattern allowances, which will be explained later in this chapter.

-   Prepare the mould in a moulding flask by placing the pattern in the moulding sand. Remove the pattern from the mould.

-   Install a gating, runner and riser system.

-   Pour the molten metal in the mould cavity and allow it to solidify and cool.

-   Break the sand mould carefully, and take out the casting from the mould.

-   Cut off the runner and riser and remove any sand that might be sticking to the casting.

A simple example is given here to explain the actual procedure involved in sand casting of a component.

Step 1   Make a pattern of the desired product [Figure 3.1(a)]. This pattern is a replica of the product, but made in wood or some other material. As will be explained later in this chapter, the pattern is made slightly larger than the product size to allow for contraction of the molten metal as it solidifies and cools to room temperature. In addition to contraction allowance, other allowances are also provided on the pattern. Place the pattern on a flat wooden or metallic plate (called pattern plate) [Figure 3.1(b)].

Step 2 On the pattern plate, place a square (or rectangular) open flask of steel around the pattern. Fill the space around the pattern completely with moulding sand by suitably ramming it [Figure 3.1(c)]. This assembly is termed as the *drag*.

Step 3 Turn the drag through 180° (i.e., upside down) and put it aside. Remove the pattern carefully by taking every precaution not to damage the mould cavity [Figure 3.1(d)].

Step 4 Carve out a channel (termed as the feeding-in gate) in the sand to provide a passage through which the molten metal can flow into the mould cavity [Figure 3.1(d)]. For this purpose, a hand trowel can be used.

Step 5 Take another steel flask and a pattern plate identical to the one used in Step 2. Place two tapered wooden plugs in position so that one will in due course align with the feeding-in gate in the drag flask and the other will align with the main mould cavity [Figure 3.1(e)]. Fill and ram the moulding sand in the flask. Take out the wooden plugs leaving the vertical holes in the moulding sand. This assembly is termed *cope* (or top box or top flask).

Step 6 Remove the two plugs from the cope carefully. Two tapered holes are thus formed in the rammed or compacted sand. The one that will align with the feeding-in gate, called the sprue, will be used for pouring the molten metal into the mould cavity. The other hole that will align with the main mould cavity is called the riser. Make several fine holes (called vents) in the sand body so as to facilitate escape of air and gases.

Step 7 Gently place the cope onto the drag in such a way that there is correct alignment between the two. This can be ensured with the help of locating pins [Figure 3.1(f)]. The interface between the cope and the drag is called *parting line*.

Step 8 Clamp the cope and the drag together and put some weight on the cope. Weighting is necessary to prevent the separation of the two halves of the mould, which might occur under the pressure of the molten metal when it is poured into the mould cavity.

Step 9 Bring the molten metal in a ladle close to the mould. Pour it into the mould through the sprue hole, and continue to do so until it rises sufficiently in the riser hole. This ensures complete filling of the mould cavity with the molten metal. Allow the metal to solidify and cool.

Step 10 Break the mould and take out the casting [Figure 3.1(g)] by using a mechanical shaker. Perform the *fettling* operation, that is, cut off the runner and riser with a chisel, and remove any sand that might be sticking to the surface of the casting either with a wire brush or by the shot blasting process. The casting is now ready to be sent for inspection, heat treatment or machining as desired.

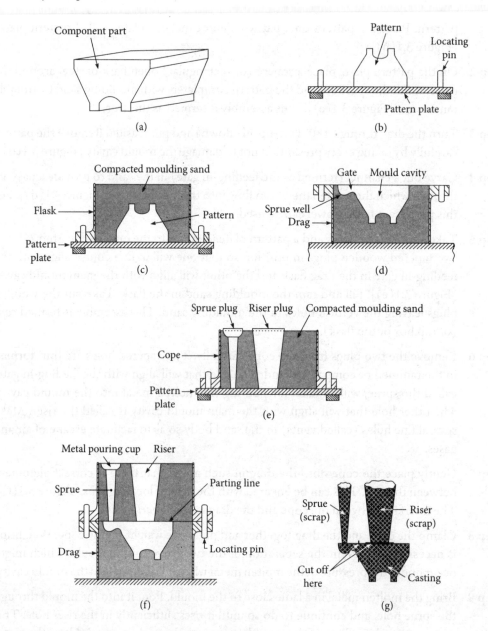

Figure 3.1 Procedure for making a sand casting

3.2.1 Characteristics of sand casting

1. Almost all commercially available metals and alloys can be sand cast.

2. Small, medium and even large size parts can be sand cast.

3. Intricate shapes (such as engine blocks, machine tool beds, parts of hydraulic turbines and large propellers for ocean liners) can be sand cast.

4. The surface of a sand casting is generally rough (in the range of 10 to 20 microns); the finish depends on the quality of sand used in making the mould.

5. The dimensional accuracy and precision are poor.

Sand casting of metals is an ancient process that dates back to the Bronze and Iron Ages. The most ancient castings so far discovered are known to have been produced by pouring molten metal into an open mould. Ancient spears were produced in two-part closed moulds with the use of cores to form sockets, similar to the way we do it today. Our great forefathers were also able to make large size castings. The largest bronze statue in the world is that of the Sun Buddha (at Nara, Japan), cast in the eighth century. This statue is about 20 m high and weighs nearly 5×10^5 kg.

Various elements of sand casting such as pattern, mould, core, metal melting and solidification will now be explained in detail.

3.2.2 Pattern for sand mould

All casting processes that require a new mould for each casting (i.e., expendable mould casting processes) need a pattern. A pattern may be considered as a duplicate of the part to be cast, and can be defined as 'a model around which sand or any other moulding material is packed to get a cavity, called mould'. It is a replica of the desired casting with minute dimensional modifications (to incorporate allowances). Later on, this cavity is filled with molten metal, and after solidification, a reproduction of the pattern is obtained, which is called casting.

Requirements of a good pattern   The requirements of a good pattern are that it should have the following characteristics.

1. Facilitate getting the casting of desired size and shape
2. Be simple in design and easy to fabricate
3. Be smooth and wear resistant
4. Be light in weight and convenient to handle
5. Be strong and have the ability to retain its dimensions, that is, it should have a long life in terms of number of moulds it can make
6. Be able to withstand rough handling

Materials for pattern   The following factors should be considered while selecting the material for a pattern.

1. The number of moulds to be made
2. The desired dimensional accuracy and surface finish of the final casting
3. The intricacy of shape of the final casting
4. The nature of mould, that is, sand mould, plaster mould, shell mould, and so on
5. The method of moulding, that is, hand moulding, or machine moulding
6. Cost

The materials generally used for fabrication of patterns are the following:

1. Wood
2. Metal
3. Plastic
4. Plaster of Paris
5. Wax

Wood is the most commonly used pattern material because it is inexpensive, light in weight, fabrication and repair of pattern is easy, and it gives a reasonably good surface finish. However, wooden patterns are susceptible to shrinkage and swelling, have poor wear resistance, and are weak compared to metallic patterns.

Metal patterns are usually used in machine moulding. They have the advantages of being stable, strong, and having a longer life compared to wooden patterns; they do not absorb moisture and warp, have better surface finish and greater resistance to abrasion, and can withstand rough handling. Metal patterns, however, are heavier, expensive, and do not have as good workability and repairability as wooden patterns. Where a large number of castings are to be produced, the pattern may be made of cast iron, aluminium or brass.

Plastic patterns are light in weight, durable and resistant to wear, water and corrosion. They are strong and have good surface finish. Epoxy resin is one of the commonly used materials for making plastic patterns.

Plaster of Paris and gypsum have also been used to make patterns for small and intricate castings. These patterns are easy to make and possess adequate strength.

Patterns made from wax or frozen mercury are used in the investment casting process. They are very easy to make and have an excellent surface finish. The typical unique advantage of patterns made from wax or frozen mercury is that the patterns need not be taken out from the mould cavity like other patterns; they are drained out of the mould simply by heating, thus eliminating any chance of damaging the mould cavity when the pattern is withdrawn from it.

Types of pattern   For different applications, different types of patterns are used. Some commonly used pattern types are listed as follows:

One piece pattern	Loose piece patterns
Split patterns	Sweep patterns
Match plate patterns	Skeleton patterns
Cope and drag patterns	Segmental patterns
Gated patterns	Follow board patterns

1. **One piece pattern** It is also called a solid pattern and generally has no joints, [Figure 3.2(a)]. It is easy to fabricate. This type of pattern is used for simpler component

shapes. The stuffing-box and the gland of a steam engine are typical examples of castings made by using single-piece patterns.

2.   **Split pattern** A two-piece pattern can be made in such a way that each part contributes to the formation of a portion of the cavity in the mould, thus facilitating mould making and easy production of complicated shaped castings. The two parts of the pattern are aligned by making use of dowel pins [Figure 3.2(b)]. A multi-piece pattern can have three or more pieces to construct mould cavities having more complex shapes. Bearings, pulleys, wheels, spindles, cylinders, valve bodies, water taps and the like, are some examples of castings made by using split patterns.

3.   **Loose piece pattern** Patterns that have complex contours cause difficulty while removing them from the mould. The troubling portions of the pattern are held as loose pieces and attached to the pattern by dowel pins [Figure 3.2(c)]. The loose piece is taken out after the main pattern has been removed, so that there is sufficient room for loose piece removal. Moulding with loose piece pattern is difficult, requires more time and a skilled operator.

4.   **Cope and drag pattern** Cope and drag pattern is a variation of the split pattern where the cope and drag portions of the pattern with gating and runner systems are fitted separately to metal or wooden plates. They are aligned with the help of alignment pins. The cope and drag moulds are prepared separately and later assembled to form a complete mould. This type of pattern is used for large-scale production of heavy castings.

5.   **Match plate pattern** Match plate patterns are further extensions of the cope and drag patterns. Here, the cope and drag patterns along with the gating and risering systems are screwed on the two sides of a single plate called the match plate; the match plate is made of wood or aluminium [Figure 3.2(d)].

   This type of pattern is used for small precision castings that are to be produced in large numbers. Several patterns may be attached to a single match plate. Usually, plaster moulds are prepared but sand moulds can also be prepared using match plate patterns.

6.   **Gated pattern** While making a mould, the gating and runner system is ordinarily cut manually, which consumes a lot of time and may also cause damage to the mould. To enhance the productivity of the mould making, the gating and runner system is made part of the pattern itself. During mass production, a number of small size castings may be produced in a single multi-cavity mould prepared by joining a group of patterns that has a common gating and runner system [Figure 3.2(e)].

7.   **Follow board pattern** This type of pattern uses a follow board for supporting a pattern that is very thin or fragile and which may otherwise sag or break under the force of ramming of the sand. The board is made to exactly match the bottom of the pattern and acts as a seat for the same.

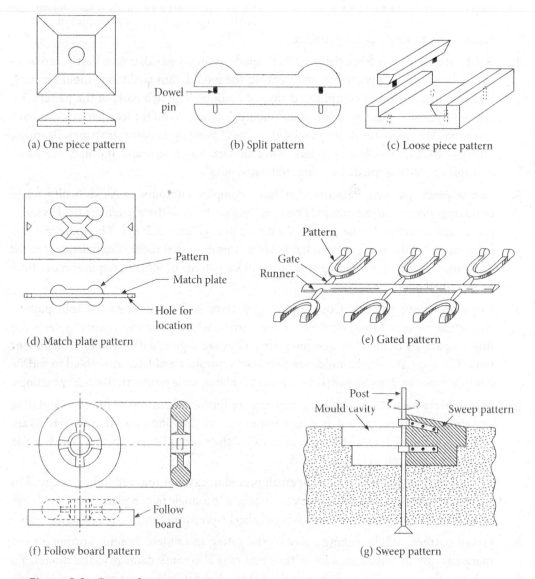

(a) One piece pattern

Dowel pin

(b) Split pattern

(c) Loose piece pattern

Pattern

Match plate

Hole for location

(d) Match plate pattern

Pattern

Gate

Runner

(e) Gated pattern

Follow board

(f) Follow board pattern

Post

Mould cavity

Sweep pattern

(g) Sweep pattern

Figure 3.2   Types of pattern

Follow board is required only in the drag flask and not in the cope flask since the sand in the drag box will support and act like a follow board to the cope pattern. [Figure 3.2(f)].

8. **Sweep pattern** In case of an axi-symmetrical or prismatic casting, sweep pattern can serve as an economical substitute for the expensive full size pattern. Here, a board cut to the shape matching the desired mould shape is given sweep, that is, rotated about a central axis (with the use of a post or spindle) so as to generate the desired mould cavity [Figure 3.2(g)].

9. **Skeleton pattern** To fabricate a full size solid pattern for a big casting, a huge volume of material would normally be required. In order to save material, a skeleton pattern is

prepared, which has the required surface and contour from outside but is hollow inside. Such a skeleton pattern can also be made as a ribbed structure that is initially hollow inside and later filled with some low cost filler material. Usually, this pattern is built in two halves, one each for the cope and the drag flasks. Boxes, pipes, pipe bends, valve bodies and so on are cast using skeleton patterns.

10. **Segmental pattern** Segmental patterns or part patterns are used for circular castings such as gears, wheels and rims. Their use saves pattern material and at the same time avoids the need to handle bulky patterns. To make the mould, a vertical spindle is fixed in the drag flask and a segmental pattern is mounted on it. Moulding sand is rammed and the impression of the pattern is obtained on the mould. Subsequently, the impression of pattern is copied further by rotating the spindle to make the complete mould.

Pattern allowances As mentioned earlier, a pattern is a replica of the desired casting with minute dimensional differences to incorporate various allowances such as shrinkage, machining and rapping. These allowances are detailed as follows.

1. **Shrinkage allowance** Most metals contract or shrink during cooling (with some exceptions such as bismuth). The contraction in casting is of three kinds, viz., liquid contraction, solidifying contraction and solid contraction. The first two are compensated by proper design of gates and risers; the solid contraction is taken care of by making a correspondingly (slightly) bigger pattern, that is, by providing an adequate shrinkage allowance on the pattern. The amount of this allowance depends mainly on the metal being cast, although various other factors such as mould material, pouring temperature, moulding method, and the like may also influence it. Table 3.1 gives the shrinkage allowances for some common engineering materials.

Table 3.1 Shrinkage allowance for some metals

Metal	Cast iron	Steel	Brass	Aluminium	Magnesium
Shrinkage allowance (%)	0.8 to 1	1.5 to 2	1.5	1.0 to 1.3	1.0 to 1.3

All the dimensions are altered evenly for an unconstrained casting, but care must be taken in case of any restrained part in the casting. Although the contraction of metal is volumetric, shrinkage allowance is always expressed in percentage or as a linear measure, that is, as mm/metre and applied to all linear dimensions. Pattern makers normally use *shrink rules* (for different casting metals) that are longer than a standard rule by specific shrinkage allowances.

If a core is to be used to form an internal cavity or a hole, it should also be made oversized to compensate for shrinkage, as all the metal surrounding the cavity will contract, thereby making the cavity smaller.

2. **Machining allowance** Finishing or machining of sand castings is often essential because they generally have a poor surface finish and are not dimensionally accurate.

Moreover, scales (metal oxides) are found on the surface of ferrous castings. Thus, extra material is required to be provided on the casting, which means that the pattern has to be made oversized. The amount by which the pattern is made larger than the desired size of casting (to account for material removal while machining of casting) is called machining allowance. The amount of this allowance depends on the degree of finish required, method of machining, casting process, size, shape and material of casting and so on. In general, it is 3 mm on a sand cast surface. Die castings and investment castings are sufficiently smooth and require very little or no machining. The designer must keep in mind the casting process while providing finishing allowance and also remember that draft allowance may partly or completely provide the extra metal required for machining.

3. **Shake or rapping allowance** While withdrawing the pattern from the mould, it is rapped or shaken by striking it all around. This action facilitates easy removal of the pattern from the adjoining sand wall, but in the process of rapping, the mould cavity size enlarges and to compensate for the same, pattern size is reduced, that is, a negative allowance is provided on the pattern. However, this allowance is applied to only those dimensions that are parallel to the parting line.

4. **Draft allowance** All surfaces of a pattern that are parallel to the direction of pattern withdrawal are provided a small taper to facilitate easy removal of the pattern from the mould and to avoid damaging of the mould. This taper is known as draft allowance. If this taper is not provided, the friction between the pattern and the mould or any horizontal movement of the pattern during its withdrawal can damage the mould. The draft on internal surfaces of the pattern is always more than that on external surfaces.

    The amount of draft depends on the size and shape of the pattern, the pattern material, the method of withdrawing the pattern, the depth of the cavity, the mould material, and the moulding method. Draft allowance is expressed in terms of degrees or in linear measure. The average value of draft is between 1 and 2 degrees. By increasing the draft on a pattern, we will need to do less shaking of the pattern and hence, ensure less shake allowance. However, since draft allowances tend to increase the size of a pattern and thereby, the size and weight of a casting, it is desired that these are kept to the minimum so as to permit satisfactory pattern withdrawal.

5. **Fillet and radii** Fillet and radii are provided to round-off the corners where two surfaces meet at an angle. This facilitates smooth flow of molten metal in the mould and eliminates stress concentration at the corners of the casting. The radius of the round shape at the corners of the pattern should be ample without damaging the function and appearance of the component.

6. **Distortion allowance** Though not very common, distortion is sometimes observed in castings of irregular shapes, particularly on sections which have long flat portions such as T, L, V and U sections with long arms. The distortion appears in the form of the vertical leg being slightly inclined. This occurs mainly due to internal stresses on account of unequal cooling of different sections of the casting and also due to hindered

contraction. One way to overcome the distortion problem is to let the pattern of U, V, T or L shape have legs converging slightly inwards so that the casting, after distortion will have its sides vertical. Alternatively, distortion problem in castings can be prevented by the following methods:

- Modifying the design of the casting

- Providing sufficient machining allowance to cover the distortion effect

The amount of this allowance is best decided by the pattern designer, based on his or her experience.

7. **Special allowances** Special allowances are given depending upon the need. For example, if the mould is heated before pouring the molten metal, the mould dimension will change, for which the mould cavity dimensions have to be modified.

Figure 3.3 is an illustration of the application of various allowances.

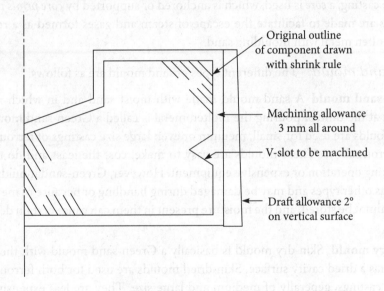

Figure 3.3   Application of various pattern allowances

Colour coding for patterns   It is a common practice to paint the pattern by adopting a colour code just to help the mould maker understand the use of various parts of a pattern. Painted wooden patterns have the additional advantage that they are protected against moisture. The following colour code is generally adopted.

Red: Surface to be machined

Black: Surface not to be machined

Yellow: Core prints

Red strips on yellow: Seats for loose pieces

No colour: Parting surface

3.2.3 Sand mould

A mould may be defined as a block of metal or a mass of refractory material, into which a cavity (of the size and shape of the desired product) has been made. The molten metal is poured into the cavity and allowed to solidify.

A sand mould can be defined as a mass of sand in which a pre-formed cavity exists. Molten metal is poured into the cavity and allowed to solidify to form what is termed as *casting*. The sand mould is destroyed after the casting is removed from it. Various features of a sand mould are illustrated in Figure 3.1(f). As shown, there are two flasks called the *cope* and the *drag*, which cover the cavity at the top and the bottom, respectively. Additional flasks may be used, if necessary. A *pouring basin* and a *sprue* are made so that molten metal when poured in the pouring basin will reach the runner and the gate system. This system helps the molten metal to enter and fill the mould cavity. Riser supplies the additional metal required to compensate for shrinkage and also indicates that the cavity has been completely filled. To form a hollow region in the casting, a *core* is used, which is anchored or supported by *core prints* made in the mould. *Vents* are made to facilitate the escape of steam and gases formed as a result of the contact of molten metal with moulding sand.

Types of sand mould   The different types of sand mould are as follows.

1. **Green-sand mould** A sand mould made with moist sand and in which moisture is present at the time of pouring the molten metal is called a Green-sand mould. Green-sand moulds are used for small, medium or even large size castings of ferrous as well as non-ferrous alloys. These moulds are easy to make, cost the least and do not require any baking operation or expensive equipment. However, Green-sand moulds are not as strong as other types and may be damaged during handling or because of metal erosion. They cannot be stored, and the moisture present in them can cause certain defects in the casting.

2. **Skin-dry mould** Skin-dry mould is basically a Green-sand mould with the difference that it has a dried cavity surface. Skin-dried moulds are used for both ferrous and non-ferrous castings, generally of medium and large size. They are less expensive to make than dry-sand moulds but more expensive than Green-sand moulds of a given size. They are not as strong as dry-sand moulds and cannot be stored for later pouring because moisture can migrate through the dry skin with the passage of time.

3. **Dry-sand mould** Dry-sand mould is a sand mould made entirely with sand. It uses a binder that does not require moisture to develop strength. Carbon dioxide setting sand mould is an example of this mould. Steel castings of small to medium size are mostly made with dry-sand moulds. Moulds made through this process are stronger; resistant to metal erosion, eliminate any possibility of moisture-related casting defects from occuring, and can be handled more easily. However, they are more expensive when compared to Green-sand or skin-dried moulds.

4. **Cement-bonded mould** Cement-bonded mould is a mould made of sand with Portland cement as binder. Dried in air, cement-bonded moulds are used for large-sized castings of steel, particularly when the pit moulding method is employed or where baking is not possible. Due to the use of slow air-drying system, more storage space is generally required.

Sand moulding methods Methods of sand mould making are as follows:

1. **Bench moulding** In bench moulding, the moulds are prepared on benches by the mould maker usually in a standing posture. This method is generally employed for small and light-weight castings of non-ferrous metals in Green-sand moulds.

2. **Floor moulding** In floor moulding, the floor itself is used as the drag and thus, only one flask is used. Sometimes, even the cope flask is not used, and runners and gating are made in the floor itself; the mould in this case is termed as an 'open mould'. Floor moulding is used for making large and medium size rough castings, where the surface finish is not very important or when the castings are difficult to mould otherwise. Normally, dry sand is used in floor moulding.

3. **Pit moulding** Here, the drag mould is prepared in a large pit that is dug in a square or rectangular shape in the floor and then lined with brick work or concrete. The bottom is particularly strengthened with concrete so as to be able to bear heavy metal pressure. A levelled bed is prepared at the bottom of well-rammed cinder to allow for the escape of gases. The cope is placed over the pit and moulding sand is rammed around the pattern and in the cope. Gates are cut in the cope after removing it. A crane may be used for lifting and positioning the cope over the pit. Pit moulding is used for very large-sized casting, when it is not feasible to prepare the mould in flasks.

4. **Machine moulding:** For mass production, manual moulding is neither economical nor efficient; hence, machine moulding is adopted. Though a number of operations such as ramming of sand, forming of gating system, withdrawing of pattern, rapping of pattern, and so on, can be performed with a machine, there are operations that do require human intervention.

   Sand moulding machines Hand moulding is suitable for large-sized castings, which have to be produced in small numbers. For mass production of relatively small-sized parts, it is necessary, from the economics' point of view, to use some mechanical aid or machine. The most important basic function performed by a moulding machine is the ramming or compaction of moulding sand. Mechanized mould making offers several advantages, such as greater and uniform strength of mould, greater production rate, less-skilled labour requirement, and better component dimensional tolerances.

   Mould making machines are basically of three types: (i) squeezing, (ii) jolting and (iii) sand slinging. Hardness isofirms of the mould achieved when ramming of mould is done by hand and by a machine is depicted in Figure 3.4. The following is a brief description of the different types of moulding machines.

Squeeze moulding machine utilizes pneumatic pressure for ramming the sand in the mould. The pressure is applied through a plate or a squeeze head, as shown in Figure 3.4(b). The moulding flask is placed on the match plate pattern; it is then filled with moulding sand, and a squeeze plate or platen, which is attached to the machine, is allowed to come on top of the moulding flask. The size of the squeeze plate is slightly smaller than the inside dimension of the moulding flask. A uniform pressure is applied on the plate by either moving it down inside the flask or by moving the match plate–flask assembly upwards. The moulding sand in the flask is compressed uniformly. The compactness of sand is highest at the surface of the plate and reduces towards the pattern [Figure 3.4(b)]. In order to achieve almost uniform compactness of sand around the pattern, the squeeze plate may be provided with contour. Sometimes, a diaphragm is used to obtain uniform sand compactness around the pattern [Figure 3.4(c)]. Both parts of the mould can be formed at the same time if the depth is not too great. This type of machine is useful for small castings where shallow flasks can be used, unless it is combined with jolting.

Jolt moulding machine provides jolts to the machine table. A match plate pattern is fitted to the machine table, on which a moulding flask is placed. Sand from a hopper fills the flask and the machine is started. The machine table (along with a pattern plate and sand-filled moulding flask) rises to a certain height and is allowed to free fall onto the base of the machine. This jolting action forces the sand to get compacted into the mould. The lifting and falling action is repeated till the required mould hardness is achieved. The sand near the pattern gets greater compactness compared to sand in the top layers [Figure 3.4(d)]. This type of moulding machine is useful for ramming when the pattern has many horizontal surfaces. The machine operation is quite noisy.

Sand slinger is a moulding machine in which particles of moulding sand are thrown on the pattern with a certain velocity (up to 50 m/s). The prepared moulding sand is picked up by elevator buckets from the sand bin and dropped onto the belt conveyor. From there it is made to fall on to rotating impeller blades and a high velocity is imparted to the particles. High speed particles are passed through a tube that is directed towards the pattern. In this way, the mould is prepared layer-wise with uniform ramming. The mould has uniform high hardness [Figure 3.4(e)]. The force of ramming is controlled by the speed of the impeller and the process is quite fast. This type of moulding machine is best adapted to components ranging from medium to very large size. Figure 3.5 shows mould hardness variation with flask depth for the three mould making methods.

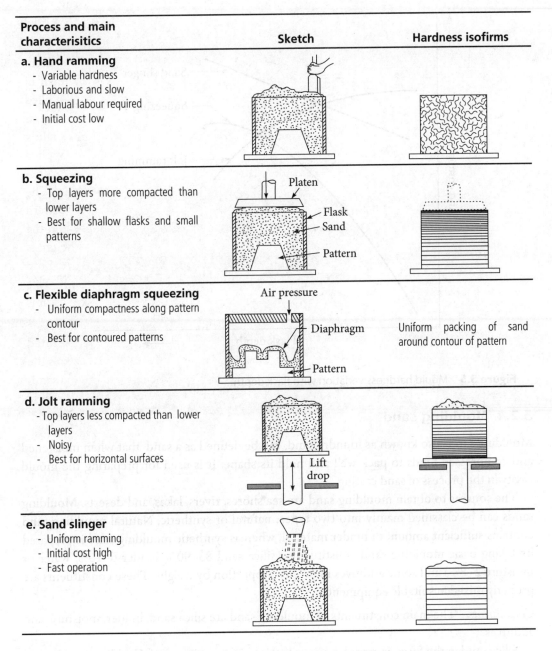

Process and main characterisitics	Sketch	Hardness isofirms
a. Hand ramming - Variable hardness - Laborious and slow - Manual labour required - Initial cost low		
b. Squeezing - Top layers more compacted than lower layers - Best for shallow flasks and small patterns	Platen Flask Sand Pattern	
c. Flexible diaphragm squeezing - Uniform compactness along pattern contour - Best for contoured patterns	Air pressure Diaphragm Pattern	Uniform packing of sand around contour of pattern
d. Jolt ramming - Top layers less compacted than lower layers - Noisy - Best for horizontal surfaces	Lift drop	
e. Sand slinger - Uniform ramming - Initial cost high - Fast operation		

Figure 3.4   Schematic of different mould making processes, their main characteristics and the hardness isofirms of the mould made by each process

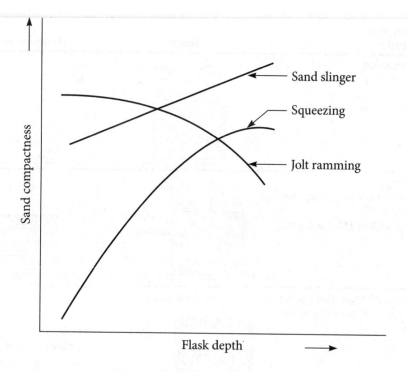

Figure 3.5   Mould hardness variation with flask depth

3.2.4 Moulding sand

Moulding sand, also known as foundry sand, can be defined as a sand that when moistened and compressed tends to pack well and hold its shape. It is used for preparing the mould cavity in the process of sand casting.

The sources to obtain moulding sand are sea shores, rivers, lakes, and deserts. Moulding sands can be classified mainly into two types: natural or synthetic. Natural moulding sand contains sufficient amount of binder material, whereas synthetic moulding sand is prepared by taking basic moulding sand constituents (silica sand 85–90%, binder 6–10%, water or moisture 2–8%) and some additives in proper proportion by weight. These constituents are properly mixed in suitable equipment.

Constituents   The main constituents of moulding sand are silica sand, binder, moisture and additives.

Silica sand in the form of granular quarts is the main constituent of moulding sand having enough refractoriness which can impart strength, stability and permeability to the moulding sand. Along with silica small amounts of iron oxide, alumina, lime stone ($CaCO_3$), magnesia, soda and potash may be present as impurities. The silica sand can be specified according to the size and the shape (angular, sub-angular and rounded) of the particles.

Binders can be either inorganic or organic substance. Binders included in the inorganic group are clay sodium silicate and port land cement. The clay may be Kaolinite, Limonite,

Bentonite, Ball Clay, or Fire Clay. Binders included in the organic group are dextrin, molasses, cereal binders, linseed oil and resins (such as phenol formaldehyde, urea formaldehyde etc.) Binders of organic group are mostly used for core making. Among the various binders, the bentonite variety of clay is the most commonly used.

Moisture content in the moulding sand varies from 2 to 8%. This amount is added to the mixture of clay and silica sand for developing bonds by filling the pores between the particles of clay without separating them. This amount of water is mainly responsible for developing the strength in the moulding sand.

To improve the moulding sand characteristics some other additional materials, known as additives, are added to the basic constituents. Some commonly used additives are coal dust, corn flour, dextrin, sea coal, pitch, wood flour, silica flour.

Coal dust is added mainly for producing a reducing atmosphere during casting process. This reducing atmosphere helps to avoid oxidation of the metal. It is usually added in the moulding sands for making moulds for production of grey iron and malleable cast iron castings.

Corn flour belongs to the starch family of carbohydrates and is used to increase the collapsibility of the moulding sand. It is completely volatilized by heat in the sand mould, thereby leaving space between the sand grains. This permits free movement of sand grains, which gives rise to mould wall movement and decreases the mould expansion and hence reduces defects in castings. Dextrin also belongs to starch family of carbohydrates that behaves also in a manner similar to that of the corn flour. Dextrin increases dry strength of the mould.

Sea coal is the fine powdered bituminous coal which positions itself among the pores of the silica sand grains in the moulding sand. When heated, sea coal changes to coke which fills the pores and is unaffected by water. Because to this, the sand grains become restricted and cannot move into a dense packing pattern. Thus, sea coal reduces the mould wall movement and the permeability in moulding sand and makes the mould surface clean and smooth.

Pitch is distilled form of soft coal. It can be added from 0.02 % to 2% in the moulding sand. Pitch enhances hot strength and surface finish on mould surfaces, and behaves exactly in a manner similar to that of sea coal.

Wood flour is a fibrous material that prevents the sand grains from making contact with one another. Wood flour can be added from 0.05% to 2% in the moulding sand. On heating, wood flour volatilizes thus allowing room to the sand grains to expand. Addition of wood flour increases mould wall movement and decreases expansion defects. Wood flour also increases collapsibility of the mould.

Silica flour, also called pulverized silica, can be added up to 3% to obtain increased hot strength and finish on the surfaces of the mould. It also reduces the metal penetration in the walls of the mould from making contact with one another. Wood flour can be added from 0.05 % to 2% in the moulding sand. Upon heating, wood flour volatilizes thus allowing room to the sand grains to expand. Additions of wood flour increases mould wall movement and decreases expansion defects in casting. Wood flour also increases collapsibility of the mould.

Silica flour, also called pulverized silica, can be added up to 3% to obtain increased hot strength and finish on the surfaces of the mould. It also reduces the metal penetration in the walls of the mould.

Characteristics of moulding sand   The characteristic requirements of moulding sand are as follows:

1. **Refractoriness** Refractoriness is the ability of sand to withstand high temperatures without breaking down or fusing. The degree of refractoriness depends on the SiO_2 content as well as the shape and size of the sand particles. The higher the SiO_2 content and rougher the granular structure of particles, the more the refractoriness.

2. **Permeability** Permeability is the ability of sand to permit easy escape of air, gas or moisture present or generated in the mould, when molten metal is poured in the mould cavity. Permeability is affected by the size and shape of sand particles, moisture and clay content in the moulding sand. The extent of ramming also affects permeability of the mould. If the sand is less permeable, that is less porous, the chances of the casting becoming defective increase.

3. **Green strength** Green strength of moulding sand refers to its strength when it is in a moist state. Green sand (i.e., moist sand) must have sufficient strength and toughness to permit making and handling of the mould. To achieve this, the sand should have good (i) *adhesiveness*, so that it clings well to the sides of the moulding box, and (ii) *cohesiveness*, so that upon taking out the pattern, the mould does not break or collapse. The green strength depends on the sand grain size and shape, type and amount of clay and the moisture content.

4. **Dry strength** Dry strength of moulding sand refers to its strength when in dried state. The sand of the mould gets dried when it comes in contact with the molten metal. This dry sand should have sufficient strength to prevent erosion of mould wall and enlargement of mould cavity due to metallostatic pressure of the liquid metal.

5. **Flowability** Flowability is the property of moulding sand due to which it behaves like a fluid; so that when rammed, it will flow all around and distribute the ramming pressure evenly in the mould. Flowability increases with decreasing green strength, reducing sand grain size and increasing moisture content.

6. **Collapsibility** Collapsibility is the ability of moulding sand to allow free contraction of the metal during solidification, thereby preventing tearing or cracking of the solidifying metal. This ability of sand also facilitates easy breaking of mould after the molten metal poured in it has solidified.

7. **Reusability** From an economical point of view, the moulding sand should be reusable.

Apart from the aforementioned properties, moulding sand should not react chemically with the metal. It should also not stick to the walls of the moulding box or to the casting.

Types of moulding sand   There are three main types of moulding sand: (i) Green moulding sand, (ii) CO_2 setting sand (dry sand) and (iii) core sand.

1. **Green moulding sand** Green moulding sand is the main type of moulding sand used in sand casting. (The term *Green* does not refer to its colour – it is actually black.) The main constituents are silica sand (SiO_2) about 90%, nearly 3% coal dust (which gives it its characteristic black colour), 6% clay and 3.5% water. Additives like molasses, wood flour and chromite are mixed with the sand to condition and enhance mould properties such as high heat transfer and low thermal expansion. Silica sand is mostly used due to the fact that it is inexpensive, has good permeability and other useful properties.

2. **Dry moulding sand** Dry moulding sand is also silica sand but instead of the use of any water-based binder, sodium silica binder is used. This binder chemically hardens when it comes in contact with CO_2. The mould is prepared in a similar fashion as Green sand mould but at a faster rate to avoid hardening of the mould due to the presence of CO_2 in the air. When CO_2 gas is passed through the mould, a much harder mould is obtained.

3. **Core sand** Core sand is used to make cores. It does not contain any water-based binder such as clay; rather, a resin binder is used that hardens with the application of heat. This makes the core stronger during the process of casting. In order to withstand the forces imposed by the molten metal during pouring, thin cores may be further strengthened by inserting reinforcement in the form of steel wires.

Testing of moulding sand Periodic testing of moulding sand is necessary because its properties can change by contamination from foreign materials. Contaminations in moulding sand are undesirable as they can affect the quality of the castings produced. A random representative sample of sand is taken by mixing all the three samples – taken one each from the front, centre, and rear of the sand heap, at a depth not less than 15 cm. Several tests can be performed on the representative sand sample. Some tests require a standard test specimen to be prepared from the sand sample while other tests do not have any such requirements.

Standard Sand Test Specimen Preparation Many characteristics of moulding sand depend to some extent on the degree of ramming; it is essential that the test specimen be prepared under standard conditions. A commonly adopted test specimen is a cylindrical one, 50.8 mm dia. × 50.8 mm long. A steel tube of 50.8 mm internal diameter closed at one end with a pedestal is taken for this purpose. A known amount (150 to 175 g) of sand is filled in the tube and a weight of 6 kg is allowed to fall on the sand three times from a height of 50 mm. The specimen thus produced has the standard dimensions. Depending upon the test to be performed, the test specimen may be retained in the tube or removed from it with the help of a stripping post already fitted in the test tube. If required, the specimen may be dried in an oven.

   Some or all of the following tests are conducted in quality-conscious foundries for the purpose of determining the properties of the moulding sand.

Clay content test This test determines the percentage of clay (by weight) present in the moulding sand. A 50 g sample of moulding sand in a dried state is placed in a mixing pot and treated with a standard solution of sodium hydroxide. After thorough washing, the residue is dried in a dryer (Figure 3.6) and then re-weighed. The amount by which the dried residue is less than 50 g is the measure of clay content in the sand. This can be expressed as per cent by weight.

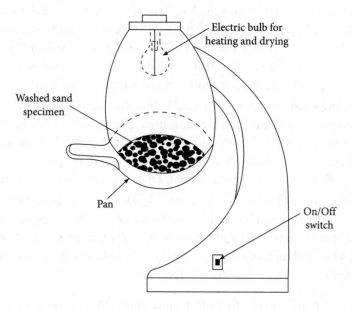

Figure 3.6   Dryer for removing moisture from sand sample

Grain fineness test   This test determines the percentage distribution of grain sizes in the sand. An apparatus consisting of a set of standard sieves (Figure 3.7) is used to perform this test. There are 11 sieves with different mesh sizes and a pan, as described in Table 3.2. The sieves are stacked according to mesh size with the sieve of AFS (American Foundrymen Society) mesh #6 at the top and pan at the bottom. The stack can be vibrated with a motor driven shaker.

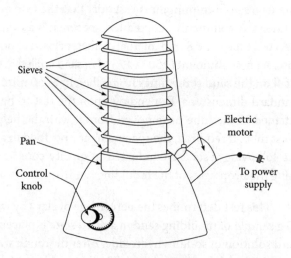

Figure 3.7   Test apparatus for determining sand grain fineness number

Table 3.2   Different sizes of sieves according to mesh size

AFS mesh number	6	12	20	30	40	50	70	100	140	200	270	Pan
Mesh opening (mm)	3.327	1.651	0.833	0.589	0.414	0.295	0.208	0.147	0.104	0.074	0.053	
Multiplier	3	5	10	20	30	40	50	70	100	140	200	300

To perform the test, a clay-free, dried-sand sample (say 100 g) is taken and placed on the coarsest sieve at the top. The shaker is then switched on. After 15 minutes, the shaker is switched off and the weight of the sand retained on each sieve and pan is carefully determined. These weights are converted to percentages. The American Foundrymen Society *fineness number* can be determined as

$$\text{AFS fineness number} = \Sigma\, P_i N_i \,/\, \Sigma P_i$$

where P_i is the percentage of sand retained at the ith sieve, and N_i is the multiplier for the ith sieve. This number indicates the average grain size and corresponds to a sieve number through which all the sand grains would have passed through, if they all were of the same size. This number is a useful index for comparing different foundry sands.

Example 3.1

A sample of 50 g of a sand was taken and placed on the top sieve of a standard stack of sieves in a shaker device. After shaking the sieve-set for 15 minutes, the amount of sand retained in each sieve and pan is given in the following table. Determine the AFS number of this sand.

AFS mesh number	6	12	20	30	40	50	70	100	140	200	270	Pan
Multiplier	3	5	10	20	30	40	50	70	100	140	200	300
Sand weight retained	0	0	2	3	2.5	5	6	5	14	4	3	5

Solution

First of all, it is necessary to find the retention of sand at each sieve in units of percentage of sand sample before the formula for AFS fineness number can be applied.

AFS mesh number	6	12	20	30	40	50	70	100	140	200	270	Pan
Multiplier	3	5	10	20	30	40	50	70	100	140	200	300
% Sand weight retained	0	0	4	6	5	10	12	10	28	8	6	10

AFS fineness number = $\Sigma P_i N_i / \Sigma P_i$

$$= [0 \times 3 + 0 \times 5 + 4 \times 10 + 6 \times 20 + 5 \times 30 + 10 \times 40 + 12 \times 50 + 10 \\ \times 70 + 28 \times 100 + 8 \times 140 + 6 \times 200 + 10 \times 300] / [0 + 0 + 4 + 6 + 5 \\ + 10 + 12 + 10 + 28 + 8 + 6 + 10]$$

$$= 102.3$$

Moisture content test   The requirement of moisture content in foundry sand varies according to the type of moulds being made and the metal being cast. In general, it varies from 2% to 8%. The apparatus used to determine the moisture content is called a moisture teller. It consists of an electric heating unit and a blower. A 50 g sample of sand is taken in a filter pan. Hot air from the apparatus is blown into the sample. After it is completely dried, the sand sample is weighed again. The difference between the initial and final readings gives the amount of moisture present. This can be expressed as the per cent by weight.

Permeability test   Permeability is an essential property of moulding sand by virtue of which it permits the escape of steam and gases. It is affected by a number of factors such as size and shape of sand particles, moisture content and binder content. Coarse-grained sand is more permeable, but when coarse grains are added to fine-grained sand, the permeability first decreases and then increases.

The permeability number of sand can be determined with the help of an apparatus (Figure 3.8) in which the time taken by a given quantity of air to pass through a standard sample of sand under standard conditions is noted. To conduct the test, a standard cylindrical specimen of sand (50 mm dia. × 50 mm length) is prepared and confined in a tube. Time (in minutes) is noted for 2000 cc of air at a pressure of 1 kPa to pass through the sample.

Permeability number $P = 50/t$, where t is time in minutes.

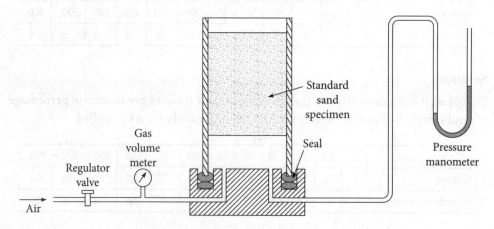

Figure 3.8   Test apparatus for determining permeability of moulding sand

Strength tests Strength of sand is a measure of the holding power of the binder in Green and dry sand. The usual practice is to measure the sand strength in compression and shear. A standard cylindrical specimen of sand (50 mm dia. × 50 mm length) is prepared and tested on a universal sand strength testing machine (Figure 3.9). The compression strength is obtained by applying a uniformly increasing load on the specimen until it fractures [Figure 3.10(a)]. The indicator on the dial of the machine directly shows the compressive strength. It is generally in the range 50 to 150 kPa.

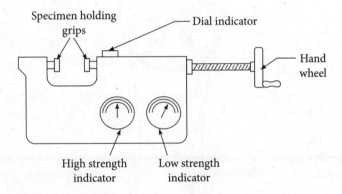

Figure 3.9 Universal sand strength testing machine

The shear strength test is carried out in much the same way and by changing the holding devices so that the load is applied on the upper half of the specimen at one end and on the lower half at the other end [Figure 3.10(b)]. The load is uniformly increased till the specimen fails. The shear strength of Green sand is generally in the range 10 to 50 kPa. The tensile strength of sand is determined on a different shaped specimen [Figure 3.10(c)], but on the same universal sand strength testing machine.

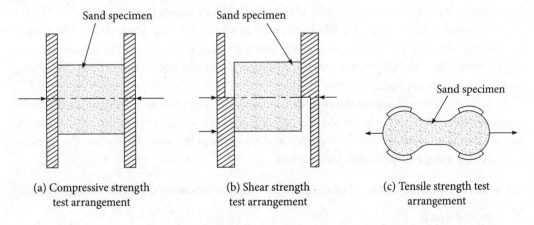

(a) Compressive strength
test arrangement

(b) Shear strength
test arrangement

(c) Tensile strength test
arrangement

Figure 3.10 Testing of sand strength

Hardness test The hardness test apparatus (Figure 3.11) uses a steel ball with a mass of 0.9 kg, which is indented into the standard specimen. The reading on the apparatus dial directly gives the mould hardness on a scale of 0 to 100. The reading 0 indicates sinking of the ball into the sand, that is, there is no hardness, while reading 100 indicates no penetration, that is, it is extremely hard.

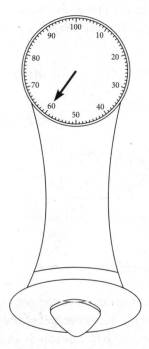

Figure 3.11 Moulding sand hardness test apparatus

3.2.5 Core

When metal is poured in a sand mould, all the empty spaces, where there is no sand and which are connected to each other, are filled with molten metal. If a hole is needed in the casting, we have to put a body of sand (called *core*) having the shape and size of the required hole at the location where the hole is needed. For instance, if a square hole is required in the casting, a sand mass (core) of square section would be placed at the desired location in the mould.

In order to correctly locate the core in the mould, and to prevent it from being displaced when molten metal enters the mould, the core is placed in specially recessed areas made in the mould. These recesses are called *core prints* and are made at the same time when the mould is prepared by using a suitably designed pattern.

Characteristics of core The core should have the following desirable characteristics.

• Be well dried.

• Be able to sustain the high temperatures of molten metal.

- Not react with molten metal nor generate any gas.

- Have a smooth outer surface to give a good finish to the casting.

- Have good permeability to allow escape of gases.

- Have adequate Green and dry strength to withstand the force of molten metal.

- Have good collapsibility to allow shrinkage in the casting during solidification; otherwise, a defect called *hot tears* can occur in the casting.

Types of core   Cores can be classified according to the sand used – *Green sand cores* and *dry sand cores*. Cores can also be classified according to their shapes and positions in the mould, as follows.

Horizontal core   A core of any size or shape, when placed horizontally in the mould, is called a horizontal core. Supported at the ends, it is held on the parting line in such a way that one half of it lies in the cope and the other half in the drag flask [Figure 3.12(a)].

Vertical core   A vertical core is held with its axis placed vertically in the mould and rests on the seats provided in the cope and drag flasks [Figure 3.12(b)]. The top end of the core is provided with more taper than the bottom end for easy fixing in the cope flask. Vertical cores are so positioned that a larger volume of it remains in the drag flask.

Balanced core   Horizontal and vertical cores are used to produce through holes only. A balanced core is used to produce a blind hole [Figure 3.12(c)]. Mounted horizontally, it is positioned as a cantilever with some over-hanging length; the amount of over-hang is kept equal to the depth of blind hole required. A long core print is provided to balance the over-hanging length of core. If over-hang is too long, the core is supported by means of chaplets. A balanced core is preferred when a casting needs an opening only on one side and only one core print is available on the pattern.

Hanging or cover core   A hanging core is one that hangs vertically in the mould without any support at the bottom. Obviously, the entire mould cavity will be formed in the drag only.

The core is fastened with a wire or rod that extends through the cope for fastening on the top side of the cope, Figure 3.12 (d). If supported on a seat provided on the parting surface in the drag, this core is called a *cover core*.

Saddle or drop core   When a hole in the casting is required to be produced at a position which is either above or below the parting line, then the core will have one of its portions inside the mould cavity and the other portion acts as a stop off [Figure 3.12(e)]. Such a core is called a *saddle core*.

Core making   The basic steps in core making are as follows:

   Core sand preparation   The core sand contains dry silica sand, binders and additives for achieving specific properties. Since the core has to be stronger than the mould,

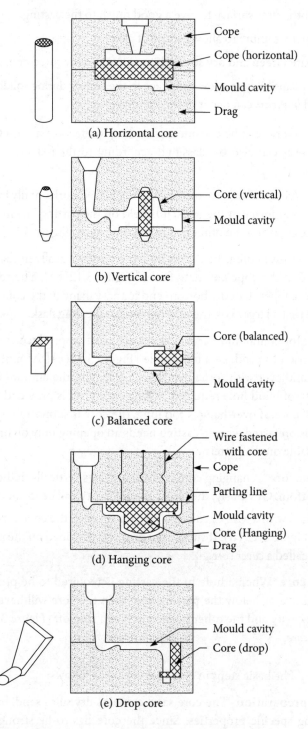

(a) Horizontal core

(b) Vertical core

(c) Balanced core

(d) Hanging core

(e) Drop core

Figure 3.12 Types of core

normal clay binders that are organic in nature are not used as they would burn away with the heat of the molten metal. The binders used are generally core oil, resins and molasses. Core oil is a mixture of linseed oil, fish oil, soya oil, petroleum oil and coal tar. The process of mixing the constituents is generally mechanized by using roller mills in order to achieve uniform and efficient mixing.

Core preparation Sand, when prepared using the aforementioned process is packed in a wooden or metallic die, called core box. The core box has the cavity of the size and shape of the core to be made. Different types of core boxes are used according to the need of the applications such as half core box, dumpy core box, split core box, loose piece core box, right and left hand core box. Cores thus prepared are baked in an oven.

Cleaning Cores taken out of the oven are cooled, cleaned and rubbed to obtain good surface finish and the required dimensions.

3.2.6 Chaplets

Chaplets are small metallic props (Figure 3.13) placed in the mould cavity to support big or uneven cores that cannot be supported at their own core prints.

Chaplets can be of flat or curved top surface depending upon the need. Chaplets of appropriate size and shape are taken and properly positioned between the mould surface and the core in such a way that the core gets proper support. Finally, when the chaplets come in contact with molten metal, they get fused with it and become part of the casting. It is, therefore, necessary that the material of the chaplets is the same or almost similar to the material of casting. Chaplets are cleaned thoroughly of dust, grease and so on, and dried before they are placed in the mould as they have to become part of the casting itself.

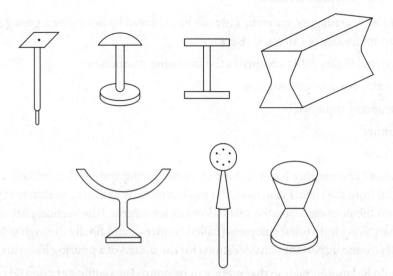

Figure 3.13 Some typical shapes of chaplets

3.2.7 Chills

Chills are metal inserts used to increase the solidification rate by carrying heat away from the solidifying metal at a rapid rate. They are placed in critical regions of the mould where either faster metal solidification is required for reducing shrinkage or for any other reason. They are usually made of the same material as of the casting and are left in the casting. Proper fusion of the chills with the casting can sometimes be a problem.

3.2.8 Gating and risering system

The gating system includes all the passageways through which molten metal enters the mould cavity while the riser is a reservoir attached to the mould cavity to compensate for the shrinkage of molten metal during solidification.

Gating system   The requirements of a good gating system are as follows:

- *Prevention of erosion of mould and core.* This can be achieved by designing a gating system that will provide low velocity of flow of molten metal as it enters the mould cavity.

- *Prevention of oxidation of molten metal.* This can be achieved by designing a gating system that will prevent turbulence in molten metal flow and thus aspiration of mould gases with the molten metal. Turbulence may be reduced by the following methods:
    - Use a sprue base well
    - Fill the mould from the lowest point upward
    - Avoid sharp directional changes of flow of molten metal
    - Use proper size of in-gate so that the mould is filled quickly and at the same time laminar flow is maintained

- *Prevention of wastage of material.* This can be achieved by designing a gating system that uses optimum size of gates and risers.

A gating system (Figure 3.14) comprises the following components:

1. Pouring basin or pouring cup
2. Sprue and sprue-well
3. Runner
4. In-gate

Pouring basin The pouring basin is the part of the gating system that initially receives the molten metal from the ladle. From here, the molten metal is delivered to different parts of the mould. From the pouring basin, the metal flows down a sprue (the vertical part of the gating system), then along horizontal channels (called runners), and finally through gates, into the mould cavity. Some important considerations for the design of a pouring basin are as follows:

- It should be large enough so that metal can be poured at a sufficient rate and cast quickly.
- It should be sufficiently deep.

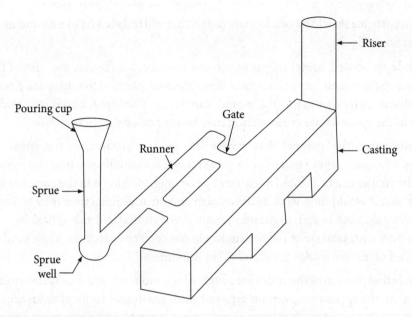

Figure 3.14 A typical gating system

- It should be located strategically so that the ladle can be brought near it and the metal poured easily.

Sprue and sprue-well Sprue is a vertical passage through the cope that connects the pouring basin to runners and finally to the in-gates. Some important aspects of sprue design are as follows:

- Size of the sprue: The size of a sprue decides the rate of metal flow; therefore, its size should be kept small so as to allow the metal to flow at less speed. At the same time, it should be large enough to fill the cavity properly and quickly without causing casting defects such as misruns. More than one sprue may be used for large-sized castings.

- Shape of sprue. The metal accelerates as it falls in the sprue, and due to the increase in velocity, the downstream part of the metal contracts. This contraction creates a partial vacuum between the mould walls and the metal stream, causing air aspiration in the metal stream. In order to prevent air aspiration, the sprue is made in a tapered shape instead of a cylindrical one so that the metal will not lose contact with the sprue walls and the air will not aspirate.

    The size of a sprue can be approximately estimated by using the following equation:

$$A_1 / A_2 = \sqrt{(Z_2 / Z_1)}$$

where A_1 = Cross-sectional area of sprue at the top

A_2 = Cross-sectional area of sprue at the bottom

Z_1 = Depth of metal in pouring basin

Z_2 = Distance between metal level in pouring basin and sprue base

- Sprue entrance should be of adequate radius that will reduce turbulence and increase the metal flow velocity.

- Provide sprue-well. Metal attains maximum velocity as it reaches the base of the sprue; also since there is an abrupt change in flow direction (vertical to horizontal), turbulence, which can cause damage to the mould, can occur. Therefore, a well is provided at the base of the sprue whose cross-section may be kept twice that of the sprue.

Runner   Runner is the channel that carries the molten metal from the sprue base and distributes it to one or more gates (or in-gates) made for metal entry into the mould cavity. Though the runner can be located in either cope or drag, locating it in the cope has the added advantage that it would then work as a riser also and no additional riser may be required. In case of casting aluminium and magnesium, runners are located in the drag flask because when such metals are cast, sand sinks and the runner in the cope can catch the loose sand. Runners may be tailed off to trap oxides, sand and other impurities.

In-gate   It is that portion of the runner through which molten metal enters the mould cavity. Depending on the application, various types of gates are in use; some of them are described here:

- **Top gate**   Here the molten metal flows down directly from the pouring basin into the mould cavity. The use of a top gate has the advantage that the hottest metal remains at the top of the casting and proper temperature gradients required for directional solidification are set up. On the other hand, the use of a top gate is also undesirable because it can result in erosion of the mould due to free falling of metal. Thus, when using the top gate, mould cavity needs to be hard and strong to resist the metal impact. Slit or pencil gate, wedge gate, top gate with strainer are some of the variations of the top gate.

- **Parting line gate**   These gates get their name from their location at the parting surface of the mould. They are simple in construction. These gates facilitate the use of *skim bob* (enlargement in the gating to trap slag or foreign material) and *choke* (contraction in gating to regulate metal flow rate). In cases where the mould cavity is deep at the bottom, these gates are not suitable since the metal has to fall from a considerable distance, which may cause erosion of the mould.

- **Bottom gate**   When bottom gates are used, the metal enters the mould cavity from the bottom and, thus, mould erosion and turbulence in metal flow are minimal. However, locating the riser at the entrance of bottom gates is difficult. Further, since the hottest metal is at the bottom, proper directional solidification of casting is difficult to achieve.

- **Step gate**   Step gates are used mainly to serve the need of directional solidification. Metal fed in the uppermost gate is the hottest; it loses heat and becomes less hot in successive gates, and finally, is least hot in the lowest gate. Therefore, use of step gates helps in hot metal being continuously fed at the top of the casting to facilitate directional solidification.

Risering system There are two main requirements of a good and effective riser.

- **Volume** It should have sufficient volume so that it
  - can feed metal to the solidifying metal in the mould cavity.
  - can provide enough feeding pressure.
  - solidifies only after the entire casting has been solidified. This will help to develop temperature gradients suitable for directional solidification.
- **Location** It should be located closest to the thickest section of the mould.

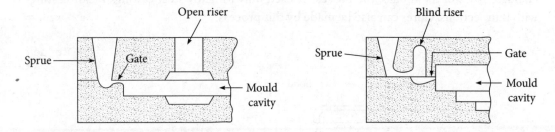

Figure 3.15 Types of risers

Types of risers Two types of riser are in use: *open riser* and *blind riser* (Figure 3.15).

- **Open riser** An open riser has its top surface exposed to the atmosphere. It is commonly placed at the topmost portion of the casting. Feeding pressure is developed due to atmospheric pressure and the gravity force on the metal contained in it. However, when a certain thickness of metal has solidified at its top, the effect of atmospheric pressure reduces.

- **Blind risers** A blind riser is surrounded by the moulding sand and is in the form of a rounded cavity. It may be located at the top or at the side of the mould cavity. Atmospheric pressure is ineffective since the end is closed. To make it more effective, a vent may be provided at its top, which extends to the top of the mould, thus allowing atmospheric pressure to exert some feeding pressure. A permeable dry sand core may sometimes be placed in this vent through which it is connected to the atmosphere.

3.3 Carbon Dioxide Mould Casting

Carbon dioxide mould castng is somewhat similar to Green sand mould casting with the difference that in this process, a much hardened mould is used. The dry silica sand is thoroughly mixed with 2% to 4% sodium silicate, an inorganic binder, which is a viscous fluid. The sand particles get coated with a thin film of the binder. The sand mix is packed around the pattern in a flask in the usual manner. It remains soft and mouldable until it is exposed to CO_2 gas, when it hardens in a fraction of a minute. The following reaction takes place.

$$Na_2SiO_3 + CO_2 \rightarrow Na_2CO_3 + SiO_2 \text{ (colloidal)}$$

The sand then becomes so hard that mould collapsibility, shake-out and core removal become difficult. Precautions are taken to avoid the carbon dioxide in the air from hardening the sand before the mould is complete. When molten metal is poured, the heat of the metal makes the mould even stronger. In some cases, additives that will burn out during metal pouring are added in the sand to improve collapsibility of moulds.

A schematic of the procedure involved in the carbon dioxide moulding process is given in Figure 3.16. Moulds are very hard but because of the costs involved and the use-only-once characteristics of the mould, the process is used only for alloy steel castings or for castings with thin sections. Cores can also be made by this process.

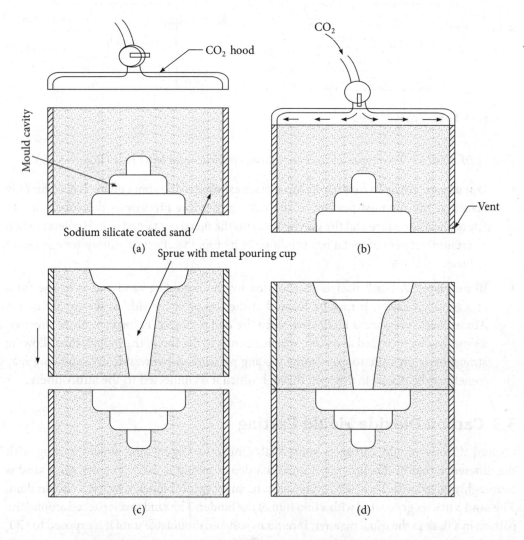

Figure 3.16   Steps involved in carbon dioxide moulding process

3.4 Shell Moulding

The shell moulding process was introduced in 1947 and was named after its inventor as the Croning process. It has been used since then for the production of components that require a high degree of accuracy and surface finish.

In this process, a pair of strong thin-walled shells, just about 5 mm thick, replaces the cope and drag of the normal sand mould. The shells are made from a mixture of dry silica sand and a thermosetting resin binder, which becomes hard when exposed to heat, and cannot be remoulded. When clamped together, the shells make up a mould, that is, produce an envelope whose internal cavity corresponds to the shape of the required casting.

3.4.1 Pattern for shell moulding

Patterns used in shell moulding process are made of metal since they have to be heated to a temperature that is about 200 – 300°C (melting point of resins). Since a hard shell is to be built around the pattern, ejector pins are provided on the pattern for the easy removal of the shell. Gate, runner and risers are also fabricated on the pattern so that these will be built in the shell.

3.4.2 Shell making procedure

The shell making procedure can be described step-wise as follows:

1. A metal pattern, attached to a pattern plate, usually made of cast iron [Figure 3.17(a)], is uniformly heated in an oven to nearly 200° C.

2. The pattern–pattern plate assembly is taken out from the oven and sprayed with a lubricant. It is then clamped onto the top of a container (called dump box). The dump box contains resin-coated sand [Figure 3.17(b)].

3. The dump box is rotated through 180° so that the coated sand falls on the hot pattern [Figure 3.17(c)].

4. By giving enough contact time, a partially cured layer (shell) of about 5 to 10 mm thickness is allowed to be formed around the pattern. The box is now rotated to its original position. The unused sand falls back to the bottom of the box while the shell (often called biscuit) remains sticking to the pattern [Figure 3.17(d)].

5. The pattern plate is de-clamped from the dump box. For the purpose of curing the resin completely, the pattern–pattern plate assembly is put in an oven at 350 – 400°C for 1 to 5 minutes, depending upon the thickness of the shell. Over-curing may cause the mould to develop cracks or even break, whereas under-curing results in low strength shells and may even cause blowholes in the casting.

6.   The pattern plate is removed from the oven and the shell is carefully stripped from the pattern using ejector devices [Figure 3.17(e)]. The shell is ready for use or for storage (for later use).

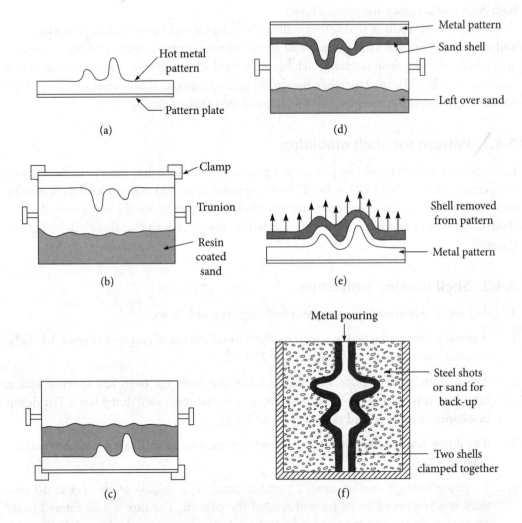

Figure 3.17   Shell moulding process: (a) Typical metal pattern with pattern plate; (b) Pattern–pattern plate assembly clamped onto the top of the dump box containing resin-coated sand; (c) Dump box rotated through 180° so that the coated sand falls onto the hot pattern; (d) Dump box rotated to its original position. The sand shell remains sticking to the pattern; (e) Sand shell carefully stripped from the pattern using ejector devices; and (f) Shell mould prepared by gluing two half-shells

When casting is to be done with shell moulds, the two half-shells are glued, clamped or wired together. The shell mould is now ready for pouring. Alternatively, for larger moulds, the shells are placed in a container and given outside support with cast iron shots or moulding sand [Figure 3.17(f)]. As the molten metal is poured into the shell mould, the heat of the metal burns off the resin binder slowly but the shells do not disintegrate until the metal has solidified enough to retain the shape of the casting during the cooling down process. Sand shells are then removed easily from the surfaces of the casting.

Advantages and disadvantages   Shell mould casting has the following advantages.

1.   The amount of sand used is quite small, only one-twentieth of the sand used in sand casting.

2.   Shell moulding can be easily adapted to mass production using automatic equipments that will require minimum skilled labour.

3.   Shell moulds can be kept for a long time because cured resins do not absorb moisture. This allows a more flexible production schedule to be followed.

4.   Shell moulds have relatively smooth walls, offering low resistance to the flow of molten metal and producing castings with sharper corners, thinner sections and smaller projections than are possible to achieve in case of Green sand moulding.

5.   As a result of the relatively smooth walls of shell moulds, castings with a very smooth surface can be obtained. A roughness value of the order of 3 to 5 microns is common.

6.   Use of cores is eliminated by forming internal cavities in the shell mould itself.

7.   Almost all metals can be cast by this process.

8.   Complex shapes can be produced by employing relatively less labour.

9.   Castings are more accurate and have closer tolerances. In most cases, tolerance values range between ± 0.20 to ± 0.35 mm.

10.   High quality of casting produced leads to savings on cleaning, machining and other finishing operation costs.

Shell mould casting has the following disadvantages.

1.   The sand used is very fine and therefore has lower permeability than the sand used in Green sand moulding. Further, the decomposition of the shell sand binder produces a high volume of gas; trapped gas can cause serious problems in ferrous castings.

2.   The size of the casting is generally a limitation. However, castings up to 500 kg can be shell moulded nowadays.

3.   The cost of pattern, resin, and other equipment is high. Generally, this process is economical only if more than 15,000 castings are to be produced.

Applications   Common applications include casting of small mechanical parts requiring high precision such as gear blanks, chain seat brackets, crank shafts (small), automobile transmission parts, cylinder and cylinder head for air cooled IC (internal combustion) engines.

3.5 Plaster Mould Casting

In plaster mould casting, the mould is made of plaster of Paris (gypsum or calcium sulphate). Various materials such as silica flour, lime, cement, glass fibres and talc are added to the plaster to improve the properties. Addition of talc and magnesium oxide helps to reduce the setting time of plaster and prevent cracking; cement or lime helps to control expansion during the process of baking; and silica flour or glass fibres help in enhancing both green and dry strength. The process involves the following steps:

1. **Pattern making**   The pattern is made of thermo-setting plastic, brass, zinc alloy, or aluminium alloy. Wood is not used as pattern material since the pattern might expand when it repeatedly comes in contact with water-based plaster slurry during usage.

2. **Plaster slurry making**   Gypsum is added to water in the ratio 1:1.6. Then, as the mixture is stirred, silica flour and other additives are added to the slurry. It is important to control the rate of mixing; slow mixing causes the slurry to harden prematurely while rapid mixing causes air entrapment in the slurry.

3. **Mould making**   A parting agent such as oil or grease is applied over the pattern surface. Plaster slurry is poured over the pattern and allowed to initially set in atmosphere, which may take nearly 15 minutes. The pattern is then carefully removed from the mould. The mould is dried in an oven at 150 – 250°C. The mould halves are then assembled to form the mould cavity soon after they are taken out from the oven.

4. **Casting**   Molten metal is poured in the hot mould cavity. Since plaster moulds have very low permeability, the gases produced during solidification of the metal cannot escape. It is essential, therefore, to feed the metal under pressure or in vacuum. Alternatively, an attempt can be made to increase mould permeability by some technique.

Advantages and limitations   Plaster mould casting has the following advantages.

1. Castings with as thin section as 1 mm can be cast.
2. Castings with minute surface details can be cast.
3. Castings have high dimensional accuracy.
4. Castings have excellent surface finish.
5. Castings have uniform grain structure.

Plaster mould casting process has the limitation that only low melting point non-ferrous metals and alloys (such as aluminium, magnesium, zinc and copper based alloys) can be cast by this process. This is because plaster mould can withstand temperatures only up to 1200°C. At higher temperatures, the plaster would undergo a phase transformation and then melt. The size of castings is generally limited to 5 kg.

Antioch mould casting   It is a variation of plaster mould casting and uses a mould material that consists of 50% plaster and 50% sand. The other operational details of this process are the same as of conventional plaster moulding. The main advantages of this process are greater mould permeability, relatively faster cooling of the casting and higher strength casting. The only limitation of this process is the relatively longer time needed to make the mould.

3.6 Ceramic Mould Casting

Ceramic mould casting process is similar to the plaster mould casting process, with the difference that ceramic mould is made of a refractory material, thereby making the mould suitable for casting ferrous and other high-temperature alloys. The commonly used mould material is a slurry consisting of fine-grained zircon $(ZrSiO_4)$, aluminium oxide and fused silica to which some bonding agents are added. The process of ceramic moulding involves the following steps:

1.   **Pattern making** The pattern may be made of wood, thermo-setting plastic, brass or aluminium alloy.

2.   **Slurry making** A mixture of fine-grained zircon $(ZrSiO_4)$, aluminium oxide and fused silica is prepared. Bonding agents are mixed thoroughly to the mixture to form homogeneous slurry.

3.   **Mould making** The pattern is placed in a flask. Some parting agent such as oil or grease is applied over the pattern surface. The slurry is poured over the pattern. Enough number of coatings of slurry is applied so that the mould (also called ceramic facing) is about 5 mm thick. After initial setting in the air, the ceramic facing is removed from the pattern and placed in an oven for drying and baking. The mould halves are clamped firmly as soon as they are taken out from the oven so that molten metal can be poured while the mould is hot.

     In another similar process, called the Shaw process, the assembled ceramic facings are placed in a flask. The empty space around the assembled facings is filled with fire clay as back-up material to give support and strength to the mould.

4.   **Casting** Molten metal is poured in the hot mould cavity. Stainless steels, tool steels and other ferrous alloys can be cast as the refractory moulding materials have high-temperature resistance.

Advantages, limitations and applications   It is possible to produce intricate shaped castings in a wide range of sizes weighing up to 500 kg. The castings produced have good dimensional accuracy and surface finish. The main limitation of this process is that it is relatively expensive. Typical parts made by this process are dies for metal working, dies for making plastic and rubber components, impellers and components of tanks and gas engines.

3.7 Investment Casting

The investment casting process uses a pattern that is usually made of low melting point wax (or it can also be made of plastic, such as polystyrene). A mould is prepared around the pattern and the pattern material is then melted out by heating before pouring the molten metal. The process is also known by other names: the lost wax casting process or the precision casting process.

The process involves the following steps:

1. **Pattern making** A metal die, usually of aluminium, having the cavity shape corresponding to the shape of the pattern is taken and molten wax is injected into it [Figure 3.18(a)]. When the wax solidifies, the die is opened and the pattern is removed. From economic considerations, it is a usual practice to make a gated pattern by assembling several wax patterns in a tree-like structure onto a central runner or sprue [Figure 3.18(b)]. Use is made of a heated tool called *spatula* for assembling wax gates and sprue to the wax pattern.

2. **Pattern investment** The multi-pattern assembly is covered in a permeable container [Figure 3.18(c)]. A fine ceramic based slurry known as *investment* is poured into the container [Figure 3.18(d)] while the whole assembly is given low frequency vibrations. (The name of the casting process is derived from this process). The fineness of the slurry is important as it determines the surface finish of the final castings. After this, the investment around the gated pattern is allowed to dry in the container itself. Alternatively, the gated pattern with a thin coating of investment on it is taken out and after drying of this initial coating, the pattern is re-coated many times with a coarse refractory powder until a coating thickness of 5 to 10 mm has been built up over the entire wax pattern assembly.

3. **Pattern melting and removal** After the investment has set around the pattern tree and dried, it is heated to a temperature of 100 – 150°C by holding it in an inverted position for the wax pattern tree to melt and run out (de-waxing), Figure 3.18(e).

4. **Investment hardening** The mould of investment material is fully hardened by placing it for about 2 hours in an oven at a temperature of 700 – 1000°C, depending on the metal to be cast. This also burns off any residual wax in the mould cavities.

5. **Metal pouring and fettling of castings** As soon as the mould is removed from the oven, the molten metal is poured into the hot mould [Figure 3.18(f)]. When solidified, the cast tree of the components is retrieved by breaking the mould made of the brittle investment material [Figure 3.18(g)]. Each component is then carefully cut from the tree and fettled.

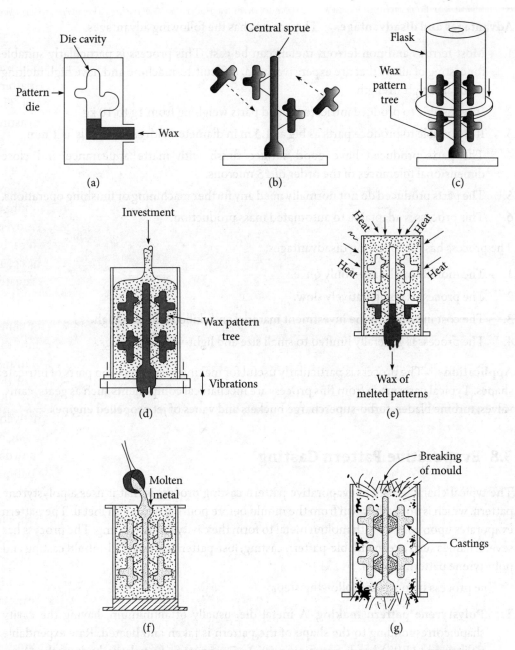

Figure 3.18 Investment casting process: (a) Wax injected into the cavity of pattern die to make a pattern; (b) Several patterns and gates made of wax joined to a central sprue; (c) A metal flask placed around pattern cluster; (d) Flask filled with investment slurry; (e) Wax patterns, sprue etc. melted out of mould; (f) Hot moulds being filled with molten metal; and (g) Mould material broken to obtain castings

Advantages and disadvantages   The process has the following advantages.

1.   Most ferrous and non-ferrous metals can be cast. This process is particularly suitable for casting of alloys that are expensive, hard, difficult-to-machine and have high melting point and high strength.

2.   It is possible to produce intricate shaped parts weighing from 1g to 10 kg.

3.   It is possible to produce parts as big as 1.5 m in diameter with as thin walls as 1 mm.

4.   The parts produced have good surface finish with matte appearance and close dimensional tolerances of the order of ±5 microns.

5.   The parts produced do not normally need any further machining or finishing operations.

6.   This process is adaptable to automated mass production.

The process has the following disadvantages.

1.   The moulds can be used only once.

2.   The process is comparatively slow.

3.   The cost incurred on the investment material and skilled labour is high.

4.   The process is generally limited to small size and light-weight castings.

Applications   The process is particularly useful for making small precision parts of intricate shapes. Typical parts made from this process are mechanical components such as gears, cams, valves, turbine blades, turbo-supercharge buckets and vanes of jet propelled engines.

3.8 Evaporative Pattern Casting

The typical characteristic of evaporative pattern casting process is that it uses a polystyrene pattern, which is not withdrawn from the mould before pouring of molten metal. The pattern evaporates upon contact with molten metal to form the cavity for the casting. The process has several names such as expendable-pattern casting, lost-pattern casting, full-mould casting and polystyrene pattern process.

The process involves the following steps:

1.   **Polystyrene pattern making**   A metal die, usually of aluminium, having the cavity shape corresponding to the shape of the pattern is taken and heated. Raw expendable polystyrene (EPS) beads containing 5% to 7% pentane (a volatile hydrocarbon) are introduced in the die. Upon heating the die, the polystyrene in it expands and takes the shape of the die cavity; more heat is applied to fuse and bond the beads together. The die is cooled and the polystyrene pattern is taken out. Complex shaped patterns are made by joining various individual pattern sections with adhesive. The runner, risers and feeding in-gate system, which are also made from polystyrene, are joined to the pattern with adhesive [Figure 3.19(a)].

2. **Mould making** The pattern together with the runner, riser and feeding in-gate system is coated with a water-based refractory slurry and dried. It is then placed in a one-piece moulding box. The space around the pattern is filled with loose fine sand, with or without bonding material [Figure 3.19(b)].

3. **Metal pouring** Without removing the polystyrene pattern, the molten metal is poured into the mould cavity [Figure 3.19(c)]. All polystyrene in the path of the metal flow de-polymerizes due to heat and the degradation products are vented into the surrounding sand. The cavity left by the vaporizing pattern is filled with molten metal.

4. **Metal solidification and production of casting** The metal flow velocity in the mould depends on the rate of degradation of the polystyrene pattern. It is usually in the range of 0.1 to 1.0 m/s. The velocity can be controlled by using a pattern having hollow regions in it. Since considerable energy is used to degrade the polymer, large thermal gradients are present at the metal–polymer interface affecting the metal fluidity. After solidification and cooling, the casting is taken out from the one-piece moulding box.

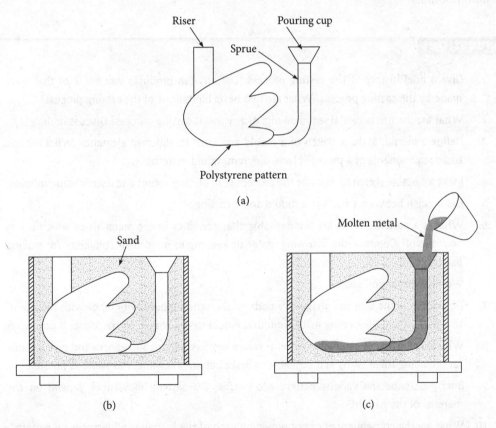

Figure 3.19 Schematic of evaporative pattern casting process: (a) Polystyrene pattern with sprue, pouring cup and riser; (b) Water-based refractory-coated dried pattern placed in a flask and filled with loose sand; and (c) Molten metal poured into the mould without removing the polystyrene pattern

Advantages and applications The evaporative pattern process has the following advantages.

1. The process is simple. There are no parting lines, cores or riser system.
2. The mould is simple and inexpensive.
3. The pattern material (polystyrene) is inexpensive and can be easily processed into patterns of any shape and size.
4. The castings produced are of high quality; thus, the cost of cleaning, machining and other finishing processes is low.
5. Almost all metals can be cast by this process.
6. Complex shapes can be cast by employing relatively less labour.
7. The process can be easily adapted to mass production using automatic equipment.

Typical applications of this process are for making crankshafts, brakes and other components of automobiles.

Questions

1. Give a brief history of the casting process. List any ten products you know of that were made by the casting process. What are two basic limitations of the casting process?
2. What are the fundamental requirements of any metal casting process? Discuss in detail.
3. Define a mould. Make a sketch of a mould and label its different elements. What are the basic requirements of a mould? Name different mould materials.
4. Make a suitable sketch to describe the procedure of placing sprues and risers in sand moulds.
5. Distinguish between a pattern, a mould and a casting.
6. What is a pattern? What are the desirable characteristics of the materials of which it can be made of? Compare the following materials keeping in mind their suitability for making patterns:
    Wood, Aluminium, Steel.
7. Do you think the size and shape of a pattern, the sand mould cavity made with the use of that pattern and the casting made from that mould cavity should be the same? If not, why?
8. Why are allowances given on a pattern? Name any five pattern allowances and give reasons for providing them. Why is it desirable to make pattern allowances as small as possible?
9. Briefly describe the various pattern allowances. Do pattern allowances depend on the material of the pattern?
10. What are the consequences of not providing each of the following allowances on pattern?
    a. Draft allowance   b. Shrinkage allowance
    c. Machining allowance

11. What is a shrink rule? Where is it used and why? When is it necessary to provide double shrinkage allowance?

12. Name the different types of patterns. Where would you use a split pattern? Give a typical example.

13. Give two examples of the castings for which you will prefer the use of (i) a sweep pattern, (ii) a gated pattern?

14. What are the requirements of a good gating system? Sketch a gating system and show its various parts. Explain the functions of different elements of the gating system.

15. Describe any four types of gates. Differentiate between runners and risers.

16. What is the main function of a riser? Give any five important characteristics of a riser. Explain the difference between an open riser and a blind riser.

17. In sand casting, the volume of the mould cavity takes up a certain proportion of the total sand volume. How is this proportion of mould cavity to total sand volume decided?

18. What are the essential properties of a moulding sand? Briefly explain them.

19. Select any component. Suppose a wooden pattern of this component is given to you and you are asked to prepare its mould in Green sand. Write the step-wise procedure of making the mould.

20. What is the function of a core? What are core prints? What is the relation between core and chaplets? Should the material of the core be the same as that of the chaplet? Give reasons for your answer.

21. What are the characteristics of core? Briefly explain the various types of core.

22. Give techniques by which you can (i) reduce core shifting and (ii) improve the surface finish of castings when expendable mould casting processes are used.

23. Discuss a method to speed up the mould making operation in the sand casting process. What factors determine the time at which the casting should be removed from the mould?

24. Name the various sand moulding machines and describe any one of them.

25. Discuss the differences in permeability of a mould when it is prepared using a jolting, squeezing and sand slinging machine. What differences can be expected in the casting surface due to change in the type of sand moulding machine?

26. Give the step-wise procedure for making a sand casting.

Fill in the Blanks

1. _____ is a model around which sand or any other moulding material is packed to get a mould.

2. Shrinkage in castings is of three kinds: _____ contraction, _____ contraction and _____ contraction.

3. Patterns made from _____ are susceptible to shrinkage and swelling.

4. Patterns made of _____ are usually used in machine moulding.

5. Patterns made of _____ are light in weight, durable and resistant to wear, water and corrosion.

6. Patterns made of _____ are used in investment casting.

7. For mass production of small castings, _____ patterns are mostly used.

8. _____ and _____ are provided on the pattern to facilitate easy flow of molten metal in the mould and eliminate stress concentration at corners of the casting.

9. Expendable moulds are mostly made of _____.

10. _____ functions to supply the additional metal required to compensate for shrinkage and also signals that the cavity has been completely filled up.

11. _____ is used to form a hollow region in the casting.

12. Core is anchored or supported by _____ made in the mould.

13. _____ are provided to remove steam and gases formed as a result of molten metal contact with moulding sand.

14. _____ is the property of moulding sand to withstand high temperatures without breaking down or fusing.

15. _____ is the property of moulding sand to behave like fluid so that when rammed it will flow all around and distribute the ramming pressure evenly in the mould.

16. The property of moulding sand by virtue of which it allows free contraction of the metal during solidification thereby preventing tearing or cracking of the solidifying metal is known as _____.

17. Mould making machines are basically of three types: (i) _____, (ii) _____ and (iii) _____.

18. Core is correctly located in the mould in recesses called _____.

19. _____ are small metallic pieces used to support big and uneven cores which cannot be supported by their own core prints in the mould.

20. _____ are metal inserts placed at critical regions in the mould to increase the solidification rate by carrying heat away from the solidifying metal at a more rapid rate.

21. In general, moisture content in Green sand varies from _____% to _____ %.

22. _____ is located at the top portion of a mould, into which molten metal from ladles is poured to reach different parts of the mould.

23. Sprue entrance should be given adequate radius which will reduce _____ and increase _____ of molten metal.

24. _____ takes the molten metal from the sprue base and distributes it to one or more gates made for molten metal entry into the mould cavity.

Choose the Correct Answer

1. An expendable mould casting process that employs single-use pattern is
   a. investment casting.
   c. ceramic mould casting.
   b. plaster mould casting.
   d. die casting.

2. Which one of the following is not a moulding process?
   a. green sand moulding
   c. plaster moulding
   b. red sand moulding
   d. carbon dioxide moulding

3. Compared to many casting processes, the dimensional accuracy and surface finish of the parts produced by sand casting process is
   a. poor.
   c. very good.
   b. good.
   d. excellent.

4. The surface finish of components produced by sand casting is generally in the range of
   a. 0.1 to 1 micron.
   c. 50 to 100 microns.
   b. 10 to 20 microns.
   d. 100 to 200 microns.

5. A pattern is
   a. a duplicate of the part to be cast.
   b. a cavity made in the sand in which molten metal is poured.
   c. the part produced when molten metal is poured and allowed to cool in a cavity made in the sand.
   d. the details of the markings made on the casting.

6. For large size casting, the pattern material preferred is
   a. ceramics.
   c. metal.
   b. rubber.
   d. wood.

7. For large-scale production of components, use is made of moulding machines that employ which one of the following pattern materials?
   a. wax.
   c. metal.
   b. plastics.
   d. wood.

8. In investment casting, the pattern is made of
   a. wax.
   c. plaster of Paris.
   b. plastics.
   d. ceramics.

9. Which of the following materials is generally not used for fabrication of patterns?
   a. cement concrete.
   c. aluminium.
   b. wood.
   d. plaster of Paris.

10. Wood is the most commonly used pattern material because
    a.   it is weak compared to metal.
    b.   it is susceptible to shrinkage and swelling.
    c.   it has high wear resistance.
    d.   it has good workability.

11. Patterns made from wax or frozen mercury are used in
    a.   investment casting.   c.   die casting.
    b.   centrifugal casting.   d.   continuous casting.

12. For axi-symmetrical or prismatic castings, it is economical to use a
    a.   gated pattern.   c.   sweep pattern.
    b.   match plate pattern.   d.   cope and drag pattern.

13. Which of the following is not a type of pattern?
    a.   gated pattern   c.   sweep pattern
    b.   match plate pattern   d.   orthogonal pattern

14. Patterns which have very complex contours can cause difficulty while withdrawing them from mould. Such patterns are often made as
    a.   gated patterns.   c.   loose piece patterns.
    b.   match plate patterns.   d.   cope and drag patterns.

15. In order to enhance the productivity of mould making, when gating and runner system is made in the pattern itself, the pattern is called
    a.   gated pattern.   c.   skeleton pattern.
    b.   match plate pattern.   d.   runner and riser pattern.

16. Pattern makers normally use *shrink rule*, which is
    a.   longer than a standard rule by specific shrinkage allowances.
    b.   shorter than a standard rule by specific shrinkage allowances.
    c.   standard rule that shrinks due to heat of the molten metal.
    d.   standard rule with Vernier scale marked on it.

17. When a core is to be used to form an internal cavity or a hole, it should be made
    a.   equal to the size of the hole or cavity desired.
    b.   undersized to compensate for shrinkage.
    c.   oversized to compensate for shrinkage.
    d.   undersized or oversized, depending upon whether it is circular or non circular.

18. Which of the following materials is not used for pattern making?
    a.   mica   c.   wood
    b.   wax   d.   plaster of Paris

19. Draft allowance is given to a pattern to
    a. facilitate improving the surface finish of casting.
    b. facilitate easy removal of pattern from the mould without damaging it.
    c. facilitate easy flow of molten metal in the mould and eliminate stress concentration at the corners of the casting.
    d. make it strong and wear resistant.

20. Which one of the following is the negative allowance given to a pattern?
    a. draft
    b. fillet and radii
    c. shake or rapping
    d. shrinkage

21. In order to form a hollow region in the casting,
    a. pattern is placed in the mould.
    b. pattern is given allowances.
    c. pattern is made hollow.
    d. core is placed in the mould.

22. Pitch obtained as a by-product of coke is used in moulding sand for improving its
    a. hot strength.
    b. green strength.
    c. permeability.
    d. dry strength.

23. The typical identification of chromite sand is its colour, which is
    a. white or light brown.
    b. greenish gray.
    c. black.
    d. white brown.

24. The clay material having highest dry compressive strength is
    a. calcium carbonate.
    b. calcium bentonite.
    c. sodium bentonite.
    d. fire clay.

25. Normal percentage of moisture content in Green moulding sand is
    a. 2 to 8.
    b. 10 to 15.
    c. 16 to 20.
    d. 20 to 25.

26. Grain fineness number of sand is an indicator of
    a. maximum grain size.
    b. minimum grain size.
    c. average grain size.
    d. ratio of minimum grain size to maximum grain size.

27. With increase in the grain size of sand, the refractoriness of moulding sand
    a. increases.
    b. decreases.
    c. first increases and then decreases.
    d. is not affected.

28. Saw dust or wood flour is added as additive to the moulding sand to
    a. increase density of moulding sand.
    b. increase hot strength.
    c. decrease metal penetration.
    d. decrease expansion defect in casting.

29. Mould wash is applied after removal of pattern from the mould in order to
    a.   prevent metal penetration.
    c.   clean the mould.
    b.   remove impurities from mould.
    d.   increase the strength of mould.

30. Which of the following acts as a reservoir to supply the additional metal required to compensate for shrinkage and also signals that the mould cavity has been completely filled up?
    a.   sprue
    c.   runner
    b.   gate
    d.   riser

31. Which of the following helps to remove steam and gases formed as a result of molten metal contact with moulding sand?
    a.   riser
    c.   gating system
    b.   vents
    d.   core prints

32. Core is anchored or supported in the mould at
    a.   core box
    c.   core vents
    b.   core prints
    d.   core flats

33. Which one of the following is not the basic requirement of moulding sand?
    a.   permeability
    c.   red strength
    b.   green strength
    d.   dry strength

34. Which one of the following is not the basic requirement of moulding sand?
    a.   flowability
    c.   collapsibility
    b.   permeability
    d.   red strength

35. *Chaplets* are small metallic pieces
    a.   which are formed when castings are cleaned with chisels and other sharp tools.
    b.   which are introduced in the castings to improve their strength and ductility.
    c.   which are used to decrease the solidification rate of molten metal in the mould.
    d.   which are used to support big and uneven cores in the mould.

36. *Chaplets* are small metallic pieces
    a.   placed in the mould cavity to support big and uneven cores which cannot be otherwise supported.
    b.   dropped in the molten metal in order to remove gases from it.
    c.   placed properly in the core to increase its strength.
    d.   used for making small holes in the sand mould for the escape of hot gases.

37. Which of the following is not a type of core?
    a.   horizontal core
    c.   follow board core
    b.   vertical core
    d.   hanging core

38. A balanced core is used to produce
    a.   blind cavity in the casting.
    c.   blowholes in the casting.
    b.   through hole in the casting.
    d.   spherical casting of high quality.

39. Which one of the following is not used as a binder in the preparation of core sand?

    a. core oil

    b. linseed oil

    c. vegetable oil

    d. molasses

40. Chills are small size metal inserts used to

    a. make small holes in the sand mould for the escape of hot gases.

    b. support big and uneven cores that cannot be otherwise supported.

    c. increase the fluidity of molten metal.

    d. increase the solidification rate by carrying heat away from the solidifying metal at a more rapid rate.

41. Erosion of mould and core can be prevented by

    a. designing the gating system that uses optimum size of gates and risers.

    b. providing low velocity of flow of molten metal as it enters the mould cavity.

    c. providing sharp directional changes of flow of molten metal.

    d. using proper size of in-gate so that mould is filled quickly and at the same time molten metal flow is turbulent.

42. For heavy and large size casting, the gating system used is

    a. step gate.

    b. bottom gate.

    c. parting gate.

    d. top gate.

43. For deep moulds, it is recommended to use

    a. top gate.

    b. bottom gate.

    c. parting gate.

    d. step gate.

44. Top gates are not used for castings to be made of

    a. steel.

    b. steel alloys.

    c. cast iron.

    d. non-ferrous alloys.

45. The insulation provided at the top of an open riser is generally made up of

    a. plaster of Paris.

    b. glass.

    c. wood.

    d. asbestos sheet.

46. Which one of the following does not form a part of the gating system?

    a. pouring basin.

    b. sprue and sprue base well.

    c. runner.

    d. riser.

47. If A_1 = Area of sprue at entrance; A_2 = Area of sprue at base; Z_1 = Depth of metal in pouring basin; and Z_2 = Distance between metal level in pouring basin and sprue base, which of the following equations can determine the size of the sprue?

    a. $A_1/A_2 = \sqrt{(Z_2/Z_1)}$

    b. $A_1/A_2 = (Z_2/Z_1)$

    c. $A_1/A_2 = (Z_1/Z_2)$

    d. $A_1/A_2 = \sqrt{(Z_2 \times Z_1)}$

48. Sprue is made tapered because tapering
    a. gives greater strength.
    b. maintains constant velocity of molten metal.
    c. prevents air aspiration.
    d. regulates flow of molten metal.

49. Sprue base well is provided at the end of sprue to
    a. reduce erosion of mould cavity.
    b. supply molten metal during solidification.
    c. prevent slag inclusion.
    d. increase its strength.

50. Which one of the following is not a type of gate?
    a. top gate
    b. bottom gate
    c. laminar gate
    d. parting line gate

51. The main advantage of using carbon dioxide moulding is that
    a. gases can be made to escape more easily.
    b. much hardened mould is obtained.
    c. gases formed react with carbon dioxide to form a colloidal solution.
    d. carbon % in the molten metal can be increased.

52. Permeability of moulding sand refers to its property by which
    a. it can withstand high temperatures.
    b. it allows escape of air or gas.
    c. it behaves like fluid so that when rammed, it will flow all around.
    d. it allows free contraction of the metal during solidification,

53. In squeeze moulding machine, the
    a. sand in the mould is rammed by applying uniform pressure with the help of a plate,
    b. compactness of sand is lowest at the surface of the plate while it increases towards the pattern,
    c. metal in the mould is introduced under pressure,
    d. machine table is vibrated so that the mould is squeezed,

54. The sand is sprayed with great force in which type of machine moulding?
    a. jolting
    b. jolt squeezing
    c. squeezing
    d. sand slinging

55. Sand slingers are moulding machines in which
    a. metal in the mould is introduced under pressure,
    b. carbon % in the molten metal can be increased,

c.   the machine table is jolted to obtain uniform compactness of sand,

d.   particles of moulding sand are thrown on the pattern with a certain velocity,

56. In carbon dioxide moulding, the binder material used in the moulding sand is

a.   sodium silicate,   c.   dextrin,

b.   sodium carbonate,   d.   molasses,

57. To prevent slag and dirt from entering mould cavity, the pouring basin is provided with

a.   sprue,   c.   skim core,

b.   on–off valve,   d.   strainer core,

Answers

1. a.	2. b.	3. a.	4. b.	5. a.	6. d.	7. c.	8. a.	9. a.	10. d.
11. a.	12. c.	13. d.	14. c.	15. a.	16. a.	17. c.	18. a.	19. b.	20. c.
21. d.	22. a.	23. c.	24. c.	25. a.	26. c	27. a.	28. d.	29. a.	30. d.
31. b.	32. b.	33. c.	34. d.	35. d.	36. a.	37. c.	38. a.	39. c.	40. d.
41. b.	42. a.	43. b.	44. d.	45. d.	46. d.	47. a.	48. c.	49. a.	50. c.
51. b.	52. b.	53. a.	54. d.	55. d.	56. a.	57. c.			

4

Permanent Mould Casting Processes

LEARNING OBJECTIVES

After reading this chapter, you should be able to understand the following:

- Die casting: process and its types – gravity die casting and pressure die casting.

- Die casting machines – hot chamber and cold chamber machines.

- Centrifugal casting: process and its different variants; advantages, limitations and applications.

- Slush casting: process and applications.

- Squeeze casting: process and its advantages/applications.

- Continuous casting: process and its advantages/applications.

One thing common among all the expendable mould casting processes described in the previous chapter is that all of them require a new mould for every casting. Such a wasteful proposition is acceptable if only a limited number of identical parts are to be produced; but when parts are required in large quantities, great savings can be made and are actually made by using moulds that are re-usable again and again, that is, permanent moulds, or dies.

The question arises as to what the permanent mould should be made of so that it is able to withstand the melting point of metals. For casting of non-ferrous metals and cast iron (melting point up to 1200°C), we use dies made of steel. In case of casting of cast iron, frequent smoothing (redressing) of the die profile is necessary. For casting of steels (melting point nearly 1550°C), we use graphite dies, although machining of complex profiles in graphite dies is difficult. For this reason, non-ferrous die casting is much more common than steel die casting.

4.1 Die Casting Process

The die casting process uses a reusable mould, that is, a metallic die and, therefore, it is classified as a permanent mould process. The gating and riser systems are machined into the die itself and in order to produce internal cavities in the casting, metallic or sand cores are placed in the die. The molten metal is introduced into the die under the force of either gravity or an external pressure. Hence, the die casting process is of two types: *gravity die casting* and *pressure die casting*.

Die casting process is suitable for the production of components in large quantities at low cost. Depending upon the metal to be cast, the pressure die casting process uses any of the two types of die casting machines – cold chamber die casting machine or hot chamber die casting machine. The only difference between the two is that in case of the hot chamber die casting machine, the metal melting furnace is an integral part of the machine, while it is not so in the case of the cold chamber die casting machine.

4.1.1 Gravity die casting process

Gravity die casting is the simplest form of die casting process in which a reusable mould is used. The two halves of the mould are preheated and clamped shut against each other under a heavy clamping force. The mould cavity is filled with molten metal flowing under gravity. After solidification has taken place, the mould is opened and the casting is taken out. For the next casting, the mould halves are again reclosed, and the metal is poured as the heat from the previous cast is generally sufficient to maintain the required mould temperature.

Most commonly cast nonferrous alloys are of aluminium due to their low melting point. Alloys of magnesium, lead, tin, zinc and copper can also be cast by this process. For casting of iron and steel, graphite is used as the mould material but the mould life tends to be very short.

Mould Material for the mould depends upon the material to be cast. Generally, a mould is made of alloy steel because of its excellent refractory properties and good resistance to erosion. Fine grained gray cast iron and Mehanite with large graphite flakes have also been used because these materials are easy to machine and have high resistance to thermal shock. Moulds can also be made of aluminium alloys with an anodized surface because anodizing yields Al_2O_3, which is highly refractory and resistant to abrasion. Aluminium alloys have better chilling properties and are easy to machine.

The mould life is short due to thermal fatigue and erosion by the molten metal. The following parameters affect the mould life.

1. **Material of the mould** The greater the resistance of the mould material to thermal fatigue, the greater is the mould life.

2. **Temperature of the mould** The larger the temperature differential between the mould and the pouring metal, greater will be thermal shocks in the mould material and shorter the mould life.

3.   **Material being cast**   The higher the melting point of the cast metal, the shorter is the mould life

4.   **Pouring temperature**   The higher the pouring temperature, the shorter is the mould life.

To increase the life of a mould, the face of the cavity is generally coated with some refractory material that performs the following functions:

• It minimizes thermal shock to the die surface.

• It prevents sticking of molten metal on the die surface.

• It controls the rate and direction of metal solidification.

• It serves as a parting agent.

• It fills up surface imperfections, if any.

The mould material offers no collapsibility to compensate for shrinkage of the casting. A common practice followed to circumvent this problem is to open the two halves of the mould and remove the casting as soon as solidification is complete. Also, as the mould material offers no permeability, provision is made for the escape of trapped air by forming very fine vent holes between the mould halves.

Directional solidification of castings can be promoted either by selectively heating or chilling various portions of the mould or by varying the thickness of the mould wall. Solidification can also be controlled by varying the coating thickness; for portions of casting where slow solidification is required (such as runners, risers, sprue and thin sections), the thickness of coating on the mould wall is increased.

As the flow of the molten metal into the mould cavity is due to gravity, risers are provided in the mould to compensate for shrinkage. Cores made of either sand or retractable metal can be used to create hollow regions in the castings. Mould life is usually of the order of 30,000 shots.

Advantages   Compared to sand casting, permanent mould casting has the following advantages.

1.   The components have closer dimensional accuracy (within 0.25 mm).

2.   The components have better surface finish (of the order of 4 microns) and closer tolerances.

3.   The components have better mechanical properties and fewer defects.

4.   The components are fine grain structured, sound and strong.

5.   The components can have directional solidification either by selectively heating or chilling different regions of the mould or by varying the thickness of the mould walls.

6.   The requirement of floor space is quite less.

7.   The requirement of skilled labour is quite less.

Limitations   The main limitations of the gravity die casting process are as follows:

1.   Uneconomical process for small quantity jobs due to high cost of die.
2.   Maximum size of casting is limited to a casting of about 50 kg due to limitation of the equipment size.
3.   Yield rate is low – seldom beyond 60%.
4.   Mould life is low, particularly when casting high melting point metals such as steel.
5.   Chilling effect of the metal moulds creates metallurgical and stress problems.
6.   Highly complex castings are difficult to obtain due to the difference in contraction of rigid mould and that of molten metal.
7.   All alloys cannot be gravity die cast.

4.1.2 Pressure die casting process

Pressure die casting is so widely used that it is common to refer to the process as *die casting* – the word *pressure* is omitted. The process uses a permanent mould, called die, and molten metal is introduced into it under the influence of an external pressure. Depending upon the magnitude of the pressure used, this process can be classified into low pressure die casting and high pressure die casting.

Low pressure die casting process

In the low pressure die casting process, a metal die is mounted over a sealed induction furnace [Figure 4.1(a)]. An inert gas under pressure is applied to force the molten metal in the furnace to rise up in the heated refractory *stalk* and fill the die cavity [Figure 4.1(b)]. As the solidification of metal in the die is completed, the inert gas supply is stopped, the die halves are made to separate and the casting is removed [Figure 4.1(c)]. Vacuum pumps are used to remove the entrapped air from the die and facilitate faster die filling. Small castings may be cooled in the die itself for a minute or less, but castings weighing up to 20 kg may need a cycle time of nearly 3 minutes.

Castings produced are dense. They have good dimensional accuracy and surface finish. The scrap rate is extremely low. The process is generally economical if the production rate is 10,000 parts per year or more.

High pressure die casting process

In the high pressure die casting process, the pressure is exerted either hydraulically or through a pneumatically operated piston–cylinder arrangement. The high pressure allows the production of narrow sections and complex shapes with fine surface details. A complete cycle comprises closing and clamping the two halves of the die, injecting molten metal under pressure into the die, opening the die after the metal is solidified and ejection of casting.

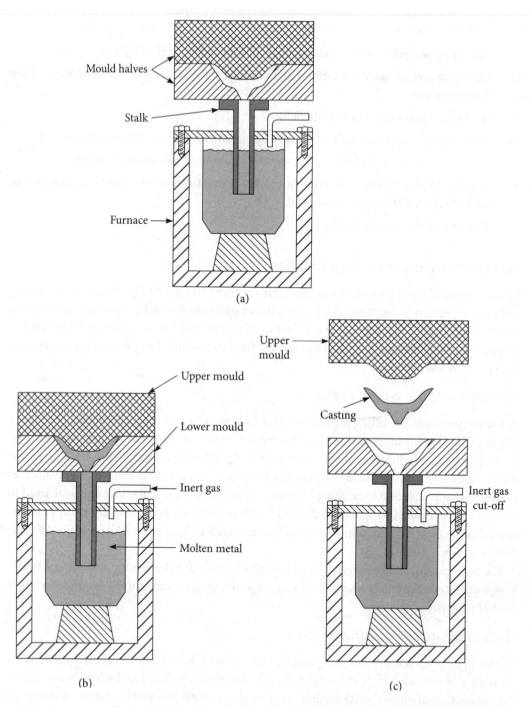

Figure 4.1 Schematic of low pressure die casting process: (a) Dies in closed position; (b) Metal injected into the mould cavity by inert gas pressure; and (c) Dies opened and casting taken out

Die Casting Machines

High pressure die casting is done on a machine. There are two types of machines: the *hot chamber* and the *cold chamber* die casting machines. A hot chamber die casting machine has an inbuilt metal melting furnace within the machine and is used for casting low melting point alloys. The cold chamber die casting machine uses a separately installed furnace for melting the metal; molten metal is brought in a ladle to the die casting machine for pouring. High melting point materials are generally die cast with the help of a cold chamber machine.

Hot Chamber Machine The essential parts of a hot chamber die casting machine are a container for the molten metal, a heating chamber, an arrangement to force the metal into the die, a mechanism for opening and closing dies and a mechanism for ejecting the casting. Two models of hot chamber machines are popular: (i) Hydraulically operated plunger type machines [Figure 4.2(a)] in which pressure of the order of 35 MPa can be obtained; and (ii) Compressed air operated machines [Figure 4.2(b)], where relatively less pressure is obtained.

In the plunger type machine, a 'gooseneck' tube is used, which remains partially submerged in a reservoir of molten metal. One end of this tube houses a plunger, as shown in Figure 4.2(a), and just below the plunger, the tube has a port (i.e., an opening) through which molten metal enters the tube. The other end of the tube is connected to the sprue of the cover die through a nozzle. The hydraulic system inside the machine operates to open and close the dies and also to give reciprocation motion to the plunger. To begin the cycle, the molten metal enters the tube through the port. As the plunger moves downward, the port in the tube closes and the entrapped metal is injected into the die cavity through the gooseneck and the nozzle. The metal is held under pressure (ranging between 10 and 35 MPa) until it solidifies in the die so as to obtain a dense metal structure in the casting. After the metal in the die is solidified, the plunger is brought back, the dies are forced open and ejecting pins are pressed to remove the casting. Finally, the sprue is detached from runner and the casting.

In the compressed air operated machine [Figure 4.2(b)], the gooseneck tube is operated with the help of links and a lifting mechanism. To begin with, the tube is submerged in the molten metal where it gets filled up, as in the case of the plunger type machine. The gooseneck is then raised so that the nozzle fixed at the other end of it can be locked to the sprue at die opening. The molten metal is forced into the die opening by directly applying the compressed air. When the metal in the die is solidified, air pressure is turned off and the gooseneck tube is lowered to receive more metal for the next casting. Systems for opening of dies and ejecting of casting are similar to those of the plunger type machine.

The hot chamber machine offers fast cycle times – nearly 15 cycles per minute. Average size of zinc castings can be produced at a rate of 4 to 5 castings per minute, whereas very small components can be cast at a rate of nearly a piece per second. Low-melting point alloys such as lead, tin, zinc and magnesium are usually cast using this process but it is not suitable for aluminium and its alloys.

Cold Chamber Machine High-melting point alloys like aluminium, copper, brass and magnesium in liquid state can react with the material of the gooseneck, which is either grey iron or cast steel. Also, these alloys cannot be melted in the machine container since in that case, the container will have a very short life. For casting of these metals and alloys, a cold chamber machine is used in which a separately located furnace is used to melt the metal. The molten metal is transported to the die casting machine [Figure 4.3(a)], where a measured quantity is poured into the injection cylinder, called *shot chamber*. The hot metal is forced into the die cavity under hydraulic pressure (in the range 20 to 100 MPa) [Figure 4.3(b)]. The pressure is maintained, rather, increased during the solidification process. The shot chamber is not heated; hence, the term *cold chamber*.

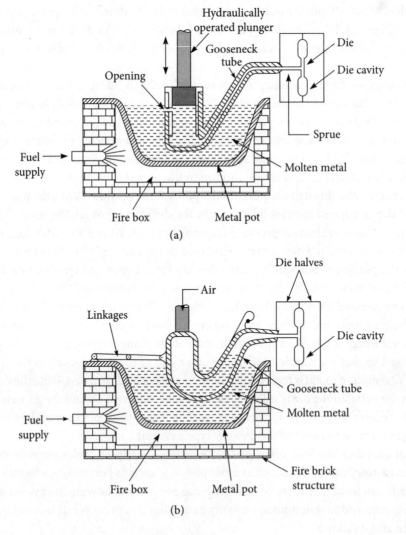

Figure 4.2   Schematic of hot chamber type die casting machines: (a) Plunger type; and (b) Pneumatic type

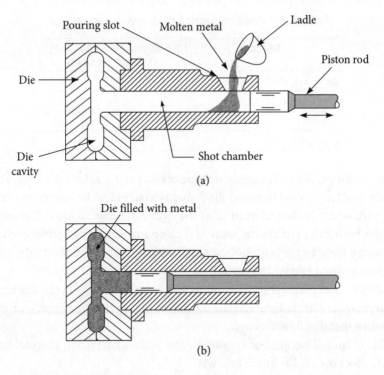

Die cavity

Figure 4.3 Schematic of cold chamber die casting machine: (a) Molten metal is transported to the die casting machine; and (b) Hot metal is forced into the die cavity under hydraulic pressure

The cycle time when the cold chamber die casting machine is employed is relatively longer than when the hot chamber die casting machine is employed because of the time taken to transfer the molten metal to the shot chamber in every cycle. Cold chamber die casting machines are designed and built very strong and rigid to withstand heavy pressure. The step-wise procedure followed for die casting with a cold chamber machine is as follows:

- The dies are closed under pressure; if necessary, cores are positioned, and the ladle containing molten metal is brought near the pouring slot.
- The molten metal is poured in [Figure 4.3(a)] and the piston rod is moved inward to force the metal into the dies where solidification of metal takes place under pressure [Figure 4.3(b)].
- Cores are withdrawn and dies are opened.
- Casting is ejected out from the movable half of the die with the help of an ejector rod.

Sand cores cannot be used in pressure die casting because the high pressures and flow rates of the molten metal can either disintegrate them or cause metal penetration. For this reason, metallic cores are used, which are retracted before the die is opened to withdraw the casting.

The minimum section thickness of casting depends upon the type of metal. Table 4.1 lists the minimum section thickness for some materials.

Table 4.1 Minimum section thickness of die castings

Metal	Minimum thickness of cast section (mm)
Aluminium alloys	1
Magnesium alloys	1.25
Zinc alloys	0.65
Brass and bronze	1.25

Dies The die set for pressure die casting is made of two parts – a stationary and a moving part. The stationary part, also called the *cover die*, remains fixed in the die casting machine, whereas the moving part, which is also referred to as the *ejector die*, can be moved in and out. There is provision for both halves of the die set to: (i) close and tightly fit against each other under a heavy clamping force to prevent molten metal seeping out at the joint line, and (ii) easily open after every pour to release the casting produced.

Metallic dies are not permeable. In order to prevent gas porosity in the castings produced, very fine vent holes are made between the die halves that permit the escape of air but do not allow the molten metal to flow through.

The die life is limited because of erosion by the molten metal and thermal fatigue. Other factors which affect the die life are as follows:

- **Melting temperature of material being cast** Higher the melting point of the material, shorter the die life.

- **Pouring temperature** Higher pouring temperatures reduce the die life.

- **Die material** Dies have a longer life if they are made from a material that has greater resistance to thermal shocks.

- **Die configuration** Dies having highly varying section thickness will produce larger temperature differences and thus, have lower life.

To increase the life of a die, the face of the cavity is generally given a coating of some refractory material, which performs the following functions:

- Minimizes thermal shock to the die surface
- Prevents sticking of molten metal on the die surface
- Controls rate and direction of metal solidification
- Serves as a parting agent
- Fills up surface imperfections, if any

As the coating has to provide insulation and lubrication, it is a refractory slurry, consisting of materials such as sodium silicate, clay, soap stone and talc. Coating is applied by either spraying or brushing and its thickness is kept to less than one millimetre. Solidification can also be controlled by varying the coating thickness; for portions of casting where slow solidification is required (such as runners, risers, sprue and thin sections), the coating thickness can be increased.

By varying the thickness of walls of the die, the designer can ensure progressive solidification of molten metal. In case it is required to expedite solidification at a particularly heavy portion of the casting, the thickness of the die wall can be decreased in that area, ensuring greater heat flow. Heavy air blast or circulation of cooling water inside the cooling channels can also serve this purpose.

The dies used for pressure die casting process are either single-cavity or multiple-cavity ones (Figure 4.4). They are produced from forged blocks of hot work steel with 5% chromium. The ratio of die weight to part weight is typically 1000:1. The wear of die increases with the increase in temperature of the molten metal. Surface cracking from repeated heating and cooling of the die, called *heat checking*, is a common problem. Materials that are resistant to thermal fatigue such as low carbon steels and high chromium steels give better die life.

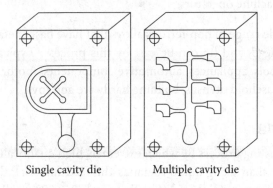

Single cavity die   Multiple cavity die

Figure 4.4 Types of dies

The life of dies generally depends on the metal being cast; it is around 10,000 shots for brass; nearly 150,000 shots for aluminium alloys; and some 1,000,000 shots for zinc alloys.

Advantages   Some important advantages of pressure die casting are as follows:

1. Components with thin sections and complex shapes can be cast since molten metal is injected at high pressure.

2. High precision of the cast components.

3. Much closer dimensional tolerances (of the order of 3 mm/m).

4. Improved surface finish (of the order of 1 micron).

5. Greater soundness and compactness of casting. Therefore, there are fewer defective castings. Reduction in defective castings adds to increased production rate.

6. Better mechanical properties of the casting due to the fine-grained skin formed during the solidification process.

7. Requires less work training; therefore, low labour cost per casting.

8.   Requires less floor space compared to other casting processes for the same production rate.

9.   Process can be easily automated.

Limitations   Some important limitations of pressure die casting process are as follows:

1.   Cost of dies and equipments is high.

2.   Maximum size of casting is limited due to limited machine capacity.

3.   Entrapment of air in the die cavity while injecting the molten metal is a serious problem.

4.   Die life decreases with an increase in the molten metal temperature.

5.   Metallic parts having a larger coefficient of contraction need to be removed quickly from the die; otherwise, removal of casting from the die becomes difficult.

6.   Maintenance and supervisory staff need to be skilled, though special skills are not required from machine operators.

Applications   A wide range of non-ferrous alloys that have base metals as zinc, aluminium, copper, magnesium, lead, and tin can be cast by this process. Typical applications are for the casting of hand tools, appliances, automotive components, motor frames and housings, plumbing fixtures, household utensils, building hardware and toys.

4.1.3 Thixocasting

This is a special die casting process by which extremely high quality aluminium components are produced. Rather than using liquid metal as the feed material, the process uses semi-solid, high viscosity feed material that is partially (nearly 25–50%) solid and partially (nearly 50–75%) liquid. A pre-cast billet with a non-dendritic microstructure that is produced by vigorously stirring the melt while the billet is being cast, is used. The billet is re-heated by induction heating to the semi-solid temperature range. The semi-solid material at a specific liquid fraction is then injected into dies fitted in the die casting machine. After the die is filled, high pressure is maintained on the material in the die.

The high viscosity feed material together with the use of controlled die-filling conditions ensure that the semi-solid metal fills the die in a non-turbulent manner so that unwanted gas porosity is eliminated.

Advantages   The main advantages of this process are the following: (i) Parts produced have consistent excellent mechanical and functional properties due mainly to the shaping of a primary alpha phase and extremely low porosity; (ii) Lower processing temperatures reduce the thermal shock on the die, raising the die life and allowing the use of non-traditional die materials; and (iii) Reduced solidification shrinkage; therefore part dimensions closer to near net shape can be obtained thus eliminating the need for machining or other finishing operations.

Disadvantages The main disadvantages of this process are the following: (i) High manufacturing cost as the process uses expensive billets; (ii) Only aluminium and aluminium alloys can be cast by this process; (iii) Scrap (runner etc.) cannot be directly recycled; and (iv) Accurate control of the temperature is required as the solid fraction and viscosity in the semi-solid state are highly dependent on temperature.

4.1.4 Rheocasting

Unlike thixocasting in which the billet is reheated, rheocasting develops the semi-solid slurry from the molten metal adjacent to the die casting machine. The liquid metal is cooled into the semi-solid range while simultaneously generating the globular microstructure. As soon as the metal is cooled to the correct temperature, the semi-solid slurry is transferred to the shot sleeve of the die casting machine, and injected into the die under controlled conditions similar to those observed in thixocasting.

Advantages The main advantages of rheocasing are as follows: (i) Low manufacturing cost, as the semi-solid feed material is produced in close proximity to the die-casting machine directly from the liquid. This allows the process to use less expensive conventional ingot material. (ii) Scrap can be put back directly into the casting stream, thus reducing the cost.

Disadvantage The main disadvantage of rheocasting is concerned with the consistency of the product. This is because rheocasting uses single shot liquid dosing (i.e., a single shot of metal is poured to produce each casting) and it is difficult to maintain exactly the same level of slurry concentration each time.

4.2 Centrifugal Casting

Every casting process uses some driving force for feeding the molten metal into a mould or die cavity. Gravitational force is used in all expendable mould casting processes as well as in the gravity die casting process. Compressed air pressure or mechanical ram pressure is used in pressure die casting. Centrifugal casting, as its name implies, uses centrifugal force for this purpose.

The principle of the centrifugal casting process is simple: the molten metal is poured into a sand, metal or graphite mould, which is rotated at high speed. The centrifugal force due to rotation of molten metal acts to push the molten metal against the mould wall, where it is allowed to remain until it cools and solidifies. The casting produced has dense grain structure, which is virtually free of porosity.

There are three variants of this process: true centrifugal casting, semi-centrifugal casting, and centrifuging.

4.2.1 True centrifugal casting

The main characteristics of true centrifugal casting are that the axis of rotation of the mould coincides with the axis of the casting (Figure 4.5). The axis of rotation of the mould, in

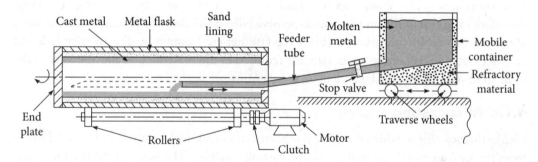

Figure 4.5 Schematic of true centrifugal casting (horizontal)

most instances, is horizontal but it can also be at an angle or even vertical for small-sized workpieces. The speed of rotation can vary between 30 and 3000 rpm (appropriate speed can be determined). As the molten metal is introduced into the rotating mould, it gets thrown onto the inside surface of the mould where it is allowed to solidify under the action of the centrifugal force. The formation of a central hole (which is always of round profile) in the casting is by the action of the centrifugal force and not by the use of any central core.

Centrifugal force can be estimated by the simple equation

$$F = \frac{mv^2}{R}$$

where F is in N; m is mass in kg; v is velocity in m/s; and R is the inside radius of the mould in m. The force of gravity is the weight of mould, $W = m.g$, where g is acceleration due to gravity, given as 9.81 m/s^2.

A term called G factor (GF) is usually used in centrifugal casting. This term can be defined as the ratio of centrifugal force divided by weight.

$$GF = \frac{mv^2}{Rmg} = \frac{v^2}{Rg}$$

Taking $v = [2\pi.R.N/60]$, where N is the rotational speed of the mould in rpm, and $D =$ inside diameter of the mould $= 2\,R$, we can write

$$GF = \frac{D}{2g}\left[\frac{\pi N}{30}\right]^2 \quad \text{or} \quad N = \frac{30}{\pi}\left[\frac{2gGF}{D}\right]^{\frac{1}{2}}$$

The value of GF is critical for centrifugal casting. The appropriate value of GF for most metals has been empirically found to lie in the range 60 to 80. If the actual value is much smaller than the appropriate value, the liquid metal in the mould will not remain forced against the mould wall during the upper half of the circular path; the liquid metal will tend to 'rain' inside the mould. This will occur as a result of the slipping action taking place between the molten metal and the mould wall, which indicates that the rotational speed of the metal is less than that of the mould.

The mould is made of iron, steel or graphite, and may be lined with some refractory material to enhance its life. Gates and risers are not needed, which means there is saving of material. The thickness of the casting is controlled by the volume of metal fed into the mould. The external profile of the casting is generally round (as with pipes and gun barrels), but square, hexagonal or any other symmetrical shape is also possible by giving an appropriate outer shape to the mould. The inner surface is always cylindrical when rotation is about the horizontal axis, but when the axis of rotation is vertical, gravitational force and centrifugal force act together to make the shape of the inner surface somewhat like part of a parabola. There is directional solidification of casting; the metal density differences can be observed across the cross-section; lighter elements such as slag, impurities or pieces of refractory lining tend to come to the inner surface of the casting.

This process is most suitable for the production of hollow cylindrical parts, such as hollow shafts, water supply and sewerage pipes, cylinder liners, bushes, brake drums, bearing rings, gun barrels, pressure vessels and street lamp-posts. The castings produced are dense and sound, have high dimensional accuracy and possess good quality external surface details. Cylindrical parts ranging from 10 mm to 3 m in diameter, up to 15 m in length and with thickness ranging from 3 mm to 100 mm can be cast.

Example 4.1

Horizontal true centrifugal casting process has been decided for the production of 1000 pieces of lead pipes. Each pipe is to have a length of 65 cm, outside diameter 75 cm and wall thickness of 10 mm. Estimate the rotational speed of the mould if it is desired to have GF of 60.

Solution

Here we have

$$L = 0.65 \text{ m}; \quad D = 0.75 \text{ m}; \quad GF = 60; \quad N = ?$$

We know that $N = \dfrac{30}{\pi}\left[\dfrac{2gGF}{D}\right]^{\frac{1}{2}}$

$$= \dfrac{30}{\pi}\left[\dfrac{2 \times 9.81 \times 60}{0.75}\right]^{\frac{1}{2}} = 378.3 \text{ rpm, say } 380 \text{ rpm}$$

Example 4.2

Copper tubes of length 800 mm, outside diameter 300 mm and wall thickness 10 mm are required to be produced. The production manager has recommended horizontal centrifugal casting process for this with a mould rotational speed of 750 rpm. Determine (a) whether the mould rotational speed is appropriate and (b) what volume of molten metal will be required to be poured into the mould if solidification and contraction after solidification are taken into account?

Solution

Copper tube dimensions are: Length l = 800 mm = 0.8 m; Outside diameter D = 0.30 m; Inside diameter d = 0.30 – 2 (0.010) = 0.28 m.

Mould rotational speed N = 750 rpm

We need to find out GF to decide whether the mould rotational speed recommendations are okay.

$$GF = \frac{D}{2g}\left[\frac{2\pi N}{30}\right]^2 = 94.34$$

This value is beyond the recommended range 60–80. Therefore, suggested speed is high. If we use the value of GF as 70, the mould rotational speed can be determined as

$$70 = \frac{0.30}{2\times9.81}\left[\frac{2\pi N}{30}\right]^2, \text{ or } N = 646 \text{ rpm, say } 650 \text{ rpm}$$

Volume of molten metal required to be poured in the mould = Volume of casting + volumetric solidification shrinkage + volumetric contraction from solidification temperature to room temperature.

$$\text{Volume of casting } \frac{\pi}{4}(D^2 - d^2)l = \frac{\pi}{4}[(0.3)^2 - (0.28)^2] \times 0.8 = 0.00729 \text{ m}^3$$

The following properties of copper can be taken from Table 5.1:

Volumetric contraction due to solidification shrinkage = 4.5%

Volumetric contraction due to solidification temperature to room temperature = 7.5%

$$\text{Volume of molten metal required for pouring} = 0.00729\frac{100}{100-12} = 0.0828 \text{ m}^3$$

Vertical true centrifugal casting

The effect of gravitational force acting on the liquid metal in case of vertical true centrifugal casting would be to produce a casting wall that is thinner at the top than at the bottom. The difference in the inside radius (or diameter) at the top and bottom depends on the rotational speed of the mould, as

$$N = \frac{30}{\pi}\left[\frac{2gL}{R_t^2 - R_b^2}\right]^{1/2}$$

This relation can be written in a simplified manner as

$$N = \frac{30}{\pi}\left[\frac{8gL}{D_t^2 - D_b^2}\right]^{\frac{1}{2}} = 42.8\sqrt{L/(D_t^2 - D_b^2)}$$

where N is the rotational speed (rpm); L is the vertical length of the casting (m); D_t is the inside diameter of the casting at the top (m); and D_b is the inside diameter of the casting at the bottom (m). It can be seen from the equation that to obtain $D_t = D_b$ in the vertical centrifugal casting, speed of rotation N needs to be infinite, which is, of course, not feasible.

Parts such as bushings, if produced by vertical centrifugal casting process, are generally subjected to machining operations in order to obtain the desired dimensional accuracy. In practice, length of a part produced by this process is generally not more than twice the diameter.

Example 4.3

Vertical true centrifugal casting process has been recommended for the production of brass tube sections of 250 mm length. Other dimensions of the tube are OD = 150 mm, and ID = 120 mm at the top and 100 mm at the bottom. Determine the speed of rotation of the mould for the process.

Solution

Here, length of tube section, $L = 0.250$ m; OD = 0.150 m; $D_b = 0.100$ m; and $D_t = 0.120$ m.

We know that for vertical centrifugal casting operation, the speed of rotation of the mould

$$N = 42.78\sqrt{L/(Dt^2 - Db^2)} = 42.78[0.25/\{(0.12)^2 - (0.10)^2\}]^{\frac{1}{2}} = 322\,\text{rpm}$$

Example 4.4

Brass tubing of length 350 mm and OD 200 mm is being produced in large quantities by the vertical true centrifugal casting process. The final casting weighs 70 kg. If the process used rotational speed of 800 rpm during solidification, determine the inside diameters at the top and bottom of the tubing.

Solution

Here, OD = 0.2 m; $L = 0.35$ m; $N = 800$ rpm; W = 70 kg; diameter at the bottom of the tubing, $D_b = ?$; diameter at the top of the tubing, $D_t = ?$

We know the density of brass $\rho = 8.55$ g/cm³ (8550 kg/m³); therefore, volume of tube = 70 ÷ 8550 = 0.0082 m³. Volume of a solid of length 0.35 m and diameter 0.2 m = 0.011 m³. Therefore, volume of hollow portion of tube = 0.011 – 0.0082 = 0.0028 m³

Also, we know that for vertical true centrifugal casting process,

$$N = 42.78\sqrt{L/(Dt^2 - Db^2)}$$

$$800 = 42.78 \left[0.35 / (D_t^2 - D_b^2) \right]^{\frac{1}{2}}$$

or, $(D_t^2 - D_b^2) = 0.001$ (4.1)

Volume of frustum of cone $= \frac{1}{12} \pi L (D_t^2 + D_b^2 + D_t \cdot D_b) = 0.0028$

or, $(D_t^2 + D_b^2 + D_t \cdot D_b) = 0.03051$ (4.2)

Solving equations (4.1) and (4.2), we can find the values of D_t and D_b.

4.2.2 Semi-centrifugal casting

Semi-centrifugal casting process is also known as profiled centrifugal casting. In this process, the mould is rotated about its vertical axis. The centre of the casting is mostly solid, but a central core can be used if a central hole is needed (Figure 4.6); in which case, the metal is poured around it. The centrifugal force generated due to the rotation of mould helps in radial outward flow of molten metal from a central reservoir to produce a structure which is denser than that obtained in conventional sand casting. The central reservoir also acts as a riser and must be made large enough to assure that this solidifies last. The rotational speeds are often much lower than the ones used for true centrifugal casting.

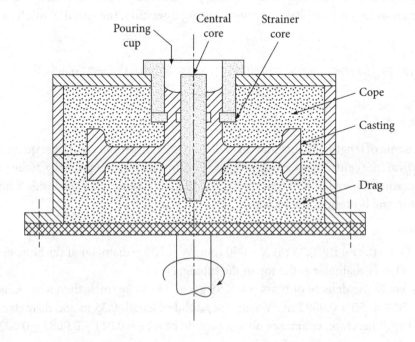

Figure 4.6   Schematic of semi-centrifugal casting

Stack moulding can be used to cast many parts at the same time. As the lighter impurities concentrate in the central region, the process is best suitable for the production of parts having shapes that are symmetrical about the central axis and where the central region will ultimately be hollow such as wheels, pulleys, gears, etc.

4.2.3 Centrifuging

In centrifuging, several mould cavities (of any shape) are placed at a certain distance from the axis of rotation (Figure 4.7). Thus, the axis of rotation does not coincide with the axis of the mould; but it does coincide with the axis of the entire assembly. As the whole assembly is rotated about the central sprue axis, the molten metal is fed into mould cavities from the central sprue through radial gates under the influence of centrifugal force. The process uses relatively low rotational speeds and is adaptable to stack moulding.

Centrifuging is used for casting of parts of non-symmetrical or irregular shapes. The properties of the metal of castings vary with the distance from the axis of rotation. Common parts produced by centrifuging include plugs, valve bodies, valve bonnets and jewellery.

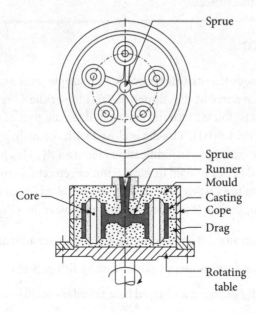

Figure 4.7   Schematic of centrifuging

Advantages   Some of the useful characteristics of castings produced by centrifuging are as follows:

1. Castings have directional solidification.
2. Castings are sound and dense with physical properties comparable with those of forgings.
3. Castings need less fettling and cleaning of surface.

4. Castings with thin sections or fine outside surface details can be readily produced.

5. Less percentage of defective castings and, therefore, high casting yield.

4.3 Slush Casting

The principles of the slush casting process are simple. Molten metal is poured into a metallic die. At the interface of the molten metal–die cavity surface, a thin layer of the molten metal solidifies (i.e., skin is formed) first, which becomes thicker with time. As soon as the desired thickness of the solidified skin is obtained, the die is inverted so as to drain out the remaining liquid metal. The die halves are then opened and the casting is taken out to be cooled in open air.

Applications   The process of slush casting finds application in producing small batches of hollow castings with thin walls. Ornamental and decorative parts such as flower vases, lamp bases and toys made of low melting point metals like lead, tin, zinc and their alloys are commonly produced by this process.

4.4 Squeeze Casting

The principles of the squeeze casting process are simple and schematically shown in Figure 4.8. There are two parts of die: upper die and lower die (Figure 4.8(a)). A precise quantity of molten metal is poured into the pre-heated female part of a metallic die kept in a horizontal position (Figure 4.8(b)). The die is closed with the male part and a high pressure is applied throughout the duration of solidification (Figure 4.8(c)). The pressures applied are lower than those required in hot or cold forging. Sand or retractable metal cores may be used to create hollow regions in the casting. The casting can be taken out of the die with the help of an ejector pin when the upper die is withdrawn from the lower die (Figure 4.8(d)).

Advantages and applications   The process has the following advantages and applications.

*   Both ferrous and non-ferrous metals can be cast by this process.

*   Parts produced under pressure and rapid heat transfer conditions have
    *   fine microstructure
    *   very low gas and shrinkage porosity
    *   excellent mechanical properties
    *   near-net-shape with fine surface details
*   Weight of the cast parts can be up to 50 kg with any shape complexity.

Most applications of this process are generally for manufacturing of automotive components.

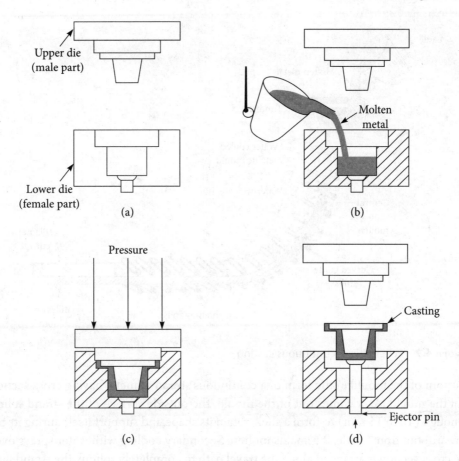

Figure 4.8 Schematic of squeeze casting process

4.5 Continuous Casting

A standard practice followed for steel production for a long time has been to cast ingots of steel. However, during the last two to three decades, continuous casting, also known as *strand casting,* has acquired unprecedented popularity across the world as it is more efficient and the most cost-effective process of steel production. Like all casting processes, continuous casting starts with molten metal as the source material but, unlike other casting processes, it is not poured into a mould. Instead, it is poured into a refractory lined intermediate reservoir/settling tank called *tundish,* where the metal is held for about 10 minutes, to permit any slag or impurities to be skimmed off. The use of tundish, which can hold nearly 3,000 kg of metal at a time, is necessary for the simple reason that this process requires a continuous stream of molten metal, the supply of which is practically not possible from any melting furnace.

From the bottom of the tundish, a steady stream of molten metal flows downward into a water-cooled mould made of copper or its alloy (Figure 4.9). This mould has no bottom. The liquid metal flows into the mould from above. Because of the very quick and efficient cooling action around the copper mould walls, partially solidified metal can be taken out of

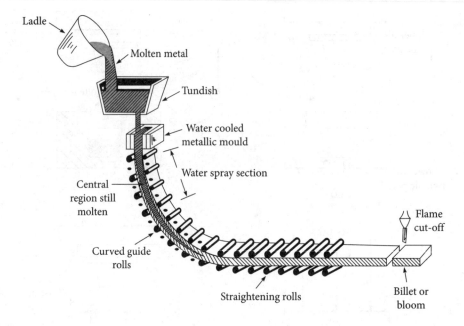

Figure 4.9   Schematic of continuous casting

the bottom of the mould in the form of a continuous strand of metal having cross-section as that of the mould. As it comes out of the mould, the outside surface of the strand solidifies just enough (10 to 15 mm) to form a shell, retain its shape and support itself during its travel downward; but from inside, it remains molten. Secondary cooling with water sprays over its whole cross-section is arranged along the travel path to completely solidify the strand.

The mould is often coated from inside with a solid lubricant such as graphite in order to reduce friction and adhesion at the mould–metal interface. In some cases, the mould is vibrated so as to reduce friction and eliminate any chance of the metal sticking to the mould surface.

Finally, the continuously cast metal strand passes through guide and straightening rolls to an oxy-gas flame cutter, which cuts it into desired lengths (Figure 4.9). Generally, the cut pieces are directly fed into a rolling mill for shape-rolling of products such as sheets, I-beams, and channels. This practice is quite useful as while the strand is still at a sufficiently high temperature, hot working can be performed, thereby avoiding wastage of heat in first cooling down and then again heating the metal later for rolling.

The modern trend is to produce a thinner strand as this reduces the number of rolling operations required and improves the overall economy of the process.

Advantages   Compared to ingot casting, continuous cast metals have the following advantages.

1.   More uniform composition and properties of cast metal.

2.   The process is less expensive as compared to other processes.

3.   The process lends itself to automation.

Questions

1. What differences, if any, can be expected in the properties of castings made by a permanent mould as compared to those of castings made by expendable moulds?

2. What advantages, if any, are derived from pre-heating the moulds used in permanent mould casting prior to metal injection?

3. Explain with a suitable sketch the gravity die casting process. Compare this process with pressure die casting.

4. Compare the hot chamber and cold chamber method of die casting. For casting of which materials would you recommend the use of hot chamber die casting machine?

5. What do you understand by 'heat checking' of dies? How can this be avoided?

6. Discuss the advantage, limitations and applications of permanent mould castings.

7. Give a comparative analysis of low and high pressure die castings.

8. Is there any difference between the materials used for making dies for gravity die casting process and pressure die casting process? Why?

9. Give reasons for the common practice of removing the castings from the permanent mould as soon as solidification has completed.

10. In permanent mould casting processes, explain (i) How venting is provided? (ii) Can sand cores be used? (iii) Are risers provided?

11. Make a sketch to describe the centrifugal casting process. Should the speed of rotation of mould have any effect on the cast structure? Give reasons for your answer. Compare the structure and properties of the material at the outer and inner surfaces of a centrifugal casting.

12. In reference to the centrifugal casting process, discuss the importance of G-factor. What is the appropriate value of this factor?

13. Distinguish between semi-centrifugal casting and centrifuging as regards their areas of application. In the semi-centrifugal casting process, why are metals such as aluminium generally spun in a horizontal plane, while platinum is usually spun in a vertical plane? Support your answer with reasons.

14. What is squeeze casting process? Can cores be used in this process? Give the advantages and applications of this process.

15. Describe the slush casting process. Give some typical applications of this process.

16. Describe the continuous casting process. Write a note on the current trends in the application of this process.

Exercise Problems

1. Steel rings with the following dimensions are to be produced by horizontal true centrifugal casting process. Length = 80 mm; outside diameter = 600 mm; and inside diameter = 500 mm.

Determine (a) the speed of rotation of the mould that will provide a G-factor of 65; (b) If the material of ring is changed to copper, the ring dimensions remaining the same, will the speed of rotation of the mould remain the same to obtain the same G-factor of 65?

2. Horizontal true centrifugal casting operation has been decided for the production of aluminium tubes of 80 mm length. The outside and inside diameters of the tube are 25 mm and 22 mm respectively. If you decide to use a G-factor of 65, what rotational speed would be given to the mould?   Ans. 682 rpm

3. Brass bushings are to be produced by the horizontal true centrifugal casting process. The dimensions of the bushing are: length = 115 mm, inside diameter = 100 mm and wall thickness = 12 mm.

   a. Determine the necessary rotational speed of the mould in order to obtain a G-factor of 68 or very close to 68.

   b. Estimate the centrifugal force that would be imposed by the molten metal on the inside wall of the mould, if the rotational speed as determined in (a) is used.

4. The production engineer has recommended horizontal true centrifugal casting process to make large diameter copper tubes. The tubes have outside diameter of 300 mm, wall thickness 15 mm and length 900 mm.

   a. If the process employs 720 rpm as the rotational speed of the mould, what would be the G-factor on the molten metal?

   b. Is 720 rpm rotational speed sufficient to avoid 'rain' of molten metal?

   c. What volume of molten metal would be necessary for pouring into the mould to achieve a good quality casting when solidification shrinkage and contraction after solidification are taken into account?

5. A rotational speed of 550 rpm has been used during solidification of aluminium bushing in a vertical true centrifugal casting process. The bushing is 240 mm long and has an outside diameter of 200 mm. If the inside diameter at the bottom is 140 mm, determine the inside diameter at the top of the bushing.

Fill in the Blanks

1. Dies made of _____are usually used for small volume production of aluminium and magnesium castings.

2. Metal melting furnace is an integral part of _____ chamber die casting machine.

3. To increase the life of a die, the face of the cavity is generally coated with _____ material.

4. Copper alloys are not preferably cast by _____ die casting process because they have relatively poor fluidity and high melting point.

5. For casting of high-melting point metals and alloys, _____ chamber die casting machine is used.

6. Semi-centrifugal casting process is best suitable for the production of parts with shapes that are symmetrical about _____ axis.

7. In case of centrifugal casting process, the appropriate value of G-factor for most metals lies in the range _____ to _____.

8. The term G-factor usually used in centrifugal casting is defined as the ratio of _____ divided by weight.

9. Slush casting process is commonly used for producing _____ castings.

10. The use of tundish in continuous casting is necessary for the reason that _____.

Choose the Correct Answer

1. The material of mould used in the die casting process is generally made of
   a. plaster of Paris.
   c. sand mixed with some binder.
   b. some metal.
   d. thermosetting resin.

2. In case of hot chamber die casting machine,
   a. the furnace is an integral part of the machine.
   b. the furnace is not an integral part of the machine.
   c. the chamber of the machine is actually not heated.
   d. aluminium and its alloys can be cast at a very fast rate.

3. In gravity die casting process,
   a. casting comes out of the die under the gravitational force.
   b. die is made to fall under the force of gravity before it is filled.
   c. die cavity is filled with molten metal flowing under the influence of gravity.
   d. die as well as casting are constantly under the influence of gravity.

4. The following parameter does not affect the mould life in gravity die casting:
   a. size of the mould
   c. pouring temperature of the metal
   b. material being cast
   d. material of mould

5. In gravity die casting, the life of the mould can generally be increased by coating the face of the cavity with some
   a. oil or grease,
   c. refractory material.
   b. thermosetting resin.
   d. meehanite with large graphite flakes.

6. In gravity die casting,
   a. risers are provided in the die to compensate for metal shrinkage.
   b. risers cannot be provided in the die to compensate for metal shrinkage.
   c. retractable metal cores are used to compensate for metal shrinkage.
   d. metal shrinkage is compensated by selectively heating or chilling various portions of the die.

7. High melting point materials are generally die cast with the help of

    a.   hot chamber machine.   c.   cold chamber machine.

    b.   hot cum cold chamber machine.   d.   chamber-less machine.

8. A cold chamber machine used for die casting is one in which

    a.   the chamber is water cooled.

    b.   a separately located furnace is used to melt the metal.

    c.   the temperature of the chamber is never allowed to rise above 200°C.

    d.   the temperature of the chamber is always maintained below 100°C.

9. In die casting, progressive solidification of molten metal can be achieved by

    a.   coating the face of the cavity with some refractory material.

    b.   varying the thickness of walls of die.

    c.   using material for the die that has varying hardness.

    d.   using material for the die that has varying resistance to abrasion.

10. For manufacturing precision investment castings, the sand generally used is

    a.   zircon sand.   c.   chromite sand.

    b.   silica sand.   d.   olivine sand.

11. For making vanes or blades of a turbine, the recommended method of casting is

    a.   shell moulding.   c.   precision investment casting.

    b.   permanent mould casting.   d.   die casting.

12. Which one of the following is not a variant of centrifugal casting process?

    a.   true centrifugal casting   c.   semi-centrifugal casting

    b.   false centrifugal casting   d.   centrifuging

13. In which one variant of centrifugal casting process, the axis of rotation of the mould coincides with the axis of the casting?

    a.   true centrifugal casting   c.   semi-centrifugal casting

    b.   false centrifugal casting   d.   centrifuging

14. In which one variant of centrifugal casting process, the centre of the casting is mostly solid, but central core can be used if central hole is needed?

    a.   true centrifugal casting   c.   semi-centrifugal casting

    b.   false centrifugal casting   d.   centrifuging

15. In which one variant of centrifugal casting process, the axis of rotation does not coincide with the axis of the mould but it coincides with the axis of the whole set-up?

    a.   true centrifugal casting   c.   semi-centrifugal casting

    b.   false centrifugal casting   d.   centrifuging

16. Which one variant of centrifugal casting process uses relatively low rotational speeds and is adaptable to stack moulding?
    a. true centrifugal casting
    b. false centrifugal casting
    c. semi-centrifugal casting
    d. centrifuging

17. In centrifugal casting, the term G-factor can be estimated as
    a. ratio of inside dia. of mould to outside dia. of mould
    b. difference of inside dia. of mould to outside dia. of mould
    c. ratio of weight of mould to weight of casting
    d. ratio of centrifugal force to weight of casting

Answers

1. b.	2. a.	3. c.	4. a.	5. c.	6. a.	7. c.	8. b.	9. b.	10. a.
11. c.	12. b.	13. a.	14. c.	15. d.	16. d.	17. d			

5

Metal Melting, Pouring and Solidification

LEARNING OBJECTIVES

After reading this chapter, you should be able to understand the following:

- The requirements of a metal melting furnace.
- The important factors in the selection of a furnace.
- The construction, working and areas of application of different furnaces.
- The metal pouring operation.
- The events that take place during metal solidification and the subsequent cooling of casting to room temperature.

5.1 Metal Melting

Metal melting is an important activity of casting operation that directly affects the quality of castings. It is done in a furnace and there are many requirements which the furnace must meet. These are as follows:

1. It should provide an adequate amount of molten metal.
2. It should provide molten metal at the desired temperature.
3. It should be able to hold molten metal for an extended period of time without deterioration of quality.
4. It should not pollue the environment.
5. It should be economical to operate and maintain.

Foundries use many types of furnaces – pit furnace, open hearth furnace, arc furnace, induction furnace, cupola furnace and so on. The selection of a furnace for specific applications generally depends on several factors:

1. Metal/alloy to be melted and the form of available raw material for charging into the furnace.

2. Desired degree of superheat.

3. Variety of metals or alloys to be melted.

4. Required capacity and rate of melting.

5. Melting requirements, whether continuous or in batches.

6. Desired quality of molten alloy.

7. Degree of control of furnace atmosphere to avoid contamination of the alloy.

8. Power supply – cost and availability.

9. Environmental pollution – both air and noise.

10. Cost – initial, operating, and maintenance costs.

5.2 Melting Furnaces

5.2.1 Pit furnace

Pit furnace, also called a *crucible furnace*, is built in a pit. It operates on the heat obtained from burning of a combustible gas [Figure 5.1(a)] or coke [Figures 5.1(b) and 5.1(c)] with a blast of air. The melting of alloy takes place in a pot-like structure, called the crucible. The crucible, with the metal charge in it, is placed in the furnace. The hot blast of air from the firebox heats the crucible and melts the metal charge contained in it. When the metal reaches the right temperature (as seen by lifting the cover of the pit), the air blast is cut off. The crucible is taken out and used as a ladle to pour the molten metal in moulds.

Crucible furnaces are mostly used for melting relatively small quantities of non-ferrous metals and alloys with low-melting point. Control of temperature and chemistry of the molten metal is poor. The main advantages of these furnaces are that their fabrication, operation and maintenance are easy and the capital cost is low.

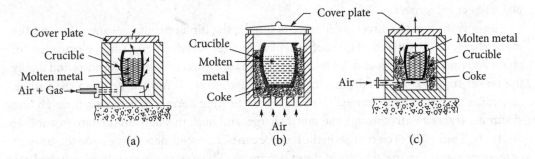

Figure 5.1 Schematic of some types of crucible furnace or pit furnace

5.2.2 Open hearth furnace

This furnace is a squat, rectangular brick structure having a shallow hearth that holds the metal charge. There is a combustion chamber where powdered coal, gas or oil is burned. The hot gases from the burning fuel are directed to the hearth where they heat and melt the metal charge (Figure 5.2). They also heat the lining of the hearth. which, in turn, makes the heat reverberate and helps the metal to melt before they leave the furnace through the chimney.

The open hearth furnace is commonly used for melting non-ferrous metals and steel in batch quantities. It is also used for holding cast iron that has been melted previously in a cupola furnace. The open hearth furnace is generally of much larger capacity than the crucible furnace. It is not as popular as the electric arc furnace.

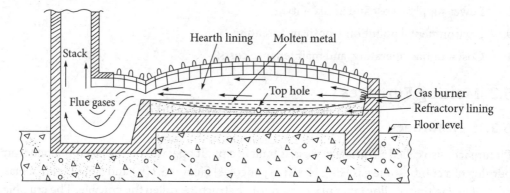

Figure 5.2   Schematic of open hearth furnace

5.2.3 Electric arc furnace

An arc furnace is used to melt ferrous alloys, especially steel. The popularity of arc furnaces is because of their (i) high melting rates, (ii) high pouring temperature, (iii) ability to produce high quality metal of almost any desired composition and (iv) ability to hold the molten metal at constant temperature for longer periods of time. Figure 5.3(a) gives a schematic of a three-phase direct arc furnace.

The operation of the direct arc furnace is simple; the furnace roof is swung aside and the metal charge is introduced. The roof is replaced; after which three carbon electrodes (of about 700 mm in diameter and 1.5 to 2 m in length) are lowered into the furnace; and finally the power supply is switched on. A continuous electric arc is formed between the carbon electrodes and the metal charge. The path of the heating current is generally through one electrode, across an arc, through the metal charge, and back through another arc to another electrode. The height of electrodes in the furnace can be adjusted, depending upon the amount of metal present. The metal melts in about two hours. The power supply is then switched off, the electrodes are raised, and the furnace is tilted to get the molten metal in a ladle.

A direct arc furnace has a thermal efficiency of up to 70%. The composition of melt can be kept within accurate limits and temperatures as high as 1900°C can be generated. Direct arc furnaces are available in capacities up to 100 tonnes, and up to 20 tonnes of metal per hour can be melted in batch operations.

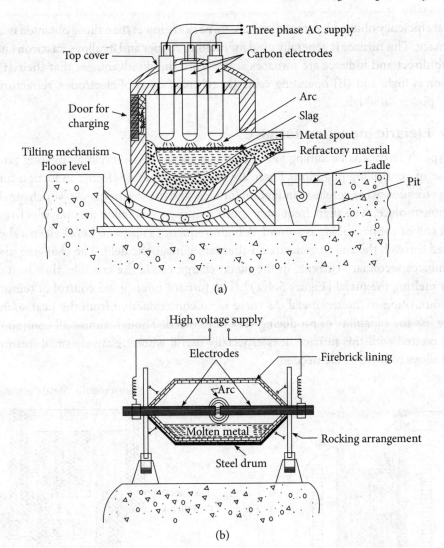

Figure 5.3 Schematic of electric arc furnaces: (a) Direct arc type; and (b) Indirect arc type

In an indirect electric arc furnace [Figure 5.3(b)], the electric arc is struck between two graphite electrodes and the metal charge does not form a part of the electric circuit. The furnace rocks back and forth so that the metal charge comes in contact with the hot refractory lining and picks up heat for melting. In addition, the radiations from the arc and the hot refractory lining of the furnace help the metal charge to melt. While the furnace rocks, metal charge constituents get mixed up thoroughly, melting is faster, molten metal gets stirred up, and over-heating of the refractory lining is avoided, which eventually leads to its extended life. The angle of rocking of furnace is adjusted in such a manner that the liquid metal level remains below the pouring spout. When the metal has completely melted, the furnace is tilted in order to allow the liquid metal to flow out of the tap hole. The temperatures and the thermal efficiency obtained in an indirect arc furnace are lower than those obtained in a direct arc furnace. This furnace is generally used for melting copper and its alloys, cast iron and steel.

Both direct and indirect arc furnaces suffer from the disadvantages that their (i) noise pollution is high, and (ii) operating costs (in terms of costs of electrodes, refractories and electric power) are high.

5.2.4 Electric induction furnace

This type of furnace is becoming very popular because of (i) very high melting rates, and (ii) ease of controlling pollution. There are two basic types of electric induction furnaces: the high frequency (or coreless) induction furnace, and the low frequency (or channel-type) induction furnace. The high frequency unit comprises a crucible around which a water-cooled coil of copper tubing is wound. A high frequency (up to 10 kc/s) electrical current is passed through the coil to generate an alternating magnetic field. The changing magnetic field induces secondary currents in the metal charge inside the crucible, thus heating and rapidly melting the metal [Figure 5.4(a)]. The furnace offers good control of temperature and composition of molten metal. As there is no contamination from the heat source, the furnace has the capability of producing very pure metal. Though almost all common alloys can be melted with this furnace, it is especially useful where relatively small quantities of special alloys of any type are needed.

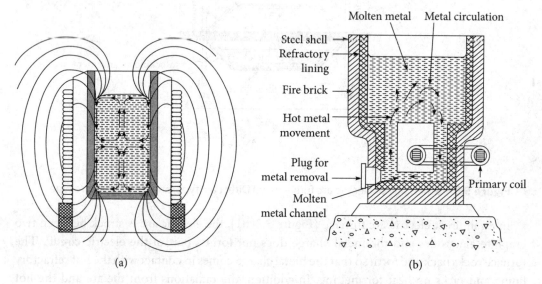

Figure 5.4   Schematic of induction furnaces: (a) Coreless induction furnace showing lines of magnetic force; and (b) Low frequency induction furnace

Furnaces using low frequency (50 c/s) currents are successfully employed for composition-controlled melting. Here, only a small channel [Figure 5.4(b)] is surrounded with the primary (current-carrying) coil. The secondary coil is formed by the channel of the molten metal, and the metal gains heat when it passes through the channel. Sufficient amount of molten metal is put in the furnace to fill the secondary coil, with the remainder of charge taking different forms. As the power supply is switched on, high heating rate is obtained with the possibility of accurately controlling the temperature.

This type of furnace finds applications as a holding furnace, where the molten metal is to be retained at a constant temperature for a sufficiently long time.

5.2.5 Cupola furnace

Cupola furnace is widely used for melting grey, nodular and white cast iron as its operating efficiency is higher than any other foundry metal melting method due to the counter-movement of hot gases with respect to the charge.

Construction The cross-sectional view of a cupola is shown in Figure 5.5. It consists of a vertical shell made of 5 to 6 mm thick mild steel plates that are either riveted or welded at the seams. The interior is lined with refractory bricks to protect the shell from becoming over-heated.

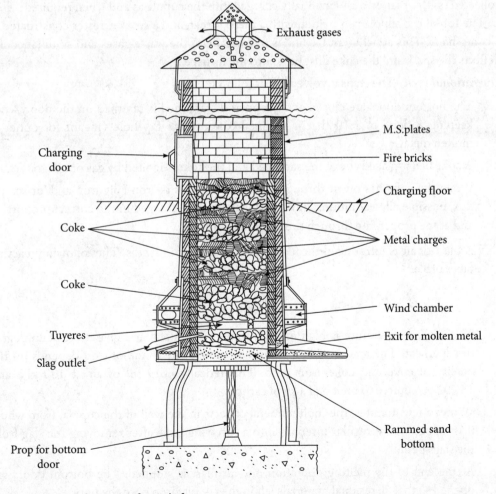

Figure 5.5 Schematic of cupola furnace

There is a door at the bottom of the shell, either in one piece hinged to a supporting leg, or in two pieces having each piece hinged separately to the two opposite legs. Before the cupola is put into operation, the bottom door is closed with the support of a *prop* so that it may not collapse due to the heavy weight of the charge, coke, etc. A rammed sand bed that provides the necessary refractory bottom for the molten metal and the coke is prepared. Just above the sand bed is the *metal tapping spout*. This spout (or opening) is initially closed with clay till the molten metal is ready for tapping. Just above the metal spout but on the opposite side is the *slag spout*, through which the slag produced during the melting process can be removed.

A wind chamber or wind belt encircles the cupola shell at a place little above the bottom of the shell. This wind chamber is connected to an air blower by means of a pipe. The required amount of air under pressure enters the furnace from the chamber through openings called tuyeres, which are provided all around the shell. A charging door is located at a suitable height above the charging platform. This platform is of robust mild steel construction, and is supported on four strong steel legs. Weighed quantities of metal, coke, scrap and flux are collected on this platform and manually charged into the cupola as and when required.

The top of the cupola is provided with a mesh screen and a spark arrester constructed in a cone shape. This attachment facilitates free escape of the waste gases and simultaneously deflects the spark and the coke dust back into the furnace.

Operational cycle   The steps involved are as follows:

1.   The bottom doors are closed and propped. A sand bed is rammed on the floor, while keeping a slope of 1:10 that is inclined towards the tap hole (meant for outlet of molten metal).

2.   A coke bed is placed above the sand bed and the coke is ignited by gas or oil igniters.

3.   When the coke has burnt through, alternating layers of iron (pig iron and/or scrap), flux, possible alloy additions and additional coke are charged in the correct proportion and at the proper rate through the charging door.

4.   A blast of air is introduced through the wind box and tuyeres. The following reaction takes place:

$$C + O_2 \rightarrow CO_2 + \text{heat}$$

The flame temperature is high enough to melt the metal and give it a certain degree of superheat. The amount of air required to melt one tonne of iron depends on the quality of coke and coke–iron ratio. Theoretically, 3.19 m^3 of air at 100 kPa and 15.5°C is required to melt half a kg of carbon.

5.   Within a few minutes, the molten metal collects in the well of the cupola, from where it is tapped out at regular intervals into a receiving ladle after removing the slag from the slag spout.

6.   At the end of the melting operation, the air blast is stopped. The bottom doors are opened so that all residual materials left in the cupola drop onto the floor.

Charge and charge calculations The charge required to produce cast iron comprises pig iron, cast iron scrap (sprues, risers and scrapped castings) and steel scrap. The proportion of these constituents of charge depends on their chemical compositions as also on the desired final composition of cast iron. The fluxes are added in the charge to protect the iron from oxidation as well as remove oxides and other impurities present in the metal. Limestone ($CaCO_3$), fluorspar (CaF_2) and soda ash (Na_2CO_3) are the commonly used fluxes added in quantity that is nearly 20% of the coke charge by weight. Iron/coke ratio of 6:1, 8:1 or 10:1 by weight are commonly used.

An approximate amount of losses and pick-ups of different elements occurring during melting operations are as under:

- Carbon up to 4.2% (maximum) balances out. The loss due to oxidation gets compensated through pick-up from the coke.

- Silicon up to 3% (maximum) is desirable. Oxidation loss of 10% that occurs is generally compensated by the addition of ferrosilicon or silicon briquettes.

- Manganese generally varies between 0.5% and 0.75%. The losses due to oxidation and reaction with sulphur are nearly 20% of the original amount. Compensation can be made by adding ferro-manganese or manganese briquettes.

- Phosphorus up to 1% (maximum level) is tolerable. The amount of phosphorus in the charge is almost entirely retained during melting, since its oxidation is negligible.

- Sulphur is undesirable and only up to 0.1% is permitted. Its oxidation loss is almost negligible, while its pick-up is from the coke and the metal charged. Coke normally contains 0.5% sulphur and the pick-up during metal melting is almost 4% of this amount.

The foundry manager is always keen to determine the final composition of the metal being produced. This can be found by knowing what is contained in each of the charge constituents and the possible losses and pick-ups occurring during metal melting in the cupola. The following example will further clarify this point.

Example 5.1

Analysis of the charge of a cupola furnace is given in the following table. As a manager of the foundry, what composition of the molten metal would you expect at the metal spout of the cupola?

Charge constituent	% of charge	Carbon %	Si %	Mn %	S %	P %
Pig iron 1	30	3.2	2.4	0.5	0.1	0.6
Pig iron 2	30	3.4	2.0	0.5	0.05	0.8
C.I. scrap	40	3.2	2.5	0.7	0.08	0.7

Solution

Let us assume that the amount of losses of different elements during the melting operation are as under: Carbon 0.1%; Silicon 10%; Manganese 20%; Sulphur (-) 0.02%; Phosphorus 0%.

Considering 1000 kg of charge, the amount of various elements present in the charge can be found. The loss of elements during the metal melting operation can then be considered, to arrive at the final composition.

	Mass of charge (kg)	Carbon %	Carbon kg	Si %	Si kg	Mn %	Mn kg	S %	S kg	P %	P kg
Pig iron 1	300	3.2	9.6	2.4	7.2	0.5	1.5	0.1	0.3	0.6	1.8
Pig iron 2	300	3.4	10.2	2.0	6.0	0.5	1.5	0.05	0.15	0.8	2.4
C.I. Scrap	400	3.2	12.8	2.5	10.0	0.7	2.8	0.08	0.32	0.7	2.8
Total	1000		32.6		23.2		5.8		0.77		7.0
Change in metal melting			(–) 0.0326		(–) 2.32		(–) 1.16		(+) 0.0015		(–) 0.00
Net amount			32.567		20.88		4.64		0.7715		7.0
% in molten metal			3.2567		2.088		0.464		0.07715		0.7

Advantages and disadvantages   Cupola is widely used for melting cast irons because of the following advantages:

- It is simple and easy to operate.
- It is available in a wide range of capacities.
- It can be operated continuously or as a batch-type furnace.
- It is possible to control the melt composition to obtain cast iron of required quality.
- It is possible to control the temperature.
- It has low cost of installation, maintenance and operation.

The main disadvantage of the cupola furnace concerns its noise and air pollution. Air pollution control is difficult and costly. Several methods can be used to improve the economy of operation and increase the metal melting rate. In one of the methods, exhaust gases are passed through a heat exchanger where the incoming air is pre-heated to a temperature as high as 600°C. In another method, oxygen-enriched air blast is used to further increase the temperature and accelerate the rate of metal melting.

From environmental considerations, there is an increasing trend to use horizontal rotary cupolas. These are oil-fired and produce less pollution. They use compressed air to atomize the fuel and are capable of producing up to 20,000 kg of molten grey iron per day. They can also utilize scrap as small as machine turning chips. Their initial and maintenance costs are not too high.

5.3 Metal Pouring

The molten metal is taken from the melting furnace to the moulds with the help of a container called a ladle. Two important requirements of this activity are that (i) proper pouring temperatures are maintained, and (ii) only high quality metal is introduced into the moulds. The choice of the size of the pouring ladle depends on the maximum volume of the metal required to be held at a given time.

There are several types of ladles. In small foundries, simple clay–graphite crucibles [Figure 5.6(a)] are mostly used for non-ferrous metals. Their only limitation is that they are quite susceptible to breakage; they are otherwise resistant to most metals. Care has to be taken to avoid their picking up moisture. Their popularity is due to the fact that they can hold molten metal for a sufficiently long time under normal conditions. In large foundries, where big-sized castings are made by pit moulding, a bottom-pour ladle [Figure 5.6(b)] or teapot type ladle [Figure 5.6(c)] is used. The bottom-pour ladle has a plug at the bottom and it can be used where the moulds move past the pouring station on a conveyor. By extracting metal from the bottom of the ladle, slag and other impurities that float on top of the melt cannot enter the mould. The lip-pouring or the teapot ladles are the easiest to pour, clean out and re-line. Ladles used for pouring ferrous metals are lined with a high alumina-content refractory material and pre-heated with gas flame to about 1450°C before filling. Once the ladle is filled, it is continuously used until the entire metal quantity is exhausted.

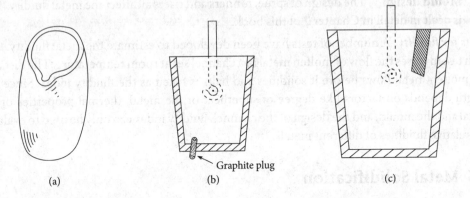

Figure 5.6 Some types of ladle: (a) Clay–graphite crucible; (b) Bottom-pour ladle; and (c) Teapot type ladle

5.4 Metal Fluidity

When any molten metal is poured into a mould, it must flow and fill all the regions of the mould before starting to solidify. This capability of the molten metal has been given the term *metal fluidity*. If the metal has insufficient fluidity, it will begin to solidify before it has filled the mould completely, resulting in defects like cold shut and misrun in the casting. One important factor influencing metal fluidity is the degree of superheat (defined by the difference between the temperature at which metal is poured and its melting temperature). Greater the degree of superheat, more is the fluidity of metal. Neither too high nor too low degree of superheat is desirable. When a molten metal with a high degree of superheat is poured into a sand mould, metal–mould reactions are accelerated and chances of the metal entering into small voids between the sand particles at the mould surface increase. The surface of the cast product may then have sand particles embedded in it. This is a casting defect known as *penetration.*

Other characteristics of molten metal influencing its flow or fluidity are its viscosity and surface tension. Lesser the viscosity of molten metal, greater is its fluidity. Similarly, lesser the surface tension of the liquid metal, higher is its fluidity. Besides, there are certain casting parameters, which also influence metal fluidity. Prominent among them are as follows:

- **Rate of pouring of metal** If the rate of pouring of molten metal into the mould cavity is slow, the fluidity decreases due to faster rate of cooling.

- **Mould material** The higher the thermal conductivity of mould material, the lesser is the metal fluidity.

- **Mould heating** Heating the mould improves metal fluidity.

- **Mould surface characteristics** The rougher the mould cavity surface, the lesser is the metal fluidity.

- **Mould design** The design of sprue, runners and risers all affect the metal fluidity. This is dealt in detail in Chapter 7 of this book.

Tests for fluidity A number of tests have been developed to estimate the metal fluidity. One such test involves the flow of molten metal in a channel set at room temperature. The distance the molten metal flows before it solidifies and halts is taken as the fluidity index. Since this length depends on factors like degree of superheat of the metal, thermal properties of the metal and the mould, and the design of the channel, fluidity index can only be used to evaluate the relative fluidities of different metals.

5.5 Metal Solidification

When any molten metal is poured into a mould, a number of events take place during its solidification and subsequent cooling to room temperature. These events affect the size, shape, uniformity and chemical composition of the grains formed, and thereby, control the quality and characteristics of the cast product. The factors that strongly influence these events are the type of metal and the cooling rate, which in turn depend on the thermal properties of both the metal and the mould, and the volume–surface area relationship of the casting.

Type of metal In case of a pure metal, solidification takes place at a constant temperature at which the complete latent heat of fusion is given off. The solidification begins at the mould wall where the temperature differential is the greatest, and as the time passes, the solid–liquid interface moves through the molten metal in towards the centre. Cooling of the solidified metal occurs as soon as it is formed. The solidified mass of metal, called the casting, is generally removed while it is still very hot from the mould. It is then allowed to cool in the open to bring it to room temperature.

The grain structure of a pure metal cast in a mould is given in Figure 5.7. Because of the largest temperature differential at the mould walls, the solidification starts there with the formation of a solidified shell having fine equi-axed grains. The growth of grains continues at the mould wall in a direction opposite to that of the heat transfer from the mould. The grains that have favourable orientation will grow in a columnar fashion as shown in the figure.

In case of some materials, new crystals can nucleate in the interior of the casting. These crystals then start growing to produce another region of randomly oriented spherical crystals, known as the equi-axed zone. This is preferred over the columnar structure and to promote this, techniques such as the use of low pouring temperatures and addition of alloying elements

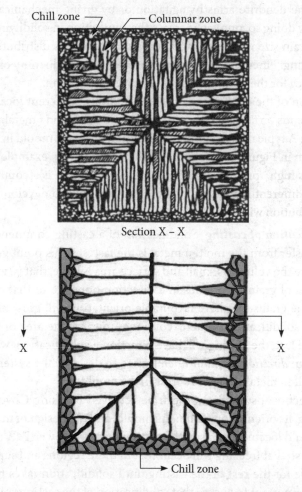

Chill zone

Columnar zone

Section X – X

Chill zone

Figure 5.7   Cast structure of a pure metal [Source: Kalpakjian and Schmid, *Manufacturing Engineering and Technology*, Pearson Education Asia.]

and inoculants are adopted. Castings having equi-axed zones possess isotropic properties (i.e., uniform properties in all directions).

In case of alloys, solidification starts as soon as the metal temperature falls below the liquidus, T_L, and is complete when it reaches the solidus, T_S. Within the range T_L to T_S, called the freezing range, the alloy is in a semi-solid or a pasty state with columnar dendrites. Aluminium and magnesium alloys have a wide freezing range and so these alloys remain in a mushy (liquid plus solid) state throughout the solidification process. Interestingly, ferrous alloys have relatively narrow freezing range. Alloys with wider freezing range are less preferred because of their tendency to develop casting defects like segregation and micro-porosity.

Cooling rate   The cooling rate of a metal has an important effect on the developed cast structure and the resulting grain size. Slow cooling rates ($\approx 10^2$ K/s) result in coarse dendritic structures that have a large spacing between the dendrite arms, while faster cooling rates ($\approx 10^4$ K/s) result in finer structures having smaller dendrite arm spacing. It is, however, possible to break the dendrite arms by agitation or by giving mechanical vibrations to the solidifying metal. By doing so, one can increase the convection in solidifying liquid metal and, thus, obtain finer grain size with equi-axed non-dendritic grains distributed more uniformly throughout the casting. Finer grain size promotes strength and ductility of the cast metal and reduces any tendency for the casting to crack during solidification.

Precise estimation of the cooling rate or the heat flow at different locations in the mould is not easy as it depends on several factors pertaining to the casting metal, the mould and the process parameters. A typical temperature distribution in a sand mould in which liquid metal is solidifying is given in Figure 5.8. In casting a thin section, for example, where the surface area to mass ratio is high, premature chilling and solidification is a common phenomenon. Uneven cooling in different regions of mould causes castings to develop non-uniform grain size and grain distribution with *anisotropic* properties.

Directional solidification of casting   Solidification of a casting commences from the point where the heat transfer from the molten metal is the fastest. This point generally lies in that area of casting where the volume is small and surface area is large, that is, where there is a thin section. The growth of grains continues in a direction opposite to that of the heat transfer from the mould. The grains that have favourable orientation will grow in columnar fashion (Figure 5.7). If the solidification of metal continues towards the area of large mass and the riser solidifies at the last, the casting will have directional solidification, which is desirable in most cases. The term *directional solidification* is used to describe the systematic way in which solidification of molten metal should progress in the mould.

The desired directional solidification can be achieved by using Chvorinov's rule in the design of the casting, its orientation within the mould, and the design of the riser system. This implies that we should locate sections of the casting that have lower V/A ratios to be farthest away from the riser so that freezing will occur first in these regions and supply of liquid metal will remain available for the rest of the casting until solidification takes place in the bulkier sections. Also, it is important to ensure that solidification of the sections of the mould that are in close proximity to the riser takes place last.

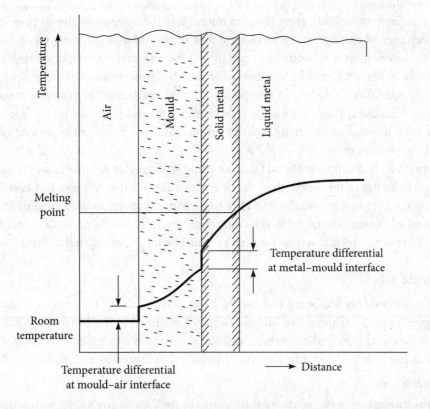

Figure 5.8 A typical temperature distribution in a sand mould

A practice followed in some industries for achieving directional solidification is by the use of *chills*. Chills are external heat sinks that cause fast freezing. Depending upon the location of their use, they may be internal or external. *Internal chills* are small metal pieces (of the same metal as of the casting) placed inside the mould cavity before pouring. Upon pouring, the molten metal will solidify first around these chills. On the other hand, *external chills* are metal pieces that are inserted in the walls of the mould cavity. When the molten metal is poured, these chills help to remove heat from the molten metal more rapidly than the surrounding sand thereby encouraging fast freezing in these areas while the connection to liquid metal of the riser still exists.

Metal solidification time When molten metal is poured into the mould, a thin layer of metal at the cool mould surface begins to solidify first; this layer thickens with the passing of time. With flat mould walls, the thickness of this solidified skin of metal at any point of time is proportional to the square root of time since the initiation of solidification. According to *Chvorinov's rule*, the solidification time is related to the volume of the casting and its surface area according to the following relation

$$\text{Solidification time} = c \, [\text{volume/surface area}]^n \quad \text{or,} \quad T = c \, [V/A]^n$$

where T is the total solidification time, minutes; V is the volume of the casting, cm³; A is the surface area of casting, cm²; n is an exponent whose value is generally taken as 2; and c is the mould constant with units min/cm², if volume and surface area of casting are taken respectively in cm³ and cm². In fact, the value of c depends on the particular conditions of the casting operation, including (a) properties of mould material (for example, specific heat, thermal conductivity, heat of fusion); (b) thermal properties of cast metal (for example, specific heat, thermal conductivity, heat of fusion); and (c) degree of superheat of molten metal at the pouring time.

Chvorinov's rule supports the fact that a casting with greater volume to surface area ratio cools and solidifies more slowly than the one with a lower ratio. We use this knowledge in designing the riser in a mould. For the riser to perform its function of feeding molten metal into the mould cavity, the metal in the riser must remain in the liquid state longer than the casting. That is, solidification time for the riser must be far greater than that for the casting.

Example 5.2

Three components are being cast out of a non-ferrous alloy. These components are designed in such a manner that all have the same volume but their shapes are different: one is a cube, the second is a sphere, and the third one is a cylinder with the diameter same as the length. Determine the order in which these three components will solidify.

Solution

Let the volume of each component be unity. From Chvorinov's rule, by taking $n = 2$

Solidification time is proportional to $1/(\text{surface area})^2$

Let us now determine the (surface area)² of each component.

Cube Let each side of the cube be equal to a.

$$\text{Volume} = a^3 = 1$$
$$\text{Surface area} = 6\,a^2 = 6$$
$$(\text{Surface area})^2 = 36$$

Sphere Let the radius of the sphere be equal to r.

$$\text{Volume} = 4/3\,\pi r^3 = 1$$
$$r = [(3/(4\pi)]^{1/3}$$
$$\text{Surface area} = 4\,\pi r^2 = 4\,\pi\,[3/(4\,\pi)]^{2/3} = 4.84$$
$$(\text{Surface area})^2 = 23.5$$

Cylinder Let d and h be the diameter and height respectively of the cylinder. Also, $d = h$.

$$\text{Volume} = ¼\,\pi\,d^2\,h = ¼\,\pi\,d^3 = 1$$
$$d = (4/\pi)^{1/3}$$
$$\text{Surface area} = 2.\,¼\,\pi\,d^2 + \pi\,d\,h = ½\,\pi.d^2 + \pi\,d^2 = (3/2)\,\pi\,(4/\pi)^{2/3} = 5.54$$
$$(\text{Surface area})^2 = 30.5$$

It is clear that the cube-shaped casting will solidify first, and then the cylinder. The last to solidify will be the sphere-shaped casting.

Shrinkage during solidification   Most metals shrink during solidification; exceptions are grey cast iron and some aluminium alloys which actually expand. There are three types of shrinkage:

1.   Shrinkage of molten metal as it cools *before* the start of solidification.

2.   Shrinkage of the metal *during* solidification (i.e., during phase change from liquid to solid).

3.   Shrinkage of the metal *after* it has solidified, and is getting cooled to room temperature.

Out of these three, the largest amount of shrinkage (or contraction) occurs during cooling of the solidified metal (casting) to room temperature. Table 5.1 gives the amount of shrinkage during solidification and after solidification of some engineering materials. From the data of Table 5.1, we see that grey cast iron does not shrink during solidification; rather it expands. This is because graphite (an element in grey cast iron) has a relatively high specific volume, and when it precipitates as graphite flakes during solidification, it causes a net expansion of the metal.

Table 5.1   Amount of shrinkage during solidification and solid contraction of some engineering materials

Metal/alloy	Volumetric contraction due to	
	Solidification shrinkage, %	Solid thermal contraction, %
Aluminium	7.0	5.5
Magnesium	4.2	3.0
Grey cast iron	up to 2.5	3.0
Carbon steel	3.0	7.0
Bronze	5.5	6.0
Copper	4.5	7.5

In addition to dimensional changes, shrinkage can also cause porosity and cracking (hot tearing). A shrinkage cavity can form if the solidification is not directed. Voids caused by shrinkage occur in the region of highest temperature and where the metal stays in molten state for the longest period. The mould design must be modified so as to allow them to occur in the risers or sprue. Though the use of shrink rule (while making pattern for casting) takes care of dimensional changes, porosity in castings is undesirable as it makes them permeable and weak. When the location of the riser is not proper, thicker sections of the casting can develop porous regions at their centres because of contraction as the surfaces begin to solidify first. Porosity caused by shrinkage can be reduced in several ways. One way is to locate the runner properly so that adequate supply of liquid metal is provided to the region solidifying last. Another technique followed for reducing porosity is by increasing the solidification rate, which may be achieved by using internal or external chills in critical regions, or by making the temperature gradient steep with the use of mould material that has high thermal conductivity.

When liquid metal solidifies, the gases dissolved in it are released to either accumulate in regions of existing porosity or cause micro-porosity in the casting. This phenomenon is particularly predominant while casting copper, aluminium and grey cast iron.

Questions

1. What are the requirements of a metal melting furnace? Discuss the factors that influence the selection of a furnace for use in a foundry.

2. Explain the construction of a cupola furnace. What types of metals are generally melted in cupolas and why?

3. Describe an electric arc furnace and name some attractive features of this furnace.

4. What is the principle of an induction furnace? Distinguish between high frequency and low frequency induction furnaces as regards their working principle and areas of application.

5. What do you understand by the term *fluidity* of molten metal? What are the factors that influence it? Discuss them. Give a simple method to evaluate the relative fluidities of different materials.

6. What is the effect of the cooling rate of molten metal on the structure of the casting? How can the cooling rate be controlled?

7. Name the three types of shrinkage that most molten metals undergo when they are solidified and brought to room temperature. Discuss some effects of shrinkage on the quality of castings.

8. Name a metal or alloy that expands rather than shrinks when it is solidified from the liquid state. Give reasons for that.

9. When molten metal is poured into a mould, a number of events take place during its solidification and subsequent cooling to room temperature. What are these events, and what factors influence these events?

10. Give a typical temperature distribution in a sand mould in which liquid metal is solidifying.

11. What do you understand by directional solidification of casting? Is it advantageous? How? Explain methods by which it can be achieved.

Fill in the Blanks

1. Solidification time of a casting is inversely proportional to the square of its _____.

2. For melting of relatively small quantities of non-ferrous metals and alloys, the furnace commonly used is _____.

3. Temperature and chemistry control of molten metal in a crucible furnace is _____.

4. _____furnace can also be used for maintaining the molten cast iron at constant temperatures for longer time.

5. _____ furnaces are popular in foundries because of their (i) high melting rates, (ii) high pouring temperature, (iii) ability to produce high quality of metal of almost any desired composition and (iv) ability to hold the molten metal at constant temperature for longer periods of time.

6. The frequency of alternating electrical current that is passed through the coil to generate an alternating magnetic field in case of an induction furnace is of the order of _____ c/s.

7. _____ furnace is widely used for melting grey, nodular and white cast irons.

8. In a cupola furnace, silicon loss due to oxidation is generally of the order of _____ %.

9. The main disadvantage of cupola furnace is _____.

10. Most metals shrink during solidification; the exception is _____.

11. _____ during solidification of metal castings is undesirable as it makes them permeable and affects their strength.

Choose the Correct Answer

1. Which one of the following is generally not considered as a requirement of metal melting furnace?
   a. It should provide adequate alloying of molten metal.
   b. It should provide molten metal at the desired temperature.
   c. It should be able to hold the molten metal for an extended period of time without deterioration of quality.
   d. It should not cause pollution of environment.

2. Which one of the following is not a metal melting furnace?
   a. pit furnace
   b. split furnace
   c. arc furnace
   d. induction furnace

3. Pit furnace is also named as
   a. arc furnace
   b. induction furnace
   c. cupola furnace
   d. crucible furnace

4. The furnace generally used for melting relatively small quantities of low-melting point non-ferrous metals and alloys is
   a. arc furnace.
   b. induction furnace.
   c. cupola furnace.
   d. crucible furnace.

5. The furnace commonly used for melting of non-ferrous metals and steel in batch quantities is
   a. open hearth furnace.
   b. induction furnace.
   c. cupola furnace.
   d. crucible furnace.

6. The furnace that has high melting rates, high pouring temperatures, ability to produce high quality of metal of almost any desired composition and ability to hold the molten metal at constant temperature for longer periods of time is

   a. open hearth furnace.   c. cupola furnace.
   b. electric arc furnace.   d. crucible furnace.

7. A direct arc furnace has a thermal efficiency of nearly

   a. 30 percent.   c. 70 percent.
   b. 50 percent.   d. 95 percent.

8. The furnace that rocks back and forth so that the metal charge comes in contact with the hot refractory lining and picks up heat for melting is

   a. open hearth furnace.   c. cupola furnace.
   b. indirect electric arc furnace.   d. crucible furnace.

9. Which one of the following furnaces suffers from the main disadvantage that the noise pollution is high?

   a. open hearth furnace   c. cupola furnace
   b. electric arc furnace   d. crucible furnace

10. The type of furnace which is becoming very popular because of very high melting rates, and less pollution is

   a. electric induction furnace.   c. cupola furnace.
   b. electric arc furnace.   d. crucible furnace.

11. For melting cast iron, the commonly used furnace is

   a. pit furnace.   c. rotary furnace.
   b. open hearth furnace.   d. cupola furnace.

12. The most commonly used flux in cupola furnace is

   a. dolomite.   c. lime stone.
   b. calcium carbide.   d. borax.

13. The required amount of air under pressure enters the cupola furnace from the air chamber through openings, which are called

   a. limbs.   c. goose necks.
   b. tuyeres.   d. sprues.

14. Molten metal after being taking from the furnace, is stored in

   a. pouring basin.   c. ladle.
   b. sprue.   d. riser.

15. In a foundry, the molten metal is taken from the melting furnace to the moulds with the help of a container called

   a. ladle.   c. slinger.
   b. sprue.   d. runner.

16. One important factor influencing the molten metal fluidity is its
    a. hardness.
    c. degree of superheat.
    b. brittleness.
    d. ability to get oxidized.

17. The solidification of alloys starts as soon as the metal temperature falls below the
    a. liquidus.
    b. solidus.
    c. freezing range.
    d. average of melting temperatures of the constituent metals.

18. If c and n are constants, according to *Chvorinov's rule*, the solidification time is related to the volume of the casting and its surface area as
    a. Solidification time = c [volume/ surface area]^n
    b. Solidification time = c/n [volume/surface area]
    c. Solidification time = [volume/surface area]$^{c/n}$
    d. Solidification time = $c.n$[surface area/ volume]

19. Most metals shrink during solidification; exception is
    a. copper.
    c. manganese.
    b. grey cast iron.
    d. silver.

20. Three components are being cast out of a non-ferrous alloy. These components are designed in such a manner that they all have the same volume but their shapes are different: one is a cube, the second is a sphere, and the third one is a cylinder with the diameter same as the length. Identify the correct statement.
    a. Cube will solidify first.
    c. Cylinder will solidify first.
    b. Sphere will solidify first.
    d. All the three will solidify at the same time.

Answers

1. a.	2. b.	3. d.	4. d.	5. a.	6. b.	7. c.	8. b.	9. b.	10. a.
11. d.	12. c.	13. b.	14. c.	15. a.	16. c.	17. a.	18. a.	19. b.	20. a.

6

Casting Cleaning, Inspection and Repairing

LEARNING OBJECTIVES

After reading this chapter, you should be able to understand the following:

- The operations involved in fettling of castings.

- The reasons for giving heat treatment to castings.

- The various methods of destructive and non-destructive testing of castings.

- The various casting defects.

6.1 Cleaning of Castings (Fettling)

After removal from the mould, most castings need some cleaning and finishing (also called fettling) operations to be performed on them. These operations include the following:

1. Removal of sand cores

2. Removal of gates and risers

3. Removal of fins and flash

4. Cleaning of surface

5. Repairing of defects, if any

Since these operations are time consuming and expensive, it is essential to try to eliminate or at least minimize their need when designing the product and choosing the specific casting method. Besides, possibilities should also be explored for automation of these operations.

Sand cores are removed from castings usually by mechanical shaking, hydro blasting or at times by chemical dissolution depending upon the size, complexity and hardness of the core. Gates and risers are either knocked off or cut-off by an abrasive wheel or a power saw. Alternatively, they are removed by melting them away with an oxy-acetylene flame. The casting surface, from where the gates and risers have been removed, is generally rather rough. Small projections may easily be chipped off with the help of either hand tools or pneumatic chisels. To remove fins, flash and sand that might be sticking to the surface of castings, a process called *tumbling* is employed. In the tumbling process, castings together with abrasive material (in the form of broken grinding wheels), cleansing fluid and metal shots are loaded in a horizontal barrel and given a slow rotary motion. The castings rub and strike against each other as well as against the abrasive grinding wheel pieces. Alternatively, castings may be subjected to *sand blasting*, *shot blasting* or *vibratory finishing* process.

Parts with surface flaws such as cracks, voids and laps may not be rejected, particularly when they are large enough in size and small enough in quantity to not warrant any change in the pattern, die or process. In such situations, it may be economically more attractive to repair the parts. If the material of casting is weldable, repairs can be carried out by removing the defective region (either by chipping or grinding) and then filling the void formed with weld metal deposition. Blowholes or fine pores that exist at the surface can be filled with some resin by a process called *impregnation*.

6.2 Heat Treatment of Castings

Mechanical and metallurgical properties of metal castings can be altered with heat treatment processes. These processes involve controlled heating and cooling of castings without major change in their shape. Heat treatment is mostly carried out to improve the product performance by increasing the strength or other desirable characteristics such as hardening or softening of material. For example, steel castings may be *annealed* to reduce the brittleness (and hardness) or the internal stresses that might have resulted due to rapid uneven cooling in some previous operation. Ferrous castings may be *tempered* for enhancement of toughness. The form of graphite in ferrous castings may be made either nodular or spheroidal so as to make the cast metal more ductile and shock-resistant. The structure of white cast iron is very hard, wear-resistant and brittle. It can be annealed in an atmosphere of carbon monooxide and carbon dioxide at 800 – 900°C to convert it into malleable iron. Non-ferrous castings can also be heat treated to provide stress relief.

6.3 Inspection and Testing of Castings

Inspection and testing of castings is necessary in order to determine their quality and the presence and extent of any defect in them. Inspection and testing are essential as they save time and money, since by doing so, the components found defective at an early stage can be discarded and further value addition on them will not be done.

Techniques of testing can be divided into two groups: destructive testing and non-destructive testing. Table 6.1 gives the advantages and limitations of both the techniques of testing.

Table 6.1 Destructive versus non-destructive testing

Destructive testing	Non-destructive testing
The component is destroyed either during the test or when preparing the test specimen	There is no damage to the component being evaluated
Advantages	**Advantages**
1. Provides more reliable measurement of how a component will behave in service conditions. 2. Provides direct and quantitative results that can be used for design. Interpretation of results is easy.	1. Can be applied on specimen, irrespective of the quantity of components available. 2. Can be applied on specimen without regard to the component cost. 3. Can often be applied on components when they are in use. 4. Can be applied on all components of production lot when results on a sample of components show high variability, or on a representative sample if results show sufficient uniformity. 5. Different tests can be performed on the same specimen. 6. A test may be repeatedly carried out on the same specimen. 7. Little or no specimen preparation is needed. 8. Machinery and equipment needed for a test are portable and relatively less costly. 9. Labour costs involved in a test are generally low.
Limitations	**Limitations**
1. Applied to a sample. The sample must be representative of the lot. 2. Tested part becomes useless for future use. 3. Generally, it is not possible to repeat a test on the same sample. 4. Generally, it is not possible to use the same sample for multiple tests. 5. Not recommended for few-in-number parts or costly parts. 6. Cannot be applied to parts in use. If done, testing will terminate the useful life of the part. 7. Generally, extensive machining or preparation of test specimen is required. 8. Cost of machinery or equipment needed for a test is generally high. 9. Labour costs involved in a test are generally high.	1. Interpretation of results is generally necessary by skilled and experience personnel. 2. Different persons may interpret the test results differently. 3. Test results are measured indirectly and they are often qualitative.

Destructive testing techniques As the name suggests, here the sample casting gets destroyed during testing and it becomes useless for future service. There are three classes of such tests:

1. Tests to investigate internal characteristics. The sample casting may be dissected or sectioned for the test.

2. Tests to determine leaks or weak sections. The sample casting is tested with water or other fluid under pressure.

3. Tests to determine some mechanical properties, such as tensile strength, percentage elongation and so on. Test specimens are taken out from various sections of the sample castings to perform the test in which the specimen fails.

Non-destructive testing (NDT) techniques Non-destructive testing techniques are used where we cannot afford to destroy the sample castings for any reason. The tests are carried out in such a way that the integrity and surface texture of casting do not change. The techniques require considerable skill of the technician, and interpreting test results may be difficult because the results are mostly subjective.

Human error can, however, be reduced by using computer graphics and other advanced techniques. The characteristic features of some commonly used non-destructive testing techniques are given here.

- **Optical or visual inspection** This is the simplest and most frequently used technique in which outward surface and appearance of the casting is inspected for surface defects and aesthetics by visual inspection with or without the use of optical aids such as mirrors, magnifying glasses and microscopes. Video cameras and computer systems can be used to automate the inspection. Borescopes or similar devices can be used to get accessibility to otherwise inaccessible locations.

- **Dimensional inspection** Using metrological instruments, various features and dimensions on a casting, such as linear and circular dimensions and squareness can be checked.

- **X-ray and gamma-ray inspection** These techniques involve the use of radiography to detect internal flaws such as cracks and porosity in a casting. The principle involved is the indication of difference of density by different shades of colour on the X-ray film. When a ray penetrates the casting, the metal surrounding the defect, being denser, shows up as a lighter-shaded area while internal defects like voids and cracks show up on the film as dark areas. Trained personnel are required for the conduct of such inspections and for proper interpretation of results. The equipment needed for these inspections is generally expensive.

- **Magnetic-particle inspection** Magnetic-particle inspection is based on the principle that ferromagnetic materials (such as iron, steel, nickel and cobalt alloys), when magnetized, will have distorted magnetic fields in the vicinity of material defects, as shown in Figure 6.1(a). Surface and sub-surface flaws, such as cracks [Figure 6.1(b)] and inclusions [Figure 6.1(c)], can produce magnetic anomalies that can be detected with the aid of magnetic particles. To carry out the test, the specimen must first be washed and dried. Fine ferromagnetic particles (either in dry form or in a liquid carrier)

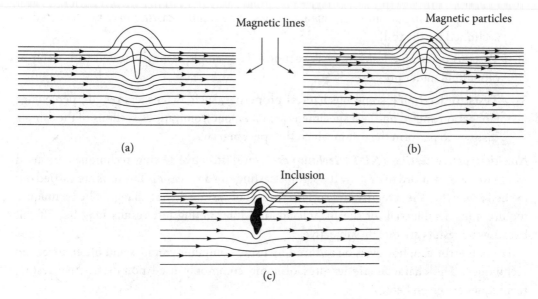

Figure 6.1 Schematic of magnetic particle inspection: (a) Surface crack causing disruption of magnetic field; (b) Magnetic particles spread on the test-piece surface are preferentially attracted to the magnetic field leakage; and (c) Sub-surface inclusion causing magnetic field disruptions that can be detected at the test-piece surface

are placed on the surface of the casting. A magnetic field is applied to magnetize the part. Any discontinuity in the form of surface or sub-surface cracks will interrupt the magnetic field and concentrate the particles along the contours of the defects [Figure 6.1(b)]. The particles may be coloured with pigments for better visibility on metal surfaces. It may be noted that for a flaw to be detected by this inspection technique, it must produce a significant disturbance of the magnetic field at the surface of the part. To illustrate, let us take an example of a steel bar. When placed within an energized coil, a magnetic field will be produced with its lines of flux travelling along the axis of the bar, as shown in Figure 6.2(a). Any defect perpendicular to this axis will disturb the field significantly and can be detected by this technique. However, if the crack or the defect runs along the axis of the specimen, the lines of flux will not be disturbed sufficiently, with the result that the defect may go undetected.

In order to detect axially-located defects, the same sample may be magnetized by passing a current through it, as shown in Figure 6.2(b). The axial defect will now become a significant perturbation and get detected, while the defect located perpendicular to the axis may go undetected. It follows from this that a series of inspections with different forms of magnetization may be required to completely inspect a given component. This test is applicable only on parts made of ferromagnetic materials, and it is advised that the parts be de-magnetized and properly cleaned after the test.

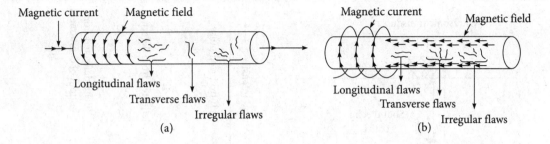

Figure 6.2 Schematic of magnetic particle inspection: (a) A bar positioned within a magnetizing coil will have an axial magnetic field. Defects in the bar located parallel to this field may go unnoticed whereas those that disrupt the magnetic field and are close to the test-piece surface will be detected; and (b) The bar, when magnetized by a current passing through it, will have a circumferential magnetic field. Flaws located longitudinally and at 45° will get detected, while transverse flaws may go unnoticed

- **Fluorescent penetrant inspection** Fluorescent penetrants are used to detect extremely minute and open pores and cracks on the casting surface. The part to be tested is first subjected to a thorough cleaning and then dried prior to the test. Figure 6.3(i) shows the initial surface with an open crack. The penetrant is applied to the surface of the part by brushing or spraying and allowed to seep into cracks or pores present, if any [Figure 6.3(ii)]. Excess penetrant is then wiped off or washed away with a solvent [Figure 6.3(iii)]. A developing agent is applied so that the penetrant seeps back to the surface by capillary action [Figure 6.3(iv)]. The size and location of defects become apparent when the surface is examined under fluorescent light.

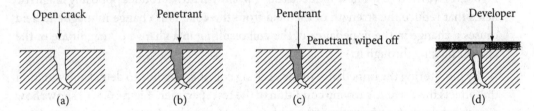

Figure 6.3 Schematic of penetrant inspection: (a) Initial surface with open crack; (b) Penetrant applied at the surface gets pulled into the crack by capillary action; (c) Excess penetrant is removed; and (d) Developer is applied on the surface, some penetrant is extracted, and the test-piece surface is inspected

- **Ultrasonic inspection** A sound signal of known frequency (higher than audible range) is applied at the casting surface, which is reflected after a short time interval. An internal defect such as a crack or blowhole interrupts the signal beam and reflects a portion of the ultrasonic energy, which can be recorded with the help of special instruments (Figure 6.4). Analysis of data helps to indicate the location and size of any defect in the casting. In case of large size parts, the ultrasonic beam can be passed on to the part from several directions in order to get a complete picture of the inside of the casting.

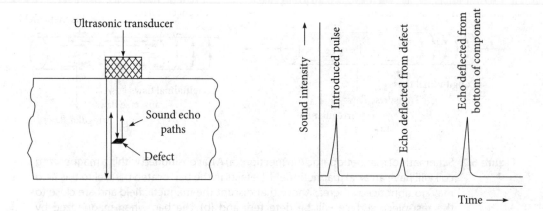

Figure 6.4 Schematic of ultrasonic testing

- **Acoustic emission inspection** This process of inspection involves the detection of high-frequency stress wave signals generated by the cast component during plastic deformation, crack initiation and propagation, phase transformation and abrupt reorientation of the grain boundaries occurring in it. To perform the test, the cast part is elastically stressed by applying a force, and acoustic emissions from the part are detected by using sensors made of piezoelectric ceramic elements.

- **Eddy current testing** Whenever an electrically conductive material is exposed to an alternating magnetic field such as the one generated by a coil of wire carrying an AC current, small electric currents are induced on or near the surface of the material. Refer to Figures 6.5(a) and (b). These induced *eddy currents*, in turn, produce opposing magnetic fields that reduce the strength of the field from the coil. This change in magnetic field causes a change in the impedance of the coil resulting in a change of magnitude of the current flowing through it.

  By monitoring the impedance of the exciting coil, it is possible to detect any situation that affects the current-carrying condition of the test specimen. Figure 6.5(c) shows how a crack would change the paths of the eddy currents, thereby changing the characteristics of the induced magnetic field in that region.

  Eddy current testing has been used to detect surface and sub-surface defects, such as cracks, voids and inclusions, although the technique is not as sensitive as penetrant testing or magnetic particle testing.

- **Pressure testing** Only those castings that are to be used for transporting liquids or gases are subjected to this test. The castings are tested for leakage, pressure tightness or impermeability. The test may be carried out with pressurized air or water. In the case of water pressure testing, water at a certain pressure (depending upon the conditions under which the casting has to be used) is passed through the casting. By keeping the outer surface of the casting dry initially, the presence of water at the outer surface during the test will show the presence of any leakage. In the pressurized air test, a soap solution is applied on the surface of the casting. Upon subjecting the casting to pressurized air, bubbles will appear on the surface at the location of the leakage.

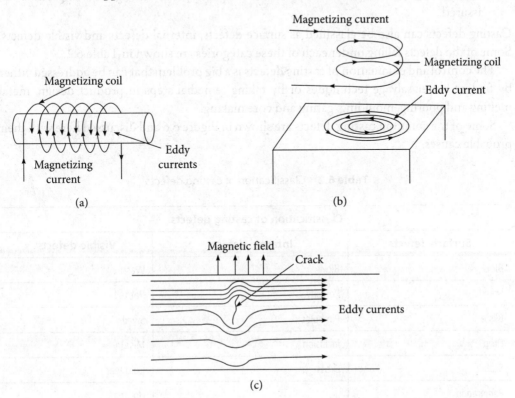

Figure 6.5 Schematic of eddy current testing. Eddy currents induced in work material change the magnitude of magnetizing current whether: (a) Magnetizing coil is placed around the workpiece, or (b) Magnetizing coil is placed close to the workpiece; and (c) Presence of any crack in the workpiece changes the magnetic field in that region, and thus can be detected

6.4 Defects in Casting

A casting defect can be defined as a deficiency or imperfection in the casting that makes the casting unacceptable with respect to the design and service requirements.

Casting defects can be classified into three categories:

1. Major or most severe defects, which result in scrapping of the casting. For example, a casting may be scrapped, if:
    - It fails to meet functional requirements because of porosity and/or improper shrinkage.
    - It fails to meet the physical requirements due to misruns, cold shut, metal penetration or rough surfaces that hamper machining and finishing operations.

2. Intermediate defects, which allow salvaging of the casting, provided the cost of repair does not exceed a certain limit.

3. Minor defects, which permit easy and economical repair or salvage so that profit is still assured.

Casting defects can also be classified as surface defects, internal defects and visible defects. Some of the defects falling under each of these categories are shown in Table 6.2.

The control and elimination of casting defects is a big problem that can be addressed either by finding better salvage techniques or by taking remedial steps in product design, metal melting and pouring, moulding, gating and core making.

Some of the common casting defects are shown in Figure 6.6 and discussed here with their probable causes.

Table 6.2 Classification of casting defects

Classification of casting defects		
Surface defects	**Internal defects**	**Visible defects**
Blow	Blow	Wash
Scar	Porosity	Rat tail
Blister	Pin holes	Swell
Drop	Inclusion	Misrun
Scab	Dross	Cold tear
Penetration		Hot tear
Buckle		Shrinkage/Shift

Blow hole and Pin Hole Blowholes, gas holes or gas cavities are significant-sized, well rounded shaped cavities having a clean and smooth surface. They may appear either on the surface of a casting or inside. When they appear on the casting surface, they are also called open cavities. The main cause of their occurrence is excessive gases in the mould that could not escape from it. The gases are formed in the mould due to the burning of combustible material in the moulding sand and core by the heat of the molten metal. The moisture present in the sand becomes steam as it takes heat from the hot metal. Also, as the molten metal solidifies, the dissolved gases try to come out. If these gases and steam are not able to escape through the mould, they collect into a bubble at the high points or spread in the form of several fine bubbles throughout the molten metal in the cavity and prevent the liquid metal from filling that space. As a result, blowholes and pin holes are formed in the casting. These defects can be prevented by taking all precautions to avoid (i) too less venting of the mould;

(ii) insufficient drying of mould and cores; (iii) excess moisture content in the moulding sand, moisture on chills or chaplets; (iv) too hard ramming, which reduces mould permeability; (v) excess carbonaceous or other organic materials in mould or in core sand; and (vi) excess gas dissolved during metal melting, which is rejected during solidification.

Blister and scar A scar is a shallow blow that normally occurs on a flat surface, whereas a blow occurs on a convex casting surface. A blister is also a shallow blow but covered with a thin layer of metal. Both are caused by the gases evolved in the mould.

Scab This is a rough irregular projection on the surface of a casting, sometimes containing embedded sand. It occurs when a portion of the face of a mould lifts or breaks down and the recess is filled by metal.

Shift This is a mismatch of the two halves of the casting at the parting line of the casting due to misalignment of pattern parts, misalignment of cope and drag parts or due to improper handling and fitting of the mould, see bottom of Figure 6.7. It could also be caused by worn-out or bent clamping pins or even faulty core boxes. A shift of small magnitude may be rectified by repairing, but if there is a large shift, the casting may be scrapped.

Core shift This defect occurs as a consequence of a cored hole, either of the wrong shape or at the wrong location. Core shift due to wrong shape of the core can severely alter the dimensions of hole/cavity, which are dependent on the core position. When caused by incorrect positioning of core, undersized or oversized core prints, use of incorrect sized chaplets, dislodging of the core from its position by the inrush of molten metal during pouring or due to misalignment of cores during assembling of moulds, core shift can make a casting unserviceable.

Swell Swell is a localized or general enlargement of casting caused due to enlargement of the mould cavity by metal pressure. Swell may be caused due to: (i) improper ramming, (ii) too large sprue that results in higher metal pressure or (iii) rapid pouring of the molten metal.

Sponginess Sponginess or honey-combing is a surface defect in the form of a number of small cavities in close proximity. It is caused by dirt or inclusions held mechanically in suspension in the molten metal as a result of imperfect skimming of slag in the ladle or incorrect gating design. The impurities, being lighter than the metal, rise to the upper part of the mould cavity, and if venting is inadequate, the trapped gas in the form of bubbles also accompanies the impurities to cause this defect.

Shrinkage A void or a sump on the casting surface, termed as shrinkage defect, is caused mainly due to concentrated contraction of the metal during solidification. Other reasons could be improper size and location of gates and runners, absence or inadequacy of risers, abrupt changes in the thickness of casting, inadequate or insufficient radiusing or filleting of corners.

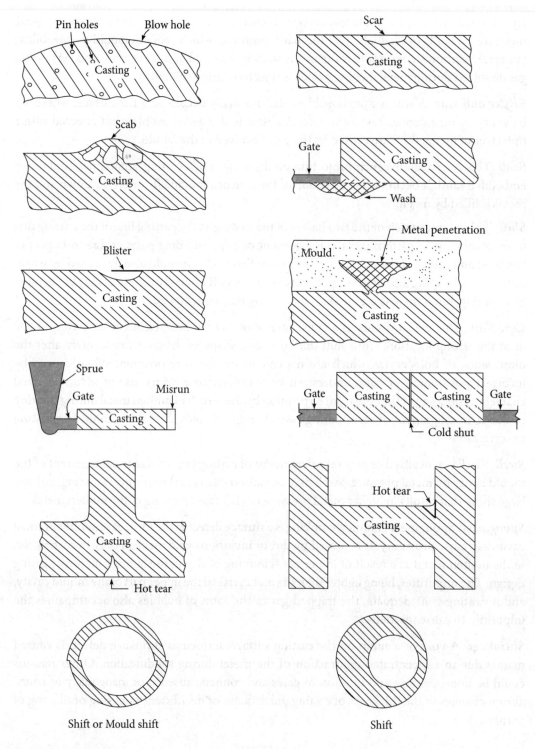

Figure 6.6 Some common defects in sand castings

Hot tear It is a torn discontinuity within the metal casting, present internally or externally. It is caused due to obstructed contraction during solidification occurring as a result of poor mould design. Abrupt changes in section thickness or inadequate filleting of inside corners give rise to extra stresses on some parts of casting leading to hot tears. Improper pouring temperature control and inaccurate placement of gates and risers also cause hot tears.

Cold cracks Quite similar to hot tears, cold cracks are less torn discontinuity and they usually occur at temperatures lower than 250°C. Reasons for cold cracks are similar to those for hot tears in addition to mishandling of castings prior to stress relieving, poor part design features, sudden chilling due to early removal of casting from the mould and water spraying on hot castings.

Misrun and cold shut Misrun occurs when a mould cavity is not completely filled, whereas a cold shut is an extreme limit of misrun, which is seen as a discontinuity within the casting as a result of cast parts not fusing into each other. Low pouring temperatures and low metal fluidity are the chief causes of misruns and cold shuts. Either of these causes can result in thin sections solidifying before the mould is completely filled and/or two molten metal streams meeting at too low a temperature so that they are not able to fuse together properly. Other reasons that contribute to these defects are slow pouring, small gates, too low sprue height, improperly placed gates and runners, more number of thin sections, and the like.

Pour short When the mould cavity is not completely filled due to insufficient metal, it results in a defect called pour short. It is caused due to interruption during the pouring operation that may occur for any reason, including insufficient metal in the ladle.

Metal penetration or wash When the metal being cast penetrates the interstices of the sand grain and forms a fused aggregate of sand and metal on the surface, it is called metal penetration or wash. Metal penetration defect is generally bigger in size than wash. Factors which promote metal penetration and wash are soft rammed sand in localized areas, too coarse moulding and core sand, excessive metal temperature, and too high fluidity of the metal.

Runout or bust out Drainage of molten metal from the cavity to the flask walls is called runout or bust out. This generally results in incomplete casting. The causes for this defect could be one or more of these: (i) too large mould cavity, which is close to flask walls; (ii) out of parallel or uneven match plate surfaces, which results in poor parting plane; (iii) inadequate mould weights or clamps to cause cope-lift and then runouts; (iv) improper sealing of mould joints; (v) excessive pouring pressure; and (vi) misalignment of cope and drag.

Inclusion Any separate non-metallic foreign material present in the cast metal is called inclusion. It may be in the form of oxides, dirt, slag or sand. The main causes of inclusions are faulty gating, faulty metal pouring, inferior moulding or core sand.

Rough surface finish Rough surface or micro irregularities on the surface of the casting occur due to poor ramming, coarse sand, too high metal fluidity or improper use of mould and core washes (mould or core washes are coatings applied to improve surface finish of castings).

Fin   This is a thin metal projection (flash) occurring around the casting at the parting line. The main causes for fins are poor fitting of cope and drag, damaged mating surfaces of cope and drag, high metal fluidity, high metal pressure due to too high sprue and insufficient mould clamping. The defect can be removed by shot blasting.

Hard spots   This defect occurs as a result of different hardness values at different areas of casting surface. The main causes for this defect are too rapid cooling in localized areas generally in thin sections, and incorrect use of chills.

Rat tail or buckle   When molten metal is poured at high temperature, it causes the thin outer layer of moulding sand to expand appreciably. When this layer fails to compress back, and get separated from the sand behind it, it remains over the surface of the casting and finally appears as an irregular line on the surface of the casting. The defect is called rat tail. A buckle is a more severe failure of the sand surface under compression.

This defect can be avoided by providing for proper expansion of mould.

Drop   A drop is the casting defect that occurs when the cope surface cracks or breaks and a piece of sand falls into the molten metal. The main causes of drop are low green strength of moulding sand and core, soft ramming and inadequate reinforcement of sand projections and core.

Fusion   This defect appears as a rough glossy surface over the casting and is caused due to melting of the sand with the heat of the metal and later getting fused to the casting surface. This defect can be prevented by using sand of higher refractoriness and by keeping pouring temperatures low.

6.5 Repair of Casting Defects

Casting defects are inevitable even for the best manufacturer. It is appropriate that defects in castings are identified and located at the product manufacturing site than passing the defective product to the user, who may not have the facilities and expertise to repair them. Common defects of castings include dross and inclusions, blowholes, shrinkage porosity, shrinkage cracks, cold shuts, hot cracking, hot tearing, hot shortness, misruns and so on. Such defects affect the surface roughness and also the strength of the castings. Hence, all foundries producing quality products do their best to implement zero defect policy; alternatively, they try to solve the problem of casting defects by repairing them suitably.

There are two basic methods used to solve the problem of casting defects.

1.   Take necessary actions before casting: This means

  - Improve the gating system to promote progressive solidification during casting
  - Control the suitable metal temperature during casting
  - Improve the melting technology to reduce the amount of dissolved gases and formation of metal oxide
  - Ensure enough feeding channels

2. After casting, if the products are found to have defects, they may be repaired by suitable methods that depend upon the nature of defects. Some of these methods are described here:

-   **Use of glues** To mend small blowholes or pin holes and shrinkage areas in grey cast iron castings, cast iron glue can be applied. The glue has quite high hardness and strength, so it does not affect the usage of cast component. It must be remembered that glue repairing should be applied to rough surfaces, and not to the machined surfaces.

-   **Healant repairing** Healant repairing involves the application of a kind of metallic glue as substitute of the traditional weld repairing. Such metallic healant is used to repair castings that are made of steel, iron, aluminum and bronzes. This repairing process does not cause damage to the castings due to the absence of residual stresses that are usually present when a defective part is subjected to weld repairing.

-   **Weld repairing** Welding is one of the most common methods of repair of castings – both ferrous and non-ferrous.

    -   Electrical welding is widely used for repairing surface defects such as large air holes and cracks. These defects are repaired by weld filling some materials inside the cavities. It is worth noting that weld repair requires professional welders, and it takes time and costs to carry out this activity. Welding may also introduce undesirable residual stresses in the casting. Sometime, due to the special material of castings, weld repair might cause more defects in the castings. In that case, the casting may have to be scraped, resulting in high financial losses.

    Weld repairing involves the following steps:

    -   Fix the place, size and the types of defects.
    -   Dig certain areas around the defects. Grind or machine suitable welding grooves.
    -   Choose suitable weld materials. Usually the welding material is the same or similar as the casting. But for some special casting materials, such as the manganese steel, it becomes necessary to choose higher quality welding materials (weld material should be with lower stress) to ensure the weld quality.
    -   Choose the right welding speed and welding type according to the size, depth and types of defects. The final welds should be raised from the casting surface.
    -   Machine the repaired surface appropriately. If necessary, grinding tools may be used.

    The casting surface thus weld repaired must be subjected to NDT to ensure that there is no weld cracks or undercut defects.

    For the repair of surface defects on a casting consisting essentially of a non-weldable alloy or a difficult-to-weld alloy, a method involving the following steps may be used:

- Form a cavity in the casting by removing the defect.
- Place filler material in the cavity; the filler material should have a strength that is less than or about equal to the strength of the alloy.
- Fusion weld the filler material in the cavity; fusion welding may produce surface cracks on the casting and sub-surface cracks in the casting near the cavity.
- Braze the surface crack on the casting.
- Process the casting with a hot isostatic pressure (HIP) process to close the sub-surface cracks in the casting.

Hot isostatic pressing (HIP) is a process used to reduce the porosity of metals. In this process, the component is subjected to both high temperature and an isostatic gas pressure in a high pressure containment vessel. The pressurizing gas most widely used is argon, an inert gas, so that the metal and inert gas do not chemically react. The chamber is heated, causing the pressure inside the vessel to increase. Pressure is applied to the material from all directions (hence, the term *isostatic*). When castings are treated with HIP, the simultaneous application of heat and pressure eliminates internal voids and micro-porosity through a combination of plastic deformation, creep and diffusion bonding. HIP also improves fatigue resistance of components.

- **Vacuum impregnation**   Vacuum impregnation is the process by which leak-proof functionality of castings can be achieved by sealing the porosity without changing their dimensional or functional characteristics. The vacuum component of the process removes air that occupies the migration path commonly known as porosity in castings, and the impregnation part of the process involves replacing the void with a durable and stable material suitable for the application or field of use.

  Vacuum impregnation prevents the migration of fluids or gases out of or into a casting, such as from contained areas to the atmosphere as in hydraulic pumps and transmissions; from adjacent independent passages as in oil and water circuits in an engine and graphite plates used in fuel cells; and from atmospheric conditions to the internals of a component as in insert or over-moulded plastic connectors, wire, cable and connector assemblies.

  Vacuum impregnation is claimed to be a preferred process to guarantee the pressure-proof, leak-proof and corrosion-proof requirements of parts and components used in critical operations. Castings or powdered metal components used in the following systems and products are reported to have been successfully impregnated: (i) engines; (ii) compressors; (iii) fuel systems; (iv) gear housings; (v) hydraulic systems; and (vi) gas and steam engine fittings.

Questions

1. What are the typical operations involved in fettling of castings? How are these operations done?

2. How can X-rays and gamma rays be used for inspection of castings? What kind of defects can be detected by the use of these rays?

3. How might defective castings be repaired to make them suitable for use in their intended applications?

4. What do you understand by magnetic particle inspection of castings? What is the precaution to be observed for this type of inspection?

5. What kinds of defects are detected by using fluorescent penetrants? Explain the procedure of making such an inspection.

6. What kinds of casting defects are detected by using ultrasonic waves? Explain the procedure of making such an inspection.

7. Classify casting defects. Name any five casting defects and give reasons for the occurrence of each of them.

8. Why do we need to conduct destructive tests on castings? Give any two destructive tests and the defects for which each is conducted.

9. Describe the procedure for repairing a defect in a casting consisting essentially of a non-weldable alloy.

10. Does the procedure of weld repairing a defect in a casting differ if the casting is made of a weldable alloy or a non-weldable alloy? How?

Fill in the Blanks

1. Mechanical and metallurgical properties of metal castings can be altered by _____.

2. _____ and _____ are the chief causes of misruns and cold shuts.

3. When the metal being cast penetrates the interstices of the sand grain and forms a fused aggregate of sand and metal on the surface, the defect caused is called _____.

4. Irregular-shaped holes running into and/or through the casting, when present inside the casting, are called _____.

5. An unwanted thin metal projection occurring around the casting at parting line is called _____.

6. Different levels of hardness at different areas of surface of casting is a defect called _____.

7. In _____ inspection of castings, a sound signal of known frequency (above audible range) is applied at the surface, which gets reflected back after a short interval of time.

8. Fins, flash and sand that might have been sticking to the surface of castings, can be removed by a process called _____.

9. A process used to reduce the porosity of metal castings by subjecting them to both a high temperature and an isostatic gas pressure in a high pressure containment vessel is called _____.

10. Vacuum impregnation is the process by which leak-proof functionality of castings can be achieved by _____ without changing their dimensional or functional characteristics.

Choose the Correct Answer

1. Fettling is a foundry operation during which
   a. core is given adequate support in the mould.
   b. molten metal is poured in the mould.
   c. casting is cleaned and finished.
   d. casting is inspected for any defect.

2. Fettling is a
   a. casting method.
   b. casting defect.
   c. cleaning process of castings.
   d. method of stirring the molten metal.

3. Tumbling is a process used in the foundry by which
   a. pattern is given a small motion and then taken out from the mould.
   b. core is given adequate support in the mould.
   c. fins, flash and sand that might have been sticking to the surface of castings are removed.
   d. the mould is given a shake after pouring the molten metal in the mould.

4. Sand blasting is a process used in the foundry by which
   a. different ingredients of moulding sand are mixed together.
   b. moulding sand is thrown on a metallic pattern in machine moulding.
   c. fins, flash. and sand that might have been sticking to the surface of castings are removed.
   d. dry sand is applied at the parting surface between cope and drag.

5. The brittleness of steel castings may be reduced by the heat treatment process called
   a. annealing.
   b. tempering.
   c. carburizing.
   d. quenching.

6. Which one of the following is not the cause of formation of blowholes in the castings?
   a. moisture on chills or chaplets
   b. venting of the mould
   c. carbonaceous or other organic materials in the mould
   d. insufficient drying of mould and cores

7. Blowholes or pin holes are produced due to
   - a. higher grain size.
   - b. lower percentage of clay.
   - c. higher moisture content.
   - d. all of the above.

8. The defect *blowhole* occurs in a casting mostly on a
   - a. convex casting surface.
   - b. flat casting surface.
   - c. concave casting surface.
   - d. vertical casting surface.

9. Chilling of a casting produces a defect known as
   - a. fusion.
   - b. cold shuts.
   - c. hot tears.
   - d. hot spot.

10. A mismatch of the two halves of the casting at the parting line of the casting is called
    - a. scab.
    - b. shift.
    - c. blister.
    - d. blowhole.

11. A localized or general enlargement of casting caused due to enlargement of mould cavity by metal pressure is called
    - a. scab.
    - b. swell.
    - c. blister.
    - d. blowhole.

12. Abrupt changes in section thickness or inadequate filleting of inside corners give rise to extra stresses on some parts of casting leading to a defect called
    - a. scab.
    - b. swell.
    - c. hot tears.
    - d. cold shuts.

13. When the metal being cast penetrates the interstices of the sand grain and forms a fused aggregate of sand and metal on the surface, the defect is called
    - a. wash.
    - b. dry clean.
    - c. rat tails.
    - d. fins.

14. A casting defect caused due to lack of molten metal fluidity prohibiting the molten metal from reaching the designated portion of the mould cavity, is called
    - a. misrun.
    - b. mismatch.
    - c. scab.
    - d. blister.

15. Turbulence of molten metal in the mould cavity can occur due to
    - a. use of core in the mould.
    - b. moisture on chills or chaplets.
    - c. absence of slag in the molten metal.
    - d. faulty molten metal pouring technique.

16. *Shift* is a metal casting defect that occurs due to
    - a. shifting of runner location to the location of riser.
    - b. entrapment of hot gases in the mould.

    c.   mis-alignment of pattern parts or mis-alignment of cope and drag.

    d.   too much metal fluidity that shifts the location of riser from its true position.

17. Ultrasonic inspection can be used to obtain information about

    a.   location of any defect in a casting.

    b.   amount of porosity in a casting.

    c.   number of cracks on the casting surface.

    d.   presence of magnetic particles in a casting.

18. Hot isostatic pressure process may be used on a casting for the purpose of

    a.   closing sub-surface cracks in the casting.

    b.   heating the casting to a uniform elevated temperature.

    c.   giving heat treatment to the casting.

    d.   introducing fine air holes in the casting.

19. Vacuum impregnation is the process used for repairing a metal casting to

    a.   withstand extremely low pressure.   c.   examine its impregnation capacity.

    b.   seal porosity.   d.   introduce shine on its surface.

20. To mend small air holes and shrinkage areas in grey cast iron castings, the recommended method will be to

    a.   use electric welding.   c.   apply cast iron glue.

    b.   use submerged arc welding.   d.   apply ultrasonic vibrations of low amplitude.

Answers

1. c.	2. c.	3. c.	4. c.	5. a.	6. b.	7. c.	8. a.	9. d.	10. b.
11. b.	12. c.	13. a.	14. a.	15. d.	16. c.	17. a.	18.a.	19. b.	20. c.

7

Casting Design Principles

LEARNING OBJECTIVES

After reading this chapter, you should be able to understand the following:

- The principles involved in the design of the gating and risering system.
- The basic design considerations in castings.
- The need for taking safety precautions in foundry operations.

7.1 Design of the Gating and Risering System

7.1.1 Design of gating system

The basic features of a casting system are shown in Figure 7.1. As the molten metal is poured into the pouring basin, it flows through the other parts of the gating system (sprue, runner and gates) and finally fills the mould cavity. The design of the gating system should ensure the following:

- The necessary amount of molten metal is able to flow through the system.
- The flow of molten metal into the mould cavity is at an appropriate speed and non-turbulent.
- While flowing through the gating system, the molten metal
  - does not lose much heat.
  - does not form an oxide by exposure to the environment.
  - does not allow contaminants (such as inclusions and oxides) to get introduced into the molten metal entering the mould cavity.

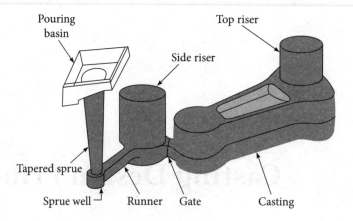

Figure 7.1   Basic features of a casting system

The rate of flow of molten metal in the gating system must be appropriate. If it is slow, high eat losses can take place with the result that casting will have defects like misruns and cold shuts. On the other hand, if the flow is fast, there can be erosion of the gating system and the mould cavity causing entrapment of mould material in the casting. The flow of molten metal can be regulated by appropriately selecting the cross-sectional areas of the various channels of the gating system. Further, the flow of molten metal in the gating system should not be turbulent; rather, it should be laminar. *Reynolds number,* Re, which represents the ratio of the *inertiato* the *viscous forces* in fluid flow, can be used to quantify the characteristics of flow. An Re value of up to 2,000 represents laminar flow; above 2,000 and up to 20,000 represents a mix of laminar and turbulent flow. In fact, the range of Re from 2,000 to 20,000 is acceptable in most gating systems. The value of Re above 20,000 represents turbulence, which is considered harmful because it promotes air entrainment and the formation of dross as a result of reaction between molten metal and air/other gases. Turbulence can be generally avoided by designing the gating system in such a way that there are minimum sudden changes in the direction of metal flow and geometry of channel cross-section.

The heat loss from molten metal can be controlled by appropriately designing the shape and length of the channels in the gating system. For instance, short channels with round or near-round cross-sections lose relatively less heat.

Let us consider different elements of a gating system.

1. **Pouring basin**   It is a cup-like cavity formed at the top of the sprue into which the molten metal is poured. Rectangular-shaped poring basins are desirable as they prevent vortex formation. Round pouring basins are very common as they are easy to form.

2. **Sprue**   It is a vertical channel through which the molten metal flows downward from the pouring basin. Short sprues are desirable, since their use reduces the distance through which the metal must fall when entering the runner. A tapered sprue, as shown in Figure 7.1, is preferred as it prevents vortex formation. The size of the tapered sprue can

be determined by using standard Bernoulli's theorem and equation of mass continuity, as under.

Bernoulli's theorem

$$h + p/\rho g + v^2/2g = \text{constant} \qquad (7.1)$$

where h is the height above a certain reference plane, p is the pressure at that height, v is the velocity of the fluid at that height, ρ is the density of the fluid and g is the gravitational constant.

Mass continuity equation

$$M = A_1 v_1 = A_2 v_2 \qquad (7.2)$$

where A and v are respectively the area of cross-section and velocity at any section. Let us denote 1 and 2 to respectively represent the planes at the top and bottom of the sprue, and assume that the metal pressure at the top of the sprue is the same as that at the bottom of the sprue. Neglecting frictional losses, if any, we can derive the following relation from Equations (7.1) and (7.2)

$$[A_1/A_2]^2 = h_2/h_1 \qquad (7.3)$$

We can thus determine the decreased cross-section at the bottom of sprue, as we move from top to bottom.

3. **Sprue-well** It is a depressed area formed at the bottom of the sprue to which the runner is connected. A big sprue-well helps to dissipate the kinetic energy of the falling metal stream. However, a too large sprue-well is not desirable as it reduces the casting yield.

4. **Runner** It is the channel that carries the molten metal from the bottom of the sprue to the mould cavity, or connects the sprue to the gate. Flat runners are easy to form. Too long runners can cause unnecessary cooling of the molten metal and therefore should be avoided.

5. **Gate** It is that portion of the runner through which molten metal enters the mould cavity. Gates that exit from the lower portion of the runner are desirable as they will not allow the dross to enter the mould cavity.

The specific design details of a gating system are influenced by the metal being cast. For example, for casting of turbulent-sensitive metals, such as aluminium, magnesium and their alloys, gating systems are designed to ensure non-turbulent metal flow and complete trapping of dross. On the other hand, for casting of turbulent-insensitive alloys such as cast iron, steel, and most copper alloys, gating systems are designed with short and open channels that permit quick filling of the mould cavity.

7.1.2 Design of riser

A riser is a sort of reservoir added in a mould for the purpose of feeding liquid metal to the solidifying casting so as to prevent shrinkage during solidification. It is, therefore, necessary that the riser must not solidify before the casting. Imagine what will happen if the riser solidifies before the casting: liquid metal from the casting would flow into the solidifying riser with the consequence that the casting shrinkage would be even more. Essentially, this implies that casting should be so designed that there is directional solidification starting from the extremities of the mould cavity toward the riser. In such a situation, the riser can feed molten metal continuously and will compensate for the solidification shrinkage of the whole casting. If, for any reason, this type of solidification cannot be achieved, multiple risers may be used with various sections of the casting solidifying toward their respective risers.

The design of rise is concerned with the functioning of a riser that will use minimum liquid metal. This would mean achieving a greater *yield of casting*. Yield of a casting can be defined as the ratio of casting weight to the total weight of the metal poured, that is, sum of the weights of the casting, sprue, gate and riser. The design of a riser, therefore, involves proper considerations to its location, shape and size.

- **Location**   The location of a riser should promote directional solidification of casting. In other words, solidification should start from the extremities of the mould and continue toward the riser. As the thickest sections of a casting will be the last to freeze, the risers should, therefore, ideally be located close to those sections of the casting.

- **Shape**   The best shape of a riser, according to Chvorinov's rule, is the one that has a long freezing time, that is, the one that has minimum surface area per unit volume. Though a spherical shape of riser would be ideal, the pattern maker and the mould maker would face practical problems with such a shape. The most common shape of a riser is a cylinder, whose height to diameter ratio is selected depending on the location of the riser, size of the flask, type of casting alloy, and other variables.

- **Size**   There are several methods to estimate the riser size, but one simple method is based on the basic requirement that total solidification time for the riser must be greater than the total solidification time of the casting. According to Chvorinov's rule, the total solidification time t_s is given by

$$t_s = B\,(V/A)^n \tag{7.4}$$

where n is a constant whose value is 1.75 to 2.0; V is the volume of the casting; A is the surface area; and B is the mould constant. Since the cavity for the riser and the cavity for the casting are in the same mould and they are filled by the same metal, the mould constant B will be the same for both regions. If we assume $n = 2$ and allow solidification time of the riser to be 30% greater than that of the casting, we have

$$t_{riser} = 1.30\,t_{casting} \tag{7.5}$$

or $[(V/A)^2]_{riser} = 1.30 [(V/A)^2]_{casting}$ (7.6)

Taking the riser geometry to be cylindrical with diameter d and height h, the square of the ratio of volume to surface area of the riser is

$$[(V/A)^2]_{riser} = [(d^2.h.\pi/4)/\pi (d.h + d^2.\pi/2)]^2$$

$$= [(d^2.h)/2(2 d.h + d^2)]^2$$ (7.7)

Further, if we fix the ratio of riser height to riser diameter, we will be left with only one unknown parameter. Let us take $h = 4 d$, and put this in Equation (7.7). We get

$$[(V/A)^2]_{riser} = 0.05 d^2$$ (7.8)

Knowing the value of $1.30 [(V/A)^2]_{casting}$ and equating it to $0.05 d^2$, we can find the value of d, the diameter of the cylindrical riser.

Note   If there happens to be a common surface between the riser and the casting (as in the case of a blind top riser), that common surface has to be subtracted from both riser and casting surface areas since this surface does not contribute to heat loss from either.

Example 7.1

A steel rectangular plate of size 80 mm × 150 mm × 18 mm is being cast by the sand moulding process in a foundry. Past data indicates that total solidification time for this casting is 2.0 minutes. For the mould of this casting, design a cylindrical riser with height/diameter ratio 1.2.

Solution

Let V, A and T respectively denote volume, surface area and total solidification time. Also, let D and h denote the diameter and height of the cylindrical riser.

We will first find the V/A ratio for the casting.

The volume $V = 8 \times 15 \times 1.8 = 216$ cm^3

The surface area $A = 2[8 \times 15 + 1.8 \times 15 + 1.8 \times 8] = 322.8$ cm^2

$V/A = 216/322.8 = 0.669$ cm

We know the solidification time of casting $T_c = 2.0$ min. We can use Chvorinov's rule. The mould constant c can be determined using the value of exponent $n = 2$.

$$c = \frac{T_c}{\left(\dfrac{V}{A}\right)^2} = 2/0.669^2 = 4.47 \, \text{min/cm}^2$$

To be effective, the total solidification time of riser T_r must be greater than that of the casting. Let us take $T_r = 2.5$ minutes. We are given h/D ratio for the cylindrical riser = 1.2.

Let us first find the V/A ratio for the riser and then use Chvorinov's rule.

Volume
$$V = \frac{\pi}{4}D^2h = \frac{\pi}{4}D^2(1.2D) = 0.3\pi D^3$$

Surface area
$$A = \pi Dh + 2\frac{\pi}{4}D^2 = 1.2\pi D^2 + \frac{\pi}{4}D^2 = 1.7\pi D^2$$

$$V/A = \frac{0.3}{1.7}D$$

We know that $(V/A)^2 = \frac{T_r}{c}$;

$$\left[\frac{0.3}{1.7}D\right]^2 = \frac{2.5}{4.47}$$

$$D^2 = 17.95, \text{ or } D = 4.24 \text{ cm}$$

$$h = 1.2\,D = 5 \text{ cm}$$

7.1.3 Design of castings

In order to produce best quality products at lowest possible cost, it is essential that the product designer gives due considerations to the various requirements of the manufacturing process and, if possible, work closely with the production engineer. Experience shows that minor changes or modifications made in the design of the product can greatly facilitate and simplify the manufacturing of a product. While this is true for all manufacturing processes, it is particularly important for products to be manufactured by casting process. The following are some of the basic design considerations in castings.

Expendable mould casting

1. Use appropriate material of casting. Designers have a tendency to over-design the product by specifying an unnecessarily expensive high-strength metal. For the functions that the product has to perform under the given set of conditions and for the quantity in which it is needed, it is important to use the least expensive metal and the most economical casting method that will meet the required specifications. Cast iron is the least expensive and easily castable metal for which various grades are available with ultimate tensile strength in the range 150 to 400 MN/m². If a component has to bear compressive but not shock loads, C.I. can probably be the best choice. Steels should be considered as casting material only if the part has to be much stronger because it is more

expensive and difficult to cast than C.I. All non-ferrous metals can be cast, but they are generally expensive; they should be preferred only when the component weight is small and the quantity of components needed is large.

2. Use appropriate pattern allowances. Although this is taken care of by the pattern maker, it is important to ensure that the necessary pattern allowances such as shrinkage allowance, machining allowance, draft, and distortion allowance are given on all patterns.

3. Avoid sharp corners. This implies that sharp corners are to be replaced by fillets (inside radii) and outside radii of ample size (Figure 7.2), because sharp corners cause localized stress concentration and may even lead to cracking and tearing of the casting during solidification. Rounded corners facilitate mould making and ensure proper flow of molten metal during the pouring process. However, excessive fillets can cause a different type of problem, called *hot spots*.

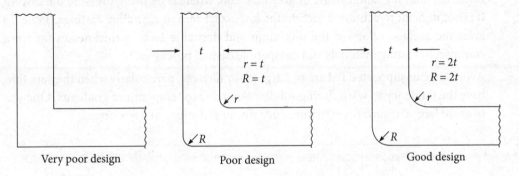

| Very poor design | Poor design | Good design |

Figure 7.2 Sharp corners should be rounded by radii and fillets of adequate size

4. Avoid sharp change in section thickness. Though desirable, it may not be always possible to completely disallow change in section thickness; sharp changes can, however, be avoided (Figure 7.3) by a smooth blending of the unequal sections into each other.

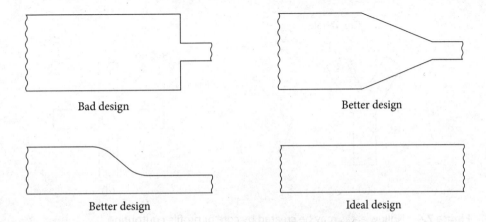

Figure 7.3 Sharp changes in section thickness should be avoided

5. Avoid heavy sections in localized areas. Localized thick sections tend to exist where sections of castings intersect. These thick sections cool more slowly than the others and tend to be areas of localized, abnormal shrinkage. In order to overcome uneven solidification problems, heavy sections in localized areas (called hot spots) can be avoided by minor design changes in component design. For example, as shown in Figure 7.4, hollow areas may be created by the use of core or profile contouring, if the design permits. Where component design requires the existence of heavy sections, an adjacent riser can be used to feed the section during solidification and shrinkage. By designing the riser properly, the shrinkage can be brought totally out of the casting, that is, within the riser, to be removed later.

6. Avoid too thin section thickness as also too small section thickness than permissible for the casting process and the casting material. For example, 3 mm is the minimum thickness limit for sand casting of grey cast iron, whereas by using pressure die casting, it is not difficult to achieve a section thickness of 1 mm of zinc alloy castings. Table 7.1 gives the average values of the minimum and desirable section thicknesses for some commercial casting materials and compatible casting processes.

7. Avoid large unsupported flat areas. Large plain surfaces, particularly when they are thin, have the tendency to warp during solidification due to temperature gradients. One way to avoid large flat surfaces is to introduce ribs or serrations at a few areas.

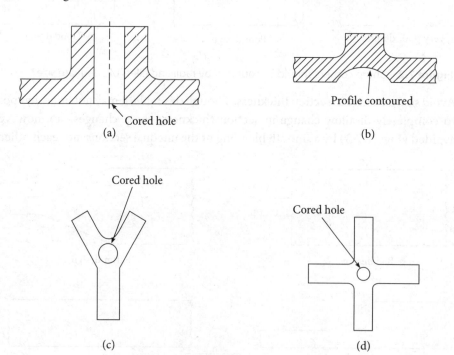

Figure 7.4   Hollow areas may be created by core or profile contouring

Table 7.1 Minimum and desirable section thicknesses for some engineering metals and casting processes

Material	Minimum thickness (mm)	Desirable thickness (mm)	Casting process
Steel	4.5	> 6.5	Sand casting
Grey cast iron	3.0	> 5.0	Sand casting
Malleable iron	3.0	> 5.0	Sand casting
Aluminium	3.0	> 4.5	Sand casting
Magnesium	4.5	> 6.5	Sand casting
Aluminium alloys	1.25	> 1.5	Die casting
Magnesium alloys	1.25	> 1.5	Die casting
Zinc alloys	0.5	> 0.75	Die casting

8. Choose appropriate location of parting line. The selection of the line (i.e., plane) that separates the upper and lower halves of mould is important because it affects: (i) the ease of moulding; (ii) the shape and number of cores; (iii) the method of supporting the cores; (iv) the use of effective and economical system of gating, runner and riser; (v) the final dimensional accuracy; and (vi) the weight of the final casting. Since closure of two parts of the mould may not always be consistent, component dimensions across the parting plane are likely to have more variation than other dimensions. In general, it is desirable to have the parting line along a flat plane, rather than contoured. Whenever possible, the parting line should be at the corners or edges of castings, rather than on flat surfaces in the middle of the casting, so that the flash that may be produced at the parting line is easily removable or at least may not be as visible and may go largely unnoticed.

Permanent mould casting

The design principles for expendable mould castings by and large also apply to permanent-mould castings. However, the designer should give considerations to the following:

1. Avoid heavy sections: Heavy sections in a die cast part should be avoided in order to save cost and weight. The more metal a part has, the more time it will take to fill the die cavity and to cool the metal prior to ejection. The designer can aim to replace them by introducing pockets to make the cross-section thinner; ribs may be used to strengthen the part, if necessary. The locations of pockets need to be considered carefully, as they can sometimes cause non-constant shrinkage, which may affect accuracy of cast parts.

2. Choose parting line for better productivity: A line that splits the component part and creates a contact surface between two or more die parts is called parting line. The location of this line is important and depends on the geometrical shape and the tolerances on the different surfaces. The parting line can be straight or broken. If the customer has his own

requirements of the casting design and the surface tolerances, there may not be more choices available to decide on the location of parting line. Otherwise, while deciding on the parting line, the designer should give considerations to the following:

a. Die cost. The designer should always aim for a straight parting line to reduce the cost of the die.

b. Machining: If the component needs some machining after casting, it would be better to place the parting line on the surface that is otherwise to be machined. This is because the surface at the parting line generally has poor finish than the other surfaces.

c. Metal flow and solidification: The inlet for molten metal has to be in the parting line. The placement of the inlet affects the die filling and metal solidification process and thereby the quality of the die cast part. The designer should aim to place the parting line that would enable as smooth die filling as possible

d. Cores: The location of the cores decides where to put the parting line.

e. Knockout: Depending on where the parting line is located, the requirement of force to knockout the cast component from die is affected.

3. Avoid the use of side core: The designer should try, if possible, to avoid holes and undercuts that are parallel to the parting line. To achieve these undercuts and holes, use is made of the side core, called 'slider', which is generally costly. The designer and die caster should work together to simplify the design of castings and avoid the use of sliders [Figure 7.5(a)]. In general, deep cavities that require cores should be avoided.

4. Blend differing sections into one another with generous radii: Sharp corners cause uneven cooling, while rounded corners permit uniform cooling with much less stress. Sharp corners are therefore undesirable because they become localized points of heat and stress buildup in the die material that can cause die cracking and early failure. Radii and fillets should therefore be as generous as possible, preferably at least 1.5 times wall thickness [Figure 7.5(b)].

5. Design for uniform wall thickness: The easiest die casting to make and the soundest in terms of minimum porosity is one that has uniform wall thickness. The ratio maximum wall thickness to minimum wall thickness should preferably be < 4 [Figure 7.5(c)]. When a heavy section seems to be indicated, the designer should core out the underside or introduce pockets, if possible, refer Figure 7.5(c)

6. Design with as thin a wall thickness as possible: In most cases, it is found that maximum *strength/weight* ratio can generally be achieved with 1.0–1.5 mm wall thickness. The minimum wall thickness allowable for different metals is given in Table 7.2.

7. Design the casting with generous drafts: Greater the draft, easier is the withdrawal of cast part from the die [Figure 7.5(d)]. The draft starts from the parting line and the value of draft should not be < 1–2°

8. Design for metal flow: The designer should aim for easy flow of molten metal in the die. This will ensure that the whole die is filled before the metal starts to solidify. If the whole die is not filled before the start of metal solidification, there is a good chance of cold shuts in the casting. Condition of easy metal flow can be achieved by avoiding (i) abrupt section changes; and (ii) sharp corners in the part design [Figure 7.5(b)].

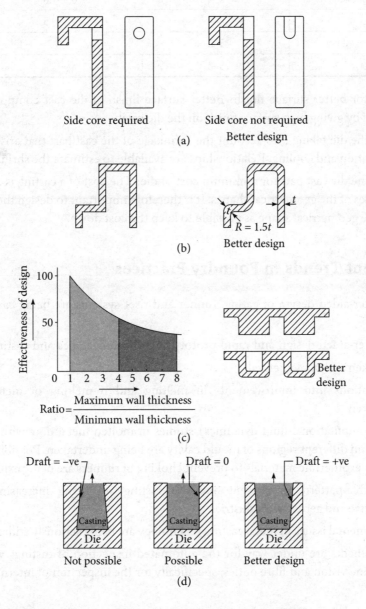

Figure 7.5 Design considerations for permanent mould casting

Table 7.2 Recommendations on wall thickness in die casting

Material	Recommended minimum wall thickness (mm)	
	Gravity die casting	High pressure die casting
Aluminium	2–4	0.5–1.0
Magnesium	2–4	0.5–1.0
Zinc	–	0.3–0.5
Grey cast iron	3–5	–
Steel	5–8	–

9. Design for better surface finish: Better surface finish of die cast components can be achieved by giving high surface finish on the die cavity.

10. Design the die taking into account the shrinkage of the cast part that arises during the solidification and cooling. Relationships are available to estimate the shrinkage.

11. Design the die cast part for minimum cost of die: The cost of a casting is related to the difficulties of the geometrical shapes. It is therefore important to design the casting with as simple geometrical shape as possible to keep the cost down.

7.2 Current Trends in Foundry Practices

- Computer-aided design of gating, runner and riser systems are being carried out at a fast rate

- Computer-aided design and rapid prototyping of moulds, dies and castings are being undertaken and implemented

- Investigations into improvements in melting and re-melting of metal are being undertaken

- CFD (computational fluid dynamics) studies in molten metal flow within the gating system and different regions of mould cavity are being undertaken. Possibilities of using different exothermic materials to prevent choking of runners are being explored

- Expendable-pattern, investment and die casting are being increasingly used in automotive and aerospace industries

- Environmental issues in metal casting technology are being seriously addressed

- Developments are under way for the automated inspection of castings with the help of machine vision and fibre optics, specifically for the inspection of internal surfaces of castings

- Robots are being increasingly used for foundry automation in carrying out operations like venting moulds, drying moulds, coating cores, lubricating dies, filling moulds with molten metal and removing gates and runners.

Questions

1. What features make a good design of gating system for mould? Discuss them in brief.

2. What can happen if the rate of flow of molten metal in a gating system is (a) too slow, (b) too fast?

3. Should the flow of molten metal in the mould be laminar or turbulent? Can you represent the flow of metal by any number? What can happen if the flow is turbulent?

4. Why is Bernoulli's equation important in metal casting?

5. Give any five design considerations in expendable mould casting.

6. What is the function of a sprue-well? Why is it not desirable to have a too big sprue-well?

7. What is a parting line? Why is it so important to choose its proper location?

Fill in the Blanks

1. A Reynolds number of up to _____ represents a laminar flow of molten metal.

2. The value of Reynolds number above _____ represents turbulence in flow.

3. Too large size of sprue-well reduces the _____.

4. According to Chvorinov's rule, the total solidification time of a casting is a function of the ratio of _____.

5. The location of riser should promote _____ solidification of casting.

6. The best shape of a riser is the one that has _____ freezing time.

7. The function of a sprue-well is to _____.

8. The runner is the channel that carries the molten metal from _____ to _____.

9. The rate of flow of molten metal in the gating system must not be too slow because _____.

10. The rate of flow of molten metal in the gating system must not be too high because _____.

Choose the Correct Answer

1. The flow of molten metal in a gating system should be such that the corresponding *Reynolds number* is

    a. less than 1000.
    b. between 20,000 and 30,000.
    c. between 30,000 and 40,000.
    d. more than 40,000.

2. The rate of flow of molten metal in the gating system must not be turbulent because if it is turbulent, it promotes

    a. air entrainment and the formation of dross.
    b. formation of defects like cold shuts.
    c. directional solidification of casting.
    d. slow filling of the mould cavity.

3. Which one is not an element of a gating system?

   a. sprue   c. runner

   b. sprue-well   d. riser

4. The runner is the channel that connects the

   a. sprue to the gate.   c. mould cavity to the riser.

   b. pouring basin to the sprue-well.   d. pouring basin to the riser.

5. Gate is that portion of the runner through which the molten metal

   a. enters the mould cavity.   b. flows downward from the pouring basin.

   c. is poured from the crucible.   d. allows the dissolved gases to escape.

6. Riser allows

   a. quick filling of the mould cavity.

   b. flow of molten metal from the bottom of the sprue to the mould cavity.

   c. flow of molten metal in the gating system to remain laminar.

   d. feeding of liquid metal to the solidifying casting.

7. Casting should be so designed that

   a. there is directional solidification starting from the extremities of the mould cavity toward the riser.

   b. solidification takes place simultaneously at all the locations in the mould cavity.

   c. solidification starts from the bottom of the riser to the thinnest section in the mould cavity.

   d. fastest cooling section is as close to the riser as possible.

8. Yield of a casting is defined as the

   a. ratio of casting weight to the total weight of the metal poured.

   b. ratio of the weight of gate, runner and riser to the weight of the casting.

   c. ratio of the pattern weight to the casting weight.

   d. product of the weight of casting and the weight of the runner and the riser.

9. According to Chvorinov's rule, the best shape of a riser is one that

   a. has the shortest freezing time.   c. is of cylindrical shape.

   b. is of spherical shape.   d. is of conical shape.

10. The minimum thickness limit for sand casting of grey cast iron is

   a. 0.5 mm.   c. 3 mm.

   b. I mm.   d. 5 mm.

Answers

1. b.   2. a.   3. d.   4. a.   5. a.   6. d.   7. a.   8. a.   9. b.   10. c

8

Metal Forming and Shaping Processes

LEARNING OBJECTIVES

After reading this chapter, you should be able to understand the following:

- The fundamentals of a metal working or forming process.

- The changes a metal undergoes when it is deformed.

- The classification of metal forming processes.

- The difference between workability and formability of metals.

- Cold working of metals: its meaning, advantages, disadvantages and main applications.

- Hot working of metals: its meaning, advantages, disadvantages and main applications.

- Warm working of metals: its meaning and comparison with hot and cold working processes.

8.1 Introduction

Several manufacturing processes are available to produce a part. Each of these processes has different degrees of suitability for the same part. While selecting an appropriate manufacturing process, not only economy but other aspects such as the desired life, strength, surface quality, appearance, repairability and use of the product must also be given due considerations.

Metal working or metal forming is a process wherein the desired shape and size of a product are obtained by deforming the metal plastically. Stresses experienced by the material during the deformation process are greater than the yield strength but less than the fracture strength of the material. Molten metal is first cast into ingots, slabs, rods or pipes, which are then converted to wrought structures by deformation processes. These processes exploit a remarkable property of metals, which is the ability to flow plastically in the solid state without any major loss to any of their other properties. With the application of suitable pressures, the material is moved or displaced to obtain the desired shape with almost no wastage. The pressures required are generally high and a major part of the input energy is efficiently utilized to enhance the material strength by strain hardening.

As a metal is deformed (or formed, as it is often called) into a useful shape, it experiences stresses such as tension, compression, shear or any combination of these.

Figure 8.1 illustrates these states of stresses. To understand the forming of metal, one should have the knowledge of the structure of metals. Metals are crystalline in nature and consist of irregularly shaped grains of various sizes. Each grain is made up of atoms in an orderly arrangement, known as a lattice. The orientation of atoms in a grain is uniform but differs in adjacent grains. When a force is applied to deform a metal or alter its shape, many changes occur in the grain structure, including grain fragmentation, movement of atoms and lattice distortion. Slip planes develop through the lattice structure at points where the atoms' bonds of attraction are the weakest and whole blocks of atoms are displaced. The orientation of atoms, however, does not change when a slip occurs.

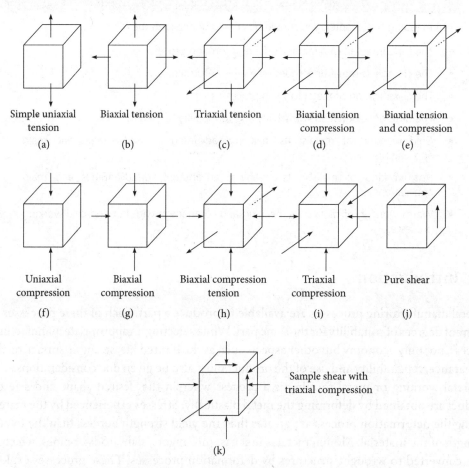

Figure 8.1   State of stresses metals undergo during deformation

The amount of deformation that a metal can undergo at room temperature (in cold state) depends on its ductility. The higher the ductility of a metal, the more the deformation it can undergo. Metals having large grains are more ductile than those having smaller grains. Pure metals can withstand a greater amount of deformation than metals having alloying elements, since alloying increases the tendency and rapidity of strain hardening.

When a metal is deformed in cold state, severe stresses known as *residual stresses* are set up in the material. These stresses are often undesirable, and to remove them, the metal is heated to temperatures below its recrystalline temperature range. In this temperature range, the stresses are removed without any appreciable change in the physical properties of the metal or its grain structure.

Flow stress behaviour of a material differs distinctly when it is heated to a temperature called the recrystallization temperature. At this temperature, new fine grains are formed in the material. The value of recrystallization temperature is different for different materials; it is affected by factors such as the amount of internal stress that exists in the material prior to heating, alloying elements in the material and the melting point. As an approximation, its value can be taken as about 40% to 50% of the melting temperature.

Due to different flow stress behaviour of materials at different temperatures, forming processes are broadly classified into three groups depending upon the temperature at which they are performed [Figure 8.2]. The three groups are: (i) cold working processes; (ii) hot working processes; and (iii) warm working processes. Forming processes can also be classified according to the product type they produce: continuous or discrete products. Rolling, extrusion and drawing processes produce continuous long products of different cross-sections such as plates, sheets, bars and tubes whereas forging, bending, shearing and powder metallurgy processes produce discrete products such as gears, sprockets, crankshafts hand tools and different sheet metal products.

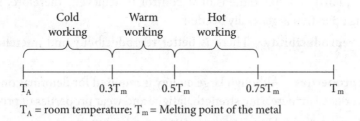

Figure 8.2 Classification of forming processes according to range of temperature at which they are performed.

Workability and *formability* are the two important terms used in metal forming processes. *Workability* generally refers to bulk deformation processing of materials such as forging, rolling and extrusion. Basically, it refers to the ease with which a material can be formed without defects such as cracks. Ductility of the material plays an important role in workability – a high ductile material is expected to have good workability. There are two important factors that decide workability. One is the material factor – ductility, microstructure, grain size and so on. The other is the process factor – geometry of die, size and shape of material, friction at die–work material interface, and so on. The term *formability* is associated with the deformation processing of materials such as sheet metal processing. An important criterion for formability is the fracture of material during deformation. Deformation is limited by fracture. If a material has high ductility, fracture may be delayed so that the material could be worked to greater levels of deformation. Fracture may occur on the surface, or internally within the deforming material or it could occur at the die–material interface.

Some common metal forming processes are shown in Figure 8.3 along with the state of stress(es) experienced by the metal during each process.

8.2 Cold, Hot and Warm Working of Metals

8.2.1 Cold working

Plastic deformation of metals performed generally at room temperature (i.e., below their recrystallization temperatures) is known as *cold working*. In some cases, slightly elevated temperatures may be used to provide increased ductility and reduced strength. Cold working offers a number of distinct advantages, and for this reason various cold-working processes have become extremely important. Significant advances in recent years have led to their greater use, and the trend appears likely to continue.

Advantages In comparison with hot working, the advantages of cold working are as follows:

1. **Cost** No heating is required and thus cold working is less costly
2. **Surface quality** There is no scale formation on the metal. No post-process cleaning of the product is required and a better surface finish is obtained
3. **Product quality** Better dimensional control is achieved; therefore, no secondary machining operation is generally needed
4. **Product reproducibility** There is better reproducibility and interchangeability of parts
5. **Product properties** Although large energy is required for deformation, a part of this energy is utilized in increasing strength, fatigue and wear properties of products
6. **Material properties** Directional properties can be imparted
7. **Material quality** No decarburization of the surface occurs. There is no loss of material; also there are negligible contamination problems
8. **Material handing** Almost no handling problems exist with cold metal

Disadvantages Some disadvantages associated with cold working processes are as follows:

1. **Type of materials** Brittle materials cannot be cold worked
2. **Type of products** Big and bulky parts cannot be easily formed. Strain hardening occurs (may require intermediate annealing)

Metal forming process	Process sketch	State of stress in material during forming
Rolling	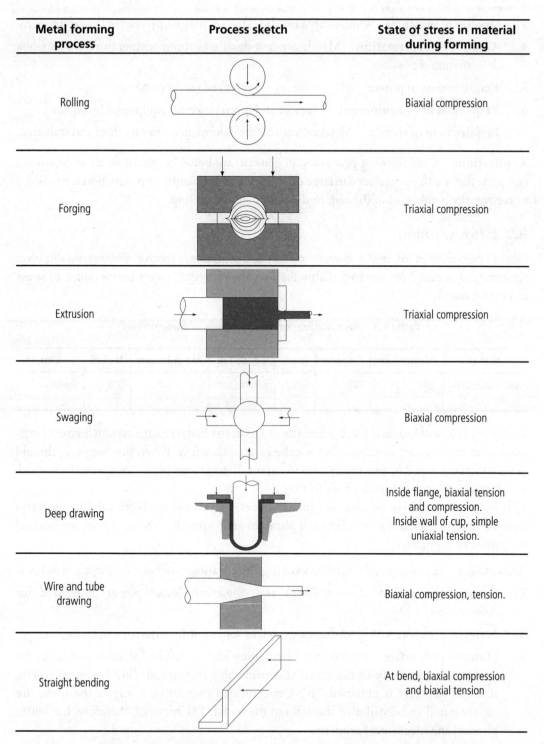	Biaxial compression
Forging		Triaxial compression
Extrusion		Triaxial compression
Swaging		Biaxial compression
Deep drawing		Inside flange, biaxial tension and compression. Inside wall of cup, simple uniaxial tension.
Wire and tube drawing		Biaxial compression, tension.
Straight bending		At bend, biaxial compression and biaxial tension

Figure 8.3 Common metal forming processes along with the state of stress experienced by the metal part

3. **Quality of products**   Undesirable residual stresses may be present in the component
4. **Amount of deformation**   Metals are less ductile at room temperature and, so, less deformation is possible
5. **Requirement of power**   Higher forces are required for deformation
6. **Requirement of equipment**   Heavier and more powerful equipment is required
7. **Requirement of surface**   Metal surfaces before deformation must be clean and scale-free

Applications   Cold forming processes, in general, are better suited to small and medium size parts that are to be produced in large quantities. Large quantity of production is necessary to recover the higher cost of the required equipment and tooling.

8.2.2 Hot working

Plastic deformation of metal carried out at a temperature above the recrystallization temperature is called *hot working*. Table 8.1 lists the recrystallization temperature of some important metals.

Table 8.1   Recrystallization temperatures of some metals

Metal	Aluminium	Copper	Iron	Lead, Tin	Magnesium	Nickel	Zinc
Recrystallization temperature °C	150	200	450	Below room temperature	150	590	Room temperature

Under the action of heat and force, when the atoms of the metal reach a certain higher energy level, new crystals start forming. This is called *recrystallization*. When this happens, the old grain structure formed by previously carried out mechanical working no longer exists; instead, new crystals which are strain-free are formed.

In hot working, the temperature at which the working is completed is critical since any extra heat left in the material after working will promote grain growth, leading to poor mechanical properties of the material.

Advantages   In comparison with cold working, the advantages of hot working are as follows:

1. **Power requirement**   Lesser forces and, therefore, lesser power is needed for deformation
2. **Material requirement**   All ductile as well as some brittle materials can be formed
3. **Material properties**   (i) No strain hardening and no residual stresses remain in the material. (ii) Porosity of the metal is considerably minimized. (iii) Favourable grain size and structure is obtained. (iv) Concentrated impurities, if any in the metal are disintegrated and distributed throughout the metal. The material, therefore, has better physical and mechanical properties
4. **Deformation amount**   Greater ductility of material is available and, therefore, more deformation is possible. Bulky jobs can be worked upon

Disadvantages   Some disadvantages associated in the hot working of metals are as follows:

1. **Power requirement**   Heat energy is needed; it adds to the cost
2. **Limited materials**   Materials which become brittle at higher temperatures cannot be hot worked
3. **Material loss**   Scale formation causes loss of material
4. **Surface quality**   Poor surface finish due to scale formation
5. **Surface degradation**   Surface of ferrous metals is rapidly oxidized. Strength and hardness at the surface may be poor, which can be disadvantageous when the part is put to service
6. **Product quality**   The weakening of the surface layer may give rise to fatigue cracks which may ultimately result in fatigue failure of the part
7. **Accuracy and dimensional tolerances**   There is poor accuracy; close dimensional tolerances cannot be maintained in parts
8. **Reproducibility**   Poor reproducibility and interchangeability of parts
9. **Equipment**   Tooling and equipment have lower life
10 **Material handling**   Handling and maintaining of hot metal is difficult and troublesome

8.2.3 Warm working

Metal deformation carried out at temperatures below the recrystallization temperature but above the room temperature (in the range 30% to 50% of melting point) is called *warm working*.

Advantages   Compared to cold forming, warm forming offers the following advantages:

1 **Power requirement**   Lesser forces and hence lesser power is required for deformation
2 **Ease of operation**   Lesser number of annealing operation (because of less strain hardening)
3 **Type of products**   Greater metal ductility and, thus, relatively bigger parts can be produced

Compared to hot forming, warm forming offers the following advantages:

1 **Energy requirement**   Lesser amount of heat energy is required
2 **Accuracy and precision**   Better precision and dimensional control
3 **Surface quality**   Better surface finish
4 **Product quality**   Lesser scaling on parts and lesser decarburization of parts
5 **Tool life**   Lesser thermal shock and thermal fatigue to tooling, and so greater life of tooling

Questions

1. Describe hot and cold working as applied to manufacturing of engineering products from metals. List the advantages and disadvantages of each. Give the effect of cold working on the metallurgical properties of steels.

2. In what ways do metal deformation processes bring about improvement in the finished product? Give examples.

3. By looking at a sheet metal product, can you make out whether it is produced by hot working or cold working? How? Name some typical important products made by hot working and cold working.

Fill in the Blanks

1. State of stress in a material while being forged in a die is _____.

2. To deform a metal permanently, the stress must exceed _____ of the metal.

3. Pressure needed to deform a material in cold state is _____ than that needed when it is in a hot state.

4. When metal is formed in cold state, there is no _____ of grains and thus recovery from grain distortion or fragmentation does not take place.

5. When metal is formed in cold state, hardness and strength of metal _____, and the metal contains _____ stresses.

6. The extent of deformation that a metal can undergo at room temperature depends on its _____.

7. The temperature at which hot working of metal is completed is critical because _____.

8. Warm forming is metal deformation carried out at temperatures _____.

Choose the Correct Answer

1. Workability of a metal
   a. is same as its formability.
   b. depends upon metallurgical factors such as grain size and grain distribution.
   c. refers to the sheet metal processing.
   d. is known to be higher in case of coarse-grained structures.

2. Stresses experienced by the material during metal working process are
   a. greater than the yield strength but less than the fracture strength of the material.
   b. greater than the tensile strength but less than the compressive strength of the material.
   c. greater than the compressive strength but less than the tensile strength of the material.
   d. greater than the tensile strength but less than the shear strength of the material.

3. In a metal working process,
    a. no change in the material strength takes place.
    b. the material strength improves by strain hardening.
    c. the material strength deteriorates by strain hardening.
    d. the material strength deteriorates by atom dislocation.

4. As a metal is deformed into the desired shape, it experiences
    a. only tensile stresses.
    b. only tensile or compressive stresses.
    c. only tensile, compressive or shear stresses.
    d. various combinations of tensile, compressive and shear stresses.

5. The orientation of the atoms in a grain
    a. is uniform but differs in adjacent grains.
    b. is uniform and the pattern of orientation remains same throughout the material.
    c. is non-uniform and this variation is uniform in all grains of a material.
    d. is non-uniform and the orientation differs from one grain to another.

6. The amount of deformation that a metal can undergo at room temperature depends on its
    a. tensile strength.   c. hardness.
    b. compressive strength.   d. ductility.

7. The amount of deformation that a metal can undergo
    a. is more when it is in pure state than when it is alloyed with other elements.
    b. is less when it is in pure state than when it is alloyed with other elements.
    c. is not affected whether it is in pure state or it is alloyed with other elements.
    d. depends upon the alloying elements in it as alloying decreases the tendency and rapidity of strain hardening.

8. When a metal is deformed in cold state, severe stresses are set up in it. These stresses are called
    a. residual stresses.   c. biaxial and triaxial stresses.
    b. recrystalline stresses.   d. microscopic stresses.

9. Cold working is the name given to the process of plastic deformation of metals performed generally at
    a. zero degree centigrade.
    b. zero degree Kelvin.
    c. below the recrystallization temperature of metal.
    d. above the recrystallization temperature of metal.

10. Directional properties can be imparted to the metal in
    a. cold working.
    b. hot working.

    c.   warm working.

    d.   both hot and cold working but not in warm working.

11. Probability of residual stresses being present in the component is more when it is manufactured by

    a.   cold working.

    b.   hot working.

    c.   warm working.

    d.   both hot and cold working but not in warm working.

12. Hot working is the name given to the process of plastic deformation of metal carried out at a temperature

    a.   hundred degree centigrade.

    b.   hundred degree Kelvin.

    c.   above the recrystallization temperature of metal.

    d.   below the recrystallization temperature of metal.

13. Recrystallization temperature of a metal is the one at which

    a.   its atoms reach a certain higher energy level and new crystals start forming.

    b.   its crystals start recirculating around the atoms.

    c.   its crystals reunite to become bigger in size.

    d.   its crystals cease to reunite.

14. In warm working of metals, the metal deformation is carried out at temperatures

    a.   above the recrystallization temperature.

    b.   above the recrystallization temperature but below the crystallization temperature.

    c.   below the recrystallization temperature but above the room temperature.

    d.   below the recrystallization temperature but above the crystallization temperature.

15. In which metal working process does the surface finish of material become poor due to scale formation?

    a.   cold working   c.   lukewarm working

    b.   warm working   d.   hot working

16. Formability refers to

    a.   sheet metal processing.   c.   hot working of metals.

    b.   bulk metal processing.   d.   cold working.

Answers

1. b.   2. a.   3. b.   4. d.   5. a.   6. d.   7. a.   8. a.   9. c.   10.a.

11. a.   12. c.   13. a.   14. c.   15. d.   16. a.

9

Metal Rolling Process

LEARNING OBJECTIVES

After reading this chapter, you should be able to understand the following:

- The process of metal rolling.

- The force required in metal rolling and the method of determining it.

- The effect of rolling force and the methods of reducing rolling force.

- The defects that occur in rolled products.

- The various variants of rolling practice, such as ring rolling, thread rolling and gear rolling.

- The various types of rolling mills, such as two-high rolling mill, three-high rolling mill, four-high rolling mill, cluster mill and planetary rolling mill.

- The material used for rolls and the need for lubrication in the rolling process.

9.1 Introduction

The mechanical working of metal is defined as the plastic deformation of metals under the action of externally applied forces. Depending upon whether the metal is worked above or below the recrystallization temperature, the product quality differs in terms of surface finish and precision, grain structure and residual stresses in it. Metal working processes can be classified according to the shape and size of the products they produce. Common metal working processes are rolling, forging, swaging, coining, extrusion and drawing. These processes are generally carried out in hot state of metals mainly because of the several advantages in hot working, as explained in Chapter 8. These processes will be described in this and the following chapters.

9.2 Rolling

Rolling is generally the first process that is used to convert material into a finished wrought product. Basically, it is a process of reducing the thickness of a long workpiece by compressive forces applied through a set of rolls (Figure 9.1). Large size starting stock (called *ingot*) is rolled into *blooms, billets* or *slabs*. Slabs can be further rolled to produce *plates, sheets* and *strips*. These hot-rolled products are mostly the starting material for subsequent processing such as cold forming, machining or welding.

Bloom	A bloom has a square or rectangular cross-section, with a thickness equal to or greater than 150 mm and width ranging between 150 mm and 300 mm.
Billet	A billet is smaller than a bloom and has a square cross-section of 40 mm × 40 mm or more but less than bloom size.
Slab	A slab has a rectangular cross-section with the width greater than thrice the thickness. Generally, it is of 250 mm width × 40 mm thickness but can also be larger.
Plate	A plate is a solid of rectangular cross-section having thickness greater than 6 mm but less than 150 mm.
Sheet	A sheet is generally less than 6 mm thick.
Foil	A foil is a thin sheet (less than 0.01 mm thick).

One important effect of the hot rolling process is the *grain refinement* brought about by recrystallization, as shown in Figure 9.1(a). The coarse grain structure of the original product

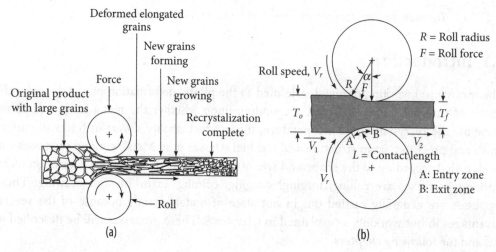

Figure 9.1   Metal rolling process

is broken up into thin elongated grains by the force applied by rolls. Because of the elevated temperature, recrystallization starts immediately and small grains begin to form. These grains grow rapidly until recrystallization is complete. If further working is not done on the metal, growth of the grains continues until the lower temperature of the recrystalline range is reached.

9.2.1 Process details

As shown in Figure 9.1(b), heated metal is passed through two rolls that rotate in opposite directions. The gap between the rolls is kept somewhat less than the thickness T_o of the metal entering the gap, so that it acquires the thickness T_f as it comes out of the rolls $(T_f < T_o)$. The surface speed of rotation V_r of the rolls being greater than the speed V_1 of the incoming metal, friction along the roll–metal contact interface acts to push the metal forward. Under the pressure of the rolls, the thickness of metal decreases, and therefore, its length increases if width increase (called *spreading*) is not permitted. The amount by which the thickness is decreased, that is $(T_o - T_f)$, is called the *draft*. Refer to Figure 9.1(b). If we apply the law of conservation of material, we get the following equations:

$$T_o . w_o . L_o = T_f . w_f . L_f \tag{9.1}$$

where w_o and w_f are respectively the widths of the work material before and after the process of rolling; and L_o and L_f are respectively the lengths of the work material before and after rolling.

Also, $T_o . w_o . V_1 = T_f . w_f . V_2$ $\qquad$ (9.2)

where V_1 and V_2 are respectively the entering and existing velocities of the work material.

The contact of the rolls with the work material is along a length L defined by the angle α (called the *angle of contact* or *angle of bite*). Each roll is of radius R and has surface velocity V_r due to the rotation. This velocity V_r of the rolls is more than the entering speed V_1 of the work material and less than the exiting speed V_2 of the work material. As the flow of material through the rolls is continuous, there is a gradual change in the velocity of the material as it moves between the rolls. There is one point along the arc of contact, where the velocity of the work material is equal to the roll velocity. This is called the *neutral point* or the *no-slip point*. The characteristic feature of this point is that on either side of this point, friction and slipping take place between the work material and the roll.

Forward slip   The amount of slip between the work material and the rolls can be estimated from the following equation:

$$\text{Forward slip} = \frac{V_2 - V_r}{V_r} \tag{9.3}$$

where V_2 and V_r are respectively the exit velocity of the work material and the speed of the roll in m/min.

Friction   The friction force between the rolls and the work material (which is the product of the coefficient of friction and compression force of the rolls) is greater on the entrance side of the neutral point and acts in one direction whereas it is smaller and acts in the opposite direction on the exit side. The net force is responsible for pulling the work material through the rolls. In case of rolling of the flat work material, it is possible to estimate the maximum possible reduction in thickness d_{max} by using the following relation:

$$d_{max} = \mu^2 R \tag{9.4}$$

where d_{max} is the maximum draft (mm), μ is the coefficient of friction and R is the roll radius (mm). It may be noted that μ depends on the surface condition as well as the temperature of the work material. Generally, in cold rolling, μ is taken as 0.1; in warm rolling, it is taken as 0.2, and in hot rolling, its value is taken as 0.4.

Rolling force and power requirements   Provided that the coefficient of friction is sufficient to permit rolling operation, the roll force F required to maintain separation between the two rolls is given by

$$F = \sigma. w . L$$

where σ is the average flow stress (MPa) experienced by the work material in the roll gap, and $w. L$ is the roll–work material contact area (mm²). The length of the roll–work contact L can be approximately expressed by the following relation.

$$L = [R (T_o - T_f)]^{\frac{1}{2}}$$

If it is assumed that the roll force F is centred on the work as it passes between the rolls, and that the roll force acts with a moment arm of $\frac{1}{2} L$, we can estimate the torque in rolling as

$$T = F. \frac{1}{2} L$$

The power P (Newton-metre/min.) required to drive each roll can be estimated as torque × angular velocity. That is,

$$P = T. 2 \pi N$$

where N is the rotational speed of the roll (rev/min.). As there are two powered rolls in a rolling mill, the total power required to run the rolling mill will be $2P$.

Rolling temperatures   Temperature control is very important for the quality of hot-rolled product. The material to be rolled should be heated to a uniform elevated temperature. If, for any reason, the temperature of the material is not uniform, the deformation cannot be expected to be uniform. For example, consider a situation where the material is being heated prior to rolling, and insufficient time is allowed in the furnace. The exterior portion will be hotter than the interior mass of the material. During rolling, the hotter exterior metal will flow in preference to the interior metal, which is cooler and stronger. Consider another situation where the material is taken out in a hot state from the furnace and left outside in the air prior to rolling. If the rolling operation is carried out after some time, the cooler outer surface will tend to resist deformation as compared to the hotter and more ductile inner mass of material. In both the situations, cracking and tearing of material is likely to occur in the rolled product.

A good practice, generally followed in hot rolling, is to complete the operation before the temperature falls to about 50 to 100°C above the recrystallization temperature of the material. This assures uniform grain size and prevents the possibility of unwanted strain hardening of the material.

Example 9.1

A 200 mm wide × 22 mm thick strip of metal is fed through a pair of powered rolls to reduce its thickness to 18 mm in one pass. The rolls are of 500 mm diameter and rotating at 60 rpm. If the coefficient of friction between the rolls and the work material is taken as 0.15, determine whether or not the rolling operation is possible. If it is possible, calculate the roll force. State the assumptions made.

Solution

The reduction in thickness desired, d = 4 mm. We can determine the maximum permissible reduction in thickness d_{max} as

$d_{max} = \mu^2 . R$, where μ is the coefficient of friction and R is the roll radius.

$$= (0.15)^2 (250) = 5.625 \text{ mm}$$

Since $d_{max} > d$, the rolling operation is feasible.
To calculate the roll force, we need to know the contact length L and the average flow stress of the material.

$$L = [R(T_o - T_f)]^{\frac{1}{2}}$$

where R is the roll radius, T_o is the initial thickness and T_f is the final thickness of the work material.

$$L = [(250)(22 - 18)]^{\frac{1}{2}} = 31.6 \text{ mm}$$

Assuming average flow stress, σ as 150 MPa, the rolling force F is estimated as

$$F = w . L . \sigma = (200)(31.6)(150) = 948 \text{ kN}$$

Example 9.2

A strip of brass 200 mm wide and 20 mm thick is rolled at room temperature to a thickness of 16 mm in a single pass. The roll radius is 300 mm and the rolls rotate at 120 rpm. Taking the true stress of brass in the unstrained condition as 200 MPa and in the strained condition as 300 MPa, calculate the roll force required. How much will be the torque on the roll? Also determine the power requirement. State any assumptions made.

Solution

Assuming a frictionless situation, the roll force can be found from the relation

$$F = L w \, \sigma_{avg}$$

where L is the contact length between the strip and the roll, w is the width of the strip, and σ_{avg} is the average true stress of the strip in the roll gap.

The contact length L is approximately equal to $[R(T_o - T_f)]^{1/2} = [300(20 - 16)]^{1/2} = 34.65$ mm

$w = 200$ mm and $\sigma_{avg} = \frac{1}{2}(300 + 200) = 250$ MPa. F is thus equal to 1.73 MN

Assuming that the force acts in the middle of the arc of contact, the torque per roll

$T = F(\frac{1}{2} L) = 30$ kNm and power per roll is 753 kW

For the two rolls, total power required for the rolling operation is approx. 1500 kW.

Example 9.3

A brass plate of thickness 40 mm is to be rolled to 10 mm on a two-high rolling mill. The diameter of each roll of the mill is 100 mm. Based on the surface condition of the plate, if the coefficient of friction is assumed to be 0.35, estimate the minimum number of passes required to achieve the desired reduction in thickness.

Solution

Total desired reduction in thickness = 40 – 10 = 30 mm; roll radius $R = 50$ mm; $\mu = 0.35$
Maximum reduction possible in one pass can be determined by Equation (9.4), as

$$d_{max} = \mu^2 R = (0.35)^2 (50) = 6.125 \text{ mm}$$

Therefore, assuming that friction conditions remain the same in each pass, minimum number of passes required to achieve a reduction of 30 mm thickness = 5.

9.2.2 Rolling force: effects and methods of its reduction

Rolling force can cause deflection of rolls and, in extreme situations, it can even cause flattening of rolls. If this occurs, the rolling operation is adversely affected. Too large roll forces may stretch the whole roll stand, including the housing and the bearings to the extent that the gap between the rolls opens up appreciably.

It is possible to reduce roll forces by:

1. Reducing friction between the work metal surface and the roll surface.
2. Using rolls of smaller diameter so that contact area is reduced.
3. Taking smaller reduction per pass of the stock material so that contact area is reduced.
4. Rolling at higher temperatures so that the stock material is more ductile.

Another effective method of reducing roll forces, particularly when rolling high strength materials, is to apply longitudinal tension to the metal stock during rolling. This action reduces the compressive force required to deform the material plastically. Tension can be applied to the metal stock either at the entry (where it enters the roll gap) or at the exit (where it comes out of the roll gap) or both at the entry and at the exit. When rolling is carried out by applying tension to the stock material at the exit, with no power given to the rolls, the process is called *Steckel rolling*.

9.2.3 Rolling practices

Hot and cold rolling   Rolling is mostly carried out on materials in the hot state. When carried out at room temperature, it is called cold rolling. Compared to hot rolling, cold rolling produces plates and sheets with far superior surface finish (due to lack of scale formation), dimensional tolerances, and mechanical properties of material (as a result of strain hardening). However, in cold rolling, the reduction in thickness of stock material per pass through rolls is limited.

Pack rolling   In this practice of rolling, two or more layers of metal are rolled together to achieve greater process productivity. This practice is mostly followed in the production of foils.

Aluminium foil, for example, is pack rolled in two layers. The two sides of the foil get different finish; the foil-to-foil side has a matte or gloss finish while the foil-to-roll side has a shiny finish due to contact with the polished roll.

Temper rolling   This practice of rolling is followed for thin sheets to remove any surface irregularities caused due to previous rolling operations. The sheet metal is given a light pass of 0.5% to 1.5% reduction. It is mostly the final operation.

Ring rolling   Ring rolling is the name given to the process used to manufacture seamless rings of different sizes from a few cm to over 6 m in diameter and face heights up to 2 m. The starting material for ring rolling is a hollow circular pre-form that has been upset and pierced. This thick-walled ring is placed between the two rolls (shown as A and B in Figure 9.2). Here, A is the driving roll that rotates about a fixed horizontal axis while B is the pressure roll that rotates freely about the horizontal axis, the height of which can be adjusted. The pressure roll is raised to come closer to roll A so that the two rolls grip the ring. While roll A is rotated, the roll B is slowly and continuously brought further closer to A. This causes rotation of the ring due to friction and simultaneous continuous reduction in its thickness and increase in the circumference. The process is continued until the desired thickness or desired diameter of ring is achieved. In order to ensure that a circular ring is rolled, a single or a pair of correctly positioned guide rolls must be used.

Ring rolling can be done in both hot as well as cold state of the workpiece material depending on its size, strength and ductility. Specific texture or shape on outer and/or inner cylindrical surface can be given by using a roll of corresponding surface texture or shape.

Advantages   Compared to other manufacturing processes that are capable of producing the same part, this process has many advantages such as (i) low set-up time; (ii) short production time; (iii) saving of material (pre-form typically utilizes up to 95% of the starting billet); (iv) close dimensional tolerances; (v) favourable grain flow in the material and excellent mechanical properties; (vi) low tooling cost; (vii) rolled sections require little or no machining.

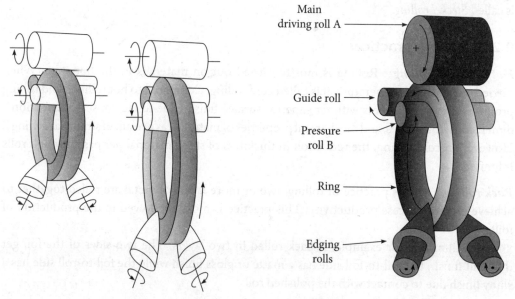

Figure 9.2   Schematic of ring rolling operation

Applications   Rings formed by this process find many applications such as steel tyres of railway car wheels, rings of jet engines, rockets and turbines, and races of ball and roller bearings.

Thread rolling Thread rolling is a cold forming process by which straight or tapered threads are formed on round parts by passing them between a set of flat reciprocating dies (Figure 9.3). As the component part rolls between the pair of dies, it is threaded. One stroke of the dies produces one part. Typical products of this process are bolts, screws and almost all types of threaded fasteners. The process has also been used to generate grooves and various gear forms on surfaces. Internal threads can be rolled with fluteless-forming tap in a similar fashion as external thread rolling.

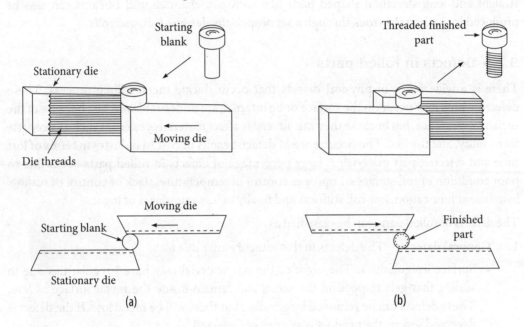

Figure 9.3 Schematic of thread rolling operation: (a) Before thread rolling; and (b) After thread rolling

The thread rolling process of generating threads on surfaces has many advantages such as absence of scrap generation, greater strength of part due to cold working, greater fatigue life of part due to induced compressive residual stresses, greater strength of threads due to better grain flow pattern along the threaded contour, and excellent surface finish.

The process has a limitation that it can be used on metals only in the soft condition on account of the ductility requirements. If needed, the parts may, however, be heat treated subsequently. Lubrication is necessary as it helps to improve surface finish and surface integrity, and to minimize defects.

Because of their complex shape, dies are made from hardened carbon steel rather than cemented carbides. These are normally not reground but discarded after they are worn out. Use of lubricants helps to achieve increased die life, sufficient to thread several million parts.

Gear rolling Spur and helical gears can be manufactured by cold rolling process in the same way as thread rolling. The process is carried out on solid cylindrical metal pieces or on pre-cut gears. Rolled gears have the advantage of greater strength and fatigue life, and excellent surface finish. For this reason, rolled gears find extensive applications in transmissions and power tools.

9.2.4 Rolling products

In addition to flat products like plates, sheets and foils, the rolling process can also be used to produce various shaped products such as seamless rings, gears and threaded parts. Various straight and long structural shaped parts like railroads, channels and I-beams can also be produced by passing the stock through a set of specially designed shaped rolls.

9.2.5 Defects in rolled parts

There is a wide range of physical defects that occur during metal rolling process. These defects, which may occur on the surface or be internal, are undesirable not just because of the surface appearance, but because they can adversely affect material properties such as strength, formability, and the like. The occurrence of defects results in cost to industry in terms of lost time and rejected part material. A large percentage of defects in rolled parts occur due to poor condition of roll surfaces, improper control of temperatures, lack of control of scaling, insufficient lubrication, low roll stiffness and finally to less soundness of ingot.

The defects in rolled parts can be classified as

1. **General defects** The defects in this category arise due to
    - Surface irregularities: The ingot or the raw material may have irregularities due to scaling that gets trapped in the metal and remain inside the metal surface as *laps*. These defects can be removed by grinding but there will be metal loss. If the defect is deep and severe, the product may even get rejected.
    - Non-metallic inclusions: The inclusions may result from oxides, nitrides or silicates present in the molten metal, especially steel. If the inclusions are less in volume, they may cause small cracks in the metal, and if these are more in volume, they can cause severe cracks called crocodile cracks separating the product into two halves.
    - Internal pores: There may be pores in the product due to the presence of gases like hydrogen, oxygen, nitrogen, etc. When too large volume of gases is present in the metal, the rolled product becomes weak as a result of elongation of the pores. Sometimes even separation may take place resulting in cracks.
2. **Structural defects** The defects in this category are wavy edges, zipper cracks, edge cracks, alligatoring, barreling, and laminations. These defects can be further classified into the following:
    - **Defects due to bending of rolls** Rolls act as straight beams loaded transversely (with rolling loads) and undergo deflection. As a result, the edges of the strip get compressed more than the central portion, that is, the edges become thinner than the central portion. Since the reduction in thickness is converted into increase in length

of the strip, the strip elongates more at the edges than at the centre. However, as the material is continuous, there is adjustment of strains within the material. On the edges, the material experiences compressive strains while at the centre, the material experiences tensile strains [Figure 9.4(a)]. Since the edges are restrained from expanding freely in the longitudinal (rolling) direction, *wavy edges* are formed on the sheet [Figure 9.4(b)].

Zipper cracks that occur in the central portion of the strip [Figure 9.4(c)] are caused due to differential strain distribution at the edges and at the centre of the strip on account of greater elongation of the material at the edges than at the centre coupled with restraint on the material from expanding freely in the longitudinal direction. Another cause of occurrence of zipper cracks is the poor ductility of the material at room temperature.

These two defects can be controlled to some extent by providing *camber* to the rolls, that is, the diameter of the rolls is slightly increased at the centre with respect to that at the ends. Under load conditions, the rolls will provide a straight uniform gap to the strip.

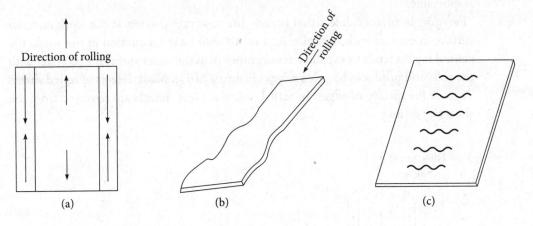

Figure 9.4 Schematic illustration of typical defects in flat rolled work material: (a) Type of strain in different regions of rolled metal; (b) Wavy edges; and (c) Zipper cracks in the central region of the strip

- **Defects due to inhomogeneous deformation** *Edge cracks* are formed mainly due to this cause. As the material is compressed under the rolls, there is a proportionate decrease in thickness with simultaneous increase in its length and width (lateral spread). The lateral spread is countered by the inward shear/frictional forces. The net effect is that the elements near the centre of the sheet experience less lateral spread when compared to those near the edges. As a result, the decrease in thickness for the elements near the centre will be mainly converted into increase in length while for the elements at the edges, a part of the decrease in thickness is converted into increase in length and the remaining decrease in thickness is converted into lateral spread. Consequently, the increase in length at the centre will be greater than that at the edges making the ends of the sheet rounded [Figure 9.5(a)]. Due to continuity of material elements, the material near the edges will be under tension while that around the centre will be under compression. This can lead to the formation of edge cracks [Figure 9.5(b)], or under severe conditions, there can even be a centre-split in the sheet [Figure 9.6(a)].

There can be rolling conditions such that only the surface of the workpiece is deformed; the middle portion is less deformed as compared to the outer surface. The cross-section of the slab is deformed into a shape like the one shown in Figure 9.6(b). The reason for this may be a variation in temperature in the metal; surface temperature being more than the inside temperature of the slab. Another common defect, which is called *alligatoring,* is caused due to metallurgical weakness in the metal (due to the presence of inclusions) along the centre line of the slab. This results in the separation of the layer giving rise to opening of the slab, which looks like an alligator mouth in the opening position. The defect has therefore acquired this name [Figure 9.6(c)]. Alligatoring is actually a complex phenomenon for which a number of factors are responsible.

Barreling is another defect that occurs due to severe friction at the work material surface in contact with the rolls. As a result with heavy reduction in the work, the central region tends to expand laterally more than the outer surfaces in contact with the rolls and produces barreled edges [Figure 9.6(d)]. Most defects of rolled sheets degrade the quality of edges. In actual practice, these defects are removed from the sheets by slitting.

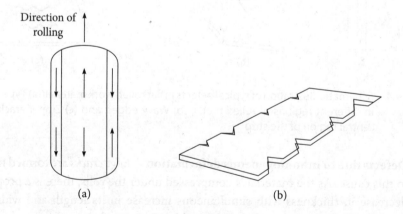

Figure 9.5 Typical defects in flat rolled work material caused due to inhomogeneous deformation: (a) Length of central region is greater than that at the edges; and (b) Cracks or material rupture at edges due to severe tension in material in that zone

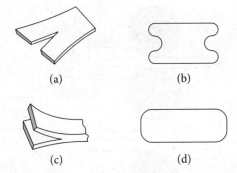

(a)   (b)

(c)   (d)

Figure 9.6   Defect in rolled products: (a) Center-split; (b) Non-uniform deformation; (c) Alligator crack; and (d) Barreling

9.3 Rolling Mills

The machines used for performing rolling operations on metals are called rolling mills. Different designs of rolling mills use different arrangements of rolls. Rolling mills for hot and cold rolling are basically the same; for hot rolling, the roll material, lubricants, and cooling system used are different. The following designs of rolling mills are commonly used in industries.

1. **Two-high rolling mill**   It is the most simple, robust and widely used design. As shown in Figure 9.7(a), it has two rolls, each of which rotates about the horizontal axis and in a direction opposite to each other. The lower roll is fixed while the upper one can be raised or lowered to vary the gap between the rolls. For successive reductions, the material is brought to the entrance of the rolls, the gap between the rolls is reduced, and the stock is fed through the rotating rolls. In case the material requires several reductions, handling time can be saved by using a *two-high reversing mill*, in which the direction of rotation of the two rolls can be reversed. After each pass of the material, the roll gap is reduced and the direction of rotation is reversed. The material is thus made to reciprocate many times between the rolls till the desired thickness of material is achieved.

    The first rolling of metal ingot into blooms and slabs is generally done on two-high rolling mills. Both hot and cold rolling can be done on these mills. The roll diameters range from 0.2 m to 1 m.

2. **Three-high rolling mill**   This design of rolling mill has three rolls arranged in a single vertical plane, each roll having a constant direction of rotation [Figure 9.7(b)]. The direction of movement of material is reversed after each pass by raising it to the upper roll-gap, and then again lowered to the lower roll-gap. The top and the bottom rolls are drive rolls and the middle roll rotates by friction. A three-high rolling mill has higher productivity than a two-high rolling mill. For handling of material, use is made of elevators and various manipulators. These mills are employed as blooming mills.

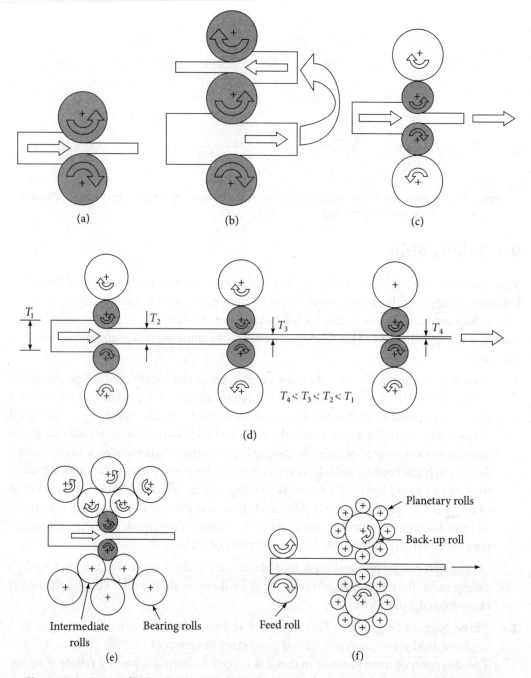

Figure 9.7   Types of rolling mills: (a) Two-high rolling mill; (b) Three-high rolling mill; (c) Four-high rolling mill; (d) Tandem rolling mill; (e) Cluster rolling mill; and (f) Planetary rolling mill

3.   **Four-high rolling mill**   A four-high rolling mill is basically a two-high rolling mill with the difference that the work rolls used are of smaller diameter and each work roll has a

back-up roll. The use of small diameter rolls has many advantages like lower roll forces and power requirements, lesser lateral spread of stock material during rolling, lower cost, and ease in replacement when worn or broken. The only disadvantage of the small diameter rolls deflecting or bending more under roll forces due to their low strength and rigidity is taken care of by providing two large diameter back-up or support rolls (one for each work roll), as shown in Figure 9.7(c). The support rolls can have a diameter up to 3 times that of work rolls.

Four-high rolling mills are reversing mills, used for cold rolling thin sheets of high strength metals having width in the range 0.5 to 1.5 m. When a series of four-high rolling mills are installed to continuously decrease the thickness of a strip [Figure 9.7(d)], the process is called *tandem rolling*.

4. **Cluster mill** It is also called the Sendzimir or Z mill. With the use of small diameter work rolls having the support of large size back-up rolls (diameter limited to 3 times the diameter of work rolls), when material reduction per pass is increased, the rolling loads also increase. A stage may be reached when the rolling loads are so large that the back-up rolls themselves start to bend and need to be supported. This is what is precisely done in the cluster mill, as shown in Figure 9.7(e).

    There are two work rolls, each supported by a pair of intermediate rolls. This pair of rolls is further supported by three bearing rolls. The intermediate rolls are the driving rolls that provide motion to all the other rolls including the work rolls. The bearing rolls support the driving rolls, as shown in Figure 9.7(e).

    Cluster mills are well suited to rolling of thin sheets or foils made of high strength metals and alloys in width up to 2 m and of thickness as small as 1 micron. The products produced have exceptionally good accuracy.

5. **Planetary rolling mill** This design of rolling mill has a pair of heavy backing rolls surrounded by a large number of small diameter planetary rolls [Figure 9.7(f)]. This design of mill is used to achieve very heavy reduction in cross-sections, say, for reducing a slab to a thin plate. Each pair of planetary rolls gives an almost constant reduction to the slab as it sweeps out a circular path between the slab and the backing roll. The total reduction is the sum of several small reductions that follow each other in rapid succession.

9.3.1 Rolls

Rolls are made of cast iron, cast steel or forged steel, depending on the required strength and allowed resistance to wear. Small diameter rolls, such as the work rolls used in a cluster mill, may be made from tungsten carbides. Forged-steel rolls have greater strength, stiffness and toughness than cast iron rolls but are more expensive. As per the need, the surface of rolls may be ground, honed or polished.

Rolls designed for cold rolling operation should not be used for hot rolling, because cracks can develop from thermal cycling.

9.4 Lubricants

The main functions of a lubricant in any metal forming process are lubrication, cooling and protection against corrosion. The overall goal is to ensure that the components of the rolling machine will work to produce the maximum rolled products with a minimum amount of maintenance due to degradation from excessive heat, wear and corrosion. Metal-forming fluids generally are categorized into four main types: water-based, oil-based, synthetic (or semi-synthetic) and solid (dry) film.

Water-based or soluble oils contain emulsions (or micro-emulsions). They offer great cooling characteristics but lack lubricity. These lubricants are ideal for high-speed applications and are commercially available in concentrates.

Oil-based lubricants provide great lubricity characteristics and long service life but sometimes lack additive solubility.

Synthetic and semi-synthetic lubricants are designed to deliver very high cooling capabilities. Synthetic lubricants can be emulsified with water (sometimes known as neo-synthetics) to offer better lubricity.

Solid (or dry) film lubrication makes use of solid materials (such as graphite) in conjunction with or without oil or water. The best applications are in extreme conditions such as low roll speeds, high and low temperatures, and high pressures.

Proper selection of lubricant should also be based on certain parameters such as the metal being rolled, the quality of water (such as in water-based fluids), requirements of the formed metal before and after the process, as well as customer preferences.

Cold rolling of steel is generally carried out with water-soluble oils or low viscosity lubricants, such as mineral oils, emulsions, and paraffin. Hot rolling of ferrous alloys can be done with or without the use of a lubricant. When it is required to break-up the scale formed on the rolled material, graphite or some water-soluble oil may be used. Hot rolling of non-ferrous alloys is done with fatty acid or emulsion as lubricant. In rolling of billets and slabs, the heating medium (such as salt) used in their heat treatment can also serve as a lubricant.

Questions

1. The thickness of plates and sheets is reduced by rolling operation. Do you think it would be feasible to reduce the thickness of a flat metal piece simply by stretching? Explain.

2. Can the application of external tension affect the flat rolling process? How?

3. What are the various technical and economic reasons for taking larger rather than smaller reductions per pass in flat rolling?

4. With the help of a suitable sketch describe the operation of a *two-high reversing mill*. What are its applications?

5. Discuss Steckel rolling. How is it different from conventional metal rolling?

6. What is tandem rolling? Why is it critical to control the roll speeds, roll gaps, temperature and other process variables in this process?

7. Name any five products that you have used, which were made by rolling process. Give a list of five products that have been made by thread rolling process.

8. Differentiate between:
   i. A bloom, a slab, and a billet.
   ii. A plate and a sheet.
   iii. A two-high rolling mill and a four-high rolling mill.
   iv. A cluster mill and a planetary rolling mill.

9. Rolls for metal rolling can be made of several metals and alloys. Name these materials and discuss which one you would prefer for which design of the rolling mill and why.

10. Write short notes on
    a. Lubricants used in rolling mill operations
    b. Planetary rolling mill

Fill in the Blanks

1. In a rolling operation, considering an ideal frictionless situation, if L is the contact length between strip and roll, w is the width of the strip, and σ is the average true stress of the strip material in the roll gap, the roll force can be determined from the relation _____.

2. In flat rolling, *spreading* _____ with decrease in width-to-thickness ratio of the entering material.

3. _____ is used as a lubricant for hot rolling of ferrous alloys.

4. _____ is a defect in plates caused due to bending of rolls.

5. Billets have cross-sectional area _____ than those of blooms.

Choose the Correct Answer

1. The type of forces generally applied to the metal during the process of metal rolling when carried out in hot state is
   a. tensile.
   b. shear.
   c. compressive.
   d. tensile and compressive both.

2. In the process of metal rolling, the thickness of sheet is
   a. increased.
   b. decreased.
   c. not affected.
   d. increased or decreased depending upon the type of forces applied.

3. In the process of metal rolling, if V_1 is the velocity of the strip at its entry into the roll gap and V_2 is its velocity at the exit from the roll gap, then
   a. $V_1 = V_2$
   b. $V_1 > V_2$
   c. $V_1 < V_2$
   d. V_1 may be less or more than V_2 depending upon the roll diameter and thickness of strip.

4. In the process of metal rolling, if V_1 is the velocity of the strip at its entry into the roll gap and V_r is the surface velocity of the roll, then
   a. $V_1 = V_r$
   b. $V_1 > V_r$
   c. $V_1 < V_r$
   d. V_1 may be less or more than V_r depending upon the roll diameter and thickness of strip.

5. In the process of metal rolling, if V_2 is the velocity of the strip at the point of exit from the roll gap and V_r is the surface velocity of the roll, then
   a. $V_2 = V_r$
   b. $V_2 < V_r$
   c. $V_2 > V_r$
   d. V_2 may be less or more than V_r depending upon the roll diameter and thickness of strip.

6. A bloom is a solid mass of metal having square or rectangular cross-section with thickness
   a. equal to 50 mm.
   c. less than 150 mm.
   b. equal to or greater than 100 mm.
   d. equal to or greater than 150 mm.

7. A billet has dimensions
   a. same as those of a slab.
   c. smaller than those of a bloom.
   b. same as those of a bloom.
   d. bigger than those of a bloom.

8. A plate is a solid mass of material having thickness
   a. less than 3 mm.
   c. more than 6 mm but less than 10 mm.
   b. more than 3 mm but less than 6 mm.
   d. more than 6 mm but less 150 mm.

9. A foil is a thin sheet generally having thickness less than
   a. 1 mm.
   c. 0.01 mm.
   b. 0.1 mm.
   d. 0.001 mm.

10. In the process of metal rolling, along the arc of contact in the roll gap
   a. there is relative sliding motion between the roll and the strip in the direction normal to the roll axis.
   b. there is no relative sliding motion between the roll and the strip in the direction normal to the roll axis.

c. there is relative sliding motion between the roll and the strip in the direction parallel to the roll axis.

d. there is no relative sliding motion between the roll and the strip in the direction parallel to the roll axis.

11. In the process of metal rolling, along the arc of contact in the roll gap

   a. the velocity of the strip is the same as that of the roll.

   b. the velocity of the strip is inverse of the velocity of the roll.

   c. there is a region where the velocity of the strip is the same as that of the roll.

   d. there is a point where the velocity of the strip is the same as that of the roll.

12. In the process of metal rolling, along the arc of contact in the roll gap there is a point called the neutral point.

   a. On one side of this point, the work material is in tension, and on the other side, the work material is in compression.

   b. On one side of this point, the work material has velocity greater than that of the roll, and on the other side, it has velocity lesser than that of the roll.

   c. On one side of this point, the work material has a rough surface finish, and on the other side, the work material has a very fine finish.

   d. At this point, there is no increase in material width, but on either side of the neutral point, the material width increases.

13. If L is the length of contact between the strip and the roll, w is the width of the strip, and σ_{avg} is the average true stress of the strip in the roll gap, the roll force can be determined as

   a. $\sigma_{avg} . L . w$

   c. $\dfrac{1}{w}\sigma_{avg} . L$

   b. $1/[\sigma_{avg} . L . w]$

   d. $\dfrac{1}{L.w}\sigma_{avg}$

14. The roll force can be reduced by

   a. using rolls of larger diameter so that contact area is increased.

   b. taking greater reduction per pass of the stock so that contact area is increased.

   c. reducing friction between the metal stock and roll surface.

   d. reducing the temperatures of rolling so that stock material does not become more ductile.

15. The roll force can be reduced by

   a. using rolls of larger diameter so that contact area is increased.

   b. taking greater reduction per pass of the stock so that contact area is increased.

   c. applying longitudinal tension to the metal stock during rolling.

   d. reducing the temperatures of rolling so that stock material does not become more ductile.

16. Steckel rolling is the rolling process carried out by applying
    a. tension to the work material stock at the roll-gap exit, with no power given to the rolls.
    b. compressive force to the work material stock at the roll-gap exit, with no power given to the rolls.
    c. tension to the work material stock at the roll-gap exit, with usual power given to the rolls.
    d. compressive force to the work material stock at the roll-gap exit, with usual power given to the rolls.

17. In pack rolling,
    a. two or more layers of metal are rolled together.
    b. rolls used are of unequal size.
    c. a large reduction of thick sheets can be obtained.
    d. it is mostly possible to remove any surface irregularities caused due to previous rolling operation.

18. Temper rolling is the practice of rolling followed to
    a. decrease the stresses in the work material.
    b. remove any surface irregularities caused due to previous rolling operation.
    c. achieve a large reduction of thick sheets.
    d. increase the strength of rolls so that their life is increased.

19. Zipper cracks occur
    a. in the central portion of the strip that is produced by rolling operation.
    b. at the edges of the strip that is produced by rolling operation.
    c. anywhere on the strip that is produced by rolling operation.
    d. on the surface of rolls used in rolling operation.

20. Cluster mill is also known by the name
    a. Z mill.   c. T mill.
    b. C mill.   d. M mill.

21. Cluster mill is mostly used for rolling
    a. thick plates of relatively ductile metals .
    b. thin sheet or foil made of high strength metals and alloys.
    c.. round and spherical components.
    d. complex shaped components.

22. In tandem rolling,
    a. the thickness of the strip is successively decreased at several stages.
    b. round and spherical components can be easily produced.

c.   complex shaped components can be easily produced.

d.   two or more layers of metal are rolled together.

Answers

1. c.	2. b.	3. c.	4. c.	5. c.	6. d.	7. c.	8. d.	9. c.	10. a.
11. d.	12. b.	13. a.	14. c.	15. c.	16. a.	17. a.	18. b.	19. a.	20. a.
21. b.	22. a.								

10

Metal Forging Processes

LEARNING OBJECTIVES

After reading this chapter, you should be able to understand the following:

- The fundamentals of the metal forging process.

- The different forging processes such as drop forging (open-die hammer forging, impression-die drop forging, upset forging), swaging (rotary forging), press forging and roll forging.

- The force required in metal forging.

- The metallurgical effects of forging.

- The details about special forging processes, such as auto-forging, roll forging, coining and piercing.

- The recent trends in metal forging practice, such as net-shape forging, isothermal forging and incremental forging.

- The forging machine: requirements, design features and common types; comparison between hammers and presses; factors involved in the selection of a forging machine.

- The dies and lubricants used in forging practice.

- The common defects in forged parts: causes and remedies.

10.1 Introduction

Forging is a deformation process in which the material is shaped by the application of localized compressive forces exerted either manually or with power hammers, presses or special forging machines. In other words, the pressures applied may be either gradual or by sudden impact. The process may be carried out on materials in either hot or cold state. When forging is done cold, processes have been given special names. Therefore, the term 'forging' usually implies hot forging carried out at temperatures which are above the recrystallization temperature of the material. Table 10.1 gives the hot forging temperature for some important metal alloys.

Table 10.1 Temperature range for hot forging

Alloy	Temperature range (°C)
Aluminium alloys	400–550
Magnesium alloys	250–350
Copper alloys	600–900
Carbon and low alloy steels	850–1250
Titanium alloys	700–950
Molybdenum alloys	1150–1350
Tungsten alloys	1200–1300
Nickel-based super alloys	1050–1200

Forging is an effective method of producing many useful shaped parts. In contrast to *rolling*, the end product of which is a long length of metal deformed into the desired shape, forging produces discrete parts of shape as close to the desired final shape as possible. Typical forged parts include rivets, bolts, crane hooks, engine crankshafts and connecting rods, gears, turbine shafts, hand tools, railroads and a variety of structural components used in manufacturing machinery. The forged parts have excellent strength and toughness; they can be used reliably for highly stressed and critical applications.

The materials for forging must have the important property of ductility, that is, the ability to sustain substantial plastic deformation without fracture. Low and medium carbon steel can be easily forged but high carbon and alloy steels are difficult to forge. Common forgeable materials are steel, wrought iron, copper-base alloys, nickel alloys, aluminium alloys and magnesium alloys.

10.2 Forging Processes

A variety of forging processes have been developed that can be used for producing either a single piece or for mass producing hundreds of identical parts. The forging processes can be classified in the following ways.

- **Based on working temperature**   (i) Hot forging; (ii) Warm forging; (iii) Cold forging.
- **Based on kind of pressure applied**   (i) Impact: examples are drop forging, swaging; (ii) Gradual: typical example is press forging.
- **Based on the degree to which the flow of work metal is constrained by the dies** (i) Open die forging; (ii) Impression die forging; (iii) Flash-less forging.

The following are some common forging processes:

1. Drop forging.
   i. Open-die hammer forging
   ii. Impression-die drop forging
   iii. Upset forging
2. Press forging
3. Swaging (rotary forging)
4. Roll forging

10.2.1 Open-die hummer forging

It is the simplest forging process and is quite flexible. Being a slow process, it is not suitable for large-scale production. The resulting size and shape accuracy of the forging are dependent on the skills of the operator.

The process is simple. The workpiece material is heated in an open furnace until it is well above its recrystallization temperature (for steel, this is ~1200°C). The operator obtains the desired shape of forging by manipulating the work material between repeated blows of a hammer (Figure 10.1). Use may be made of some specially shaped tools or a simple shaped die for shaping the required sections (round, concave or convex), making holes or performing cut-off operations. One common open-die forging operation is known as *upsetting*. In this operation, the height of the workpiece is reduced and its cross-section increased. Other operations that belong to open-die forging are fullering, edging and cogging.

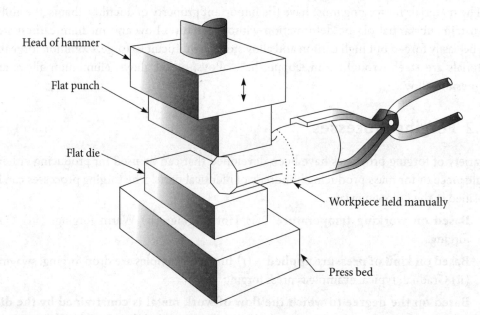

Figure 10.1 Schematic of open-die hammer forging

As can be seen in Figure 10.2, the fullering operation is used to reduce the cross-section of the workpiece. The operation is performed with the dies having convex surfaces. Edging operation is similar to fullering, except that the dies have concave surfaces. Cogging operation involves a series of forging compressions along the length of a workpiece to achieve reduced cross-section and increased length. It is used in the steel industry to produce blooms and slabs from cast ingots. Incremental forging (described later in this chapter) is a type of cogging operation.

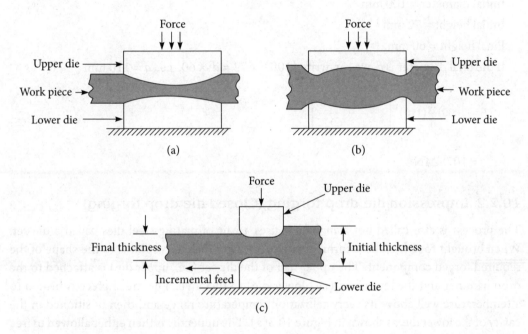

Figure 10.2   Schematic representation of open-die forging operations: (a) Fullering; (b) Edging; and (c) Cogging

Open-die forging process is most often used to make a rough or near-final shape of the part; some further operations may be done on the job to get the final shape. It is quite a cost-effective method for making small quantities of medium size parts.

Forging force   In the open-die forging operation, the forging force F, to be applied on a solid cylindrical component, can be determined from the relation

$$F = \sigma_f \frac{\pi}{4} d^2 \left(1 + \frac{\mu d}{3h} \right) \tag{10.1}$$

where σ_f is the flow stress of the material, μ is the coefficient of friction, and d and h are respectively the final diameter and height of the workpiece.

Example 10.1

Using an open-die forging operation, a solid cylindrical piece of stainless steel having 100 mm dia. × 72 mm height is reduced in height to 60 mm at room temperature. Assume that the coefficient of friction is 0.22 and the flow stress for this material at the required true strain is 1000 MPa. Calculate the forging force at the end of the hammer stroke.

Solution

Initial diameter = 100 mm

Initial height = 72 mm

Final height = 60 mm

If the final diameter is d, we can write $(100)^2 \times 72 = d^2 \times 60$, i.e., $d = 110$ mm

$$F = (1000)\frac{\pi}{4}(110)^2 \left(1 + \frac{0.22 \times 110}{3 \times 60} \right)$$

$$= 1078 \text{ MN}$$

10.2.2 Impression-die drop forging (Closed-die drop forging)

The process is also called hot *stamping*. It uses a pair of mating steel dies called a die set. When brought together, these form an enclosed cavity that corresponds to the shape of the required forged component. The upper half of the die set (i.e., upper die) is attached to the drop hammer and the lower half (i.e., lower die) to the anvil. The metal piece is heated to a temperature well above its recrystallization temperature range and then positioned in the cavity of the lower die, as shown in Figure 10.3(a). The upper die is then either allowed to free fall or is forced down by pneumatic or mechanical means onto the lower die. The hot metal is thus forced to deform and fill the cavity by hammering, as shown in Figure 10.3(b). Excess metal is squeezed out around the periphery of the cavity to form flash, as shown in Figure 10.3(c). On completion of forging, the flash is trimmed off with the help of a trimming die.

Most impression-die sets contain several cavities. The work material is given the final desired shape in stages as it is deformed in successive cavities in the die set. The shape of the cavities cause the metal to flow in the desired direction, thereby imparting the desired fibre structure to the component.

Drop forging is a flexible process; to produce a different component, only the die set has to be changed. The main limitation of the process is that it cannot produce close tolerance work, and machining or other finishing operations are often required to achieve the desired shape and dimensional accuracy.

The process is mostly used for copper and copper alloys, steel, titanium and refractory alloys.

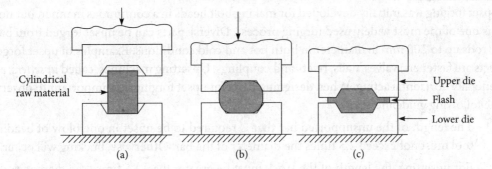

Figure 10.3 Schematic representation of the sequence in impression-die forging: (a) Cylindrical raw material placed in the lower die, and upper die coming down to touch the top of the raw material; (b) The upper die comes further down, applies force on the raw material and compresses it; and (c) The upper die closes on the lower die under force to form flash in the gap between lower and upper dies

10.2.3 Upset forging

Upset forging involves increasing the cross-section of a component at the expense of its height (volume of the stock remains the same). The process can be done either through open-die forging [Figure 10.1] or through closed-die forging [Figure 10.4]. The portion of stock that is not to be upset is clamped in a clamping die, while the portion to be upset projects out [Figure 10.4(a)]. Lengthwise impact pressure is applied to forge the projected portion into the required shape [Figure 10.4(b)].

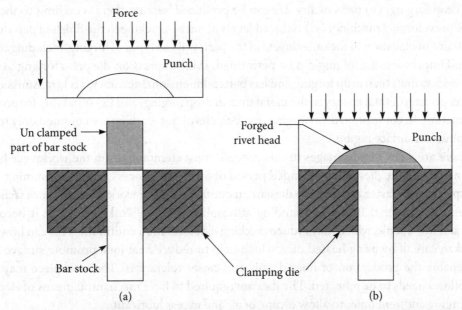

Figure 10.4 Schematic of upset forging of a rivet head at the end of a bar: (a) Before forging; and (b) After forging

Upset forging was initially developed for making bolt heads in a continuous manner, but now it is one of the most widely used forging process. Diverse parts can be upset forged from bars or rods up to 200 mm in diameter in both hot and cold conditions. Examples of upset forged parts are fasteners, valves, nails, rivets and couplings. Upsetting machines, called *upsetters*, are generally horizontal acting. When designing parts for upset forging, it is important to observe the following guidelines.

1.   The length of the unsupported bar that is required to be upset in one blow of heading tool must not exceed 2.5 times the diameter of the bar. Otherwise, bucking will occur.

2.   For upsetting, the length of the stock must be greater than 2.5 times the diameter; the cavity diameter must not exceed 1.5 times the diameter of the bar.

10.2.4 Closed-die pressure forging (Press forging)

Press forging does not rely upon kinetic energy from repeated hammer blows to achieve the required metal deformation; rather a gradual, steady and controlled pressure, typically 1000 MPa, is applied to the hot metal with the help of a hydraulic press. The metal experiences slow and squeezing action; it has time to flow as it is pressed resulting in uniform deformation throughout the entire depth of the workpiece. The press forging operation can be done either cold or hot.

The entire operation is completed in one go and is, therefore, quicker and cheaper than drop forging. Other benefits include the following: (i) improved quality of product shape; (ii) better dimensional accuracy; (iii) uniform metallurgical properties because the forging force is transferred to the bulk of the material uniformly and gradually; (iv) quieter operation than drop forging; (v) parts of any size can be produced because there is no limit to the size of the press forging machine; (vi) reduced levels of micro-cracking in the finished part due to constraint of oxidation to the outer layers of the part; (vii) all types of forging, including open-die and impression-die forging can be performed; (viii) impression-die press forging usually requires less draft than drop forging and has better dimensional accuracy; (ix) transmission of greater portion of total energy to the metal than in drop forging; and (x) suitability for process automation. In contrast, in drop forging, the benefits of hot working are confined only to the component's surface region.

There are a few disadvantages to this process, most stemming from the workpiece being in contact with the dies for an extended period of time. The process is time-consuming. The workpiece cools faster because the dies are in contact with the workpiece; the dies facilitate more heat transfer than the surrounding atmosphere. As the workpiece cools it becomes hard and less ductile, which may induce cracking if deformation continues. This can however be taken care of by using heated dies, which help to reduce heat loss, promote surface flow and enable the production of finer details and closer tolerances. The workpiece may also sometimes needs to be reheated. The dies are required to have mechanical means of ejecting the forging and vent holes to allow escape of air and excess lubricant.

Hydraulic presses are available in the capacity range of 5 MN to 500 MN. However, 10 MN to 100 MN capacity presses are more common.

Forging force The forging force, F, required to forge the material by impression-die forging operation can be determined by the relation

$$F = k\,\sigma_f\,A$$

where k is a constant whose value can be taken from Table 10.2, σ_f is the flow stress of the material at the forging temperature and A is the projected area of the forging including the flash.

In hot forging of most non-ferrous metals and alloys, the forging pressure is generally in the range of 500 MPa to 1000 MPa.

Table 10.2   Range of value of k

Simple shape of part, no flash produced	3 to 5
Simple shape of part, flash produced	5 to 6
Intricate shape of part, flash produced	8 to 12

10.3 Other Forging Operations

10.3.1 Swaging

This process is also known as *rotary swaging* or *radial swaging*. In this process, the diameter of a rod or a tube is reduced by forcing it into a confining die. A set of reciprocation dies provides radial impact forces to cause the metal to flow inward and acquire the form of the die cavity. The die movements may be of in-and-out reciprocatory or rotary. The latter type of die movement is obtained with the help of a set of rollers in a cage, similar to the action in a roller bearing. The workpiece is held stationary and the dies rotate as well as strike the workpiece at a rate as high as 10–20 strokes per second. Figure 10.6 shows the schematic of the process of swaging of round parts.

Screwdriver blades and soldering iron tips are some common examples of flat swaged products. In tube swaging, the tube thickness and/or internal diameter of the tube may be left uncontrolled as shown in Figure 10.5(a) or it may be controlled with the use of an internal mandrel as shown in Figure 10.5(b). For small-diameter tubing, a thin rod can be used as a mandrel; even internally shaped tubes can be swaged by using mandrels [Figure 10.5(c)].

The process is quite versatile. The maximum diameter of the workpiece that can be swaged is limited to about 150 mm; workpieces as small as 0.5 mm diameter have been swaged. The production rate can be as high as 30 parts per minute, depending upon the complexity of the part shape and the part handling means adopted.

The parts produced by swaging have improved mechanical properties and tolerance in the range ± 0.05 mm to ± 0.5 mm. Use of lubricants helps in obtaining better work surface finish and longer die life. Materials such as tungsten and molybdenum are generally swaged at elevated temperatures as they have low ductility at room temperature. Hot swaging is also used to form long or steep tapers, and for large reductions. One major concern about swaging is that it is a noisy operation. The level of noise can, however, be reduced by proper mounting of the machine or by using some kind of enclosure around the machine.

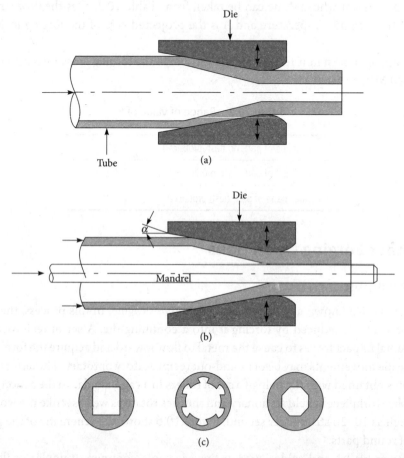

Figure 10.5 Schematic of swaging process for round parts: (a) Swaging of tubes without a mandrel. Wall thickness is more in the die gap; (b) Swaging of tubes with a mandrel. The final wall thickness of the tube depends on the mandrel diameter; and (c) Typical cross-sections of tubes produced by swaging with shaped mandrels

10.3.2 Roll forging

This process is used to reduce the thickness of round or flat stock of material with corresponding increase in length. Examples of products produced by this process include leaf springs, axles and levers.

The forging operation involves a heated bar being fed into a pair of cylindrical rolls that have the shape of the required component cut into their surface. Upon feeding of stock, the rolls are rotated for half a revolution, at the end of which the forged part is ejected.

Depending on the component complexity, each roll may have a series of shaped grooves on it so that as the stock comes out from one set of grooves, it is inserted between the next set of smaller grooves on the roll and the process is repeated till the desired shape and size are achieved. In this way, the material is progressively squeezed and shaped (Figure 10.6).

Figure 10.6   Roll forging machine

10.3.3 Auto-forging

This is a modified form of impression-die forging used mainly for non-ferrous metals. Here, a cast pre-form, taken out from the mould while hot, is finish-forged in a die. The flash formed during die forging is trimmed later in the usual manner. As the four steps of the process – casting, transfer from mould to the forging die, forging and trimming – are completely mechanized in most applications, the process has acquired the name auto-forging.

10.3.4 Coining

Coining is a severe metal squeezing operation in which the flow of metal occurs only at the top layers of the material and not throughout the material. The operation is carried out in closed dies mainly for the purpose of producing fine details such as that needed in minting coins, and in making medals or jewellery.

The blank is kept in the die cavity and pressures as high as five to six times the strength of material are applied with a press. Depending upon the details required to be coined on the part, more than one coining operations may be done.

The difference between coining and sheet metal embossing is that the same design is created on both sides of the sheet in embossing (one side depressed and the other raised), whereas in coining operations, different designs can be created on each side of the workpiece.

10.3.5 Piercing

It is a process in which the surface of a forged workpiece is indented with a punch so as to produce a shallow cavity or an impression. The workpiece may just be kept unconstrained or held in a die cavity or a vice. If a hole is required in the workpiece at a location, piercing is followed by punching operation.

The force required for piercing depends on the tip geometry of the punch, cross-sectional area of the punch, and the strength of the workpiece material.

10.3.6 Net-shape forging (Precision forging)

The modern trend in forging is toward economy and greater precision of components. The metal is deformed in the die cavity so that no flash is formed and the final dimensions are very close to the desired component dimensions. There is minimum wastage of material and subsequent machining operation is not necessary.

The process uses special dies having greater accuracies than those in impression-die forging. The equipment used is also of higher capacity. The forces required for net-shape forging are high. Aluminium and magnesium alloys are more suitable, although steel can also be precision-forged. Typical precision-forged components are gears, turbine blades, fuel injection nozzles and bearing casings. Because of the greater cost of tooling and machines, precision forging is preferred over conventional forging only where the volume of production is extremely large.

10.3.7 Isothermal forging

Heat transfer from the hot workpiece to the relatively cool die surfaces causes thermal gradients in the workpiece material. The cooler areas of the work material at the die interface surfaces undergo less plastic flow than the hotter core areas, resulting in non-uniform plastic flow. In the isothermal forging process, which is also known as *hot die forging*, the dies are heated to the same temperature as the workpiece material. By maintaining both at that temperature, the forging operation is completed. In doing so, heat transfer from the workpiece material to the die surfaces is avoided.

Aluminium alloys are usually forged by using a hydraulic press under isothermal or near isothermal conditions at around 425°C. At that temperature, conventional die materials do not undergo any significant loss of strength or hardness. Steels and alloys of titanium and nickel are forged in the range 925–1260°C. Isothermal forging of these alloys requires special tooling materials such as nickel-based super alloys and molybdenum alloys for dies, and lubricants that can perform adequately at these temperatures. It is important to use a surrounding atmosphere of inert gas or vacuum to protect both the dies and the workpiece from oxidation.

Advantages   The main advantages are (i) complex parts with good dimensional accuracy can be forged to near-net shape by just one stroke of the press, resulting in reduced machining and material costs; (ii) reduction in the number of pre-forming and blocking operations, resulting in reduced processing and tooling costs; (iii) reduction in cross-section of up to 70% can be achieved in a single forging operation, thus facilitating the forging of parts with thin fins and ribs; and (iv) possibility of the use of slow ram speeds/ lower forging pressures and smaller machines.

Disadvantages   The main disadvantages are related to costs, due to (i) need for more expensive die materials; (ii) need for uniform and controllable die heating systems; (iii) need for an inert atmosphere or vacuum around the dies and workpiece to avoid oxidation of the dies; and (iv) low production rates as proper die filling takes time at low forging pressures.

The process can however be economical for intricate forgings made of materials such as titanium and super alloys, provided the quantity required is high enough to justify the die costs. The process is gaining increasing acceptability for parts used in automotive and aircraft industries.

10.3.8 Incremental forging

It is a technique in which a big workpiece is forged by working on different regions of the workpiece to give them the required shape, one at a time. Since only a limited volume of material is worked at any specific time, the forging equipment can be of smaller capacity. Huge parts can thus be forged on presses of modest capacity.

One major drawback of this technique of forging is that the workpiece material tends to cool below the forging temperature as it moves from one incremental step to another. Reheating the part to its original forging temperature can destroy the thermo-mechanical work already done on it. Therefore, as the workpiece temperature falls below the forging temperature, the workpiece is progressively reheated to a lower temperature, or alternatively, the heat loss may be prevented by covering the areas of workpiece that are not being worked on with some thermal insulating coating. Parts for the bulkhead of the Airbus aircraft are reported to have been made by this technique of forging.

10.4 Forging Equipment

Requirements of forging machine

The forging machine must be compatible with the requirements of the given forging process with respect to load, energy, time and accuracy characteristics. Recent developments in the forging machine building industry are getting influenced by the requirements for manufacturing ever larger and more complex parts out of difficult-to-forge materials. The forging machine and a set of dies comprise the forging equipment. There is a large variety of designs of forging machines available, differing in range of speeds, speed-stroke characteristics and power rating.

Classification

Forging machines can be divided into two basic categories: (i). Energy-restricted machines, and (ii). Stroke-restricted machines.

In energy-restricted machines, the amount of deformation that can be achieved during each stroke or blow of the machine is limited by the energy or maximum force available. If the energy or force capacity is less than that required for deforming the part, then more than one stroke or blow is applied. Machines that fall into this category are hammers, friction screw presses and hydraulic presses.

In stroke-restricted machines, the amount of deformation that can be achieved is fixed by the stroke of the machine. If sufficient force or energy to carry out the operation is not available, then the machine will stall; implying that a larger machine should be used. Mechanical presses fall into this category, as crank length or eccentricity determines the amount of ram movement.

We shall now learn about some important forging machines.

10.4.1 Hammers

Hammers are the most versatile and least expensive of forging machines. They are used for both open-die and impression-die forging, and are generally considered the most flexible as they can be used to perform a variety of forging operations. Hammers are preferred for small to medium batches because of quicker tool setups and lower overall costs.

A hammer has four main parts: (i) falling weight or ram; (ii) lifting mechanism for the ram; (iii) anvil or base; and (iv) frame or guide for the ram. The hammer derives its energy from the potential energy of the heavy ram, which is converted into kinetic energy; hence, it can be called an *energy restricted* equipment. The upper die is fastened to the bottom of the ram while the lower die is fitted on the top of the anvil. The work material is positioned in the bottom die and shaped by the die fitted to the falling ram. The ram is lifted up to a certain height and then allowed to fall by gravity or accelerated by other means onto the workpiece. Hammers apply energy and cause deformation at very high rates. The hammer frame guides the ram, but is essentially not stressed during forging.

Hammers are suitable for alloys that can be deformed rapidly without forming cracks or splits in the workpiece. Aluminium alloys and most magnesium alloys are not forged by hammers for this reason.

Hammers can be classified according to the way in which the ram is raised and whether it falls freely or is driven.

- **Gravity drop hammers**   The ram is raised mechanically to a predetermined height, which cannot be varied between blows, but can be reset between jobs. The energy imparted to the workpiece for forging is derived from a free-falling ram [Figure 10.7(a)]. The amount of available energy in each blow can be approximately estimated from the product of the ram's mass and the height of its fall. The range of the ram's weight in hammers is generally from 200 kg to 4000 kg. The anvil serves as an inertia block and usually weighs 10 to 20 times as much as the hammer. Hammers have high cycle rates – up to 60 per minute. They are available in a range of blow energies from 0.5 kNm to 400 kNm.

- **Power drop hammers**   In this type of hammers, the ram is raised either by steam or air, and is powered down onto the workpiece by pressurized steam or air, adding controlled energy and speed beyond gravity. Striking force can be varied on each stroke over the entire range from a light tap to full power. The complete control of each work stroke places higher requirements on the operator's skills. However, the current trend is to use programmable systems for control.

Steam and air hammers are the most powerful of conventional forging hammers, and typically range in weight from 500 to 20,000 kg. Double-frame hammers for open-die forging have been built to 100,000 kg, but 10,000 kg is the usual maximum size. Anvils weigh 10 to 20 times as much as the hammer ram, and require massive underground installation.

- **High energy rate hammers** In this type of hammers, the ram is accelerated by inert gas at high pressures and the workpiece is forged in just one blow at a very high speed of the ram. These hammers have found limited use in industry because of various problems associated with their operation and maintenance such as die breakage and safety. Speed range of different types of hammers is shown in Table 10.3.

Table 10.3 Speed range of different types of hammers

Hammer	Speed range (m/s)
Gravity drop hammer	3.5 to 5
Power drop hammer	3 to 9
High energy rate hammer	10 to 20

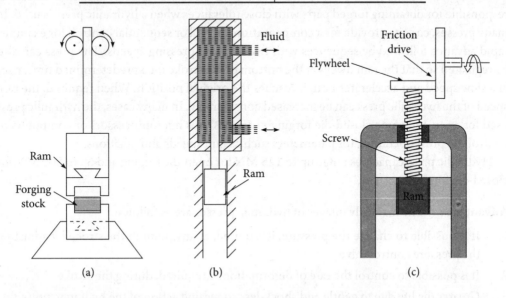

Fluid

Friction drive

Flywheel

Screw

Ram

Ram

Ram

Forging stock

(a)   (b)   (c)

Figure 10.7 Schematic of forging machines: (a) Gravity drop hammer; (b) Hydraulic press; and (c) Friction screw press

10.4.2 Presses

Forging presses are another group of forging machines commonly used in impression die and large open-die forging processes. They are generally classified as mechanical or hydraulic, based on the means used to deliver energy. Hydraulic presses are essentially energy-restricted machines; that is, their capability for carrying out a forging operation is limited mainly by the maximum load capacity. Mechanical presses are stroke-restricted machines, since the length of the press stroke and the available load at various stroke positions represent the capability of these machines. In general, presses deliver energy more slowly than hammers do. They can be used for all alloys, and are preferred to hammers for alloys that require slow deformation rates, such as aluminium alloys and magnesium alloys. Similar to hammers, they usually operate vertically. The upper die is attached to the ram, and the downward stroke of the ram exerts force on the workpiece.

Hydraulic presses

Hydraulic presses are slow moving compared to mechanical and screw presses, and perform squeezing action rather than impacting action on the workpiece. The ram of the hydraulic press is operated by a large piston driven by a high-pressure hydraulic or hydro-pneumatic system [Figure 10.7(b)]. In operation, hydraulic pressure is applied to the top of the piston, moving the ram downward. When the stroke is complete, pressure is applied to the opposite side of the piston to raise the ram. Hydraulic pressures and thereby speeds of the ram can be closely controlled, permitting accurate control of metal flow in the die. This feature is responsible for obtaining forged parts with close tolerances when a hydraulic press is used. In many presses, circuits provide for a compensation control or sequential control; for example, rapid advance followed by sequences with two or more pressing speeds. The press can also be regulated so that the ram dwells at the bottom of the stroke for a predetermined time, rises at a slow speed and accelerates until it reaches the original position. When required, the ram speed of the hydraulic press can be increased considerably. In many cases, the hydraulic press used for open and some closed-die forging processes uses microprocessors or computers to control the press operation, for parameters such as ram speeds and positions.

Hydraulic press capacities range up to 125 MN for open-die forging and up to 500 MN for closed-die forging.

Advantages   The main advantages of hydraulic presses are as follows:

1. It is possible to change the pressure, if required, at any point in the stroke by adjusting the pressure control valve.
2. It is possible to control the rate of deformation, if required, during the stroke.
3. Greater die life due to gentle and shock-less squeezing action of the hydraulic press.
4. Lower die maintenance cost.
5. Higher accuracy and close tolerance on forged parts.
6. Low maintenance cost as compared to mechanical presses.

Disadvantages   Some disadvantages of hydraulic presses are as follows:

1.   High initial cost as compared to the cost of mechanical presses of equivalent capacity.

2.   Slower action as compared to mechanical presses.

3.   Slower action of hydraulic press means longer contact between the dies and the workpiece, resulting in greater heat transfer from the hot workpiece to the dies; this can consequently lead to lower die life.

4.   Slower action of hydraulic press tends to cool the workpiece rapidly while being forged unless the dies are heated.

Mechanical presses

Mechanical presses typically store energy in a rotating flywheel, which is driven by an electric motor. The flywheel is engaged and disengaged to a mechanical drive such as a crankshaft, eccentric shaft, eccentric gear or knuckle levers, which convert flywheel rotation to reciprocatory vertical motion. The upper die is fitted to the bottom of the ram, while the bottom (or stationary) die is clamped to the die seat of the main frame of the press. The ram stroke is shorter than that of a hydraulic press or a forging hammer. The speed of the ram is highest at the centre of the stroke, but force is highest at the bottom of the stroke. The speed, length and duration of the stroke are generally fixed for a press. Capacity of a mechanical forging press is given in terms of the maximum force it can apply, and ranges from 2 MN to 100 MN.

Mechanical forging presses are similar to the mechanical presses used for forming sheet metal, but differ with respect to the following:

1.   **Strength and robustness**   Forging presses are built stronger.

2.   **Delivery of maximum force**   Forging presses deliver their maximum force within 2 to 3 mm of the end of the stroke. This is because maximum pressure is needed to form the flash.

3.   **Ram velocity**   The ram velocity of a forging press is greater than that of a press used for sheet metal deep drawing. This is because in case of forging, it is desirable to complete the forging in less time to minimize the time of contact of hot metal with the dies.

Advantages   Some advantages of mechanical forging presses are as follows:

1.   High productivity and accuracy than with forging hammers.

2.   Consistent forging results.

3.   Dies are less bulky because of less impact compared to hammers; dies are less expensive too.

4.   Dies have longer life; they can be of greater hardness because presses deliver a less severe impact blow.

5.   High skill of operator is not required.

Limitations   Some disadvantages of mechanical forging presses are as follows:

1.   High cost of mechanical forging press compared to hammer; it is 3 to 5 times the cost of a hammer that will produce the same forged part.

2.   Less suitable for (i) forging asymmetrical workpieces; and (ii) preliminary shaping operations such as fullering because a press delivers consecutive strokes of equal force.

Applications   Mechanical presses are best suited for small to medium size simple profile forgings because of their short stroke.

Upsetters

Upsetters are basically double-acting mechanical presses operating in a horizontal plane. They were originally developed to upset metal for bolt heads and similar shapes, and are sometimes referred to as *headers* or simply *forging machines*. They are used to gather or upset (i.e., laterally displace) material, either at the end of the feedstock, between the ends, or at several places of the feed stock. They are often used to gather metal prior to forging operations on other equipment, or to produce complex, finished configurations with precision such as gear blanks, bearing races and spindles.

Forging machines employ a flywheel, air clutch and eccentric shaft to operate the heading ram (or slide). In operation, the bar stock, either heated or in cold state (at room temperature), is placed against the stationary die. The grip-die moves laterally against the stationary die, gripping the stock tightly. The heading die with its attached heading tool (die) then moves forward against the end of the workpiece and displaces the stock into the die impression [Figure 10.4]. As the ram recedes, the grip-die retracts and releases the workpiece to perform subsequent forging operations. In some cases, the forging is punched or sheared off of the bar stock in the final step.

Forging machines are specified according to the maximum bar size for which they can provide an upset head. For example, a 10 mm upsetter could theoretically head bolts or form features in sizes up to 10 mm stem diameter.

Screw presses

A screw press uses a mechanical screw to translate rotational motion into reciprocatory vertical motion. The ram acts as the nut on a rotating screw shaft moving up or down depending on the screw rotation. Energy is either delivered from a flywheel, which is usually coupled with a torque-limiting (slipping) clutch, or by a direct drive reversing electric motor. The screw presses are energy-restricted machines. They can be considered similar to hydraulic and mechanical presses since their frames are subject to loading during the forging stroke. The main advantage of screw presses over crank-type mechanical presses is in the better control of the final thickness of the workpiece when the dies impact each other.

There is another type of screw press, called friction screw press, in which the flywheel is driven by rotating friction discs. The rotary motion of the flywheel is transformed into linear motion by the multiple screw threads on the spindle and a nut [Figure 10.7(c)]. At the top of the ram stroke, the flywheel contacts the friction disc near the centre [Figure 10.8]. As the ram moves downward, the contact point between the flywheel and the friction disc moves towards the outer edge of the friction disc; thereby, rotational speed of the flywheel increases. As soon as the die attached to the ram touches the workpiece, the flywheel speed reduces sharply and its energy is dissipated in the process of deformation. If the dies do not close at the end of the cycle, the operation is repeated until the forging is completed.

Screw presses are used for various open-die and closed-die operations. They are generally suitable for small production quantities and precision parts. They are rated by spindle diameter or by the maximum force they can exert. They are available in a capacity range of 1 MN to 250 MN.

Figure 10.8   Pictorial view of a friction screw press

10.4.3 Selection of forging machine

There are many factors which should be considered when selecting a forging machine. Some of these are as follows:

1.   Strength and ductility of the workpiece material.

2.   Size, shape and complexity of the forging, that is, the load and energy requirements for a given product geometry.

3.   Desired dimensional accuracy of the forging.

4.   Desired production rate of the forging.

5.   Available operator's skill.

6.   Cost.

7.   Noise level permitted.

Presses are generally preferred for components that are to be made from aluminium, brass, bronze, magnesium and beryllium, whereas hammers are generally preferred for components that are to be made from copper, steel, titanium and refractory metal alloys. Depending on the shape complexity of the forged part, the initial rough shape may be given by using a hammer; then, a press may be used to get the final accurate shape. For the same shape, forgings can generally be produced at a higher rate by hammers than by presses. Further, presses are relatively more costly, need higher operator skills, and are less noisy to operate.

10.5 Dies and Lubrication

10.5.1 Dies

Most medium and large-sized forged parts are produced at elevated temperatures. The die materials must therefore possess the following properties:

1.   High strength and toughness at elevated temperatures (high hot hardness and toughness).

2.   High resistance to thermal and mechanical shocks.

3.   High resistance to wear, particularly abrasive wear because of the presence of scale on the hot metal of the forging.

Forging dies are generally made from tool and die steels containing nickel, chromium, molybdenum and vanadium. To make the die, a forged die block is taken and the desired shape of the cavity, hardness and surface finish are achieved by carrying out machining, heat treatment and finishing operations on the die block.

10.5.2 Lubrication

Use of lubricant in forging practices is necessary as it serves numerous functions such as the follows:

•   Reduces friction, and thereby reduces the forging force requirement.

•   Reduces wear, and thereby increases die life.

- Acts as a thermal insulation between the hot workpiece and the relatively cooler dies. This reduces the rate of cooling of the hot workpiece and, thereby, improves metal flow in the die.

- Acts as a parting agent, that is, does not allow the forging to stick to the die. This is necessary for the release of forging from the die.

A variety of lubricants are used in forging practice. For hot forging, graphite and molybdenum disulphide are quite common, while for cold forging, mineral oils and soaps are mostly used. The method of applying a lubricant for hot forging differs from that for cold forging. The lubricant is applied to the dies in case of hot forging; while in case of cold forging, it is applied to the workpiece.

10.6 Metallurgical Effects of Forging

The grain flow pattern in the material of forged parts is similar to that in the parts produced by rolling. The mechanical properties vary with grain direction (called *anisotropy*). In case of forged components, the grain structure tends to follow the physical shape of the component [Figure 10.9(a)]. As a result, the forged component has increased strength in the area where the highest stresses are likely to occur in its use, for example, at corners and section changes. For this very reason, high performance components like engine crankshafts and crane hooks are forged rather than cast. On the other hand, in case of a machined component, as shown in Figure 10.9(b), the grain flow lines follow the direction of rolling operation, to which the material has been subjected to before machining. In case of a casting, the grain structure is almost random as shown in Figure 10.9(c).

The designer must be careful in specifying the production process for critically stressed components. By specifying forging rather than casting for such components, the risk of failure of component during use reduces. If such parts have to be produced from rolled bars or sheets, the designer should ensure that the direction of grain flow of the part is such that the maximum load is taken up by the strongest section of the component.

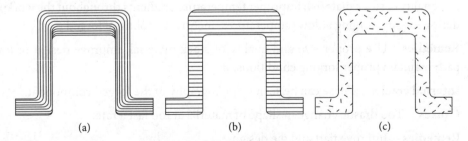

(a)	(b)	(c)

Figure 10.9   Grain flow patterns in products manufactured by different processes: (a) Forging; (b) Machining from bar stock; and (c) Casting

During forging as well as rolling processes, any slag inclusion present in the material gets broken into very small pieces and then dispersed in the total large volume of the material.

However, these processes suffer from one major limitation and that is the work hardness of the material, which occurs particularly at the surface. This occurs specially if the process is carried out in cold condition of material, that is, at room temperature. The resulting hard skin makes subsequent machining quite difficult; although in some applications, it can be advantageous also, particularly where a component is required to be shock-resistant and/or hard and tough at the surface.

10.7 Forging Defects and their Removal

Defects in forging are undesirable as these can cause fatigue failures, and can lead to problems such as corrosion and excessive wear during the service life of the forged component. It is important that for critical applications, forged components are subjected to proper inspection. Forging defects can occur due to several causes, such as poor quality of stock material, incorrect forging conditions, incorrect forging method or technique, improper material flow pattern in the die or incorrect die design, and uneven cooling of forgings after they are taken out from dies. Some common defects in forgings with possible causes and suggested remedies are given here.

1. **Laps or cold shuts**   These look like big cracks or unfilled gaps on the surface.

    Causes   Metal surface folding against itself during forging; insufficient volume of material to fill the die cavity; buckling of part of the workpiece in the die during forging; insufficient number of blows during forging at low temperature of material.

    Remedies   Improve ductility of the material by heating to proper temperatures; improve die design to avoid hindrance to material flow; use adequate number of blows for forging.

2. **Surface cracks**   These occur in a longitudinal or transverse direction on the surface of the forged part.

    Causes   Excess stock material that flows past the already formed part of the forging; bad quality of stock material; improper temperature gradients throughout the workpiece during forging; forging at low temperatures; incorrect cooling of forged part.

    Remedies   Use proper size and quality of stock material; improve design of forged part; maintain proper forging conditions.

3. **Internal cracks**   These can be seen by radiography of the forged component.

    Causes   Too drastic change in shape of material at too fast a rate.

    Remedies   Improve part and die design.

4. **Die shift**   Two parts of the forged component are mismatched at the parting line.

    Causes   Misalignment between the top and the bottom forging dies due to loose wedges.

    Remedies   Maintain proper fitting of dies.

5. **Incorrect size and finish on part**   The dimensions and surface quality of forging do not match with those specified in the drawing.

   Causes   Worn out dies; at times, incorrect dies.

   Remedies   Use proper dies.

6. **Pits**   Shallow depressions at the surface of the forged part, which appear when the forgings are cleaned.

   Causes   Scale, if not removed from the die cavities, gets worked into the surface of the part during forging.

   Remedies   Maintain proper furnace environment; clean the dies frequently.

7. **Dents**   Irregular depressions on the surface of the forged part.

   Causes   Incorrect forging conditions and forging methods

   Remedies   Use proper conditions and method of forging.

8. **Burnt and overheated metal**   Discoloured and disfigured components.

   Causes   Overheating and soaking of stock material for too long a period.

   Remedies   Keep stock temperatures within proper range.

9. **Ruptured fibre structure**   Discontinuity in the flow lines of forging.

   Causes   Working too fast during forging; inadequate stock size.

   Remedies   Use proper stock size, forging technique and die design.

10. **Slag, sand and porosity**   Part looks shabby due to fine holes at the surface; lumps of metal oxide or other foreign material inside the forging.

    Causes   Defective stock material.

    Remedies   Inspect the stock material before forging.

11. **Decarburization**   Degradation of surface of forging made out of high carbon steels.

    Causes   Soaking of stock material at too high temperatures for too long periods.

    Remedies   Heat stock material to proper temperature and forge it soon after.

10.7.1 Defect removal from forgings

Some forging defects such as deep cracks and cavities, decarburization and burnt surface cannot be removed. Other defects, such as shallow or hair cracks, coarse grain structure, distortion and internal stresses can be cured, as under:

1. Decarburized areas and shallow hair cracks on surface can be removed by grinding.
2. Shallow cracks and cavities can be removed by chipping with a pneumatic chisel.
3. Distorted forgings can be straightened in presses.
4. Internal stresses in the forgings can be removed by heat treatment operations such as annealing and normalizing.

Questions

1. Differentiate between
   i. Drop forging and press forging.
   ii. Grain flow patterns of cast, forged and rolled products.
   iii. Isothermal forging and incremental forging.
2. Why is it necessary to control the volume of blank in closed-die forging?
3. Name any five forging defects. Also give their causes and remedies.
4. What is meant by flash in impression-die forging process? What purpose does it serve?
5. Why is the use of lubricant in forging practice necessary? Name the lubricants used for hot forging and for cold forging.
6. Compare mechanical and hydraulic forging presses w.r.t. their principle of operation, working and the range of products for which they are suitable.

Fill in the Blanks

1. In forging, the term 'flash' refers to the metal _____.
2. In upset forging, the cross-section of a component _____ at the expense of its _____.
3. Some typical parts made by upset forging operation are _____, _____ and _____.
4. When designing parts for upset forging, in order to avoid buckling, the length of unsupported bar that can be upset in one blow of heading tool should not exceed _____ times the diameter of the bar.
5. In case of forged components, the grain structure tends to follow the _____.
6. _____ is a family of metal working processes in which deformation of the workpiece is carried out by compressive forces applied through a set of dies.
7. _____ is a process in which a solid rod or a tube is reduced in diameter by the reciprocating radial movement of a set of two or four dies.
8. The lubricant is applied to the _____ in case of hot forging; while in the case of cold forging, it is applied to the _____.
9. For _____ forging, graphite and molybdenum disulphide are quite common lubricants.
10. Forging machines generally preferred for components that are to be made from aluminium, brass, bronze, magnesium, and beryllium are _____, whereas _____ are generally preferred for components that are to be made from copper, steel, titanium and refractory metal alloys.

Choose the Correct Answer

1. Forging is a process in which material is shaped by the application of localized
   a. compressive forces.
   b. tensile forces.

    c.   compressive or tensile forces depending upon the requirement.

    d.   shear forces.

2.   Forging is a process which is carried out on materials in their

    a.   hot state.   c.   either hot or cold state.

    b.   cold state.   d.   neither hot nor cold state.

3.   Hot forging is carried out at a temperature which is

    a.   above the crystallization temperature of the material.

    b.   below the crystallization temperature of the material.

    c.   below the recrystallization temperature of the material.

    d.   above the recrystallization temperature of the material.

4.   For successful upsetting operation, the length of the unsupported bar that can be upset in one blow of the heading tool should

    a.   exceed 2.5 times the diameter of the bar.

    b.   not exceed 2.5 times the diameter of the bar.

    c.   be equal to 5 times the diameter of the bar.

    d.   be less than 5 times the diameter of the bar.

5.   In case of forged components, the grain structure of the work material

    a.   is almost random.

    b.   is unidirectional.

    c.   tends to follow the physical shape of the component.

    d.   cannot be determined.

6.   The forging process in which a set of reciprocating dies provides radial impact forces to cause the metal to flow inward and acquire the form of the die cavity is

    a.   auto-forging.   c.   coining.

    b.   swaging.   d   embossing.

7.   Materials such as tungsten and molybdenum are generally swaged at elevated temperatures because they have

    a.   high ductility at room temperature.

    b.   low ductility at room temperature.

    c.   high porosity at elevated temperatures.

    d.   low porosity at elevated temperatures.

8.   The name of the forging operation in which a heated metal bar is fed into a pair of cylindrical rolls that have the shape of the required component cut into their surface is

    a.   swaging.   c.   roll forging.

    b.   cylindrical forging.   d.   auto-forging.

9. The forging operation that is carried out in closed dies and in which the flow of metal occurs only at the top layers of the material but not throughout the material is called

   a. swaging.
   b. roll forging.
   c. coining.
   d. incremental forging.

10. The forging operation in which the metal is deformed in the die cavity so that no flash is formed and the final dimensions are very close to the desired component dimensions is called

    a. swaging.
    b. coining.
    c. roll forging.
    d. net shape forging.

11. The forging operation in which the dies are heated to the same temperature as the workpiece material and both are maintained at that temperature till completion of the forging is called

    a. swaging.
    b. coining.
    c. isothermal forging.
    d. incremental forging.

12. Titanium and high temperature resistant nickel-based alloys, which have high flow stress are generally forged by a process called

    a. swaging.
    b. coining.
    c. isothermal forging.
    d. incremental forging.

13. The forging process in which a big workpiece is forged by working different regions of the workpiece into shape one at a time is called

    a. swaging.
    b. coining.
    c. thermal forging.
    d. incremental forging.

14. In the hot forging process, lubricant

    a. is not applied to work metal nor to dies.
    b. is applied to work metal.
    c. is applied to dies but not to work metal.
    d. is applied to both work metal and dies.

Answers

1. a. 2. c. 3. d. 4. b. 5. c. 6. b. 7. b. 8. c. 9. c. 10. d.
11. c. 12. c. 13. d. 14. c.

Metal Extrusion and Drawing

LEARNING OBJECTIVES

After reading this chapter, you should be able to understand the following:

- The metal extrusion process.

- The direct extrusion process and the process variables.

- The force required for extrusion and its determination.

- The indirect extrusion process and its comparison with direct extrusion.

- Hot extrusion versus cold extrusion.

- Continuous versus discrete processing.

- The impact extrusion process, its advantages, limitations, and applications.

- The process of drawing: rod, wire and tube.

- The force required for metal drawing and its determination.

11.1 Extrusion

Extrusion is a process in which high compressive pressure is applied on a billet of ductile metal to force it through an orifice of required shape in a steel die. The extrusion process is analogous to squeezing toothpaste from its plastic tube. It may be carried out in either hot or cold state, that is, above or below recrystallization temperature. Extrusion is mostly carried out on ductile non-ferrous metals such as aluminium, magnesium, zinc and copper alloys. Other metals can also be extruded; the force required is high even when they are hot extruded. Because the orifice geometry is unchanged throughout the operation, extruded products have a constant cross-section.

There are several advantages of the extrusion process. Some of these are as follows:

(i)   Component cross-section. A variety of cross-sectional shapes of products are possible, especially with hot extrusion; the only limitation is that the cross-section of the part must be uniform throughout its length. Further, the shape or the cross-section produced can be easily changed simply by changing the extruding die.

(ii) Grain structure and strength properties of metal. Extruded products have improved grain structure and mechanical properties, particularly in case of cold and warm extruded products.

(iii) Dimensional accuracy and tolerances on extruded parts. Fairly good accuracy and close tolerances can be achieved, especially in cold extrusion.

(iv) Metal scrap. There is little or no wastage of material.

Extrusion can be classified in three ways:

- By working temperature
  - Cold extrusion
  - Warm extrusion
  - Hot extrusion
- By performance technique
  - Continuous extrusion
  - Discrete extrusion
- By physical configuration
  - Direct extrusion
  - Indirect extrusion

11.1.1 Hot versus cold extrusion

As stated in the beginning of the chapter, extrusion can be performed either in hot or cold state of the material. The choice is largely dependent upon the work material and the amount of strain to which it can be subjected during deformation. There are some metals such as aluminium, copper, zinc, tin, magnesium and their alloys, which can be extruded in both hot and cold states. Among these, aluminium is the most extensively used for extruded products.

Hot extrusion involves prior heating of the billet to a temperature well above the recrystallization temperature of the metal. At the elevated temperature, the metal is softened and its ductility is increased, permitting (i) low ram forces, (ii) increased ram speeds, and (iii) more complex shapes to be produced in the process. Lubrication in hot extrusion of certain metals such as steels is essential. Glass is often used as a lubricant in hot extrusion. Other lubricants for hot extrusion are graphite and molybdenum. Lubrication serves three functions: (i) to reduce friction and wear, (ii) to reduce extrusion force and (iii) to provide effective thermal insulation between the hot billet and the relatively cool extrusion chamber.

Cold extrusion and **warm extrusion** are generally used for producing discrete parts, mostly in finished (or nearly finished) form. Other advantages of cold extrusion are: (i) higher strength of extruded part due to strain hardening of material; (ii) better surface finish; (iii) absence of oxide layer and defects in extruded parts due to it; (iv) better dimensional accuracy and close tolerances; and (v) high production rates. In addition, cold extrusion carried out at room temperature does not require heating of material prior to start of the process.

11.1.2 Continuous versus discrete processing

An ideal continuous process operates in a steady-state mode for an infinite long period. In reality, there exists no such process. However, there are some extrusion operations that produce very long extruded parts in one cycle; the length is limited by the size of the billet that can be loaded into the extrusion chamber. These operations can rightly be called semi-continuous. The long length of the extruded part is actually cut into desired usable lengths in a subsequent shearing operation.

A discrete extrusion operation produces a single part in each cycle. A typical example of a discrete extrusion process is the impact extrusion.

11.2 Direct Extrusion

Direct extrusion is also called *forward extrusion*. The process uses a cylindrical chamber to which a die is fitted at one end. The orifice shape of the die corresponds to the cross-section of the required extruded product. A round billet of hot metal is placed in the chamber, where a hydraulically-driven ram forces it out through the die orifice to produce a length of extruded product having the required cross-section, as shown in Figure 11.1(a). As the ram approaches the die, a small portion of the billet left in the chamber cannot be forced through the die opening. This extra portion, called the *butt*, is separated from the extruded part by cutting it just beyond the exit of the die.

A serious problem experienced in direct extrusion is due to the significant friction that exists between the chamber walls and the billet surface as the billet is pushed to slide towards the die opening. This friction is responsible for the high ram force required in direct extrusion. The friction problem becomes more serious when a metal-oxide layer is present on the surface of the hot billet. The oxide layer can cause defects in the extruded part. This problem can however be overcome to some extent by introducing a dummy block between the ram and the work material billet, as shown in Figure 11.1(b). The diameter of the dummy block is made slightly smaller than the billet diameter. In this way, although relative motion between the billet surface and the container wall during extrusion is eliminated, a thin shell of work metal (comprising mostly of metal-oxide layer) is left in the chamber and the extruded part is free of oxide.

Hollow sections (such as tubes) can also be produced simply by inserting a mandrel through the centre of the ram. Figure 11.1(c) shows a schematic of the process. An axial hole is first made in the starting billet, which serves as a passage for the mandrel. A dummy block may also be inserted. On the application of ram force, the billet material is pushed through the gap between the mandrel and the die opening. As a result, the extruded part becomes tubular. Some common hollow sections produced by the direct extrusion process are shown in Figure 11.1(d).

Process variables and force required in direct extrusion

As shown in Figure 11.1(a), the process variables are the die angle a, the extrusion ratio R (ratio of the cross-sectional area of billet A_o to that of the extruded product A_f, i.e., A_o/A_f), the temperature of the billet, the ram speed, and the type of lubricant used. Under ideal conditions (no friction and no redundant work), the extrusion force F can be estimated from the following relation

$$F = \sigma_f A_o \ln(A_o/A_f)$$

where σ_f is the average flow stress of work material during deformation, and A_0 and A_f are the billet and extruded product areas of cross-section respectively. The values of σ_f for some metals are given in Table 11.1.

The ratio A_o/A_f is called extrusion ratio and it is an important process parameter. Under the assumption of ideal deformation (no friction and no redundant work), true strain in extrusion can be estimated from the relation $\varepsilon = \ln(A_o/A_f)$.

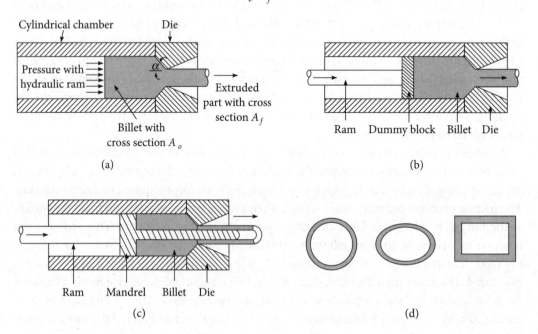

Figure 11.1 Schematic of direct extrusion process: (a) Without the use of dummy block; (b) With dummy block; (c) With dummy block and mandrel for producing hollow sections; and (d) Some typical hollow sections

Table 11.1 Values of average flow stress for some metals

Metal	Temperature range (°C)	Flow stress σ_f (MPa)
Aluminium	300–400	80
	401–500	70
Copper	500–600	220
	601–700	210
	701–800	200
70–30 Brass	500–600	380
	601–700	300
	701–800	220

It must be remembered that direct extrusion is not a frictionless process; friction exists not only at the interface between the billet surface and the chamber wall but also at the interface between the die and the work material surface as the billet is compressed and material is forced to pass through the die opening. Therefore, these equations grossly underestimate the strain and the force because the effect of friction is to increase the extrusion force and the strain experienced by the work material.

Actual true strain in extrusion can however be estimated by the Johnson empirical formula

$$\varepsilon_a = a + b \ln A_o/Af$$

where ε_a is the actual extrusion strain; and a and b are empirical constants whose values vary (increase) with die angle α. Typical values of these constants are: $a = 0.8$ and $b = 1.2$ to 1.5.

Example 11.1

A billet of metal 800 mm long × 150 mm diameter is to be extruded into a cylindrical component. Direct extrusion process is to be used. If the estimated extrusion ratio is 4.0 and the average flow stress experienced by the metal during deformation is 100 MPa, calculate the true strain and the force necessary for the extrusion process. State any assumption made.

Solution

Here, extrusion ratio $A_o/A_f = 4.0$ and $\sigma_f = 100$ MPa

Assuming ideal deformation conditions (i.e., no friction and no redundant work),

True strain $\varepsilon = \ln(A_o/A_f) = 1.3863$

Force $= \sigma_f \, A_o \ln(A_o/A_f)$

$$= 100 \times 10^6 \left[\frac{\pi}{4} \times \left(\frac{150}{1000} \right)^2 \right] \times 1.3863$$

$$= 2.45 \text{ MN}$$

11.3 Indirect Extrusion

Indirect extrusion is also called *backward extrusion* or *reverse extrusion* and can be carried out in both hot and cold state of the work material. The process is similar to direct extrusion except that the die is mounted to the ram end rather than at the opposite end of the chamber. A schematic of the process is shown in Figure 11.2. Both solid and tubular parts can be produced by this process. When solid extruded parts are to be produced, a hollow ram is used, which presses into the billet material to force the extruded part back through the centre of the hollow ram as shown in Figure 11.2(a). For producing hollow or tubular parts, a solid ram is used. The ram together with the die fitted at its front is pressed into the billet to force the material to flow around the die and take the tabular shape [Figure 11.2(b)]. One major advantage of indirect extrusion is that less ram force is required as there is no frictional resistance between the chamber and the billet surfaces because there is no relative motion between them.

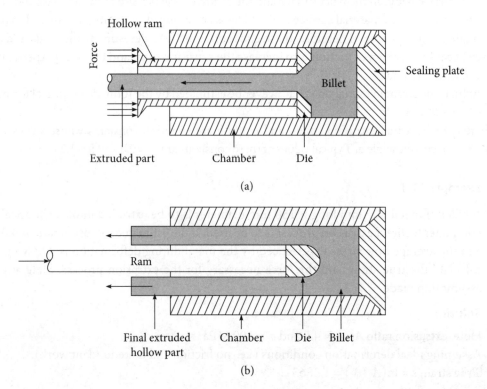

Figure 11.2 Schematic of indirect extrusion: (a) For solid parts; and (b) For tubular parts

A comparison of direct and indirect extrusion processes on the basis of their salient features is given in Table 11.2.

Compared to direct extrusion, indirect extrusion is less popular because of the following:

- Longer extruded lengths are not possible to produce because it is relatively difficult to adequately support the ram, when hollow or tubular parts are to be produced. The extruded solid part as it comes out of the die orifice is also difficult to support in the hollow ram; this is particularly difficult when the extruded part is long.

• Hollow ram is less rigid and also relatively more difficult to manufacture.

Table 11.2 Comparison of direct and indirect extrusion processes

Forward or direct extrusion	Reverse or indirect extrusion
1. Simple. The work material must slide along the chamber wall.	1. Work material does not slide along the chamber wall but die moves inside the work material.
2. High friction forces, which must be overcome.	2. Low friction forces, as whole mass of work material does not move.
3. High extrusion forces are needed.	3. Extrusion force required is about 30% lesser than direct extrusion.
4. Service life of the container and liner is short due to sliding contact of billet.	4. Longer service life of the container and liner.
5. Lower extrusion speed.	5. Higher extrusion speed.
6. Lesser uniform metal structure over the extruded length.	6. More uniform metal structure over the extruded length.
7. Size tolerance varies over the length of the extruded product.	7. Closer tolerances over the entire length of the extruded product.
8. Thick butt ends that lead to high scrap or material waste; as much as 20 to 25% material goes waste.	8. Thinner butt ends. Scrap or material waste is quite low; only 2 to 5% material goes waste.
9. Ram used is solid.	9. Ram used is hollow. High extrusion forces cannot be applied, even if needed.
10. Support to extruded part, if needed, can be easily applied.	10. Support of extruded part is needed as it comes out of die.
11. Cross-section of extruded part is not a limitation.	11. Cross-section of extruded part is limited with the bore of the hollow ram

11.4 Some Special Extrusion Processes

11.4.1 Extrusion with active friction forces (EAFF)

This process, which is still not fully commercialized, is an improved version of the indirect extrusion process. A schematic of the process is given in Figure 11.3. As can be seen in this figure, there is additional movement of the container or die relative to the motion of the ram. The frictional forces at the billet–container interface are in the direction of the metal flow, thereby allowing acceleration of peripheral flow and deceleration of central flow. This results in uniform distribution of the longitudinal speed component in the reduction zone across the billet's cross-section. As a result of change in mechanics in this process, EAFF has several advantages over direct and indirect extrusion processes. These are as follows:

- Higher extrusion speeds. Achievable extrusion speed in EAFF is 2 to 3 times greater than indirect extrusion, and 2 to 4 times greater than direct extrusion.

- Increased yield due to reduced scrap.

- Better surface finish, grain structure and corrosion resistance; product has better mechanical properties.

- Better quality of rods, bars and other shapes of products from harder metals and alloys.

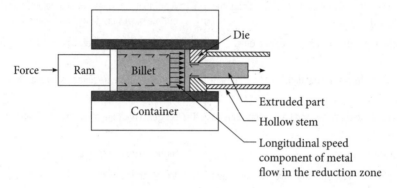

Figure 11.3   Schematic of extrusion with active friction forces process. ⟶ represents direction of friction force

11.4.2 Hydrostatic extrusion

Hydrostatic extrusion is an improved version of the direct extrusion process by which the problem of friction at the billet–chamber interface is taken care of. The billet is surrounded by a fluid inside the extrusion chamber and the pressure required for extrusion is supplied through the fluid medium as shown in Figure 11.4. The pressure used is of the order of 1000–1500 MPa, which is responsible for low friction at the die surface and no friction inside the chamber. Consequently, ram force is significantly smaller than conventional direct extrusion. The process is known by this name as the fluid pressure acts on all the surfaces of the billet.

Hydrostatic extrusion process can be done hot, warm or cold; however, the temperature is limited by the stability of the fluid used. At room temperature, the process can be carried out by using some vegetable oil as the fluid. Castor oil is found to be a good fluid for hydrostatic extrusion because its viscosity does not change much with the increasing applied pressure; it is a good lubricant as well. For carrying out hydrostatic extrusion at elevated temperatures, polymers, waxes and glass can be used as fluid. These materials also serve as thermal insulators.

Advantages   The advantages of this process are as follows:

- Extrusion force required is low because of no friction and no sliding motion between the container and the billet. This ultimately allows for faster speeds, higher reduction ratios, and lower billet temperatures.

- Large billets and large cross-sections can be extruded.

- Brittle materials can be successfully extruded because hydrostatic pressure on the work material increases its ductility.

- Ductile metals can also be extruded hydrostatically, of course, with large reduction ratios.

- The process permits a uniform and even flow of material through the die.

- The process permits the use of small die angles.

- No billet residue is left on the container walls.

Disadvantages   The disadvantages of hydrostatic extrusion are as follows:

- There is need for special preparation of the starting work billet. One end of the billet has to be tapered to properly match the die entry angle. This is done to avoid leakage of the fluid from the die opening when the chamber is pressurized.

- The complete billet is required to be machined for the removal of surface defects.

- It can be difficult to contain the high pressure fluid (pressure may be sometimes up to 2 GPa).

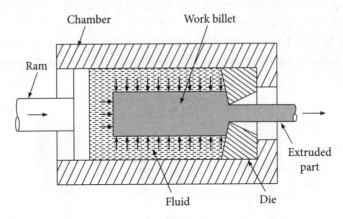

Figure 11.4   Schematic of hydrostatic extrusion process

Limitations   There are a number of limitations in the hydrostatic extrusion process, especially when a large volume of fluid is used in comparison with the billet volume, which is to be extruded. These limitations are:

- Lot of handling for the injection and removal of the fluid for every extrusion cycle.

- Decreased control of speed of the billet, and stopping because of potential stick-slip and enormous stored energy in the compressed fluid. (This limitation can however be minimized with the use of viscous dampers and also with the improvement in lubrication at the billet–die interface. Alternatively, the amount of pressurizing fluid to be maintained can be reduced to an absolute minimum.)

- Decreased process efficiency in terms of billet-to-container volume ratio.

- Enhanced complications, when extrusion is done at elevated temperatures.

11.4.3 Impact extrusion

Impact extrusion is a cold extrusion process and is similar to indirect extrusion. It is special because it is performed at higher speeds and with shorter strokes than conventional extrusion. In this process, a slug of metal at room temperature is placed at the bottom of a die. A punch descends rapidly on the metal blank with a force that is sufficient to force the metal to flow [Figure 11.5(a)] and fill the annular space between the punch and the die [Figure 11.5(b)]. The stripper plate acts to strip off the extruded part from the punch during upward stroke [Figure 11.5(c)]. Since the volume of the metal remains constant, the thickness of the tubular extruded section is a function of the clearance between the punch and the die cavity. The base thickness depends on the adjustment of the bottom position of the punch ram. This should ideally be 15–20% greater than the side wall thickness.

The speed of the impact is such that there is instant temperature rise in the metal piece as the punch strikes the metal, thus allowing a much greater degree of deformation with this process compared to what would normally be expected in cold working. The process is used to make individual components. Metals suited to impact extrusion are softer and more ductile, such as aluminium, copper and brass. Low and medium carbon ductile steels are also extruded now-a-days by this process. Depending upon the principal direction in which the metal is to flow upon being struck by the impacting punch, impact extrusion can be reverse, forward or a combination of both [Figure 11.6].

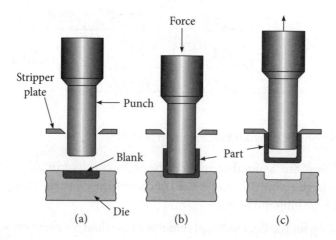

Figure 11.5 Schematic representation of the impact extrusion process. The extruded part tends to stick to the punch, which is stripped by a stripper plate

Reverse impacting extrusion   This process is used to produce specific shell configurations with extruded side walls and a forged base. The cold metal billet inside the die cavity is struck by a punch or ram. The metal is forced to flow upward around the punch through an opening between the die and the punch. The opening between the die and the punch decides the wall thickness of the shell.

Applications of reverse impact extrusion include products of configurations like internal or external rib, multi-shell walls, square and circular, oval, rectangular and other cross-sections.

Forward impact extrusion   This process closely resembles the conventional extrusion. Though the billet is, as usual, placed in the die, the force of the punch pushes the metal through the orifice of the die. This causes the metal to flow in the direction of the punch. There is no escaping of the metal backwards as the punch fits the wall of the die very closely.

Applications of forward impact extrusion include products such as straight, round, non-round and ribbed rods, thin walled tubing with one or both ends open, and with tapered or parallel side walls.

Combination impact extrusion   The punch in this process permits both forward as well as reverse metal flows. The process is best suited for the formation of complex-shaped parts. Here the metal is allowed to flow upward into the punch, until the cavity is filled. This is done by incorporating a lower punch and a cavity in the upper punch. Punch movements cause forward extrusion of the remaining metal and results in the formation of a web.

Advantages and Limitations   The advantages as well as limitations of the impact extrusion are as follows:

- The parts produced by impact extrusion are light in weight because the work material used is generally of low density.
- The parts produced by impact extrusion have (i) high toughness; (ii) good corrosion resistance; and (iii) highly uniform grain refinement.
- The process has high repeatability. It can be automated for high speed production of tubular components involving large reductions.
- Close tolerance on components can be achieved, though it varies with work material and component design. 0.05–0.10 mm tolerance is easily achievable.
- Cycle times of less than 1 s are common.
- Large length-to-diameter ratios are possible to achieve. Diameter of the parts can be up to 150 mm.
- Parts with very thin walls can be made. Thickness-to-diameter ratio as small as 0.005 is achievable.
- Process is cost competitive. The tooling cost is low; almost no scrap is produced, and there are hardly any defective parts.
- Symmetry of the part and the concentricity of the punch and blank are essential.

Applications   Typical products made by impact extrusion process are tubular components like collapsible tubes (such as for cream or toothpaste as shown in Figure 11.6), spark plug bodies, lipstick cases, flashlight cases, battery cases, cover cases for electronic components and cans for food and beverages.

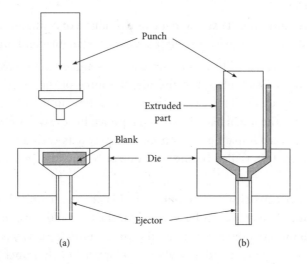

Figure 11.6   Schematic of impact extrusion of a collapsible tube

11.4.4 Comparison of impact extrusion with other manufacturing processes

Impact extrusion versus deep drawing

Impact extrusion process is a far superior process compared to the deep drawing process when the part design requires: (a) the base to be thicker than the side walls; and (b) when the shell length is more than twice the diameter. Deep-drawn parts are typically limited to a 1:1 wall/bottom thickness ratio and a length/width ratio of 2:1. The impact extrusion process can typically produce a wall/bottom thickness ratio of 1:2 with a length/width ratio of 8:1 in aluminum and a 4:1 ratio in steel in a single operation. Further processing can triple these ratios. High cost savings are realized in impact extrusion through the elimination of excess handling, lower tooling costs and reduced labour costs. The material yield is much greater when using the impact extrusion process; it is typically greater than 90%, whereas it is 80% or less when using the deep drawing process.

Impact extrusion versus forging

Impact extrusion process is a better choice than forging when the design of the part requires that it be strong, lightweight with minimal draft angles, and there is a need to maintain close tolerances. The impact extruded parts have a surface area/volume ratio of 16:1 whereas this ratio is 6:1 for forgings. This allows impact extruded parts to have a much thinner wall section than a forging, resulting in a lighter weight part that exceeds or is comparable in strength to a forging. Another advantage of the impact extrusion process is its capability to consistently maintain tolerances in the 0.15 mm range versus 1.5 mm for forgings. The close tolerance capability of impact extrusion in many cases eliminates the need for costly secondary machining operations.

Impact extrusion versus casting

Impact extrusion process is preferred to casting when the design of the part requires it to be light in weight yet strong with smooth surfaces. In addition, thin wall parts can be easily produced using the impact extrusion process while they would be difficult or impossible to cast. Parts produced from the impact extrusion process are 3% more dense for aluminum and 8% more dense for steel over the casting process. Further, it is often not necessary to perform secondary machining operations on impact extruded parts since the impact extrusion process has the capability to maintain closer tolerances compared to casting.

The raw material cost for the parts manufactured using the impact extrusion process is generally two to three times more than the cost of material used in the casting process. This additional cost is attributed to the cost of additional labour to convert bars into slugs. However, the higher raw material costs are offset by savings in the tooling costs.

Impact extrusion versus stamping

Impact extrusion process offers significant advantages over the metal stamping process by providing the capability of increased complicated geometry, multiple wall thickness, and the elimination of sub-assemblies. Due to the limitation of the stamping process to produce parts with complex geometry, assembly operations often are required to produce a final part.

11.5 Extrusion Dies

There are three important factors to be considered in the design of dies for extrusion process. These are (i) die material, (ii) die angle and bearing length and (iii) orifice shape. For hot extrusion, the die material often used is die steel or high carbon high chromium steel. One important requirement is that the material must have high thermal conductivity so that heat can be easily removed from the process. Also, it should be able to withstand the high temperature of the process without softening (the property called *hot hardness*) and wear less. For cold extrusion, the die materials commonly used are tool steels and cemented carbides. The materials must have high wear resistance and the ability to retain shape under high stress. Dies made of carbides last longer and provide excellent dimensional control.

The die angle affects the extrusion force. If the die angle (in Figure 11.1(a), α is a half die angle) is too small, surface area of the die contact becomes large, leading to more friction at the die–billet interface and hence, the requirement of larger ram force. If, on the other hand, the die angle is too large, it will cause more turbulence in the metal flow during reduction resulting in the need for increased ram force. Therefore, there is an optimum die angle (usually in the range 45 to 60°); actual value, however, depends upon several factors such as the type and temperature of work material, and the type of lubrication.

The effective bearing length of extrusion dies controls the metal flow through the die. The aim is to have all parts of the product profile emerge from the die at the same speed. The longer the bearing length, the greater is the resistance to the flow of metal; and the shorter the bearing length, the lesser is the resistance to flow. Through proper design, the thick parts of a profile can be slowed through the use of longer bearings to match the speed of the thinner parts with short bearings.

The shape of the die orifice affects the ram force required for extrusion. Circular orifice needs the minimum extrusion force while orifice of any other shape will need greater extrusion force. Greater the shape complexity (determined by *shape factor*), larger is the force requirement. The shape factor is defined as the ratio of the parameter of the extruded cross-section to the parameter of a circular cross-section of equal area.

Special wear resistant coatings can be applied on the die surfacer to enhance the life of the die.

11.6 Extrusion Presses

Both horizontal and vertical types of extrusion presses are in use; however, horizontal type is more common. The choice depends upon the orientation of the work axis. The drive for presses employed for direct as well as indirect extrusion is mostly hydraulic because of the ease of control of the stroke and the speed of operation. A hydraulic press is capable of applying a constant force over a long stroke and therefore, is useful for extruding long billets. Hydraulic presses are available with a ram-force capacity up to 100 MN. Mechanical drive is more common for presses used for cold extrusion of small size individual parts (i.e., for impact extrusion).

11.7 Defects in Extruded Parts

Extruded parts can suffer from any of the following defects owing to non-homogeneous deformations generally associated with the extrusion process.

1. **Centre burst**   This defect is also known by the names *arrowhead fracture, chevron crack* and *centre cracking*. As shown in Figure 11.7(a), it is an internal crack. It develops as a result of tensile stresses that may act on the material along the centre line of the part during the extrusion process. Although extrusion is a compression process, material along the central axis of the part can experience tensile stresses under conditions that cause large deformation in the regions of the work material away from the centre line of the part. The large deformations in those regions tend to cause stretching of the material along the centre line of the part, and when stresses become too large, bursting can take place. Conditions that promote centre burst are (i) large die angle, (ii) small extrusion ratio, (iii) high friction and (iv) impurities in the billet that act as a nucleus for crack formation. Being in the central region of the extruded part, the defect is generally not detectable by visual observation, and therefore causes serious difficulty in the quality control of extruded products.

2. **Piping**   This defect is also known by the name *tailpipe* or *fishtailing*. It occurs in parts that are produced by the direct extrusion process. As shown in Figure 11.7(b), this defect is in the shape of a deep depression in the centre, at the end-face of the billet. It occurs due to inhomogeneous deformation. Material at the centre of the billet comes across least resistance compared to the material near the die wall. As a result, rapid flow happens at the centre. After one third of the billet is extruded, the material from the periphery gets entrained towards the centre and flows rapidly. Oxides present in the peripheral layers are also entrained. These oxides form internal stringers near the centre. Towards the end of the process, rapid flow of material at the centre will result in pipe formation. Although, the defect cannot be completely eliminated, it can be reduced if during the extrusion process, a dummy block is used whose cross-section is slightly smaller than that of the billet.

3. **Cracks**   Cracks are sometimes seen to occur on the surface of extruded parts, as shown in Figure 11.7(c). These can develop due to (i) high temperature of the material, (ii) high frictional conditions and (iii) high extrusion speeds. High extrusion speed that causes high strain rates and the associated high heat generation is the primary cause of surface cracks. These cracks are inter-granular, that is, along the grain boundaries and occur especially in aluminium, zinc and magnesium and their alloys. The chances of occurrence of surface cracks can be reduced by reducing the extrusion speed and lowering the billet temperature.

   At times, surface cracking may also occur at lower work material temperatures especially in hydrostatic extrusion where pressures are very high. The cause, in that case, is the periodic sticking of the extruded product along the land of the die. As the extruded product sticks to the die land, the extrusion pressure rises abruptly. Soon after, as the product moves forward, the pressure is released. The cycle may repeat continuously resulting in periodic circumferential cracks on the surface of the extruded product. Due to resemblance of these cracks to the surface of a bamboo stem, the defect is known as *bamboo* defect.

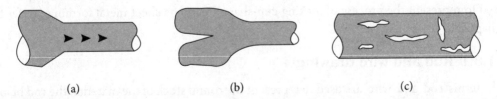

(a)   (b)   (c)

Figure 11.7   Some common defects in extrusion: (a) Centre burst; (b) Piping; and (c) Surface cracks

11.8 Drawing

Drawing is a process in which the cross-section of a round rod, wire or tube is reduced by pulling it through a die opening as shown in Figure 11.8. As can be seen, the general features

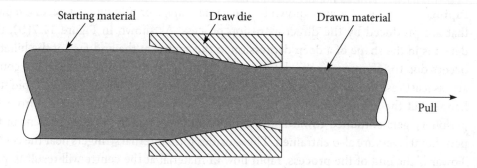

Figure 11.8 Schematic of drawing of rod or wire

of the drawing process are similar to those of direct extrusion. The difference lies in the type of force applied; in case of drawing, the work material is pulled through the die, whereas in case of extrusion, it is pushed through the die. In addition to the tensile stresses to which the work material is subjected to in drawing, compression also plays an important role because the work material is squeezed down as it passes through the die opening. Drawn rods have many uses such as machine spindles, shafts and small pistons. Small-sized drawn rods or wires are extensively used as raw material for the production of fasteners such as screws, rivets and bolts. Apart from a circular profile, the process can also be used to produce long sections of other profiles.

Drawn wires are also used in the industry for several applications, including welding electrodes, springs, spokes for bicycle wheels, cables, windings of electromagnets and transformers, tension-loaded structural members and string members of musical instruments. Drawing of tubes and tubular parts is also carried out by pulling through a die when it is desired to reduce either their diameter or their thickness, with or without the use of an internal mandrel.

The parameters which affect the drawing process are percent reduction in cross-sectional area per pass, friction at workpiece–die interface, die angle and drawing speed. The die angle is important because it influences the quality of the drawn product. The term *drawing* is also used to represent the process of making cup-shaped parts by sheet metal forming (Refer to Chapter 12).

11.8.1 Rod and wire drawing

The terms 'rod' and 'wire' are used to represent the round stock of the material; the rod being larger in cross-section than the wire. In literature, wire is generally defined as a rod that has been drawn through a die at least once.

Drawing is basically the process of reduction of cross-section of a round rod by pulling it through a die (Figure 11.8). For a successful drawing operation, it is necessary to make a proper selection of process parameters and give due consideration to important factors. Drawing speeds depend upon the ductility of the material and on the percentage of reduction in cross-sectional area; for rods, the range may be 1 m/s to 10 m/s, while for wires, the range may be from 20 m/s to as high as 50 m/s. At high drawing speeds, the temperature of the material can rise substantially, making cooling of the die and the work material essential for getting good quality products.

Terms related to wire drawing:

$$\text{Draft} = D_o - D_f$$

$$\% \text{ reduction in area} = \frac{A_o - A_f}{Af} \times 100 = \frac{D_o^2 - D_f^2}{D_f^2} \times 100$$

$$\% \text{ elongation} = \frac{L_f - L_o}{L_o}$$

where D_o, D_f, L_o and L_f are respectively the original and final diameter and length, and A_o and A_f are respectively the original and final cross-sectional area of wire.

Reduction in cross-section per pass ranges from 15% to 45% with the thumb rule being, 'smaller the initial cross-section, the smaller is the percentage of reduction per pass'. Fine wires are, therefore, usually drawn at 15% to 25% reduction per pass, and thick wires and rods at 25% to 45%. Reduction of more than 45% per pass can result in lubricant breakdown and damaged surface finish of the drawn product.

Wire drawing is primarily the same as rod drawing except that it involves smaller diameter material that can be coiled and is generally performed as a continuous operation on a draw bench as shown in Figure 11.9.

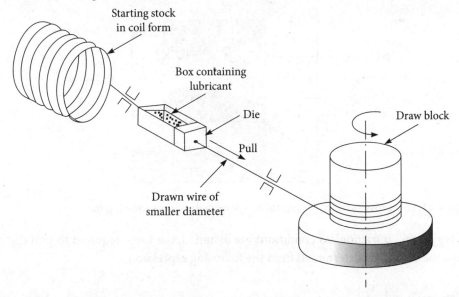

Figure 11.9 Wire drawing on a continuous draw block. The rotating draw block provides a continuous pull on the incoming wire

Here, a long coil of hot rolled material of nearly 10 mm diameter is subjected to preparation treatment before starting the actual drawing process. The preparation treatment for steel wire consists of:

- **Cleaning**   Any rust, scale or dirt on the wire is removed by a series of operations comprising acid pickling, rinsing and drying. Mechanical methods can also be used for cleaning the wire.

- **Neutralization**   If acidic treatment has been given to the raw material for cleaning, any remaining acid on it is neutralized by immersing it in a lime bath. A thin layer of lubricant may also be applied to protect it against corrosion.

To begin the drawing process, one end of the coil is reduced in cross-section up to a certain length, fed through the drawing die, and then gripped for applying the necessary pull force. A wire drawing die is generally made of tungsten carbide with the configuration shown in Figure 11.10. For drawing a very fine wire, a diamond die is preferred.

A small diameter wire is generally drawn on tandem machines that consist of a series of dies, each of them held in a water-cooled die block. Each die reduces the cross-section by a small amount so as to avoid excessive strain in the wire. Intermediate annealing of material between different states of wire may also be done, if needed.

For a single cold-drawing pass, the percentage of area reduction depends upon several factors such as the type of material, its size, initial metallurgical condition, the final size and mechanical properties desired, die design and lubrication efficiency.

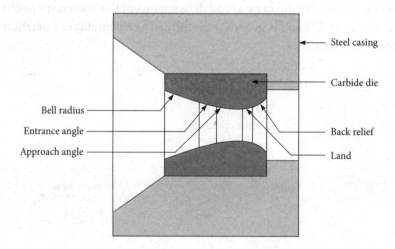

Figure 11.10   Cross-section of a typical tungsten carbide wire drawing die

Drawing force   If frictionless conditions are assumed, the force required to pull the stock through the die can be determined from the following expression.

$$F = \sigma_{avg} \, A_f \ln\left(\frac{A_o}{A_f}\right)$$

where F = force required to pull the stock through the die, that is, drawing force

σ_{avg} = average true stress of the material in the die gap

A_o, A_f = original and final areas of cross-section of material

Note This expression is similar to the one for extrusion. The force increases with increasing friction at the workpiece–die interface; lubrication is therefore necessary.

Alternatively, the following expression can be used for the estimation of drawing force.

$$F = c \, \sigma_t \, (A_o - A_f)$$

where c is a constant whose value is in the range 1.5 to 3.0, depending upon the percentage of area reduction (lower value for higher percent reduction), and σ_t is the tensile strength of material before drawing. The pull force determines the machine capacity needed.

11.8.2 Tube drawing

Tube drawing is a process of reducing the diameter or wall thickness of tubes that have been already produced by extrusion or any other process. The process of tube drawing [Figure 11.11] is similar to that of wire or rod drawing [Figure 11.8], except that it usually requires a mandrel of the requisite diameter to form the internal hole. Tube drawing operation when carried out without mandrel causes problems of lack of control over the inside diameter and wall thickness of the tube. Tubes as large as 300 mm in diameter can be drawn by this process.

11.8.3 Drawing equipment

Drawing equipment can be classified into two basic types: Draw bench and Bull block. A draw bench [Figure 11.8] uses a single die and the pulling force is supplied by a chain drive or by hydraulic means. Draw bench (Figure 11.11) is used for single length drawing of the rod or the tube with diameter greater than 20 mm. Length can be as much as 30 m. The drawing speed attainable on a draw bench ranges from 5 m/min to 50 m/min. Draw benches are available with capacities to provide a pull force of up to 1 MN.

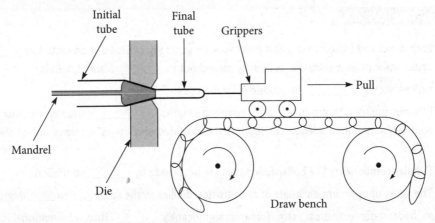

Figure 11.11 Schematic of tube drawing process on a draw bench

Bull block or rotating drum is used for drawing rods or wires of very long lengths.

Questions

1. Describe the process of extrusion as applied to metals. Give suitable sketches of both the forward and backward extrusion processes. Compare the two processes with respect to the length of extruded part and the force required for extruding. Can spur gears be produced by direct extrusion? If yes, how and if not, why?

2. A round billet of aluminium at 350°C is extruded. If the initial billet diameter is 120 mm and the extruded part has 40 mm diameter, determine the extrusion force required.

3. Calculate the extrusion force for a round billet of copper at a temperature of 650°C, provided the billet diameter is 125 mm and the extrusion ratio is 20.

4. Will the force vary as the billet gets shorter and shorter in (a) direct extrusion, (b) indirect extrusion? Support your answer with reasons.

5. With the help of suitable sketches, explain the process of impact extrusion. Give advantages and a few typical applications of this process. What is the purpose of a stripper plate in this process?

6. Discuss the factors which affect the extrusion force. How does change of die angle affect the extrusion process?

7. Compare hot extrusion with cold extrusion. What is the purpose of using lubricant in the extrusion process? Name some lubricants used for hot and cold extrusion processes.

8. What defects are generally possible in extruded parts? Briefly describe these defects.

9. Sketch the hydrostatic extrusion process. Compare it with the direct extrusion process.

10. Differentiate between draw bench and rotating block for the drawing operation.

11. Describe the processes of wire drawing and tube drawing with suitable sketches. What changes would you expect in the strength, hardness and ductility of a metal after it has been drawn through dies at room temperature?

Fill in the Blanks

1. Both direct and indirect extrusion processes are generally carried out on metals in _____ state, while impact extrusion is usually carried out in _____ state of metals.

2. Hollow sections _____ be produced by direct extrusion.

3. It is not possible to produce longer extruded lengths in _____ extrusion because it is relatively difficult to adequately support the extruded section as it comes out of the die orifice.

4. Tubular components like collapsible tubes are best made by _____ extrusion.

5. The value of optimum die angle of an extrusion die lies in the range ____ to ____ degrees.

6. In hydrostatic extrusion, ram force is significantly _____ than conventional direct extrusion.

7. If in wire drawing, D_o and D_f are respectively the original and final diameter of wire, the *draft* is given by_____.

8. The difference between rod drawing process and direct extrusion lies in the _____ applied.

9. An extrusion process in which fluid pressure acts on all the surfaces of the billet is known by the name _____.

10. Impact extrusion process is a far superior process over the deep drawing process when the part design requires the base to be thicker than the _____.

11. In _____ extrusion process, the die is mounted at the ram end rather than at the opposite end of the chamber.

Choose the Correct Answer

1. In backward extrusion process, the type of pressure applied on a billet of ductile metal to force it through the die orifice is
   a. tensile.
   c. shear.
   b. compressive.
   d. tensile, compressive and shear.

2. Impact extrusion is mostly carried out in which state of work metal?
   a. cold
   b. warm
   c. hot
   d. any one of the above depending upon the need

3. Direct extrusion process can produce
   a. only solid round shaped parts.
   c. only round parts whether solid or hollow.
   b. only round hollow parts.
   d. parts of any cross-section.

4. At the end of an extrusion operation, a small portion of the billet left in the extrusion chamber that cannot be forced through the die opening is called
   a. lap.
   c. corner.
   b. butt.
   d. snug.

5. A serious problem experienced with direct extrusion (as compared to other extrusion processes) is due to
   a. friction at the billet–extrusion chamber surfaces.
   b. solid ram, which is heavier and therefore requires more force for extrusion.
   c. hollow ram, which is light in weight and therefore buckles.
   d. metal-oxide layer that gets into the billet and causes defects in the extruded parts.

6. The speed of impact extrusion is

   a. higher than the speed at which direct extrusion is usually carried out.

   b. lower than the speed at which indirect extrusion is usually carried out.

   c. same as the speed at which direct extrusion is usually carried out.

   d. same as the speed at which hydrostatic extrusion is usually carried out.

7. The stroke of punch in impact extrusion is generally

   a. shorter than the stroke of ram in direct extrusion.

   b. longer than the stroke of ram in indirect extrusion.

   c. same as the stroke of ram in direct extrusion.

   d. same as the stroke of ram in indirect extrusion.

8. Parts with very thin walls (thickness to diameter ratio as small as 0.005) can be made by

   a. direct extrusion.   c. impact extrusion.

   b. indirect extrusion.   d. hydrostatic extrusion.

9. Discrete parts with relatively short lengths are generally made by

   a. direct extrusion.   c. impact extrusion.

   b. indirect extrusion.   d. hydrostatic extrusion.

10. The extrusion ratio is defined as the ratio of

   a. the cross-sectional area of the billet to that of the extruded product.

   b. the length of the billet to the length of the extruded product.

   c. the cross-sectional area of the extruded product to that of the billet.

   d. the length of the extruded product to that of the billet.

11. Under ideal deformation conditions, true strain experienced by the material in extrusion can be found from the following relation, where A_o and A_f are, respectively the cross-sectional area of the billet and the extruded part.

   a. $\varepsilon = \ln(A_f / A_o)$ c. $\varepsilon = \ln(A_o / A_f) + \text{constant}$

   b. $\varepsilon = \ln(A_o / A_f)$ d. $\varepsilon = \ln(A_f / A_o) + \text{constant}$

12. The extrusion force required is

   a. less in indirect extrusion due to low friction resistance, as compared to direct extrusion.

   b. more in indirect extrusion because of high friction resistance, as compared to direct extrusion.

   c. same for indirect extrusion as for direct extrusion because it does not depend upon friction resistance.

   d. same for indirect extrusion as for direct extrusion because friction resistance is same in both cases.

13. Which one of the following is not a factor to be considered in the design of extrusion dies?

    a. component material   c. die material

    b. orifice shape   d. die angle

14. If the extrusion die angle is small,

    a. surface area of die contact with billet increases.

    b. there is greater resistance to metal flow during reduction of cross-sectional area.

    c. the extrusion force required is also small.

    d. lubrication problems are reduced.

15. Compared to direct extrusion, indirect extrusion is less popular because

    a. longer extruded lengths cannot be produced.

    b. solid ram used in indirect extrusion is heavy.

    c. lubricants used in indirect extrusion are very costly.

    d. extrusion force required in indirect extrusion is more.

16. Impact extrusion is generally

    a. cold working process.

    b. hot working process.

    c. hot or cold working process depending upon the material on which it is performed.

    d. hot or warm working process depending upon the material on which it is performed.

17. Typical products made by impact extrusion process are

    a. strips and sheets.   c. tubular components.

    b. solid wires and rods.   d. circular rings.

18. The most common type of extrusion press used for direct and indirect extrusion process is the

    a. hydraulically operated horizontal press. c. mechanically operated horizontal press.

    b. hydraulically operated vertical press.   d. mechanically operated vertical press.

19. Centre burst is a common defect in extruded parts. This defect is also known as

    a. arrow-head fracture.   c. arrow and crow.

    b. arrow and bow.   d. pipe.

20. Piping is a type of defect found in extruded parts. This defect is also known as

    a. fish-tailing.   c. hollow sphere.

    b. snake tail.   d. stick and pick.

21. Chances of surface cracks in aluminium extruded parts

    a. decrease at high extrusion speeds that cause high strain rates.

    b. increase at high extrusion speeds that cause high strain rates.

   c.   increase with the size of extruded part.

   d.   decrease with higher billet temperatures.

22. In hydrostatic extrusion,

   a.   the extruded part as it comes out from the die is surrounded by a fluid.

   b.   the ram force required is significantly larger than in conventional direct extrusion.

   c.   the extrusion pressure is supplied through a fluid medium.

   d.   the static charge on the work material is suppressed by hydrogen gas.

23. Collapsible tubes used for toothpaste are often produced by

   a.   direct extrusion.   c.   impact extrusion.

   b.   indirect extrusion.   d.   hydrostatic extrusion.

24. By drawing operation, the diameter or thickness reduction of tubular parts

   a.   cannot be carried out.

   b.   can be carried out only when mandrel is used.

   c.   can be carried out only when mandrel is not used.

   d.   can be carried out with or without the use of mandrel.

25. By drawing operation, the range of reduction in cross-section per pass is generally

   a.   from 5% to 10%.   c.   from 15% to 45%.

   b.   from 5% to 20%.   d.   from 40% to 75%.

Answers

1. b. 2. a. 3. d. 4. b. 5. a. 6. a. 7. a. 8. c. 9. c. 10. a.
11. b. 12. a. 13. a. 14. a. 15. a. 16. a. 17. c. 18. a. 19. a. 20. a.
21. b. 22. c. 23. c. 24. d. 25. c.

12

Sheet Metal Forming and Shaping Processes

LEARNING OBJECTIVES

After reading this chapter, you should be able to understand the following:

- The basics of sheet metal forming process.
- The formability of a material and methods of its determination.
- The various sheet metal cutting operations, such as shearing, blanking and punching, piercing, trimming, notching, nibbling and perforating.
- The various sheet metal forming operations, such as bending, deep drawing, spinning, stretch forming and embossing.
- The equipment needed for sheet metal working.
- The classification of metal working presses and the factors to be considered during selection of a press for a given application.
- The comparison between mechanical and hydraulic presses.
- The press feeding devices.
- The types and details of dies and punches used for sheet metal working.

12.1 Sheet Metal Working

There are a large number of items of daily use that are made by sheet metal forming and cutting operations. Some examples are almirahs, filing cabinets, fan wings, bodies of automobiles, refrigerators and water coolers, computer desktop bodies, household appliances and utensils, beer and soft drink cans. Sheet metal parts (also called *stampings*) have several advantages over those made by casting or by forging, such as low cost, light weight, high strength, good dimensional accuracy, good surface finish, and possibility of a large variety of shapes. Typical sheet metal thickness varies from 0.5 mm to 6 mm. When the thickness is less than 0.5 mm, it is considered as a leaf or foil but when it is more than 6 mm, the stock is generally referred to as a plate rather than a sheet. The most commonly used sheet material is mild steel or low carbon steel because it is low cost and has good strength and formability characteristics, although for aircraft and aerospace applications, aluminium and titanium are the common sheet materials. Sheet metal processing is generally carried out at room temperature (cold working), although some processes may be carried out in the warm state of the sheet metal especially when it is brittle or when the deformation required is large. The tooling used for sheet metal processing is called a die-and-punch, and the machine tool on which these processes are carried out is called the stamping press. In the following sections, we shall study the following:

- **Formability of materials**   definition and various tests for its estimation.

- **Sheet metal cutting operations**   shearing, blanking, punching, piercing, trimming, notching, nibbling and perforating.

- **Sheet metal forming operations**   bending, drawing and embossing.

- **Equipment for sheet metal working**   presses – classification and selection; feeding devices; dies – essential features and various types.

- **High energy rate sheet metal forming processes**   explosive forming; electro-magnetic forming; and electrohydraulic forming (explained in Chapter 13)

12.1.1 Sheet metal formability

Formability of a sheet metal may be defined as 'the ease with which sheet metal may be forced into a permanent change of shape without undergoing localized necking or excessive thinning or fracture'. It is important for the product designer to know the extent to which a material can deform before designing a reproducible forming operation. Formability of a material depends on several factors. The important ones are related to the properties of the material such as yield strength, strain hardening rate and ductility. These metal properties are greatly temperature dependent. With an increase in temperature of the material, its yield strength and rate of strain hardening progressively reduce while its ductility increases. Hot working of metal, therefore, permits a relatively large amount of deformation before cracking. It is worth mentioning here that the formability of sheet metals (particularly deep drawing) is also affected by *anisotropy*, that is, the variation of material properties with respect to directions, due to variations in microstructure introduced in forming operations such as rolling.

Formability tests

There are many cupping tests of formability for sheet materials, such as the Swift test, Olsen and Erichsen tests and Fukui test. It is important to understand that none of these tests correlate well with sheet metal behaviour in all forming processes. One reason is that the relative amounts of drawing and stretching vary from test to test and process to process. Other reasons are insufficient size of the penetrator, inability to prevent inadvertent drawing in of the flange, and inconsistent lubrication.

In *Swift flat bottom draw test* [Figure 12.1], different diameters of circular blanks with constant thickness are drawn into cups until fracture is observed in the cup. The test uses a flat bottom cylindrical punch and the blank holder. The maximum diameter of blank that gives successful formation of cup without fracture is evaluated. This would mean that any diameter of blank greater than that will produce fracture in the cup. The maximum diameter of blank is used to determine the *limiting drawing ratio*, which is defined as the ratio between the maximum diameter of blank for successful formation of cup to the diameter of punch. The larger the value of limiting drawing ratio, the better is the formability of the sheet metal as per Swift cup drawing test.

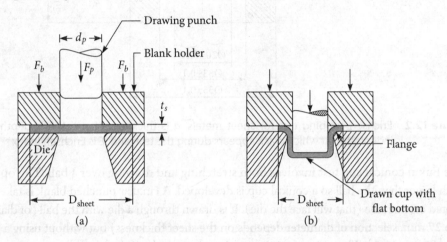

Figure 12.1 Swift cup test: (a) At the start of test; (b) At the end of test. D_{sheet} = dia. of blank; d_p = dia. of punch; t_s = thickness of sheet; F_p = force on punch; F_b = force on blank holder

Olsen and Erichsen cupping tests are basically similar in nature. Both are ductility tests, in which a cup is formed by stretching the material over a hemispherical tool. The flanges are very large and clamped so little drawing occurs. The results depend on the stretchability of the material rather than its drawability. The Olsen test is used in America and the Erichsen test in Europe.

Figure 12.2 shows the setup for the Erichsen test, and Table 12.1 gives dimensional difference between the two tests. The test consists of placing a sheet metal on the die cavity and clamping the flanges. An indentation is formed in the sheet when a punch having a hemispherical end is pressed into the sheet by using hydraulic force until a through crack forms on the sheet metal [Figure 12.2]. The depth of the cup h is measured and taken as an index of formability.

Table 12.1   Dimensional difference between Olsen and Erichsen cupping tests

	Cylindrical punch diameter	Gap diameter in die
Erichsen test	20 mm	27 mm
Olsen test	0.875″	1.00″

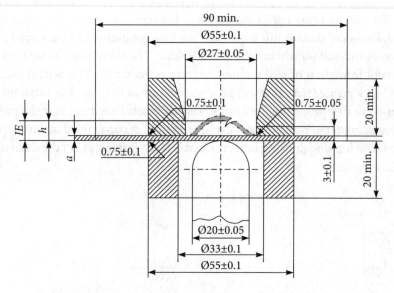

Figure 12.2   Erichsen cupping test for sheet metals. *a* is thickness of sheet; *h* is depth of indentation at which crack appears during the test; and *IE* is Erichsen index

The Fukui conical cup test involves both stretching and drawing over a ball. The opening is much larger than the ball so a conical cup is developed. A circular punched blank is taken and lubricated on one side (that will face the die). It is drawn through a die with the ball (of diameter 12.5 to 27 mm, selection of diameter depends on the sheet thickness) but without using a blank holder [Figure 12.3]. The ratio of minimum diameter at which the crack does not appear to the initial diameter of the blank is taken as a measure of formability of the sheet metal.

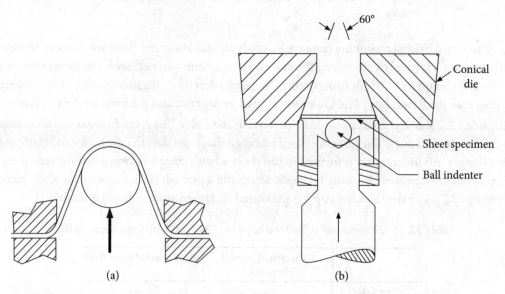

Figure 12.3   Schematic of the Fukui test

It may be noted that the flanges are allowed to draw in. A failed Fukui cup is shown in Figure 12.4 and a comparison of the relative amounts of stretch and draw in these tests is shown in Figure 12.5.

An alternative method to the Fukui test has been developed. The travel of the punch between the initial contact with the specimen and the onset of a drop in the punch load, which corresponds to the formation of visible crack, is determined and used instead of the ratio of the diameters. This value, termed as the formability index, correlates well with the uniform elongation of low carbon steels.

By using formability prediction techniques, designers and fabricators are able to make a wiser choice of metals and obtain data quickly on newer metals. The essential data can be obtained before the die is designed.

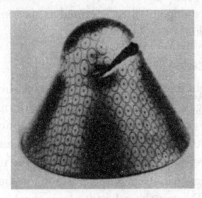

Figure 12.4 Failed Fukui cup [Courtesy of *Institut de Recherches de la Side´ rurgie Franchaise*]

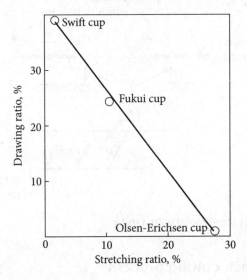

Figure 12.5 Relative amounts of stretching and drawing in the Swift, Fukui and Olsen/ Erichsen cupping tests

12.2 Sheet Metal Cutting

Sheet metal cutting involves separating a piece from a big sheet or strip by applying a force that causes the material to fail. The most common sheet metal cutting processes are performed by applying a shearing force, and are therefore sometimes referred to as shearing processes. When the applied shearing force exceeds the ultimate shear strength of the material, the material fails and separates at the cut location. The shearing force is applied by two tools, one above and the other below the sheet. The sheet rests over the lower tool and a quick downward blow is applied through the upper tool. A small clearance present between the edges of the upper and lower tools facilitates the fracture of the material.

Depending upon the thickness and shear strength of the material, sheet metal cutting may be done by using hand tools (called tin snips) or power tools. Further, the cutting may be along a straight line (edge to edge of sheet) termed as *shearing*, or along a desired shape, termed as *blanking* and *punching*.

12.2.1   Shearing process

This process produces straight line cuts to separate pieces of sheet metal along straight lines running between parallel edges. The shearing process is performed on a shear machine that can be operated manually (by hand or foot) or by hydraulic, pneumatic, or electric power. A typical shear machine consists of a table with support arms to hold the sheet, stops or guides to secure the sheet, the lower straight-edge blade or die, the upper straight-edge blade or shearing punch and a gauging device to precisely position the sheet. As shown in Figure 12.6, small pieces such as A, B, C, D... may be cut from a large sheet by shearing action.

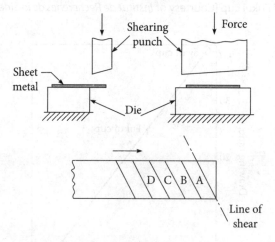

Figure 12.6   Cutting of sheet metal with a shear

12.2.2 Die-and-punch cutting process

Cutting of sheet metal along a desired contour is performed with a die-and-punch. The cutting takes place as a result of shearing action between two sharp cutting edges. To understand the process, refer to Figure 12.7. As the punch starts to press into the sheet metal, plastic deformation occurs in the surfaces of the sheet around the punch [shown as A, B, C and D in Figure 12.7(a)]. With further movement of punch into the sheet metal, cracks start forming on both the top and bottom edges [marked T and T' in Figure 12.7(b)(i)]. As the punch descends further, these cracks grow and if the clearance between the punch and the die is correct, the cracks eventually meet each other [Figure 12.7(b)(ii)] resulting in separation of the slug from the sheet.

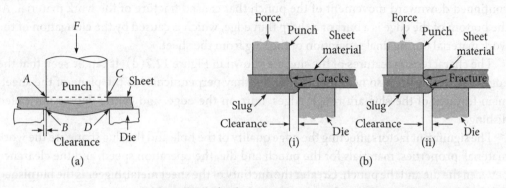

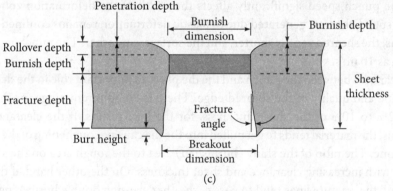

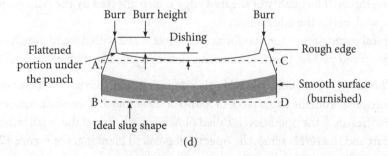

Figure 12.7 Sheet metal cutting operation with a punch and die: (a) Punch begins to push into sheet, causing plastic deformation; (b) Cracks and fracture develop at the opposing cutting edges that separate the sheet; (c) Characteristic features of the sheared edges of the sheet; and (d) Characteristic features of the slug

The sheared edges of the sheet have characteristic features as shown in Figure 12.7(c). At the top of the sheared surface is the rollover region up to a small depth. This corresponds to the depression made by the punch in the work material during the initial plastic deformation. Below the rollover is the burnish region, which corresponds to the penetration of the punch into the work material before the fracture begins. The burnish region is quite shiny in appearance. Just below the burnish region is the fracture zone. The surface of this zone is rough in appearance. This zone is relatively much larger in depth and is the result of the continued downward movement of the punch that caused fracture of the work material. At the bottom of the edge is a burr or a sharp thin edge, which is caused by the elongation of the work material during final separation of the slug from the sheet.

The characteristic features of the slug are shown in Figure 12.7(d). It can be seen that the edges of the slug are also not smooth, nor are they perpendicular to the plane of the sheet; main features of the slug are rough edges, burr on the edge, and centre-depression called dishing.

The significant factors affecting the edge quality of the hole and the slug shape are the work material properties, materials for the punch and die, the operation speed, and the clearance between the die and the punch. Greater the ductility of the sheet metal, bigger is the burnished depth. The punch speed significantly affects the width of the deformation zone. At higher punching speed, the heat generated due to plastic deformation remains confined to a smaller zone. Thus, the sheared zone is shorter, and the surface smoother. The punching speeds may be as high as 10 m/s.

The clearance between the punch and the die plays an important role in the determination of the shape and quality of the sheared edge. There is an optimum range for the clearance, which is 2% to 10% of the sheet thickness, for the best results. If the clearance increases beyond this, the material tends to get pulled into the die causing roughening of the edges of the sheared zone. The ratio of the shiny (burnished) area to the rough area on the sheared edge decreases with increasing clearance and sheet thickness. On the other hand, if the clearance is too small, the fracture lines tend to pass each other, causing double burnishing and hence, larger cutting forces. The quality of sheared edge is also affected by the punch speed; greater the punch speed, better the edge quality.

Some typical cutting operations performed on sheet metal with die and punch are punching, blanking, cut-off and parting, piercing, trimming, slotting, notching, nibbling and perforating.

Punching/blanking Punching or blanking is a stamping operation in which the punch removes a portion of material from the larger piece or a strip of sheet metal. If the small removed piece is of no use and is discarded, the operation is called punching, whereas if the small removed piece is the useful part and the rest is scrap, the operation is called blanking, see Figure 12.8.

The clearance between the die and punch can be determined as $c = k \cdot t$, where c is clearance (mm), k is a constant (also called clearance allowance) and t is sheet thickness (mm). The value of constant k is different for different materials. For example, for aluminium alloys, $k = 0.045$; for soft cold rolled steel and for soft stainless steel, $k = 0.060$; for half hard cold rolled steel, and for half hard and full hard stainless steel, $k = 0.075$. The die opening is always larger than the punch size by an amount equal to $2c$.

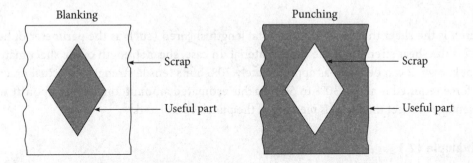

Figure 12.8 Comparison of basic stamping operations. In punching, the metal piece inside the part becomes scrap and is removed; in blanking, the metal piece around the part becomes scrap and is removed

For blanking operation Die size determines the blank size, and punch is made smaller by an amount equal to $2 \times$ clearance.

For punching operation Punch size determines the hole size, and die opening is made larger by an amount equal to $2 \times$ clearance.

An angular clearance of 1° to 2° is given at the die opening so that the slug or blank can easily drop through the die. See Figure 12.9. Both the die and the punch are made from tool steel or carbide.

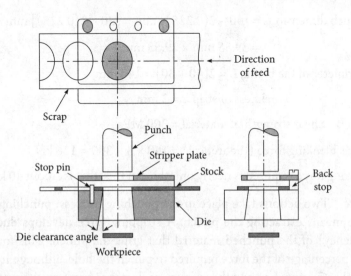

Figure 12.9 Blanking punch and die

The maximum force P required to be exerted by the punch to shear out a blank from the sheet can be estimated as

$$P = t L \zeta$$

where t is the sheet thickness, L is the total length sheared (such as the perimeter of hole) and ζ is the shear strength of the sheet material. In case, shear strength of the sheet material is not known, it can be taken as approximately 70% of its tensile strength. In actual practice, the force required is about 30% to 50% of this estimated amount, depending upon at what percentage of sheet thickness is piercing of the punch completed.

Example 12.1

A rectangular shape of blank 40 mm × 30 mm is to be cut from a half hard cold rolled steel strip of 3 mm thickness. Determine (a) the dimensions of the punch and die, and (b) the blank force. Take shear strength of strip material as 300 MPa.

Solution

(a) As the material of strip is half hard cold rolled steel, the constant k can be taken as 0.075. Given thickness of strip, $t = 3$ mm

Clearance = $k\, t = 0.075 \times 3 = 0.225$ mm

We know that for blanking operation, die size is the blank size.
Therefore,

Die opening dimensions = 40 mm × 30 mm

Punch dimensions = $[40 - 2(0.225)]$ mm × $[30 - 2(0.225)]$ mm

= 39.55 mm × 29.55 mm

(b) The perimeter of the blank, $L = 2[40 + 30] = 140$ mm

Thickness of strip, $t = 3$ mm

Shear strength of material = 300 MPa

Therefore, blanking force (theoretical) = $140 \times 3 \times 300 = 126$ kN

Actual blanking force required is nearly one-third of this, that is, about 40 kN.

Stripping force   Two actions take place in the punching process: punching and stripping. Stripping here means extracting the punch. A stripping force develops due to the spring back (or resiliency) of the punched material that grips the punch. This force is generally expressed as a percentage of the force required to punch the hole, although it varies with the type of material being punched and the amount of clearance between the cutting edges. The following simple empirical relation can be used to find this force.

$$SF = 0.02 \, L \, t \, \zeta$$

where SF = stripping force, kN; L = length of cut, mm; ζ = shear strength of material, MPa; and t = thickness of material, mm.

Example 12.2

A circular blank of 30 mm diameter is to be cut from a 2 mm thick 0.1 percent carbon steel sheet. Determine the die and punch sizes. Also estimate the punch force and the stripping force needed.
Following can be assumed for the steel:
Tensile strength: 410 MPa; shear strength: 310 MPa

Solution

For cutting a blank, die size = blank size = 30 mm diameter
For the sheet material, we can assume the value of constant $k = 0.06$

$$\text{Clearance} = k \, t = 0.12 \text{ mm}$$

Punch size = die size – 2 clearance = $30 - 2 \times 0.12 = 29.76$ mm diameter

Punch force needed (theoretically) = $L \, t \, \zeta = (\pi \times 30) \times 2 \times 310 = 58.5$ kN

Punch force needed (actually) = $0.3 \, L \, t \, \zeta = 20$ kN nearly

Stripping force needed = $0.02 \, L \, t \, \zeta = 0.02 \times 3.142 \times 30 \times 2 \times 310 = 1.17$ kN

Cut-off and parting   Cut-off is an operation in which blanks are taken away from a sheet metal strip by cutting the opposite sides of the part in a sequence as shown in Figure 12.10(a). Typically, a new part is produced with each stroke of the punch and no scrap is produced (the blanks are nested within each other). In a cut-off operation, the cutting edge is not necessarily straight whereas conventional shearing operation, as shown in Figure 12.7, is carried out with a straight cutting edge.

Parting is a sheet metal cutting operation [Figure 12.10(b)] that is similar to the cut-off operation but produces scrap since the shape of the part does not permit perfect nesting of the blanks on the strip.

Piercing   Piercing is an operation by which a hole is cut (or torn) in the sheet metal. This operation is different from punching in the sense that piercing does not generate a slug. Instead, the metal is pushed back to form a jagged flange on the back side of the hole.

A pierced hole looks somewhat like a bullet hole in a sheet of metal.

Trimming   When parts are produced by die casting or drop forging, a small amount of extra metal gets spread out at the parting plane. This extra metal, called flash, is cut off before the part is used, by an operation called trimming. The operation is also used to cut and remove any extra metal from a sheet metal formed part. The operation is very similar to blanking and the dies used are also similar to blanking dies. The presses used for trimming have, however, a relatively larger table.

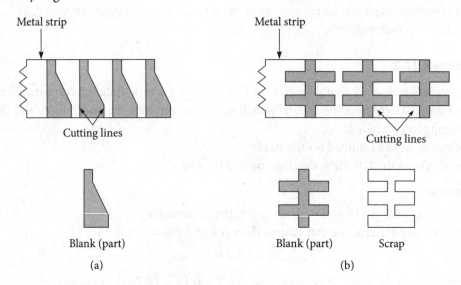

Figure 12.10 Sheet metal shearing operations: (a) Cut-off; and (b) Parting

Slotting   It is a punching operation by which an elongated or rectangular hole is cut out from the sheet metal as shown in Figure 12.11(a).

Notching   It is an operation in which a specified small amount of metal is cut off from a blank. Notching is different from punching in the sense that in notching, the cutting line of the slug formed must touch one edge of the blank or strip [Figure 12.11(b)]. A notch can be made in any shape. The purpose of notching is generally to release the metal for fitting up.

Nibbling   It is a variation of notching, with overlapping notches being cut into the metal. Nibbling operation may be performed to produce any desired shape, such as flanges, collars, and so on.

Perforating   Perforating is an operation in which a large number of uniformly spaced holes are punched in a sheet of metal as shown in Figure 12.11(c). The holes may be of any size or shape. They usually cover the entire sheet of metal.

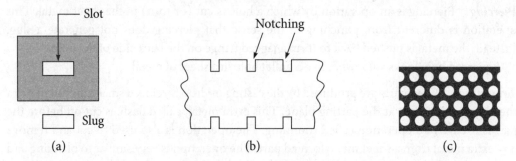

Figure 12.11 Sheet metal cutting operations: (a) Slotting; (b) Notching; and (c) Perforating

12.3 Sheet Metal Forming

12.3.1 Sheet metal bending

Bending is a very common sheet metal forming operation in which the metal is plastically deformed around a straight axis. The operation is used to create shapes like seams, corrugations and flanges. It may also be used to provide stiffness to the part (by increasing its moment of inertia).

As a sheet metal is bent [Figure 12.12], its fibres experience distortion – those nearer its outside convex surface are forced to stretch and experience tension, while the inner fibres experience compression. Somewhere in the cross-section, there is a plane that separates the tension and compression zones. This plane is parallel to the surface around which the sheet bends, and is called the *neutral axis*.

The position of the neutral axis depends on the radius and the angle of bend. Further, because of Poisson's ratio, the width of the part L in the outer region is smaller, and in the inner region, it is larger than the initial original width. Bending produces little or no change in the thickness of the sheet metal.

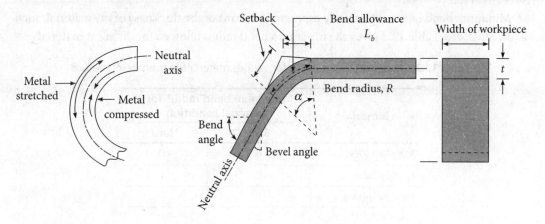

Figure 12.12   Sheet metal bending. The bend radius is measured at the inner surface of the bent part

Bend allowance   Bend allowance is the length of the neutral axis in the bend, as can be seen in Figure 12.12. This determines the blank length needed for a bent part. It can be approximately estimated from the relation

$$L_b = \alpha \left(R + k\, t \right)$$

where L_b = bend allowance (mm); α = bend angle (radian); R = bend radius (mm); t = thickness of sheet (mm), and k = constant, whose value may be taken as $1/3$ when $R < 2t$, and as $1/2$ when $R \geq 2t$. This assumes that stretching occurs only if bend radius is small relative to thickness of sheet.

Example 12.3

A 20 mm wide and 4 mm thick low carbon steel sheet is required to be bent to 60° at bend radius 10 mm. Determine the bend allowance.

Solution

Here, bend radius $R = 10$ mm, sheet thickness $t = 4$ mm and $a = 2\pi \times \dfrac{60}{360}$ radians
Since $R > 2t$, we can take $k = 0.5$

$$\text{Bend allowance} = \left(2\pi \times \frac{60}{360}\right)(10 + 0.5 \times 4)$$

$$= 12.56 \text{ mm}$$

Minimum bend radius   As the ratio of the bend radius to the thickness of sheet (i.e., R/t) decreases, the tensile strain on the outer fibres of the sheet increases. If (R/t) decreases beyond a certain limit, cracks start appearing on the surface of the material. *Minimum bend radius* for a material is defined as the limiting bend radius beyond which cracks start developing in the sheet material.

Minimum bend radius is generally expressed in terms of the thickness of the material, such as $2t$, $3t$, $4t$, etc. Table 12.2 gives the minimum bend radius allowed for different materials.

Table 12.2   Minimum bend radius for various materials at room temperature

Material	Minimum bend radius for material condition	
	Soft	Hard
Aluminum alloys	0	6t
Beryllium copper	0	4t
Brass, low-leaded	0	2t
Magnesium	5t	13t
Steels		
Austenitic stainless	0.5t	6t
Low-carbon, low-alloy	0.5t	4t
Titanium	0.7t	3t
Titanium alloys	2.5t	4t

Springback   At the end of the deformation operation, as soon as the bending force is removed, the elastic energy, which is there in the bent part, causes it to recover its original shape to some extent. This elastic recovery is called *springback*, and it can be defined as the increase in the included angle of the bent part with respect to the included angle of the forming tool (or die) after the bending pressure is removed. By referring to Figure 12.13, springback SB can be expressed as

$$SB = \frac{\alpha - \beta}{\beta}$$

where β is the included angle of the bending tool, degrees [Figure 12.13(a)]; and α is the included angle of the bent sheet metal part, degrees [Figure 12.13(b)]. It has been observed that springback increases with modulus of elasticity as well as yield strength of the work material. Two methods used to compensate for springback are overbending and bottoming. Overbending involves the use of a bending tool of *smaller than the specified* angle so that after springback, the final sheet metal part is of the desired included angle. Bottoming involves squeezing the sheet metal component at the end of the tool stroke so that the component is plastically deformed in the bend region and no elastic recovery takes place.

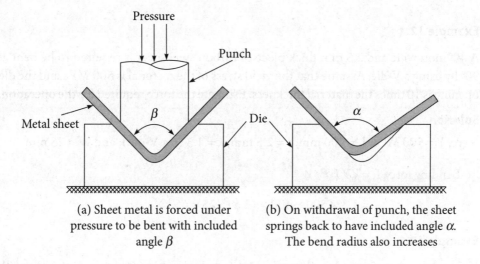

(a) Sheet metal is forced under pressure to be bent with included angle β

(b) On withdrawal of punch, the sheet springs back to have included angle α. The bend radius also increases

Figure 12.13   Springback in bending causes increase in bend angle as well as bend radius

Bending Force   There are two general types of die bending: V-die bending [Figure 12.14(a)], and wiping die bending also called *edge bending* [Figure 12.14(b)]. V-die bending is used extensively in brake die operations and stamping die operations. The bending force can be estimated from the following simple relation.

$$P = k\,Y\,L\,t^2/W$$

where P is the bending force, N; Y is the yield stress of the material, MPa; L is the bend width (bend allowance), mm; t is the sheet thickness, mm; W is the die opening, mm; and k is a constant whose value can be taken as 1.33 for a V-die and 0.33 for a wiping die.

Bending force varies as the punch progresses through the bending operation. The force is zero in the beginning, it rises and reaches the maximum value as the punch progresses and reaches the bottom of the stroke.

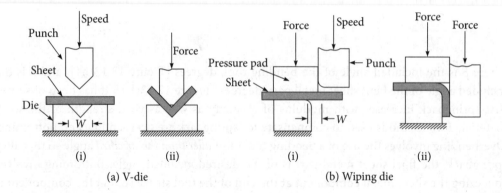

(a) V-die   (b) Wiping die

Figure 12.14   Die bending operations

Example 12.4

A 400 mm wide and 2.5 mm thick piece of carbon steel sheet is required to be bent at 90° by using a V-die. Assume that the yield stress of the material is 500 MPa and the die opening is 10 times the material thickness. Estimate the force required for the operation.

Solution

Here, $Y = 500$ MPa; $L = 400$ mm; $t = 2.5$ mm; $k = 1.3$ (for V-die); and $W = 25$ mm

Bending force $P = k\,Y\,L\,t^2/W$

$$= 1.3 \times 500 \times 400 \times (2.5)^2/25 = 65 \text{ kN}$$

Example 12.5

If the material mentioned in Example 12.4 is to be bent at 90° using wiping die with radius = 3.75 mm, what will be the force requirement?

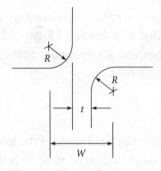

Figure 12.15   Wiping die dimensions

Solution

Here, $Y = 500$ MPa; $L = 400$ mm; $t = 2.5$ mm; $k = 0.3$; and $W = 2.5 + 3.75 + 3.75 = 10$ mm (Figure 12.15)

Bending force $P = k\,Y\,L\,t^2/W$

$$= 0.3 \times 500 \times 400 \times (2.5)^2/10 = 37.5 \text{ kN}$$

Different sheet metal bending processes

Beading   It is one of the common sheet metal processes used to form the working structure of parts, such as hinges. In this process, a curl is formed over the edge of sheet on a straight or curved axis. There are different techniques for forming a bead. Some techniques form the bead progressively in multiple stages, using several same or different die arrangements [Figure 12.16(a)], while it is also possible to form a bead with a single die.

Hemming   It is an edge bending process in which the edge of the sheet is bent completely over itself. It can be of flat type or open type [Figure 12.16(b)].

Corrugating   It is a bending process in which a symmetrical bend is produced across the width of sheet metal and at a regular interval along its entire length. Corrugating can be of different shapes, but all have the same purpose, to increase the rigidity of the sheet metal and increase its resistance to bending moments. The bend geometry [Figure 12.16(c)] is achieved by work hardening of the metal. Corrugated sheets are very useful in structural applications and are widely used in the construction industry.

Seaming   It is a sheet metal joining process in which the edges of two parts are bent on each other [Figure 12.16 (d)]. As the bends are locked together, each bend helps resist the deformation of the other bend, providing a good joint structure. Watertight or airtight joints between sheet metal parts can be produced by double seaming.

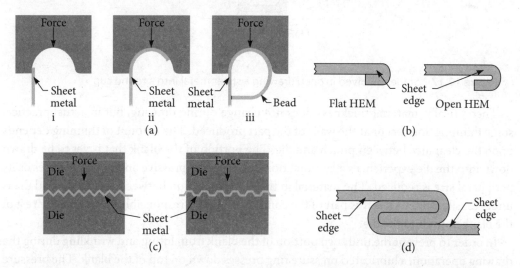

Figure 12.16   Sheet metal bending operations: (a) Bead formation on the edge of sheet in multiple stages; (b) Hemming operation; (c) Corrugating sheet metal; and (d) Seaming operation for making sheet metal joint

12.3.2 Sheet metal drawing

Sheet metal drawing is a process of cold forming a flat blank of sheet metal into a hollow vessel without much wrinkling, trimming or fracturing. The process involves forcing the previously cut sheet metal blank into a suitably shaped steel die with a punch mounted in a press. The punch exerts sufficient force and the metal is drawn over the edge of the die opening and into the die [Figure 12.17]. The blank is mostly held down flat against the die by the pressure exerted by the blank holder. In forming a cup, however, the metal goes completely inside the die. Typical sheet metal parts made by the drawing process include ammunition shells, cooking utensils, sinks and automobile body panels.

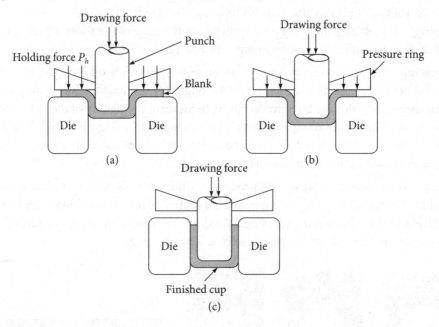

Figure 12.17   Stages involved in deep drawing a sheet metal into a round cup

Theoretically, material thickness does not change during drawing, but in actual practice, some thinning does occur at the walls of the part produced. The amount of thinning depends upon the clearance between punch and die. The portion of the blank that is yet to be drawn down into the die experiences a combination of heavy compressive and tensile stresses as its peripheral size is reduced. The material in the vertical portion between the punch and die is under tensile stress as it is this part of the component that is responsible for pulling the rest of the blank down into the die.

In order to prevent the undrawn portion of the blank from lifting and wrinkling during the drawing operation, a lubricated pressure ring presses down on top of the blank. The pressure exerted by this ring has to be sufficient to prevent the blank from wrinkling, but at the same time, it must not be too large that the blank is prevented from being drawn down into the die.

Some lubricant may be used over the face of the blank to reduce friction and thereby reduce drawing load. Deep drawing operation is mostly used for the production of circular shaped parts; though shapes other than circular ones can also be drawn. The term *shallow drawing* is used when the height of the cup formed is less than half its diameter. But if the height of the cup formed is equal to or greater than half its diameter, it is termed as *deep drawing*. While deep drawing is a much faster process, it should only be commercially considered if production quantities are sufficient to justify the initial high cost of the die. Drawing process is generally considered to be more complicated than cutting or bending. For circular components, spinning is generally chosen as an alternative to deep drawing.

Measures of drawing The severity of a deep drawing operation can be estimated with the help of any or all of the three measures – drawing ratio, thickness-to-diameter ratio, and per cent reduction.

Drawing ratio, DR, for a cylindrical shaped part can be defined as the ratio of blank diameter D to the punch diameter d.

$$DR = \frac{D}{d}$$

The greater the drawing ratio, the more severe is the operation. Generally, DR should not exceed 2, though the limiting value of DR depends on many factors such as corner radii on die and punch, depth of the draw, friction conditions and physical properties of the sheet metal.

The thickness-to-diameter ratio is another measure of drawing severity. The ratio (the thickness of the starting blank divided by blank diameter) should be more than 1%. If the ratio $\frac{t}{d}$ is less than 1%, the tendency for wrinkling on the surface increases.

The per cent reduction r is defined as

$$r = \frac{D-d}{D} \times 100$$

The value of r should not exceed 50%.

If the design of the drawn component is such that the drawing ratio, thickness-to-diameter ratio and per cent reduction exceed their limits, it becomes desirable to complete the operation in two or more steps, preferably by performing some stress relieving operation on the material (such as annealing) in between steps.

Example 12.6

A cylindrical cup is to be formed from a 2.5 mm sheet metal by drawing operation. The cup dimensions are: height 60 mm and inside diameter 80 mm. If the starting blank diameter is 155 mm, determine the operation feasibility.

Solution

The feasibility of defect-free drawing operation can be checked by determining the drawing ratio, per cent reduction and thickness-to-diameter ratio.

$$DR = \frac{155}{80} = 1.94 \qquad \text{(It is less than 2.0)}$$

$$\% \text{ reduction} = \frac{155-80}{155} \times 100 = 48.4\% \qquad \text{(It is less than 50\%)}$$

$$\frac{t}{d} = \frac{2.5}{155} \times 100 = 1.6\% \qquad \text{(It is more than 1\%)}$$

Based on these measures, it is seen that the drawing operation is feasible.

Blank size   It is generally difficult to find the exact size of the blank needed for drawing a given cup because of thinning and thickening of the metal sheet during the drawing operation. The following simple relations can be used to approximately determine the blank diameter D:

$$D = \sqrt{d^2 + 4dh} \qquad \text{when } d \geq 20r$$

$$= \sqrt{d^2 + 4dh - 0.5r} \qquad \text{when } d \text{ is between } 15r \text{ and } 20r$$

$$= \sqrt{d^2 + 4dh - 5r} \qquad \text{when } d \leq 10r$$

where d = inside diameter of cup; h = height of cup and r = corner radius on punch.

Drawing force   In case of deep drawing cylindrical shells having a circular cross-section, the maximum drawing force P can be determined from the relation

$$P = k \pi d t Y$$

where d = inside diameter of cup; t = thickness of material; Y = yield strength of material; and k = factor whose value is approximately equal to $[D/d - 0.6]$, where D is blank diameter.

The holding force P_h can be roughly estimated from the relation:

$$P_h = 0.015 . Y [D^2 - (d + 2.2 t + 2 R_d)^2$$

where R_d is the die corner radius in mm.

Defects in drawn parts   Some of the defects that commonly occur in a drawn part are:

1.   **Wrinkling**   This defect appears in the form of a series of ridges. As shown in Figure 12.18(a), this defect generally occurs on the wall or flange of the drawn component. The flange of the blank undergoes radial drawing stress and tangential compressive stress during the drawing process, which sometimes results in wrinkles. The main cause for this defect is the improper application of holding force, or too less holding force. Another cause is related to the clearances between the blank, blank holder, punch and die cavity. Factors,

such as die temperature and the metal alloy of the blank, can also affect the drawing process and a variation in any of these factors influences the potential for wrinkling in the deep-drawn part. In general, wrinkling is preventable if the deep drawing system and stamped part are designed properly.

2. **Tearing** This defect is in the form of an open crack on the walls of the drawn component. It usually occurs near the base of the component as it is at this location that the material experiences high tensile stresses and also thinning as shown in Figure 12.18(b). When stresses exceed the limit, material failure can take place, particularly when the punch or die has a sharp corner. One main cause for this defect is the application of excessive blank holding force.

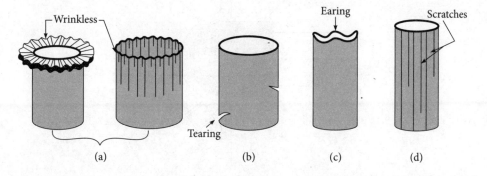

Figure 12.18   Some typical defects in drawn parts: (a) Wrinkling – in the flange or on the end of the wall; (b) Tearing on the wall at the base of the part; (c) Earing; and (d) Scratches on the surface of the wall

3. **Earing** This defect is in the form of a series of irregularities (or wavy edges) appearing at the upper edge of a deep drawn cup [Figure 12.18(c)]. One major cause of this defect is the anistropy (i.e., directional property) in the sheet metal.

4. **Scratches** Shallow scratches appear on the surface of the drawn component [Figure 12.18(d)] when the surfaces of the die and punch (particularly die) are not smooth. The tendency to form scratches decreases if the die and punch surfaces are adequately lubricated.

12.3.3 Sheet metal spinning

Spinning process is performed on sheet metal to form axially symmetrical cup-type components when the quantity of components required is small and the use of expensive deep drawing dies cannot be justified. Basically, the process involves forming of the sheet metal over a shaped wooden or steel former. A circular blank of sheet metal is taken and pressed (with a pressure pad) against the former (also called forming block) held inside the chuck of a heavy duty centre lathe. With the high speed rotation of the headstock spindle of the lathe, the former and the blank rotate together. Sheet metal is made to flow over the former when a roller (or rounded tool) is pressed against the revolving blank in a series of sweeping strokes until ultimately the blank acquires the shape of the former, as can be seen in Figure 12.19. The tool is either hand held or gripped in the tool holder of the lathe, depending upon the ductility and strength of the blank material and the component size. The pressure applied through the tool is highly localized (almost a point contact), and an important feature of the process is that the thickness of the initial blank remains essentially the same throughout its transformation into the finished part.

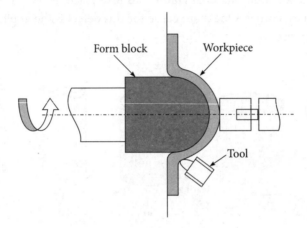

Figure 12.19   Schematic of spinning process

Advantages   There are several advantages of sheet metal forming by spinning process.

There are several advantages of sheet metal forming by spinning process.

1. Better mechanical properties: The mechanical working of the metal during the spinning process provides a refined and strengthened grain structure. The heavy pressures used to achieve plastic flow of the metal during the process cause an orientation of grain parallel to the principal axis. Cold working of the metal also increases tensile strength appreciably.

2. Several operations can be performed on one setup.

3. Several workpiece profiles are possible.

4. Seamless objects, such as circular cans and gas cylinders can be produced using a single piece of material.

5. Environment friendly process with few emissions and negligible amount of material wastage compared to other metal working methods.

6. Economical process, since the tooling and production costs are comparatively low.

7. High production rate, if the process is automated.

8. Short lead times.

Disadvantages/Limitations

Some limitations of sheet metal spinning process are as follows:

1. Products produced by spinning are limited to concentric and axially symmetric shapes.

2. Cracks and dents in the component during production are irreparable for all practical purposes. Repairing the defective component is generally not cost-effective.

3. Maximum practical diameter of the components produced is limited due to the size of the available metal spinning equipment.

4. Production volume constraint: The process requires component-specific tools suited to the desired geometry. From an economic viewpoint, this makes it impractical for a manufacturer to produce low volumes of a component with a unique geometry.

5. Manual spinning requires that operators have a high level of skill as well as a fair amount of strength, as the process is physically demanding.

6. Compared to similar metal-shaping techniques – such as press forming – manual metal spinning takes more time to produce a component.

Applications   Sheet metal spinning is used for producing a large number of products, including hemispheres, parabolas, Venturi – hourglass shaped parts, cookware, bells, cans, cones, flowerpots, lampshades, funnels, gas cylinders, dished heads and trash bins.

12.3.4 Sheet metal stretch forming

Stretch forming is a metal forming process in which a piece of sheet metal is stretched and bent simultaneously over a form die (called a form block or a former) so as to form large contoured parts. The material is stressed beyond the elastic limit and into the plastic range so that it is permanently deformed. There is no tendency to spring back. The process is performed on a stretch press, in which a piece of sheet metal is securely gripped along its edges by gripping jaws. Each of the jaws is attached to a carriage that is pulled by pneumatic or hydraulic force to stretch the sheet. The stretch forming process subjects the metal blank to both plastic and elastic deformation.

The only tooling used in this process is a form die, which is a solid contoured piece, as shown in Figure 12.20. The surface of the forming block must be highly smooth and lubricated.

The process is performed on vertical or horizontal stretch presses. Thinning and strain hardening of material are inherent in stretch forming. Reduction in thickness should not exceed 5% of the original thickness. The force needed in stretch forming can be estimated by using the relation

$$P = L \cdot t \cdot \sigma_f$$

where P = stretching force, N; L = length of the sheet in the direction perpendicular to the stretching, mm; t = instantaneous thickness of sheet, mm; and σ_f = flow stress of sheet metal, MPa.

The process is also used for the manufacture of large parts such as aircraft leading edges, door panels and nose sections.

There are two variants of stretch forming: (i) stretch forming, as shown in Figure 12.20(a) and (ii) stretch-wrap forming, as shown in Figure 12.20(b).

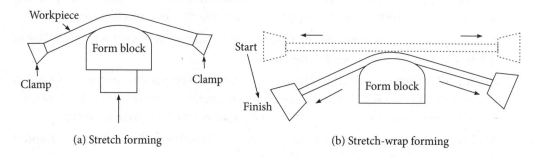

(a) Stretch forming   (b) Stretch-wrap forming

Figure 12.20 Two variants of stretch forming

In stretch forming, the two ends of the sheet metal are firmly gripped in jaws and stretching is accomplished by driving the forming block with a hydraulic piston onto the sheet. On the other hand, in stretch-wrapping, first, the two ends of the sheet metal are firmly gripped and stretched beyond its yield point while it is straight. The metal is then wrapped around a forming block. Stretch-wrapping process has been used for making long sweeping bends on tubes and other extruded shapes.

Advantages and applications   Stretch forming on sheet metal has many advantages. Some of these are as follows:

1. Parts produced have better shape and surface quality than rolled or drawn parts.

2. Low tooling costs – only one forming block is needed – it can be made of wood, cast iron, or zinc alloy.

3. Fast production process, well suited to higher volume output.

A typical application of this process is for making prototype models of aircraft and automotive parts. Stretch formed aluminium parts are widely used in the automobile industry and as household appliances. Titanium parts have been produced by this process for aerospace applications.

12.3.5 Sheet metal embossing

Embossing is an operation in which sheet metal is drawn to shallow depths with male and female matching dies [Figure 12.21]. The metal experiences some stretching and thinning. The embossing operation may seem to be similar to the coining process but it is not so. Embossing dies possess matching cavity contours, that is, the punch contains the positive contour and the die contains the negative; whereas coining dies generally have quite different cavities in the two die halves. Therefore, embossing involves less severe metal deformation than coining. The operation is carried out mostly to stiffen flat panels. It is also sometimes used for making decoration items like number plates or name plates, jewellery, and so on.

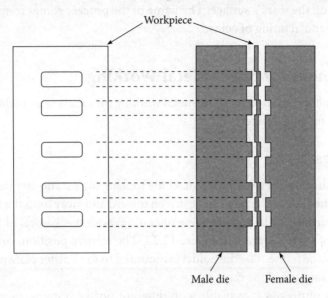

Figure 12.21 Embossing operation with male and female dies. Letters, numbers and designs on sheet metal parts can be produced by this operation

12.3.6 Coining

Coining is a flashless precision forging process in which a workpiece is subjected to a sufficiently high stress to induce plastic flow on the surface of the material. The process is used to create very fine and intricate details on the surface of the workpiece [Figure 12.22].

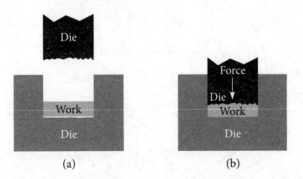

Figure 12.22 Schematic of coining process: (a) Before the upper die presses the work material; and (b) The upper die presses the work material to complete the process

The plastic flow of material reduces surface grain size and work hardens the surface, while the material deeper in the part retains its toughness and ductility. Due to the required high shape accuracy in the process, it is performed cold. Lubrication is not used since any substance between the die and the work would hinder the reproduction of the most accurate details that are to be formed on the work's surface. The name of the process comes from the initial use of the process for manufacturing of coins.

12.4 Equipment for Sheet Metal Working

The main equipments required for sheet metal working on a mass scale include press, die and punch, and press feeding devices.

12.4.1 Presses

A press used for sheet metal working is a machine tool having a stationary bed and a powered ram (also called the slide). The ram can be driven toward and away from the bed to enable the performance of various cutting and forming operations with mechanical or hydraulic power. A simple sketch of a press is given in Figure 12.23. The relative positions of the bed and ram are established by the frame. The die holder is mounted to the bolster plate of the bed and the punch holder is mounted in the ram.

A large variety of presses is available with different power systems, capacities and frame types. The power system of a press refers to the source of power and the type of drive used to deliver the power to the ram. The capacity of a press refers to the force and energy that can be delivered by it for carrying out the metal forming or cutting operation. The type of press frame refers to the design and other physical features of the press.

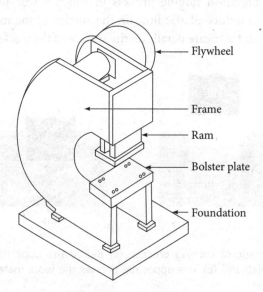

Figure 12.23 Schematic of a stamping press

Classification of Presses

Presses for sheet metal working can be classified by one or a combination of characteristics, including source of power, number of slides, type of frame and construction, type of drive and intended applications.

Classification on the basis of source of power

- **Manual presses**   Manual presses are either hand or foot operated through levers, screws or gears. A common press of this type is the arbor press used for assembly operations.

- **Mechanical presses**   Mechanical presses utilize flywheel energy, which is transferred to the workpiece by gears, cranks, eccentrics or levers. These presses develop very high forces at the bottom of their strokes, and are therefore more suitable to blanking and punching operations.

- **Hydraulic presses**   Hydraulic presses provide force when fluid pressure is applied on a piston through pumps, valves, intensifiers and accumulators. These presses generally provide longer ram strokes than mechanical presses and also develop full force throughout the entire stroke. One important limitation of hydraulic presses is that they are slower. These presses have better performance and reliability than mechanical presses.

- **Pneumatic presses**   Pneumatic presses utilize the air cylinders to exert the required force. These presses are generally smaller in size and capacity than hydraulic or mechanical presses and, therefore, find use for light duty operations only.

Classification on the basis of number of slides

- **Single action presses**   A single action press has one reciprocating slide that carries the tool for the metal-forming operation. The press has a fixed bed. It is the most widely used press for operations like blanking, coining, embossing and drawing.

- **Double action presses**   A double action press has two slides moving in the same direction against a fixed bed. This press is more suitable for drawing operations than a single action press. For this reason, its two slides are generally referred to as outer blank holder slide and inner draw slide. The blank holder slide is hollow rectangular, while the inner slide is solid rectangular that reciprocates within the blank holder. The blank holder slide has a shorter stroke and dwells at the bottom end of its stroke till the punch mounted on the inner slide draws the workpiece. In this way, practically the total capacity of the press is available for drawing operation.

  Another advantage of double action press is that the four corners of the blank holder are individually adjustable. This permits the application of non-uniform forces on the sheet metal, if needed. A double action press is widely used for deep drawing operations and irregular-shaped stampings.

- **Triple action presses**   A triple action press has three moving slides. Two slides (the blank holder and the inner slide) move in the same direction as in a double action press and the third or lower slide moves upward through the fixed bed in a direction opposite to that of the other two slides. This action allows reverse-drawing, forming or bending operations against the inner slide while both upper slide actions are dwelling.

Cycle time for a triple action press is longer than for a double action press because of the time required for the third action.

Classification on the basis of frame design and construction

- **Arch frame presses**   Arch frame presses, with their frame in the shape of an arch, are usually not very common.

- **Gap frame presses**   Gap frame presses have a C-shaped frame. These are the most versatile and common in use, as they provide unobstructed access to the dies from three sides and their backs are usually open to eject stampings and/or scrap.

- **Straight side presses**   Straight side presses are stronger than other presses since heavy loads can be taken in a vertical direction by the massive side frame and there is little tendency for the punch and die alignment to be affected by the strain. The capacity of these presses is usually greater than 10 MN.

- **Horn presses**   Horn presses generally have a heavy shaft projecting from the machine frame instead of the press bed. These presses are used mainly on cylindrical parts involving punching, riveting, embossing and flanging edges.

Figure 12.24 shows typical frame designs.

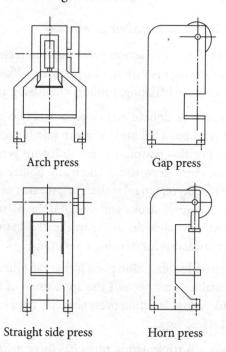

Arch press   Gap press

Straight side press   Horn press

Figure 12.24   Some typical designs of frames of power presses

Press Selection

Proper selection of a press is necessary for successful and economical operation. The press is a costly machine, and the return on investment depends on how well it performs its job. There is no single press that can provide maximum rate of production as well as prove to be economical for all applications. When a press is required to be used for several widely varying jobs, compromise is generally made between economy and productivity.

Important factors to be considered during the selection of a press are size, force, energy and speed.

Size   The bed and slide areas of the press should be of the right size so as to accommodate the dies to be used and also to ensure adequate available space for die changing and maintenance. Stroke requirements are related to the height of the parts to be produced. A press with a short stroke should be preferred because it will permit faster operation and greater productivity. The size and type of press to be selected also depend upon the method and nature of part feeding, the type of operation and the material being formed.

Force and energy   The press selected should have the capacity to provide the force and energy necessary for carrying out the operation. The major source of energy in mechanical presses is the flywheel, which is driven by means of a motor. The energy available is a function of mass of flywheel and square of its speed.

Speed   Fast speeds are generally desirable, but they are limited by the operations performed. High speed may not, however, be most productive or efficient.

Size, shape and material of the workpiece, die life, maintenance costs and other factors should be considered while attempting to achieve the highest production rate at the lowest cost per piece.

Mechanical versus hydraulic presses

Mechanical presses are widely used for sheet metal blanking, forming and drawing operations. For certain operations, which require very high force, hydraulic presses are more advantageous. Table 12.3 gives a comparison of the salient characteristics and preferred applications of the two types of presses.

Table 12.3   Comparison of mechanical and hydraulic presses

Characteristic	Mechanical presses	Hydraulic presses
Force	Depends upon slide position	Does not depend upon the slide position. Relatively constant
Stroke length	Short strokes	Long strokes, even as much as 3 m
Slide speed	High: Highest at mid-stroke. Can be variable	Slow: Rapid advance and retraction. Different speeds. Uniform speed throughout stroke
Capacity	About 50 MN (maximum)	About 500 MN, or even more

Contd.

Table 12.3 Contd.

Characteristic	Mechanical presses	Hydraulic presses
Control	Full stroke generally required before reversal	Adjustable, slide reversal possible from any position
Applications	Operations requiring maximum pressure near bottom of stroke; cutting operations (blanking, shearing, piercing), forming and drawing to depths of about 100 mm	Operations requiring steady pressure throughout stoke; deep drawing; drawing irregular shaped parts; straightening; operations requiring variable forces and/or strokes

12.4.2 Die and punch

Most sheet metal operations are carried out on a press with a punch and die, simply called a *die* or a *die set*. The term *stamping die* is sometimes used for a high production die. A typical die and punch set used for blanking operation is shown in Figure 12.9. The sheet metal used, called stock, is generally in the form of a strip.

The working parts of a die set are the punch and the die, which actually perform the cutting /forming operation. Other parts of the die set are as follows:

Punch holder It holds the punch and is bolted to the ram of the press.

Die holder It is also called the die shoe. The die shoe holds the die and is bolted on to the bolster plate.

Stop pin It is also called guide pin and acts as a gauge for the purpose of setting the advance of the strip between the press cycles. The strip stock is held butted against the back of the stop pin as the punch strikes the strip stock.

Guide pin (or post) and bushing These ensure proper alignment between the punch and the die during the stamping operation as shown in Figure 12.25.

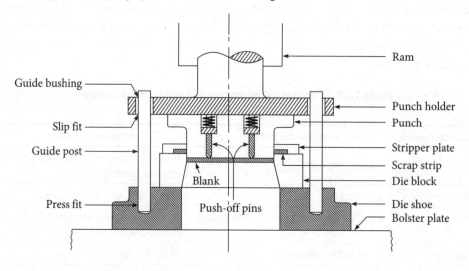

Figure 12.25 Schematic of a blanking die

Stripper plate As the punch pierces through the stock strip, the hole formed is of the same size as the punch. Therefore, the scrap strip tends to cling to the punch on its withdrawal. The stripper plate, which is attached to the die, simply holds the scrap strip so that the punch can be pulled out of the hole after the operation. It is a simple plate with a hole slightly larger than the punch cross-section.

Push-off pins These help to free the blank in instances where the strip material clings to the bottom of the punch. Their use is vital when the strip is thin or where lubricants are used on the strip.

The die opening is given an angular clearance to permit escape of the cut part (blank). The clearance angle provided on the die [Figure 12.9] depends on the material as well as the thickness of the stock. For thicker and softer materials, generally higher angular clearance is given. In most cases, up to 2 degrees of angular clearance and 3 mm of height of cutting land are generally sufficient.

A *blanking die* in the conventional closed position is shown in Figure 12.25. Sometimes, the positions of the die and the punch may be interchanged. This may become necessary when the opening in the bolster plate is too small to permit the finished product to pass through the bolster opening. Figure 12.26 shows such a die – it is also called an *inverted die*.

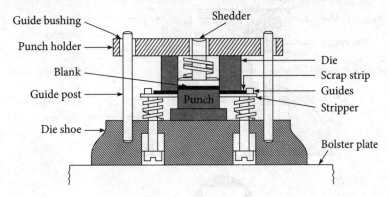

Figure 12.26 Schematic of an inverted die

An *inverted die* is designed in such a way that the die is fastened to the punch holder and the punch fastened to the die shoe. During the downward stroke of the ram, the blank is sheared from the strip. The blank and shedder are forced back into the die opening, which loads a compression spring in the die opening. At the same time, the punch is forced through the scrap strip and a spring attached to the stripper is compressed and loaded. On the upstroke of the ram, the shedder pushes the blank out of the die opening and the stripper forces the scrap to strip off the punch. The finished part (blank) falls or is blown out from the rear of the press.

Types of stamping dies

Stamping dies can be classified on the basis of the number of operations they perform with each stroke of the press. Accordingly, these are *single operation dies* and *multi-operation dies*.

With every press stroke, single operation dies perform one operation whether it is cutting, bending or drawing. As the die shown in Figure 12.25 performs a single blanking operation with each press stroke, it belongs to the category of single operation dies.

Multi-operation dies include compound dies, combination dies and progressive dies. These dies are relatively more complex than the single operation dies.

Compound die

A *compound die* [Figure 12.27] combines the principles of the conventional and inverted dies in one station. This type of die is used to produce a workpiece that requires two operations (such as blanking and punching, or drawing and blanking) to be performed at one station and in single operation. For the workpiece shown in Figure 12.27, the piercing punch is fastened in the conventional way to the punch holder. Its matching die opening for piercing is machined into the blanking punch. The blanking punch and the blanking die opening are mounted in an inverted position. The blanking punch is fastened to the die shoe and the blanking die opening is through the punch holder.

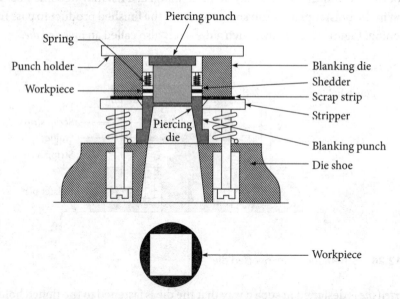

Figure 12.27 Schematic of a compound die

Combination die

A *combination die* performs two operations at two different stations in the die. Though these dies are not very popular, some typical examples of their application include blanking two different parts, or blanking a part and then bending the same part at the next station.

Progressive die

Progressive die is made with two or more stations arranged in a sequence. Each station performs an operation on the workpiece – or provides an idler station – so that the workpiece is completed when the last operation has been carried out. Thus, after the fourth stroke of a four-station die, each successive stroke will produce a finished part. Operations that are usually carried out at different stations in a progressive die are piercing, notching, bending, forming, drawing, blanking and so on. The number and types of operations that may be performed in a progressive die depend upon the ingenuity of the designer.

Figure 12.28 shows a four-station progressive die. The die block is made up of four sections and fastened together in the die shoe. This permits easy replacement of broken or worn die blocks. The sheet metal stock is fed from the right and registers against a finger stop (not shown). The first stroke of the press [Figure 12.28(a)] produces a square hole and two notches. These notches form the left end of the first piece.

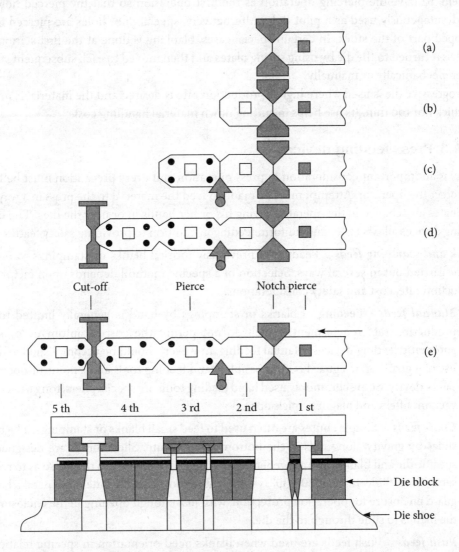

Figure 12.28 Schematic of operations on a progressive die

During the upstroke of the ram, the stock is moved to the next station against a finger stop (not shown). The stock is positioned for the second stroke. The second station is an idler [Figure 12.28(b)]. The right end of the first piece, the left end of the second piece, and a second square hole are pierced.

The ram retracts and the scrap strip is moved to the third station against an automatic stop, as can be seen in Figure 12.28(c). This stop picks up the notched V and positions the scrap strip. The third stroke of the ram pierces four holes, as shown in Figure 12.28(c). The fourth stroke [Figure 12.28(d)] cuts off and forms the radii at the ends of the finished piece. Thereafter, every stroke produces a finished part, as can be clearly seen in Figure 12.28(e).

In a progressive die, the cut-off or blanking operation is often the last operation. It is useful to have the piercing operation as the first operation so that the pierced hole can be advantageously used as a pilot hole. Alternatively, special pilot holes are pierced in the scrapped part of the stock. In certain special cases, blanking is done at the first station; the blank is returned to the die by using spring plates and then moved to each subsequent station either mechanically or manually.

Progressive die is used where higher production rate is desired and the material is neither too thick nor too thin. Its use helps in cutting down material handling costs.

12.4.3 Press feeding devices

Safety is an important consideration in press operation and every precaution must be taken to protect the operator. Attempt must be made to feed the material to the press in a way that eliminates any chance of the operator having his or her hands in or near the dies. The use of feeding devices allows faster and uniform feeding in addition to providing safety features.

Blank and stamping feeds Feeding of previously formed blanks or stampings to presses can be carried out in several ways. Selection of a specific method depends upon factors like production rate, cost and safety considerations.

- ***Manual feeds*** Feeding of blanks or stampings by hand is generally limited to low production rate requirements which do not permit the cost of automatic or semi-automatic feeding devices. Manual feeding, however, should be accomplished with the use of a guard or, if a guard is not possible, hand feeding tools and a point-of-operation safety device. Some commonly used hand feeding tools are special pliers, tongs, tweezers, vacuum lifters and magnetic pick-ups.

- ***Chute feeds*** Simple chutes are often used to feed small blanks or stampings. The blank slides by gravity along rails in the bottom of the chute. Slide chutes are designed for specific die and blanks, and are generally attached permanently to the die so as to reduce setup time. Slide angle of 20°–30° is sufficient in most cases. Chute feeds need a barrier guard enclosure for operation protection, with just enough opening in the enclosure for the blanks to slide through to the die.

- ***Push feeds*** Push feeds are used when blanks need orientation in specific relation to the die. The workpiece is manually placed in the nest in a slide, one at a time. The slide is then pushed until the piece falls into the die. An interlock is provided so that the press cannot be operated until the slide has correctly located the part in the die. To increase the production rate, push feeds can be automated by actuating the feed slide through a mechanical attachment to the press slide.

- *Lift and transfer devices*   In some automatic installations, vacuum or suction cups are used for lifting of blanks one at a time from stacks to be moved to the die by transfer units. Separation of the top blank from a stack is achieved by devices that are operated magnetically, pneumatically or even mechanically.

- *Dial feeds*   Dial feeds consist of rotary indexing tables (also called turntables) on which the fixtures are fitted for holding the workpieces as they are taken to the press tooling. Parts are placed in the fixtures at the loading station (which are located away from the place of press operation) manually or by other means including chutes, hoppers, vibratory feeders and robots. Dial feeds are increasingly being used because of the higher safety and productivity associated with them.

- *Coil stock feeds*   Automatic press feeds for the coil stock are slide (or gripper) and roll feeds. Both of these may be press or independently driven.

- *Mechanical slide feeds*   Press-driven slide feeds have a gripper arrangement which clamps and feeds the stock during its forward movement and releases it on the return stroke. The material cannot back up during the return stroke of the gripper because of a drag unit that acts like a frictional brake. Grippers reciprocate on rods or slides between adjustable positive stops to ensure accuracy. Slide feeds are available in a variety of sizes and designs. These are mostly used for narrow coil stock and short feed lengths.

- *Hitch-type feed*   This feed differs from the press-driven mechanical slide feed with respect to actuation, which is by a simple flat cam attached to the ram or punch holder. On the downward stroke of the ram, one or more springs are compressed by the cam action, and on the upstroke, the springs provide the force to feed the stock into the die.

  These feeds are best suited for coil stock of small to medium thickness and for relatively short feed progression. They are one of the oldest and least expensive feeding devices that are still widely used. Due to their low cost, they are generally left permanently attached to the dies, thus reducing the setup time.

- *Pneumatic slide feeds*   Pneumatic slide feeds are similar to mechanical slide feeds as both have grippers or clamps that reciprocate on guide rails or slides between adjustable positive stops to push and/or pull stock into a die. However, these feeds differ from mechanical slide feeds with respect to the source of power for actuating. A pneumatic slide feed is powered by an air cylinder, with actuation and timing of valves done by cam operated limit switches.

  These feeds are best suited for short progression, and find wide applications in job shops because of their low cost and versatility.

- *Roll feeds*   In roll feeds, the coil stock is advanced by the pressure exerted between intermittently driven, opposed rolls. These rolls allow the stock to dwell during the working part of the press cycle. Intermittent rotation (or indexing) of the feed rolls, with the rolls rotating in only one direction, is accomplished in many ways. In one common design, the rolls are indexed through a one-way clutch by a rack-and-pinion mechanism that is actuated by an adjustable eccentric on the press–crankshaft.

These feeds are available in several types and sizes to suit almost any width and thickness of stock. Although their initial cost is slightly higher, they are preferred because of their greater durability and lower maintenance cost.

Questions

1. A circular part having 80 mm diameter is to be cut from a 2.00 mm thick cold rolled (half hard) steel sheet by blanking operation. Determine

   i. The appropriate sizes of the punch and die.

   ii. Theoretical and actual blanking force.

   You may take shearing strength of the material as 300 MPa.

2. Determine the feasibility of using a 2.5 mm sheet metal to form a 50 mm high cylindrical cup with inside diameter 70 mm. The starting blank is of 140 mm diameter.

3. Differentiate between

   i. Piercing and punching operation of making a hole in sheet metal

   ii. Piercing, punching and blanking operations

   iii. Coining and embossing

4. What do you understand by formability of a material? Describe any cupping test to determine the same.

5. Explain the process of sheet metal shearing operation done with a punch and die. What is the importance of giving proper clearance between the punch and the die?

6. Explain with the help of suitable sketches the difference between punching and perforating operations. Give applications of the two operations.

7. Describe the blanking operation with a die and punch. Can a better component layout yield maximum number of parts with minimum scrap? Give an example to prove your answer.

8. A hole, 50 mm in diameter, is to be punched in an MS plate 5 mm thick. Piercing is complete at 40% penetration of the punch and the radial clearance on the tooling being 8% of the material thickness. Take ultimate shear stress of the material as 500 MN/m^2 and capacity of the available press as 200 kN. Determine

   i. Suitable punch and die diameters.

   ii. Shear angle necessary if the aforementioned press is to be used.

9. What do you understand by minimum bend radius for a sheet material?

   A 25 mm wide, 150 mm long and 4 mm thick mild steel sheet is required to be bent at the middle of its length at 60° and at a bend radius of 10 mm. Determine the bend allowance.

Fill in the Blanks

1. The formability of material depends on properties of material such as _____, _____ and _____.

2. As the temperature of material is increased, _____ and _____ of material reduce while the _____ of material increases.

3. In blanking operation, the clearance between the die and punch is a function of _____ of the sheet and _____ of sheet material.

4. For blanking operation, die size is _____ blank size, and the punch is made _____ by the amount of clearance.

5. As a sheet metal is bent, its fibres at the outside convex surface come in _____, while the inner fibres come in _____.

6. In sheet metal bending operation, *bend allowance* is the length of the _____ in the bend.

7. In sheet metal bending operation, *minimum bend radius* depends on the sheet material, its thickness and _____.

8. _____ is a severe metal squeezing operation in which the flow of metal occurs only at the top layers of the material and not throughout the material.

Choose the Correct Answer

1. Formability of a material may be defined as the
   a. ease with which material may be given a shape within the elastic limit of the material.
   b. ease with which material may be given a shape beyond the elastic limit of the material.
   c. force with which material may be given a shape within the elastic limit of the material.
   d. force with which material may be given a shape beyond the elastic limit of the material.

2. Formability of a material does not depend on
   a. its yield strength.
   b. its strain hardening rate.
   c. its ductility.
   d. its thickness.

3. For sheet metal cutting operations, the clearance between the punch and the die should be
   a. 1 to 2 mm.
   b. 2 to 5 mm.
   c. 1 to 2% of punch diameter.
   d. 2 to 10% of sheet thickness.

4. In sheet metal cutting operations, if the clearance between the punch and the die is less than optimum value,
   a. the cutting force required is also less.
   b. the heat generated is less.
   c. the slug formed has double burnishing on the sheared edge.
   d. there is an increase in the size of the blank.

5. In sheet metal cutting, the quality of sheared edge is affected by
   a. punch speed.
   b. punch diameter.
   c. punch material.
   d. sheet thickness.

6. In sheet metal cutting operations, if the punch speed increases
   a. there is corresponding increase in the die speed.
   b. there is improvement in the edge quality.
   c. there is deterioration in the edge quality.
   d. there is no effect on the edge quality.

7. In sheet metal cutting operation, the punch removes a small portion of material from a larger piece. If the small removed piece is the useful part and the rest is scrap, the operation is called
   a. blanking.
   b. punching.
   c. nibbling.
   d. piercing.

8. In sheet metal working with a punch and die, a stripping force develops due to the
   a. springback (or resiliency) of the punched material.
   b. high ductility of the punched material.
   c. high hardness of the punched material.
   d. high tensile strength of the punch material.

9. In sheet metal blanking operation, the blank size equals
   a. die opening size.
   b. punch size.
   c. die opening size plus clearance between the punch and die.
   d. punch size plus clearance between the punch and die.

10. A die and punch has been used for punching operation on a sheet metal of thickness t. The hole size is equal to the
    a. die opening size + t.
    b. punch size.
    c. die opening size plus clearance between the punch and die.
    d. punch size plus clearance between the punch and die.

11. In the calculation for force required for a sheet metal cutting operation, if the shear strength of material is not known, a general practice is to take it as
    a. 30% of its tensile strength.
    b. 50% of its tensile strength.
    c. 70% of its tensile strength.
    d. equal to its tensile strength.

12. The process by which a hole is cut in the sheet metal in such a way that no slug is formed, is called
    a. punching.
    b. blanking.
    c. piercing.
    d. trimming.

13. The name given to the operation by which a small amount of extra metal on casting or forging, called flash is cut off, is
    a. punching.
    c. piercing.
    b. blanking.
    d. trimming.

14. A sheet metal deformation process by which cup-type components are formed by pressing the sheet metal blank against a rotating wooden or metallic forming block of desired shape and applying a series of tool strokes to press the revolving sheet against the former block till the blank acquires the shape of the forming block is called
    a. stretch forming.
    c. stretching.
    b. spinning.
    d. drawing.

15. An operation by which a number of uniformly spaced holes are punched in a sheet of metal is called
    a. blanking.
    c. perforating.
    b. piercing.
    d. nibbling.

16. The operation in which a specified small amount of metal is cut from a blank in such a way that the cutting line of the slug formed necessarily touches one edge of the blank or strip is called
    a. blanking.
    c. piercing.
    b. notching.
    d. nibbling.

17. In a sheet metal deformation operation, as soon as the applied force is removed, the elastic energy in the component causes it to recover its original shape. This elastic recovery is called
    a. honey-combing.
    c. earing.
    b. strain hardening.
    d. springback.

18. If D is the blank diameter and d is the punch diameter, the drawing ratio DR of a cylindrical shaped part is given by
    a. $\dfrac{D-d}{D}$
    c. $\dfrac{d}{D}$
    b. $\dfrac{D-d}{d}$
    d. $\dfrac{D}{d}$

19. Which one of the following is not a defect found in sheet metal drawn parts?
    a. tearing.
    c. earing.
    b. smearing.
    d. scratch.

20. The name given to a sheet metal deformation operation by which different indentation and raised sections can be formed on the two faces of the component, is
    a. coining.
    c. stretching.
    b. embossing.
    d. trimming.

21. Most sheet metal forming operations are carried out with a punch and die commonly termed as
    a. embossing die.
    b. coining die.
    c. compound die.
    d. stamping die.

22. A die that combines the principles of conventional and inverted dies in one station is called
    a. progressive die.
    c. compound die.
    c. complicated die.
    d. solvent die.

23. The cutting force in a sheet metal blanking operation depends on the following mechanical property of the metal
    a. compressive strength.
    b. modulus of elasticity.
    c. shear strength.
    d. tensile strength.

24. Springback in a sheet metal bending operation is the result of
    a. elastic recovery of the metal.
    b. overbending.
    c. overstraining.
    d. yield strength of the metal.

Answers

1. b.	2. d.	3. d.	4. c.	5. a.	6. b.	7. a.	8. a.	9. a.	10. b.
11. c.	12. c.	13. d.	14. b.	15. c.	16. b.	17. d.	18. d.	19. b.	20. a.
21. d.	22. b.	23. c.	24. a.						

13

High Energy Rate Metal Forming Processes

LEARNING OBJECTIVES

After reading this chapter, you should be able to understand the following:

- The basic principles of high energy rate metal forming processes.

- The explosive forming process: its definition, applications and the various techniques by which it is carried out.

- The electro-magnetic forming process – process details and applications.

- The electro-hydraulic forming process – process details and applications.

- The basic principles of high velocity metal forming processes.

- The pneumatic – mechanical forming process.

- The internal combustion forming process.

13.1 Introduction

High energy rate forming (HERF) and high velocity forming (HVF) processes can be differentiated from conventional metal forming processes by their higher speeds of forming. The range of speeds for conventional forming is 0.3 to 5 m/s whereas this range is 30 to 300 m/s in HERF and HVF processes. HVF processes were developed from the principle of the proportionality of kinetic energy of hammers to the square of the velocity. That means high kinetic (mechanical) energy can be delivered to the metal to deform it by using a small weight ram or die at high velocity. This has led to the development of high speed hammers of smaller size (resulting in reduced cost) and shorter stroke (giving higher rate of production). The velocity achievable from these high speed hammers is in the range of 5 to 60 m/s, only limited by the inertia of the moving parts.

The need for forming metals at velocities higher than those available from HVF hammers (or presses) has led to the development of systems that produce high energy at very short times (i.e., high energy rates), such as energy developed when an explosive material is detonated, when interaction of magnetic fields takes place, and when sudden electric discharge occurs in a fluid. The high energy thus produced is transferred directly to the metal to be deformed. As a result, the following HERF processes have emerged.

- Explosive forming

- Electro-magnetic forming

- Electro-hydraulic forming

There are several advantages of using HERF processes of forming: (i) the die costs are low; (ii) the cost of equipment and tooling required is low; (iii) the production cost of components made by such processes is therefore low; (iv) the production rates of parts are higher; (v) parts can be produced within close tolerances; (vi) it is possible to form most materials including titanium and tungsten alloys; (vii) large workpieces out of difficult-to-form metals can be easily formed; (viii) the processes are suitable for a range of production volume such as small numbers, batches or mass production; and (ix) the material does not show any springback effect. The reasons for non-occurrence of springback are: (a) high compression stresses are set up in the work material when it is forced into the die and (b) some small deformation of the die takes place under high pressure that results in a slight over-forming of the workpieces and it thus only appears that no springback has occurred.

There are some limitations of using HERF processes of forming though. These are: (i) there is need for skilled personnel; (ii) highly brittle materials are difficult to form; (iii) controlling the application of high energy is difficult and the die or work may develop cracks; (iv) dies need to be much bigger to withstand high energy rates and shocks and to prevent cracking; and (v) governmental regulations/procedures/safety norms must be followed for handling the source of energy (chemical explosive or electrical).

Applications of HERF processes are many. Some of them are for: (i) bending of thick tubes/pipes (up to 25 mm thick); (ii) crimping of metal strips; (iii) fabrication of radar dishes; (iv) fabrication of elliptical domes used in space applications; (v) making of large plates/parts (up to 25 mm thick) used in ship building; and (vi) cladding of two large plates of dissimilar metals.

Factors to be considered while selecting an HERF process include (a) size of workpiece; (b) geometry of deformed part; (c) behaviour of work material under high strain rates; (d) cost of tooling/die; (e) cycle time; (f) overall capital investment; (g) safety considerations; and (h) energy requirements/source

We shall discuss these processes in detail in the following sections.

13.2 High Energy Rate Forming (HERF) Processes

13.2.1 Explosive forming

Explosive forming is distinguished from conventional forming in the sense that the punch is replaced by a diaphragm and an explosive charge. The charge comprises high-explosive chemicals like TNT, RDX and dynamite, gaseous mixtures or propellants. Explosive forming can be carried out by any of the two techniques: the standoff technique (called unconfined type) and the contact technique (called confined type).

Standoff technique   In this technique, the metal is deformed inside a water tank. The sheet metal blank (workpiece) is clamped over a die and the assembly is lowered into a water tank. The height of water level in the tank should be approximately 2 m above the workpiece surface. The air in the die is pumped out. At some distance from the workpiece, a definite quantity of explosive charge is placed suitably in the water medium, as can be seen in Figure 13.1(a). When the explosive is detonated, a pressure pulse (or a shock wave) of very high intensity is produced [Figure 13.1(b)].

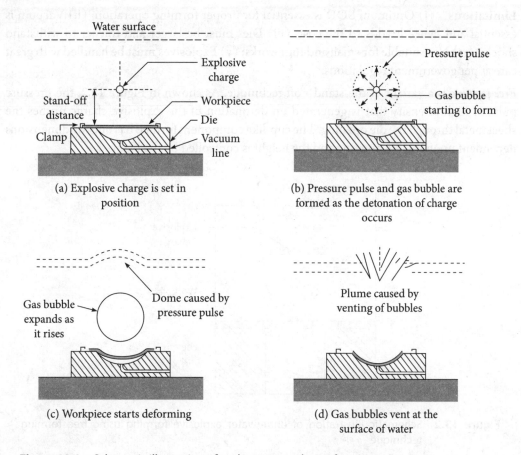

Figure 13.1   Schematic illustration of underwater explosive forming

A gas bubble is also produced, which expands spherically [Figure 13.1(c)] and then collapses. When the pressure pulse impinges against the workpiece, the metal sheet starts deforming into the die with as high velocity as 100 to 120 m/s. A plume is formed with the collapse of the gas bubble, and by then, the component is deformed into the die [Figure 13.1(d)]. The amount of the explosive charge and the distance at which it is placed above the workpiece (i.e., stand - off distance, SOD) is a matter of art and experience. The vacuum is necessary in the die to prevent adiabatic heating of the work that may lead to oxidation or melting.

The water performs numerous functions in the process: (i) It acts as the energy transfer medium; (ii) it ensures a uniform transmission of energy; (iii) it muffles the sound of the explosive blast; and (iv) it ensures smooth application of energy on the workpiece without direct contact.

Advantages (i) A large variety of shapes can be formed; (ii) There is virtually no limit to the size of the workpiece; (iii) It is equally suitable for low as well as high quantity production; (iv) Large and thick parts can be easily formed; (v) Economical for large parts, when compared to using a hydraulic press.

Limitations (i) Optimum SOD is essential for proper forming operation; (ii) Vacuum is essential and hence it adds to the cost; (iii) Dies must be larger and thicker to withstand shocks; (iv) Not suitable for small and thin works; (v) Explosives must be handled with great care as per government regulations.

Free forming is a variant of the stand - off technique. As shown in Figure 13.2, the pressure pulse of high intensity that is generated on detonation of the explosive charge pushes the sheet metal through the die opening. The cup-like component formed has outside dimensions dependent upon the die opening and the height is controlled by the blank size.

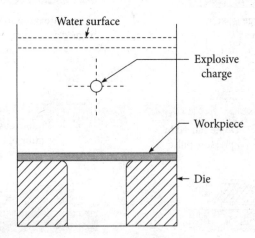

Figure 13.2 Schematic illustration of underwater explosive forming using free forming technique

Applications The process has been successfully used to form steel plates of up to 25 mm thickness and 400 mm length/diameter.

Contact technique The explosive charge in the form of a cartridge is held in direct contact with the workpiece (usually tubular) while the detonation is initiated. The energy is thus directly applied on the work without any water medium. The detonation builds up extremely high pressures (up to 30,000 MPa) on the surface of the metal workpiece, resulting in its instant collapsing into the die cavity. Sometimes, the metal may even fracture. The process is often used for bulging and flaring of tubes, as shown in Figure 13.3.

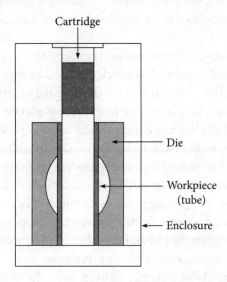

Figure 13.3 Schematic illustration of contact technique of explosive forming

Advantages (i) Entire shock wave front is utilized as there is no loss in water; (ii) More efficient as compared to unconfined type; (iii) Local bulging of tubes is possible; (iv) The required final shape/dimensions are obtained in one stroke (or step), thus eliminating intermediate forming steps and pre-forming dies.

Disadvantages (i) More hazard of die failure; (ii) Vacuum is required in the die; (iii) Air present in the workpiece (tube) is compressed leading to heating; (iv) Not suitable for large and thick plates.

Applications Explosive forming is mainly used for large parts, typically those used in the aerospace industry but it has also found successful applications in the production of automotive components. The process has great potential for prototype forming and for forming of large-sized components for which conventional tooling costs are prohibitively high.

Precautions All production personnel must follow the safety precautions. Explosive forming operations should be carried out away from the main production shop.

13.2.2 Electro-magnetic forming (EMF)

The process, also called *magnetic pulse forming*, is mainly used for swaging type operations, such as fastening the fittings on the ends of tubes and crimping the terminal ends of cables. Other applications include blanking, forming, embossing and drawing.

Principle   The electro-magnetic field of an induced current always opposes the electro-magnetic field of the inducing current. When a large capacitor bank is discharged, it produces a current surge in the coil. If the coil is placed close to the workpiece (i.e., within a conductive tube, around a cylinder or adjacent to a flat sheet of a metal), the discharge induces a secondary current in the workpiece, causing it to be repelled from the coil and conformed to a die or a mating workpiece.

To understand the principle of electro-magnetic forming more clearly, let us consider a bank of capacitors connected in parallel in which electrical energy is stored. Also consider a tubular workpiece mounted on a mandrel having the die cavity corresponding to the shape to be produced on the tubular workpiece. The workpiece is placed into or enveloping a coil [Figure 13.4]. The amount of electrical energy stored in the capacitor bank can be increased either by adding capacitors to the bank or by increasing the voltage. When the charging is complete, which takes very little time, a high voltage switch triggers the stored electrical energy through the coil. A high-intensity magnetic field is established that induces eddy currents into the conductive workpiece, resulting in the establishment of another magnetic field. The forces produced by the two magnetic fields oppose each other with the consequence that there is a repelling force between the coil and the tubular workpiece that repels the work tube causing it to collapse into the die cavity, assuming its shape.

Either permanent or expandable coils may be used. Since the repelling force acts on the coil as well as on the work, the coil itself and the insulation on it must be capable of withstanding the force, or else they will be damaged. Expandable coils are less costly and are preferred when high level energy is needed. The coil can be designed depending upon the application. The same power source can be used for different coils.

Magnetic forming can be accomplished in any of the following three ways, depending upon the requirements.

- **Coil surrounds the workpiece**   When a tube, say, part x is to fit over another part say y, shown as insert in Figure 13.4(a), the coil is designed to surround x so that when energized, it will force the material of x tightly around y to obtain the necessary fit.

- **Coil is placed inside the workpiece**   A collar is fixed on a tube-like part, as shown in Figure 13.4(b). The magnetic coil is placed inside the tube-like part, so that when energized, it will be able to expand the material of the part into the collar.

- **Coil is placed on a flat surface**   A flat coil having a spiral-shaped winding can be designed to be placed either above or below a flat workpiece. For a more detailed overview, see Figure 13.4(c). These coils are used in conjunction with a die in order to form, emboss, blank or dimple the workpiece.

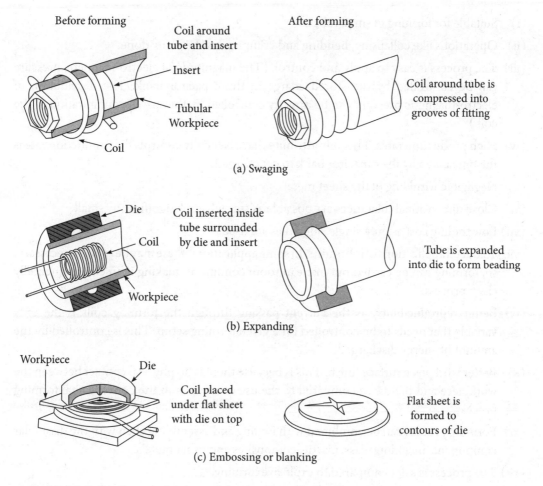

Figure 13.4 Various applications of electro-magnetic forming process

In EMF, the initial gap between the workpiece and the die surface, called the *fly distance*, must be enough to permit the material to deform plastically. From energy considerations, the ideal pressure pulse should be of just enough magnitude to accelerate the part material to some maximum velocity and then let the part come to zero velocity when it has covered the full fly distance.

Precautions All production and maintenance personnel need to strictly follow the safety precautions because extremely high voltages and currents are involved. It is to be noted that all forming coils fail; though, expandable coils fail faster than non-expandable coils.

Advantages The electro-magnetic forming technology has a unique advantage in forming light weight metals such as aluminium because it leads to improved formability and mechanical properties, strain distribution, reduction in wrinkling, control of springback, minimization of distortions at local features, local coining, and need of only a simple die. Other advantages are the following:

(i) Suitable for forming of small tubes.

(ii) Operations like collapsing, bending and crimping can be easily done.

(iii) The process is easy to apply and control. (The magnitude of electro-magnetic pressure can be controlled by the stored charge in the capacitor bank. The distribution of electro-magnetic pressure can be directly controlled by the spatial configuration of the coil.)

(iv) High production rates. The only attribute that essentially controls the production rate is the time taken by the capacitor bank to get charged.

(v) Negligible wrinkling of the sheet metal.

(vi) Close dimensional tolerances are possible as springback is significantly small.

(vii) Low tooling cost as only single sided dies are used.

(viii) Reduced applications of lubricants. In some applications, these may be even unnecessary; so, forming can be carried out in clean room conditions, making it an environmentally clean process.

(ix) Better reproducibility, as the current passing through the forming coils is the only variable that needs to be controlled for a given forming setup. This is controlled by the amount of energy discharged.

(x) Better workpiece surface finish. This is because there is no physical contact between the workpiece and the die as compared to the use of a punch in the conventional forming process.

(xi) Forming process can be combined with joining and assembling even with the dissimilar components including glass, plastic, composites and other metals.

(xii) The process is safer compared to explosive forming.

Limitations   Some limitations of EMF process are:

(i) Applicable only for electrically conducting materials.

(ii) Not suitable for large workpieces.

(iii) Rigid clamping of primary coil is critical.

(iv) Shorter life of the coil due to large forces acting on it.

Applications   The EMF process has a wide variety of forming and assembly applications. Some of these are as follows:

(i) Fabrication of hollow, non-circular and asymmetrical shapes from tubular stock.

(ii) Fabrication of compression, tensile and torque joints, and sealed pressure joints by swaging.

(iii) Fastening components together. For example, clamping of compression bands or shrink rings on other components.

(iv) Fabrication of stretch (internal) and shrink (external) flanges on ring- and disc-shaped work pieces.

(v) Fabrication of components by using operations such as shearing, piercing and riveting.

(vi) Fabrication of high-lift wing panels for Boeing aircraft using permanent coils; it is reported that these products have shown lifetime fatigue resistance.

13.2.3 Electro-hydraulic forming (EHF)

Electro-hydraulic forming (EHF), also known as *underwater electro spark forming*, is a process in which electrical energy is converted into mechanical energy to form metallic parts. A bank of capacitors is first charged to a high voltage. It is then discharged across a gap between two electrodes, inside the hollow workpiece, which is filled with some suitable medium, generally water. The spark produced across the electrodes creates shock waves or pressure pulses that propagate radially in all directions at high velocity until they meet some obstruction. If the discharge energy is sufficiently high, the hollow workpiece is deformed. The deformation can be controlled by applying external restraints in the form of a die or by varying the amount of energy released, as shown in Figure 13.5. The air between the workpiece and the die is usually evacuated before the discharge is allowed. This is done to prevent the possibility of *puckering* due to entrapped air.

The characteristics of this process are similar to those of explosive forming. The major difference, however, is that the chemical explosive is replaced by a spark that creates a shock wave or pressure pulse. The energy released through the spark is much lesser than that released by the detonation of explosive in explosive forming.

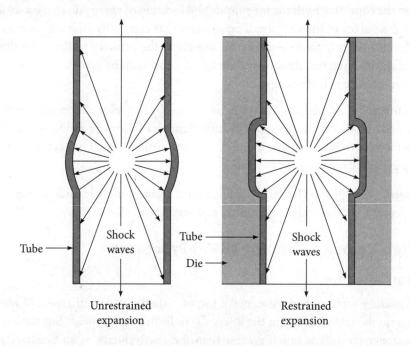

Figure 13.5 Unrestrained and restrained electro-hydraulic forming process

Advantages   Some important advantages of EHF are:

(i)   Better control of the pressure pulse as source of energy is electrical – this can be easily controlled.

(ii) Hollow shapes can be formed quite easily and at quite less cost as compared to other high velocity forming techniques.

(iii) More safe and adaptable to automatic production compared to other high energy rate forming techniques.

(iv) More suitable if the work size is small to medium, not having excessive energy requirements. Parts up to 1 m diameter have been formed.

(v)   Thin sheets can be deformed with smaller amounts of energy.

(vi) The process does not depend on the electrical properties of the work material.

(vii) The process need not be performed in remote areas.

Limitations   Some limitations of the EHF process are as follows:

(i)   Suitable only for smaller workpieces.

(ii) Need for vacuum makes the equipment more complicated.

(iii) Proper SOD is necessary for better process efficiency.

Accuracy of parts produced   The accuracy of the electro-hydraulically formed parts depends on the control of both the magnitude and location of energy discharges as also on the dimensional accuracy of the dies used. Equipment that can easily control the energy within specified limits precisely are now available; therefore, the primary factor is the dimensional accuracy of the die. External dimensions on tubular parts can be achieved within ± 0.05 mm with the current state of technology.

Materials formed   All materials that can be formed by conventional forming processes can also be formed by EHF. These materials include aluminium alloys, nickel alloys, stainless steels and titanium. Materials having low ductility or those with a critical impact velocity less than 30 m/s are generally not suitable for EHF.

Applications   The process has many applications. Some of these include forming of smaller radar dish, cone and other shapes in thinner and small parts.

13.3 High Velocity Forming (HVF) Processes

13.3.1 Introduction

The high velocity forming processes make use of a single or several repeated blows of the upper die onto the material held in the lower die to form a component. But the velocity with which the upper die falls is much greater than the ram velocity of an ordinary press and, therefore these two processes can be considered as high velocity forming processes. The ability of the processes to deliver energy rapidly is responsible for inducing higher strain rates than those associated with conventional techniques. This results in greater formability limits and correspondingly increased mechanical properties, thereby allowing more intricate shapes to be formed than those possible with the conventional metal deformation techniques. The two common HVF processes are described hereunder.

13.3.2 Pneumatic-mechanical forming

In the pneumatic-mechanical forming process, use is made of a pneumatic-mechanical press that can be installed among the more conventional metal-forming equipment, unlike explosive forming which requires a remote work area. The lower die is clamped to the bolster plate of the press bed. The upper die is connected to a reciprocating piston. Gas at pressure p_1 is applied to the bottom of the piston, which holds it up against a small-area seal. On the other side of the seal, gas at pressure p_2 $(p_2 >> p_1)$ is then applied. Pressure p_2 is steadily raised until the force due to p_2 far exceeds the force due to p_1 and the seal is broken. At that instant, the entire area of the piston is exposed to the gas at high pressure p_2, and the piston moves downward at high speed, causing the sheet metal on the lower die to be formed by the upper die.

13.3.3 Internal combustion forming

The internal combustion forming process uses an engine for obtaining high speed and force needed by the upper die to strike the material held in the lower die and form the component part. The lower die is clamped to the bed of a press while the upper die is connected to the piston that reciprocates in a cylinder. Combustion of a gaseous mixture is allowed to occur in the cylinder, which causes the piston to be driven downward at a high speed (up to 20 m/s) with cycle rates up to 60 strokes per minute. A couple of blows are generally sufficient to form a part.

Questions

1. What is the basic principle of high energy rate forming processes? Name and briefly explain the main three high energy rate forming processes. Why is springback too less in high energy rate forming?

2. Distinguish between explosive forming and conventional forming of sheet metal. Explain with suitable sketches, the stand-off technique of explosive forming. Why are the stand-off distance and the location of the explosive charge important for the success of the operation? What functions does water perform?

3. Explain the principle of electro-magnetic forming with the help of a sketch. Give advantages, limitations and various applications of this process.

4. Explain the principle of electro-hydraulic forming process. Compare this process with electro-magnetic forming with respect to advantages, limitations and applications.

5. Write a short note on the accuracy of shapes formed in the electro-hydraulic forming process.

Fill in the Blanks

1. Explosive forming can be carried out by two techniques: (i) _____ technique; and (ii) _____ technique.

2. In stand-off explosive forming, the pressure pulse impinges against the workpiece and the metal is deformed into the die with as high velocity as _____ m/s.

3. In under-water explosive forming, the water performs three main functions: (i) _____, (ii) _____ and (iii) _____.

4. In contact technique of explosive forming, the detonation builds up extremely high pressures of the order of _____ MPa on the surface of the workpiece.

5. From energy considerations, the ideal pressure pulse in electro-magnetic forming should be of just enough magnitude that accelerates the part material to _____ velocity and then let the part come to _____ velocity by the time it completely covers the fly distance.

Choose the Correct Answer

1. Explosive forming is distinguished from conventional forming in that the
   a. punch is replaced by a diaphragm and an explosive charge.
   b. die is replaced by a diaphragm and an explosive charge.
   c. die is replaced by an explosive charge.
   d. punch and die both are replaced by a diaphragm and an explosive charge.

2. High energy rate forming is especially useful to form
   a. small and thin workpieces of any soft material.
   b. large and complex shape workpieces of any soft material.
   c. small and micro-size workpieces out of ductile materials.
   d. large workpieces out of difficult-to-form metals.

3. In high energy rate forming, almost negligible springback is seen because
   a. workpiece material is usually thick.
   b. high compressive stresses are set up in the work material and the die itself expands a bit.
   c. cracks are formed in the workpiece material.
   d. die and punch are not used.

4. The technique of high energy rate forming in which the explosive charge is placed at a distance from the workpiece is called
   a. stand-off technique.   c. pressure technique.
   b. standstill technique.   d. up and down technique.

5. In high energy rate forming using explosives, the work material is deformed into the die at a velocity, which is generally of the order of
    a. 5 to 10 m/s.
    c. 100 to 120 m/s.
    b. 50 to 60 m/s.
    d. 1000 to 1100 m/s.

6. In high energy rate forming using explosives, the height of the water level above the workpiece surface in the tank is generally of the order of
    a. 10 mm.
    c. 500 mm.
    b. 100 mm.
    d. 2000 mm.

7. The high energy rate forming process using explosives is carried out in a water tank. The water functions as
    a. the energy transfer medium.
    b. the lubricating agent.
    c. the transparent medium useful for monitoring the process.
    d. the work material stretching device.

8. The technique of high energy rate forming in which the explosive charge in the cartridge is placed in direct contact with the workpiece is called
    a. contact technique.
    c. Kelvin technique.
    b. cartridge technique.
    d. Parkinson technique.

9. In electro-magnetic forming, the initial gap between the workpiece and the die surface is called the
    a. crow distance.
    c. magnetic gap.
    b. fly distance.
    d. back-to-back distance.

10. Electrohydraulic forming process is also known as
    a. electro spark forming process.
    c. hydro forming process.
    b. electro energy forming process.
    d. hydro mechanical forming process.

11. A high energy forming process in which electrical energy is converted into mechanical energy for the forming of metallic parts is called
    a. electro spark forming process.
    c. hydro forming process.
    b. electro energy forming process.
    d. hydro mechanical forming process.

12. Electro-hydraulic forming is mainly used for the production of
    a. small size parts out of metals with low ductility.
    b. small to intermediate size parts out of metals with high ductility.
    c. large size parts out of hard and brittle metals.
    d. large and complex shape parts out of brittle metals.

13. The following is not a high energy rate or a high velocity forming process:
    a. electro spark forming process
    c. hydro forming process
    b. electro chemical forming process
    d. internal combustion forming process

14. Magnetic pulse forming process is also known as

   a.   explosive forming process.

   b.   inside–outside forming process.

   c.   electro-magnetic forming process.

   d.   AC–DC pulse forming process.

Answers

1. a.   2. d.   3. b.   4. a.   5. c.   6. d.   7. a.   8. a.   9. b.   10. a.

11. a.   12. b.   13. b.   14. c.

14

Powder Metallurgy

LEARNING OBJECTIVES

After reading this chapter, you should be able to understand the following:

- The principle of the powder metallurgy forming process and the typical characteristics of the parts produced by it.

- The advantages, limitations and applications of powder metallurgy as a process of forming metal parts.

- The different steps involved in forming parts by powder metallurgy.

- The various secondary or finishing operations that can be performed on parts made by powder metallurgy.

- The various metal powders used in powder metallurgy and their methods of production.

- The various design considerations of parts to be produced by powder metallurgy.

14.1 Introduction

Powder metallurgy (PM) is a metal working process that forms precision metal components from metal powders. The process is simple to understand, but not so easy to carry out because in order to get consistent product quality, specialized equipment, thorough knowledge of the process, and an extensive amount of experience is required. In simple words, the process has three steps. In the first step, fine metallic and/or non-metallic powder(s) required to give the end product its desired properties are taken and mixed together. The powder mix is introduced into a metal die. In the second step, the powder mix is compressed with high pressure in the die (the operation is called compaction) to produce what is called a *pre-form*. In the third step, this pre-form is heated to a high temperature (the operation is called sintering) in an oven having vacuum or a controlled atmosphere for a finite period to get the final product. A detailed description of the process follows.

14.2 Powder Metallurgy Process Details

Production of parts by the PM process requires the following steps to be carried out in sequence:

- Mixing and blending of metal powders.
- Die filling and powder compacting.
- Sintering.

Powder mixing and blending   A single powder may not fulfil all the requisite properties and hence, powders of different materials with a wide range of mechanical properties are blended to form a final part. A typical example is tungsten carbide–cobalt matrix, which is a material used for cutting tools. It is necessary that powders are properly mixed together. The surface friction properties of the powders to be mixed significantly affect the properties of the mixture. If the powders differ too much in density, segregation of the heavier powder may occur because gravitational forces may be stronger than the frictional forces.

Blending is carried out for several purposes: (i) it permits addition of binders to the mixture of the powder particles to enhance the green strength during the powder compaction process; (ii) it permits mixing of powder particles with alloying elements in a homogeneous form so that a fully pre-alloyed powder has the initial particle hardness and work hardening rate both increased by the alloying addition; (iii) it permits addition of lubricants to (a) improve the flow characteristics of the powder particles (and therefore, even out density variations during compaction), (b) reduce friction between particles and dies, (c) reduce ejection forces, and (d) minimize the tendency for cracking during ejection of the compact.

The temperature during the mixing operation also affects the friction between powder particles. With increasing temperatures, the friction coefficient between materials generally increases and the flow of powders is impaired. It is therefore desirable to maintain lower mixing temperature.

Additives that may be added during mixing and blending of powders seek to meet specific requirements. These additives are:

(i)   *Solid lubricants*, such as graphite and stearates of zinc and aluminium, in small amounts, generally 0.5% to 1% by weight, help in thorough intermingling of the powder particles. The use of lubricant is also necessary to reduce friction between the compact being pressed and the walls of the die and core rod. The actual quantity of lubricants to be used is carefully decided as it affects the flow and apparent density of the powder mixture. Excessive use of lubricants reduces the green strength of the green compact. It is important to note that most of the lubricants get burnt off during sintering, leaving voids, which add to the porosity in the PM product.

(ii) *Blenders*, which help to impart greater strength in the green compact.

(iii) *Deflocculants*, which help to impart better flow characteristics to the metal powder during subsequent compacting.

There are several methods for mixing and blending. Some commonly used methods are shown in Figure 14.1. For best mixing results, these containers should not be filled to more than 50% of their capacity.

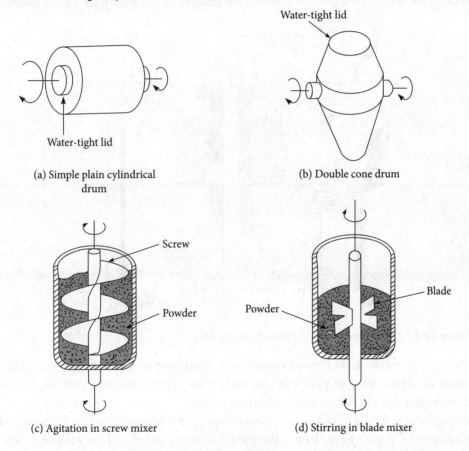

Figure 14.1 Schematic representation of methods of mixing and blending of powders: (a) and (b) show two types of drums; and (c) and (d) show two types of blades used for mixing

Die filling and powder compacting A controlled amount of the mixed powder is introduced into a hardened steel die and then subjected to one of the two processes: (i) it is compressed under high pressure in the range 100 MPa to 1000 MPa with the punch to reduce it to half its original volume or even less; (ii) the die is vibrated to ensure complete die filling. The first of the options is called compacting and is carried out either cold or hot, while the other option is called pressureless forming. The compacted mass of the mixed powder is called a *compact* (or *pre-form*).

The compaction activity results in the following effects: (i) Reduces voids between the power particles and enhances the density of the consolidated powder; (ii) Facilitates plastic deformation of the powder particles to conform to the final desired shape of the part; (iii) Enhances the contact area among the powder particles and facilitates the subsequent sintering process. Some organic binder is usually required to hold the hard particles together after pressing until the sintering process is performed. Figure 14.2 gives a schematic view of the tooling required for the powder compaction process for the manufacture of a bushing.

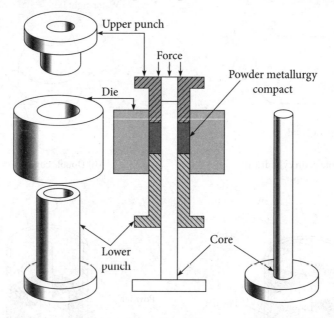

Figure 14.2   Typical set of powder metallurgy tools

The average density in a compact depends, in addition to other factors, on the width and thickness of the component part. For obtaining good compaction, the ratio of *thickness to width* of the part should not exceed 2, wherever possible.

In compaction, the use of a lubricant plays an important role in reducing the friction between powder particles and between the powder particles being pressed and the walls of the die and the core rod. The required compacting pressure depends on the specific characteristics and initial shape of the particles, the method of blending and the application of the lubricants. Extremely hard powders are slower and more difficult to press. The capacity (kN or MN) of the vertical press required for compacting can be estimated simply by multiplying the pressure needed to compact the given metal powder (MPa) by the projected area (mm^2) of the PM part in the horizontal plane, that is,

$$F = p_c . A_p$$

where F = force required to be applied by press, MN; p_c = compaction pressure required to be applied onto the powder, MPa; and A_p = projected area of the part, mm^2. Compaction pressures typically range from 70 MPa (for aluminium powder) to 700 MPa (for iron/steel powders).

Any of the following practices can be followed to produce a compact.

1. ***Cold compacting*** This is the most common practice. Here, the powder mix, at room temperature, is subjected to high compressive pressure. Cold welding between the powder particles occurs, and gives sufficient green strength to the resulting compact so as to permit its removal as one piece from the die. This avoids the need to put the die into the sintering oven. The magnitude of the applied compacting pressure has a major effect upon the tensile strength of the final PM product.

   Figure 14.3 illustrates the compacting cycle for a bushing, which involves the following steps:

   Step 1 The upper punch is in its fully raised position. The lower punch is in its pre-set upper position. The core is held in position. The powder feed chute reaches just over the die opening as shown in Figure 14.3(a), and delivers the required quantity of powder mix.

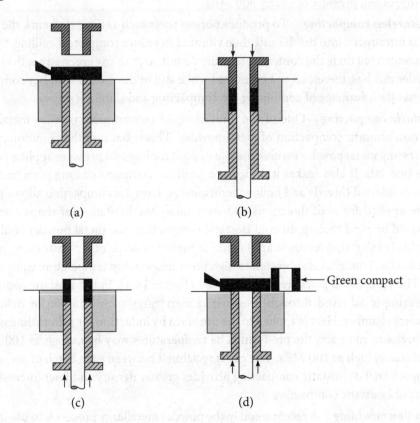

Figure 14.3 Powder metallurgy compacting cycle steps for a typical component

Step 2   The lower punch is brought to the pre-set lower position. The die cavity is filled with the metal powder mix up to the die top. Extra amount of powder mix is removed. The upper punch descends and compresses the powder by a certain definite amount as shown in Figure 14.3(b).

Step 3   The upper punch moves up to its raised position, and the lower punch rises to eject the green compact as shown in Figure 14.3(c).

Step 4   The lower punch reaches its top position. The green compact is out of the die. The powder feed chute reaches the die opening for the next cycle while its front edge clears the compact out of the pressure area of the upper punch as shown in Figure 14.3(d), and delivers the powder mix required for the next cycle. The next cycle can now continue.

   This compacting cycle is almost the same for any shape or size of the product.

2. **Hot compacting**   Some hard metals cannot be cold compacted satisfactorily and must be compacted hot. Compacting and sintering are, thus, combined into one operation. The die material has to withstand typical sintering temperature of 1000°C or more and a compression pressure of nearly 800 MPa.

3. **Pressureless compacting**   To produce porous parts such as filter elements, the powder mix is introduced into the die and then vibrated to ensure complete die filling. Since it is not compacted then, the contents of the die do not acquire any green strength at all. The powder mix has, therefore, to be sintered while still in the die. As with hot compacting, this has the advantage of combining the compacting and sintering steps.

4. **Isostatic compacting**   One of the limitations of conventional powder metallurgy is the non-uniform compaction of metal powder. This is because the common methods of pressing metal powder involve the use of rigid tooling and pressure application along only one axis. It also makes it difficult to produce compacts of long parts and shapes such as internal threads and hollow hemispheres. Isostatic compacting allows pressure to be applied from all directions and overcomes the limitation of shape constraints imposed by rigid tooling. In cold isostatic compacting, the metal powder is filled into moulds (of slightly oversize shape) made of rubber or some other elastomeric material. The flexible container is subjected to high pressures at room temperature using water or oil. The compacted parts are then removed [Figure 14.4]. In hot isostatic compacting, squeezing is achieved through pressurized inert gases such as argon or helium in a pressure chamber. Heat is applied to the pre-form by induction for a short time while the gas pressure compacts the pre-form. The temperatures may be as high as 1000°C and pressures as high as 100 MPa. The gas is reclaimed between each batch of pressings. In comparison, hot isostatic compacting provides greater density and finer microstructure than cold isostatic compacting.

5. **Injection moulding**   A recent trend in the powder metallurgy process is to use injection moulding in place of compaction, particularly when complex-shaped products are to be made. Up to 50% by volume of a thermoplastic material is added to the ultrafine

(< 10 micron size) metal or ceramic powder mix. The mixture is heated in a container to achieve a paste-like consistency. This is then injected into the mould cavity and a necessary pressure (about 70 MPa) is applied. The compact in green state is ejected out of the die.

The binder material and lubricant, initially added in the metal powder, are removed by solvent extraction technique or by evaporation (by heating to the volatilization temperature). The main advantages of injection moulding are: (i) relatively much higher density (>95% of ideal), (ii) uniformity of higher density throughout the component and (iii) close tolerances (< 0.5%). The compact is thereafter subjected to conventional sintering.

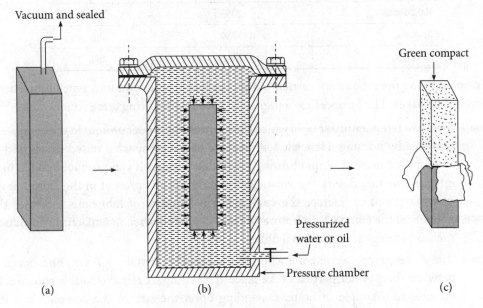

Figure 14.4   Isostatic compacting. (a) Powder mix is filled inside a flexible container; vacuum is applied; container is sealed. (b) Powder filled container is placed in a pressure chamber into which pressurized water or oil is pumped. (c) Container is removed; stripped off to obtain green compact

Sintering   During this step, the green compact or the pre-form is heated in a furnace to a suitable temperature, which is below the melting point of the metal. The furnace has a protective atmosphere. Typical sintering atmospheres are endothermic gas, exothermic gas, dissociated ammonia, hydrogen and nitrogen. Vacuum sintering is common for stainless steel, titanium and refractory metals. Sintering temperature varies from metal to metal; typically, these are within 70% to 90% of the melting point of the metal or alloy. If the component part is composed of more than one material, the sintering temperature may even be above the melting temperature of one or more constituent materials. The lower-melting temperature materials, in that case, melt and flow into the voids between the particles of remaining powder. Table 14.1 gives the general guidelines for sintering temperature and time used for various metals. In actual practice, sintering time varies with the size of the part.

Table 14.1   Temperature and time for sintering various metal powders

Material	Sintering temperature (°C)	Time (minutes)
Copper, brass, bronze	760–900	10–40
Nickel	1000–1150	30–40
Stainless steel	1100–1290	30–60
Ferrites	1200–1500	10–600
Tungsten carbide	1430–1500	20–30
Molybdenum	2050	120
Tungsten	2350	480
Tantalum	2400	480

Most sintering operations are carried out in batches or in continuous type atmosphere-controlled furnaces. The furnaces are designed to have the following three zones.

Zone 1 It is a low temperature zone in which the lubricant or binder present in the compact is removed by burning. Here the temperature of the compact is raised slowly and in a controlled manner. Rapid heating is avoided because it can produce sudden high internal pressure due to the volatilization of lubricants present in the closed pores that may swell or fracture the compact. The removal of lubricants increases the porosity of the compact – a feature which is exploited when manufacturing products such as bearing races and metal filters.

Zone 2 It is a high temperature zone where the desired solid-state diffusion and bonding between the powder particles take place. The compact remains in this zone for 15 minutes to a couple of hours depending upon the size of the compact and the characteristics of the metal powders of which the compact is made of.

Zone 3 It is the cooling zone where the temperature of the product is slowly brought down under a controlled atmospheric condition. This zone is responsible for preventing (i) thermal stresses and strains, and (ii) oxidation of the part.

The structure and porosity obtained in a sintered compact depends on the sintering temperature, time and processing details. It is not possible to completely eliminate porosity because voids cannot be completely closed by compaction. Further, gases formed during sintering need to escape through the voids.

14.3 Secondary and Finishing Operations

Sometimes, additional operations called secondary operations are carried out on sintered PM parts in order to further improve their properties, precision or to impart special characteristics. Some common secondary operations are as follows.

- **Coining and sizing** These are high pressure compacting operations, and are carried out to impart: (i) greater dimensional accuracy to the sintered part; and (ii) greater strength and better surface finish by further densification. The need for these operations arises because during sintering, shrinkage of part occurs (due to densification). Further, warping or distortion can also occur as the part cools down from a high sintering temperature.

- **Forging** The sintered PM parts may be hot or cold forged to obtain the exact shape, better surface finish, better dimensional tolerances, and a uniform and fine grain size. The changes are basically derived from the plastic flow of the metal that occurs during the operation. Forging also increases the density of the part, often up to 99% of theoretical density and appreciably improves the mechanical properties. Forged PM parts are being increasingly used for such applications as highly stressed components of jet engine, turbine and automobiles.

- **Impregnation** The inherent porosity of PM parts is utilized for impregnating them with a fluid such as an oil or grease. A typical application of this operation is for sintered bearings and bushings that are internally lubricated with up to 30% oil by volume by simply immersing them in heated oil and applying pressure. Such components have a continuous supply of lubricant by capillary action during their extended lifetime of operation. The universal joint is a typical grease-impregnated PM part. PM parts have also been impregnated with fluorocarbon resin (such as teflon) in order to improve the strength and reduce the surface friction.

- **Infiltration** The pores of the sintered part are filled with some low melting point metal with the result that the part's hardness and tensile strength get improved. A slug of metal to be impregnated is kept in close contact with the sintered component and together they are heated to the melting point of the slug. The molten metal infiltrates the pores by capillary action. When the process is complete, the component has greater density, hardness and strength. Copper is often used for the infiltration of iron-based PM components. Lead has also been used to infiltrate into components like bushes for which lower frictional characteristics are needed. Infiltration may also be used to seal pores prior to plating or to make the part gas or liquid tight.

- **Heat treatment** Sintered PM components may be heat-treated for obtaining greater hardness or strength in them. Use of protective atmosphere is necessary when heat treating low density PM parts. Special care must be exercised while selecting liquid quenching media for heat treatment of PM parts.

- **Machining** The sintered component may be machined by turning, milling, drilling, threading, grinding, etc., to obtain accurate geometric features. Machining is rarely done to size the part but to create features that are not possible to achieve by pressing, such as internal and external threads, side holes, etc.

- **Finishing**   Almost all commonly used finishing operations can be carried out on PM parts. Some of these operations are plating, burnishing, coating and colouring.

   - *Plating*   For improved appearance and resistance to wear and corrosion, the sintered compacts may be plated by electroplating or other plating processes. To avoid penetration and entrapment of plating solution in the pores of the component, an impregnation or infiltration treatment is often necessary before plating. Copper, zinc, nickel, chromium and cadmium plating can also be done on PM parts.

   - *Burnishing*   To work-harden the surface or to improve the surface finish and dimensional accuracy, burnishing may be done on PM parts. It is relatively easier to displace metal on PM parts than on wrought parts because of surface porosity in PM parts.

   - *Coating*   PM sintered parts are more susceptible to environmental degradation than cast and machined parts. This is because of interconnected porosity in PM parts. Coating can be done on PM parts to fill in the pores and seal the entire reactive surface.

   - *Colouring*   Ferrous PM parts can be applied colour for protection against corrosion. Several methods are in use for colouring. One common method to blacken the ferrous PM parts is to do it chemically using a salt bath.

- **Joining**   PM parts can be welded by any conventional method. Electric resistance welding is better suited than oxy-acetylene welding and arc welding because of oxidation of the interior porosity. Argon arc welding is commonly used for joining stainless steel PM parts.

14.4 Metal Powders for Powder Metallurgy

Metal powders play an extremely important role in powder metallurgy. The particle size, shape and size distribution of the metal powder affect the characteristics and properties of the compacted product. A large number of types and grades of powders are available that enable the production of a wide variety of components to meet the numerous performance requirements. All metals can be produced in powder form but not all of them have the desired properties that are necessary for economical production. Some widely used metal powders for manufacturing PM parts are listed in Table 14.2.

Table 14.2 Some widely used metal powders

Pure metals		Alloys	Compounds
Aluminum	Molybdenum	Aluminium–iron	Borides (chromium, tungsten, etc.)
Antimony	Nickel	Brass	Carbides (molybdenum, tungsten, etc.)
Beryllium	Precious metals (gold, silver)	Copper–zinc–nickel	Molybdenum disilicide
Bismuth	Rhenium	Nickel–chromium	Nitrides (silicon, titanium, etc.)

Contd.

Table 14.2 Contd.

Pure metals		Alloys	Compounds
Cadmium	Silicon	Nickel–chromium–iron	Zirconium hydride
Chromium	Tantalum	Nickel–copper	
Cobalt	Tin	Nickel–iron	
Copper	Titanium	Silicon–iron	
Iron	Tungsten	Lead–tin	
Lead	Vanadium	Stainless steel	
Manganese	Zinc		

14.4.1 Powder production

All metal powders, because of their individual physical and chemical characteristics, cannot be produced in the same way. There are several methods for producing metal powders, each of which results in different size and structure of the particles. Table 14.3 gives the important characteristics of powders produced by some commercial methods. A brief description of some of these methods follows.

Automization It is an excellent and widely used method of producing metal powders. Atomization involves the disintegration of a thin stream of molten metal through the impingement of high energy jets of a fluid (liquid or gas). The technique for ferrous metals is different from that for non-ferrous metals. For ferrous metals, water is the most commonly used liquid in atomization. Water atomized iron powders have irregular particle shape and therefore, offer good green strength. The individual powder particles do not contain internal porosity and, therefore have superior compressibility. Water atomized powders are usually the choice where high green density is needed in PM structural parts.

Table 14.3   Metal powder characteristics

- **Apparent density** The apparent density or specific gravity of a powder is expressed in kg/m³. It should generally remain constant. This means that the same amount of powder should be fed into the die every time.

- **Chemical properties** These properties include the purity of the powder, amount of oxides permitted and the percentage of other elements allowed.

- **Compressibility** Compressibility is the ratio of the volume of initial powder to the volume of the compressed piece. It varies considerably and is affected by the particle shape and size distribution. Compressibility affects the green strength of a compact.

- **Fineness** Fineness refers to the particle size and is estimated by passing the powder through a standard set of sieves or by microscopic measurement.

- **Flowability** The flowability is the characteristic of a powder that permits it to flow readily and conform to the mould cavity. It can be estimated by the rate of flow through a fixed orifice.

- **Particle-size distribution** Particle-size distribution refers to the amount of each standard particle size in the powder. It influences the flowablity and apparent density as well as porosity of the product.

- **Sintering ability** Sintering ability refers to the suitability of a powder for bonding of particles by the application of heat.

Non-ferrous metal powders are produced by a variety of means, the most significant one uses an inert gas as the atomizing fluid. In inert gas atomization, the particle shape produced is dependent on the time available for surface tension to take effect on the molten droplets prior to solidification and, if a low heat capacity gas is used (nitrogen and argon are most common), this time is extended and spherical powder shapes result. Spherical powders are particularly useful in hot isostatic pressing, where green strength is not an issue but initial packing density of the powder in the die is significant. Spherical metallic powders of titanium and other metals can also be produced by plasma atomization process, which uses argon plasma torches at >10,000°C to melt and atomize the metal into fine droplets. The process has the distinction of producing highly flowable high temperature metal powder using wire as its feedstock. This method ensures a high level of traceability allowing the production of parts for applications in the biomedical and aerospace sectors.

Another branch of the 'atomization family' comprises a number of centrifugal atomization processes. There are essentially two types of such processes – in the first type, a cup of molten metal is rotated at high speed or a molten stream of metal is allowed to fall onto a rotating disc or cone; in the second type, the rotating electrode process (REP), a bar of metal is rotated and the free end is progressively melted by an arc from a tungsten electrode. If a plasma arc is involved, the process is known as PREP (plasma rotating electrode process) and this is the best method for titanium powder production.

Electrolysis   Electrolysis is a common technique of producing powders of copper, silver and several other metals. In this technique, powders are produced by following the principles used in electroplating, with the conditions changed to produce a loose powdery deposit rather than a smooth adherently solid layer. The formation of powder deposits that adhere loosely to the cathode is favoured by low metal ion concentration in the electrolyte, high acid concentration and high cathode current density. The starting material is a pure metal anode.

Reduction   In this process, the metal oxide is reduced to metal powder through contact with a reducing gas at a temperature below the melting point of the metal. For example, in case of iron, the iron oxide is crushed and passed through a furnace. The hydrogen atmosphere in the furnace reacts with the oxygen of iron oxide at a temperature of nearly 1050°C and pure iron with a sponge-like structure is obtained. Other metal powders produced commercially through this method are those of nickel, cobalt, molybdenum and tungsten.

The carbonyl process has been used for the production of fine nickel or iron powders. In this process, the crude metal is reacted with CO under pressure to form the carbonyl, which is gaseous at the reaction temperature, but decomposes to deposit the metal on raising the temperature and lowering the pressure.

Machining and grinding   Machining has been used to produce coarse magnesium powder. Milling and grinding processes utilize various types of rotary mills, stamping mills, crushers and grinders to break down brittle metals into powders of almost any fineness; but, the particles are of irregular shape.

Metal powders can also be produced by several other methods that employ precipitation, condensation and other chemical processes.

14.5 Advantages of Powder Metallurgy

Metal in its powder form is more expensive than in its solid form. Further, expensive dies and equipment needed to use this process imply that the process has to be justified by the unusual properties obtained in the products. Powder metallurgy offers the following specific advantages:

- **Composition variety** Parts can be made from a variety of compositions. Bi-metallic products, sintered carbides and porous bearings can be produced only through this process.

- **Refractory metals** Parts can be produced from high melting point refractory metals with relatively less difficulty and at lesser cost.

- **Impregnation and infiltration** Parts can be produced with impregnation (by oil or plastic) and infiltration with other materials so as to obtain the special characteristics needed for specific applications.

- **Controlled porosity** Parts with controlled porosity can be produced. Porosity up to 50% is possible.

- **Surface finish** Most sintered parts have a very good surface finish and accuracy and do not require any post-sintering operation. This is advantageous as some material combinations like diamond matrices and the hard metal carbides of tungsten and titanium are extremely difficult to machine.

- **Desirable properties** By changing the composition of the part, it is far easier to have parts of desired mechanical and physical properties such as density, hardness, toughness, stiffness, damping and specific electrical or magnetic properties. Damping of noise and vibration can be tailored into a PM part.

- **Near-net shape** Near-net shape components can be produced. The dimensional tolerances on components are mostly such that no further machining is needed.

- **Post-process operations** PM parts can be forged, electroplated heat treated or machined if needed.

- **Low scrap** Scrap is almost negligible. About 95% of the starting powders are converted into product.

- **Low cost** Skilled machinists are not needed, so labour cost is low. Since material scrap is low, overall product cost is also low.

- **High production rate** Production rates are high even for complex parts. Component uniformity and reproducibility are among the highest in manufacturing. This is primarily because of the use of automated equipment in the process.

14.6 Limitations of Powder Metallurgy

Powder metallurgy has the following limitations:

- **High cost of powder**   Metal powders have a high cost compared to the cost of raw material used for casting or forging a component. A few powders are even difficult to store without some deterioration.

- **High tooling and equipment cost**   The cost of tooling and equipment is high. In case of small production volumes, the product cost may become quite high.

- **Not all shapes and sizes**   Parts of large sizes or complex shapes are difficult to produce. Re-entrant shapes or cored holes normal to the axis of compaction are not possible. Component thickness to width ratio is limited to 3:1. Thin vertical sections are difficult to produce.

- **Part weight limitation**   Although, parts weighing up to 20 kg can be produced, most PM parts are less than 2 kg in weight.

- **Lower corrosion resistance**   PM products are porous, and therefore have larger exposed surface to any corrosive atmosphere than solid metal products.

- **Lower properties**   Parts have lower ductility and impact strength than those produced by forging. Sintered parts can be brittle.

- **Non-uniform density**   Parts of uniformly high-density are difficult to produce. The non-uniform product density results in property variation throughout the part.

- **Fire and health hazard**   Some powders (such as aluminium, magnesium, titanium and zirconium) in a finally divided state present fire hazard and risk of explosion. Some metal powders are difficult to store and handle. Fine particles of metal can also remain airborne for considerable amount of time and cause lung problems to workers.

- **Sintering difficulties**   Low melting point metal powders (such as those of zinc, tin, cadmium) give thermal difficulties during the sintering operation. This is because most oxides of such metals cannot be reduced at temperatures below their melting point.

14.7 Applications of Powder Metallurgy

There is a great variety of components that can be produced by powder metallurgy. Most of these parts are put to use without any machining or finishing operation carried out on them. While most PM products are less than 50 mm in size, several products have been produced with a weight up to 40 kg and linear dimensions up to half a metre. Following are some of the prominent powder metallurgy products along with their applications.

Porous products   Under this category, filters and bearings are quite common. Filters made by powder metallurgy have greater strength and shock resistance than ceramic filters. Powder metallurgy filters can be made with pores of almost any size, some as small as 0.005 mm. Fibre metal filters, having porosity up to 95% are used for filtering or separating air and fluids. These filters also find use in dehydrators for diffusing moisture-laden air around some drying agent such as silica gel as shown in Figure 14.5. Use can be made of metal filters in petrol/diesel engines for separating dirt and moisture in the fuel system. Other applications of metal filters are for arresting flame and for attenuating sound.

Oil-impregnated bearings are very common PM products. Bearing and bushes used with rotating parts are made from copper powder mixed with graphite. In small quantities, lead, tin or Babbitt metal may also be added for obtaining better wear resistance. After sintering, the bearings are sized and then impregnated with oil by vacuum treatment. Such bearings have large applications for automobile and aircraft engines. Porosity in the bearings may be as high as 40% of the volume.

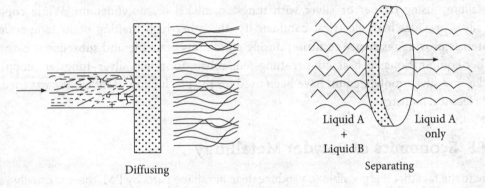

Diffusing   Separating

Figure 14.5 Applications of powder metallurgy parts. Filters can be used for diffusing or for separating

Several machinery parts including gears, rotors and sprockets are made by powder metallurgy from the mixture of metal powders and graphite. Addition of graphite provides desired carbon content in the product. The parts generally have nearly 20% porosity. The pores of the parts, whose surfaces are to rub against the surface of another part, are impregnated with oil to promote quiet operation.

Parts of complex shape   When made by other manufacturing processes, complex-shaped parts require considerable amount of machining. Powder metallurgy parts have relatively greater accuracy and surface finish, and therefore need no further processing. Several complex-shaped parts of small size are made by powder metallurgy process. Examples of such parts are clutch plates, brake drums, ball retainers and cams.

Parts made from materials that have high melting point or are difficult to machine Common products of this category are cutting tools and dies. Cemented carbide cutting tool inserts are produced by PM from tungsten carbide powder mixed with a cobalt binder. These cutting tools find extensive applications in machine shops. Cemented carbide dies are extensively used in press shops as they have a comparatively long life.

Friction materials   Powder metallurgy process can be used to produce (i) friction materials in the form of bi-metal powder materials that are bonded to a steel base and (ii) aluminium-based antifriction materials containing iron, copper and graphite.

Magnets   Small magnets can be produced from different compositions of powders of iron, aluminium, nickel and cobalt. The magnets produced by PM have shown far superior performance as compared to those produced by casting or other manufacturing processes.

Electrical parts   Some electrical contact parts are required to have excellent electrical conductivity, good wear resistance and sufficient refractoriness. The possibility of combining several metal powders and maintaining characteristics of each has promoted powder metallurgy for production of such parts. Copper and graphite are frequently combined in such applications as motor/generator bushes, copper providing the current carrying capacity while graphite providing the lubrication. Electrical contacts are mostly made by powder metallurgy using copper or silver with tungsten, nickel or molybdenum. While copper or silver provides high electrical conductivity, the other high melting point temperature materials provide resistance to fusion during conditions of arcing and subsequent closure. Other combinations such as copper–tungsten, cobalt–tungsten, silver–tungsten, copper–nickel and silver–molybdenum have been used for the production of different parts used in the electrical industry.

14.8 Economics of Powder Metallurgy

Due to the fact that it is possible to produce near-net shape parts by PM, there is usually very little scrap and, correspondingly, no need for secondary manufacturing or finishing operations, PM is becoming increasingly competitive to conventional manufacturing processes like forging, casting and machining. The high initial cost of dies, punches and equipment for PM processing however, requires sufficiently high production volume to make this process cost-effective. Generally, minimum quantities of 10,000 units are suggested, although exceptions exist.

14.9 Design Considerations for Powder Metallurgy Products

The following recommendations regarding the shape of the part should be kept in mind while designing parts to be made by PM. The shape and size of the component part should be so designed that they:

- do not require the powder to flow into thin walls, narrow passages or sharp corners.
- permit ejection from the die; perpendicular side walls are preferred.
- permit construction of strong and rigid tooling.
- take into account the length to which the thin-walled portion of the part can be compacted.

- have the fewest possible changes in section thickness.
- are compatible with the equipment available.
- take advantage of the fact that certain shapes can be produced by powder metallurgy that are either impractical or uneconomical to produce by any other manufacturing process.
- take into account the compensation for the dimensional changes that normally occur after compaction; for example, the shrinkage of size and warping during sintering.
- take into account product tolerances; greater precision and repeatability may be expected in the punch pressing direction (axial) than in the radial or perpendicular direction.

Questions

1. Describe a suitable process for the manufacture of a range of metallic oil filter elements.
2. List the advantages, disadvantages and limitations of PM products as compared to those of products manufactured by closed-die forging.
3. Compare the scope of PM process with that of investment casting.
4. Describe any three methods of producing metal powders.
5. Should green compacts of PM parts be heated up to the sintering temperature slowly or rapidly? Give reasons for your answer.
6. Why do the compacting pressure and the sintering temperature depend on the type of metal powder?
7. For what types of parts is powder metallurgy injection moulding recommended? Why?
8. Why is it necessary to provide protective environment during sintering? What can happen if sintering is done in the normal environment?
9. Powder metallurgy products have low strength. How serious is this limitation? What can be done to overcome this?
10. Discuss the three stages commonly associated with the sintering operation.
11. What are the changes that can occur to the PM compact during sintering operation? Describe the three zones of furnaces used for sintering PM compacts.
12. Discuss the effect of addition of a lubricant to the metal powder mix on (i) compressibility, and (ii) green strength of PM compact. What special effect does the graphite lubricant have over other lubricants used in PM?
13. What is pressureless compacting? Discuss its applications in PM.
14. Discuss the similarity and differences between *impregnation* and *infiltration*, the terms as used in PM.
15. Is it possible to infiltrate PM parts with various metals as well as resins? What possible applications can there be from resin infiltration? Explain.
16. It is possible to impregnate PM parts with a fluid. What possible applications can there be for oil impregnated parts? Explain.

17. Describe any three methods by which metal powders for PM are manufactured.

18. Give advantages and limitations of powder metallurgy.

19. Sometimes, additional operations called secondary operations are carried out on sintered PM parts in order to further improve their properties, precision or to impart special characteristics. Briefly explain any five secondary operations and give their specific usages.

20. Write short notes on:
    i.   Applications of PM parts.
    ii. Pressureless forming of PM products.
    iii. Design considerations for PM parts.
    iv. Economics of powder metallurgy.

Fill in the Blanks

1. Cold compacting of metal powders in PM is usually carried out in the pressure range of _____ to _____ MPa.

2. Physical and mechanical properties of PM parts mainly depend on _____ of PM parts.

3. The bigger the particle size of metal powder, the more _____ will be the PM part.

4. _____ is a process of metal powder production in which a stream of molten metal is forced through a small nozzle and then disintegrated by a jet of water or gas.

5. Pressureless forming is particularly used for the manufacture of _____ parts.

6. Component thickness to width ratio of PM parts is generally limited to _____.

7. Powder metallurgy is the manufacturing process in which scrap produced is of the order of_____%.

8. Bearings and bushes are generally manufactured by PM wherein _____ is generally combined with iron or copper, or the mixture of the two metals such as tin and copper.

9. _____ is the process by which a lower melting point metal is introduced into a PM product with or without the use of pressure.

10. _____ is the process by which oil or some other liquid is forced into the porous PM product.

11. _____ is an operation in which the pressed-powder compacts are heated in a controlled atmosphere so as to achieve solid-state diffusion.

12. Injection moulding of PM products involves application of pressure of the order of _____ MPa.

13. Uniform compaction of metal powders can be promoted by increasing the amount of _____ in the powder.

14. Compacting pressures of metal powder generally range between _____ MPa to _____ MPa.

15. When added in a metal powder, _____ plays a dual role, serving as a lubricant during compacting, and a source of carbon in the alloy material of the PM part.

16. Sintering operation and subsequent cooling of a PM product is done in a controlled-atmospheric environment in order to prevent _____.

Choose the Correct Answer

1. In the powder metallurgy process, a powder mix is compressed in a die under heavy pressure to produce what is called
   a. soft part.
   c. sintered part.
   b. powder metallurgy product.
   d. pre-form.

2. The lubricants used in the powder-mix should not generally exceed
   a. 0.5% to 1% by weight.
   b. 5% to 10% by weight.
   c. 10% to 20% by weight.
   d. 20% to 30% by weight.

3. In powder metallurgy process, the compacting of powder
   a. must be done under pressure only at room temperature.
   b. must be done under pressure only at high temperature.
   c. may be done under pressure at room temperature or higher temperatures.
   d. may be done under pressure or no pressure at room temperature or higher temperatures.

4. In the powder metallurgy process, the sintering of pre-form must be done
   a. only in factory environment.
   b. only in vacuum environment.
   c. only in atmospheric-controlled environment.
   d. only in vacuum or atmospheric-controlled environment.

5. During the sintering operation of powder metallurgy, rapid heating of pre-form is avoided because
   a. it increases the cost.
   b. it can produce sudden high internal pressure due to volatilization of lubricant.
   c. it can lead to evaporation of liquid lubricant present in the pre-form.
   d. it can create diffusion of particles of metal powder.

6. After the sintering operation of powder metallurgy, rapid cooling of pre-form is avoided because
   a. it prevents thermal stresses and strains.
   b. it creates diffusion of particles of metal powder.

c.   recycling of heat becomes difficult.

d.   handling of hot parts can cause accidents.

7.   Sintered powder metallurgy components

a.   cannot be forged.

b.   can be only hot forged, if forging is to be done on them.

c.   can be only cold forged, if forging is to be done on them.

d.   can be hot forged or cold forged.

8.   The process by which liquid oil or grease is filled in the pores of a sintered powder metallurgy product is called

a.   infiltration.

b.   impregnation.

c.   infusion.

d.   integration.

9.   The process by which some low melting point metal is filled in the pores of a sintered powder metallurgy product is called

a.   infiltration.

b.   impregnation.

c.   infusion.

d.   integration.

10.   Sintered powder metallurgy components

a.   cannot be coated.

b.   cannot be electroplated.

c.   cannot be welded.

d.   can be coated, electroplated or welded.

11.   For joining of powder metallurgy components, the best suited process is

a.   oxy-acetylene welding.

b.   arc welding.

c.   electric resistance welding.

d.   thermit welding.

12.   Which one of the following is not a method of powder production?

a.   atomization

b.   electrolysis

c.   reduction

d.   oxidation

13.   PM products are porous, and therefore

a.   they have high resistance to corrosion.

b.   they have low resistance to corrosion.

c.   they cannot be forged.

d.   they cannot be electroplated.

14. Which of the following shape of powder particles would tend to have the lowest inter-particle friction?

a. spherical

b. flaky

c. cubic

d. triangular

Answers

1. d.   2. a.   3. d.   4. d.   5. b.   6. a.   7. d.   8. b.   9. a.   10. d.

11. c.   12. d.   13. b.   14. a.

15

Introduction to Joining Processes

LEARNING OBJECTIVES

After reading this chapter, you should be able to understand the following:

- The various joining processes.

- The adhesive bonding process: procedure, advantages, limitations and applications.

- The mechanical fastening process: advantages, limitations and applications.

- The brazing process: procedure, types, advantages, limitations and applications.

- The filler metals and fluxes used in brazing.

- The various methods of brazing.

- The soldering process: procedure, various characteristics and applications.

- The details of solder materials and fluxes used in the soldering process.

- The welding process: advantages and limitations, metallurgy of welding and heat affected zone.

- The types of fusion welds and weld joints.

- The classification of welding processes and the factors affecting the selection of an appropriate welding process.

15.1 Introduction

A majority of the products that we use and see around us every day, whether they are industrial products, home appliances or even products of personal use, are created by assembling a number of component parts. Depending upon the need, the component parts are joined together either permanently or in such a way that they can be subsequently dissembled for maintenance, repair or other purposes. It is very important that engineers should be aware of the large variety of available joining processes and understand the fundamental principles involved in each process. They should also appreciate the advantages and limitations of each process so that better products can be produced at low cost and made available to society.

Different joining processes employed in manufacturing are as follows:

- Adhesive bonding
- Mechanical fastening
- Thermal joining
  - Soldering
  - Brazing
  - Welding
  - Shrink fitting

15.2 Adhesive Bonding

In current times, adhesives are increasingly being used to produce reliable joints on metals and non-metals. The term *adhesive bonding* refers to a joining process in which a filler material (called adhesive), in the form of liquid or a semi-solid state material, is applied between the faying surfaces of the workpieces (adherends) to be joined. Either heat or pressure or both are applied to bond the surfaces. To make an effective adhesive joint, the procedure involves four essential steps. These steps are: (i) preparation of the surfaces; (ii) application of the adhesive on to the mating surfaces; (iii) assembly of workpieces/parts; and (iv) curing the joint.

Surface preparation   Cleanliness of the joining surfaces of workpieces is very important as this directly affects the adhesion between the adhesive and the adherent, and hence, the strength of the joint. There are many methods for cleaning the surface of a part. One common method used for both metallic and non-metallic parts involves solvent wiping followed by abrasion of the surface, carried out by sandblasting or some other process. Abrasion increases the roughness of the surface which is necessary for good adhesion.

The prepared surfaces can be tested for their affinity to be wetted by water. The test is called water-break test. Smooth and uniform spread of water on the surface is an indication that the surface is chemically clean while a collection of droplets indicates the possibility of an oil film on the surface.

Adhesive application   Soon after the joining surfaces of the adherents are prepared, adhesive is applied to one or both faying surfaces. This can be accomplished in a number of ways such as brushing, spraying, silk screening and manual or mechanized rolling.

Assembly of workpieces   After the application of adhesive, the workpieces are assembled and held together by means of clamps, fixtures, tack welds or other means. During the assembly process, care should be taken so that the workpieces are put together in the proper sequence. The bonding takes place under specified environmental conditions, and the workpieces are held together until curing is complete.

Curing   It is a process during which an adhesive changes from liquid or semi-solid state to solid state, often due to a chemical reaction. During curing, the physical properties of the adhesive change such that effective bonding of the surfaces of the parts is achieved. The chemical reaction generally involves polymerization, vulcanization or condensation. Application of pressure, heat and/or a catalyst is often helpful in quickening the bonding process. The curing of adhesive takes time, known as *curing time*. It may be just a few seconds to as much as several hours. For a good joint, it is important to use a proper combination of curing temperature, time and pressure.

15.2.1 Joint strength

The strength of a joint made by adhesive bonding depends on the strength of the adhesive and on the strength of the bond between the adhesive and each of the adherends. The strength of the bond, which is basically promoted by the adhesion mechanism, can be enhanced by ensuring (i) complete cleaning of the surfaces of the adherends (any dirt, oil or oxide film must be removed so that intimate contact between adhesive and adherend surface can be achieved); (ii) adequate roughening of the adherend surface (this increases the effective contact area and promotes mechanical interlocking); and (iii) thorough wetting of the adherend surface by the adhesive in its initial liquid state. A good adhesive bonded joint is one in which, on application of high stresses, failure occurs in one of the adherends rather than at an interface or within the adhesive.

15.2.2 Adhesive types

There are a large number of adhesive types for various applications. They can be classified in a variety of ways – on the basis of their constituent sources (e.g., organic, inorganic, synthetic), their chemistries (e.g., epoxies, polyurethanes, polyimides), their form (e.g., paste, liquid, film, pellets, tape), their type (e.g., hot melt, reactive hot melt, thermosetting, pressure sensitive, contact, etc.), or their load carrying capability (structural, semi-structural or non-structural). We will take up some important types of adhesives.

- **Natural adhesives**   These are derived from natural sources (e.g., plants and animals). Examples of natural adhesives include starch, dextrin (a gummy material obtained from starch), soya flour and animal products. These adhesives are used for low-stress applications, such as for the manufacture of cardboard cartons and wooden furniture; or where large surface areas are involved (e.g., plywood).

- **Inorganic adhesives**   Examples of inorganic adhesives are sodium silicate and magnesium oxy-chloride. These are also used for low-stress applications.

- **Synthetic adhesives**   Examples of these adhesives are thermosetting polymers and thermoplastics. They provide good cohesive strength and are useful for load-bearing applications.

Synthetic adhesives can be further grouped under the following four categories:

Chemically reactive adhesives   Examples of chemically reactive adhesives are polyurethanes, polyamides, epoxies, silicones, phenolics and modified acrylics.

Pressure-sensitive adhesives   Examples of pressure-sensitive adhesives are poly-acrylates and a variety of rubbers such as natural rubber, nitrile rubber, butyl rubber and styrene–butadiene rubber.

Hot-melt adhesives   Hot-melt adhesives are thermoplastics including polyolefins, polyamides, polyester, ethylene vinyl acetate co-polymers and thermoplastic elastomers.

- **Non-structural adhesives**   They bond a range of similar and dissimilar substrates wherever load-bearing strength is not required or where joint is required only for aesthetic purposes. They are available in a variety of formats to meet specific application requirements.

- **Semi-structural adhesives**   They bond a range of similar and dissimilar substrates wherever low load-bearing strength is required or where failure would be less critical.

- **Structural adhesives**   They bond a range of similar and dissimilar substrates wherever high load-bearing strength is required. They are most common for engineering applications, and are available as pastes, liquids, films and supported films. The latter are supported on loose knit or mat scrim cloth to improve the handling properties and also to offer some measure of thickness control. They can be further classified into two groups – thermoplastic adhesives and thermosetting adhesives.

    Thermoplastic adhesives soften at high temperatures. The most commonly used thermoplastic adhesives include polyamides, vinyls and non-vulcanizing neoprene rubber. Vinyls are especially useful for structural applications. For instance, polyvinyl acetate is commonly used to form strong bonds with metals, glass and porous materials.

    Thermosetting adhesives usually do not soften at high temperatures. Once they harden, these adhesives cannot be re-melted; therefore re-bonding of a broken joint cannot be accomplished by heating. Thermosetting adhesives are available in two variants – the phenolic resin and the epoxy resin. Phenolic resins are mostly used as bonding materials for the manufacture of waterproof plywood. Epoxy resins are used to produce joints that have high strength, toughness, chemical inertness and low shrinkage. These adhesives can be cured at room temperature. Other thermosetting adhesives include melamin–formaldehyde, polyurethane, polyester, phenolic rubber and neoprene rubber.

- **Special purpose adhesives**

    Electrical conducting adhesives   Most applications of adhesive bonding are meant to achieve mechanical strength and structural integrity. However, the recent trend is to employ electrically conducting adhesives to replace lead-based soldering in the electrical and electronics industry. Since these adhesives require curing or setting temperatures that are lower than those used for soldering, they are easy to use and are economical too. Electrical conductivity in adhesives is obtained by using additives such as silver, gold, aluminium, copper, nickel and graphite. These additives are mostly in the form of flakes or particles. The current trend is to use additives in the form of polymeric particles (such as polystyrene) coated with a thin film of silver or gold. The matrix is made of polymer (generally, epoxies) and there is only a small volume (10% to 20%) of coated additive, just to make the adhesive electrically conducting. The additives that improve electrical conductivity also enhance the thermal conductivity of the adhesive. The desired electrical properties (isotropic or anisotropic) of the adhesive can be obtained by controlling the size, shape and distribution of the additive particles as well as the nature of the contact among the individual particles in the adhesive.

Most applications of electrical conductive adhesives are in the electronics industry. Typical examples of parts using these adhesives include mobile sets, pocket TV sets, liquid crystal displays and electronic assemblies.

Thread locking adhesives The use of these adhesive prevents shock and vibration loosening of metallic screwed joints. To use, the adhesive is applied to one of the metal parts, then the parts are screwed together or placed together. The adhesive starts to set as soon as the screw is turned or the nut is tightened.

Advantages There is a tendency to use adhesive bonding as a substitute to traditional joining methods such as mechanical fastening, soldering, brazing and welding due to the following advantages of adhesive bonding:

- It is often more economical.
- It can eliminate machining operations such as threading that are needed to mechanically assemble two parts.
- There is no change in material properties, surface roughness, or external appearance of the components when they are joined by adhesive.
- There is no change in structural integrity of the components, since no holes are required as in the case of mechanical fastening.
- There is load distribution at the interface; thus, part stresses are uniformly distributed over a large surface. There are no localized stresses that typically exist when components are joined with mechanical fasteners.
- It is possible to obtain a joint strength comparable to that obtained by alternative methods of joining.
- It is possible to give shock and vibration protection to the assembly by using elastomeric adhesives.
- It is possible to join heat-sensitive materials without damage. There are no heat-affected zones present in the parts or assembly.

- It is possible to join a wide variety of materials– porous materials as well as dissimilar materials. When dissimilar materials are adhered together, the adhesive bonds are able to tolerate the stresses of differential expansion and contraction.

- It is possible to join parts of different sizes and cross-sections. Very thick to very thin parts, not suitable for mechanical fastening or welding, may be adhesively bonded. Joints between very thin or delicate materials such as foils can also be made. Fragile components can be joined without any significant addition to weight.

Limitations   There are some limitations of adhesive bonding of parts. These include the following:

- **Surface cleaning and surface finish**   The surfaces that need to be joined must be properly cleaned. The finish of the surfaces to be bonded is important and the strength of the joint depends mainly on the ability of the adhesive to wet the surface without asperities or air voids.

- **Non-availability of a universal adhesive**   It is often difficult to select the right adhesive from a wide variety of available options.

- **Unfavourable properties of adhesives**   Some adhesives are toxic and flammable. Other adhesives may be unstable and have a short shelf life. High-strength adhesives are often brittle and possess poor impact properties. Some adhesives become brittle when exposed to low temperatures.

- **Difficulty in determining life expectancy**   Durability and life expectancy of adhesive bonded joints are difficult to estimate.

- **Difficulty in determining joint quality**   Traditional non-destructive techniques cannot be used to assess the quality of an adhesive-bonded joint.

- **Non-suitability for certain applications**   This refers to those applications where dis-assembling is frequent or where the joint has to bear high loads.

- **Non-suitability for high temperature applications**   Adhesive-bonded joints are generally not effective at temperatures above 200°C; in fact, the joint may start to lose its strength at much lower temperatures.

- **Non-suitability for hostile environment applications**   Degradation of adhesive-bonded assemblies can take place as a result of oxidation, exposure to ultraviolet light and other radiations, dissolution or stress corrosion.

- **Non-suitability for production applications**   Adhesive-bonded joints are not popular in high production lines, mainly because they require a high curing time. Specialized fixtures may also be needed in some cases.

- **Low joint strength**   Adhesive-bonded joints are generally not as strong as joints made by other processes, for example, welding.

- **Compatibility**   Adhesives must be compatible with materials of the adherends.

Applications   Adhesives can be usefully applied to bond a large variety of components made of similar and dissimilar metals and non-metals. These components can be of varying sizes, shapes, and thicknesses. It is possible to combine adhesive bonding with mechanical fastening in order to provide enhanced strength to the joint. A critical parameter in the use of adhesives in component manufacturing is curing time, which may be just a few seconds at high temperatures or a few hours at room temperature – this limits the rates of production. Another critical limitation in the use of adhesive bonds for structural applications is their poor strength for service above 200 °C.

Adhesive bonding has several applications. Some of these are as follows:

1. Bonding of metal to non-metals especially plastics. Teflon, polyethylene and polypropylene however are difficult to join due to their sticking inability.

2. In the aerospace industry, as an alternative to riveting for assembly of aircraft structures; for fastening of stiffeners to the aircraft skin; for assembling honeycomb structures; and in the production of helicopter blades and aircraft bodies.

3. In the automobile industry, for attaching brake lining to shoes; for rear view mirror assembly with windshields; and in the production of laminated windshield glasses.

4. In the fabrication of railway coaches, boats, refrigerators, storage tanks and microwave reflectors for radar and space communications.

15.3 Mechanical Fastening

Most of the products we see around us, whether they are consumer products or industrial products, have been manufactured by one or the other mechanical fastening method. Mechanical fastening of two (or more) parts together generally involves the use of discrete hardware components, called *fasteners*. The fasteners are added to the component parts during assembly operation. Mechanical fastening methods can be classified into two major categories: (i) Non-permanent fastening that allows for frequent disassembly and reassembly if needed (for instance, for repair and maintenance). All joints made by snap fits or by threaded fasteners such as screws, bolts and nuts belong to this category. (ii) Permanent fastening that produces a sort of permanent joint. All joints made with non-threaded fasteners such as rivets, locking pins, retaining rings, staples, wire stitches and so on belong to this category. Fastening of bushings, bearings, pins and similar other parts can however be accomplished without the use of any fastener but by shaping or reshaping of one of the components being assembled.

Selecting a suitable fastener or fastening method depends on several factors, such as:

•   The function, strength and reliability requirements of the joint.

•   The dimensions and material of the components to be joined.

•   The desirability or need for disassembly.

•   The need for resistance to adverse environment conditions (corrosive, hot, vibratory).

•   Accessibility.

- Appearance.
- Weight.
- Cost.

The most common mechanical fastening methods make use of the following:

- Threaded fasteners
- Non-threaded fasteners
- Integral fasteners

A fastening method that makes use of interference fit can also be considered to fall in this category. We shall now study these fastening devices and processes.

15.3.1 Threaded fasteners

Threaded fasteners are low-cost means of mechanically joining and holding parts together. They are used where subsequent disassembly and reassembly may be required; they can be installed by hand with common hand tools or by automated machinery. Threaded fasteners have external or internal threads and are available in a variety of sizes, thread types, thread pitch and tolerances. Important threaded fasteners include machine screws, nuts and bolts.

Screws Machine screw or a cap screw is used to assemble parts as shown in Figure 15.1(a). It passes through a clearance hole in one piece and screws into a threaded hole in the other. The head draws the parts together as the screw enters the threaded hole. Screws are available with different types of heads as shown in Figure 15.2.

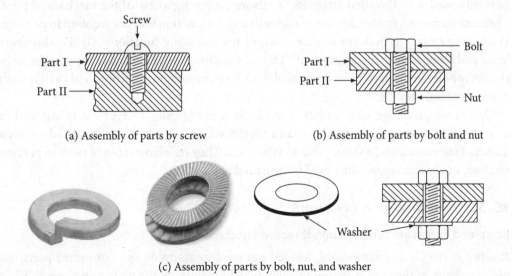

(a) Assembly of parts by screw

(b) Assembly of parts by bolt and nut

(c) Assembly of parts by bolt, nut, and washer

Figure 15.1 Assembly methods by using threaded fasteners

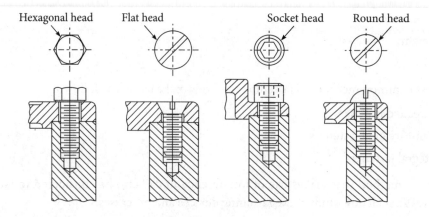

Hexagonal head   Flat head   Socket head   Round head

Figure 15.2   Screws with different types of heads

Bolt   A bolt is an externally threaded fastener that is inserted through holes into the component parts. The length of the bolt is more than the thickness of the parts such that a nut can be screwed on the opposite side, as shown in Figure 15.1(b).

Nut   A nut, as shown in Figure 15.1(b), is an internally threaded fastener. For a good assembly, the threads of the nut should match those of the bolt with respect to the diameter, pitch and thread form.

Screws, bolts, and nuts are available in a variety of materials and have a range of standard designs, sizes, shapes and threads.

Washer   A washer, as shown in Figure 15.1(c), is a flat, thin ring of sheet metal that is generally used with threaded fasteners to ensure proper tightness of the mechanical joint. There are numerous washer designs available to suit the function they are required to perform. Washers are used to perform one or more of the following functions: (i) To distribute loads and stresses over a large area; (ii) To seal the joint; (iii) To provide support for large clearance holes in the parts to be assembled; (iv) To increase spring tension; and (v) To resist inadvertent unfastening.

One common design of a washer is the lockwasher [Figure 15.1(c)]. It is installed in assemblies that are subject to shock and vibrations. Lockwashers are designed to keep threaded fasteners from loosening due to vibrations. They may have external teeth to prevent rotation. Lock washers are often used in structural applications.

15.3.2 Non-threaded fasteners

Rivets and eyelets are common non-threaded fasteners.

Rivets   A rivet is a non-threaded, headed pin used to assemble two (or more) parts. To use, the shank of the rivet is passed through matching holes in the parts to be joined. Rivet setting devices and tools are then employed to form a head (by upsetting operation) on the opposite end of the rivet, clinching the parts together. A rivet and a riveted joint are shown in Figure 15.3(a). The clearance between the hole and the rivet size is critical; if it is too small, rivet insertion becomes difficult and the time to make assembly increases. If the clearance is too large, the shank of the rivet may bend during the formation of the head on the opposite side. Riveting can be done manually or automatically. Riveted joints are mostly lap joints [Figure 15.3(b)]. Riveted butt joints have to use straps [Figure 15.3(c)]. Applications of riveted joints are quite common in the boiler and aerospace industries.

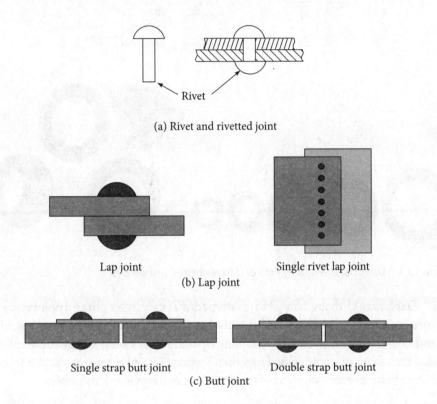

(a) Rivet and rivetted joint

Lap joint   Single rivet lap joint

(b) Lap joint

Single strap butt joint   Double strap butt joint

(c) Butt joint

Figure 15.3 Riveted joints

Eyelets An eyelet is a thin-walled tubular fastener with a flange on one end as shown in Figure 15.4. It is used to make a permanent lap joint of two or more flat workpieces. For low-stress applications, particularly for thin non-metallic parts, eyelets are preferred over rivets because their use saves material, weight and cost. To use, the eyelet is passed through the holes of the parts and the straight end is formed flat to effect assembly. Eyelets are available in different sizes, shapes and materials [Figure 15.4]. This fastening method is used widely in toys, electrical and electronics industry, and shoe industry.

Pins A fastening pin, such as a dowel pin or clevis pin, provides strength when it is used to secure materials together. Pins may be tapered or straight, with a head or without. A metal cotter pin can be bent during installation to act like a staple or spring pin. Clevis pins are primarily used as pivots and linkages. Dowel pins are used to align mating parts in precise position. A steel-grade, industrial safety pin locates, aligns and safely secures components.

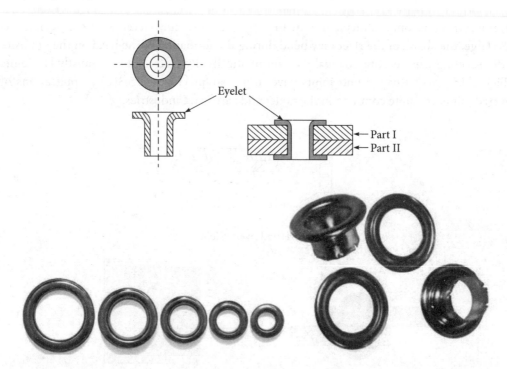

Figure 15.4 Use of eyelet and eyelets of different sizes and shapes

Staples Staples are U-shaped metal wire fasteners that vary by length and point types. These point types include: (i) Chisel point; (ii) Chisel inside bevel point; (iii) Chisel outside bevel point; and (iv) Divergent point. The stapling operation uses semi-automatic stapling guns pre-loaded with strips of staples glued together. Stapling is used extensively in the automotive and furniture industries as a method of making a sort of permanent assembly.

Stitching Industrial stitching is similar to cloth stitching but with steel wire. A series of U-shaped stitches are made through the two (or more) thin parts to be joined.

When designing joints involving fasteners, it is important that the environmental service conditions are taken into account and that the parts to be joined and the fasteners used are strong enough to cope with the service loads imposed.

15.3.3 Interference fit

The assembly of two (or more) parts can also be made by producing mechanical interference between them. Locking between parts is primarily due to friction. To effect assembly, one part is pushed into another. Typical examples of interference fits are the press fitting of a shaft into a bearing, and a bearing into its housing.

Press fit A press fit, also known as a force fit or interference fit, is an assembly in which one part is inserted tightly into a hole in another part. The inserted part is typically 0.02 to 0.03

mm larger than the mating hole. The assembly stays in place through friction, and the force required to press parts together depends on the hardness, slipperiness and surface finish of the materials; the size, thickness and geometry of the parts; and the amount of interference between them, that is, the difference in size between the inserted part and the hole. In most cases, the press fit is strong enough to stand on its own. In others, the joint is augmented by an additional assembly method, such as adhesive bonding or brazing.

Most press-fit parts are round, but they can also be oval, square, rectangular or triangular. The parts can even have a keyway. The part to be inserted can be solid like a pin or hollow like a bushing. Either way, putting a taper on the inserted part and a chamfer on the mating part will help the parts go together nicely. Press-fit parts can be metal or plastic, similar or dissimilar. However, if dissimilar materials are used, it is always preferable to choose materials with similar coefficients of thermal expansion, but different hardness ratings.

Many parts are assembled with press fits, including bushings, bearings, rotors, gears, pulleys, shaft collars and gland seals. In the automotive industry, press fits are used to assemble valve seats, fuel injectors, cylinder sleeves, muffler baffles, transmission components and impellers for water pumps.

Shrink and expansion fit Shrink-fitting is a technique in which an interference fit is achieved by a relative size change after assembly. To make a joint of two parts, a dimensional change is introduced to one or both the parts either by heating or cooling. Depending upon the need, only one part may be heated, one part may be heated and the other cooled or only one part may be cooled with respect to the other. The parts are then assembled, and normal temperature condition is restored. A strong interference fit is established.

An example is the fitting of a wrought iron tyre around the rim of a wooden cart wheel. Another example is of fitting a steel tyre to the wheel of a railway engine. In both cases, the tyre is heated to expand to a size slightly greater than the wheel's diameter, and is fitted around the wheel. After cooling, the tyre contracts, binding tightly in place. The same procedure can also be adopted to introduce a pre-stress condition in the joint.

15.3.4 Integral fasteners

Integral fasteners are formed areas designed into sheet metal products. Integral fasteners function by interlocking or interfering one component with another component during assembly. The three most common types of integral fasteners are: (i) Embossed protrusions; (ii) Edge seams; and (iii) Hemming. Embossed protrusions are formed between two sheet metal components by drawing a small cup-shaped section through them. As the metals are squeezed through the components, they impact and expand on a die, producing an interlocked button with a greater diameter than the drawn section. This process is also called clinching or clinch-joining. Edge seams interlock the edges of two sheet metal parts by folding the edges of both parts over each other. They not only reinforce the entire assembly, but also eliminate sharp edges. Hemming assembles two sheet metal components together by bending the edge of one component more than 180° over the edge of the other sheet metal component.

Figure 15.5 shows some typical integral fasteners. Though there is generally no restriction on joining dissimilar materials, care must be taken to ensure that the mating materials do not chemically react among themselves with the passage of time. One most common application of integral fasteners is in the manufacture of a beverage can.

Advantages   There are several attractive features of mechanical fastening that make it highly popular in manufacturing industries. Some of these are as follows:

- **Ease of disassembly and reassembly**   The use of threaded fasteners and sometimes, non-threaded fasteners help in quick disassembling and reassembling of the component parts.

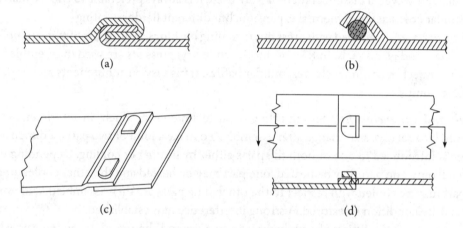

Figure 15.5   Use of integral fasteners involves some forming operation

- **Variety of size and material of components**   Mechanical fasteners can be used to join a wide variety of materials, similar or different in size, shape and properties.

- **Variety of joint designs**   Mechanical fasteners can be used to join components in a wide range of joint designs. Some of the joints made with hinges and slides even permit a small amount of relative motion between the components.

- **Little surface preparation**   The use of mechanical fasteners does not usually require any surface preparation of the component parts.

- **Little adverse effect on component material**   The use of mechanical fasteners does not affect any chemical or mechanical properties of the component material, as is often the case with joining techniques involving the application of heat and/or pressure.

- **Low cost**   The use of mechanical fasteners does not involve a high cost when compared to the cost of components being joined. Further, they are readily available in the market in standard sizes produced on a mass scale.

Disadvantages Among the disadvantages or limitations of mechanical fastening, the following are important.

- **Localized stresses** Within the joint area, localized stresses may exist, which can cause mechanical fasteners to be the location of joint failure.

- **Galvanic action** Within joints made of dissimilar metals, galvanic action can occur.

- **Fatigue failure** Vibrations can cause loosening or fatigue failure of joint.

- **Joint preparation** Some mechanical fastening techniques require joint preparation, such as drilling hole and threading.

Applications Mechanical fastening is widely used for making engineering assemblies. The main reason for the popularity of this method is that there is no restriction on the thickness of parts that can be assembled and the ease with which joints can be dismantled and then reassembled using simple tools. A classic example is the internal combustion engine where the need to strip down the engine for maintenance purposes is necessary. Mechanical fastenings are also used extensively in various devices of daily use.

15.4 Thermal Joining Processes

Thermal joining includes all processes that use heat for fastening the two parts, such as soldering, brazing, welding and shrink fitting. This method of joining is generally effective on homogeneous metal parts with similar melting points. Assemblies produced by thermal methods are very difficult to disassemble and may have aesthetic concerns such as distortion and discoloration. Manufacturers can often solve these aesthetic concerns – by grinding or sanding down the part to minimize the metal bump or by painting over the problem area to minimize discoloration. Distortion, which is caused by uneven heating and cooling of the part, is more difficult to repair.

Brazing and soldering are two joining processes that provide permanent joints and involve heating to temperatures that are not as high as those required for welding. The two processes are distinguished by the temperature involved. Brazing temperatures are higher than those used in the soldering process; therefore, the brazed joint has greater strength than the soldered joint. A filler metal in molten state is introduced in both brazing and soldering processes as in most fusion welding processes but no melting of the base metals takes place. Brazing and soldering are generally preferred over welding when

- the metals of the parts to be joined have poor weldability.

- the metals of the parts to be joined are quite different.

- there is possibility of damage to the parts due to high heat.

- there is no need for a high joint strength.

- the geometry of the joint is such that welding methods cannot be used or are difficult to use.

15.4.1 Brazing

In a brazing operation, a non-ferrous alloy (filler metal, also called the brazing metal) is introduced between surfaces of the metal pieces to be joined and the temperature is raised to melt the filler metal, but not the workpieces [Figure 15.6(a)]. The molten metal fills the closely fitting space by capillary action; upon cooling and solidification of the filler metal, a strong joint is formed. There are two types of brazing processes: (i) brazing and (ii) braze welding. In braze welding, the filler metal is melted and deposited at the point where the joint is to be made [Figure 15.6(b)]. Brazing is usually carried out in a normal atmosphere, but in case of aluminium brazing, the process is often performed in vacuum in order to prevent oxidation problems.

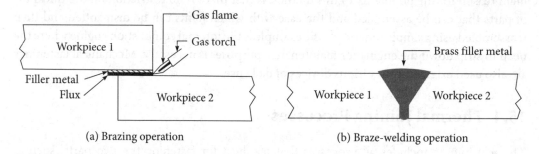

(a) Brazing operation   (b) Braze-welding operation

Figure 15.6 Schematic representation of brazing processes

Several heat sources can be used to perform the brazing process, the most common being oxy-acetylene flame torch, furnace, electrical resistance and induction heating. Flame heating, being the most flexible, is used extensively while induction heating offers the best heat control.

Filler metals The filler metals used for brazing, unlike those used for other welding processes, generally have different compositions than those of the workpiece materials to be joined. These filler metals have a melting temperature more than 450°C (lower than the melting temperature of the workpiece material). Most filler metals belong to one of the three alloy compositions: copper-based alloys, silver-based alloys and aluminium-based alloys. Copper-based alloys have a melting point range of 700–1150°C and are suitable for brazing copper and ferrous metal parts. Silver-based alloys have a melting point range of 640–850°C and are appropriate for nickel- and copper-based materials, brass and titanium. Brazing using silver-based alloys is also referred to as *silver soldering*. Aluminium-based alloys have a melting point in the range 570–620°C and are exclusively used for brazing aluminium and its alloys. It is to be noted that aluminium parts are difficult to braze as the aluminium filler metal melts at just below the melting point of the aluminium parts to be joined. Induction heating is preferred for the purpose of obtaining accurate and precise control of temperature.

Filler metal is available in a variety of shapes such as wire, rod, strip, ring, pre-form and powder. One can choose the shape to suit the joint design so as to facilitate speed in brazing. The choice of composition of the filler metal is critical because a wrong composition can cause embrittlement of the joint, formation of brittle inter-metallic compounds at the joint or galvanic corrosion in the joint. It is important to note that as a result of diffusion between the filler metal and the base metal, mechanical and metallurgical properties of joints can change during the service life of the brazed components or in subsequent processing of brazed parts. For example, if titanium is brazed with pure tin filler metal, it is possible that the tin completely diffuses into the titanium base metal by subsequent ageing or heat treatment. In that case, the joint may no longer exist.

Fluxes   The use of a flux is very important in brazing as well as in braze welding. Flux performs three main functions: (i) removing oxide films from workpiece surfaces; (ii) providing the filler metal the fluidity to wet the joint surfaces; and (iii) preventing the formation of oxides and other unwanted by-products in the brazing process. The important properties of a good brazing flux are: (i) low melting temperature; (ii) low viscosity so that it can be displaced by the filler metal; (iii) high wetting property; (iv) ability to protect the joint against oxidation until solidification of filler metal; and (v) ease of removal after the joint has been made. Brazing fluxes are generally made of borax, boric acid, borates, fluorides or chlorides. They are available in the form of powder, paste or slurry. Additional wetting agents may also be used to improve the capillary action of the molten filler metal or its wetting characteristics.

Flux removal: Some brazing fluxes are corrosive in nature and hence, flux residues must be removed from the components after they have been brazed. Most fluxes are soluble in hot water, and therefore removal is not a major problem. Simple dipping of the joined components in a hot water bath for about five minutes generally gives satisfactory results. Mechanical removal of flux is also easy, particularly when the flux is still hot.

Fluxless brazing   The application as well as removal of brazing flux is not only cumbersome but also costly, particularly in the case of complex joints and assemblies. Research in fluxless brazing is mostly directed to the brazing of aluminium because there are several important applications of aluminium due to its light weight and excellent thermal conductivity. Special filler materials have been developed that do not need the use of brazing flux. Furnaces are also available, which allow brazing operation to be done in vacuum or such environment that prevents the formation of oxides, thus, eliminating the need of brazing flux.

Brazed joint types   The types of brazed joint generally made are the lap, butt and scarf (see Figure 15.7), although numerous modifications of these shapes may be used depending upon the shape of the parts to be joined. The lap joint is most common in brazing and the strength of the joint is a function of the contact area; greater the contact area, more will be the strength of the joint. A good estimate of the correct length of lap can be made using the following relations:

$L = k \, t \, (\sigma / \zeta)$ for a flat joint, and

$L = k \, (D - t) \, (\sigma / \zeta)$ for a tubular joint

where k is the factor of safety, t is the thickness of the thinner member, mm; D is diameter of tube, mm; σ is the tensile strength of the thinner member, Pa; and ζ is shear stress of the

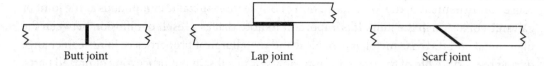

Figure 15.7   Types of joints used in brazing

braze filler metal, Pa. As a rule of thumb, length of the lap should not be less than three times the thickness of the thinner member. The brazed joints can have shear strength as high as 800 MPa when use is made of brazing alloys containing silver.

Example 15.1

Two plates of the same metal – one 0.5 mm thick and the other 0.8 mm thick – are to be lap-joined by brazing. If the ratio of tensile strength of the workpiece material to shear strength of filler material is 8, and if it is desired to have a factor of safety of 1.25, what should be the length of the lap joint?

Solution

Here $k = 1.25$, $\sigma/\zeta = 8$, $t = 0.5$ mm

$$L = (1.25)\,(0.5)\,8 = 5 \text{ mm}$$

Precautions for brazing operation   To achieve a strong brazed joint, it is important that:

- The surfaces to be brazed should have good finish. Sand blasting may be used to accomplish this.
- The surfaces to be brazed should be thoroughly cleaned using chemical or mechanical means, so that all the dirt, oil or oxides are removed. This ensures proper adhesion at the interface of the workpiece and the filler metal.
- The joint should be properly prepared by keeping an appropriate clearance between the surfaces to be brazed. The clearance between the mating surfaces is an important parameter, as it affects the strength of the brazed joint. The smaller the gap, the higher is the shear strength of the joint. However, too small a clearance can restrict the flow of molten filler metal to the entire interface. Too large a clearance reduces the capillary action and in that case, there may be areas between the parts where no filler metal can reach. An optimum gap is necessary to achieve maximum tensile strength. Typical value of joint clearance ranges between 0.02 mm to 0.2 mm.
- Flux and wetting agents should be used to improve the cleaning of faying surfaces, wetting characteristics of the molten filler metal and capillary action. Before putting the assembled component to use, it is important to thoroughly wash the joint with hot water so that flux (which is corrosive in nature) is removed.

If the joint is properly designed and the brazing operation has been properly performed, the brazed joint can be stronger than the filler metal with the help of which it has been made.

Brazing methods   Depending upon the *source of heat* used and the *method of application of heat*, there are several brazing methods. Some of these are as follows:

1. **Torch brazing**   The torch method of brazing uses a carburizing flame of oxy-acetylene gas mixture as the source of heat. The parts to be joined are first heated locally at the location where the joint is to be made, and then the brazing material is deposited in the joint. The process is suitable for part thickness in the range 1 mm to 5 mm. Although the process can be automated as a production process, torch brazing is difficult to control and often requires skilled labour. This method is commonly used in repair works.

2. **Furnace brazing**   The furnace method of brazing is carried out in a furnace. The parts to be joined are first cleaned. The right quantity of brazing metal is kept in the joint; the assembly is heated uniformly to the brazing temperature, and then cooled in the furnace. The joint is ready as the assembly comes out of the furnace. The control of temperature and atmosphere is important in furnace brazing. The furnace used may be either of continuous or of batch type.

3. **Resistance brazing**   This method of brazing uses the flow of current through the electrical resistance of the components to be brazed as the source of heat. The parts to be brazed are assembled and placed between two electrodes in such a way that when current is passed through the electrodes, the area of the joint gets heated up instantly. Either the filler metal is pre-loaded in the joint before passing the current or it is supplied externally during brazing. Parts that are commonly brazed by this method have a thickness ranging from 0.1 mm to 10 mm. The main advantages of this method are that it is fast, the heating zone can be confined to very small areas and the process can be easily automated to achieve joints of uniform quality. The process is used for relatively small parts.

4. **Induction brazing**   This method of brazing uses induction heating by high frequency (5 kHz to 5MHz) AC current as the source of heat. The filler metal is preloaded in the joint and the parts are instantly heated when placed near the induction coils. The use of flux is necessary unless the process is carried out in a protective atmosphere. Parts that are commonly brazed by this method have a thickness ranging from 0.1 mm to 3 mm. This process can be easily automated for mass production.

5. **Dip brazing**   This method of brazing is carried out by dipping the assemblies of parts to be brazed into a molten filler metal bath that serves as the source of heat. All the workpiece surfaces are thus coated with the filler metal. For small and simple assemblies made of sheet metal of less than 3 mm or 5 mm thickness or diameter, dip brazing is useful as a production process. In case of complex assemblies of different thicknesses, molten salt baths, which also contain fluxes are used as the source of heat. Fixtures are employed to braze as many as 1000 parts at a time; the number depends on the size of

the parts and the bath. Dip brazing is particularly suitable when it is required to braze many joints on a single part.

6. **Infrared brazing**   The infrared method of brazing uses high intensity infrared lamp or microwaves as the source of heat. The radiant heat is focused on the area where the joint is to be made and the brazing process is carried out. Very thin parts can be brazed by this method, with their thickness ranging from 0.1 mm to 1 mm. The process is slower than other brazing processes.

7. **High energy beam brazing**   The high energy beam brazing method uses an electron beam or laser beam as the source of heat. This method finds applications for brazing of precision components made from high-strength and high-melting point metals and alloys.

Advantages, limitations and applications

Brazing has many advantages compared to welding. Some of them are as follows:

i.   Both similar and dissimilar metals can be joined.

ii.   Metals that are difficult to weld can be joined.

iii. Operation times are low, leading to high production rates.

iv.   Operation lends itself to automation.

v.   Joints are neat looking, which require minimum additional finishing.

vi.   Very thin-walled parts that cannot be welded can be joined.

vii. It requires less heat and power than required in fusion welding.

viii. Problems like heat affected zones (HAZs) in the base metals near the joint are minimal.

ix.   Joint areas that are inaccessible by many welding processes can be brazed since molten filler metal is drawn into the joint by capillary action.

Some of the limitations of the brazing process are as follows:

i.   Strength of a brazed joint is less compared to a welded joint.

ii.   Strength of a brazed joint is less than that of base metals, although it may be more than that of the filler metal.

iii. Hot service environment may weaken a brazed joint.

iv.   Colour of the brazing metal does not generally match the colour of base metals – an aesthetic limitation.

The process finds wide commercial use in the making of small assemblies and electrical parts. It also finds applications in the assembly of pipes to fittings, carbide tips to tool shanks, heat exchangers, radiators, bicycle frames and jewellery making. The process is used extensively for repair and maintenance work across all industries.

Braze welding

Braze welding is a process that combines the techniques of brazing and fusion welding. The filler materials for the joint as well as the temperatures involved are the same as that for brazing.

The filler metal is deposited into the joint using an oxidizing flame of an oxy-acetylene torch (as in fusion welding) rather than by capillary action (as in brazing). A better quantity of filler metal is deposited as compared to brazing. The use of flux is essential. The main advantage of this process is that there is negligible distortion to the component. Applications of the process are mainly for repair of ferrous parts. Dissimilar metals can be joined with good joint strength. Braze welding is commonly used for joints made of pieces of carbide drill bits and joints made of carbide bits with steel tool shanks. Automated braze welding has been successfully used for mass production.

15.4.2 Soldering

Soldering (also known by the term 'soft soldering') is a process in which two thin pieces of metal are joined with the help of a filler metal (known as solder). Solder is heated and applied in a molten state between the two pieces to be joined; it fills the closely fitting joint by capillary action in the same way as in brazing. There is no melting of the workpiece material; the solder wets and combines with the workpiece material to form a metallurgical bond. Typical clearance between the parts to be joined by soldering ranges from 0.08 to 0.15 mm. The solder melts at a temperature below 450°C.

The molten solder is applied to the joining surfaces by using heat from a gas torch. Alternatively, use is made of a soldering iron (Figure 15.8). This is a hand-held type device having either a copper bit or a plated-iron bit at one end. The bit can be heated by electric resistance heating or in a furnace.

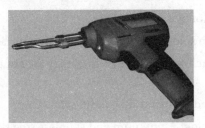 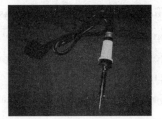

Figure 15.8   Soldering iron

The steps required to join two pieces by the soldering process are as follows:

1. **Surface preparation** This involves thorough cleaning of the joining surfaces mechanically as well as chemically. It is important that joining surfaces are free of oxides and oily films.

2. **Application of flux**   The joining surfaces are covered with flux.

3. **Application of solder**   The bit of the soldering iron is heated to about 300°C, dipped into the flux, and a small quantity of solder is melted by placing it on the bit. The molten solder is then applied to the surface of the parts prepared by using the soldering iron. At the joint, the solder enters the clearance by capillary action, spreads itself between the closely fitting parts, and forms the joint after solidification.

4. **Removal of flux**   The flux residue must be removed after the solder has solidified.

The strength of the joint depends on the adhesive quality of the solder, which never reaches the strength of the materials being joined.

Hard soldering is a process which is similar to soft soldering but the filler material used has a melting temperature greater than 450°C. Typical example of hard soldering is 'silver soldering' in which an alloy containing silver is used as filler material. Silver provides free flowing characteristics but silver solder is not good at gap filling, therefore, use of a flux is a must in silver soldering. Silver soldering is a useful process for doing odd repair works and for fabricating small fittings.

Advantages, limitations and applications

The soldering process has the following advantages:
- Easy to perform.
- Low cost.
- Reversibility.
- Thin parts of various metals can be joined by soldering. Copper parts can be easily joined with parts made of silver or gold.
- Low energy requirement compared to brazing and fusion welding.
- Good electrical and thermal conductivity in the joint.
- Capabe of making air-tight and liquid tight seams for containers.

Some of the limitations of soldering are as follows:
- Butt joints are generally not made with solder because of small faying surfaces.
- Solder joints do not generally have much strength. Therefore, they are not used on load-bearing members.
- Solder joints cannot be used in elevated temperature conditions.
- Not all metals can be joined by soldering. Aluminium and stainless steels, for example, are difficult to solder.
- Requires skill and is time consuming, although the soldering speed can be increased if automated equipment is used.

As an industrial process, soldering is widely used for joining thin sheet metals such as lips of cans. In the electronic industry, particularly in assembling printed-circuit boards, soldering finds extensive use. Soldering can also be used for preparing liquid- or gas-tight joints (for example, car radiators), provided the metal be joined is solderable and the operating temperature is well below the melting point of the solder used.

Solders and fluxes   Solders are usually alloys of tin and lead prepared in various proportions. Other compositions of solder (such as tin–zinc, zinc–aluminium, lead–silver, silver–antimony and cadmium–silver alloys) are also used for better joint strength and special applications. Tin is chemically active at soldering temperatures and promotes wetting action, which is necessary for a good joint. Table 15.1 gives the application areas of some common solders. As a result of the harmful effects of lead on the environment and lead's toxicity, lead-free solders (which are essentially tin-based solders) are now being extensively used.

Table 15.1   Areas of application of some common solders

Application area	Solder
General purpose	Tin–lead alloy
Joining aluminium parts	Tin–zinc alloy; Zinc–aluminium alloy
Joining for strength at high temperatures	Lead–silver alloy; Cadmium–silver alloy
Joining electronic parts	Tin–silver alloy; Tin–bismuth alloy; Copper–tin alloy

The soldering flux performs the following functions.

- Removes oxide film from the surfaces of workpieces.
- Promotes wetting of the faying surfaces.
- Gets readily displaced by the molten solder during the soldering operation.

The flux must melt at soldering temperatures and its residue, which is left after the joint has been made, should be non-corrosive. Unfortunately, there is no single flux that serves all these functions perfectly for all work materials. Available soldering fluxes can be classified as inorganic and organic.

- **Inorganic fluxes**   Examples of this type of fluxes are muriatic acid and salts that are combinations of zinc and ammonium chloride. They are quite effective in rapid cleaning of the surface, but after soldering, the component must be washed thoroughly with flowing water in order to remove flux residues, which may cause corrosion. The salts are less corrosive than the acids.

- **Organic fluxes**   They are made of either resin, which is not water soluble (such as gum wood) or water-soluble materials (such as organic acids and alcohols). Water-soluble type fluxes are preferred because their removal after soldering is relatively easy. Organic fluxes are generally non-corrosive and find applications in joining of electrical and electronic components.

Solderability   Solderability of material is defined as 'the ability of the material to be soldered'. Some metals such as copper, tin, brass, silver and gold are easy to solder, while aluminium, zinc-based metals and stainless steels are difficult to solder because of their thin and strong film. Iron and nickel are even more difficult to solder, unless special fluxes are used that modify the surfaces. Non-metallic materials such as ceramics and graphite may be soldered by first plating the parts with metallic elements.

Soldering methods   Different soldering methods use different sources of heat and methods of application of heat. Most of the methods used for soldering are similar to the ones used for brazing. Some of them are:

1. Iron soldering
2. Torch soldering
3. Furnace soldering
4. Induction soldering
5. Resistance soldering
6. Dip soldering

Joint design for soldering   Large contact surfaces are necessary for developing sufficient joint strength. In several cases, the joint strength can be improved when sheet parts are mechanically joined prior to being soldered. Figure 15.9 shows some commonly used solder-joint designs.

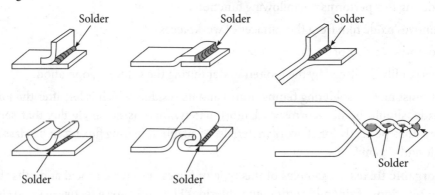

Figure 15.9   Some commonly used solder-joint designs

15.4.3 Welding

Joining of metal parts by welding involves heating the parts at their contacting surfaces with or without the application of pressure. Many welding processes are accomplished by heat alone; a few others by a combination of heat and pressure; and there are others which are completed by pressure alone with no external heat supplied. Some welding processes require the addition of a filler material in the joint for better joint strength while the others do not require it. Welding is mostly associated with metallic parts, but the process can also be used for joining of plastic parts. For the parts that cannot withstand high temperatures, or those that are delicate or intricate (such as electronic components), joining processes other than welding are employed.

In order to obtain a perfect metallurgical bond, it is essential that: (a) surfaces of the parts where the joint is to be made are perfectly smooth and free of any contaminant such as oxide, grease and so on; and (b) there are no internal impurities in the metal of the parts. While these conditions are difficult to obtain in normal situations, different welding processes have been developed to overcome these difficulties. For example, surface roughness is overcome either by application of force, causing plastic deformation of the metal asperities, or by melting the two surfaces, facilitating fusion. In pressure welding or solid state welding, the contaminated layers from the surfaces to be joined are removed by mechanical or chemical cleaning prior to welding, or by forcing the layer of contaminated metal to flow along the interface out of the weld. In fusion welding processes, contaminants from the pool of molten metal are removed using fluxes.

There are numerous welding processes and these differ with respect to the procedures through which temperatures and pressure are combined and applied. They can be divided into two groups: (i) fusion welding processes, and (ii) solid state or pressure welding processes. *Fusion welding* refers to the welding processes that rely upon melting to join materials of similar compositions and melting points. Due to the high temperature involved in these processes, a heat affected zone is created in the material. *Solid state welding* refers to the *welding* processes in which two workpieces are joined under pressure; an intimate contact is provided between them and at a temperature essentially below the melting point of the work materials. Bonding of the materials is a result of diffusion of their interface atoms.

Advantages and limitations of welding over other joining processes

Some advantages of joining metallic parts by welding are as follows:

- **Strength**   The joints made by welding are stronger than those made by other joining processes. The joint strength can be greater than that of work materials if the filler metal has strength properties better than those of parent materials, and proper welding technique has been used.

- **Leak proof**   Most welded joints are water leak proof. Joints made by some welding processes do not even allow air to pass through them.

- **Compact**   Welded joints are compact and do not require additional supports.

- **Light weight**   Welded products are relatively lighter in weight.

- **Corrosion resistant**   Compared to riveted and bolted joints, joints made by welding are more corrosion resistant.

- **Variety**   Several types of joints are possible when the parts are to be joined by welding. Selection can be made depending on the strength and appearance desired.

- **Application to dissimilar materials**   Parts made of dissimilar materials can be easily joined by welding.

- **Application anywhere**   Welding can be carried out not only in the factory environment but in the field also.

- **Only choice**   For very thick parts, welding is often the only choice for joining.

- **Ease**   Welding is the most rapid and easiest way of joining metal parts.

- **Economical**   Welded joints are less expensive due to reduction in weight and less cost of material.

There are some limitations of welding too. These are as follows:

- **High energy**   Most welding processes use high energy, and can at times be dangerous unless safety precautions are followed.

- **Labour intensive**   Many welding processes are performed manually and most jobs are done by skilled workers. In terms of labour cost, welding processes can be expensive.

- **Difficulty in dissembling**   Since welding accomplishes a permanent joint of the components, it cannot be employed where components require frequent disassembling (for example, for repair or maintenance).

- **Difficulty in weld defect detection**   In the absence of correct welding conditions, welded joint can suffer from quality defects, resulting in reduced joint strength. Detection of defects in welds is not so easy.

Metallurgy of welding

All welding processes, by definition, involve melting (or at least heating) and cooling of the workpiece material, resulting in the occurrence of undesirable metallurgical changes. In fusion welding processes, where the workpiece material is heated to a molten state, the thermal effects can be quite severe; in other welding processes also, adverse thermal effects do occur, though to a lesser extent. The thermal damage to the work material or to the component part caused by the welding process can be avoided or at least reduced if proper conditions are chosen.

The subject of welding metallurgy is very vast because there is a large variety of welding processes and there is also a large variety of metals that are welded. In the following paragraphs we will, however, restrict ourselves to some typical cases.

Let us first take the case of the fusion welding operation. Here, a pool of molten metal is formed. This pool comprises either only the workpiece metals or a mixture of the filler metal and the workpiece metals, as can be seen in Figure 15.10(a). When fusion welding of two parts of different metals is carried out using a backing strip of another metal and a filler rod of yet another material [Figure 15.10(b)], the molten pool will become an alloy of all the four metals. The molten metal pool is then surrounded by a solid workpiece metal while it cools to form the weld. This is analogous to casting a certain volume of molten metal in a metal mould. The resultant microstructure and the properties of the *casting* can be analyzed considering the type and volume of weld metal and the heat flow to the adjacent workpiece metals as well as to the surroundings. The grain structure of the weld zone may, therefore, be fine or coarse, equi-axed or dendrite, depending upon these parameters. Since the material and the microstructure of the *cast weld* are different from those of the workpiece material being welded, the properties and characteristics of the two cannot be expected to be the same. In order to obtain a strong weld, a common practice followed is to use filler rods or electrodes that have properties *in their as-deposited condition* that equal or excel those of the workpiece metal.

In spite of every care being taken in the selection of proper electrode material, the weld is prone to possess any or all the defects that are normally associated with metal casting, such as porosity, blowholes, cracks, shrinkage and inclusions. Since the amount of weld metal pool is mostly small as compared to the total mass of the workpiece, rapid solidification and cooling of the weld is unavoidable, with the result that entrapment of dissolved gases and problems of grain size and shape do occur.

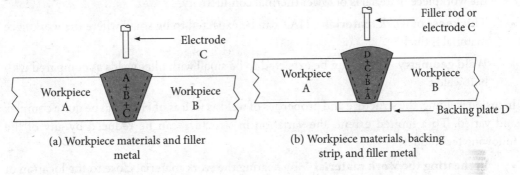

(a) Workpiece materials and filler metal

(b) Workpiece materials, backing strip, and filler metal

Figure 15.10 Weld metal pool

As can be seen in Figure 15.11, an undesirable heat affected zone (HAZ) is present between the fusion zone and the area where the workpiece metal has experienced too little heat from the welding process. As the name suggests, the workpiece material in the HAZ is subjected to high temperatures for a short duration, but no melting of metal takes place. Due to exposure to high heat, the metal in the HAZ experiences changes in structure and properties such as phase transformation, grain growth, re-crystallization, embrittlement and even cracking.

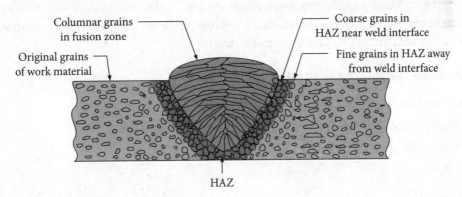

Figure 15.11 Heat affected zone

Experimental results have shown that a metal in the HAZ undergoes wide ranging changes in its microstructure. The properties and behaviour of the material in the HAZ are, therefore, different from those of the parent workpiece material or solidified weld metal. In several cases, the HAZ is the weakest region of the weld joint and forms the nucleus for most welding failures, except for those cases where the solidified weld has more serious defects.

The size of the HAZ depends on the following:

- **Welding process employed**   Processes with low rate of heat input tend to give high total heat content into the work material and produce large HAZ.
- **Welding speed**   Higher welding speeds produce smaller HAZ.
- **Thermal conductivity of the work material**   HAZ can be expected to be small where the workpiece material is of lower thermal conductivity.
- **Thickness of work material**   HAZ can be expected to be small where the workpiece material is thick.
- **Weld geometry**   HAZ can be expected to be small with fillet welds as compared with butt welds.

In fusion welding, the structure and properties of weld as well as of HAZ can be quite complex and varied. To a limited extent, the variation in structure can be reduced by any of the following techniques.

- **Preheating the work material**   By heating the work material close to the location of joint before starting the welding operation, it is possible to reduce the cooling rate of the weld deposit as well as that of the metal in the HAZ. This also helps in avoiding any drastic change in the microstructure and metallurgical stresses.
- **Heat treatment to the work material**   By heat treating the complete workpiece after the welding operation is over, it is possible to reduce the variation in the microstructure of the weld metal in comparison to that of the workpiece metal. This technique is, however, limited to situations where the component size is small.

In cases of non-fusion welding processes, where the joint is obtained by applying considerable pressure to the heated metal (as in resistance welding processes), the weld region experiences deformation with little or no change in microstructure.

Types of fusion welds and weld joints

Fusion weld types   There are four types of fusion welds:

- Bead welds.
- Groove welds.
- Fillet welds.
- Plug welds.

Bead welds   Bead welds are also called surfacing welds because the weld is made directly onto a flat surface. These types of welds are applicable to thin sheets of metal and, therefore, have only small penetration depth. Generally, no edge preparation is needed. The main use of bead welds is to build surfaces and to deposit hard facing materials such as stellite. Figure 15.12(a) shows a typical bead weld.

Groove welds   Groove welds, also called butt welds, are used for joining thicker metals. Edge preparation of the sheets or plates to be joined is necessary to form a groove between the abutting surfaces. Depending upon the thickness of the plate, the welding process to be used, and the position of the workpiece, either V, double V or U configurations may be prepared. The joints usually require a number of successive weld layers to build up the full weld thickness, though single-pass welding is preferred. Figure 15.12(b) shows a typical groove weld.

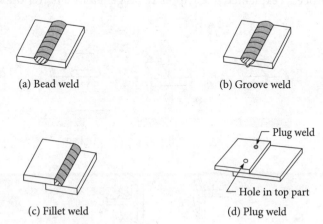

(a) Bead weld   (b) Groove weld

(c) Fillet weld   (d) Plug weld

Figure 15.12   Typical fusion welds

Fillet welds   Fillet welds are used for making tee, lap and corner joint configurations, as can be seen in Figure 15.12(c). These welds are typical of structural steel work. Filler metal is used to develop a cross-section approximating the shape of a right triangle. The size of the *fillet* is the leg of the largest right triangle that can be inscribed within the contour of the weld cross-section. As with groove welds, larger fillet welds often require multi-pass welding to reduce stress concentration. No edge preparation is necessary because, by the nature of the angular joint shape, open access is available across the entire weld thickness. Fillet welds may be either continuous or intermittent (with spaces being left between short lengths of weld) that save both time as well as weld materials.

Plug welds   Plug welds are used to attach one flat part on top of another flat part, replacing rivets or bolts. A hole is made in the plate (one part) and placed over the other part. Welding is done at the bottom of this hole to fuse the two parts together [Figure 15.12(d)].

Fusion weld joints   Five basic types of joints that can be made with the use of the aforementioned weld types are shown in Figure 15.13. These are termed as butt, tee, corner, lap and edge joints.

Butt joints   Butt joints are used to weld parts in the same plane and employ either bead or multi-pass butt welds, depending upon the part thickness.

Tee joints Tee joints are used to weld one workpiece to another at right angles. Fillet welds are used on both sides of the tee junction. Tee joints are prone to welding distortion, which can be reduced by welding both sides of the joint at the same time.

Corner joints Corner joint is similar to one-half of a tee joint and is made using fillet welds.

Lap joints As shown in Figure 15.13, all lap joints involve filling in of corners along the joint. Fillet welds are used on both sides. In case of thin sheet lap joints, use of resistance spot or seam welding process (explained in Chapter 18) is generally a better option.

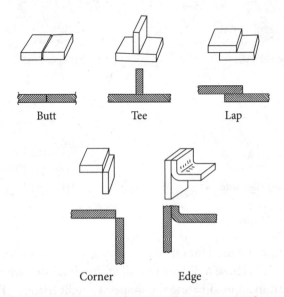

Figure 15.13 Some types of fusion weld joints

Edge joints Edge joints are used mainly on thin parts that are parallel with at least one of their edges in common. The joint is made at the common edge. Although fusion welding is commonly used for making edge joints, spot or seam resistance welding can be a better option for thin sheets. If a continuous weld is needed, then bead welds are used.

The selection of a proper type of weld joint is made by considering the type of loading that will be applied on the welded part, accessibility for welding and the actual cost. The cost comprises the expenses involved on edge preparation, weld metal and the equipment that must be used.

Classification of welding processes

Welding processes differ mainly with respect to the amount and the manner in which heat and pressure are applied to produce a joint. The quality of joint produced depends on the means used for cleaning the metal parts as also for protecting the metal from metallurgical effects. The equipment for different welding processes differs on account of these considerations.

Welding processes can be classified into two categories: pressure welding processes and fusion welding processes. *Pressure welding,* as the name indicates, requires the pressure to bring the hot surfaces of the metal parts to a state when cohesion can take place. Welding processes in this category need hammering, rolling or pressing to produce the weld. *Fusion welding* involves bringing the metal at the joint to a fluid state so that a metal pool is formed. In this metal pool, some kind of weld metal may be added but no pressure is applied. *Thermit welding* process can also be included in this category. Thermit welds are made by casting, that is, the metal is heated to a very high temperature and poured into a cavity made around the two pieces at the location where the joint is to be made. Figure 15.14 shows the important welding processes grouped into these two categories

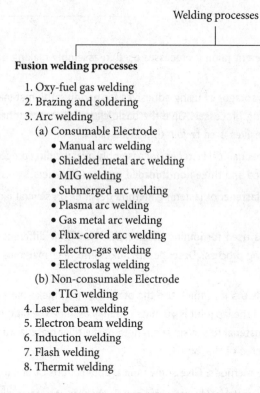

Welding processes

Fusion welding processes
1. Oxy-fuel gas welding
2. Brazing and soldering
3. Arc welding
  (a) Consumable Electrode
    • Manual arc welding
    • Shielded metal arc welding
    • MIG welding
    • Submerged arc welding
    • Plasma arc welding
    • Gas metal arc welding
    • Flux-cored arc welding
    • Electro-gas welding
    • Electroslag welding
  (b) Non-consumable Electrode
    • TIG welding
4. Laser beam welding
5. Electron beam welding
6. Induction welding
7. Flash welding
8. Thermit welding

Pressure welding processes
1. Forge welding
2. Cold welding
3. Pressure gas welding
4. Friction welding
5. Ultrasonic welding
6. Roll welding
7. Explosion welding
8. Resistance welding

Figure 15.14 Classification of welding processes

Welding process selection

Selection of an appropriate welding process can be made by giving due consideration to the following factors:

- **Cost** Costs are involved in pre-welding operations (such as edge preparation), welding and post-welding operations (such as machining and grinding).
- **Characteristics of the parts to be welded** The material, shape, size and thickness of the parts are all important factors.

- **Strength of the joint**   Depending on the service requirements, strength of joint and other parameters such as air or fluid leakage proof conditions are important to consider.
- **Welding stresses, distortion and discolouration**   Depending on the service requirements of the parts to be welded, these factors are important.
- **Quality and appearance of weld**   Depending on the usage of welded part, these factors need to be considered.
- **Ease of welding**   This is mainly dependent on the location and accessibility of the area of the component parts where welding is to be done.
- **Rate of welding**   This factor is important in achieving the specific levels of production.

Questions

1.   Name and briefly describe the different joining processes used in assembly making during manufacturing.

2.   Discuss the advantages and disadvantages of using adhesives for bonding the materials as compared with conventional joining processes. Give the basic classification of adhesives and name any three synthetic adhesives used to join thin metal parts.

3.   What are the advantages of using mechanical fasteners for assembly over welding processes? Name and sketch any three threaded and three non-threaded types of fasteners.

4.   Selection of a suitable mechanical fastener or fastening method depends on several factors. List them.

5.   Briefly explain the *brazing* process used for joining metal parts. How is it different from soldering process and braze welding process? Describe the fluxes and filler materials used in brazing.

6.   Two plates of the same metal – one 0.5 mm thick and the other 0.4 mm thick –have been lap-joined by brazing. The length of the lap joint is 10 mm. You may assume the ratio of the tensile strength of the workpiece material to the shear strength of the filler material to be 6. What factor of safety can be expected of the joint?

7.   Briefly describe the various brazing methods. Give some typical applications of brazing.

8.   What is meant by *solderability of a material*? Name some metals that are easy to solder and also some metals that are difficult to solder. Name the two basic types of fluxes used in the soldering process. Sketch any three typical joint designs used for soldering.

9.   Name the processes that can be employed to join metal parts. Define welding and list the advantages of welding over other joining processes.

10.   Define the term *heat affected zone* as used in welding. Suggest some measures to reduce its unwanted effects.

11.   What is the basic classification of welding processes? How do welding processes differ from one another? What factors should be kept in mind while selecting an appropriate welding process to join a given pair of metal parts?

12. Name any two pre-welding and two post-welding operations. Sketch different weld types and weld joints.

Fill in the Blanks

1. _____ is a natural adhesive, while _____ is an inorganic adhesive and _____ is a synthetic adhesive.

2. When using adhesive bonding for assembly, _____ is a critical parameter that limits the rate of production.

3. Welding processes can be classified into two categories: (i) _____ welding processes and (ii) _____ welding processes.

4. Wherever frequent disassembly and reassembly is needed (for instance, for repair and maintenance), the component parts should preferably be joined by _____.

5. Most common application of *integral fasteners* is in products made of _____.

6. _____ is a mechanical joining method in which a joint of two parts is made by introducing a dimensional change to one or both the parts either by heating or cooling.

7. Brazing and soldering processes are distinguished from each other by the _____ involved.

8. Brazing temperatures are _____ than those used in soldering.

9. The brazed joint has _____ strength than the soldered joint.

10. In brazing, the filler metals and the workpiece metals to be joined, generally, have _____ compositions.

11. The use of flux has three main functions in the brazing process. These are (i) _____, (ii) _____ and (iii) _____.

12. The strength of a brazed lap joint depends mainly on the _____ of the joint.

13. _____ is a brazing flux.

14. In soldering, the solder fills the joint by _____ action between closely fitting or closely placed components.

15. Solders used in the soldering process are usually alloys of _____ and _____ prepared in various proportions.

Choose the Correct Answer

1. When it is desired that no change takes place in material properties, surface roughness or external appearance of the joined components, the joining method adopted is
   a. adhesive bonding.
   c. brazing.
   b. mechanical fastening.
   d. soldering.

2. When fragile components are to be joined without any significant addition of weight, the recommended method of joining is

    a. adhesive bonding.   c. brazing.

    b. mechanical fastening.   d. soldering.

3. In most engineering applications, particularly for load-bearing applications, adhesives used for obtaining better cohesive strength of component assembly are

    a. natural adhesives.   c. organic adhesives.

    b. inorganic adhesives.   d. synthetic adhesives.

4. A critical limitation in the use of adhesive bonds for structural applications is their

    a. excellent strength for service above 500°C.

    b. poor strength for service above 200°C.

    c. electrical conductivity.

    d. pressure sensitivity.

5. Adhesive bonding

    a. is never performed automatically.

    b. may allow for disassembly.

    c. uniformly distributes stresses over a large surface.

    d. is a high cost assembly option.

6. In adhesive bonding, the term used for the parts that are joined is

    a. adherend.   c. adhesive.

    b. adherentive.   d. adhibit.

7. A good adhesive-bonded joint is one in which on the application of high stresses, the failure occurs

    a. in one of the adherends.

    b. at one of the interfaces between adhesive and adherend.

    c. at both the interfaces between adhesive and adherend.

    d. within the adhesive.

8. Wherever frequent disassembly and reassembly is needed (for instance, for repair and maintenance), the desired method of joining is

    a. mechanical fastening.   c. soldering.

    b. electrical fastening.   d. adhesive bonding.

9. Wherever frequent disassembly and reassembly is needed (for instance, for repair and maintenance), use should preferably be made of

    a. threaded fasteners or snap fits.   c. riveted joints.

    b. permanent fasteners.   d. welded joints.

10. The mechanical type of fasteners that comprise formed areas of a component, which interfere or interlock with other components of the assembly, are called

    a. lockhead devices. c. shrink and expansion fits.

    b. integral fasteners. d. leisure fasteners.

11. Integral fasteners are

    a. inserted during assembly. c. high in cost.

    b. designed into sheet metal products. d. always installed manually.

12. Threaded fasteners are

    a. a low cost means of assembly.

    b. used when disassembly is required.

    c. installed by hand or by automated machinery.

    d. all of the above.

13. Shrink and expansion fits are an important class of

    a. interference fit.. c. soldering.

    b. brazing. d. adhesive bonding.

14. In brazing operation,

    a. a filler metal of ferrous alloy is introduced between the surfaces of the metal pieces to be joined.

    b. heat is applied only to melt the filler metal, but not the workpieces.

    c. heat is applied to melt the filler metal and the workpieces.

    d. the joint strength obtained is generally the same as that obtained in the soldering operation.

15. Aluminium parts are commonly brazed in

    a. vacuum. c. oxygen-rich environment.

    b. normal environment. d. corrosive environment.

16. The filler metals used for brazing generally have

    a. different compositions than those of the workpiece materials to be joined.

    b. same compositions as those of the workpiece materials to be joined.

    c. a melting temperature of less than 450°C.

    d. a melting temperature almost the same as the melting temperature of the workpiece material.

17. A common flux used in brazing operation is

    a. sodium nitrate. c. potassium permanganate.

    b. silver nitrate. d. borax.

18. Which of the following is not a brazing method?

    a. torch brazing c. resistance brazing

    b. furnace brazing d. capacitance brazing

19. Solders used in soldering operation are usually the alloys of
    a.   tin and lead prepared in various proportions.
    b.   tin and copper prepared in various proportions.
    c.   iron and carbon prepared in various proportions.
    d.   lead and brass prepared in various proportions.

20. The use of flux is a must in brazing operations because it helps in
    a.   removing oxide films from workpiece surfaces.
    b.   giving the filler metal the necessary fluidity to wet the joint surfaces.
    c.   preventing oxidation.
    d.   all the above.

21. If k is factor of safety, t is wall thickness of thinner member in mm, σ is tensile strength of thinner member in Pa and ζ is shear stress of braze filler metal in Pa, the length L of lap for a flat lap brazing joint can be estimated by using the following relation
    a. $L = k \cdot t \cdot (\sigma / \zeta)$ c. $L = k/t \cdot (\sigma / \zeta)$
    b. $L = 1/k \cdot t \cdot (\sigma / \zeta)$ d. $L = k \cdot t \cdot (\zeta / \sigma)$

22. Braze welding and brazing
    a.   differ from each other with respect to the technique of deposition of filler metal in the joint.
    b.   differ from each other with respect to the composition of filler material used in the two processes.
    c.   differ from each other with respect to the types of joint produced.
    d.   are the two names of the same welding process.

23. Carbide tool bits are joined to steel tool shanks mostly by the process of
    a.   soldering.   c.   gas welding.
    b.   arc welding.   d.   braze welding.

24. The melting point of solder is mostly
    a.   below 450°C.   c.   between 550°C and 650°C.
    b.   between 450°C and 550°C. d.   above 650°C.

25. Another name for the process of soldering is
    a.   hard soldering.   c.   white brazing.
    b.   soft soldering.   d.   white welding.

26. Which one of the following is difficult to solder?
    a.   stainless steel   c.   copper
    b.   silver   d.   brass

27. Which of the following metals is not used in solder alloys?
    a.   antimony   c.   tin
    b.   lead   d.   iron

28. Which of the following is not a method of soldering?

    a. furnace soldering
    b. weld soldering
    c. induction soldering
    d. resistance soldering

29. In welding, the heat affected zone does not depend upon

    a. welding speed.
    b. weld geometry.
    c. thermal conductivity of work material.
    d. thermal conductivity of filler material.

30. Which one of the following is not a type of fusion weld?

    a. groove weld
    b. fillet weld
    c. plug weld
    d. socket weld

31. Bead welds are generally used for

    a. thin sheets.
    b. thick plates.
    c. circular rods.
    d. hollow rods.

32. Which of the following is not a type of weld joint?

    a. butt
    b. L
    c. N
    d. T

33. Which one of the following is generally not a factor while selecting a proper type of weld joint?

    a. material of the part
    b. type of loading on the part
    c. accessibility for welding
    d. cost of welding

34. Thermit welding is a sort of

    a. casting.
    b. forging.
    c. machining.
    d. spinning.

35. Cold welding is a process of

    a. casting.
    b. welding.
    c. press working.
    d. sand testing.

36. One-half of a tee joint is known as

    a. butt joint.
    b. lap joint.
    c. edge joint.
    d. corner joint.

37. Riveted assembly falls under the category of

    a. permanent joint.
    b. semi-permanent joint.
    c. temporary joint.
    d. no-joint.

38. Nut and bolt assembly falls under the category of

    a. permanent joint.
    b. semi-permanent joint.
    c. temporary joint.
    d. no-joint.

Answers

1. a. 2. a. 3. d. 4. b. 5. c. 6. a. 7. a. 8. a. 9. a. 10. b.

11. b. 12. d. 13. a. 14. b. 15. a. 16. a. 17. d. 18. d. 19. a. 20. d.

21. a. 22. a. 23. d. 24. a. 25. b. 26. a. 27. d. 28. b. 29. d. 30. d.

31. a. 32. c. 33. a. 34. a. 35. b. 36. d. 37. b. 38. c.

16

Gas Welding Processes

LEARNING OBJECTIVES

After reading this chapter, you should be able to understand the following:

- The various oxy-fuel gas welding processes and the equipment used.
- The oxy-acetylene gas welding, its advantages, disadvantages and applications.
- The various gas welding methods.
- The pressure gas welding process.
- The safety precautions in gas welding practices.
- The oxy-fuel gas cutting process.

16.1 Introduction

Fusion welding can be defined as the technique of joining metal pieces in which materials are melted locally at the place of joint by the application of heat. Filler materials may or may not be added to the weld area during welding. The source of heat, generally, is a gas flame or an electric arc. Fusion welds made *without* the addition of any filler material are known as *autogenous welds*.

Fusion welding processes that use gas as the source of heat are termed as gas or oxy-fuel gas welding processes. Some important oxy-fuel gas welding processes will be described in this chapter. The subject matter will cover the basic principles of each process, the equipment used, their relative advantages and limitations, their capabilities and applications.

16.2 Oxy-fuel Gas Welding Processes

Oxy-fuel gas welding (OGW) is a term used for the welding process in which oxygen and a fuel gas are combined to obtain a flame. This flame is then used to melt the metals at the joint.

The fuel gases generally used in this process are acetylene, hydrogen, propane, propylene and natural gas.

16.2.1 Oxy-acetylene welding

The oxy-acetylene welding process is the most common gas welding process in which a high-temperature flame is produced from the combustion of oxygen and acetylene gas [Figure 16.1]. The primary combustion that occurs in the inner core of the flame can be represented by the following reaction:

$$C_2H_2 + O_2 \rightarrow 2CO + H_2 + Heat$$

The process uses a device, called the welding torch, in which the supplied oxygen and acetylene gases are mixed and the gas mixture is delivered at its tip. The aforementioned reaction occurs near the tip of the welding torch and is responsible for nearly one-third of the total heat produced in the flame. The secondary combustion, which follows the primary combustion, occurs just beyond the first combustion zone and produces nearly two-third of the total heat. The following reaction represents the secondary combustion:

$$2CO + H_2 + 1\tfrac{1}{2}O_2 \rightarrow 2CO_2 + H_2O + Heat$$

As a result of these reactions, the total heat liberated is of the order of 50×10^6 J/m^3 of acetylene gas. However, due to the temperature distribution in the flame and losses to the surrounding air, thermal efficiency in oxy-acetylene welding is quite low. The temperatures developed in the flame are of the order of 3400°C. The flame is used to heat the metal at the joint to a state of fusion and, as a rule no pressure is applied to the workpieces.

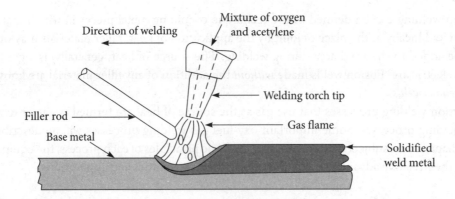

Figure 16.1   Schematic of oxy-acetylene welding process

Types of flame

By regulating the proportion of acetylene and oxygen in the gas mixture, three types of flames can be obtained. Figure 16.4 shows the three types of oxy-acetylene gas flames.

- Neutral flame
- Oxidizing flame
- Carburizing flame (or reducing flame)

Neutral flame A neutral flame is formed when the proportion of acetylene and oxygen in the gas mixture is almost 1:1 (often in the range 1:1 to 1.15:1). As we can see in Figure 16.2(a), the primary combustion occurs at the inner cone of the flame (which is bright white), while the secondary combustion is exhibited by the outer envelope (which is somewhat colourless having tinges ranging from blue to orange). The maximum temperature of the flame is at the tip of the inner cone; the flame temperature decreases outwards. During welding operation, the outer envelope touches the work surface and spreads out to shield it from the surrounding atmosphere. This flame is used for welding of most metals since it has a negligible chemical effect on the heated metal.

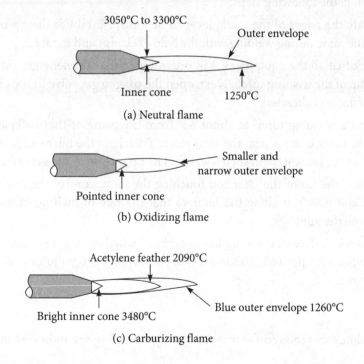

Figure 16.2 Types of oxy-acetylene gas flame

Oxidizing flame An oxidizing flame contains relatively greater amounts of oxygen than acetylene. The appearance of the flame is similar to the neutral flame, except that the inner luminous cone is much shorter and the outer envelope appears colourful. The molten metal at the joint gets oxidized when this flame is used for welding purposes. For this reason, many metals, especially steel, are *not* welded with this flame. However, copper, brass and bronze can be welded with this flame because in these cases, a thin layer of slag is formed over the molten metal that protects it from getting oxidized.

Carburizing flame A carburizing flame contains more amount of acetylene than oxygen, and is also called a reducing flame. The appearance of flame is different. There are three zones instead of two. Between the luminous cone and the outer envelope is an intermediate white-coloured cone, whose length is determined by the amount of excess acetylene. The temperature of this flame is relatively low and, therefore, it is suitable for those applications that require less heat, for example, brazing. This flame is also used to weld low-carbon steels, some types of alloy steels, nickel and Monel (a nickel–copper alloy). There is no carburization of metal but the metal is protected from oxidation.

Gas welding practice

Most ferrous and non-ferrous metals can be welded by oxy-fuel gas welding. Several types of joints can be produced by this method. The procedure for oxy-acetylene gas welding can be described through the following steps:

Step 1 Prepare the edges of the workpieces to be joined. Establish their proper position, and maintain the same during welding with the help of clamps and fixtures.

Step 2 Check that all the equipment is in order. Open the acetylene gas valve and ignite the gas at the tip of the welding torch. Next, open the oxygen gas valve to the extent that the desired type of flame is obtained.

Step 3 Hold the welding torch at about 45° from the plane of the workpiece in such a position that the inner flame is near the workpiece. Then hold the filler rod at about 30°–40° from the plane of the workpiece in such a way that its tip is close to the inner flame.

Step 4 Keeping the tip of the filler rod touching the joint, control the movement of the welding torch and filler rod along the joint so that the rate of melting of the filler rod is appropriate to fill the joint.

Step 5 Clean the surface of the solidified weld bead whether or not another layer of weld bead is required to be deposited. This is necessary to obtain a proper joint strength as well as a good appearance.

Equipment

The main equipments required for oxy-acetylene gas welding are indicated in Figure 16.3. These include:

- Blow pipe (welding torch)
- Oxygen and acetylene gases and gas cylinders
- Pressure regulators
- Pressure gauges

- Nozzle or tip
- Hose and hose fittings
- Miscellaneous items

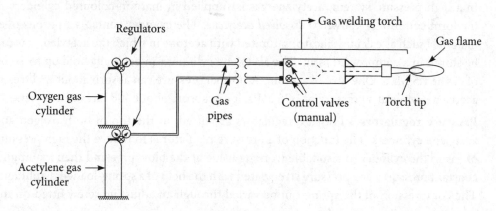

Figure 16.3 Oxy-acetylene gas welding equipment

1. **Blow pipe** The function of a blow pipe (also known as welding torch) is to mix the two gases in desired proportions and to deliver the mixture to the tip of the nozzle where it is burned. The main parts of a blow pipe are two gas inlets, each fitted with a needle type control valve, a gas mixing chamber (of the blow pipe) and a replaceable nozzle screwed at the end as shown in Figure 16.4. Depending on the thickness of material to be welded, smaller or bigger tips may be used. The blow pipe receives the gases when the two gas inlets are connected to the gas cylinders through reducing valves with the help of rubber tubes. The flow rate of each gas can be individually controlled and hence, the type of gas flame can be varied with the help of knobs fitted on the control valves. The blow pipe is available in various sizes and designs.

2. **Oxygen and acetylene gases and gas cylinders** Oxygen can be produced either by electrolysis of water or by liquification of air. Electrolysis separates water into hydrogen and oxygen, whereas liquification of air involves separation of oxygen from nitrogen. Oxygen gas is stored in black-coloured steel cylinders at a pressure of 15 MPa.

   Acetylene gas can be generated either at site in a low pressure system or obtained in cylinders at a high pressure. In a low pressure system, acetylene is generated by placing pieces of calcium carbide in water. The gas bubbles through the water, and the slaked lime is left behind in the form of a precipitate. The following reaction takes place in an acetylene gas generator.

   $$CaC_2 + 2H_2O \rightarrow Ca\,(OH)_2 + C_2H_2 + Heat$$

   The generated acetylene is supplied from a gas holder incorporated in the generator to the blow pipe at low pressure. A purifier incorporated in the system cleans the gas.

To prevent any chance of air blowing back and entering the system and causing an explosion, a back pressure valve is introduced between the blow pipe and the gas holder. The pressure of acetylene at the torch in a low pressure system is up to 0.006 MPa.

In a high pressure system, acetylene gas is supplied in maroon-coloured cylinders in the form commonly known as *dissolved acetylene*. The cylinder contains a porous filler material (such as calcium silicate) saturated with acetone in which the acetylene gas can be stored in a compressed form. The acetylene cylinder can generally hold up to 10 m³ of gas at 1.5 MPa. One litre of acetone at normal pressure can absorb about 25 litres of acetylene, while at a pressure of 1.75 MPa, it can absorb about 400 litres of acetylene.

3. **Pressure regulators**   Pressure regulators are fitted on the top of both oxygen and acetylene cylinders. The function of a pressure regulator is to reduce the high pressure of gas in the cylinder to a suitable working value at the blow pipe and then maintain a constant pressure. The pressure is regulated with the help of a spring-loaded diaphragm. The compression of the spring can be varied through an adjusting screw fitted on the regulator.

4. **Pressure gauges**   There are two pressure gauges installed in each gas cylinder, one indicating the pressure of gas inside the cylinder and the other indicating the pressure of gas being supplied to the blow pipe.

5. **Nozzle**   The nozzle or torch tip is a device screwed to the end of the blow pipe. Its function is to allow the flow of the gas mixture from the mixing chamber (of the blow pipe) to the tip of the nozzle in order to facilitate combustion of the gas mixture. Nozzles are available with different hole sizes so that the operator can select the right nozzle that will give the necessary gas flow (and hence, heat flow) to match the workpiece thickness. Each nozzle is generally stamped with the information about gas consumption in litres/hour at specific pressures and the attached table, generally supplied by the manufacturer, defines the suitability of the different nozzles for various workpiece materials and thicknesses.

6. **Rubber tubing and fittings**   The rubber tubing (hose) is used as a flexible connection between the blow pipe and outlet of the pressure reducing valve fitted at the top of the gas cylinder. For the purpose of distinction, *blue* or *black* coloured tubes are used for oxygen and *red* tubes for acetylene. In order to prevent the interchange of fittings, the oxygen gas fittings and the acetylene gas fittings have different threads.

7. **Miscellaneous items**   Other items of equipment used for gas welding are:
   - **Spark lighter**   This is used to light the gas mixture at the nozzle tip.
   - **Safety equipment**   These include face shields and goggles with shaded lenses, gloves and aprons. The use of goggles and face shield protects the operator's eyes from the heat and glare (light) coming from the flame and molten metal in the weld pool. Gloves protect the operator's hands, whereas the apron protects the operator's clothing from heat and metal splashes.

- **Chipping hammer:** A chipping hammer is used to remove metal oxides and residues of flux from the weld bead.
- **Wire brush:** A wire brush is used to clean the workpiece near the joint both before and after welding.

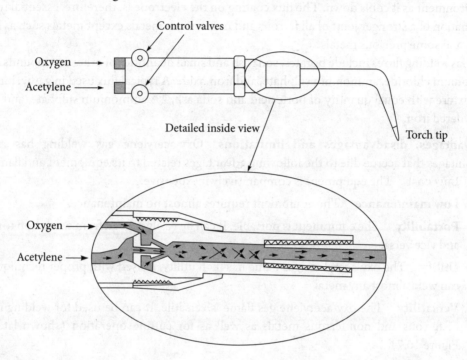

Figure 16.4 Schematic of a welding torch

Filler rods and fluxes

The welding rod or wire used as filler material supplies additional material to the weld zone during welding. The consumable filler rod generally has the same or nearly same composition as that of the workpiece material. The diameter of the welding rod selected is related to the thickness of the workpiece by the following relation:

$$d = \tfrac{1}{2} t + 1 \text{ mm}$$

where d is the diameter of the welding rod and t is the thickness of the workpiece material in mm.

The welding rod may either be bare, or it may be coated with flux. The flux coating performs the following functions:

1. Eliminating or at least reducing the oxidation of the surfaces of the workpieces being welded by producing a *gaseous shield* around the weld zone.

2. Dissolving and removing oxides and other non-desirable substances from the workpiece surfaces.

The flux coated on the welding rod must melt at a temperature lower than that of the metals being welded so that the surface oxides will be dissolved before the workpiece metal melts. The molten flux combines with metal oxides and other impurities to develop a slag that floats on the top and, thus, protects the molten puddle of metal against reaction with the environment as it cools down. The flux coating on the electrode is, therefore, essential to the formation of a stronger joint of all ferrous and non-ferrous metals except metals such as lead, zinc and some precious metals.

Gas welding fluxes include borates, soda ash and small quantities of other compounds such as sodium chloride, ammonium sulphate, and iron oxide. A typical flux used in gas welding is a mixture with equal quantity of boric acid and soda ash, 2% ammonium sulphate, and 15% powdered iron.

Advantages, disadvantages and limitations Oxy-acetylene gas welding has many advantages that accrue due to the following advantages related to its equipment and flame:

- **Low cost** The equipment is comparatively inexpensive.

- **Low maintenance** The equipment requires almost no maintenance.

- **Portability** The equipment is portable. It can be easily moved from workshop to field and vice versa.

- **Utility** The oxy-acetylene gas flame has high utility. If used with proper technique, it can weld almost any metal

- **Versatility** The oxy-acetylene gas flame is versatile. It can be used for welding most of ferrous and non-ferrous metals as well as for cutting operation (shown later in Figure 16.7).

Oxy-acetylene gas welding has the following disadvantages:

- **Slow** The process is relatively slow mainly because it is accomplished manually.

- **Thermal effects** Due to the application of heat for a prolonged period, the harmful thermal effects are aggravated. There is probability of increased grain growth, greater distortion and, in some cases, loss of corrosion resistance.

- **Safety** There are several safety problems in handling gases. For example, different screw threads are required on the acetylene and oxygen cylinders and hoses to avoid accidental connection of the wrong gases.

- **Metal protection** Shielding provided by the secondary envelope of the flame is generally not enough.

- **Hazardous** The combination of oxygen and acetylene is highly flammable, and therefore can be hazardous.

- **Uneconomical** For welding component parts thicker than 6 mm, gas welding becomes uneconomical when compared to arc welding.

- **Skill of operator** Proper training and skill of the operator are essential for good results.

Oxy-acetylene gas welding is quite widely used for low quantity work, say, in fabrication and repair work. The process is used to weld practically all metals as well as for all types of joints and in all positions.

16.2.2 Oxy-hydrogen welding

In this process, hydrogen (fuel gas) and oxygen together form the flame. Hydrogen is obtained either by electrolysis of water or by passing steam over coke. The oxy-hydrogen flame has a lower temperature (2,000°C) compared to the oxy-acetylene flame and, therefore, finds application in the welding of thin sheets or parts of low-melting point alloys. It is also used for brazing work. A reducing atmosphere is recommended. As there is no oxide formed on the weld surface, the quality of weld produced is very good.

The same torch as used for oxy-acetylene gas welding can be used for oxy-hydrogen gas welding. However, flame adjustments are more difficult because there is no colour distinction of the flame with change of gas proportions.

16.2.3 Air-acetylene welding

This process uses a torch having a similar construction as that of the Bunsen burner. Air, as needed for proper combustion, is drawn from the atmosphere into the torch. The temperature of the flame produced is quite low and, therefore, this process is used to weld parts made of lead or other low melting point metals. The air-acetylene flame can also be used for brazing and soldering operations.

16.3 Methods of Gas Welding

There are three main methods of gas welding. The selection of a particular method for a given job will depend upon the metal to be welded, its thickness and the desired quality of the welded joint. The methods of gas welding are:
*   Leftward welding
*   Rightward welding
*   Vertical welding
*   Overhead welding

Leftward Welding   The leftward welding method, which is also known as *forward welding*, requires the filler rod to be held in the left hand and the blow pipe in the right hand. The welding operation is carried out from the right-hand side towards the left-hand side, with the blowpipe following the filler rod, as shown in Figure 16.5(a). The blow pipe is given an additional short transverse (side to side) movement, while the filler rod is moved progressively along the joint. This method allows preheating of plate edges immediately ahead of the molten metal pool, and is widely used for butt welding of plates up to 6 mm thickness.

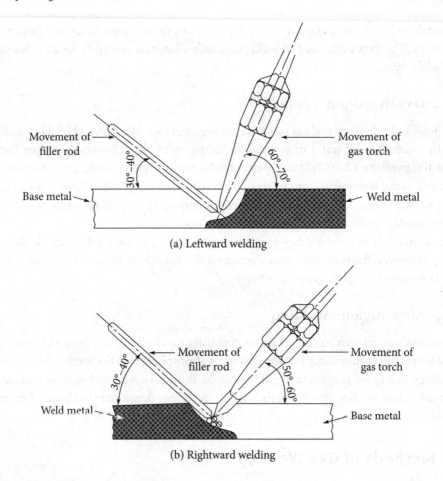

Base metal

Movement of filler rod

30°–40°

60°–70°

Movement of gas torch

Weld metal

(a) Leftward welding

Weld metal

Movement of filler rod

30°–40°

50°–60°

Movement of gas torch

Base metal

(b) Rightward welding

Figure 16.5 Welding techniques

Rightward welding The rightward welding method, which is also known as *backward welding*, also requires the filler rod to be held in the left hand and the blow pipe in the right hand. Welding operation is carried out from the left-hand side towards the right-hand side, with the filler rod following the blow pipe, as shown in Figure 16.5(b). The blow pipe points towards the direction of the completed weld so that the weld puddle is kept hot for a longer time. The inclination of the blow pipe with the plate is comparatively less. The inclination of the torch with the surface being welded depends primarily upon the thickness of the metal; larger the thickness, larger the angle of inclination. This method is widely used for butt welding of plates over 6 mm thickness. Some advantages of using rightward welding technique are:

- Welding can possibly be done faster due to an unobstructed view of the joint edge. Further, as the welding progresses, there is no need to remove the end of the filler rod to inspect the quality of weld formed. The end of the filler rod is thus not oxidized and, hence, there are less chances of getting an unfavourable weld structure.

- Thicker plates can be welded. Plates up to 9 mm thickness can be welded with a square edge preparation, whereas with the leftward technique, plates over 3 mm thickness need bevelled edge preparation.

- The heat of the flame remains confined to the weld seam and there is less spread of flame. This is due to the relatively smaller included angle between the edges being welded. As a result, this technique consumes relatively less gas (15–25%) and filler material.

- Strength and mechanical properties of weld are better. This is due to the annealing effect of the flame, which is directed towards the completed weld as the welding operation progresses.

Vertical welding The vertical welding method can be employed to weld metal plates of any thickness, but only when it is possible to put the plates in a vertical plane. Edge preparation is not required if the plate thickness is up to 15 mm. This makes the method economical as compared to other methods. Welding is started from the bottom of the plates and is continued upwards along the seam, keeping the filler rod ahead, followed by the blow pipe. The inclination of the filler rod to the plate surface is kept at about 30° while that of the blow pipe is varied as per the plate thickness; 25° for plates up to 3 mm thick, 50° for plates between 3 to 5 mm thick, and 85° for plates thicker than 5 mm. Both the blow pipe and the filler rod are moved in a zigzag manner in the transverse direction as the welding proceeds from the bottom upwards.

Overhead welding Overhead welding is performed from the underside of a joint. In overhead welding, the metal deposited tends to drop or sag on the plate, causing the bead to have a high crown. To overcome this difficulty, the molten puddle should be kept small, and enough filler metal should be added to obtain good fusion at the bead. If the puddle becomes too large, the flame should be taken away for an instant to permit the weld metal to freeze. When welding light sheets in this position, the puddle size can be controlled by applying the heat equally to the base metal and filler rod.

16.4 Pressure Gas Welding

This process differs from the conventional gas welding process because in this process, pressure is applied to complete the joint.

The main application of this process is for making butt joints between the ends of objects like pipes and rods. The ends of the parts to be joined are brought closer. The entire interface is heated uniformly with a gas flame [Figure 16.6(a)]. As a layer of molten metal appears at the interface, the flame is quickly withdrawn and the melted surfaces are *forced* together. The joint is held under suitable pressure till the interface solidifies. A flash usually appears at the joint due to the upsetting of the joined ends, as can be seen in Figure 16.6(b). No filler metal is used in pressure gas welding.

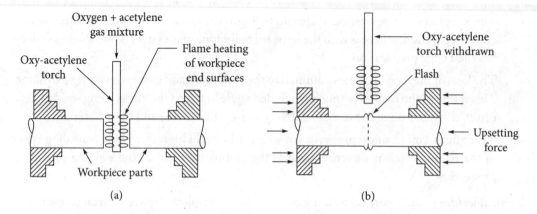

Figure 16.6 Schematic of pressure gas welding process

16.5 Safety Practices in Gas Welding

It is important to follow safety practices in gas welding. Some of these are as follows:

- Welding should be carried out at a distance from all combustible materials such as flammable fluids, vapours, gases, wood and textiles.

- Always use safety equipment such as safety goggles or safety shield, gloves and apron in order to protect the operator's eyes, face and body against sparks, spatter and infrared or ultraviolet radiations. Aids for ear protection may be used to protect the operator from excessive and prolonged noise generated by welding.

- Use proper connection of hoses to the cylinders.

- Gas cylinders should be anchored securely and should never be dropped or mishandled

- When starting the welding operation, first open the acetylene gas valve and ignite the gas at the tip of the welding torch. Thereafter, open the oxygen gas valve to an appropriate extent so as to get the desired type of flame.

- Install fire extinguishers in the area where welding is being carried out.

- Weld area should be well ventilated. Exhaust fan may be used if necessary.

16.6 Oxy-fuel Gas Cutting

Metal sheets and plates can be cut along the desired contours or straight line by means of oxy-fuel torches. The cutting is achieved basically by a thermal phenomenon. In case of non-ferrous metals, the oxy-fuel gas flame is used to first melt the metal and then blow away the molten metal to achieve the cut. But in case of ferrous metals, the cutting is achieved basically by burning (rapid oxidation) of metal at high temperatures. The following chemical equations represent the process:

$$3Fe + 2O_2 \rightarrow Fe_3O_4 + Heat$$

$$4Fe + 3O_2 \rightarrow 2Fe_2O_3 + Heat$$

For these reactions to occur, the metal has to be at around 870°C. Therefore, an oxy-fuel flame is used to first preheat the metal to an appropriate temperature at which burning can commence. The greater the carbon content of the steel, the higher is the preheating temperature. An additional stream of oxygen is then introduced into the torch (or the oxygen content in the oxy-fuel mixture is increased). Doing so oxidizes the iron. The liquid iron oxide is then expelled out from the plate by the kinetic energy of the oxygen gas stream, as can be clearly seen in Figure 16.7. The process finds applications for cutting thick cast iron and steel castings.

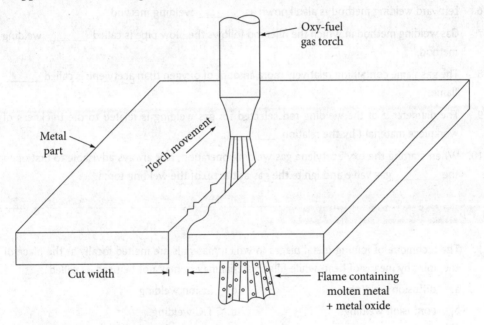

Figure 16.7 Schematic of oxy-fuel gas cutting process

Questions

1. Make sketches and describe the three types of flames used in oxy-acetylene gas welding. Give the application areas of these flames.

2. Describe the oxy-acetylene gas welding process. Describe its advantages, limitations and applications. Why is oxy-acetylene welding preferred over other oxy-fuel welding processes?

3. Discuss the various techniques of gas welding. Give the applications of each technique.

5. Describe pressure gas welding process. Discuss its areas of application.

6. What are the various important safety practices in gas welding? Discuss them in brief.

Fill in the Blanks

1. Fusion welds made _____ the addition of a filler material are known as *autogenous welds*.

2. Fuel gases that are generally used in oxy-fuel gas welding processes are _____, _____, and _____.

3. In oxy-acetylene gas welding, the primary combustion process that occurs in the inner core of the flame can be represented by the reaction: _____.

4. The temperatures developed in the oxy-acetylene gas flame are of the order of _____ °C.

5. The temperature obtained from the oxy-hydrogen flame is _____ than that from the oxy-acetylene flame.

6. Leftward welding method is also known as _____ welding method.

7. Gas welding method in which the filler rod follows the blow pipe is called _____ welding method.

8. The gas flame containing relatively more amount of oxygen than acetylene is called _____ flame.

9. The diameter d of the welding rod selected for gas welding is related to the thickness of workpiece material t by the relation: _____ .

10. When starting the oxy-acetylene gas welding operation, it is always advisable to first open the _____ gas valve and ignite the gas at the tip of the welding torch.

Choose the Correct Answer

1. The technique of joining metal pieces in which materials are melted locally at the place of the joint by means of heat, while filler material may or may not be used, is called
   a. diffusion welding.
   b. confusion welding.
   c. fusion welding.
   d. TIG welding.

2. Oxy-acetylene gas welding process is a type of
   a. diffusion welding.
   b. pressure welding.
   c. fusion welding.
   d. TIG welding.

3. In oxy-acetylene gas welding, the primary combustion process that occurs in the inner core of the flame is responsible for what proportion of the total heat produced in the flame?
   a. $\frac{1}{3}$ nearly
   b. $\frac{1}{2}$ nearly
   c. $\frac{2}{3}$ nearly
   d. $\frac{7}{8}$ nearly

4. In oxy-acetylene gas welding, the secondary combustion that follows the primary combustion and occurs just beyond the first combustion zone produces what proportion of the total heat of the flame?
   a. $\frac{1}{3}$ nearly
   b. $\frac{1}{2}$ nearly
   c. $\frac{2}{3}$ nearly
   d. $\frac{7}{8}$ nearly

5. In oxy-acetylene gas welding, which combustion is represented by the following reaction in the gas flame?

$$C_2H_2 + O_2 \rightarrow 2CO + H_2 + Heat$$

    a. primary   c. tertiary

    b. secondary   d. terra-tertiary

6. For use in oxy-acetylene gas welding, oxygen is produced by

    a. liquification of air.   c. contamination of water.

    b. electrolysis of air.   d. liquification of water.

7. The colour of steel cylinders in which oxygen gas is stored is

    a. red.   c. white.

    b. maroon.   d. black.

8. In gas welding, which gas is sometimes produced at the site by using calcium carbide?

    a. hydrogen   c. carbon dioxide

    b. oxygen   d. acetylene

9. Acetylene gas is supplied in cylinders which contain porous filler material such as

    a. calcium silicate saturated with acetone.

    b. calcium carbide saturated with acetone.

    c. potassium carbide saturated with acetone.

    d. calcium carbide saturated with benzene.

10. The acetylene cylinder can generally hold up to what quantity of gas?

    a. 5 m³ of gas at 1.5 MPa   c. 20 m³ of gas at 2.5 MPa

    b. 10 m³ of gas at 1.5 MPa   d. 30 m³ of gas at 5.0 MPa

11. Which type of flame is not used in oxy-acetylene gas welding?

    a. neutral flame   c. carburizing flame (or reducing flame)

    b. oxidizing flame   d. nitrogen flame

12. For welding of steel parts with oxy-acetylene flame, which type of the flame is not used?

    a. oxidizing flame   c. neutral flame

    b. carburizing flame   d. nitriding flame

13. If t is the thickness of the workpiece material in mm, the diameter d of the welding rod selected for welding with oxy-acetylene gas flame can be determined by the relation:

    a. $d = \frac{1}{2}t + 1$ mm   c. $d = \frac{1}{2}t + 4$ mm

    b. $d = t + 1$ mm   d. $d = t + 4$ mm

14. Gas welding flux must melt at a temperature

    a. lower than melting points of the metals being welded.

    b. that is equal to the melting point of the metals being welded.

    c.   just above the melting points of the metals being welded.

    d.   somewhat average of the melting points of the metals being welded.

15. Which one of the following is a flux commonly used in gas welding?

    a.   coke ash   c.   potassium nitrate

    b.   soda ash   d.   sodium nitrate

16. The main application of pressure gas welding process is for making

    a.   butt joints.   c.   tee joints.

    b.   lap joints.   d.   corner joints.

17. Leftward welding method is also known as

    a.   backward welding.   c.   rightward welding.

    b.   forward welding.   d.   vertical welding.

18. Which of the following gas welding technique allows preheating of plate edges immediately ahead of the molten metal pool?

    a.   backward welding   c.   rightward welding

    b.   forward welding   d.   vertical welding

19. In which one of the following gas welding methods is there no specific requirement of edge preparation?

    a.   backward welding   c.   rightward welding

    b.   forward welding   d.   vertical welding

20. In oxy-acetylene gas welding,

    a.   acetylene gas valve should be opened first and then oxygen gas valve.

    b.   oxygen gas valve should be opened first and then acetylene gas valve.

    c.   both acetylene gas valve and oxygen gas valve should be opened together.

    d.   it does not matter whether acetylene gas valve is opened first or oxygen gas valve is opened first.

21. Autogenous joint is one which

    a.   uses a filler material whose composition is the same or similar to that of the base material.

    b.   uses a filler material whose composition is different than that of the base material.

    c.   does not require the use of any filler material.

    d.   is automatically produced when electric current is passed through the workpiece sheets using a pair of electrodes.

22. Homogeneous joint is one which

    a.   uses a filler material whose composition is the same or similar to that of the base material.

    b.   uses a filler material whose composition is different than that of the base material.

c. is produced by taking heat from the surroundings; no filler material is used.

d. is produced when electric current is passed through the workpiece sheets using a pair of electrodes.

23. Heterogeneous joint is one which

a. uses a filler material whose composition is the same or similar to that of the base material.

b. uses a filler material whose composition is different than that of the base material.

c. is produced by taking heat from the surroundings; no filler material is used.

d. is produced when electric current is passed through the workpiece sheets using a pair of electrodes.

24. A gas pipe line is to be laid out. This requires butt joining of pipe lengths at several places. Which of the following joining processes will you prefer?

a. riveting

b. flange coupling

c. screw threading

d. welding

25. In oxy-acetylene gas welding, it is required to obtain complete combustion of gases. How much volume of oxygen would be required per unit volume of acetylene?

a. nearly 1

b. nearly 2

c. nearly 2.5

d. nearly 3

26. Consider the following statements:

1. Resistance welding uses no flux.

2. Fusion welding is similar to casting process.

3. Brazing and braze welding are different names given to the same process.

4. Soldering is a joining process in which melting of work material does not take place. Of these statements,

a. only 1 and 2 are true.

b. only 1 and 3 are true.

c. only 1, 2 and 4 are true.

d. only 2, 3 and 4 are true.

Answers

1. c.	2. c.	3. a.	4. c.	5. a.	6. a.	7. d.	8. d.	9. a.	10. b.
11. d.	12. a.	13. a.	14. a.	15. b.	16. a.	17. b.	18. b.	19. d.	20. a.
21. c.	22. a.	23. b.	24. d.	25. a.	26. c.				

17

Electric Arc Welding and Cutting Processes

LEARNING OBJECTIVES

After reading this chapter, you should be able to understand the following:

- The fundamentals of arc welding process and comparison with other welding processes.

- The various consumable and non-consumable electrodes used in arc welding processes.

- The equipment used in arc welding processes.

- The arc blow and methods for reducing its effects.

- The capabilities and applications of the shielded metal arc welding process, the submerged metal arc welding process, the gas tungsten arc welding process, the gas metal arc welding process, the flux cored arc welding process, the electro-slag welding process, the atomic hydrogen welding process, the plasma arc welding process and the stud welding process.

- The various arc cutting processes and their applications.

17.1 Introduction

An arc is generated when there is an electrical discharge that flows between two adjacent metal objects that are not actually touching each other. This discharge can be sustained through a path of ionized gaseous particles called plasma – the temperatures generated being over 15,000°C inside the arc and in excess of 6,000°C at the surface of the arc. Electrical currents involved in the generation of the arc are of the order of 1,000 amps, although voltages are quite low and in the range of 30 to 80 V.

Arc welding is a type of fusion welding process in which two metal pieces are joined by using the heat obtained from an electric arc that can be produced between

- a consumable electrode (which also supplies filler material) and the workpiece, or

- a non-consumable electrode (made of carbon, graphite, or tungsten) and the workpiece, or

- two non-consumable electrodes.

Depending upon the way the arc is produced, there are numerous electric arc welding processes. The most common is the one in which the arc is struck between the workpiece to be welded and the tip of a consumable metal electrode by the use of an AC or a DC power supply. The arc develops a temperature that is much higher than those developed in oxy-acetylene gas welding. A generic arc welding process is shown in Figure 17.1. The material at the tip of the electrode is heated to the liquid state by the arc and then gets deposited into the pool of molten metal formed of base metal(s). The addition of electrode material in the weld metal pool increases the volume and strength of the weld joint. Therefore, the consumable electrode is also known as a filler rod. The electrode is moved along the joint at a rate compatible with the joint design, welding parameters and weld quality desired. Upon solidification of the molten weld pool, the joint is ready. One major problem encountered in welding concerns the melting and solidification of metals in air. Molten metal gets metallurgically contaminated when exposed to the atmosphere. To overcome this problem, either arc welding must be carried out in vacuum or the molten weld pool area must be enveloped in a protective gas shield to exclude the surrounding air, until it has had time to solidify and cool down.

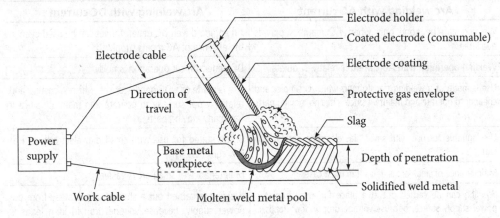

Figure 17.1 Electrode coating extends beyond the electrode core material during arc welding

17.1.1 DC versus AC arc welding

In arc welding, an arc can be created by using either DC or AC power supply. The main advantage of using DC power supply is that we can select the polarity, which means the electrode can be connected to the negative terminal or positive terminal of the power supply as desired. When the electrode is connected to the positive terminal (called 'reverse' polarity), it gets more (about ⅔rd of the total) heat, and when connected to the negative terminal (called 'straight' polarity), it gets less (⅓rd of the total) heat. Therefore, DC reverse polarity provides more penetration at a given amperage than AC. Also, DC straight polarity is more suitable for welding thinner metals than AC. Other advantages of DC welding over AC welding are as follows:

- Easier starting of arc
- Fewer arc sticking
- Smoother arc
- Less spatter and much better looking welds
- Easier vertical-up and overhead welding

However, there are a few situations where AC welding is used. These are as follows:

- When there is no choice, that is, AC mains power supply source is easily available at low cost.
- When arc blow problem occurs with DC welding.
- When welding is to be done of magnetized materials/parts.
- A comparison of AC and DC arc welding is given in Table 17.1.

Table 17.1 Comparison of AC and DC arc welding

Arc welding with AC current	Arc welding with DC current
Welding can be done only when AC mains supply is available	An engine-driven DC generator set can be used even in the absence of AC mains supply
Welding operation with AC current is relatively quieter	DC generator set operation is noisy
Use is made of a welding transformer, which is simpler and cheaper to operate and maintain since it has no moving parts	Use is made of a DC generator set, which is costlier and relatively not so easy to operate and maintain since it has many moving parts
Less suitable for use with small dia. electrode and at low currents	Better suited for use with small dia. electrode and at low currents
Maintenance of small arc is difficult in most cases	Maintenance of small arc is easier
Welding can be carried out at a place far away from the power supply source, because voltage drop in long leads is relatively less	Welding is carried out a short distance away from the power supply, because voltage drop in long leads is relatively high
Striking of arc, particularly when welding thin sheets with thin electrodes, is relatively difficult	Striking of arc is relatively easy even with thin electrodes. For welding of thin parts, it is the preferred option
Bare electrodes cannot be used	Both bare and coated electrodes can be used

17.1.2 Electrodes

There are two types of electrodes used for the purpose of heat input in arc welding: consumable electrodes and non-consumable electrodes.

When use is made of consumable electrodes, the arc is struck between the work material and the electrode tip. The arc melts both the workpiece metal and the tip of the electrode. The molten metal from the tip of the electrode and that from the work material mix under the arc to form a weld metal pool, which becomes a joint after solidification. Thus, once the arc is initiated, the electrode is continuously consumed, necessitating continuous movement of the electrode towards the workpiece in order to maintain a constant arc length. The molten metal of the electrode thus also serves as filler material for the weld joint. The electrode performs both the functions of providing heat as well as filler material. Consumable electrodes are made of a variety of materials and are available in diameters of 3, 4, 5, 6, 8 and 9 mm. Further, they are available in the form of coated sticks of lengths in the range 150–450 mm, or spools containing long lengths of bare wire. Selection of electrode for a given job is made keeping in mind the thickness and material of the job. The problem with stick electrodes is that on consumption of one electrode, changing to another electrode causes interruption and waste of time.

Coated stick electrodes are generally used for manual arc welding process. The material of coating can be selected as per the requirement. The coating on the electrode serves several functions, such as:

- **To provide an envelope of inert gas**   On coming in contact with the arc, the electrode coating burns and produces an environment of inert gases, such as carbon dioxide, to shield the molten metal pool and protect it from atmospheric oxygen, hydrogen and nitrogen pick up, thereby reducing the chances of any contamination of the weld metal.

- **To remove impurities**   The coating acts as flux to the weld metal pool, that is, it mixes with the oxides and other impurities present in the weld metal pool and forms slag. The slag, being lighter, floats on the top of the weld pool and protects it from the surrounding air during solidification. Later on, the slag is removed from the top surface of the weld bead.

- **To prevent brittleness of weld bead**   The slag covering of the weld metal pool helps the molten metal to cool down slowly and thereby prevent the formation of brittle weld.

- **To promote arc stabilization**   Materials promoting arc stabilization may be added in the coating.

- **To improve upon the strength and other properties of the weld metal**   Special alloying elements may be added in the coating to achieve this.

- **To improve arc concentration and weld metal deposition rate**   If the electrode coating is such that it is consumed at a slower rate as compared to the core material (i.e., filler material), the coating would extend beyond the core material of the electrode during the welding operation, as can be seen in Figure 17.1. This configuration is useful for concentrating the arc (to improve penetration) and directing the filler metal in the joint (to improve weld metal deposition rate).

- **To control the composition of slag**   The composition of slag (so that it is viscous or fluid) can be varied by varying the composition of the coating material. This is advantageous, for example, in cases when welding in the vertical position – viscous slag is useful as it can cover the molten weld metal pool for a longer period of time.

Coatings are generally of three types: (i) cellulosic, (ii) mineral and (iii) iron powder. The cellulosic coatings are made up of wood pulp, saw dust, cotton, etc., which burn with the heat of the arc in order to form an expanding gas that gives a digging action to the weld. The rate of burning of coating is slower than the rate of melting of the electrode material. Thus, a cup-like shape gets formed at the electrode tip that helps to direct the heat of the arc as shown in Figure 17.1. Cellulosic coated electrodes can be used for welding in any position, but are mostly used for horizontal, vertical and overhead positions. Mineral coatings are basically made of natural silicates such as clay and asbestos. Additives, such as titanium oxide, are introduced in the coatings to soften the digging action of the arc and make it less penetrating. Electrodes with mineral coatings produce a thick slag that protects the weld metal from oxidation and promotes its slow cooling. Their use is recommended for sheet metal welding where shallow penetration is desired, and for joints where fit-up is poor. They are best suited for making flat welds and those inclined at 45°. For welding of manganese, molybdenum and alloy steels, mineral coatings are especially formulated to keep the hydrogen gas formation to the minimum. Iron-powder coatings are particularly useful in producing a cup-like shape at the electrode tip when the arc is struck. This, apart from providing heat concentration, also gives an automatic consistent arc length. The slag formed over the weld is generally of the self-removing type and the weld bead appearance is excellent.

In case of welding processes that use non-consumable electrodes, the arc is struck between two electrodes and the heat of the arc is used to heat and melt the workpiece material. The filler metal is deposited in the joint through a separate filler rod. Non-consumable electrodes are made of carbon, graphite or tungsten. The carbon and graphite electrodes are used only in DC welding, whereas tungsten electrodes are used in both DC and AC welding processes. Tungsten electrodes are often alloyed with thorium or zirconium in order to obtain better current-carrying and electron-emission characteristics. When welding with non-consumable electrodes, it is important to observe the following precautions.

- The tip of the electrode should be clean and free from any surface contamination such as molten filler metal.

- The electrode should not be allowed to cool in the atmosphere at the end of the welding operation. This is to prevent oxidation of the electrode material.

- The flow of shielding gas should be maintained for some time after the arc is extinguished so that the electrode gets cooled to room temperature in a protective atmosphere.

- The electrode tip should be properly prepared. This helps in better weld metal penetration. Figure 17.2 shows some typical tip configurations.

The selection of electrode depends upon the requirements with respect to its chemical composition, mechanical properties and operating characteristics. The operating characteristics of an electrode denote its quality: (i) *fill* (i.e., the speed at which the weld metal fills the joint, or the deposition rate); (ii) *freeze* (i.e., how fast the weld metal cools down – necessary for use in specific positions); and (iii) *follow* (i.e., how fast the electrode follows, or the welding speed). The type and position of the joint decides whether the electrode should primarily have fill, freeze or follow characteristics. Fill electrodes are suited for easy-to-weld joints in a flat position. The coating on these electrodes consists mainly of iron powder, which increases the deposition rate as well as current requirements. Freeze electrodes provide low deposition rate and require lesser currents. They are suited for overhead or vertically inclined joints. Follow electrodes permit welding to be carried out at high travel speed with almost no skips or misses.

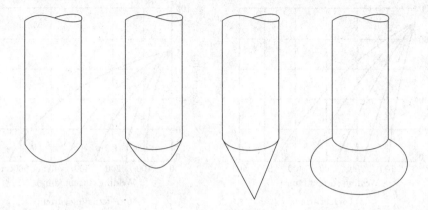

Figure 17.2   Some typical shapes of tips of non-consumable electrodes used in arc welding

Electrode wire is commercially available in the form of spools or coils of desired lengths. These are identified either by numbers and letters or by colour code as per IS specifications. Aluminium, mild steel and stainless steel wires are available in the diameter range of 0.5 to 5.0 mm. It is important that the surface of the wire is free from any lubricant or oxides. Coated stick electrodes are commercially available in a length range of 150–450 mm and a diameter range of 3–9 mm.

17.1.3 Equipment

The basic arc welding equipment consists of (i) an electric power source; (ii) power cables; and (iii) an electrode holder. The equipment is generally portable.

Arc welding power sources   Arc welding requires electric power. Depending upon the application, either AC power source or DC power source may be used.

- AC power source may be
  - A transformer (with the primary connected to the AC mains), or
  - An alternator (which may be motor or engine driven).
- DC power source may be
  - A transformer plus rectifier (with the primary of the transformer connected to the AC mains), or
  - A generator (which may be either motor or engine driven).

Power sources used for manual arc welding are required to provide a high current, which should either not change at all or change very little in magnitude as the voltage varies over a considerable range. The load voltage normally ranges between 30 to 40 V, while the actual voltage across the arc varies in the range 12 to 30 V depending on the arc length. For this reason, arc welding power sources (whether DC or AC) are designed to have *drooping voltage* characteristics (as shown in Figure 17.3) and current capacities in the range 200 to 1000

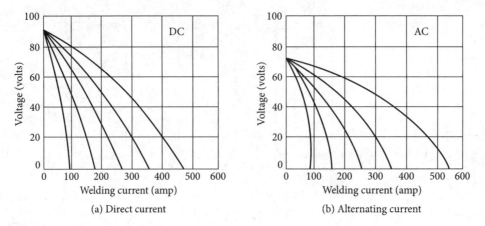

(a) Direct current   (b) Alternating current

Figure 17.3   Voltage characteristics of arc welding power sources

amperes. These characteristics assure that the current would not vary too much as the voltage varies in the usual operating range.

Direct current for welding can be obtained from a motor-generator set or a solid-state transformer-rectifier machine. Transformer-rectifier machines operate on a three-phase 440 V mains and can provide both AC and DC currents. AC welding can be performed by using a simple transformer-type machine.

Power cable and electrode holder   The power cable should be able to carry the currents used in the welding operation. Only ISI marked cables should be used for safety considerations. A good ergonomic electrode holder having a spring-controlled grip on the electrode improves the working of the welder.

17.1.4 Arc blow

When using DC current in arc welding, a phenomenon called *arc blow* is almost always present. A strong magnetic field is set up around the electrode which tends to deflect the arc as though a strong wind were blowing; hence, the phenomenon has been termed 'arc blow'. The arc may be deflected to one side but it is generally deflected either forward or backward along the direction of electrode travel. The phenomenon is particularly noticeable when the electrode reaches the end of the joint or when welding is being done at corner locations. This is because at these locations, the magnetic flux lines tend to move out of the work material, which is not possible, thus causing a high magnetic pull on the arc, thereby resulting in a backward arc blow. The effects of arc blow are: (i) excessive spatter on account of tiny droplets of weld metal getting thrown out of the joint on the workpiece material; (ii) incomplete fusion; and (iii) reduced welding speed. In case of AC arc welding, however, this phenomenon is not prominent because alternating current does not permit the formation of a strong magnetic field, as there is continuous change in the polarity.

The following steps may be taken to reduce the severity of the arc blow problem.

- Use AC current rather than DC.
- Reduce the magnitude of current. Lesser the current, lesser will be the strength of magnetic field.
- Use short arc length.
- Place metal blocks near the end of the plates being welded. This will allow the flow of magnetic field lines through the block and thus reduce the arc blow.

17.1.5 Safety in arc welding

Safety is of serious concern in arc welding. Gas tungsten arc welding, for example, done with argon gas shielding, is the highest emitter of ultra violet radiations. These radiations can burn the cornea and the skin if proper protection measures are not taken. The use of the following safety equipment is mandatory.

- **Welding helmet** A welding helmet with proper safety lens must be used when performing an arc welding operation.
- **Goggles with side shields** Goggles with proper lens and side shields under the helmet must be worn to protect the welder' eyes from harmful radiations.
- **Leather apron** Welders must wear dark coloured leather aprons for skin protection.
- **Enclosure for welder** An enclosure made of opaque material or tinted curtains of PVC plastic sheets must be provided to enclose the welder. This is necessary for protecting bystanders from exposure to harmful radiations.
- **Proper ventilation** Good natural ventilation is a must at the place of welding. In confined spaces, it may be necessary to provide forced ventilation with an exhaust fan.

17.2 Arc Welding Processes with Consumable Electrodes

17.2.1 Shielded metal arc welding (SMAW)

The shielded metal arc welding (SMAW) process, shown schematically in Figure 17.1 is mostly carried out manually. The process uses a consumable electrode, which is primarily a filler metal rod with a coating of chemicals that provide flux and shielding. The electrode is typically in the form of a stick and is made of a metal having a composition very close to that of the metal to be welded.

To start the welding operation, the bare metal end of the coated welding rod (opposite to the welding tip) is clamped to an electrode holder that is connected to the power source. The holder has an insulated handle so that it can be held and manipulated by the human welder. The other terminal of the power source is connected to the workpiece to be welded. The current, which may be AC or DC, ranges between 50 amp and 250 amp at voltages from 15 to 45 V; power requirements are often less than 10 kW. To weld thick workpieces, high AC currents with large diameter electrodes are more suitable. In case of DC current, the direction of flow, i.e., *polarity* is important and its selection depends on the metal to be welded, its thickness, required depth of heat affected zone and the type of electrode used. Straight polarity (workpiece positive; electrode negative) is preferred for thin workpieces and sheet metal because it produces shallow heat penetration. On the other hand, reverse polarity (workpiece negative; electrode positive) produces deeper weld penetration and is preferred for thick workpieces.

An electric arc is established by striking the tip of the coated metal electrode with the metal workpiece and quickly raising it through a short distance sufficient to maintain the arc. Under the intense heat of the arc (temperatures greater than 5,000°C), a small part of the work material is instantly raised to the melting point causing the formation of the weld metal pool. At the same time, the heat of the arc melts the tip of the metal electrode and small globules (or drops) of molten metal pass through the arc. These drops of molten filler metal together with the electrode coating material get deposited in the weld metal pool. The electrode coating (flux) burns to develop an envelope of a shielding gas on the weld metal pool and protects it from getting oxidized with the oxygen in the environment. Flux also helps the welding process in other ways, the most important being the enhancement of the arc stability as welding progresses so that high quality welds are produced.

After establishing the electric arc between the electrode and the workpiece surface, the welder slowly traverses the electrode along the weld path, ensuring that a constant arc gap is maintained at all times, despite a continually reducing electrode length. After a layer of weld bead has been laid, it is necessary to clean the bead surface so that the *slag* (comprising fluxes, electrode coating material and metal oxides) is completely removed.

The heat (or the temperature) generated in the arc depends upon the amount of input electric power. The following simple relation can be used.

$$H = EIT$$

where H is heat (Joules or Watts); E is voltage (Volts); I is current (amperes); and T is time (seconds).

Advantages, limitations and applications   Some advantages of SMAW process are as follows:

- The SMAW process is simple and versatile.
- It is suitable for welding of workpieces in a wide range of thickness, 3 mm to 20 mm.
- It is suitable for welding at site in remote areas where a portable fuel-powered generator can be used as the source of power supply.

The process is generally not used for joining parts made of aluminium and its alloys, copper alloys and titanium. Other limitations of SMAW are as follows:

- Low production rate. This is due to the need to change electrodes periodically as they get consumed.

- Maintenance of current levels within a safe range required during the welding.

Most applications of this process are in general fabrication and maintenance work, ship building and joining of pipelines and machinery structures. It is preferred over oxy-fuel gas welding for joining thicker parts, usually above 5 mm because of its higher power density. The metals that can be joined by SMAW include cast irons, steels, stainless steels and certain non-ferrous alloys.

17.2.2 Gas metal arc welding (GMAW)

Gas metal arc welding (GMAW) uses a consumable bare metal wire as the electrode, which is fed continuously and automatically from a reel or spool (Figure 17.4). The wire electrode passes through a gun, where a provision exists to impart an electric current to the wire. The size of the wire used depends on the thickness of the parts being joined and the desired metal deposition rate. Generally, the wire diameters range from 1 to 6 mm. The arc between the tip of the wire electrode and the workpiece is shielded under an envelope of an inert gas, which may be argon, helium or even a mixture of the two. The atmosphere or envelope of inert gas prevents contamination of the weld metal and simultaneously helps in efficient transfer of filler metal at the joint. The selection of shielding gas (or mixture of gases) depends on the metal being welded. Inert gases are generally used for welding aluminium alloys and stainless steels, whereas use can also be made of an active gas such as CO_2 for welding of low and medium carbon steels. The desirable rate of shielding gas flow depends primarily on weld geometry, speed, current and the metal transfer mode being utilized. Welding flat surfaces requires higher flow than welding grooved joints since the gas envelope is formed more

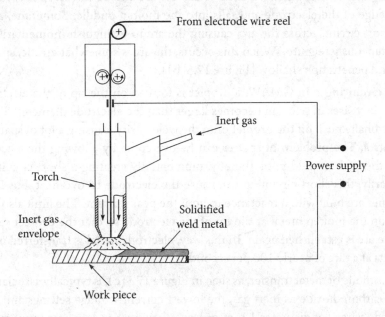

Figure 17.4 Schematic of gas metal arc welding process

quickly. Similarly, faster welding speeds will generally require more gas to provide adequate coverage. GMAW is also commonly known as *metal inert gas (MIG) welding* and CO_2 *welding*.

Power supply   Most applications of GMAW use a constant voltage power supply. As a result, any change in the arc length (which is directly related to voltage) results in a corresponding change in the heat input and current. A shorter arc length will cause a much greater heat input, which will make the wire electrode melt more rapidly and eventually restore the original arc length. This helps the welder to keep the arc length consistent even when welding manually with a hand-held welding gun.

Direct current is mostly employed and the electrode is generally connected to the positive terminal of power supply. Alternating current is rarely used with GMAW.

Metal transfer modes   Metal transfer from the electrode to the weld joint in GMAW can occur in one of the following three modes:

- **Spray transfer**   As the name indicates, small droplets of molten metal from the electrode tip are transferred to the weld area at rates as high as several hundred droplets per second, as can be seen in Figure 17.5(a). The size of the droplet is smaller than the electrode diameter. The transfer of molten metal is stable and spatter-free. This type of metal transfer occurs when typically high direct currents, high voltages and large diameter electrodes are used with argon as the shielding gas.

- **Globular transfer**   This mode of metal transfer is generally used when welding thick workpieces. Carbon dioxide or a mixture of carbon dioxide and other gases along with high currents are used, which permit larger weld penetration and higher welding speeds. In globular transfer, a molten drop forms on the end of the electrode, moves to the outer edge of the electrode and falls into the molten puddle. Sometime, a large drop will 'short circuit' across the arc, causing the arc to extinguish momentarily, and then instantaneously reignite. When this occurs, the arc is somewhat erratic, spatter level is high and penetration shallow [Figure 17.5(b)].

- **Short circuiting**   In GMAW, a droplet is formed on the tip of the electrode, which slowly increases in size and becomes larger than the electrode diameter. The forces of the arc finally push off the droplet onto the weld cavity, causing a lot of spatter and lack of control. The problem of spatter can be overcome by allowing the electrode tip to touch the molten weld pool, thereby, momentarily creating a short circuit condition. Ordinarily, this short circuiting can cause the electrode to overheat, but DC welding machines are built with a reactance to limit the peak current. The limit also has a pinch effect on the molten metal at the tip of the electrode so that the droplet separates out and the arc is established again. In this way, electrode metal is transferred in individual droplets at a rate of nearly 100 per second.

  This mode of metal transfer, as seen in Figure 17.5(c), is typically associated with the use of carbon dioxide as inert gas, the lowest current–voltage settings and the thinner electrode wires (of diameter 1 mm or less), that is when low heat input is needed for sheet metal, out-of-position work and poor fit-up applications.

- **Pulse transfer** It is a mode of metal transfer somewhat between spray and short circuiting. A power source has built into it two output levels: a steady background level, and a high output (peak) level. The later permits the transfer of metal across the arc. This peak output is controllable between high and low values up to several hundred cycles per second. The result of such a peak output produces a spray arc below the typical transition current.

  The arc is initiated by touching the wire to the work. Upon initial contact, a bit of the wire melts off to form a molten puddle. The wire feeds forward until it actually contacts the work again, as at 1 in Figure 17.5(c) and the arc is extinguished. The short circuiting current causes the wire to neck down, as shown in 1, until it melts off, as shown at 2. As soon as the wire is free of the puddle, the arc is reignited and a molten ball forms at the end of the electrode. The wire continues to move forward until it makes contact with the puddle, and the cycle is repeated.

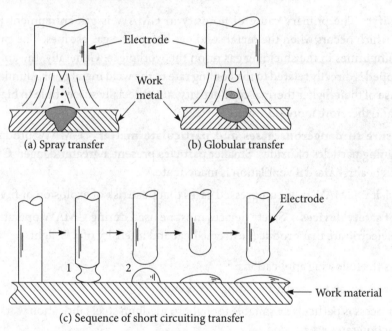

(a) Spray transfer   (b) Globular transfer

(c) Sequence of short circuiting transfer

Figure 17.5 Modes of metal transfer from electrode to weld joint in GMAW process

Advantages limitations and applications GMAW has the following advantages:

- Welding can be done at high speeds.
- Welds produced are very clean, smooth and sound.
- No flux is required and, therefore, no slag forms over the weld. This is particularly useful for multi-pass welds as no intermediate cleaning will be required.
- Weld metal penetration is exceptionally good.

- There is no frequent change of electrodes as is the case with shielded metal arc process.

- The process can be easily adapted to an automatic operation.

- The welding unit is light and compact and, thus, can be easily adopted for robotic manipulation.

- It is an economical welding process.

GMAW suffers from the following limitations:

- **Dross** This is a common problem when welding aluminium with GMAW. The cause of dross is the aluminium oxide or aluminium nitride present in the electrode or workpiece materials. The problem can be overcome by brushing the electrode and workpieces with a wire brush or treating the electrodes chemically to remove oxide from the surface. Providing sufficient flow of shielding gases also helps to overcome the problem to some extent.

- **Porosity** The primary cause of porosity in GMAW is gas entrapment in the weld joint, which occurs when the metal solidifies before the gas escapes. The gas can come from impurities in the shielding gas or on the workpiece. Generally, the amount of gas entrapped is directly related to the cooling rate of the weld metal pool. Aluminium welds, because of their higher thermal conductivity, are especially susceptible to higher cooling rates and therefore more porosity.

- **Exposure to dangerous gases and particulate matter** GMAW produces smoke containing particles of oxides. Smaller particles present a greater danger. CO_2 can be a serious health hazard if ventilation is inadequate.

- **Fire risk** GMAW uses compressed gases that pose risk of explosion or fire.

- **Use of safety devices** Safety devices must be used during GMAW operation because of the electric arc that produces extreme heat and intensity of UV light.

GMAW has the following applications:

- The process can be used for welding any metal.

- The process is particularly suitable for light to medium steel fabrication work when high production rates are needed.

17.2.3 Metal inert gas spot welding (MIGSW)

Metal inert gas spot welding (MIGSW) is an application-oriented variant of GMAW. This process is used to produce spot, plug or tack welds by an argon-shielded electric arc using a consumable metal electrode. The operator very tightly holds in his hand a small portable welding gun with pistol type grip against the workpiece. To make the weld, the operator just actuates the trigger switch and the following sequence takes place. The shielding gas flows for a short interval before wire feeding starts; wire feeding starts; the arc is initiated and continues for a pre-set time (usually a few seconds); welding current and wire feeding stops; and the shielding gas flow continues for a short interval before it automatically stops. One major advantage of this equipment is that spot welds can be made on thin sheets from one side of the workpiece. Large and irregular-shaped assemblies, which are difficult to weld with the resistance welding equipment, can be easily welded using this low-cost process.

17.2.4 Pulsed gas metal arc welding (GMAW-P)

This process is a variant of the GMAW process in which a low-welding current is initially used to generate a molten globule at the tip of the electrode wire. Immediately thereafter, a burst of high current is applied, which 'explodes' the globule into a spray, thus, transferring the molten metal across the arc into the joint. By alternating the low and high currents at some rate (which may be as high as 100 times/s), the filler metal is transferred into the joint in a series of rapid bursts. By controlling the alternating current, the desired shape of the weld bead and depth of penetration can be achieved.

Advantages The GMAW-P has the following advantages over the GMAW process:

- Faster process.
- More economical because of lower energy or power requirements.
- Less spatter and, therefore, cleaner welds.
- Low weld temperature and less heat input to the workpiece material because of pulsed form of metal transfer.
- Possibility of welding thinner sections.
- Less distortion of workpiece.
- external cooling of electrode.
- Fine microstructure of weld pool.

17.2.5 Submerged arc welding (SAW)

Although shielded metal arc welding (SMAW) is a flexible general purpose method of joining components of ferrous metals, it is difficult to obtain consistently high quality welds for which three basic requirements are vital: (i) maintenance of a constant gap between the workpiece and tip of electrode across which the arc is struck; (ii) maintenance of a uniform speed at which the electrode is traversed along the weld path; and (iii) need for continuous welding of complete weld run, that is, welding once started should continue uninterruptedly till the end of weld run.

In any manual arc welding, the first two requirements are difficult to meet, especially when we know that the consumable electrode becomes increasingly smaller as the operation progresses and the welder is required to constantly view the workpiece through a darkened shield or goggles. For an appreciable length of weld run, the third requirement is also difficult to meet, particularly if the length of weld run is appreciable, because the length of the electrode rod is mostly limited to 400 mm. Whenever more than one electrode rod is used to complete the weld, more than one *start and stop* sequence will be introduced and the weld quality is affected.

The aforementioned limitations of manual arc welding are taken care of in a mechanized form of arc welding called submerged arc welding (SAW). The schematic of the process is shown in Figure 17.6. In SAW, use is made of a mechanically propelled welding head through which a consumable 2 to 10 mm diameter bare electrode wire is continuously supplied automatically through a tube (called welding gun). The need to replace rods during a weld run is, thus, eliminated. The electrode wire has necessarily to be free from surface imperfections and contaminants.

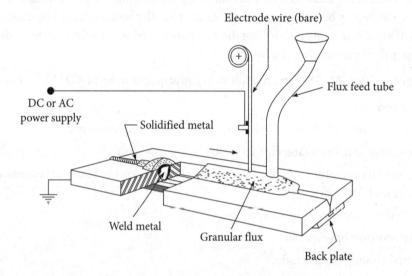

Figure 17.6 Schematic of submerged arc welding process

The arc between the tip of the electrode wire and the workpiece is completely submerged under a heap of granular flux made up of several elements such as lime, silica, calcium fluoride and magnesium oxide. The molten weld metal pool is thus entirely covered under a thick layer of flux and oxidation of weld metal is prevented. In addition, spatter and sparks are prevented while fumes and UV radiations are suppressed. The flux also acts as a thermal barrier, enabling faster weld pool formation. The flux is fed into the weld zone by a gravity flow through a nozzle that delivers it ahead of the welding electrode. The portion of the flux closest to the arc is melted. It mixes with the molten weld metal to remove impurities, and then solidifies on top of the weld joint to form a glass-like slag. The slag and unfused flux granules on the top provide good protection from the surrounding atmosphere and good thermal insulation for the weld area. As a result of slow cooling, a high quality weld joint is obtained. After welding, the unfused flux can be recovered, treated and then reused.

The power source used with SAW can be either AC or DC. Both constant voltage and constant current type machines can be employed. The electric currents range between

250 amp to 2500 amp. Higher the current, higher is the burn-off rate for a given electrode wire diameter and material. The burn-off rate for steel wire electrodes is depicted in Figure 17.7. At high values of current, high welding speeds of the order of 3 to 4 m/min and high metal deposition rates of the order of 10 to 15 kg/h can be achieved. Welding current higher than what is required should not be used as it would give out additional heat as well as filler metal into the weld joint resulting in larger heat affected zones (HAZs) and unnecessary reinforcement of the weld joint. On the other hand, use of lesser welding current than necessary would result in lesser deposition of filler metal and hence, weak joints. The joint design and edge preparation used with SAW are somewhat different from other arc welding processes because of relatively higher deposition rates and deeper penetrations involved. Figure 17.8 shows some typical edge preparations used in this process.

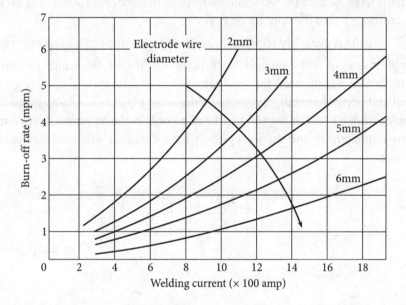

Figure 17.7 Burn-off rate for steel electrodes in submerged arc welding process

The amount or the size of the heap of flux used has a bearing on the quality and appearance of the weld. If the amount of flux is less, it would not cover the arc completely, thus, resulting in oxidation of the weld metal as well as flashing and spattering. Similarly, if the amount of flux is too much, the weld gases generated during the process would not be able to flow out, resulting in porosity in the weld metal.

Advantages, limitations and applications The SAW process has several advantages. They are as follows:

- It is simple and versatile.
- It can easily weld low-carbon, low-alloy and stainless steels.

- It has high productivity. Weld metal deposition rates are 5 to 10 times to the rates of the SMAW process. Welding speed as high as 5 m/min can be achieved.
- It produces very high quality weld. The toughness and uniformity of weld metal properties are exceptionally good.
- It can weld a large variety of sheet and plates of carbon and alloy steels.
- It can be automated for greater economy.

Some limitations of SAW are as follows:

- The process is not suitable for the welding of some materials such as high carbon steels, tool steels and most non-ferrous metals.
- The parts to be welded by SAW must always be in horizontal position. This is because granular flux is fed to the joint by gravity.
- A back-up plate is generally required beneath the joint during welding operation.

Typical applications of SAW include thick plate welding of ships and pressure vessels. The process is also widely used for steel fabrication of structural shapes (e.g., I-beams); longitudinal and circumferential joints of large diameter pipes. It is advantageous to traverse the workpiece under a stationary welding head to obtain the required relative movement between the welding head and the workpiece. Circumferential welds can be made on pipes in this manner.

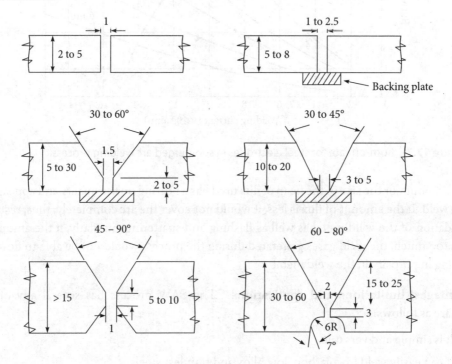

Figure 17.8   Some typical edge preparations used in submerged arc welding process

17.2.6 Flux-cored arc welding (FCAW)

Flux-cored arc welding (FCAW) utilizes a continuously-fed tubular electrode, electrical power to melt the electrode, and may or may not use shielding gas from an externally supplied source when depositing material in the weld joint. The tubular electrode has a metal sheath with central area (i.e., core) filled with flux material, which is mostly mineral compounds and powdered metals. The electrodes are available in different configurations as shown in Figure 17.9 and in long lengths (in coil form).

The weld bead produced is covered by a residual slag (melted and solidified flux), which helps to protect and shape the finished weld, and is generally easily removable upon completion of the weld.

There are two versions of FCAW. These include the (i) gas-shielded and (ii) self-shielded versions. The first version uses flux-cored electrodes with separate shielding gases, and can be considered as a hybrid of SMAW and GMAW. It combines the advantages of shielded arc welding (SMAW) together with the continuous and automatic feeding feature of GMAW.

Self-shielded flux-cored electrodes do not require shielding from any external gas. During welding, the ingredients mixed with the flux in the electrodes burn in order to create a shield of inert gas around the weld area that protects it from getting contaminated by the surrounding atmosphere.

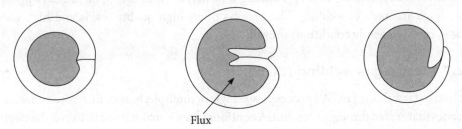

Flux

Figure 17.9 Different configurations of flux-cored electrodes used in flux-cored arc welding process

Advantages, limitations and applications   The main advantages of FCAW are:

- High-quality weld deposit with excellent appearance.
- Deposition rate is up to four times greater than that achieved in manual arc welding.
- Excellent weld penetration leading to simplified joint design.
- Can be used to join many types of metals (especially carbon and alloy steels, stainless steels, cast iron and nickel based alloys) over a wide thickness range.
- Because of its greater tolerance for base plate contamination, less pre-cleaning needed than metal inert gas (MIG) welding.
- Process offers great ease with which specific weld-metal chemistry can be obtained by adding alloying elements to the flux core. This feature has made the process known for achieving virtually any alloy composition of the weld metal at the joint.

- The use of self-shielded electrodes eliminates the need for flux handling or gas apparatus, and is more tolerant of windy conditions present in outdoor construction than gas-shielded processes.

- Flux-core welding does not need a high skill level to perform.

FCAW has the following limitations:

- Most non ferrous exotic metals (including aluminium) cannot be welded.

- Limited to flat and horizontal positions generally.

- Process produces a slag covering that must be removed.

- Weld produced has porosity, because the gases (specifically those from the flux core) do not escape the welded area before the metal hardens, leaving holes in the welded metal.

- Electrode wire is more expensive on a weight basis than solid electrode wires, except for some high alloy steels.

- Equipment is more expensive and less mobile; however, increased productivity usually compensates for this.

- In general, more fume is generated than with MIG welding.

FCAW is primarily used in the ship building industry, as ships are made of heavy plate, and require huge amounts of welding. The process offers high quality welds and high welding speeds even when windy conditions prevail.

17.2.7 Electro-gas welding (EGW)

The electro-gas welding (EGW) process uses single or multiple, bare or flux-cored consumable electrodes that are fed through a conduit. A continuous arc is maintained between the electrode tip and the workpiece that is shielded with an inert gas (such as carbon dioxide, argon or helium) as per the need of the material being welded. The shielding gas may be provided from an external source, or it may be produced from burning of the ingredients mixed in the flux in the flux-cored electrode. Electric currents used are in the range of 300 to 600 amp for cored electrodes and up to 400 amp for solid electrodes while power requirements are in the range 15–25 kW.

The main application of this process is for butt welding the edges of workpieces vertically in one pass. The weld metal is deposited into the cavity formed between the two pieces to be joined by enclosing the space with two water-cooled copper shoes, thereby preventing the molten slag from running off. The welding process requires special equipment that has the mechanical drive for upward movement of the shoes. Circumferential joints such as on pipes or pressure vessels can also be welded by rotating the workpieces. Aluminium alloys and almost all types of steels up to 70 mm thickness can be welded by this process. In addition to butt welding, it can also be used for fillet and groove welds, but always with vertical orientation of parts.

17.2.8 Electro-slag welding (ESW)

Electro-slag welding is mostly used for welding very thick components or plates (of as much as 40 to 500 mm thickness) where the joint to be welded is in a vertical position. The process is schematically shown in Figure 17.10. The components to be welded are set in the required vertical position with the necessary gap between the butted edges. A backing plate is tacked at the bottom. Water-cooled copper shoes which can travel along the joint are initially located at the lowermost position. These shoes close off the space between the parts to be welded so that a U-shaped starting block is formed, which prevents the slag and molten metal from spilling out of the pool.

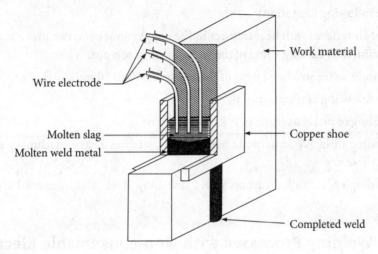

Figure 17.10   Schematic of electro-slag welding process

To start the welding operation, an arc is created between the tip of the consumable electrodes and the bottom plate Upon the introduction of granular flux into the joint, an approximate 3–4 mm thick layer of molten slag starts floating at the top of the weld metal pool. As the molten slag reaches the tip of the electrode, the arc is extinguished and current is conducted directly from the electrode wire to the base metal through the conductive slag. Thereafter, the high electrical resistance of the slag causes most of the heating required for welding, that is, for melting the wire electrode and the workpiece metal. As the welding progresses, single or multiple electrode wires along with flux are continuously fed into the molten slag pool confined between the copper shoes. The slag, being lighter than the molten metal, remains on top to protect the weld metal pool. The shoes are made to slide upwards along the joint at a speed determined by the speed at which the electrode and the work material at the joint are melted. The lower part of the weld metal bath is solidified as heat is conducted away by the copper shoes and the work material. The welding operation takes place at 40–50 V, and the current requirements are 500–600 amp, although higher currents are used for very thick plates.

Advantages, limitations and applications   ESW has the following advantages:

*   Thick metals can be welded in a single pass.
*   Almost no joint preparation is required.
*   Heating is uniform, therefore, there is good stress distribution across the weld; distortion is also less.
*   The weld quality is good as the weld metal is protected at all times from contamination.
*   The weld speed is good, as much as 15–40 mm/min.
*   The process is almost automatic; once started, it keeps going until the job is completed.

ESW has the following limitations:

*   The scale interferes with heat transfer to the copper shoes and can prevent a good fit-up of the joint, thus causing some of the weld metal to run out.
*   Uneconomical for welding plates of thickness less than 20 mm.

ESW has the following applications:

*   For welding of plates as thick as 1/2 m in one pass.
*   For welding of heavy structural steel sections, such as heavy machinery and nuclear-reactor vessels.
*   For welding of hot rolled carbon steels, low-alloy steels and quenched and tempered steels.

17.3 Arc Welding Processes with Non-consumable Electrodes

17.3.1 Gas tungsten arc welding (GTAW)

In gas tungsten arc welding (GTAW), also known as *TIG welding*, a tungsten electrode is held in a water-cooled holder through which an inert gas (or a mixture of two inert gases) flows to provide a protective environment around both the arc and the molten weld metal pool, as can be seen in Figure 17.11. The shielding gas is usually CO_2, argon, helium or a mixture of argon and helium. As the electrode material is not consumed at the temperature of the arc, the latter is stable and a constant arc length is easy to maintain.

The kind of current to be employed is dependent on the metal to be welded. Direct current with reverse polarity is rarely employed as it tends to melt the tungsten electrode, whereas DC with straight polarity is common for cast iron, mild steel, stainless steel, titanium, high temperature refractory metals and copper alloys. Alternating current (ac) is preferred for the welding of aluminium and magnesium because the cleaning action of the ac removes surface oxides and improves the weld quality.

The process is used with or without filler metal, depending upon the workpiece material, its thickness, and joint configuration. When a filler metal is used, it is added to the weld pool from a separate rod or wire, being melted by the heat of the arc rather than transferred across the arc as in consumable arc welding processes. The filler metal should match the chemistry of the metal being welded. The deposition rate of the filler metal can be increased by oscillating the filler wire side to side while the welding operation is being carried out. Filler metal wire may not be used where a close fit exists at the joint or when thin sheets are to be welded to close tolerances. The electrode material may be one of the three types: pure tungsten, thoriated tungsten or zirconiated tungsten, and the size may vary from 0.5 mm to 10 mm. The oxides of thorium and zirconium help the electrodes to maintain their shape at the tip for a longer time and improve the ease of electron emission. There is hardly any wear loss of tungsten since its melting point is quite high (3410 °C).

Welding voltage is 20 to 40 V and the weld current varies between 100 to 500 amperes.

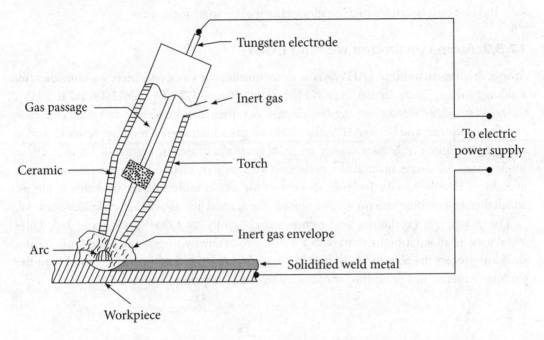

Figure 17.11   Schematic of gas tungsten arc welding process

Advantages, limitations and applications   The advantages of GTAW are as follows:

- Operating costs are low.
- Very high quality of welds.
- There is no spatter (unwanted small droplets of weld metal) because the filler metal is not transferred across the arc gap. Thus, there is no need for post-welding cleaning, grinding or finishing operation. This is an important feature when welding is done in hard-to-reach locations.
- A variety of metals (both ferrous and non-ferrous) especially aluminium, magnesium, titanium and refractory metals can be welded. The process is particularly suitable for welding highly alloyed metals where weld purity is essential.

The limitations of GTAW are as follows:

*   Tungsten electrode cannot be allowed to touch the work metal because some tungsten may get deposited.

*   Cast iron, wrought iron and lead are difficult to weld by this process.

*   For welding of steel, the process is slower and more costly than consumable electrode arc welding.

GTAW has the following applications:

*   The process is best suited for parts made of aluminium and stainless steel.

*   It is also best suited for high quality welding of thinner workpieces.

17.3.2 Atomic hydrogen welding (AHW)

Atomic hydrogen welding (AHW) is a non-consumable electrode inert gas shielded arc welding process. There are two major differences between GTAW and AHW: (i) In AHW, the arc is struck between two tungsten electrodes rather than between a tungsten electrode and the workpiece; and (ii) in AHW, the shielding gas is hydrogen, which is reactive in nature compared to argon or helium, which are inert gases. As shown in Figure 17.12, in AHW, a single-phase AC arc is maintained between two tungsten electrodes and hydrogen gas is introduced into the arc. As the hydrogen enters the arc, its molecules are broken into atoms, which then re-combine into molecules outside the arc and just above the workpiece material.

This reaction is exothermic and temperatures as high as 6,000°C are generated. Filler metal may be added into the joint with a welding rod. The hydrogen gas, besides acting as a shield to protect the electrodes and molten metal from oxidation, breaks the oxides on the workpiece metal, thus promoting the formation of a high quality clean weld.

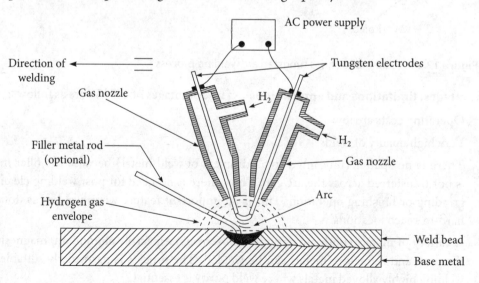

Figure 17.12   Schematic of atomic hydrogen welding process

The AHW setup comprises a welding torch, a hydrogen gas cylinder and a single-phase AC power source. Although DC power source can also be used, it is not recommended because of high electrode wear. The voltage requirements are in the range 50 V to 75 V and the current requirements vary from 15 amp to 150 amp. The welding torch accommodates two tungsten electrodes and has a provision for changing the distance between them. In operation, the welding torch is seen as a mobile tool that travels without the arc getting extinguished.

Advantages The process provides high heat concentration. The hydrogen provides protection for the molten metal and the electrodes.

Applications AHW finds applications for welding of various tool steels and alloys that are difficult to weld by other processes. The process is used for hard surfacing and repairing of dies and moulds. AHW is mostly used for welding in flat positions only.

17.3.3 Plasma arc welding (PAW)

Plasma, considered as the fourth state of matter, is a glowing, partially ionized gas produced by the passage of gas through an electrical field, which separates it into free electrons, neutrons and ions. The energy required for this dissociation of gas is very high but as the atoms recombine, the process releases extremely high latent heat and temperatures as high as 30,000°C are generated. Plasma, which is electrically conducting, is always present in between the electrodes whenever an arc is formed.

PAW and GTAW resemble each other in the sense that both use non-consumable tungsten electrodes and shielding gas. The construction of the welding torch is however different in the two cases. The plasma torch is of two types: transferred arc type and non-transferred arc type. In case of the non-transferred type, both electrodes are inside the torch, while in the case of the transferred arc type, the arc is struck between the negatively charged electrode (which is in the torch) and the positively charged workpiece. Figure 17.13(a) shows a schematic of GTAW torch in comparison with two types of plasma arc torches – transferred arc type as shown in Figure 17.13(b) and non-transferred arc type as shown in Figure 17.13(c). The transferred arc is better since it transfers more energy at the workpiece and is less susceptible to magnetic deflection; but it can be used only with conductive work materials.

As can be seen in Figure 17.13 (b) and (c), PAW uses a tungsten electrode that is contained in a specially designed torch. A high-velocity stream of gas (argon or argon–hydrogen mixture) is introduced into the region of the arc to form a high-velocity, intensely hot plasma. For the purpose of arc shielding, the gases used are argon, helium, and argon–helium mixture. The reason for higher temperatures in PAW compared to those in GTAW lies in the constriction of the arc, which produces a plasma jet of small diameter and very high energy density.

There are two types of PAW – one uses low operating currents while the other type uses high operating currents. The low-current plasma arc welding operates in the transferred arc mode and uses current in the range 0.1 to 10 amperes. It is also known as micro-plasma welding. The collimated shape of the arc has a needle-like appearance and permits sufficiently large arc length variation, and hence, is easily adapted to automated equipment. The low-current PAW is suited for thin sheet components up to 1 mm thick such as radiators, air ducting and exhaust manifolds. The concentrated heat with an associated narrow weld puddle makes the process best suited for welding instrument parts.

The high-current plasma process is associated with a 'keyhole' effect. This means that a keyhole is formed at the leading edge of the weld puddle, where the forces of the plasma jet displace the molten metal to permit the arc to pass completely through the work material. As the plasma torch moves forward, the molten metal under the influence of surface tension flows in behind the keyhole to make the weld bead. The keyhole ensures full penetration and uniformity of weld bead formation.

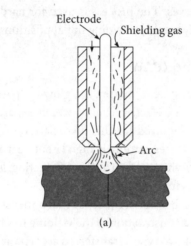

(a)

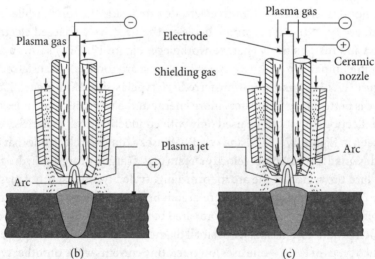

(b)   (c)

Figure 17.13   Schematic comparison between a GTAW torch and the two basic types of plasma torches used in plasma arc welding process: (a) GTAW torch; (b) Transferred arc type plasma torch; and (c) Non-transferred type plasma torch

Advantages, limitations and applications   The low-current PAW has the following advantages and applications:

- The arc is collimated. The total divergence is only about 5°, whereas it is nearly 45° in case of GTAW.
- The collimated arc allows large variation in arc length without seriously affecting the weld quality.
- The collimated arc causes very small HAZ.
- The process is easily adaptable to automation because any variation in arc length is less critical.

The process is best suited to the welding of thin complicated structures such as instrument panels, radiators and exhaust manifolds.

The high-current PAW has the following advantages and applications:

- PAW is less sensitive to workpiece edge mismatch as compared to the GTAW process.
- The plasma arc allows deep penetration and, therefore, welds with depth-to-width ratio of up to 20:1 are possible.
- Welding speed is almost twice of what is attainable in GTAW.

The process is suitable for welding of workpiece of varying thickness because it is less sensitive to stand-off distance. Any metal weldable by GTAW process can also be welded by this process.

The only limitations of the PAW are that the process is noisy and the cost of equipment is very high, almost four to five times of that of GTAW.

17.3.4 Stud welding (SW)

Stud welding, also known as stud arc welding, is a special purpose arc welding process, which is used to join a stud (or a fastener) to a flat surface of another piece of metal. The stud acts as one of the electrodes and the workpiece as the other electrode. The polarity used in stud welding depends on the type of metal being welded. Welding aluminum, for example, would usually require direct current electrode positive (DCEP). Welding steel parts would normally require direct current electrode negative (DCEN). The process uses a type of flux called *ferrule*. It is a ceramic ring that concentrates the heat generated, prevents oxidation and retains the molten metal in the weld zone.

A portable stud welding machine called a gun, similar to the one schematically shown in Figure 17.14 is used. The stud to be welded is held in the holder of the gun and its tip is brought to the spot where it is to be welded on the base metal surface. Upon energizing the stud gun, the solenoid in the gun withdraws the stud from the base metal through a short distance at which a DC arc is established between the tip of the stud and the workpiece surface [Figure 17.15 (i)]. The arc heats and melts the base metal as well as the tip of the stud.

After a specified time interval, a mechanical spring is released, which forces the stud into the molten pool of the workpiece surface under light pressure [Figure 17.15 (b)]. The current is switched off and the stud is held in place until the metals re-solidify and the stud gets welded to the workpiece [Figure 17.15 (c)]. The ceramic ferrule is now removed. The length of the stud is shortened as a result of its tip being melted; due consideration is therefore given to this fact while selecting the original length of the stud.

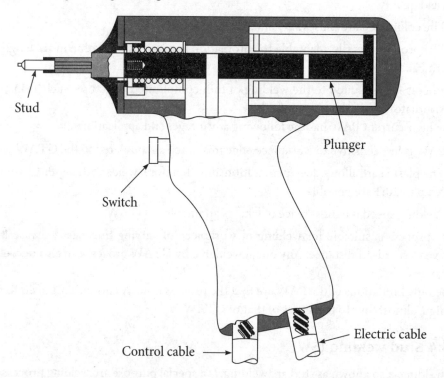

Figure 17.14   Welding gun used in stud welding process

Stud welding is versatile and easy. The process requires almost no skill on the part of the welder. As soon as the stud is inserted in the gun and held in the holder, the gun is positioned on the workpiece. Upon triggering the gun, the welding cycle is completed automatically in just a few milliseconds. Automatic equipment controls the intensity and duration of arcing as well as the amount and duration of pressure application. The process can be used to weld 500 to 1000 assemblies per hour.

Typical applications include welding of threaded fasteners to attach handles on cookware, welding of radiation fins on machinery, automobile body building, ship building, electrical panels and building construction. Stud welding has been used in ship building since ages but in other manufacturing industries, its use for a variety of purposes is rather recent.

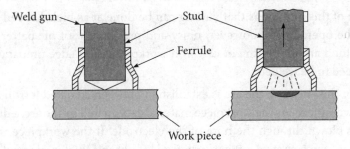

(a) Stud is positioned in the gun and arc is established between
stud and work piece so that a molten metal pool is formed

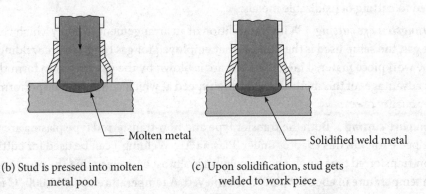

(b) Stud is pressed into molten
metal pool

(c) Upon solidification, stud gets
welded to work piece

Figure 17.15 Schematic of stud welding process

17.4 Arc Cutting

All metals can be cut using an electric arc. The procedure is simple; the material is melted by the intense heat of the arc and then allowed to be blown away by the force of the arc, or pushed to flow away from the region by the flow of some gas. There are several methods of cutting with an arc; most of them are just a simple adaptation of the arc welding procedures described earlier in this chapter. A brief description of the methods follows.

Shielded metal arc cutting In this method, the arc from a shielded metal electrode is used to melt the metal. The molten metal is then pushed away from the workpiece either by the force of the arc or by the force of gravity in order to form the cut. The method is employed in job shops where workpiece cutting is not a regular operation, for example, in garages.

Air carbon arc cutting In this method, the arc is established between a carbon electrode and the workpiece. The metal melted by the arc is pushed away from the workpiece by directed high velocity jets of air from holes in the electrode holder. Some oxidation of the metal does take place but the main function of the air is to blow the molten metal from the region to generate the cut.

The main advantage of this method is that cutting can be done at as high a speed as half a metre per minute. The operation is, however, noisy and produces a lot of spatter. Main applications of this method are for cutting of cast iron workpieces and edge preparation of thick steel plates that need to be welded.

Oxygen arc cutting   In this method, the arc is established between a coated ferrous metal tube electrode and the workpiece. As the workpiece material gets melted by the arc, a directed stream of oxygen gas is blown through the bore of the electrode. If the workpiece is made of some oxidizable metal – such as steel – it gets oxidized locally and then is expelled by the oxygen stream to form the cut.

The main advantage of this method is that the cut formed is clean; but, it is generally limited to cutting of oxidizable metals.

Gas tungsten arc cutting   With the addition of an arrangement to apply a high velocity jet of some gas, the setup used is the same as that employed for gas tungsten arc welding. The zone of the workpiece material melted by the arc is blown by the gas stream to form the cut. The main advantages of this method are the high speed at which cutting can be performed and the better quality of cut.

Plasma arc cutting   Both the transfer type and non-transferred type plasma arc torches (as described earlier in this chapter under 'Plasma Arc Welding') can be used for cutting. In case of non-transferred type torch, the arc column is almost entirely within the nozzle of the torch, and a temperature of about 16,000°C is achieved. A temperature up to 33,000 °C is, however, possible in case of a transfer type torch where the arc is maintained between the electrode and the workpiece. In either case, the temperatures are so high that virtually any metal can be cut by melting it locally and then blowing the molten metal from the workpiece.

The quality of cut formed by a plasma arc torch can be improved by using a constricting arc with the help of some arrangement such as radial impingement of water around the arc or by using a magnetic field. This method of cutting has several advantages such as:

- It is economical (compared to the oxy-fuel method of cutting).
- It is versatile, that is, it can be used to cut virtually any metal.
- It gives very high cutting speed (typically, five to six times faster than oxy-fuel method of cutting).
- It can be easily integrated with robots or CNC machines.
- The width of the kerf is small.
- The cut surface is spatter-free.
- The heat affected zone is small, just one-third to one-fourth as much as that produced in case of the oxy-fuel method of cutting.

Questions

1. Briefly discuss the three basic types of current and polarity used in arc welding.

2. Describe the manual flux-coated electrode arc welding process. Name one major limitation of this process and describe how it may be overcome.

3. Why is it necessary to use a flux in some arc welding processes but not in others? Name one major disadvantage of the use of flux in the production of multi-layer welds.

4. Differentiate between a consumable and a non-consumable electrode. Describe any arc welding process that uses a non-consumable electrode.

5. Explain the similarities and differences between consumable and non-consumable electrode arc welding processes.

6. What are three main types of metal transfer that can occur during arc welding? Describe them briefly with suitable sketches.

7. Define polarity as applied to DC arc welding. How is this advantageously used?

8. What do you understand by the term 'arc blow'? What can be done to reduce its effects?

9. What functions does the electrode coating perform in shielded metal arc welding?

10. What are the functions of the slag that forms over a shielded metal arc weld?

11. Why is iron powder introduced in the coating of shielded metal arc electrodes that are to be used for welding ferrous metals?

12. Why are the electrodes used in shielded arc welding process generally limited in length, making the process an intermittent operation?

13. Discuss some of the attractive features of gas tungsten arc welding process. What are the various gases used in this process? What techniques can be used to increase the rate of filler metal deposition during welding by this process?

14. Why is it generally necessary to use a filler metal in gas tungsten arc welding process? Give reasons for your answer.

15. Compare the two major inert gas shielded arc welding processes with respect to advantages, limitations and applications.

16. What could be the reasons for preferring gas metal arc welding over shielded metal arc welding for production work?

17. What is the advantage of putting flux in the centre of an electrode (as in flux-cored arc welding process) as compared to putting flux on the outside surface of an electrode (as in shielded metal arc welding process)?

18. Describe with a suitable sketch the submerged arc welding process. Give various advantages and limitations of this process.

19. Explain why the electro-slag welding process is suitable for thick plates and heavy structural parts.

20. Describe with suitable sketches the plasma arc welding process. Define the various attractive features of this process. Differentiate between the plasma arc welding and the plasma arc cutting process.

21. What are two major methods used to constrict the arc in plasma arc cutting for the purpose of a cleaner, narrower and more controlled cut?

22. Compare the size of the heat affected zone obtained in different cutting processes: oxy-fuel, arc and plasma. Give reasons for the same.

23. Briefly describe the various methods available for arc cutting of metals. Compare these with respect to applications and quality of cut obtained.

24. How is a pulsed gas metal arc welding process different from an MIG welding process? Give advantages of the pulsed gas metal arc welding process.

Fill in the Blanks

1. In arc welding processes, electrical currents used are of the order of _____ amps, and the voltages used are in the range of _____ to _____ V AC.

2. The electrodes used in arc welding are basically of two types: _____ electrodes, and _____ electrodes.

3. When DC current is used in arc welding, the selection of *polarity* depends on (i) _____, (ii) _____ and (iii) _____ .

4. Straight polarity (workpiece positive; electrode negative) produces _____ heat penetration and is, therefore, preferred for welding of _____ workpieces.

5. Reverse polarity (workpiece negative; electrode positive) produces _____ heat penetration and is, therefore, preferred for _____ workpieces.

6. In case of arc welding with _____ current, arc blow phenomenon is not prominent because _____ current prevents the formation of strong magnetic field.

7. The shielded metal arc welding process is best suited for welding of workpieces having thickness in the range _____ mm to _____ mm.

8. The shielded metal arc welding process is especially useful for welding _____ metals. Most applications of this process are _____.

9. In shielded metal arc welding process, it is difficult to obtain consistent high quality welds because the following three basic requirements cannot be easily met (i) _____, (ii) _____ and (iii) _____.

10. The granular flux used in submerged arc welding is made up of several elements such as _____ and _____.

11. The power source used in submerged arc welding is of _____ type.

12. The electric currents used in submerged arc welding range between _____ amp to _____ amp.

13. In arc welding process, higher welding current than necessary should not be used as it would cause _____.

14. In arc welding process, use of lesser welding current than necessary results in _____.

15. Two most common arc welding processes that use the principle of inert gas shielding are (i) _____ and (ii) _____ .

16. Generally, gas tungsten arc welding is done with direct current, _____ polarity.

17. GTAW process is suited for welding of _____ workpieces rather than for welding _____ workpieces.

18. Shielded metal arc welding uses _____ electrode that is fed continuously through a gun to a contact surface that imparts an electric current to it.

19. _____ current is generally not used in shielded metal arc welding.

20. Metal transfer from the electrode to the weld joint in MIG welding can occur in any of the following three ways: (i) _____, (ii) _____, (iii) _____ .

21. The flux-cored arc welding process is limited to welding in _____ and _____ positions.

22. Electro-slag welding is mostly used for welding _____ components or plates where the joint to be welded is in a _____ position.

23. The best welding process to join 500 mm thick plates in one pass is _____.

24. _____ welding process is uneconomical for welding plates of thickness less than 20 mm.

25. In atomic hydrogen welding process, the arc is struck between _____.

26. The only welding process which uses reactive shielding gas is _____.

27. Atomic hydrogen welding process is mostly used for _____ positions only.

28. Plasma torches are of two types: (i) _____ arc type, and (ii) _____ arc type.

29. The high-current plasma process is associated with _____ effect. Accordingly, a _____ is formed at the leading edge of the weld puddle, where the forces of the plasma jet displace the molten metal to permit the arc to pass completely through the work material.

30. The _____ arc welding process is best suited to welding of thin complicated structures such as instrument panels, radiators and exhaust manifolds.

Choose the Correct Answer

1. Arc welding is a technique of joining two metal pieces in which heat can be obtained from
   a. an electric arc struck between two workpieces that are to be joined.
   b. an electric arc struck between two non-consumable electrodes.
   c. a gas flame of oxygen and acetylene.
   d. a gas flame of oxygen and hydrogen.

2. Arc welding is a technique of joining two metal pieces in which it is not possible to use the heat obtained from
    a.   an electric arc between a consumable electrode and the workpiece.
    b.   an electric arc between a non-consumable electrode and the workpiece.
    c.   an electric arc between two non-consumable electrodes.
    d.   an acetylene–oxygen flame.

3. One major problem encountered in arc welding concerns
    a.   melting and solidifying of metals in air. b.   polarity.
    c.   formation of weld pool metal.   d.   use of low voltages.

4. Arc welding of very thin parts
    a.   is not possible.
    b.   should preferably be done using AC current.
    c.   should preferably be done using DC current with straight polarity.
    d.   should preferably be done using AC current with reverse polarity.

5. The electrode performs both the functions of providing heat and providing filler material in case of
    a.   arc welding with consumable electrodes only.
    b.   arc welding with non-consumable electrodes only.
    c.   arc welding with either consumable or non-consumable electrodes.
    d.   gas welding with oxy-acetylene flame.

6. Arc welding with straight polarity means
    a.   alternating current has been used in the process.
    b.   alternating current or direct current has been used in the process.
    c.   direct current has been used in the process and electrode is connected to the negative terminal.
    d.   direct current has been used in the process and electrode is connected to the positive terminal.

7. Arc welding with reverse polarity means
    a.   alternating current has been used in the process.
    b.   alternating current or direct current has been used in the process.
    c.   direct current has been used in the process and electrode is connected to the negative terminal.
    d.   direct current has been used in the process and electrode is connected to the positive terminal.

8. In arc welding with direct current
   a. same amount of heat is produced at the electrode whether it is connected to the positive or negative terminal.
   b. same amount of heat is produced at the electrode as compared to when alternating current is used.
   c. more heat is produced at the electrode when it is connected to the negative terminal.
   d. more heat is produced at the electrode when it is connected to the positive terminal.

9. A consumable electrode used in arc welding
   a. is always bare.
   b. is always coated.
   c. is always electroplated.
   d. can be either bare or coated.

10. Identify the statement which does not represent the function of coating on arc welding electrodes.
    a. To provide envelope of inert gas.
    b. To remove impurities.
    c. To prevent brittleness of weld bead.
    d. To provide arc de-stabilization.

11. Which one of the following is not a 'type of coating' of arc welding electrodes?
    a. cellulosic
    b. exotic
    c. mineral
    d. iron powder

12. Which one of the following does not form a part of the cellulosic coatings of arc welding electrodes?
    a. natural silicate
    b. wood pulp
    c. saw dust
    d. cotton

13. Thick slag is produced with which type of coating on the electrode?
    a. mineral
    b. cellulosic
    c. iron powder
    d. exotic

14. Which one of the following materials is not used for making non-consumable electrodes?
    a. carbon
    b. copper
    c. graphite
    d. tungsten

15. Tungsten electrodes are often alloyed with which one of the following so as to obtain better current-carrying and electron-emission characteristics?
    a. thorium
    b. magnesium
    c. copper
    d. silver

16. Which one of the following factors does not determine the *operating characteristics* of arc welding electrodes?
    a. fill
    b. freeze
    c. follow
    d. hollow

17. The phenomenon called *arc blow* is almost always present
    a. when using DC current in arc welding.
    b. when using AC current in arc welding.
    c. when DC or AC current is used but filler metal is not used.
    d. when non-consumable electrodes are used.

18. Which one of the following actions does not reduce the severity of arc blow problem in arc welding?
    a. Use AC current rather than DC.   c. Increase the magnitude of current.
    b. Reduce the magnitude of current.   d. Use short arc length.

19. Which one of the following elements does not form a constituent of granular flux used in submerged arc welding?
    a. lime   c. magnesium oxide
    b. calcium fluoride   d. copper sulphate

20. In which arc welding process is current conducted directly from the electrode wire to the base metal through the conductive slag?
    a. ESW   c. GTAW
    b. SMAW   d. GMAW

21. Which one of the following arc welding processes uses an electrode consisting of continuous metal tubing containing flux and other ingredients in its core?
    a. GMAW   c. FCAW
    b. GTAW   d. SMAW

22. Which one of the following arc welding processes produces the highest temperatures?
    a. SAW   c. PAW
    b. FCAW   d. GTAW

23. Which one of the following arc welding processes uses a non-consumable electrode?
    a. FCAW   c. SMAW
    b. GTAW   d. GMAW

24. Which one of the following is not a mode of metal transfer from the electrode to the weld joint in GMAW?
    a. spray transfer   c. open circuiting
    b. short circuiting   d. globular transfer

25. When coated electrodes are used in arc welding, consider the following statements about the coating on electrodes:
    i   It provides a shielding atmosphere around the molten weld pool.
    ii   It provides flux which gets mixed with the impurities and forms slag.
    iii It helps to stabilize the arc.

Of these statements,

a. only (i) is true.

b. only (i) and (ii) are true

c. only (i) and (iii) are true

d. all (i), (ii) and (iii) are true

26. A non-consumable electrode to be used in arc welding (AC and DC)is mostly made of

a. tungsten.
c. graphite or carbon.

b. tungsten or graphite.
d. tungsten or carbon or graphite.

27. A non-consumable electrode to be used in DC arc welding is mostly made of

a. only tungsten.
c. only graphite or carbon.

b. only tungsten or graphite.
d. tungsten or carbon or graphite.

28. Consider the following statements:

i   Submerged arc welding process uses a large pool of granular flux.

ii   Electro-gas and electro-slag welding processes use consumable electrodes.

iii Atomic hydrogen welding is suitable for low temperature applications.

iv   TIG welding does not use any shielding medium

Which one of the following answers is correct?

a. Only (i) is true.

b. Only (i) and (ii) are true.

c. Only (i) and (iii) are true.

d. Only (ii) and (iii) are true.

29. In which one of the following welding processes the workpiece is not part of the electrical circuit?

a. MIG welding
c. submerged arc welding

b. TIG welding
d. atomic hydrogen welding

Answers

1. b.	2. d.	3. a.	4. c.	5. a.	6. c.	7. d.	8. d.	9. d.	10. d.
11. b.	12. a.	13. a.	14. b.	15. a.	16. d.	17. a.	18. c.	19. d.	20. a.
21. c	22. c.	23. b.	24. c.	25. d.	26. a.	27. c.	28. b.	29. d.	

18

Resistance Welding

LEARNING OBJECTIVES

After reading this chapter, you should be able to understand the following:

- The resistance welding process, its advantages, limitations and applications.
- The various advantages, limitations and applications of resistance welding process.
- The resistance spot welding, its equipment and applications.
- The resistance seam welding, its advantages, limitations and applications.
- The resistance projection welding, its advantages, limitations and applications.
- The resistance butt welding, its advantages, limitations and applications.
- The resistance percussion welding, its advantages and applications.

18.1 Introduction

Resistance welding can be considered as a solid state welding, although it is generally also classified as a fusion welding process. In the same way as any other fusion welding process, resistance welding also requires both heat and pressure in the weld area to create a satisfactory joint. All metals have finite electrical resistance that resists the flow of electrical current and, in doing so, generates heat. The resistance welding process utilizes thermal energy obtained from the flow of electrical current through the electrical resistance of the workpieces and the interface between them. By external means, pressure is applied that is varied with the progression of the weld cycle. Initially, a small amount of pressure is applied to hold the workpieces in contact, thereby controlling the electrical resistance at the interface. As the current is passed through the workpieces, a rise in temperature takes place at the interface due to the presence of high electrical resistance. As the proper temperature is attained, the pressure is increased to make the weld. Due to the application of pressure, welding occurs at a lower temperature than that required for oxy-fuel or arc welding. In many resistance welding operations, the base metal does not even melt; the required temperature is attained in just a second, making it possible to have the weld completed in a few seconds. Resistance welding is, therefore, an extremely rapid and economical process. It requires no filler metal and the tight contact maintained between the workpieces excludes air, thereby eliminating the need for any shielding gas or flux.

18.1.1 Thermal energy

The thermal energy required for resistance welding is obtained when a large electrical current (of the order of 15000 amp) at a voltage of 0.5 to 10 V is passed through the workpieces for a very short time (typically 0.2 to 0.5 s) by means of electrodes. The magnitude of heat available can be determined from the relation

$$H = k\, I^2 R\, t$$

where H: total heat generated at the joint (Joules); I: electrical current (amp); R: electrical resistance at the interface of the two workpieces (ohms); t: duration for which current flows (seconds); k: constant to account for energy losses through conduction and radiation (value of k is less than unity).

Figure 18.1 shows the circuit for spot welding, the most widely used electric resistance welding process.

The total resistance in the welding circuit is the sum of:

(i)   Resistance of the electrodes.

(ii) Contact resistance between electrodes and the workpieces.

(iii) Resistance of the workpieces.

(iv) Resistance between the surfaces to be joined. These surfaces are called the *faying surfaces.*

In order to obtain the maximum temperature at the location where the weld is to be made, it is necessary to keep resistances (i), (ii) and (iii) as small as possible. The resistance of

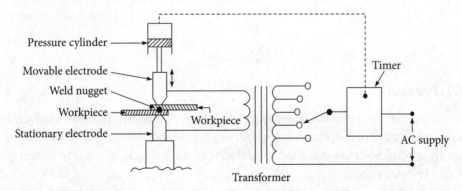

Figure 18.1   Resistance welding circuit

electrodes is minimized by making them of metals with very low resistivity, such as copper. Resistance (ii), that is, the one between the workpieces and electrodes, can be minimized by choosing an appropriate shape for the electrode tip, and by applying pressure on the electrodes to obtain an *intimate* contact with the workpieces. Resistance (iii), that is, that of the workpieces, depends upon the thickness and type of the material, and is often much smaller than resistances (i), (ii), and (iv). Resistance (iv), that is, the one between the faying surfaces, depends on the roughness and cleanliness (presence of dirt, non-conductive oxide scale, etc.) of the surfaces, and the area of contact. All these factors need to be controlled to get consistent weld quality results.

Example 18.1

A resistance spot welding operation is carried out on two thin sheet metal parts as shown in Figure 18.1. Thickness of sheet is 1.5 mm and the diameter of the electrodes is 5 mm at the contacting surfaces. If the operation uses a current of 12,000 amps for a 0.25 s duration to produce a weld nugget of 5 mm diameter and 2.5 mm thickness, calculate the thermal efficiency of the process. Assume the contact resistance of the faying surfaces as 0.0001 ohm and the unit melting energy for the workpiece metal as $U_m = 12 \, \text{J/mm}^3$.

Solution

The heat generated in the operation can be determined as $H = I^2 R t$

$$= (12{,}000)^2 \, (0.0001) \, (0.25) = 3600 \, \text{J}$$

The volume of the weld nugget $= \dfrac{\pi}{4} (5)^2 \, 2.5 = 49 \, \text{mm}^3$

The heat required to melt nugget volume of metal $= 49(12) = 588 \, \text{J}$

$$\text{Thermal efficiency of the process} = \frac{\text{Heat utilized}}{\text{Heat generated}}$$

$$= \frac{588}{3600} \times 100 = 16.35\%$$

18.1.2 Pressure

One major advantage of resistance welding is that the welds are produced at relatively lower temperatures because of the pressures applied, which promote a forging action. It is necessary to properly control both the magnitude and timing of the pressure in order to obtain quality welds. As a rule, we should

- Apply moderate pressure to hold the workpieces in place and establish the necessary resistance at the interface before switching on the power supply.

- Maintain a moderate pressure while the current is being passed.
- Raise the pressure just when adequate welding heat is obtained.
- Stop the pressure as soon as the weld is forged.

Initially, if less pressure is applied than necessary, the contact resistance will be high and the heat produced will be more, causing burning of the workpiece surface or pitting of the electrode tip. On the other hand, if pressure applied is more than necessary, the softened metal may get expelled from between the faying surfaces or there can even be an indentation mark of the electrodes on the workpieces.

Depending upon the design of the resistance welding machine, pressure application is with the help of compression springs or pneumatic cylinders.

18.1.3 Electric power supply

In addition to proper magnitude and timing of pressure, which also controls the resistance at the interface of the faying surfaces, proper control of the magnitude and duration of electric current is necessary to produce quality resistance welds. Power transformers convert the high-voltage, low-current main line power to the high-current (5,000 to 100,000 amp) low-voltage (0.5 to 10 V) power needed for resistance welding operation. Nowadays, highly precise production welding machines are available that can be programmed to supply specified cycles of needed magnitude and duration of welding current.

Advantages, limitations and applications The resistance welding processes have a number of advantages over other welding processes. Some of these are as follows:

- Rate or speed of welding is very high.
- Degree of reliability and reproducibility is very high.
- Both similar and dissimilar metals can be easily joined.
- The processes can be fully automated.
- Skilled operators are generally not needed.
- No pollution hazard.
- Saving of materials as there is no requirement of filler metal, shielding gases and fluxes.

There are some limitations of the resistance welding processes. These are:

- High initial cost of equipment.
- Not all types of joints can be made; generally only lap joints can be made.
- Welding surfaces of some materials like aluminium and magnesium have to be properly cleaned before carrying out resistance welding.
- Martensite can form in steels having more than 0.15% carbon content. Critical components are, therefore, annealed after welding in order to reduce brittleness.

- Joints have relatively lower tensile strength.

Some important applications of resistance welding are for:

- Joining thin parts of both similar and dissimilar metals.
- Assembly of parts in a wide range of industries including automobiles, transportation, electronics and communication, consumer products, defence and construction/building products.

18.2 Resistance Welding Processes

The commonly used resistance welding processes are:

- Resistance spot welding.
- Resistance seam welding.
- Resistance projection welding.
- Resistance butt welding
- Resistance percussion welding

These will be described in the following sections.

18.2.1 Resistance spot welding

Resistance spot welding is the simplest and most widely used type of resistance welding. Between two water-cooled copper electrodes, sheet materials are positioned one overlapping the other (Figure 18.2). A controlled cycle of pressure and current is applied to produce weld nuggets that are circular in shape having 3 to 10 mm diameter depending upon the electrode tip size. The steps in a spot welding cycle are shown in Figure 18.3. Upon completion of the cycle, the electrodes open out and the weld is ready. Sheet metal workpieces can either be removed or moved forward to make another weld at a different location. Normally, a series of spot welds are made at appropriate intervals along the length of the weld line.

The strength of the bond in the weld nugget depends on surface roughness as also on the cleanliness of the faying surfaces. It is essential that oil, paint and thick oxide layers are removed before welding, although the presence of a uniform, thin layer of oxide does not seriously affect the process.

All metals can be spot welded with the exception of a few. Metals that have high electrical conductivity such as silver and copper do present some difficulty. Such metals must be surface-cleaned either by mechanical or chemical means prior to welding in order to assure that the electrode-to-metal resistance is low enough to develop an adequate temperature at the interface of the faying surfaces. Additional measures, such as the use of higher welding currents and water cooling adjacent to the area where spot welding is to be done, may also be taken.

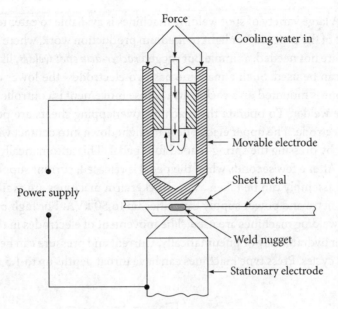

Force

Cooling water in

Movable electrode

Sheet metal

Power supply

Weld nugget

Stationary electrode

Figure 18.2 Schematic of resistance spot welding process

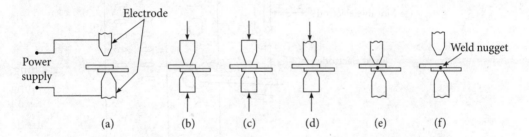

Electrode

Power
supply

Weld nugget

(a)   (b)   (c)   (d)   (e)   (f)

Figure 18.3 Resistance spot welding operation cycle: (a) Sheets to be spot welded properly placed on the stationary electrode; (b) Moveable electrode lowered to touch the upper-sheet surface; pressure applied; (c) Current switched on; pressure increased; (d) Current switched off; pressure continues until weld nugget formed; (e) Pressure released; and (f) Movable electrode raised; sheets may be moved

When the two pieces of sheet metal being spot welded are of the same thickness, each should not generally be thicker than 3 mm. Thinner sheets may, however, be spot welded to sheets or plates thicker than 3 mm. When sheets of different thickness or different materials are to be spot welded, positive results can be expected if both materials are brought to the desired temperature at the same time. This can be achieved by using a larger electrode or electrode made of higher-conductivity material against the work material of greater thickness or higher resistance.

The electric currents used are in the range 3,000 amp to 30,000 amp; the actual value depends upon the materials being welded as well as on their thicknesses.

Equipment   A large variety of spot welding machines is available to cater to different needs of industrial use of the process. For light to medium production work, where precise current–pressure cycles are not needed, a simple but rugged *rocker-arm spot welder,* like the one shown in Figure 18.4 can be used. Such a machine has two electrodes–the lower one is stationery and the upper one is mounted on a rocker arm whose movement is controlled by a foot pedal operated by the welder. To operate the machine, overlapping sheets are positioned on the lower (fixed) electrode. The upper electrode is brought down into contact with the surface of the upper sheet by pressing the spring-loaded foot pedal. This automatically switches on the current supply. After a few seconds when the pedal is released, current supply is switched off and the welded assembly can be taken away. Rocker-arm machines are available with throat depths up to 1 metre and power supply capacities up to 50 kVA. For high production work, press type spot welding machines are used. The movement of electrodes in these machines is controlled either hydraulically or pneumatically. Current and pressure can be programmed to follow specified cycles. Press type machines can have throat depths up to 1.5 m and capacities up to 500 kVA.

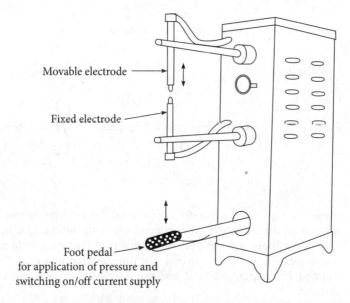

Movable electrode

Fixed electrode

Foot pedal
for application of pressure and
switching on/off current supply

Figure 18.4   Resistance spot welding machine of rocker-arm type

Applications   The maximum users of the spot welding process are those who are involved in fabricating sheet metal parts. This process finds wide applications in the automobile industry as also for the manufacture of household goods such as metal furniture, refrigerators, washing machines, desert coolers and so on. One can get an idea of the economic importance of this process by considering its application in car body manufacture. A typical car body has more than 5000 individual spot welds, and according to an estimate, several million cars are produced annually in the world.

18.2.2 Resistance seam welding (RSW)

Resistance seam welding differs from resistance spot welding with respect to (i) shape of copper electrodes–spot welding uses stick-shaped electrodes whereas seam welding uses rotating disc wheels as electrodes, and (ii) power supply –spot welding uses normal AC power supply whereas seam welding uses pulsed power supply. Otherwise, the basic equipment used for seam welding is the same as for spot welding. Resistance seam welding is of two types: the first type is used for welding overlapping sheets of metal to appear like a seam joint, that is, for making a series of overlapping spot welds, while the second type is used to produce butt welds of thick metal plates.

In case of resistance seam welding of the first type, the frequency of current pulses is so adjusted with the linear traverse rate of the workpiece (controlled by the rotational speed of electrode wheels) that a series of overlapping spot welds are made that resembles stitching. A schematic of this type of resistance seam welding is shown in Figure 18.5. If the frequency of current discharge is very small, there will be spaces between the weld spots.

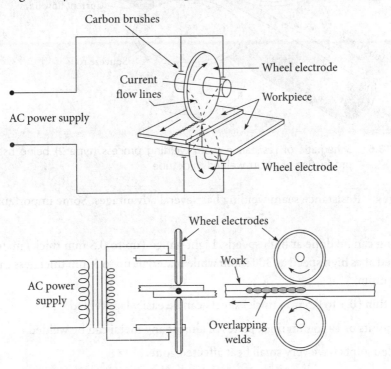

Figure 18.5 Schematic of resistance seam welding process (type 1)

Resistance seam welding of the second type is also called high frequency resistance seam welding. This process uses AC current of 10 to 400 kHz frequency. Figure 18.6 shows a pipe being formed by this process. The electrodes make contact with the work in the immediate vicinity of the weld joint. Heat is generated due to the flow of current and the resistance to the flow of the current offered by the butting metal surfaces. The heated surfaces are then welded by rapid application of an upsetting force provided by the squeeze rolls.

The power required for high frequency resistance seam welding is relatively less. The reason is that the effective resistance of the metal is very high at high frequency of the flowing current; the current required, therefore, for a given amount of heat ($I^2 R$) input is small.

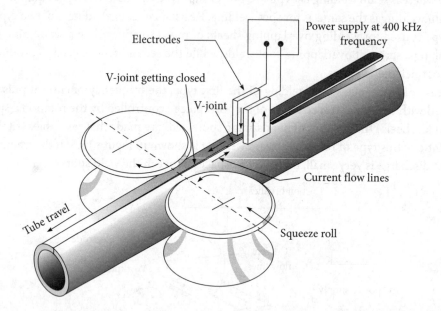

Figure 18.6 Schematic of resistance seam welding process (type 2) being used for the production of a butt-welded thick tube

Advantages Resistance seam welding has several advantages. Some important ones are as follows:

- Joining can be done at high speeds. Light-gauge (up to 0.5 mm thick) materials can be welded at as high speed as 300 mpm while materials up to 5 mm thickness can be welded at 50 mpm.

- Very thin (0.1 to 0.5 mm thick) sheets can be easily lap welded.

- Butt joints of 1–15 mm thick plates of almost any metal can be welded.

- Welded joints have very small heat affected zone.

- High conductivity metals (such as aluminium, silver, copper, and their alloys) and dissimilar metals can be welded.

- Dissimilar metals can be welded together. One typical application is in the production of band saw blades, where high-speed steel blade teeth are seam-welded to a low carbon steel backing strip.

Applications   Resistance seam welding of the first type finds wide applications in the manufacture of water-tight or air-tight sheet metal vessels such as fuel tanks, gasoline tanks, automobile mufflers, heat exchangers and different kinds of cans and drums. Resistance seam welding of the second type finds wide applications in the continuous welding of longitudinal seams of metal sheets, pipes and tubes.

18.2.3 Resistance projection welding

Two major limitations of the spot welding process that prohibit it from becoming a highly attractive process of mass production are: (i) only one spot weld can be produced at a time, that is, a pause of a certain time duration is necessary between two consecutive spot welds, and (ii) the electrode condition must be maintained at regular intervals of time. Both these limitations are overcome in a variant of resistance spot welding, which is known as resistance projection welding.

There are several forms of projection welding; a typical one is shown in Figure 18.7. Small projections are embossed (or raised) on one of the sheets (or plates) to be joined at the locations where the welds are required to be made. These projections are pressed against the matching flat sheet (or plate) by a pair of large-area copper electrodes, which are also used to transmit the electrical supply. As the electrical current flows through the points of contact, that is, the projections, heating is concentrated where the welds are required to be made. Just when the metal at the projections is heated up and becomes plastic, applied pressure causes all projection areas held between the electrodes to flatten and become welded simultaneously. The number of projections that can be welded simultaneously, however, depends on the availability of electric power and pressure.

The machine for conventional spot welding can be converted to projection welding just by changing the size and shape of the electrodes. Projections of almost any shape can be made on parts by press forming, generally along with other blanking or forming operations.

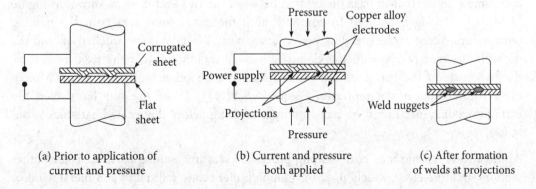

(a) Prior to application of current and pressure

(b) Current and pressure both applied

(c) After formation of welds at projections

Figure 18.7   Schematic of resistance projection welding process

Advantages   The main advantages of projection welding process are as follows:

- The welded surface is very clean. There is no indentation mark on the surface.

- The production rate is high.

Applications   Projection welding is widely used to weld nuts and bolts to other parts. Projections machined or forged onto the bolts and nuts are made to touch the sheet to which they are to be welded. Electric current is supplied and pressure is applied through electrodes to form welds. Another major application of the process is to produce welded wire products such as wire fence, shopping carts and wire mesh concrete reinforcing mats in which welding occurs at the intersection of the wires.

18.2.4 Resistance butt welding

Butt joints can be made with resistance welding in two ways: (i) Upset welding, and (ii) Flash welding.

Resistance upset welding   In this process, the metal bar stock to be welded is clamped in such a manner that the ends where the joint is to be made are in slight contact with each other as shown in Figure 18.8[a(i)]. A high-density electric current in the range 300 to 500 amp per square cm of the contact area is passed through the clamps. At the interface, a high resistance causes a corresponding rise in the metal temperature and the metal softens. Just enough force is then applied, as can be seen in Figure 18.8[a(ii)], to avoid arcing. With the application of more force, a large, symmetrical upset is made as shown in Figure 18.8[a(iii)]. There is no melting of metal, nor is there any spatter. The protruding metal may be machined off before using the welded bar stock.

Resistance flash welding   In this process, two parts of the metal bar stock to be welded are held in two clamps, one fixed clamp and the other movable clamp as shown in Figure 18.8[b(i)]. The two ends of bar stock to be joined are placed very close to each other, as shown in Figure 18.8[b(i)]. When a high density electric current is passed through the clamps, an arc (called flash) is created between the two end faces as shown in Figure 18.8[b(ii)]. Arcing is allowed to continue until the entire joint area is at the melting temperature. Some of the metal may even burn away. Power is then switched off and the movable bar part (along with the clamp) is moved rapidly towards the fixed one; thus, the two parts of the bar stock are pushed against each other with great force. Molten metal is forced out of the joint area [Figure 18.8[b(iii)]]. When the joint has cooled, the extra protruding metal must be removed by machining before the welded bar stock is put to use.

Applications   Resistance butt welding process is ideal for joining bars, tubes and other sections and, therefore, widely used for joining boiler tubes, rail tracks and metal window frame assemblies.

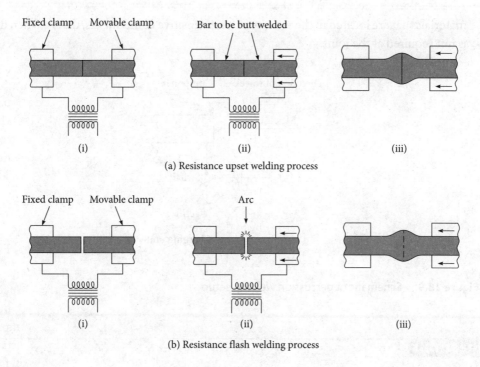

(a) Resistance upset welding process

(b) Resistance flash welding process

Figure 18.8 Resistance butt welding processes

18.2.5 Resistance percussion welding

Resistance percussive welding is a high-speed welding process that can be used to produce either a fusion or forge (solid phase) weld. A high temperature arc is generated from a short quick electrical discharge between the two surfaces to be joined say, a small workpiece, such as a wire, and a component. This is immediately followed by the application of pressure by one part against the other to form the weld. This type of joining brings the materials together in a percussive manner. The weld cycle is extremely short, generally less than 15 ms. Figure 18.9 shows a schematic of the process.

Advantages and applications   The main advantages of this process are that (i) the heat produced is very localized resulting in a shallow heat affected zone; and (ii) the weld cycle time is very short.

The process is widely used for the welding of

- electronic components having very small dimensions, for example, for attaching pins (around 2 mm or less in diameter) to components such as resistors, capacitors, etc.
- similar or dissimilar materials that have small cross-sectional areas.
- anchor points to assemblies; for example, threaded studs are welded to test structures to allow the attachment of fatigue/fracture monitoring sensors.

- materials that are located in the vicinity of heat-sensitive components, that is, when flash is not required at the joint.

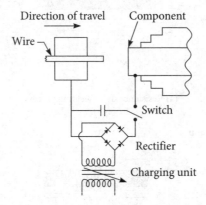

Figure 18.9   Schematic of percussion welding setup

Questions

1. Briefly discuss the essential differences between arc welding and electric resistance welding. Give three examples of applications where each would be most appropriate.

2. Give some attractive features and limitations of the electric resistance welding process. What are the metallurgical problems that might have to be faced when spot welding is done on parts made of medium or high-carbon steels?

3. What is the most appropriate sequence of pressure application during electric resistance welding? Explain the same briefly. What can happen if the most appropriate pressure-cycle is not applied?

4. What is the effect of the magnitude of pressure applied through the electrodes during resistance welding operations?

5. Describe resistance spot welding process with a schematic diagram. What is the typical size of a spot-weld nugget? On what factors does the strength of a weld nugget in resistance spot welding depend?

6. What are the major components of the total resistance between the electrodes in resistance welding? Which of these components should be high and which of them low? Suggest ways to reduce the resistance between the electrodes and workpieces?

7. What are the materials for spot-welding electrodes? How and why are the spot-welding electrodes cooled when in use?

8. Is it possible to spot weld two components which have quite different thicknesses? Explain the process?

9. Explain the working of a spot-welding gun. What is one major advantage of using this gun?

10. Give two important limitations of the spot welding process. How can these be overcome in projection welding? Describe the process of resistance projection welding.

11. What is the essential difference between the two types of resistance seam welding? Describe any one type with a suitable sketch.

12. Why is high frequency AC current generally used for resistance butt welding process?

13. Describe the procedure for resistance butt welding of two cylindrical components of different material compositions.

14. Explain resistance projection welding with a neat sketch. Give advantages and typical applications of the process.

15. What is resistance percussion welding? Give a schematic sketch and some typical applications of the process.

Fill in the Blanks

1. The resistance welding process utilizes thermal energy obtained from flowing of electrical current through resistance at the _____.

2. _____ is one metal that is most commonly welded by spot welding.

3. The practical limit of the thickness of material that can be easily spot-welded is _____.

4. In resistance projection welding, the number of projections that can be welded simultaneously depends on _____ and _____.

5. In resistance upset welding, high-density electric current in the range _____ amp per square cm is passed between the two ends of the bar stock to be welded.

6. The temperature in resistance welding can be regulated by controlling the magnitude and duration of _____.

7. In resistance spot welding, the resistance between the faying surfaces depends upon _____ and _____.

8. Resistance welds can be produced at _____ temperature than welds made by other processes.

9. In resistance welding, the total resistance between the electrodes consists of three components: _____, _____ and _____.

10. Resistance welding processes have two main limitations. These are: _____ and _____.

Choose the Correct Answer

1. The welding process that uses an electric current but no shielding gas or a flux is
   a. SMAW.   c. RSW.
   b. GTAW.   d. MIG.

2. In resistance welding process, the resistance mainly responsible for welding is the
    a. resistance of the electrodes.
    b. contact resistance between electrodes and workpieces.
    c. resistance of the workpieces.
    d. resistance between the surfaces to be joined.

3. In resistance spot welding process, the strength of the bond in the weld nugget depends on the
    a. cleanliness of the faying surfaces of workpieces.
    b. hardness of workpieces.
    c. tensile strength of the electrodes.
    d. electrical conductivity of electrodes.

4. In resistance seam welding, high frequency current is used because it
    a. is less costly than low frequency current.
    b. offers lesser resistance to flow between two faying surfaces.
    c. offers larger resistance to flow between two faying surfaces.
    d. produces lower noise.

5. Resistance welding is characterized by which one of the following?
    a. The process uses no electric current.   c. The process uses no pressure.
    b. The process uses no filler metal.   d. There occurs no fusion of parts in the process.

6. The reason for the use of high current in resistance welding is that
    a. heat required in the process is high because no pressure is used.
    b. no pressure is used in the process.
    c. resistance in the electric circuit is very low, around 0.0001 ohm.
    d. electrodes are made of highly conducting material.

Answers

1. c.   2. d.   3. a.   4. c.   5. b.   6. c.

19

Other Welding Processes

LEARNING OBJECTIVES

After reading this chapter, you should be able to understand the following:

- The electron beam welding process, its advantages, limitations and applications.
- The laser beam welding process, its advantages, limitations and applications.
- The comparison between laser beam welding and electron beam welding.
- The thermit welding process, its advantages, limitations and applications.
- The friction welding process, its advantages, limitations and applications.
- The ultrasonic welding process, its advantages, limitations and applications.
- The explosion welding process, its advantages, limitations and applications.
- The diffusion welding process, its advantages, limitations and applications.

In this chapter, certain special welding processes will be described. These processes are considered special because they cannot be classified as arc, oxy-fuel or resistance welding processes. Each of these processes use a unique technology and has special applications.

19.1 Electron Beam Welding (EBW)

Electron beam welding (EBW) is a fusion welding process that uses the heat resulting from impingement of a narrow focused beam of high velocity electrons on the workpiece to be welded. When electrons from the beam impact the surface of a solid, they collide with the particles of the solid and lose their kinetic energy. In fact, the electrons 'travel' a very small distance (a few hundredths of a millimeter) below the surface before their kinetic energy is transferred into heat. This distance is proportional to their initial energy and inversely proportional to the density of the solid.

A schematic of the electron beam gun used for the process is given in Figure 19.1. A tungsten filament is heated to about 2200°C with a high-voltage (in the range 50 to 100 kV) current, causing it to emit electrons. By using a control grid, an accelerating anode, and focusing coils, these electrons are accelerated to an extremely high speed and, in the process, form a narrow beam that can be focused to a circular spot about 1 mm in diameter on the workpiece. Unfortunately, normal atmosphere slows down the speed of the electrons to such an extent as to render the process ineffective. Therefore, to be effective as a heat source, the electron beam must be generated and focussed in a very high vacuum (say, at a pressure of 0.01 Pa). In most applications, even the workpiece to be welded is enclosed in the high vacuum chamber.

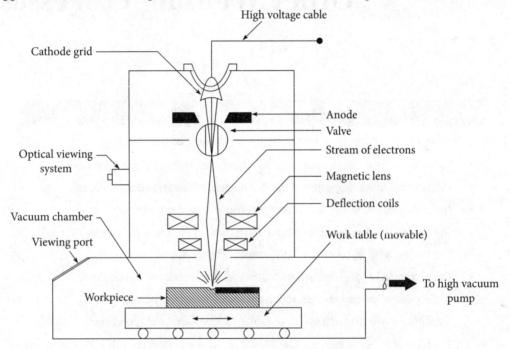

Figure 19.1   Schematic of the electron beam welding process

Advantages and limitations   The following advantages are claimed by the electron beam welding process:

- Welds are of high purity and quality, as vacuum assures both de-gasification and de-contamination.
- Welds have narrow profile with deep penetration. The fusion zone can have a depth-to-width ratio of 25:1 [Figure 19.2].
- The heat affected zone is very narrow, typically only 2–5% of that produced in arc welding processes. Therefore, distortion in the weld area is very small.
- Most metals in the thickness range of 0.2 mm to 100 mm can be butt or lap welded. Even metals such as zirconium, beryllium and tungsten, which are otherwise difficult to weld by other methods, can be welded.

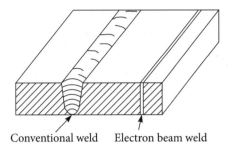

Conventional weld   Electron beam weld

Figure 19.2   Electron beam weld has narrow profile with deep penetration

- Dissimilar metals can also be welded.
- Heat-sensitive materials can be welded without any damage to the workpiece material.
- The process can be performed in any position.
- High welding speed up to 10 mpm can be achieved when parameters are precisely controlled with servo controls.
- There is no need for shielding gas, flux or any filler metal.
- No pre-welding or post-welding operations are needed since the weld is not contaminated.

The EBW process has the following disadvantages:

- All materials cannot be welded by an electron beam in a vacuum. This technology cannot be applied to materials with high vapour pressure at the melting temperature, such as zinc, cadmium magnesium and practically all non-metals.
- The process equipment is expensive.
- There is need for stringent safety measures in terms of expensive shielding, as the equipment emits harmful X-rays.
- There is need for extensive joint preparation and alignment. For welding thin-walled parts, appropriate welding aids are generally needed to provide perfect contact of the parts and prevent their movement during welding.
- There is a limit on the size of the workpiece that can be accommodated in the vacuum chamber.
- There may be some change of material properties induced by the welding process, for example due to a high cooling rate.
- Process productivity is low, as a lot of time is lost in re-establishing the vacuum every time a new job is to be loaded in the chamber.
- Not suitable for those applications where a wide gap filling is required.
- The material melted by the beam shrinks during cooling after solidification, which may cause cracking, deformation and changes of shape.

- The butt weld of two plates results in bending of the weldment because more material melts at the surface than at the root of the weld. This effect is of course not as substantial as in arc welding.

- There is possibility of cracks in the weld. If both parts are rigid, the shrinkage of the weld produces high stress in the weld, which may lead to cracks if the material is brittle.

Applications   The process is best suited for applications:

- in which thin parts have to be welded along with thick parts.

- in which other welding processes are unable to produce the required results. That is, where the quality of welds required is quite high.

- in which deep penetration is required.

- in electronics industries.

- in aircraft engine and aerospace industries. The process is used to join new and to repair used components made of titanium alloys in the aircraft industry.

- in defence industry for welding of nuclear and missile components.

- in automotive industry for welding of automatic transmission components. The range of components includes a variety of designs for shaft assemblies as well as planet carriers.

- for medical implants for which pure titanium is used. The pins of the implant are welded into the base plate by this process. The electron beam hits the pins from the flat back of the plate. For these small pin diameters, it is advantageous to deflect and move the beam in circles electronically rather than mechanically.

19.2 Laser Beam Welding (LBW)

Laser as a heat source has been used for several applications, including welding, machining, and heat treatment. Laser beam welding (LBW) is a fusion welding process that employs a focussed beam of laser that can provide a power intensity of nearly 100 W/mm^2. On striking the workpiece surface, this high-intensity beam produces a very fine column of vapourized metal surrounded by a small molten metal pool. As the laser beam is moved forward, the molten metal flows into a channel to produce a weld with a depth-to-width ratio of as much as 5:1. The weld pool, being very narrow, solidifies instantly, thus producing a negligible heat affected zone and thermal distortion. Generally, no filler metal is added, but it may be supplemented if the workpiece gap to be filled is excessive. Inert-gas shielding is optional; it may be used to protect the weld pool from oxidation. A schematic of the laser beam welding process is shown in Figure 19.3.

Laser beam welding is often compared to electron beam welding since both the processes use a stream of energy to fuse metals. Table 19.1 compares the two processes.

Advantages and limitations   Laser beam welding offers several advantages. These are:

- High controllability. The laser beam can be easily shaped, focused and directed. This makes it highly suitable for welding precision parts.

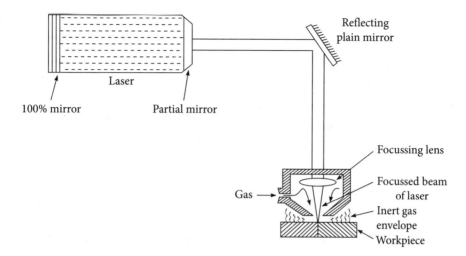

Figure 19.3 Schematic of laser beam welding process

Table 19.1 Comparison between laser beam and electron beam welding processes

Characteristic	Electron beam welding	Laser beam welding
Heat generation	Moderate	Low
Range of weld materials	Wide	Extremely wide
Range of workpiece thickness	Wide	Narrow
Range of dissimilar metals	Wide	Very wide
Maximum weld depth	50 mm	20 mm
Weld depth-to-width ratio	10:1	5:1
Need for vacuum chamber	Yes	No
X-rays emission	Yes	No
Initial cost	High	Moderate
Tooling costs	Moderately high	Moderate
Operating costs	Moderate	Low
Miniature welding	Excellent	Limited

- Non-contact process. This makes it suitable to weld workpieces even when they are located in an inaccessible location.
- Laser can be transmitted through air, so vacuum is not required.
- High melting-point metals and refractory materials that are virtually non-weldable by any other process can be fused together by laser beams.

- The heat generated in the process is highly concentrated. The physical and chemical properties of the workpiece materials are, therefore, not affected significantly.
- Filler material is not required.
- Laser beam does not generate harmful X-rays.
- Welds produced are of high quality. The weld joints are strong and free from porosity.
- Heat affected zone, workpiece distortion and shrinkage are almost negligible.

Laser beam welding has the following limitations:

- High equipment cost.
- Only thin materials can be welded. Deep welds are not possible because of low heat input (0.1 to 10 J).
- Rate of welding is slow since only limited pulse rate is possible.
- Eye protection is necessary, as reflected or scattered laser beams are dangerous.
- Compatibility between materials to be welded is essential. For example, titanium cannot be welded to stainless steel as the two are incompatible.

Applications   Laser beam welding is used in electronics industry for applications such as joining small parts or connecting wire leads to small electronic components. The process also finds applications in automotive industries to weld transmission components and body panels.

19.3 Thermit Welding (TW)

Thermit welding is the only welding process in which heat for welding is obtained from an exothermal chemical reaction. The process relies on the fact that aluminium has a great affinity for oxygen and can be used as a reducing agent for many oxides. The thermit mixture consists of aluminium powder and iron oxide mixed in the ratio of 1:3 by weight. This mixture is not explosive, but when ignited by a magnesium fuse at a temperature of about 1200°C, it reacts according to the following chemical equation:

$$8Al + 3Fe_3O_4 \rightarrow 9Fe + 4Al_2O_3 + \text{Heat}$$

The heat produced is nearly 3 MJ/mole, and in about 30 s, a temperature of about 2500°C is achieved. The resultant products of reaction are superheated highly purified iron (steel) and aluminium oxide slag. The slag floats on top and shields the molten iron from the atmosphere.

In actual practice, a wax pattern of the weld is built around the break of the part where the welding is to be done. Refractory sand is packed around the joint and provision is made for risers and gates – as in a casting – to channel the molten metal and compensate for solidification shrinkage [Figure 19.4]. A gas flame is used to melt and burn out the wax, to dry the mould and to bring the joint to a hot state.

From the crucible, in which the chemical reaction has taken place and molten metal is ready with slag floating on the top, the molten metal is tapped and allowed to flow into the mould. The slag is taken off and not allowed to enter the mould. Since the molten metal is highly superheated, it quickly fuses in the joint and a sound weld is created.

Advantages   Thermit welding has the following advantages:

1. No power supply is needed as the heat for welding is obtained from chemical reaction. This makes the process useful for field use.
2. Process can be used to weld complex shaped parts.
3. Process can be used to weld very large section parts.
4. Equipment required is simple and inexpensive.

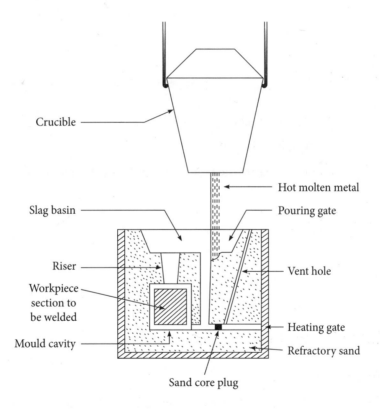

Figure 19.4   Schematic of thermit welding process

Limitations   Thermit welding has the following limitations:

(i)   Rate of welding is slow.

(ii) Cannot be used for repairing of parts made of low melting point materials such as lead, tin and zinc.

(iii) Cannot be used for repairing of parts made of reactive metals such as titanium.

(iv) High risk to operators because of high temperatures are involved.

(v) High temperature may cause distortions and changes in grain structure in the weld region.

(vi) High level of fumes

(vii) Weld may contain slag contaminations and hydrogen gas.

(viii)Needs high skill of operators.

Applications Thermit welding has been used for the welding of parts made of steel, chromium and nickel, particularly:

(i) High thickness parts

(ii) Large broken crankshafts

(iii) Broken frames of machines

(iv) Broken teeth on big gears

(v) Damaged wobblers

(vi) Rails in railways

(viii)Strengthening bars used in building construction concrete

(viii)New necks to rolling mill rolls with pinions

Typical defects The following are the typical defects found in welds produced by Thermit welding:

(i) Inclusions

(ii) Incomplete fusion

(iii) Porosity

(iv) Thermal cracks

(v) Shape defects, such as misalignment, deviation from straightness, etc.

19.4 Solid State Welding Processes

19.4.1 Forge welding

It is probably the oldest welding process. Even today, village blacksmiths can be seen performing this process to join pieces of metal into a single strong product. The parts to be welded are heated in a forge (furnace) that may be fired with coal or charcoal. Air under pressure is introduced in the fire to increase the temperature by using bellows or a motor driven fan. The parts are placed in the fire and heated to a temperature below the melting point. They are then removed from the fire and by hammering their ends, are shaped so that they can be fitted together. The ends are then re-heated to just the right temperature for welding (as judged by the blacksmith from its colour). The ends are dipped into borax (flux) and the surface is cleaned. Loose scales are removed by hammer or by striking on the anvil.

The parts are placed on an anvil with the ends that have to be joined overlapping. Hammering is done over the overlapped portion just sufficient to produce an acceptable weld [Figure 19.5]. The quality of weld depends on three things: (i) *proper heating* of individual parts to the correct temperature; (ii) *proper cleaning* to obtain scale-free surface; and (iii) *proper deformation* induced by pressing or hammering.

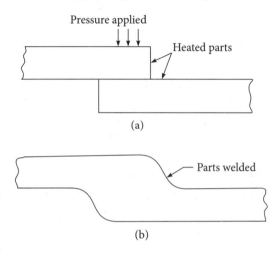

Figure 19.5 Forge welding: (a) Heated parts being hammered; and (b) Parts welded

19.5 Cold Welding

Cold welding is a variation of forge welding in which no heat is used but metallurgical bond is produced by means of cold plastic deformation. The steps involved in this process are as under.

(i)   Clean the surfaces to be joined thoroughly. This is generally done by degreasing and wire brushing. It is essential that cleaning is done just before joining.

(ii) Place the surfaces (to be joined) in close contact.

(iii) Apply localized pressure sufficient to cause about 30% to 50% localized cold working.

In the process, some heat is produced due to severe plastic deformation, but the formation of bond is primarily due to the applied highly localized pressure on the newly formed surface. It is necessary that at least one of the materials (preferably both) must be very ductile and free from work hardening.

Applications   The main application of the process is for joining of small parts made of soft and ductile materials such as soft aluminium and copper. Electrical connections are often made by this process.

19.6 Roll Welding

It is a solid state welding process in which high pressure is applied by means of rolls [Figure 19.6]. Heat may or may not be applied through external means. When external heat is applied, the process is called *hot roll welding*; when external heat is not applied, the process is called *cold roll welding*.

Applications   There are several applications of this process. Some of these are as follows:

1.   Cladding. Stainless steel may be cladded on mild steel to provide corrosion resistance.

2.   Bimetallic strips. Bimetallic strips used for temperature measurement are made by this process.

3.   Coins. Bimetallic coins, such as that of Rs. 10, are produced by this process.

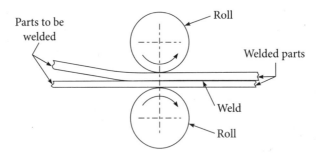

Figure 19.6   Schematic of roll welding process

19.7 Friction Welding (FW)

Friction welding is a solid-state welding process as the metal is not heated to molten state during the process. The process is mostly used to weld two end-to-end pieces of round bar stock. The heat required for welding is generated through pressure and friction at the interface of the two pieces being joined. Keeping one piece stationary, the other is rotated (generally by holding it in a chuck or a collet) at high speed; the ends of the two pieces are brought into contact under controlled axial pressure. The surface speed of rotation of the workpiece before contact may be as high as 15 m/s. As soon as enough interfacial contact is established, the rotating bar stock piece is brought to a quick stop while the axial force is increased (typically to 10 MN) to upset the joint slightly. The two surfaces get heated to a high temperature and the adjacent material becomes plastic. The flash developed during the process takes away the surface oxides and impurities from the interface so that a strong metallurgical bond is obtained. This flash may be later removed either by machining or grinding. Figure 19.7 shows the sequence of operations involved in the process of welding two round shafts. The total cycle time for these operations is about 30 s. The sequence of operations remains the same when welding tubular workpieces or even when welding rods or when tubes have to be abutted to a flat surface. An important point to be noted is that the process does not use any filler metal, flux or shielding gas.

The weld zone is quite narrow, but depends on: (i) the amount of heat generated; (ii) the thermal conductivity of the materials; and (iii) the mechanical properties of the materials at the temperature obtained in the process. It may be noted that the shape of the welded joint depends on: (i) the rotational speed of the workpiece; (ii) the thermal conductivity of the material of the bar stock; and (iii) the axial pressure applied. Figure 19.8 shows some typical joint shapes when welding at different rotational speeds and applied pressures.

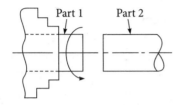

(a) Part 1 held in rotating chuck; Part 2 held stationary

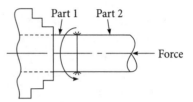

(b) Part 1 still rotating; Part 2 brought to touch Part 1 with small force

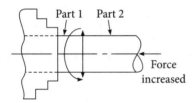

(c) Part 1 still rotating; Part 2 butting against Part 1, force increased; relative motion between the two parts reduce

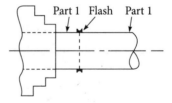

(d) Part 2 welds with Part 1, both rotate together; pressure released and rotation is stopped

Figure 19.7 Sequence of operations involved in joining two circular shafts by friction welding process

(a) High pressure, low speed

(b) Low pressure, high speed

(c) Moderate pressure and speed of rotation

Figure 19.8 Typical shapes of fusion zones in friction welding

19.7.1 Some modified friction welding processes

1. **Inertia friction welding**   In the inertia friction welding process, the part to be rotated is connected to a flywheel with the help of a coupling. The flywheel is rotated and the kinetic energy of the flywheel is used as the input energy required for friction welding. When the rotating part attains proper speed, it is made to come into gentle contact with the stationary part; then, an axial force is applied. The friction at the interface causes a rise in the temperature at the interface and slowing down of the flywheel. At this time, the axial force is raised; the weld is completed as the flywheel comes to zero speed. The timing of each element in the sequence is important to obtain quality weld.

2. **Linear friction welding (LFW)**   It is a solid state joining process in which a permanent joint between two metallic non-axysymmetric workpieces can be formed through the intimate contact of a plasticized layer at the interface of the adjoining workpieces. This plasticized layer is created through a combination of frictional heating, which occurs as a result of pushing of a stationary workpiece against one that is moving in a linear reciprocating manner, and the applied pressure, see Figure 19.9. The applied pressure, which is raised slowly can go up to 100 to 150 MPa depending upon the requirements. The friction surfaces in this process get heated up more uniformly than in friction welding with rotation in which the circumferential speed and, consequently, the temperature in heating increases with increase in the distance from the axis of rotation, from the minimum value in the centre to the maximum value on the periphery. In LFW, the welded joint, therefore, has more uniform structure and properties in comparison with friction welding with rotation.

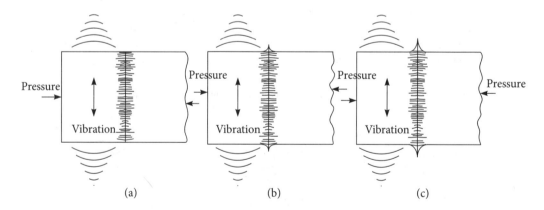

Figure 19.9   Schematic of linear friction welding: (a) Interface temperature rises due to rubbing action caused by vibrations; (b) High temperature at the interface softens the material; expulsion of material occurs; and (c) Expulsion of surface layer and fresh surfaces are joined under pressure

Advantages   LFW has many advantages. These are:

- This is a rapid, repeatable and flexible fabrication process for producing parts with a variety of geometric shapes. The process has been used to join a wide range of part geometries, such as plate to plate, tube to plate, square to square, round to square, concave to round and plate to part of any shape.
- The joints produced are of forged-quality.
- The process is at least twice – and up to 100 times – as fast as other welding techniques.
- The process can join dissimilar metals not considered compatible using conventional welding methods. This allows manufacture of bimetallic parts and near-net shape parts that use expensive materials only where needed.
- Multiple pieces can be bonded simultaneously, giving high production rate.
- Joint preparation is not very critical in this process; it lowers overall cycle time and raises throughput.
- This is an ecologically clean process that requires no consumables, flux, filler material or shielding gases to run, like conventional welding methods. It also does not emit smoke, fumes or gases that need to be exhausted.
- This is an energy efficient process. Power requirements are as much as 20% lower than those for conventional welding processes.
- There is no melting, therefore solidification defects do not occur, virtually eliminating gas porosity, segregation and slag inclusions.

3.   **Friction stir welding (FSW)**   This process is used for applications where the original metal characteristics, as far as possible, must not change due to welding. The process is primarily used on aluminium, and most often on large pieces which cannot be easily post-weld heat treated to recover temper characteristics.

The friction stir welding process uses a special tool which has a cylindrical shoulder and a profiled pin (called probe) at its one end. The pin, whose length is slightly less than the weld depth required, is introduced into the gap between the abutting workpiece surfaces; see Figure 19.10(a). The tool is rotated at a constant speed and its shoulder is kept in intimate contact with the work surface. Due to rotation and rubbing, heat is generated at the interface between the workpiece materials and the wear-resistant welding tool shoulder and pin. This heat, along with the additional heat generated by the mechanical mixing process and the adiabatic heat within the material, causes the stirred materials to soften without reaching the melting point, allowing the traversing of the tool along the weld line in a plasticized metal. As the pin is moved in the direction of welding, the leading face of the pin, assisted by a special pin profile, pushes the plasticized material to the back of the pin while a heavy forging force is applied on one workpiece against the other [Figure 19.10(b)]. The welding of the material is facilitated by the severe plastic deformation in the solid state, involving dynamic recrystallization of the work material.

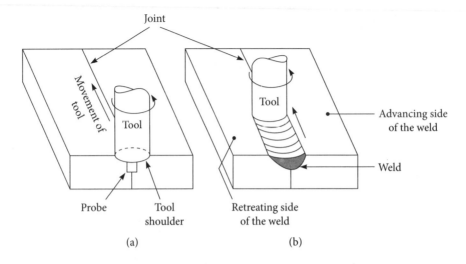

Figure 19.10 Schematic of friction stir welding process

Advantages, limitation and applications Friction stir welding process has many advantages. These include:

- It is easy to perform.
- It requires simple setup and less operator skill.
- It requires low total energy.
- It is rapid, and therefore lends itself to mass production.
- It can be easily programmed into the machine, and thus automated.
- It requires almost no joint preparation.
- It can be carried out in all positions (horizontal, vertical, etc.), as there is no weld pool formation.
- Welds produced are quite sound and are of high quality.
- Welds have good appearance so that there is no need for any post-welding finishing operation.
- Heat affected zone is small.
- There is no microstructural change in the work material since the process is completed at low temperature; also there is no appreciable distortion to the workpieces.
- There occurs no change in mechanical properties of workpiece due to welding.
- There is no need for consumables – no requirement of any filler metal or gas shield for aluminium. Only a threaded pin made of tool steel is enough to weld over 1000 m of aluminium.
- Dissimilar metals can be welded.
- Low environmental pollution.
- Improved safety as there are no toxic fumes or spatter of molten material.

Some disadvantages or limitations of the FSW process are as follows:

- Exit hole is left when tool is withdrawn.

- Large forces required for clamping of the plates to keep them together.

- Less flexible than manual arc welding processes (difficulties with thickness variations and non-linear welds).

- Weld rate is often slower than some fusion welding techniques.

- Only a few workpiece configurations can be welded.

The friction welding process finds considerable applications in welding of those parts of which at least one must be rotatable in either a chuck or other gripping fixture. Solid steel rods up to 100 mm diameter and tubes up to 200 mm outside diameter have been successfully welded by using this process. Sheets and plates from 1 mm to 25 mm thickness have been welded. Even parts made of thermoplastics have been joined using the friction welding process. Industries which have used this technology include automotive, aircraft, farm equipment, ship building, and oil and natural gas. The automotive industry uses this process to produce items such as axle casings, and transmission shafts. Components of aircraft engines such as blisks are being manufactured by friction welding blade parts to separately manufactured discs.

19.8 Ultrasonic Welding (USW)

Ultrasonic welding is a solid-state welding process by which similar or dissimilar metal parts can be joined, usually by an overlap joint. The faying surfaces of the two metal parts to be joined are held together under a modest clamping force, and subjected to static normal force and vibratory energy of high frequency (10–50 kc/s) and low amplitude (0.02–0.15 mm) with the help of the tip of a transducer, as illustrated in Figure 19.11. Oscillating shear (tangential) stresses are, thus, set up at the interface of the workpieces that cause small-scale plastic deformation and break up of surface oxides. This results in good metal-to-metal contact, permitting a strong solid-state weld nugget. No external heat is applied, although the workpiece metal gets heated up to a temperature in the range of one-third to one-fourth of the melting point of the metals being joined. There is, therefore, no melting and no diffusion. No filler metals, fluxes or shielding gases are required in USW.

A simple setup of the ultrasonic spot-type welding is shown diagrammatically in Figure 19.11. To begin with, by considering the type and thickness of the material to be joined, the operator pre-sets the machine with respect to the clamping force, time and ultrasonic frequency and power. The overlapping workpieces are then properly located on the anvil of the machine. The welding cycle starts with the lowering of the tip of the sonotrode (vibrating element) to the upper work part. The clamping force builds up to the required amount and ultrasonic power of the preset intensity is applied through the sonotrode for a pre-set time. The power is cut off automatically and the clamping force is released. The weldment can now be removed. The entire cycle takes just about a second.

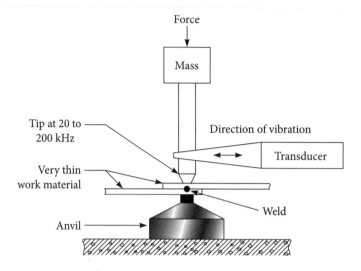

Figure 19.11   Schematic of ultrasonic welding process

When making ultrasonic continuous-seam welding, a rotating disc tip along with a counter-rotating table-type anvil is used. The entire assembly, consisting of an ultrasonic transducer, coupling system and the disc tip rotates, ensuring that the peripheral speed of the tip matches the linear traverse speed of the workpiece with almost no slippage between the tip and the workpiece.

Advantages, limitations and applications   Ultrasonic welding has the following advantages:

- The process is rapid, reliable as well as versatile.
- The process can be used to join a wide variety of metallic and non-metallic materials.
- The process can be used to join dissimilar metals. Bimetallic strips are generally made using this process.
- Thin sheets can be easily joined with thick sheets, because the thickness limitation applies only to thinner workpieces.
- Sheets of practically any thickness (up to 3 mm) can be welded by this process.
- The welds are quite sound, often superior to those obtained by other processes.

Ultrasonic welding has the following limitations:

- Welds obtained are characterized by local plastic deformation at the interface of weld materials.
- Process is limited to lap joints on soft materials such as aluminium and copper.
- Process is limited to welding of small parts.

The process finds wide applications for lap welding of sheet, foil and thin wire, so as to make small part assemblies in:

- Consumer, electrical and electronics industries.
- Automotive industry.
- Aircrafts.
- Missiles and nuclear reactors.

19.9 Explosion Welding (EW)

Explosion welding is a solid-state welding process in which a metallurgical bond between two metal surfaces is rapidly caused by the energy released from a detonated explosive. The process is generally used to bond two dissimilar metals, rather, to clad one thin metal on top of a thick base metal over large areas. As shown in Figure 19.12, a layer of explosive charge is placed over the upper plate, called the flyer plate. The base plate (mating plate) is placed at a short gap distance on a firm platform, say an anvil. Upon detonating the explosive charge, extremely high pressures develop and the kinetic energy of the flyer plate causes it to strike against the mating base plate. As the explosive charge propagates from one end of the flyer plate to the other end (shown in the lower part of Figure 19.12), a high impacting pressure progressively propels the flyer plate to collide with the base plate. As a result, severe deformation of the surfaces takes place and any oxide films present at the interface break up. The high speed collision occurring in a progressive manner causes the contact surfaces to become very soft leading to metallurgical bonding. The interface may even become slightly wavy, further aiding in strengthening the joint by mechanical interlocking of the two surfaces.

No filler metal is used in this process, and no external heat is applied. The explosive, which may be in the form of a liquid or granulated powder, is spread over the flyer metal plate. Depending on the type of explosive material and the thickness of the layer, detonation speed can be as much as 2000 to 5000 m/s, although there is a minimum detonation speed, called critical detonation speed, below which welding of the two components can not occur. The function of the anvil is to absorb the energy generated during the welding operation.

Advantages, limitations and applications   The process is advantageous because:

- It is simple as well as rapid.
- It can join dissimilar metals even when they are metallurgically incompatible.
- It is a *cold welding process*. Heat generated at the interface is small and quickly dissipated.
- The work materials undergo very little metallurgical changes, except a small variation in hardness and elongation.
- Work piece thickness can be controlled within close tolerance.
- It is relatively inexpensive since no expensive equipment is needed.
- The equipment is portable.
- Theoretically, there is no limitation of the size of the parts that can be clad or welded.

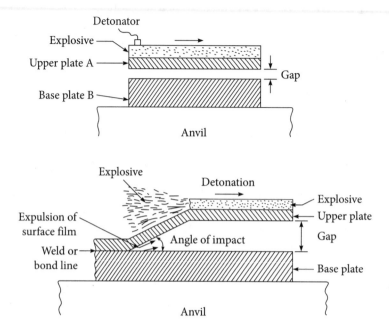

Figure 19.12   Schematic of explosive welding process

The process has the following limitations:

- It is difficult to clad very small size parts.

- It is difficult to weld complex-shaped components since it is complicated to place explosives on complex-shaped components.

- It is hard to keep the effects of the explosion confined to the areas desired.

- Materials having low melting points, low impact resistance, and strain-hardening properties cannot be welded effectively by this process.

- The process cannot be carried out in an ordinary factory environment because of the high level of noise produced. The process has to be carried out either in sound-proof areas or in remote locations far away from normal work areas.

- It requires highly skilled and trained operators.

- The process requires a high degree of safety measures.

The explosive welding process is used to clad a large area sheet on a thick plate of different metal. Areas up to 2 m by 6 m have been bonded through this process. The bonded material may then be rolled into thinner sections. In addition to area welds, seam, lap and edge welds can also be made. Even internal cladding of tubes and pressure vessels is possible. The process is also used to join tubes or pipes into holes of head plates of boilers and heat exchangers. In such applications, the explosive is placed inside the tube so that the explosion expands the end of tube to form the weld.

19.10 Diffusion Welding (DW)

Diffusion welding is a solid-state bonding process in which flat metal surfaces are metallurgically joined in an inert-gas atmosphere by applying both heat and pressure. The strength of the joint between the two metal pieces stems basically from the diffusion phenomenon, that is, as a result of movement of atoms across their interface. The plastic deformation of the faying surfaces contributes only partially towards the joint strength. The bonded interface retains the same physical and mechanical properties as those of the metal pieces.

There are three major variables that control the strength of the joint: temperature, pressure and the time of contact. Diffusion welding is completed at a temperature of about $\frac{1}{2}T_m$ (where T_m is the maximum of the melting points of the metals being welded on an absolute scale). The parts to be welded through diffusion are generally heated to the required temperature in an electrical furnace. The temperature accelerates the co-mingling of atoms at the joint interface and simultaneously softens the workpiece metal that promotes surface deformation and more intimate contact at the interface.

The pressure required varies from 50 to 350 MPa, but it is preferred that it should be just under the yield stress at the operating temperatures. The application of pressure is generally through dead weights, differential thermal expansion of the parts, or by the use of a power press. The time is controlled to be just sufficient for appropriate atomic movement across the interface. It may vary from just a few seconds to several hours. Smoothness and cleanliness of the contacting surfaces play an important role in obtaining good bond strength.

Advantages, limitation and applications   The diffusion welding process has the following advantages:

- It is economical.
- The joints are quite clean in appearance.
- The joints have high dimensional accuracy and low residual stresses.

The limitations of this method are that it is slow and expensive.

The process has several applications in high technology areas such as joining of high strength and refractory metal in the atomic energy, aerospace and electronic industries. The process is particularly useful where dissimilar metal parts have to be joined. One common application of this process is for the *coating* of cutting tools. The process is also successfully used for joining of parts made from reactive metals such as titanium, zirconium and beryllium.

Questions

1. Explain what is meant by *solid-state welding*. What are some of the attractive features of ultrasonic welding? Are there any geometric limitations of parts for ultrasonic welding? Discuss them briefly.

2. Why is a high vacuum required in the electron beam welding process?

3. Explain the process of laser beam welding. Give specific advantages and limitations of the process as compared to electron beam welding.

4. What are the main similarities between electron beam and laser beam welding? For what applications, is the laser beam welding preferable to electron beam welding? Give reasons for your answer.

5. Discuss the possibilities of butt welding two cylindrical components of different material compositions. Briefly describe any feasible method and give its advantages and limitations.

6. What is the source of heat in friction welding? With the help of a neat sketch, describe the friction welding process.

7. How does the friction stir welding process differ from the conventional friction welding? Briefly describe the friction stir welding process with a sketch.

8. How does the exothermal chemical reaction apply to thermit welding? For what types of applications might thermit welding be attractive? Do you think a thermit weld is similar to the production of a casting? Give reasons for your answer.

9. Give a suitable process to weld heavy rail sections at site. How is the heat required for the process obtained?

10. Discuss the inertia friction welding process. Give any two applications of this process.

11. Describe the difficulties one might encounter in using explosion welding in a factory environment. Explain the high-velocity jet phenomenon in this welding process.

12. Describe the process of diffusion welding. What are the conditions necessary to produce high quality fusion welds? What are the two main limitations of the process?

Fill in the Blanks

1. In electron beam welding, the heat for welding is obtained from the _____ energy of electrons.

2. Electron beam gun used for electron beam welding has a tungsten filament that is heated to about _____ °C with a high voltage (in the range _____ to _____kV) current, causing it to emit electrons.

3. Vacuum is not required in _____ beam welding.

4. By laser beam welding, a weld with depth-to-width ratio of as much as _____ can be produced.

5. In friction stir welding process, a _____ is introduced into the joint that rubs between the two contacting surfaces.

6. There are three major variables that control the strength of the joint made by diffusion welding. These are _____, _____ and _____.

7. Diffusion welding is completed at a temperature of about _____ T_m (where T_m is the maximum of the melting points of the two metals being welded).

8. The pressure required in the fusion welding process should preferably be just less than the _____ of the work material at the operating temperatures.

9. _____ welding process is generally used to bond two dissimilar metals, rather to clad one thin metal on top of a thick base metal over large areas.

10. _____ welding process has the limitation that it is used for lap joints on soft materials such as aluminium and copper.

Choose the Correct Answer

1. Electron beam welding can be classified as a
   a. resistance welding process.
   b. fusion welding process in which filler metal is used.
   c. fusion welding process in which filler metal is not used.
   d. solid-state welding process.

2. In an electron beam welding gun, the electrons are emitted from
   a. a heated tungsten filament.
   b. a laser beam.
   c. an arc produced with DC current.
   d. an arc produced with AC current.

3. In an electron beam welding process, it is
   a. necessary to emit electrons in vacuum and also keep workpieces to be welded in vacuum.
   b. necessary to emit electrons in vacuum but workpieces to be welded need not be kept in vacuum.
   c. not necessary to emit electrons in vacuum but workpieces to be welded have to be kept in vacuum.
   d. not necessary to emit electrons in vacuum nor do the workpieces to be welded have to be kept in vacuum.

4. One critical disadvantage of electron beam welding is that
   a. the equipment emits harmful X-rays.
   b. welding cannot be done at more than a few cm per minute.
   c. distortion in the weld area is too much.
   d. welds produced have shallow penetration.

5. Laser beam welding can be classified as a
   a. resistance welding process.
   b. fusion welding process in which filler metal is used.
   c. fusion welding process in which filler metal is not used.
   d. solid-state welding process.

6. In laser beam welding,
   a. inert gas shielding and filler metal usage are essential.
   b. inert gas shielding is a must but filler metal usage is optional.
   c. inert gas shielding is optional but filler metal usage is essential.
   d. inert gas shielding and filler metal usage are optional.

7. Use of vacuum chamber is an essential part of the machine for
   a. electron beam welding.   c. friction welding.
   b. laser beam welding.   d. thermit welding.

8. In friction welding process, the shape of the welded joint does not depend on the
   a. rotational speed of the rotating workpiece.
   b. thermal conductivity of the materials of the bar stock.
   c. shape of the ends of the bar stock.
   d. axial pressure applied to complete the weld.

9. In friction stir welding, what is stirred?
   a. workpiece material   c. filler material
   b. tool material   d. flux

10. Friction welding process has a limitation that
    a. it requires a costly flux.
    b. it requires large amount of power.
    c. it can weld only a few workpiece configurations.
    d. it is relatively a very slow process.

11. In which of the following welding processes, is the heat for welding obtained from an exothermic reaction?
    a. electron beam welding.   c. friction welding.
    b. laser beam welding.   d. thermit welding.

12. The thermit mixture used in thermit welding of steel parts consists of
    a. aluminium powder and iron oxide.
    b. powders of aluminium oxide and iron oxide.
    c. powders of aluminium oxide and magnesium oxide.
    d. powders of aluminium oxide and tin.

13. Which of the following is a solid-state welding process?
    a. electron beam welding.   c. friction welding.
    b. laser beam welding.   d. thermit welding.

14. In the ultrasonic welding process,
    a. no flux is used.   c. flux used is sodium carbonate.
    b. flux used is sodium chloride. d. flux used is borax powder.

15. Ultrasonic welding process is limited to
    a. lap joints on soft materials.
    c. butt joints on soft materials.
    b. lap joints on hard and brittle materials.
    d. butt joints on hard and brittle materials.

16. Which one of the following is not a major variable that controls the strength of the joint in diffusion welding process?
    a. temperature
    c. physical properties of workpiece materials
    b. pressure
    d. time of contact

17. Railroad rails are best welded by which one of the following processes?
    a. ultrasonic welding
    c. electron beam welding
    b. laser beam welding
    d. thermit welding

Answers

| 1. c. | 2. a | 3. a. | 4. a. | 5. c. | 6. d. | 7. a. | 8. c. | 9. a. | 10. c. |
| 11. d. | 12. a.. | 13. c. | 14. a | 15. a. | 16. c. | 17. d | | | |

Weld Inspection, Testing and Defect Analysis

After reading this chapter, you should be able to understand the following:

- The need for inspection and testing of welded joints.
- The various destructive and non-destructive testing techniques.
- The various weld defects, their causes and remedies.

20.1 Weld Inspection and Testing

As in all manufacturing processes, in welding too it is important to establish the quality of the welded joint by inspection and testing. For this, the finished weld needs to be inspected for undercut, overlap, surface checks, cracks or other defects. Moreover, the degree of penetration and side wall fusion, extent of reinforcement, and size and position of the welds are important factors in the determination of the quality of the weld. There are several standardized tests and test procedures established by organizations like the Indian Welding Society, American Welding Society, Indian Standards Institution, etc. There are two basic categories of tests for welded joints: Destructive techniques and non-destructive techniques. Each of these techniques has its capabilities, limitations, reliability, sensitivity and requirement of operator's skill and equipment.

20.2 Destructive Testing Techniques

These are the techniques in which the weld gets destroyed during the test. They include mechanical and metallurgical tests. Metallurgical tests involve the preparation and examination of specimens of weldment for the purpose of determining features like metallic structure, defects, extent of heat affected zone and so on. Mechanical destructive techniques include tensile, shear and bending tests, in which the test specimens are loaded until they fail.

- **Tensile test**   This test is used to measure the tensile strength of a welded joint. A portion of the welded plate is chosen so that the weld is located midway when held between the jaws of the testing machine [Figure 20.1]. The width and thickness of the test specimen are measured before testing, and the area in square mm is calculated. The tensile test specimen is then mounted in a machine that will exert enough pull on the piece to break the specimen. As the specimen is being tested in this machine, the load applied gets continuously registered on the gauge. The load at the point of breaking is recorded.

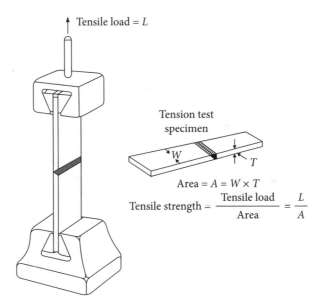

Figure 20.1   Tensile test

   The tensile strength is calculated by dividing the breaking load of the test piece by the original cross-section area of the specimen. The usual requirement for the tensile strength of welds is that the specimen shall pull not less than 90% of the base metal tensile strength.

- **Fillet weld test**   This test involves breaking a sample fillet weld that is welded on one side only. Load is applied on the sample on its unwelded side, typically in a press, and the load is increased until the weld fails. The failed sample is then inspected to establish the presence and extent of any welding discontinuities.

   Fillet weld break test provides a good indication of discontinuities within the entire length of the weld tested (normally 150 mm to 300 mm) rather than a cross-sectional snapshot. This type of weld inspection can detect such defects as lack of fusion, internal porosity and slag inclusions.

- **Tension–shear test**   Test specimens, as shown in Figure 20.2, are prepared to simulate the actual welded joint by the tension–shear test. By subjecting the specimens to tension, the shear strength of the weld metal and the location of fracture can be determined.

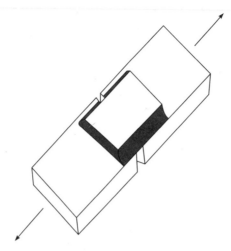

Figure 20.2 Specimen used for tension–shear test

- **Bend test**   The strength and relative ductility of a welded joint can be determined by any of the several available bend tests. In the wrap around bend test, the welded specimen is bent around a fixture, as shown in Figure 20.3(a), whereas in the three-point transverse bend test, the test for bending is accomplished for the root, face and the side [Figure 20.3(b)].

- **Fracture toughness test**   The fracture toughness test is carried out on an impact testing machine. A Charpy V-notch specimen is prepared out of the welded joint and a standard toughness test is performed. Alternatively, toughness can be estimated with the help of a drop-weight test where use is made of energy from a falling weight.

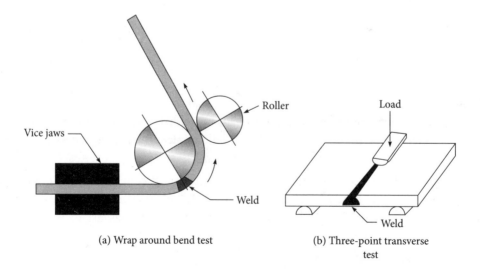

(a) Wrap around bend test   (b) Three-point transverse test

Figure 20.3 Schematic representations of bend tests

- **Corrosion and creep tests** Due to the difference in the composition and microstructure of the materials in the weld zone, preferential corrosion is likely to occur in the weld zone. When the application demands such a test, the welded joint may be subjected to corrosion and creep resistance tests.

20.3 Non-destructive Testing Techniques

In case of critical applications where failure of welded joints can be catastrophic such as nuclear power plants, pressure vessels, pipe lines and load-bearing structural members, it becomes essential to subject the welded joint to non-destructive tests (NDTs). There are several non-destructive tests, and we will study some important ones. There are many advantages of using non-destructive techniques of weld testing. These include low cost, quick identification of defects, and no power requirement. There are some disadvantages too for using NDT. These are: (i) more dependence on human training and eyesight; (ii) difficulty in properly identifying internal defects; and (iii) difficulty in correct interpretation of results.

- **Optical or visual inspection** Visual inspection is often the most cost-effective method, but it must take place prior to, during and after welding. It is necessary that it is carried out before using any other method of inspection, because there is no point in submitting an obviously bad weld to sophisticated inspection technique. Visual inspection requires little equipment. Apart from good eyesight and sufficient light, all it takes is a pocket rule, a weld size gauge, a magnifying glass and possibly a straight edge and square for checking straightness, alignment and perpendicularity.

    Before the start of welding operation, materials should be examined to see if they meet specifications for quality, type, size, cleanliness and freedom from defects. Grease, paint, oil, oxide film or heavy scale should be removed. The pieces to be joined should be checked for flatness, straightness and dimensional accuracy. Likewise, alignment, fit-up and joint preparation should be examined. Finally, process and procedure variables should be verified, including electrode size and type, equipment settings and provisions for pre-heat or post-heat. All of these precautions apply regardless of the inspection method being used.

    During the welding operation, visual examination of a weld bead and the end crater may reveal problems such as cracks, inadequate penetration and gas or slag inclusions. Among the weld defects that can be recognized visually are cracking, surface slag inclusions, surface porosity and undercut.

    On simple welds, inspecting at the beginning of each operation and periodically as work progresses may be adequate. Where more than one layer of metal filler is being deposited, however, it may be desirable to inspect each layer before depositing the next. The root pass of a multi-pass is most critical to weld soundness. It is especially susceptible to cracking, and because it solidifies quickly, it may trap gas and slag. On subsequent passes, conditions caused by the shape of the weld bead or changes in the joint configuration can cause further cracking, as well as undercut and slag trapping. Repair costs can be minimized if visual inspection detects these flaws before welding progresses.

Visual inspection at an early stage of production can also prevent under-welding and over-welding. Welds that are smaller than called for in the specifications should not be allowed. Beads that are too large increase costs unnecessarily and can cause distortion through added shrinkage stress.

After welding, visual inspection can detect a variety of surface flaws, including cracks, porosity and unfilled craters. Dimensional variances, warpage and appearance flaws, as well as weld size characteristics, can be evaluated. It is important that before inspection of surface flaws, welds must be cleaned of slag. Shot blasting should not be done before examination, because the peening action can seal fine cracks and make them invisible.

Visual weld inspection has the benefit of being able to be done in-house, causes minimal production delays and provides immediate feedback to welders and designers. The limitation of visual inspection is that only the surface defects can be detected; internal defects cannot be discovered.

- **Dimensional inspection**   Dimensional discrepancies can be found by comparing the welded structure against drawings or specifications by using some metrological instruments. Various features and dimensions of a welded joint, such as linear dimensions, squareness, etc. can be checked through this method.

  Defects that can be found include warpage, misalignment and incorrect joint preparation and weld size or profile discrepancies. These can create serious performance problems by introducing severe weld stresses where little stress is expected.

  Centerline mismatch may create a stress riser, which could exceed the design strength of the assembly. Likewise, specialized or forceful weld fixturing can be used to compensate for imprecise dimensioning. This causes high locked-in stresses in the weld itself, increasing the potential for weld failure.

  Dimensional defects can be avoided by the proper application of fixtures, welding sequences and pre-forms.

- **Hydrostatic test**   This is a nondestructive test used to check the quality of welds on closed containers such as pressure vessels and tanks. The test usually consists of filling the vessel with water and applying a pressure greater than the working pressure, of the vessel. Sometimes, large tanks are filled with water, which is not under pressure to detect possible leakage through defective welds. Another method is to test with oil and then steam out the vessel. Back seepage of oil from behind the liner shows up visibly.

- **X-ray and gamma-ray inspection**   These techniques involve the use of radiography to detect internal flaws such as cracks and porosity in the weld. The techniques exhibit the difference of metal density by different shades of colour on the X-ray film. When a ray penetrates into the weld, the metal surrounding the defect being denser shows up as a lighter-shaded area while internal defects such as voids and cracks show up on the film as dark areas. Trained personnel for proper interpretation of results and quite expensive equipment are required to conduct such inspections.

- **Magnetic particle inspection**   In this technique, fine ferromagnetic particles (either in dry form or in a liquid carrier) are sprinkled on the surface of the welded joint to be inspected. An intense magnetic field is set up in the part. Any material discontinuity in the form of surface or sub-surface cracks, voids and inclusions will cause the magnetic flux to be distorted and concentrate the particles along the contours of the defects, as can be seen in Figure 20.4. The location, size and shape of the defect can thus be known. The particles may be coloured with pigments for better visibility. This test is applicable only on parts made of ferromagnetic materials, and it is advised that the parts be de-magnetized and properly cleaned after the test.

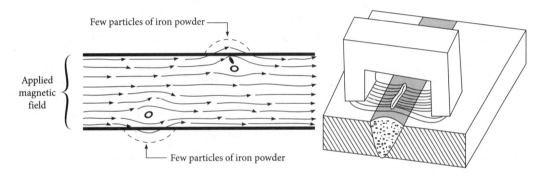

Figure 20.4   Principle of magnetic particle inspection

- **Liquid penetrant inspection technique**   The liquid penetrant inspection technique is used to detect very minute pores or crack on the surface of the weld. The surface of the weld joint to be inspected is first thoroughly cleaned. The liquid is then applied on the surface of the weld joint with the help of a brush or a spray gun, and allowed to stay there for enough time during which it seeps into surface openings, cracks, seams and pores, if any. The liquid can seep into cracks as deep as half a micron. The excess penetrant is then wiped off or washed away with some kind of solvent or water. A developing agent is applied so that the penetrant seeps back to the surface by capillary action and spreads to the edges of the openings. The size and location of defects thus become apparent when the surface is examined under fluorescent light. A schematic of the technique is given in Figure 6.3.

    Two common types of liquid used are: (i) fluorescent penetrants with different sensitivities, which shine under UV light; and (ii) visible penetrants, such as dyes that are usually red in colour, which appear as contrast bright lines on the surface of the component part. The equipment required for this technique of inspection is simple, portable as well as easy to operate. The technique is suitable for detecting a variety of surface defects but not any internal defects.

- **Acid etch test**   This test is used to determine the soundness of a weld, and is performed on the cross-section of the joint. The cross-section is polished and etched using a mild acid mixture, depending on the base material. Solutions of hydrochloric acid, nitric acid, ammonium per sulphate or iodine and potassium iodide are commonly used for etching carbon and low alloy steels. The acid etch provides a clear visual of the weld's internal structure. It reveals depth of penetration, as well as evidence (if any) of lack of fusion, inadequate root penetration, internal porosity and cracking at the fusion line (which is the transition between the weld and the base material). This type of inspection is a snapshot of the overall weld-length quality.

- **Ultrasonic inspection**   A vibratory signal of known high frequency (in the range 15–25 kHz) is applied at the weld surface to be inspected. An internal defect, such as a crack, interrupts the signal and reflects back a portion of the ultrasonic energy, which can be recorded using special instruments. The amplitude of the energy reflected and the time it has taken to return are measured with the help of a cathode ray tube. Thus, the size and location of any discontinuity (e.g., cracks, porosity, inclusions) in the weld can be precisely determined.

  The ultrasonic waves are generated with the help of piezoelectric transducers, which are made of materials such as quartz, lithium sulphate and some ceramics. These waves are transmitted from the transducer to the weld joint with the help of couplants, such as water, oil and glycerine. A schematic of ultrasonic testing is given in Figure 6.4.

  The ultrasonic inspection technique has greater accuracy than any other non-destructive techniques but requires experienced technicians to carry out the inspection and interpret the results.

- **Acoustic emission inspection**   The acoustic emission process of inspection involves the detection of high-frequency stress wave signals generated by the component itself during plastic deformation, crack initiation and propagation, phase transformation and abrupt re-orientation of grain boundaries occurring in it. To perform the test, the component part having the welded joint is elastically stressed by applying a force, and the acoustic emissions from the part are detected with the help of sensors made of piezoelectric ceramic elements. This technique is very useful for continuous surveillance of load-bearing welded structures.

- **Acoustic impact inspection**   The acoustic impact process of inspection is quite simple. Most people often use it to find out if there is any crack or discontinuity flaw in crockery, wooden parts, vitrified tiles or even concrete walls. It involves tapping at various locations of the surface of the welded joint to be inspected with a hammer. The sound emitted from the weld is carefully heard and analyzed in order to detect the location of discontinuities and flaws in the weld joint.

  Equipment are available, which use a reference standard in the form of a perfect weldment, and the sound emitted from a given component is analyzed to identify the flaws, if present.

- **Thermographic inspection** This is a safe, non-intrusive and non-contact technique of detecting relatively shallow sub-surface defects. The technique involves the use of a heat source to produce a thermal contrast between the internal defects and the weld metal. The thermal patterns at the weld surface are analyzed to identify the location of defects, if any.

  A variant of this technique involves the application of heat-sensitive paints, papers, liquid crystals or other coatings on the surface of the weld to be inspected. Defects like cracks or de-bonded regions are located from the observed changes in colour when the welded joint is heated.

- **Holographic inspection** In the holography technique, an optical system is used to prepare a 3-D image of the weld to be inspected. While the weld is being subjected to external forces or time-dependent variations, images are taken of the weld through multiple exposures. Changes in the images reveal the presence of defects in the weldment.

20.4 Defects in Welds

As a result of the heating and cooling cycle that is present in a welding operation, some amount of distortions, micro-structural changes and discontinuities are bound to occur in a welded joint. A brief discussion of such deformations is given here.

- **Distortion** Distortion or warping is almost always present in any welded part. It is usually of three types: Transverse (occurring normally on the weld line), longitudinal (occurring parallel to the weld line), and angular (occurring as a rotation about the weld line).

  Cause Uneven shrinkage due to heating and cooling of component parts.

  Remedies Distortion in welded parts can be minimized by

  - Designing the part so as to have a minimum number of welded joints.
  - Pre-set the component parts by the amount of distortion so that after welding, the welded part is shaped as per the desired proportions.
  - Assemble the parts in the desired configuration with adequate restraint.

- **Porosity** Porosity in welds is in the form of tiny voids [Figures 20.5 and 20.7], which can often be detected by the eye. It is present in most welds either in a spherical shape or in the form of an elongated pocket. The distribution of porosity in the weld zone may be either random, or it may be concentrated in a particular region. Surface porosity indicates porosity throughout the weld. A polished cross-section of a weld, when examined under a microscope, is distinguished by its 'Swiss-cheese' appearance. Minor internal porosity does not significantly affect weld performance but surface porosity is a serious condition.

  Almost all fatigue fractures begin at the surface of the metal; anything that interrupts the surface of the metal is a fatigue crack nucleation point. This would include the craters created by surface porosity.

Figure 20.5   Porosity in a welded joint

Causes   Gas bubbles trapped in the weld material cause porosity. The gas bubbles can come from low quality or gassy metals or from interaction among weld materials. However, it is commonly caused by contaminant's oil or rust on the weld surface.

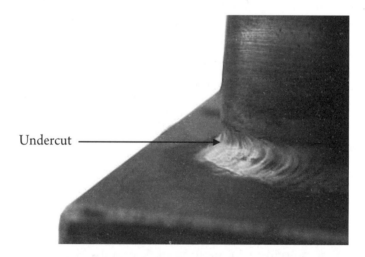

Figure 20.6   Undercut in a welded joint

Remedies   Porosity in welds can be reduced by

- Proper cleaning of the weld zone so that contaminants do not occur in the weld zone.
- Proper selection of electrodes and filler metals. Avoid sulphur content.
- Improving the welding technique by pre-heating the weld area, increasing the rate of heat input, and so on.
- Reducing the speed of welding so that gases get enough time to escape.

Welds with surface porosity should always be replaced.

- **Undercut**   Undercut is like a notch or groove in the shape of a sharp recess, as shown in Figure 20.6 and 20.7, that occurs at the weld interface. Generally, it is prominent in horizontal and vertical welding. If it is deep or sharp, it can act as a stress raiser and reduce the fatigue strength of the joint. This is critical in applications that involve impact, low temperature or fatigue conditions.

    Causes   The defect occurs as a result of melting of the base metal due to improper welding techniques, such as incorrect manipulation of the welding electrode while depositing the bead. It can also occur when using very high currents.

    Remedy   By following proper welding procedures, undercuts can be generally avoided. If it does occur, it should be repaired.

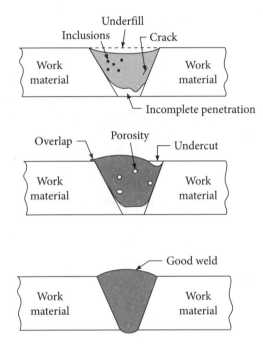

Figure 20.7   Weld defects

- **Overlap**   Overlap is a sort of surface discontinuity as shown in Figure 20.7.

    Causes   Causes for overlapping include poor welding practices and incorrect selection of electrode material.

    Remedies   Overlap can be reduced by

    - Following correct welding practices.
    - Using electrodes, the melting point of whose material is not much lower than that of the base metal.

- **Slag inclusions**   Slag is a metal oxide formed when the shielding gases used are ineffective during welding and the molten metal reacts with the environment. Slag is lighter than metal and floats on the surface of the molten weld metal pool from where it is chipped off after it solidifies. Instead of floating to the top of the weld metal pool, globules of slag can become encased during solidification of the metal as shown in Figure 20.7. These slag inclusions resemble black shards of glass on the top of the fillet. The number, size and distribution directly determine the weld strength.

Electrode flux debris and non-metallic inclusions also produce slag. These entrapped particles reduce the tensile strength of the weld and tensile ductility because of lack of metal homogeneity and lack of fusion. Lack of fusion occurs when the base metal fails to melt or mix with the weld material. Surface oxides, such as rust or scale often cause this. Unless these oxides are removed, there is every chance of lack of fusion to occur. In some cases, these discontinuities can be identified by a small gap between the fillet and the base metal or along the toe edge.

Causes   Improper welding technique can cause a high intensity arc to produce a stirring action in the molten weld metal pool that may force the molten slag to go into the weld pool. If it does not get enough time to float, it may solidify inside the fusion zone to end up as slag inclusion. Non-removal of surface oxides, such as rust or scale from the base metal is a significant cause of slag inclusion. Another cause of slag inclusion is the non-removal of solidified slag from the weld surface before depositing the next bead in multi-pass welding.

Remedies   Slag inclusions, or *slag entrapment* may be prevented by

- Properly preparing the weld surface. This may include grinding metal protrusions to ensure that no slag is caught in undercuts and gaps.
- Allowing time for the slag to rise to the surface of the molten metal. Rapid solidification is most likely to trap the inclusions.
- Using a more fluid-like flux that will enable the slag to reach the surface before the weld solidifies.
- Providing adequate shielding gas.
- Properly designing the joint that permits sufficient space for proper manipulation of the molten weld metal pool so that the arc does not produce any stirring action.
- Properly working the molten puddle to ensure that the slag comes to the surface.
- Properly cleaning the weld bead surface before depositing the next layer of beads.

- **Incomplete fusion and lack of penetration**   Incomplete fusion (or lack of proper fusion) occurs as a result of poor weld beads. Lack of penetration means that the fusion has not penetrated deeply enough into the root of the joint as shown in Figure 20.7.

Causes   The main causes of incomplete fusion are:

- Improper welding technique, such as incorrect choice of welding parameters, particularly the welding current.

- Improper cleaning of the joint that hinders the fusion of metal in the joint.
- Improper joint design.

Remedies   A better weld can be obtained by

- Heating the base metal around the joint just prior to welding.
- Cleaning the weld area just before welding.
- Providing adequate shielding of the weld area during the welding operation.
- Improving the joint design and type of electrode.

Better penetration can be achieved by

- Increasing the heat input.
- Lowering electrode travel speed during welding.
- Ensuring proper fit of the surfaces to be joined.
- Improving the joint design.

- **Cracks**   Cracks can occur in any location and direction of the weld or in the base metal adjacent to the weld. Based on their location, cracks can be classified as longitudinal, transverse, under bead and toe cracks, as shown in Figure 20.8. Cracks can also be classified as *hot cracks* and *cold cracks*. Hot cracks occur while the joint is still hot, whereas cold cracks develop after the weld has solidified and been brought to room temperature.

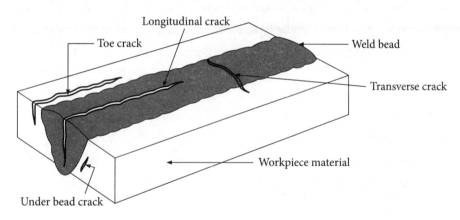

Figure 20.8   Various types of cracks in welds

In general, the different types of cracks in welds can be as follows:

- **Arc crack**   This crack appears as a depression left at the termination of the weld where the weld pool is left unfilled.

  Cause   Improper weld termination technique.

  Remedy   Fill in the crater.

- **Longitudinal crack**   It is a crack running in the direction of the weld axis. It may be present in the weld metal or the base metal.

Causes   Problems related to pre-heating of base metal or rapid cooling of the joint as soon as it is welded. Shrinkage stresses in high constraint areas.

Remedies   Welding should progress towards the areas of less constraint. Pre-heat the base metals to even out the cooling rates.

- **Transverse crack**   It is a crack running into or inside a weld in a direction transverse to the weld axis.

  Cause   Weld metal is too hard.

  Remedy   Use electrode of a softer material.

- **Crater crack**   It is a crack, generally in the shape of an 'X', which is found in a crater. Crater cracks are hot cracks.

  Cause: The centre of the weld pool solidifies before the outside of the weld pool, pulling the centre apart during cooling.

  Remedy   Fill the crater at the weld termination and/or pre-heat to even out the cooling of the puddle.

- **Throat crack**   It is a longitudinal crack located in the weld throat area.

  Causes   Transverse stresses, probably from shrinkage. Improper filler metal selection or welding procedure; propagation of crater crack.

  Remedies   Use proper filler metal and welding procedure. Improve pre-heating of base metal. Avoid formation of crater crack. Use a more ductile filler material.

- **Toe crack**   It is a crack in the base metal beginning at the toe of the weld.

  Causes   Transverse shrinkage stresses. Brittleness of metal in the heat affected zone.

  Remedies   Increase pre-heating of the base metal. Use a more ductile filler material.

- **Root crack**   It is a crack in the weld at the weld root.

  Causes   Same as for throat crack.

  Remedies   Same as for throat crack.

- **Under bead crack**   It is a crack in the unmelted base metal of the heat affected zone.

  Cause   Hydrogen embrittlement.

  Remedy   Use low hydrogen type of electrodes and/or pre-heat the base metal.

- **Hot crack**   It is a crack in the weld metal that occurs during solidification.

  Cause   Micro-stresses from weld metal shrinkage pulling apart the weld metal as it cools from liquid state to solid.

  Remedies   Pre-heat the work material before welding. Increase the weld size. Use a low tensile grade filler material.

- **Cold crack**   It is a crack that occurs after the metal has completely solidified. The most damaging form of cold cracking is hydrogen embrittlement. This occurs when hydrogen is absorbed into the metal. Hydrogen embrittlement is usually associated with dust and dirt that has accumulated on the weld surface or from using a damp electrode.

Causes   Shrinkage of weld metal in the solid state. Inability of the weld metal to contract due to excessive restraint of the workpieces being joined. Discontinuities in the weld metal. Use of damp electrode.

Remedies   Pre-heat the base metal. Weld toward areas of less constraint. Use a more ductile weld metal.

- **Lamellar tears**   These are generally noticed at the edge of the heat affected zone (HAZ) in the form of a long and continuous separation line between the base metal and the HAZ.

  Causes   A lamellar tear is caused by:

  - Elongated inclusions, such as manganese and sulphur present in the base metal.
  - Aligned non-metallic inclusions present in the base metal.
  - Shrinkage of the restrained members in the structure during the process of cooling.

  Remedies   Lamellar tears can be prevented by:

  - Providing for shrinkage of the workpieces.
  - Modifying the joint design to enable deeper weld bead penetration.

- **Surface damage**   The workpiece surface close to the joint may be damaged or spoiled during the welding operation, which is often objectionable for reasons of appearance or later use of the welded component. Severe surface damage may also adversely affect the properties of the welded component, particularly if it is made of a notch-sensitive material.

  Causes   Surface adjacent to the joint may be damaged due to:

  - Spatter that occurs during welding, causing deposition of small droplets of metal in the area.
  - Inadvertent contact of the electrode with the workpiece surface at places just close to but outside of the weld zone.

  Remedy   Surface damage can be avoided by simply following the welding procedure correctly.

- **Residual stresses**   Presence of residual stresses in a welded component is undesirable because they can cause distortion, warping, buckling or even cracking of the welded part. Residual stresses can also reduce the fatigue life of the part and are responsible for stress-corrosion cracking.

  Cause   Residual stresses in the welded part are caused by expansion and contraction of the weld area occurring as a result of localized heating and cooling during welding operation.

Remedies   The problems arising due to residual stresses, such as distortion, warping or buckling can be minimized by

- Pre-heating the parts to be welded by radiant lamps, hot air blast, electrically or any other means.
- Applying stress-relieving operations such as annealing of the welded parts.
- Plastically deforming the welded parts to a small degree.

Questions

1. Differentiate between destructive and non-destructive techniques of weld testing. Briefly explain any two techniques of each of the two types.
2. Describe how welds can be tested by using (i) ultrasonics and (ii) magnetic particles.
3. Describe the following weld defects by discussing the causes and remedies.
   i.   Slag inclusion   ii.   Porosity
   iii. Undercut

Fill in the Blanks

1. When welds are tested by X-ray, internal defects such as voids and cracks show up on the film as _____ areas.
2. By subjecting a weld to tension–shear test, it is possible to find the _____ strength of the weld metal and the location of _____.
3. Magnetic particle inspection technique of testing welds is applicable only to parts made of _____ materials.
4. Residual stresses in the welded part are caused by _____ and _____ of the weld area.
5. During a welding operation, deposition of small droplets of metal in the weld area is termed as _____.
6. Presence of residual stresses in the welded component is undesirable because they can cause _____ and _____ of the welded part.

Choose the Correct Answer

1. Weld testing techniques are commonly classified as
   a.   destructive and semi destructive techniques.
   b.   destructive and non-destructive techniques.
   c.   semi destructive and non-destructive techniques.
   d.   destructive, semi destructive and non-destructive techniques.

2. Creep test of a weld joint

    a. cannot be conducted.

    b. cannot be used to find porosity in the weld.

    c. is a non-destructive test.

    d. is a destructive test.

3. Magnetic particle test of a weld joint

    a. cannot be conducted.

    b. can be used to find only location of any material discontinuity in the weld.

    c. can be used to find only location and size of any material discontinuity in the weld.

    d. can be used to find location, size and shape of any material discontinuity in the weld.

4. Which one of the following weld test techniques involves application of force to elastically stress the component having welded joint?

    a. ultrasonic inspection   c. acoustic impact inspection

    b. acoustic emission inspection   d. holography inspection

5. In a welded joint, the term hot cracks

    a. and cracks have the same meaning.

    b. has no meaning.

    c. is used for cracks that occur while the joint is still at high temperatures

    d. is used for cracks that appear only when a welded joint is subjected to hot environment

6. In a welded joint, the term toe crack

    a. and transverse crack have the same meaning.

    b. has no meaning.

    c. is used for cracks that occur in the base metal beginning at the toe of the weld.

    d. is used for cracks that occur in the weld metal beginning at the toe of the weld.

Answers

1. b.   2. c.   3. d.   4. b.   5. c.   6. c.

21

Plastics and Shaping of Plastics

LEARNING OBJECTIVES

After reading this chapter, you should be able to understand the following:

- The advantages and limitations of plastics over metals and alloys.

- The classification and uses of plastics.

- The properties of polymers.

- Compression moulding, transfer moulding and laminating.

- The welding of plastics.

- The design considerations when designing plastic parts.

- Recent trends in plastic technology.

21.1 Introduction

The word 'plastics' is mostly used as a synonym for 'polymers', although plastics constitute only a subset of polymeric materials. In fact, the word *plastic* is from the Greek word *plastikos* which means 'able to be moulded and shaped'. Plastics can be moulded, cast, formed, machined and joined by welding operations. They have many unique and diverse useful properties due to which they are increasingly replacing metals and alloys for manufacturing of components that are used in a wide range of applications.

Advantages of plastics   The following are some important advantages of plastics over metals and alloys.

- *Density*   Plastics are light in weight.

- *Insulation*   Plastics possess good thermal and electrical insulating properties.

- *Ease in manufacturing*   Plastics get softened at a relatively low temperature range. They can thus be easily moulded and require low energy for processing.

- *Ease in handling*   Handling of plastic products during manufacturing is easy as the temperatures involved are relatively low.

- *Resistance to corrosion*   Plastics have greater resistance to corrosion and are chemically inert.

- *Strength*   Plastics have high strength-to-weight ratio, particularly when reinforced.

- *Cost* Plastic parts are generally less costly.

- *Ready to use*   Plastic parts formed by the moulding process are generally *net shape*, not requiring any further shaping.

- *Finish*   Plastic parts generally have excellent finishing. They can be given a wide range of colours and surface finishes without the use of paints or plating.

Limitations of plastics   The following are some important limitations of plastics over metals and alloys.

- *Thermal expansion*   Plastics expand more than metals. Plastic parts therefore undergo greater dimensional changes with variation in temperature when compared to metallic parts.

- *Strength*   For the same size, plastic parts are generally weaker than metal parts. Plastic parts, therefore, should not be used for applications where high stresses are likely to be encountered.

- *Ductility*   Plastics have poor ductility compared to metals. They become brittle at low temperatures.

- *Combustibility*   Plastics are combustible and produce toxic fumes when burnt, polluting the environment and posing a danger to human and wildlife.

- *Useful temperature range*   Plastics have lower useful temperature range (generally up to 300° C).

- *Resistance to creep and impact*   For most plastics, resistance to creep is poor but for some plastics, resistance to impact is somewhat comparable to that of metals.

- *Resistance to heat*   Plastic parts have lower resistance to heat than metals.

- *Stability* Plastic parts have less dimensional stability over a period of time compared to metallic parts.

- *Degradation*   When placed in sunlight or when exposed to other forms of radiations, plastics are known to degrade. Degradation also takes place when plastic parts are placed in oxygen or ozone environments.

- *Solubility*   Plastics are soluble in many common solvents unlike metals.

- *Recycling*   Recycling of plastics is difficult compared to metals.

- *Usage for eatables*   Use of plastics to store eatable items, particularly in hot environments, is harmful as this can cause diseases, even cancer.

Table 21.1 gives the typical range of mechanical properties of some engineering plastics at room temperature.

Table 21.1 Mechanical properties of some engineering plastics

Engineering plastic	Ultimate tensile strength (MPa)	Elastic modulus (GPa)	% Elongation	Poisson's ratio
ABS	28–50	1.4–2.8	70–5	–
ABS, reinforced	100	7.5	–	0.33
Acrylic	40–80	1.5–3.5	50–5	–
Epoxy	40–140	3.5–15	10–1	–
Epoxy, reinforced	80–1400	22–52	4–2	–
Fluorocarbon	7–50	0.7–2	300–100	0.46
Nylon	55–85	1.4–2.8	200–50	0.33
Nylon, reinforced	70–200	2–10	10–2	–
Phenolic	30–70	3–20	2–0	–
Polycarbonate	55–70	2.5–3	125–10	0.33
Polyster	55	2	300–10	0.35
Polyster, reinforced	100–150	8–12	3–1	–
Polyethylene	8–40	0.1–1.4	1000–20	0.45
Polypropylene	20–35	0.6–1.2	500–20	–
Polypropylene, reinforced	40–100	3.5–6	4–2	–
Polystyrene	14–80	1.5–4	50–1	0.33
PVC	7–50	0.015–4	450–50	–

Uses of plastics   Some common engineering plastics and their uses are given in Table 21.2

Table 21.2 Some commonly used engineering plastics and their uses

Plastic	Typical uses
Acrylonitrile butadiene styrene (ABS)	Keys on a computer keyboard, power-tool housing, plastic face-guard on wall sockets and LEGO toys.
Polycarbonate (PC)	Compact discs, eyeglasses, riot shields, security windows, traffic lights, lenses. A blend of PC and ABS creates a stronger plastic, which is used in many applications, e.g., car interior and exterior parts, mobile phone bodies.
Polyester (PES)	Fibers, textiles.
Polyethylene (PE)	Supermarket bags, bottles and equipment covers.
High-density polyethylene (HDPE)	Detergent bottles, milk jugs and boxes.
Low-density polyethylene (LDPE)	Outdoor furniture, siding, floor tiles, shower curtains, packaging stuff.
Polyvinyl chloride (PVC)	Plumbing pipes and guttering, shower curtains, window frames, flooring.

Contd.

Table 21.2 Contd.

Plastic	Typical uses
Polypropylene (PP)	Bottle caps, drinking straws, yogurt containers, appliances, car bumpers, pressure pipe systems.
Polystyrene (PS)	Packaging for food items such as peanuts and banana chips, food containers, plastic tableware, disposable cups, plates, cutlery, boxes for CD and cassette.
Polytetrafluoroethylene (PTFE)	An insulator in cables and connector assemblies and as a material for printed circuit boards used at microwave frequencies
Polyurethanes (PU)	Cushioning foams, thermal insulation foams, surface coatings, printing rollers, car parts
Silicone (S)	Heat resistant resin used mainly as a sealant but also used for high temperature cooking utensils.

21.2 Classification of Plastics

Plastics can be classified into two basic types: (i) thermoplastics, and (ii) thermosetting plastics (also called thermosets). The fundamental difference between the two types lies in their chemical behaviour when heated and thereafter cooled.

Thermoplastics Thermoplastics soften when heated. If further heat is applied, they eventually melt. Upon removal of the heat source, as they cool down, they regain their original hardness and strength. Thus, thermoplastics can be re-melted any number of times by successive applications of heat without risk of degradation of the material. Chemically, the material is not affected regardless of its temperature so long as it is not heated to such an extent that it is destroyed. Typical examples of thermoplastics are: acrylics (Perspex and Plexiglas), PVC, cellulosics, nylon, polystyrene, polypropylene, fluorocarbons and PTFE.

Thermosetting plastics (thermosets) When heated, thermosetting plastics undergo an irreversible change. In other words, a thermosetting plastic, after heating, is no longer chemically the same as it was initially. When heated it softens, then melts and starts hardening when still hot. Reheating of thermosetting plastics never results in re-softening nor retaining of their hardness. Further heating will only destroy them by charring and finally burning. The permanent change that occurs to thermosetting plastics when they are heated is due to a phenomenon called 'polymerization'.

Thermosetting plastics generally possess better mechanical, thermal and chemical properties, electrical resistance, and dimensional stability when compared to thermoplastics. Typical examples of thermosetting plastics are: Bakelite, polyesters, phenolic and melamine. Some common products made from this type of plastic are the handles and knobs that are used on cooking pans and electric switches.

Of the two types, usage of thermoplastics is much larger, comprising nearly 80% of the total plastics usage.

21.3 Properties of Polymer Melts

To shape a thermoplastic polymer, it has to be heated so that it softens to the consistency of a thick fluid. In this state, it is called a 'polymer melt'. There are some unique properties of polymer melt. These are:

Viscosity   Viscosity is a fluid property that relates the shear stress experienced during flow of the fluid to the rate of shear. This is an important property of polymer melt, as many polymer shaping techniques involve the flow of polymer melt through small channels in the die. As the flow rates of material in the die are generally high, the rates of shear are high and so are the shear stresses. High pressures are therefore required to accomplish the shaping processes. For a polymer melt, viscosity decreases with increase in shear rate (fluid flow rate), that means the fluid becomes thinner at higher rates of shear. This behaviour of polymer melt is termed as *pseudoplasticity*.

   Viscosity of a polymer is also affected by temperature. For some common polymers, the relation between viscosity and temperature at a shear rate of 10^3 s^{-1} is shown in Figure 21.1. This shear rate normally prevails in high speed extrusion processes and injection moulding. It can be seen from this figure that viscosity of a polymer melt decreases with increase in both the shear rate and the temperature.

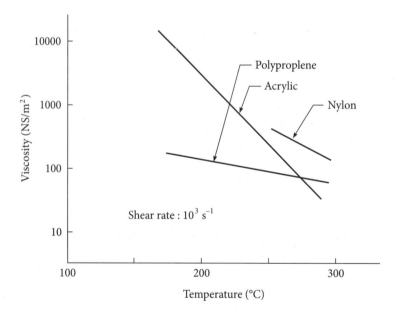

Figure 21.1   Variation of viscosity with temperature for some polymers

Viscoelasticity   This is another important property possessed by polymer melt, which can be easily explained by the *die swell* phenomenon in the extrusion process, illustrated in

Figure 21.2. As can be noticed from this figure, hot plastic expands as it comes out of the die opening. This is because the polymer was contained in a chamber of much larger cross-section before entering the narrow die opening, and the extruded material 'remembers' its earlier shape and tries to return to the same after leaving the die opening. In technical terms, what it means is that the compressive stresses that act on the polymer melt as it enters the small die opening do not relax immediately, and as the material comes out of the die opening (i.e., when the restriction is removed), the unrelaxed stresses cause the cross-section to enlarge.

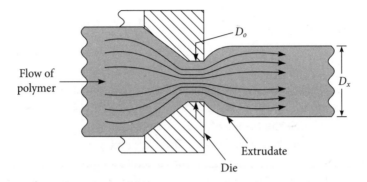

Figure 21.2   Die swell, a manifestation of viscoelasticity. The polymer expands as it comes out of an extrusion die

For a circular die opening, die swell can be measured by the *swell ratio*, given by

$$SR = D_x / D_o$$

where SR = swell ratio; D_x = diameter of the extruded cross-section; and D_o = diameter of the die opening. It has been experimentally found that the amount of die swell is a function of the time spent by the polymer melt in the die channel. The die swell can be reduced by increasing the time in the channel, say by making the channel longer.

Example 21.1

A plastic rod of circular cross-section of 11 mm diameter is being extruded by passing the polymer melt through a die having an orifice of 10 mm diameter. Determine the swell ratio.

Solution

We know that

$$SR = D_x / D_o$$

where SR = swell ratio; D_x = diameter of extruded cross-section; and D_o = diameter of the die opening.

Therefore, swell ratio in this case is 11/10 = 1.1 or 110%

21.4 Plastic Shaping Processes

Both thermoplastics when heated, and thermosets in their initial pre-polymerized form, are physically quite flexible. Both the types of plastics can therefore be moulded into a wide variety of shapes. In a way, this is quite similar to moulding of liquid metals except that plastics are not liquid when moulded. A description of some important plastic shaping processes is given here.

21.5 Plastic Shaping Processes (For Thermoplastics)

21.5.1 Extrusion

Extrusion is a continuous process, as opposed to *moulding*, which is a cyclic process. In this process, a solid thermoplastic material is converted into a viscous fluid by heating. It is then forced to flow through the orifice of a die to obtain a long continuous product (called extrudate). Upon cooling, the extrudate becomes a solid product. Depending upon the flexibility and the storage needs, it may be cut into discrete lengths, coiled or wound on a roll. Extrusion is suitable for many types of continuous plastic products that have uniform outside shape. Typical products made by the extrusion process are solid forms, pipes, bearings, brake linings, gears, structural shapes, sheets and films that are used widely in sectors such as construction, automobiles, medical and health care, packaging and sports. It is possible to achieve cross-sectional tolerance of 0.4%. The extrusion process is also used to coat electrical wires and cables with a polymer. Thermosetting polymers are generally not suitable for extrusion process as they harden very rapidly; their use is limited to the production of thick-walled tubes only.

Materials   Most thermoplastic polymers can be extruded. A material that will flow easily is generally not a good candidate for extrusion. Polymer materials that exit the die in a very stiff state are preferred for profile extrusion. This material property is expressed by a variety of terms, including drape strength, melt strength, melt stiffness, etc. An indicator of melt viscosity that is commonly reported in literature is the *melt flow rate* of the material. Polymer materials that can be extruded typically have melt flow rates less than 1 (fractional melt). It is interesting to note that the melt flow rates for materials that are good for injection moulding typically exceed 8.

In many cases, materials that are easier to extrude into profiles are those that do not change phase (solid to liquid) in the heating process. Upon heating, these materials soften just sufficiently so that they can be formed into the desired shape, but do not actually melt. This is desirable because in these cases we will not have to take so much heat energy out of the part to cool it down (freeze from liquid to solid).

Process and equipment   Thermoplastic material, in either granular or powder form, is fed through a hopper into the barrel chamber of a screw extruder. As shown in Figure 21.3, a rotating screw propels the material through the barrel, where it gets heated (by external electrical resistance or by internal heat generated through the mechanical shearing action of the rotating screw or by both of these), homogenized and compressed. The hot material is then forced to flow through the orifice of a heated die, and collected on a conveyer where it is immediately cooled by jets of air or water so that enough hardening of material takes place. The material gets cooled further as it moves over the conveyer. The extrudate is either cut into desired lengths or coiled, depending upon whether the material is rigid or flexible.

There are two main components of the extruder: the barrel and the screw. The die is not a component of the extruder; it can be changed every time a new product profile has to be produced. The barrel, which usually has an internal diameter in the range 25 to 200 mm and length-to-diameter ratio of 10 to 25, has a hopper for the feedstock located at one end while the die is fitted at the other end.

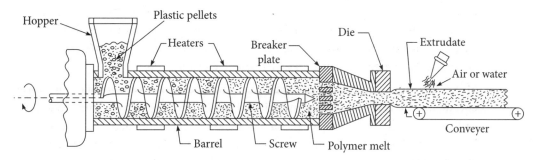

Figure 21.3 Schematic of the constructional features of an extruder for producing plastic parts

The spiral screw, which rotates at about 60 to 100 rpm, performs many functions such as feeding, homogenization, compression and pumping. The polymer moves along the barrel and finally reaches the die zone. But before reaching the die, the polymer melt is made to pass through a *breaker plate*, which consists of a series of wire meshes set into a stiff plate. Passage of the melt through the fine axial holes of the breaker plate helps to (i) filter out any contaminants or hard lumps in the melt and (ii) straighten the flow of polymer melt in order to remove its 'memory' of the spiral motion imposed by the rotating screw. It is important to note that the use of a breaker plate is vital from the view point of the polymer's viscoelastic property, which would tend to play back its history (of spiral motion inside the extrusion chamber) and twist and distort the extruded product, if the flow were not straightened.

Die configurations and extruded products   The cross-sectional shape (i.e., the profile) of the extruded part is determined by the orifice configuration of the die. We will consider the following cases: (i) solid profiles; (ii) hollow profiles; (iii) wire and cable coating; and (iv) sheet coating.

(i)   **Solid sections**   Regular cross-sectional shapes (such as rounds, squares and ovals) and irregular cross-sectional shapes (such as structural sections, door and window mouldings and automobile trims) are categorized as solid profiles. For a round shape solid profile, the die orifice is circular but for other profiles, the die orifice is designed to take care of the *die swell* phenomenon; thus, the die is slightly different from the product profile.

(ii)   Hollow sections   Extrusion of hollow sections such as tubes and pipes requires the use of a mandrel to create the hollow form. The polymer melt flows around the mandrel to produce the hollow tubular section. Sometimes, the mandrel has a provision for blowing air to maintain the hollow form of the extruded product while it is cooling and hardening. Pipes and tubes are generally cooled by pulling the soft extrudate through a water filled tank. Sizing sleeves are often fitted to obtain the desired outer diameter (OD) of the tube while air pressure maintained inside the tube controls the inner diameter (ID) of the tube.

(iii) Wire and cable coating   For providing insulation on wire or cable, a layer of polymer is coated by the extrusion process. The polymer melt is applied on the bare wire (or cable) as it is pulled at high speed through a die. A weak vacuum applied between the wire and the polymer helps in adhesion of the polymer coating. Hardening of plastic is achieved by passing the coated wire through a water tank.

(iv) Sheet coating   Extrusion is also widely used for coating flat surfaces of paper, fabrics and metal foil. A thermoplastic material is extruded through a very thin rectangular orifice of the die onto a sheet passing beneath it. The extruded sheet, while soft, blends onto the substrate and is passed over a rubber roll, which is held against a steel roll at a certain pressure. The edges of the sheet are then trimmed before being taken onto the wind-up roll. A schematic of the process is given in Figure 21.4. Vinyls, polyethylene and polypropylene are commonly used thermoplastic materials for such applications.

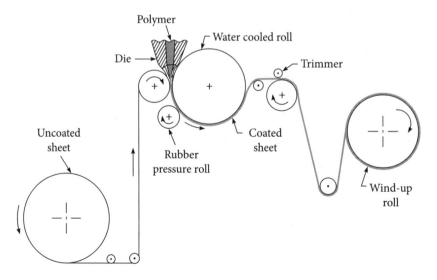

Figure 21.4   Schematic of process of sheet coating with plastic extrudate

Defects in extruded parts The failures or defects that commonly occur in extruded parts are due to three main causes: die design, material selection and processing. In some cases, certain failures occur during the extrusion process, which cause defects in extruded parts. Some important defects are: rough surface, bubbles and pits, surging (cyclic thickness variation) and material degradation.

- **Rough surface** Fine ridges or rough surface seen on an extrudate when it comes too fast out of a narrow die opening is caused due to melt toughness or melt fracture. It is quite common with polyethylene, and can be eliminated by running the melt (or the die lips) hotter, using a longer or more streamlined die, or by using a different grade of material. Use of additives can also help greatly in this regard.

- **Bubbles and pits** Pattern of dotted lines, long bubbles and pits on the extrudate are caused by moisture that is absorbed by some plastics. The moisture in the melt passes through the extruder and boils out when the pressure is relieved at the die lips. To remove moisture, the material must be pre-dried, or a vent must be used in the extruder, or both. A moisture level of 0.1% is usually low enough to avoid such visual problems. Some plastics, such as PET, nylons and polycarbonate can degrade and weaken if even a very small amount of moisture is present when they are melted. It is a usual practice to use dehumidifying dryers to bring moisture levels down to 0.01% or less.

  Bubbles and pits can also be caused by trapped air. This is not common when pelletized material is used with long extruder barrels. When the melt is pushed at a fast rate through the die, the air is trapped into the product and the surface shows bubbles and pits. Such a surface will improve if the screw is run more slowly, die-head is cooled and use is made of vents.

- **Surging** When a cyclic variation occurs in the extruded product thickness in the direction of extrusion, the defect is called *surging*. The surge cycle time is typically between 30 seconds and 3 minutes, and the cause can be inside or outside the extruder. Outside causes are easier to locate and correct.

Cause	Observation	Remedy
Take-off pull of extrudate may be irregular.	Screw rpm and ammeter readings remain steady.	Ensure uniform pull of product from extruder
Screw motor speed varies because it is not being regulated properly.	Show up as unsteady rpm of screw motor.	Correct the regulation of screw motor
The feed of plastic melt is uneven because of variation in particle size, density or bridging in the hopper or throat.	Screw rpm is steady but the ammeter shows variation of ± 5% or more.	Sometimes this can be cured by increasing the temperature of the feed to promote earlier melting. Raising the rear barrel temperature may also help.

- **Material degradation** Degradation of material can occur due to overheating, which is caused if the take-off cooling is not enough. Overheating not only causes degradation of product but can also make dimensional control and sizing difficult. When this occurs, the external source of heat to the barrel should be stopped except in the rear zone if needed for bite (input) control. The barrel may even be cooled from outside if necessary.

21.5.2 Injection moulding

The injection moulding process has seen steady improvements since its first use in the late 1860s. The technique has evolved from the production of combs and buttons to major consumer, industrial, medical and aerospace products. Injection moulding of thermoplastics is similar to pressure die casting of metals. In this process, a thermoplastic polymer is heated to a highly plastic state and a high pressure is then applied to force it to flow (i.e., inject) into a cold steel mould cavity where it solidifies under pressure. The moulded part, whose shape is almost the same as that of the mould cavity, is called a ***moulding***. The part produced, as ejected from the mould, is usually a finished product requiring no further processing before assembly or use.

The production cycle is usually of 10 to 30 seconds. To increase the production rate, the mould may be designed to have more than one cavity so that each cycle produces multiple mouldings. A moulding may be as small as of 25 g to as big as of 25 kg weight depending on the machine capacity.

Equipment   An injection moulding machine consists of two main components: (1) the plastic injection unit and (2) the mould unit (see Figure 21.5).

Injection unit   It is somewhat similar to an extruder, and is made up of a barrel and a screw. The barrel has a hopper at one end into which raw polymer (in the form of pellets) is fed. Inside the barrel is a screw that performs two functions: (i) mixing and heating the polymer; this is achieved by its rotary motion, and (ii) injecting the molten plastic into the mould; this is achieved by its linear motion, like that of a ram. Because of its dual (rotary and linear) action, it is called a ***reciprocating screw***.

During the process, the screw rotates continuously to mix and heat the polymer. It simultaneously has to-and-fro linear motion; forward motion to inject the molten plastic into

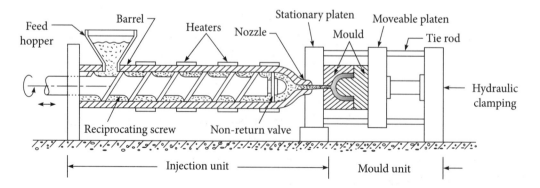

Figure 21.5   Schematic of reciprocating screw type injection moulding machine

the mould, and backward motion to return to the former position. A non-return valve is fitted near the tip of the screw, which prevents the polymer melt from flowing backward along the screw threads.

Mould unit   The mould used for injection moulding is custom-designed and fabricated for the given product. It is mostly of a two-platen configuration–to one platen is fastened one half of the mould and to the other platen is fastened the second half of the mould. The mould unit has a mechanism for opening and closing the mould halves at appropriate times during each mould cycle. The mould unit is also responsible for holding the two halves of the mould properly aligned to each other and keeping them firmly closed against the melt injection force.

The process cycle for injection moulding follows the sequence shown in Figure 21.6. Let us consider the cycle starting at the instant when the mould is open prior to being injected with polymer melt. (a) The mould halves are closed and clamping force applied. (b) A known quantity of polymer melt, which has been brought to the proper temperature and viscosity by rotation of the screw and external heating, is injected under heavy pressure into the mould cavity. As the injected plastic comes into contact with the cold surface of the mould, it starts solidifying and shrinking. Screw pressure is maintained to allow additional melt into the cavity to compensate for the shrinkage during cooling. (c) The screw is retracted. Simultaneously, the non-return valve opens to allow polymer melt to flow into the forward section of the barrel. By this time, the injected polymer in the mould has completely solidified. (d) The mould halves are separated out, and the moulding is ejected.

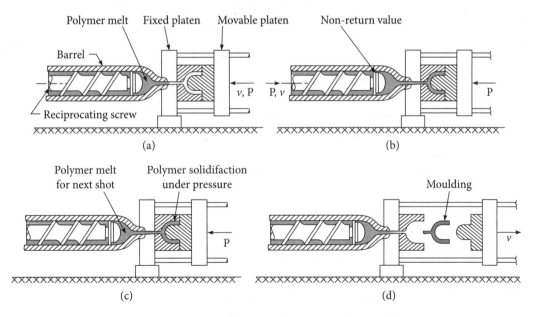

Figure 21.6   Injection moulding cycle: (a) Mould halves are closed; clamping force is applied; (b) Polymer melt is injected into mould cavity under pressure; (c) Screw is retracted; fresh polymer melt flows into forward section of barrel; (d) Mould halves are separated and moulding is ejected

Polymer shrinkage Shrinkage occurs during cooling of the polymer melt in the mould from the moulding temperature to the room temperature. It can be as high as 8% for some plastics, and is often expressed as mm/mm of the dimension under consideration. Thicker parts experience greater shrinkage. To account for the shrinkage, the dimensions of the mould cavity are made correspondingly bigger than the specified part dimensions. The following relationship can be used to find the mould dimensions.

$$d_c = d_p + d_p . S + d_p . S^2$$

where d_c = dimension of cavity; d_p = corresponding dimension of moulded part and S = shrinkage of the polymer (Refer to Table 21.3).

Table 21.3 Shrinkage values of some commonly used thermoplastics

Thermoplastic	Shrinkage (mm/mm)
ABS	0.006
Polycarbonate	0.007
Polyethylene	0.025
Polystyrene	0.004
Poly vinyl chloride	0.005

Example 21.2

A component is to be made of ABS plastic by injection moulding process. A particular portion of this component is 60 mm long. Determine the corresponding dimension of the mould cavity if you have to account for the shrinkage.

Solution

We have here $d_p = 60$ mm; $d_c = ?$ and shrinkage S for ABS plastic = 0.006

$$d_c = d_p + d_p . S + d_p . S^2$$

$$= 60 \, (1+0.006 + 0.000036) = \mathbf{60.36216 \ mm}$$

Defects in injection moulded parts Some common defects in injection moulded parts, their causes and remedies are explained in Table 21.4.

Table 21.4 Common defects in injection moulded parts, causes and remedies

Defect	Appearance	Causes	Remedies
Short shots	Incomplete moulded product because the mould cavity was not completely filled.	• Insufficient injection: Moulding machine performance (shot capacity, plasticizing capacity, etc.). • Poor material flowability due to low temperature or pressure. • Gate cross-section surface area is too small. • Moulded product thickness is too thin. • Poor gas venting.	Moulding equipment • Increase the amount of material feed. Use a larger capacity machine. • Increase the injection pressure. • Increase the injection speed • Raise the temperature of barrel as well as nozzle. • Ensure that the nozzle is not clogged. Mould • Raise the mould temperature • Increase the mould gas release. • Increase gate cross-section surface area. • Increase the moulded product thickness. Materials • Choose a low-viscosity high-flow material type. • Use surface lubricant. (Add 0.05–0.1% by weight).
Flow marks	Ring-shaped miniature bands appear on the moulded product surface around narrow sections.	The molten polymer cools rapidly within the mould and becomes highly viscous. Once that molten polymer starts to coagulate, it gets pushed by the molten polymer injected afterward and forms miniature bands.	Moulding equipment • Increase the nozzle diameter. • Increase the injection speed. • Increase the injection pressure. • Raise the barrel temperature. • Raise the nozzle temperature. Mould • Increase the mould temperature. • Increase the gate cross-section surface area. Materials • Use surface lubricant.

Contd.

Table 21.3 Contd.

| Voids | The presence of holes inside moulded products. | • Variation in density as the material changes from molten to a coagulated state.
• The surface of moulded product loses heat rapidly through the mould wall and the polymer hardens. As a result, the polymer is pulled outward, causing all shrinkage to concentrate in the thickest parts of the product leaving holes within the product.
• Air gets trapped within the molten polymer resulting in bubbles within the product. | Moulding equipment
• Increase the injection pressure.
• Increase the injection time.
• Lower the barrel temperature.
Mould
• Change the product design so that the thickness ≤ 6 mm. Enhance strength, if needed, by adding necessary number of thick, uniform ribs to the product design.
• Lower the mould temperature. Make the mould temperature uniform.
• Change the gate locations in order to prevent air leakage.
Materials
• Dry the material thoroughly.
• Choose more viscous grade. |
| Silver streaking | Streaks of a silvery white colour appear in the direction of material flow. | • Material is absorbing water.
• Material is contaminated with another type of material.
• Aeration is occurring during moulding.
• Too much additive is present in the material. | Moulding equipment
• Reduce the injection speed.
• Thoroughly clean the moulding machine barrel.
Mould
• Increase (or decrease) the size of runners and gates.
• Increase the mould temperature.
Materials
• Pre-dry thoroughly.
• Check for potential contamination. |

21.5.3 Blow moulding

Blow moulding is a process in which air is used to inflate soft plastic to fit into a die cavity. The process is used to produce *hollow shaped containers*. The basic concepts of the process have been borrowed from the glass industry. The process can be described by the following steps [Figure 21.7].

(a) A round hollow tube of required length (called a *pre-form* or *parison*) is first made by extrusion moulding (or injection moulding) process. While the pre-form is still hot, it is positioned around an air pipe, which is already located centrally between the two halves of a split die.

(b) The die halves are then closed and clamped. In doing so, the open end of the pre-form is nip-shut.

(c) Air (or any gas) is blown into the pre-form. This expands the plastic tube out to the walls of the die. The air supply is then cut-off. The die may be water-cooled so as to cool down the blown plastic part and shorten the cycle time.

(d) The die halves are separated. The moulded product is ejected out. Any flash on the product may be trimmed and re-cycled.

Most common thermoplastics used for this process are polyethylene, PVC, polypropylene and PEEK resins. Air pressures used are 300 to 700 kPa. The die is generally cast or machined out of a block of stainless steel, tool steel, aluminium, or beryllium–copper. The die material must not chemically react with the polymer being processed. It should be durable, inexpensive and of high thermal conductivity.

Applications   A large variety of products are being produced by this process. Some common products are disposable containers for packaging liquid consumer goods, large water storage drums, automotive fuel tanks, gas ducts and toys.

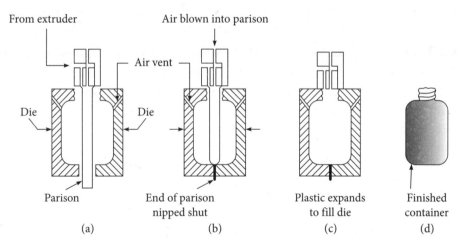

Figure 21.7   Schematic of blow moulding process: (a) A round hollow tube of a given length in hot condition is positioned around an air pipe located centrally between two halves of a split die; (b) The die halves are closed and clamped. In doing so, the open end of the pre-form is nip-shut; (c) As air or gas is blown into the plastic tube, it expands out to the die walls. Air already present in the die escapes through vent holes. The air supply is then cut-off; and (d) Die halves are separated and the finished container is ejected out

21.5.4 Rotational moulding

The rotational moulding process is an alternative to the blow moulding process for manufacturing large hollow products of thermoplastic polymers, although the process is also finding applications for thermosets. The process uses gravity inside a rotating mould to obtain the hollow form of the product rather than the use of air pressure. Small production quantities and large-sized parts with complex external geometry are typical features, which make this process more favourable than blow moulding. The process cycle is described as under.

1. **Loading** The cavity of a warm split-mould is filled with a specific quantity of thermoplastic powder or liquid.

2. **Heating and mould rotating** The mould is closed, heated and slowly rotated simultaneously about two perpendicular axes. The resin inside the mould melts and gets distributed in the form of a coating of uniform thickness over the entire surface of the die cavity.

     The length of time the mould spends in this part of the cycle is critical; if the length of time is too long, the polymer will degrade, reducing its impact strength. If the mould spends too little time here, the polymer melt may not get enough time to get properly distributed on the mould wall, resulting in large bubbles in the polymer. This can have an adverse effect on the mechanical properties of the final product.

3. **Cooling** The mould is then moved into a cooling chamber, while it is still rotating. Water or air is used to slowly bring down the temperature of the mould.

4. **Unloading** The rotation of the mould is stopped as soon as the plastic solidifies. The mould halves are opened to take out the hollow product.

Figure 21.8 illustrates the rotational moulding process cycle being carried out on a three-station indexing machine, in which loading and unloading steps are carried out at the same station. It is important to note that rotational speed of the mould seldom exceeds 20 rpm. Therefore, it is the gravitational force and not the centrifugal force which is responsible for the spread of polymer to uniform thickness inside the mould.

Advantages Rotational moulding has the following advantages.

1. The moulds used for this process are inexpensive. They are light in weight and fabricated from sheet of aluminium or stainless steel. The moulds require less tooling; they can be fabricated and put into production much more quickly compared to other moulding processes. It is therefore a highly suitable process for short run production and rush deliveries of products.

2. It is possible to obtain consistent wall thickness and strong outside corners that are virtually stress free.

3. It is possible to integrally mould metallic or ceramic inserts into the plastic products made by this process. Metallic threaded parts, internal pipes, and structures, and even different coloured plastics can be inserted into the mould prior to placing the plastic powder or pellets.

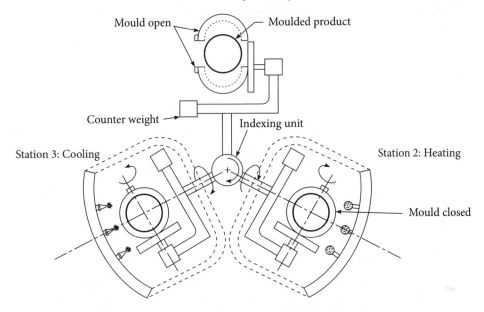

Figure 21.8   Rotational moulding cycle on a three-station indexing machine

4.   The process is economical as very little material is wasted in production. There are no sprues or runners (as in injection moulding), no off-cuts (as in thermoforming), or pinch-off scrap (as in blow moulding). Whatever small amount of material is wasted, through scrap or failed part testing, can be recycled.

Limitations   Rotational moulding has the following limitations.

1.   The cycle time is generally high–up to half a minute.

2.   Unlike other processes where only the product needs to be cooled before being removed, rotational moulding requires cooling of the entire mould. While water cooling is possible, there is a significant down time of the mould. This increases both financial and environmental costs.

3.   Some plastics degrade during the long heating cycles or in the process of turning powder into melt.

4.   The stages of heating and cooling in the process involve transfer of heat first from the hot medium to the polymer material and next from it to the cooling environment. In both cases, the process of heat transfer occurs in an unsteady regime.

5.   Being a low pressure process, sometimes the polymer melt fails to reach all areas in the mould. For example, it is not possible to make sharp threads that would be possible with injection moulding.

Applications   The process is widely used for producing hollow seamless products such as storage tanks of various sizes, buckets, trash cans, housings, toys, helmets, footballs, carrying cases and boat hulls. The process is also used to make highly specialized products, including seals for inflatable oxygen masks and lightweight components for the aerospace industry. The parts produced can be as large as 2 m × 2 m × 3 m. The wall thickness of the parts can vary from as small as 0.5 mm to as much as 20 mm.

21.5.5 Calendering

Calendering is a process used for producing continuous lengths of thermoplastic sheet. A calendering unit consists of a series of counter-rotating heated rolls through which a warm softened mass of thermoplastic material is forced to pass (Figure 21.9). As the plastic passes through a decreasing gap between the rolls, it is squeezed into a continuous thin sheet or film, which is then cooled to induce hardening. The thickness of the sheet mainly depends on the gap between the last two rolls.

The sheet may be either wound onto storage rolls or cut into pieces of specific lengths. Sheet thickness can vary between 0.2 mm and 1 mm. It is possible to produce sheets having textures or patterns on the surface by replacing the last set of rolls with rolls having specially designed surfaces.

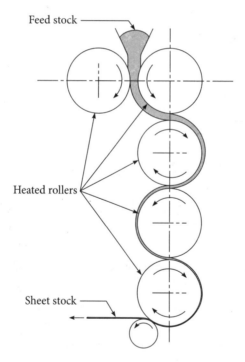

Figure 21.9 Schematic of sheet calendaring process

The best polymers for calendering are thermoplastics because they soften at a temperature much lower than their melting temperature, giving a wide range of working temperatures. They also adhere well to the rollers, allowing them to continue through the chain well; at the same time, they do not adhere too much so as to get stuck on the roller. Heat sensitive materials are also good candidates for calendering because rolls put immense pressures on the materials to work them and therefore, high temperatures are not required to process them limiting the chances of thermal degradation. This is why calendering is often done on PVC.

Calendering is the best process for producing quality sheets of plastic today, although extrusion is considered its competitor in sheet forming. There are also two disadvantages of this process. The process is quite expensive to perform, and there are difficulties when the sheet thickness is too small or too much. If the thickness is < 0.15 mm, then there is a tendency for pinholes and voids to appear in the sheets, while if the thickness is ≥ 1.5 mm, there is a risk of air entrapment in the sheet.

Applications   The products produced by calendering are finding many applications, such as rainwear, shower curtains, table covers, automotive and furniture upholstery, wall coverings, luminous ceilings, sign boards, displays, etc.

21.5.6 Thermoforming (Vacuum Forming)

The vacuum forming process is very similar to the *blow moulding process* in that both the processes involve the application of a differential pressure across the plastic raw material. A pre-heated sheet of thermoplastic polymer is placed in a one-piece die that has a sealing plate attached to it. The atmospheric air beneath the plastic sheet within the die is sucked out by means of a vacuum pump (Figure 21.10).

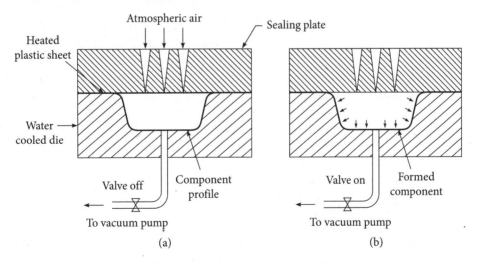

Figure 21.10   Schematic of thermoforming process cycle: (a) Pre-heated sheet of thermoplastic polymer is placed in die and sealing plate falls on the polymer sheet. The whole unit is sealed-off; (b) The atmospheric air beneath the plastic sheet is sucked out. The plastic sheet collapses onto the mould and conforms to its profile while from the sealing unit side, atmospheric air flows in to act on the other side of the sheet

As a consequence, the plastic sheet collapses onto the mould and conforms to its profile while from the sealing unit side, atmospheric air flows in to act on the other side of the sheet. When the plastic sheet has cooled down, the vacuum pump is switched off and the sealing plate is withdrawn. The finished moulding is then removed from the die. An entire cycle takes only a few minutes.

Applications   Typical products made by this process include panels for light fixtures, bath and shower cabinet mouldings, pre-formed product packaging materials and pages of Braille text for the blind.

21.5.7 Slush moulding

The process is similar to slush casting technology for metals described in Chapter 4 (Permanent Mould Casting). A liquid plastic is poured into the cavity of a heated split mould. As soon as a skin of desired thickness is formed at the inside surface of the mould cavity, the excess plastic liquid is poured off the mould. The mould is thereafter opened to remove the moulded part.

Applications   The process is widely used for encapsulation of electrical and electronic assemblies. Typical applications include plastic encasing of connectors, coils and transformers.

21.6 Plastic Shaping Processes (For Thermosets)

21.6.1 Compression moulding

Compression moulding is an old and widely used shaping process for thermosetting plastics. The process is similar to that used in non-ferrous die casting. A two-piece die is used; the die halves must be readily openable so that the component produced can be easily taken out by ejector pins without damaging the die or the component. It is important to provide mirror-finish to the die cavity so as to obtain a blemish-free surface finish on the components produced.

Process   As illustrated in Figure 21.11, the process is completed by the following sequence of steps.

(a) A precise quantity of pre-heated plastic raw material (in solid granules or pre-formed tablets of un-polymerized plastic), called the *charge*, is introduced into the cavity of a pre-heated open die.

(b) A pre-heated (120–220° C) upper die half is lowered onto the charge to close the cavity. As the plastic melts and becomes fluid, pressure is applied which forces the plastic melt to flow into all portions of the die cavity. Heat and pressure are maintained until the material has *set* (i.e., polymerized and cured) into a solidified part.

(c) The die is opened and the component is ejected from the cavity by knock-out pins. Flash, if formed, is removed by trimming.

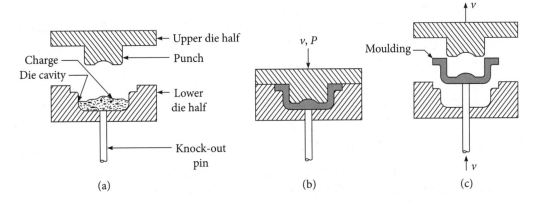

Figure 21.11 Steps in compression moulding process: (a) Charge is loaded into die cavity; (b) Pre-heated upper die half is lowered to melt the charge and force it into all portions of the die cavity; and (c) Upon solidification of plastic melt, die is opened and component is ejected

The component is still hot when it is ejected from the die, but it is able to retain its shape because of the unique characteristic of thermosets. For increasing the rate of production, the die may be designed with multiple cavities so that more than one part is produced in a single pressing. Cycle time depends upon the rate of heat transfer, complexity of the part and curing time of the polymer; it is often in the range of 1 to 20 minutes.

The process is currently being used to mould parts out of fibre-reinforced plastics, both thermoplastics and thermosets. In the thermoset family, polyesters, epoxies and phenolics are most commonly used as the base of fibre-containing sheet moulding polymer.

Advantages   Compression moulding process has the following advantages.

1. Dimensional precision and surface finish on the moulded parts are high. There is generally no need for secondary operations.
2. Residual stresses in the moulded parts are low.
3. Dies and machinery used in compression moulding are simple, require less maintenance and are generally less expensive than those used for competing processes.
4. Less scrap
5. Process is relatively economical for small production runs of parts requiring close tolerances and high impact strength.

Limitations   Compression moulding process has the following limitations.

1. Moulded parts may have thin flash, which can however be subsequently removed by trimming.
2. Not suitable for complex shaped parts and parts having thick sections (because thick parts require large curing times).
3. Cycle times are long and therefore it has lower production rates than injection moulding.

Applications   Typical parts made by compression moulding process are container caps, handles, gaskets, seals, dinnerware plates, electrical and electronic components (such as electric plugs, sockets), aircraft fairings, washing machine agitators, exterior automotive panels and refrigerator parts.

Because of low stresses in the moulded parts, the process is advantageously employed for the manufacture of relatively flat and thin parts.

21.6.2 Transfer moulding

Transfer moulding has been developed as an improved form of *compression moulding*. The process is similar to compression moulding because it uses the same type of polymer, that is, thermoset; it is also similar to injection moulding, as the charge in this process is pre-heated in a separate chamber and then inserted into the mould.

Process   The process is accomplished through the following steps and is shown in Figure 21.12(a).

i.   The raw thermosetting material is placed in a heated chamber (or transfer pot) where it is heated to molten state. The required quantity of it is then inserted into a heated closed die set through a transfer hole.

ii.   The plunger descends to force the molten plastic to flow through narrow channels (or runners) into adjoining mould cavities. Temperature and pressures are maintained until the plastic has cured completely.

iii. The die is then opened and the component is ejected and allowed to cool. The sprue, that is formed, is then removed.

The flow of polymer melt inside the die generates a certain amount of heat that raises the temperature of the melt and also homogenizes it. Because the polymer entering the die cavity is in molten state, parts with more intricate shape and better dimensional accuracy can be produced.

The process can also be used when metal or ceramic inserts are to be incorporated into the product [Figure 21.12(b)]. In this case, the inserts are placed into the die cavity prior to closing of the heated die set and their position maintained as the liquid plastic flows around them.

Advantages   Transfer moulding process has the following advantages.

1.   Parts with intricate shapes and varying wall thickness can be produced.

2.   Parts requiring high dimensional accuracy can be produced.

3.   Parts produced are consistent in size and shape.

4.   Inserts made from ceramic or metal can be introduced in the component.

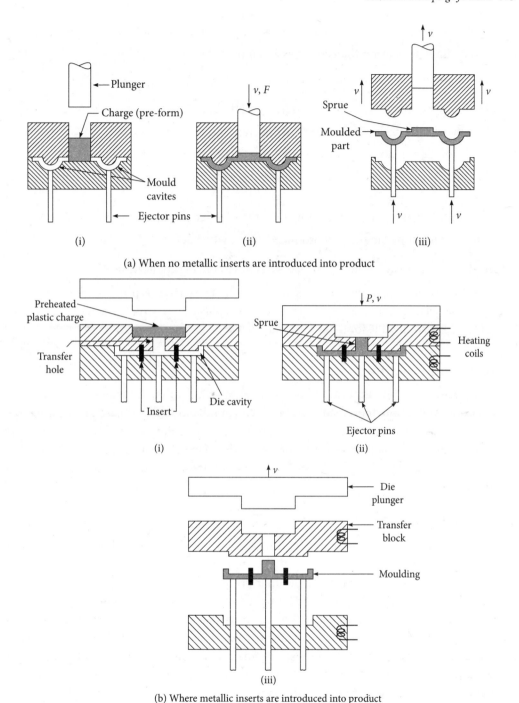

(a) When no metallic inserts are introduced into product

(b) Where metallic inserts are introduced into product

Figure 21.12 Schematic of transfer moulding process: (a) Pre-heated thermoset material is placed in transfer block; (b) Die plunger forces the hot polymer into die cavity through transfer hole; and (c) Die plunger retracts, transfer block raised, and solidified moulding is knocked out

5.   Part production rate can be increased by using die sets that contains multiple cavities.

6.   Cycle times are shorter than compression moulding.

Limitations   Transfer moulding process has the following limitations.

1.   Higher pressures are needed to uniformly fill the mould cavity.

2.   The process has a slower fill rate than injection moulding process.

3.   The moulds are more expensive than those of compression moulding.

4.   Some material which is left in the transfer hole during filling of the cavity goes waste as scrap.

5.   Greater die maintenance is required than that needed in compression moulding.

6.   Air can get trapped in the part produced, leading to a defect called 'void'.

Applications   Transfer moulding process has the following applications.

Since it is possible to mould with ceramic or metallic inserts, this process has been widely used to encapsulate items such as integrated circuits, plugs, connectors, pins, coils and studs. The process is also suitable for manufacturing television cabinets and car body shells.

21.6.3 Cold moulding

In this process, the raw thermosetting material is compressed to shape while at room temperature. After removing the formed product from the mould, it is cured by heating to a specific temperature in a separate oven. The process is economical and highly useful for short run manufacturing. It is sometimes used for testing the shape of the mould cavity. The quality of products produced by this process with respect to dimensional accuracy and surface finish is generally not good.

21.6.4 Lamination

Lamination is the technique of manufacturing a composite material by bonding more than one material in multiple layers so that the composite material achieves better strength, stability, sound insulation, appearance or other properties on account of the use of different materials. The bonding may be achieved by any combination of heat, pressure and adhesives.

Plastics have excellent attributes: Low density, attractive surface appearance, easy manufacturability, minimal post-processing, low wastage, and low cost. However, they are structurally very weak compared to most non-metals and metals. Plastic can be combined with non-metallic material(s) by the *lamination* process to produce new materials whose properties are far better than the original plastic.

The non-metallic material such as paper, woven cloth, fibreglass, etc. is taken in a roll. It is impregnated with thermosetting resin and partially dried in a hot chamber. Hot impregnated non-metallic material (generally known by the term *prepreg*) is then cut into pieces of specific length and built up in layers to the desired thickness. These layers are then compressed in another hot chamber to complete polymerization and to form a consistent texture throughout the laminate. Figure 21.13 shows a schematic of the complete process.

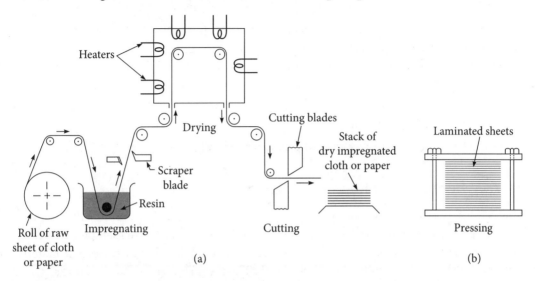

Figure 21.13 Schematic of lamination process: (a) Prepeg manufacture; and (b) Laminated sheet manufacture

Applications Laminated materials have found extensive applications in the manufacture of engineering components for aerospace and automotive industries. Vehicle windshields are commonly made by laminating a tough plastic layer between two layers of glass. This is to prevent shards of glass detaching from the windshield in case it breaks. Laminated materials also find many applications in the manufacture of office furniture and household appliances.

21.7 Welding of Plastics

Plastic components can be joined by many techniques such as by the use of adhesives and solvents, mechanical fasteners and by welding. While joints made with the use of adhesives and solvents, and mechanical fasteners have their advantages and limitations, this section will deal with thermal welding as a method of joining two plastic parts.

It is to be noted that only thermoplastic polymers can be welded since these materials do not change their properties when heated to soften or heated to melt. Thermosetting polymers, on the other hand, do not soften on heating but tend to char or burn. Since thermoplastics melt at relatively much lower temperatures, the heat requirement for welding of thermoplastics is much less than that for welding of metals.

Several steps are involved in thermal welding of thermoplastics. These are: joint surface preparation; heating; application of pressure; diffusion; and cooling. Out of these steps, surface preparation is the most important because moulded plastics are contaminated with mould release chemical compounds. Pressure may be applied manually or by mechanical means. Diffusion occurs when the interface between the parts becomes liquid before solidification takes place as the assembled part cools down.

Depending upon the source of heat used for welding, the processes used to weld plastics can be classified into two groups:

1. Processes that use frictional resistance to movement or mechanical vibrations to produce heat. Examples are friction welding and ultrasonic welding.

2. Processes that use external source of heat. Examples are hot gas welding, and resistive and inductive implant welding.

Some important processes of welding of plastics are described here.

21.7.1 Hot-plate welding of plastics

This is the simplest of the various mass production processes used for welding plastic parts. The two parts to be joined are held in fixtures. Their faying surfaces are then tightly pressed against the two opposite sides of a non-sticking heated tool till such time the plastic material at the surface has melted up to a very short depth. The pressure is removed so that a relatively thick melt layer is developed. After a pre-selected heating time, the parts are retracted from the tool and then brought together; the two molten surfaces are pressed against each other to weld and then allowed to cool. A flash may appear at the joint which may contain contaminated material present at the joining surface. If necessary, the flash is removed by trimming. A specially designed shaped tool can be used for non-flat joint profiles.

Advantages   This process of welding of plastics has the following advantages.

1. It is a simple and useful process for making butt joints. Lap seam welds on plastic sheets can also be made by applying pressure with the help of rollers after the joint area of the pair of sheets has passed over a heater.

2. It is a robust process useful for field applications.

3. Hermetic and consistent strong welds can be produced. The joint strength is often 80 to 100% of the parent material.

Limitations   This process of welding of plastics has the following limitations.

1. The process is slow–it may take ½ minute to 5 minutes per joint. Larger parts may take as much as 30 minutes.

2. Joint design is generally limited to square-butt configuration.

Applications   The process has many applications. In the automotive industry, it is widely used for fuel tank assemblies. Batteries are often assembled by the use of this process. The process has also found large-scale applications in PE pipe welding for drainage systems and gas line installations where pipes as big as 1 m diameter are welded.

21.7.2   Hot gas welding of plastics

The process is similar to oxyacetylene welding of metals to produce butt joints. Using a gas gun, a stream of hot compressed gas (air, oxygen, hydrogen or nitrogen) at about 200 to 350° C is made to strike at the joint area. The workpiece material at the joint and the tip of a thin plastic rod (filler material) get softened by the hot gas. The heated filler material is forced into the softened joint area to accomplish the joint.

Advantage   Process is simple and does not require any joint preparation.

Limitations   Process has the following limitations.

1.   The process is slow, and therefore not suitable for production applications.

2.   Joint quality is dependent on operator's skill.

Application   The process is very useful for repair of automobile parts and home appliances made of thermoplastic materials.

21.7.3   Friction welding of plastics

Friction welding of thermoplastics is a well established technique. The process uses the heat generated through mechanical friction between the workpiece surfaces in relative motion to one another. An axial force is applied to plastically displace and fuse the materials. The process has many variations such as linear, rotational, orbital, angular, and friction stir.

*   Linear friction welding (also known as vibration welding) involves rubbing one component in a linear reciprocating motion against the other stationary component under an axial force. The frequency of the vibration is generally between 100 and 250 c/s with a peak-to-peak vibration movement of 1 to 3 mm. The process is used to join a wide range of part geometries such as plate to plate, tube to plate, any shape to plate, square to square and round to square.

*   Rotational friction welding (also known as spin welding) involves rotation of one part in a continuous circular motion against the other part, under axial force. The rotation speed is generally between 1500 and 3000 rpm.

*   Orbital friction welding involves rubbing together of two plastic parts, under axial force, in an orbital motion at the interface. The frequency of motion is nearly 200 c/s with an off-axis deflection between 1 and 2 mm.

*   Angular friction welding is used for welding of circular components. The components are rubbed together in a reciprocating motion through a few degrees (typically 3 to 5°) during the welding process, giving an arc of vibration motion at the interface of components.

*   Friction stir welding, similar to the one used for metals (see Section 19.7.1, Chapter 19), involves a rotating non-consumable tool that is forced between the parts to be welded, which are held fixed. The rotary tool is given a linear motion, entering the joint from one end

and leaving the joint at the other end (Figure 21.14). In some cases, small vibrations may also be given to the tool with the vibratory motion either in line with the joint or perpendicular to it. The shoulder on the rotating probe also rubs over the workpiece top surface to provide additional heating and prevent expulsion of the softened material from the joint.

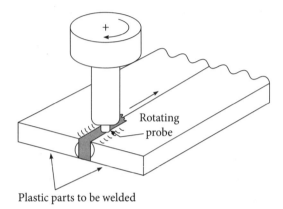

Plastic parts to be welded

Figure 21.14   Schematic of friction stir welding using rotary and linear motions to produce butt joints in plastics

Whichever friction welding process is used, the heat generated by the rubbing action must be sufficient to melt and flow the plastic at the weld interface. This is achieved by a combination of weld time, weld force and interface velocity, determined by either the reciprocating or rotational motion. The welding is carried out until either a pre-set weld time has elapsed or a pre-set material displacement has taken place.

When welding by displacement, the value of pre-set displacement is generally between 1 to 2 mm but depends on the flatness of the components being welded. Undulations in the welding interface are given due consideration when setting the weld displacement.

Application of force to the component during welding creates a pressure at the joint interface. Increasing the weld pressure beyond a certain value can reduce the strength of the weld by forcing out most of the molten plastic, resulting in a *cold weld* being formed. Typical applied weld pressure is in the range of 1–2 MPa.

A complete weld cycle consists of weld time plus cooling time. The length of time for which parts remain under pressure after the relative friction motion has ceased is termed as cooling time. Typical cooling time is in the range of 5–10 seconds.

Advantages   Friction welding of plastics has the following advantages.

1. High speed of operation (cycle time often about 10 s)
2. High reproducibility.
3. Little end preparation requirement.
4. Joint strength is good, varies between 50% and 80% of the parent material.

5. Almost all thermoplastics can be welded irrespective of whether their prior processing was injection moulding or extrusion moulding.

Limitations   Friction welding of plastics has the following limitations.

1. Joints between dissimilar thermplastics generally have quite low strengths.

2. Cost of equipment and tooling, particularly for large size components, may be very high.

3. Some materials may generate dust-like particulates during rubbing, which may give rise to problems.

Applications   The friction welding process has many applications. Some of these are in: (i) the manufacture of automotive components (for example, air intake manifolds and expansion tanks), (ii) the manufacture of household appliance components (for example, cistern ball float) and (iii) the joining of polyethylene pipes used for gas and water distribution.

In addition to the aforementioned techniques, there are several other techniques of welding of thermoplastics that make use of infrared, radio-frequency, microwave and laser heating.

21.8 Safety Precautions

The following are some general safety precautions which should be observed when shaping plastics by injection moulding/compression moulding process.

- *Proper ventilation*   Many plastics emit toxic fumes and can cause health problems if inhaled for longer periods. It is necessary to provide proper ventilation where shaping of such materials is carried out.

- *Avoid high temperatures*   Do not raise the resin temperature over 360° C. This is essential to prevent material thermal decomposition, gas emission and pressure build up in the process equipment.

- *Pre-heat equipment before start*   Before feeding pellets or rotating the screw, allow sufficient time for die or cylinder to heat and wait until the temperature reaches 300° C at least.

- *Use goggles*   Operators must wear protective goggles (especially when purging). Plastic dust remains hard when damp, unlike wood dust. Eliminate the risk of getting the plastic dust near the eyes by using goggles.

- *Use gloves*   Operators must wear protective hand gloves when handling a hot mould or when touching any part of plastic shaping machines.

- *Install fire extinguishers*   Do not leave the plastic shaping machine unattended as the plastic will melt and there could be a fire. Install fire-fighting equipment to meet any eventuality.

- When the moulding operation is to be interrupted for a short time, withdraw the injection unit to prevent the material in the nozzle section from solidifying by contact with the mould.

- When moulding operation is to be interrupted for a long time, the material in the barrel must be thoroughly purged out and the temperature be lowered to less than 280° C.

21.9 Considerations when Designing Plastic Components

It is important while designing plastic components, that the product designer is fully conversant with the useful features as well as limitations of plastic materials and the processes used for producing plastic products. Some useful tips while designing plastic parts to be produced by moulding or extrusion are as under.

Moulded parts The following considerations are important when designing parts that are to be produced by injection moulding, compression moulding or transfer moulding processes.

- *Production quantities* All moulding processes need a unique mould for a specific design of plastic part. Since the mould is generally costly, it is important from the economics point of view to consider the production quantities needed while designing a moulded part.

- *Wall thickness* The component wall must be thick and stiff enough for the job. From the manufacturing point of view, it must also be thin enough to cool faster, result in lower part weight and higher productivity. A general rule is that wall thickness should be uniform or constant throughout the part. This is because thicker sections cool slowly–cooling time is proportional to square of wall thickness. Also, a thick section shrinks more than a thin section, thereby introducing differential shrinkage resulting in warpage or sink mark. Where wall thickness variation is essential, the transition between the two should be gradual.

  If there is any thick solid section in the part, it may be made hollow by introducing a core [Figure 21.15]. This should ensure uniform wall thickness around the core. In order to increase the stiffness of a wall, ribs can be added to it. The ribs are generally made thinner than the walls they strengthen (rib thickness should be 0.5 to 0.6 times the nominal wall thickness).

- *Corner radii and fillets* Where two surfaces meet, a corner is formed, and the wall thickness increases to 1.4 times the nominal wall thickness. Sharp corners, both external and internal, should be avoided because these cause (i) differential shrinkage; (ii) moulded-in stress; (iii) longer cooling time; (iv) interruption to the smooth flow of melt; and (v) stress concentration in the finished part.

  It is recommended to have a corner radius of 0.5 to 0.6 times the wall thickness.

- *Holes* Although holes in plastic parts can be made during the process of moulding, these should normally be avoided because they tend to interrupt the polymer melt flow, complicate mould design and make part removal from the mould difficult.

Not desirable   Desirable

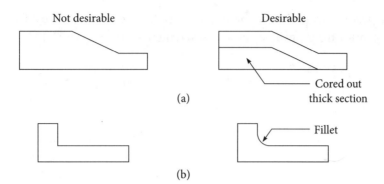

Figure 21.15   (a) Parts should have uniform wall thickness. Thicker sections can be cored out if required. (b) Sharp corners should be avoided as they act like a notch to support crack propagation

- *Draft*   Draft on both inside and outside the walls of a moulded plastic part is necessary because it facilitates removal from the mould. Although recommended value of draft varies from one plastic compound to another, generally it is ⅛° to ½° for thermoplastic polymers and ½° to 1° for thermosets.

- *Tolerances*   Shrinkage depends on process parameters and the complexity of part geometry. Moreover, the amount of shrinkage varies from one plastic compound to another. It is recommended that generous tolerances be provided on plastic moulded parts.

  Extruded parts   A large variety of plastic parts are made by the extrusion process. Although most design recommendations are similar to those for moulded parts, the following are some specific design considerations for extruded plastic parts.

- *Wall thickness*   The extruded part should have uniform wall thickness. If a part is designed with uneven wall thickness, the centre of gravity is skewed to one side or the other, causing problems with part straightness because the part will cool faster on one side than the other. Figure 21.16 illustrates how an extruded part with uneven section can cause bending.

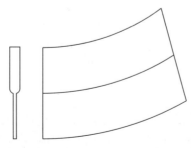

Figure 21.16   If an extruded part has uneven sections, a bow may be induced upon cooling. As the part cools, the thinner section will cool first, the thicker section later, drawing the already solidified section towards it

• *Deep grooves* Avoid grooves or an openings that are relatively deep. Due to inefficient cooling inside the groove, the groove will tend to close [Figure 21.17].

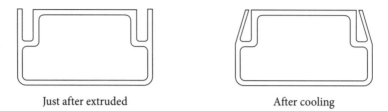

Just after extruded   After cooling

Figure 21.17 Extruded part geometry can change if different portions undergo uneven cooling

• *Hollow sections* Hollow cross-sections should be avoided, if possible. Hollow sections cause difficulties in melt flow and cooling, and complicate the die design. Problems of cooling and shaping of hollow part designs can however be handled by using vacuum sizing or vacuum calibration. In these cases, the part is run through a sizer or calibrator that is built to shape the outside walls of the part.

• *Corners* Sharp corners, whether inside and outside, should be avoided in the extruded cross-section. They cause difficulties in smooth melt flow and stress concentration in the final product. Minimum internal radii should be 1 mm. Outside radii should be equal to the internal radius plus a wall thickness.

• *Tolerances* Typical tolerances for extruded parts are ± 0.5 mm for dimensions up to 50 mm. Closer tolerances are possible where necessary, but they tend to increase the tooling cost, set up time or run speed–or all three. In most cases, ± 0.15 mm will be the tightest tolerance that can be effectively measured.

21.10 Stresses in Integrated Plastic Parts

When products are made by assembly of parts (whose materials have different coefficients of thermal expansion) in such a way that there is no relative movement between them, there is possibility for thermal stress to occur. Take the case of a non-reinforced thermoplastic part that is joined with another part of a metal that has lower coefficient of thermal expansion. We know that change in linear dimension (such as length or diameter) due to change in temperature of an object is given by the relation

$$\Delta L = a . L . \Delta T$$

where ΔL is the change in length of the part due to change in temperature ΔT, L is the original length of the part and a is the coefficient of thermal expansion. If the plastic part is restricted from expanding or contracting, strain ε will be introduced due to temperature change, given by

$$\varepsilon = \Delta L \div L = a . \Delta T$$

and the corresponding stress can be calculated by multiplying the strain ε by Young's modulus of the material.

Example

A piece of copper wire of length 8 metre is to be insulated at 20° C with a non-reinforced polymer having coefficient of thermal expansion $52 \times 10^{-6}/°$ C. Estimate the length of the insulator to ensure that at 45° C, an excess of 30 mm of insulator will be left on each end.

Solution

We know that for copper, coeff. of thermal expansion, $a = 17 \times 10^{-6}/°$ C

Due to rise in temperature from 20° C to 45° C, increase in length of copper wire, $\Delta L_c = a_c \cdot L_{c(20)} \cdot \Delta T = 17 \times 10^{-6} \times 800 \times (45 - 20) = 0.34$ cm

Thus, required length of the insulator at 45° C, $L_{p(45)} = \left[L_{c(20)} + \Delta L_c \right] + 6$ cm $= 806.34$ cm

or, the required length of the insulator at 20° C, $L_{p(20)} = 806.34 - \Delta L_p$

We can find ΔL_p as under

$$\Delta L_p = a_p \cdot L_{p(20)} \cdot \Delta T = 52 \times 10^{-6} \times L_{p(20)} \times (45 - 20) = 1.3 \times 10^{-3} L_{p(20)} \text{ cm}$$

Thus, $L_{p(20)} = 806.34 - 1.3 \times 10^{-3} L_{p(20)} = 804.95$ cm

21.11 Fibre-reinforced Plastic

Composites are combinations of materials differing in composition, where the individual constituents retain their separate identities but act together to give the necessary mechanical strength or stiffness to the composite part. For structural applications, composites are made by mixing the separate materials in such a way as to achieve controlled and uniform dispersion of the constituents. They have superior mechanical properties and in some cases, properties uniquely different from the properties of their constituents.

Fibre reinforced polymer matrix composites (called FRPs) use matrix of a polymer material; the reinforcement materials are fibres. The most commonly used polymers are: polyester, vinyl ester, epoxy, phenolic, polyimide, polyamide, polypropylene and polyether ether ketone (PEEK). The strength of a composite is greatly dependent on the ratio in which the polymer and fibres are mixed into it.

Advantages FRP composites have many advantages. They are light in weight and non-corrosive, have superior properties such as strength, stiffness, fracture resistance, abrasion resistance, impact resistance, corrosion resistance and fatigue resistance. Parts of FRP can be easily produced to satisfy specific performance requirements.

Limitations   FRP composites have the following limitations:

- Not suitable as sustainable materials, FRP composites have environmental issues, which act as a barrier to their use as sustainable materials, especially when considering fossil fuel depletion, air pollution, smog and acidification associated with their production.
- Limitation to recycling. Unlike steel and timber, structural components made from FRP composites cannot be re-used to perform a similar function in another structure.
- Low thermal resistance.
- High coefficient of thermal expansion.

Applications   FRPs are used for the manufacture of

1. Aerospace structures: The aircraft industry uses a large number of polymer composites. In commercial airlines and helicopters, their use is gradually increasing. Space shuttle and satellite systems use FRPs for many structural parts.
2. Marine: FRPs are finding applications for boat bodies, canoes and kayaks.
3. Automotive: Body panels, leaf springs, drive shaft, bumpers and doors.
4. Electrical: Panels, housing, switchgear, insulators and connectors.
5. Sports goods: Golf clubs, skis, fishing rods and tennis rackets.
6. Chemical processing equipment: Storage tanks, pressure vessels, piping, pump body and valves.
7. Biomedical applications: Medical implants, orthopedic devices and X-ray tables.
8. Civil infrastructure: Bridges made of polymer composite materials are gaining acceptance because of their low weight, high corrosion resistance, longer life cycle and low earthquake damage.

The usage of FRP composites continues to grow at an impressive rate due to the development of newer forms of FRP materials. Recent developments in high performance resin systems and new styles of reinforcement, such as carbon nanotubes and nanoparticles, have opened up new avenues for FRP usage.

21.12 Recent Trends in Plastic Technology

The search for new high performance plastics have always been one of the goals of the plastic technologists. Some newer trends currently observed in the market are:

- **Smart polymers**   These are polymers that can manipulate their dimensions according to changes in environmental parameters such as amount of heat, light, vibrations, moisture and so on. These materials are finding a large number of applications in the medical field.
- **Nanocomposites**   Attempts have been made to enhance the properties of plastics at the molecular level by combining nanotechnology with plastic engineering.

Nanocomposites generally include materials like nanotalcs, carbon nanotubes and nanoclays, which are characterized by high electrical conductivity, dimensional stability, and flame retardancy together with resistance to scratch, dent and heat. These nanocomposites are finding application in many sectors such as automotive, aerospace, electronics and military hardware.

- **Radio frequency embedded plastics**   In these resins, a plastic medium embeds a signal generator and can assume various shapes. Applications of such plastics include security system badges, hospital patient tracking, highway toll tags, cargo container seals and many more of that kind.

- **Biobased plastics**   Glass, carbon, Kevlar and boron fibers are being used as reinforcing materials in FRPs, which have been widely accepted as materials for structural and nonstructural applications. However, these materials are resistant to biodegradation and can pose environmental problems. Natural fibres from plants such as jute, bamboo, coir, sisal and pineapple are known to have very high strength and hence can be utilized for many load-bearing applications. These fibres have special advantage in comparison to synthetic fibres in that they are abundantly available from a renewable resource and are biodegradable. However, all natural fibres are hydrophilic in nature and have high moisture content, which leads to poor interface between fibre and hydrophobic matrix. Several treatment methods are being employed to improve the interface in the manufacture of natural fibre composite.

  Eco-friendly biobased plastics, which use polymer resins from plants, are finding several applications in the field of electronics, telecommunications, aerospace, automotive, biomedical and food packaging. Natural fiber composites can be used as a substitute for timber and for a number of other applications. It can be molded into sheets, boards, gratings, pallets, frames, structural sections and many other shapes. They can be used as a substitute for wood, metal or masonry for partitions, false ceiling, facades, barricades, fences, railings, flooring, roofing, wall tiles and so on. It can also be used for prefabricated housing, cubicles, kiosks, and sheds/shelters. Attempts have been made to develop plastics that will decompose with the help of bacteria.

- **Fully green composites**   A new class of fully biodegradable green composites by combining fibres with biodegradable resins is being developed. The major attractions about green composites are that they are ecofriendly, fully degradable and sustainable, that is, they are truly green in every way. Green composites may be used effectively in many applications such as mass-produced consumer products with short life cycles or products intended for one time or short time use before disposal.

Problems

1. A component is to be made of PVC plastic by the injection moulding process. The length of the mould cavity is 38 mm. What length of the moulded part would you expect? You may assume the shrinkage of PVC as 0.005.

2. A certain part is designed to be made out of polycarbonate using the injection moulding process. A particular dimension of this part is 100 mm. Calculate the corresponding dimension to which the mould cavity must be machined.

3. A particular dimension of a polyethylene part made by the injection moulding process is 100 mm. For some reasons, this part is now required to be produced out of polycarbonate. The production manager insists that the same mould be used for the new material. Estimate the expected corresponding dimension of the polycarbonate moulding.

4. A hollow copper bar bus at $20°$ C has a hole of diameter 100 mm. The designer has suggested inserting a phenolic plug of 99.80 mm diameter into it. Find the temperature at which the assembly should be maintained to guarantee a snug fit.

5. A playing ball of 300 mm outside diameter is to be produced out of polypropylene using the rotational moulding process. If the thickness of the ball is 3 mm, estimate the weight of the polymer powder to be loaded in the mould so that the required thickness of the product is ensured.

Review Questions

1. Differentiate between thermoplastic and thermosetting plastics. Give any three typical applications of each. Make a list of the processes used for shaping each of the two major types of plastics.

2. Discuss some attractive engineering properties of polymeric materials.

3. Elaborate some of the environmental conditions that might adversely affect the engineering properties of plastics.

4. List the plastic materials generally used in injection moulding. What properties make them suitable for the process?

5. Name some products for which plastics have taken over segments of markets traditionally held by metals or alloys.

6. Explain the process of extrusion. Is there any restriction on the properties of plastics for extrusion? Name any four plastic products that can be produced by extrusion.

7. Briefly describe the plastic extrusion process. What functions are performed by a screen pack or a breaker plate fitted at the end of the extruder barrel?

8. Explain the differences between the barrel section of an extruder and the barrel section of an injection moulding machine.

9. Explain with a sketch the process used for applying plastic coating on electrical wires.

10. Briefly explain the injection moulding process. Describe the two principal components of an injection moulding machine. Name any three defects that can occur in plastic injection moulding.

11. Explain with a suitable sketch the process of blow moulding. Name some products that can be produced by this process.

12. Explain with a suitable sketch the process of rotational moulding. Give its advantages.

13. Describe the process of compression moulding. Do you know why it is difficult to process thermoplastic materials by compression moulding? Explain briefly.

14. Give any two plastic products for which the manufacturer has used calendering process. What is the distinction between a plastic sheet and a plastic film?

15. Name the processes you will recommend for producing the following products: boat hulls, garbage containers, containers for packaging food, thin films, TV cabinets, plastic bottles.

16. Name the processes you will recommend for producing the following products: knobs for electrical appliances, chassis of vehicles, gasoline tanks.

17. Name plastic shaping processes that use plastic powder as raw material and the processes which use plastic pellets.

18. Using the Internet, get the necessary information and prepare reports on the following:
    - Difference between extrusion and pulltrusion.
    - Problems involved in recycling products made from reinforced plastics.
    - Availability of polymer additives for enhancing properties.

Fill in the blanks

1. Upon heating, a thermoplastic polymer softens to the consistency of a liquid. In this state, it is called a _____.

2. Bakelite is _____ plastic.

3. A process of plastic moulding that is similar to metal die casting is _____.

4. The form of starting material in thermoforming is _____.

5. _____ is a process in which a flat thermoplastic sheet is heated and deformed into the desired shape.

6. When the extrusion process is used for a plastic product, the cross-sectional shape of the product is determined by the shape of the _____.

7. Die swell in extrusion is a phenomenon due to a property of polymer melt known as _____.

8. In extrusion of plastics, the difference in the cross-section of die orifice and the desired product profile is because of _____.

9. A common defect in extruded plastic parts, in which the surface of the product becomes rough upon exiting the die, is known as _____.

10. _____ is a process in which a hot polymer is forced to flow under high pressure into a mould cavity where it solidifies.

11. A plastic shaping process which uses a reciprocating screw is _____.

12. Compression moulding and transfer moulding processes are mostly applicable to _____ polymers.

13. _____ is a plastic moulding process in which air pressure is used to inflate soft plastic into a mould cavity.

14. The plastic moulding process in which gravity is used inside the mould to achieve a hollow form is _____.

15. Disposable containers for packaging liquid consumer goods are mostly manufactured by a process called _____.

16. A negative mould has a _____ cavity, whereas a positive mould has a _____ shape.

17. A thin sheet of polymer is generally produced from _____ material.

18. Tubular plastic products are generally made by _____ process.

Multiple Choice Questions

1. Which one the following statements is not true?
   a. Plastics have lesser resistance to chemicals and corrosion.
   b. Plastics have high strength-to-weight ratio, particularly when reinforced.
   c. Plastics have low electrical and thermal conductivity.
   d. Plastics have low energy requirements for processing.

2. Upon cooling down from a molten state, if plastic regains its original hardness and strength, the plastic is
   a. thermoplastic.
   c. thermosetting plastic.
   b. non-thermoplastic.
   d. off-setting plastic.

3. Plastics which can be re-melted any number of times by successive applications of heat without risk of degradation belong to the following category
   a. thermoplastic.
   c. thermosetting plastic.
   b. non-thermoplastic.
   d. off-setting plastic.

4. Upon heating, a plastic part initially softened, and then melted. When still hot, it started hardening. What category of plastics is this?
   a. thermoplastic
   c. thermosetting plastic
   b. elasto-thermoplastic
   d. off-setting plastic

5. The permanent change that occurs to thermosetting plastics when they are heated is due to the phenomenon called
   a. hyper tension.
   c. polly effect.
   b. polymerization.
   d. halo effect.

6. A circular rod of a polymer is being extruded. If the area of cross-section of the die opening is 10 mm² and the area of cross-section of the extruded plastic rod is 11.5 mm², the swell ratio is
   a. 1.150.
   b. 0.869.
   c. 1.07.
   d. 0.932.

7. Viscosity is an important property of polymer melt in plastic shaping processes, and it depends on
    a. flow rate of polymer melt.
    b. temperature.
    c. flow rate as well as temperature of polymer melt.
    d. none of the above.

8. Which one of the following is the function of the ejection system?
    a. Move polymer melt into the mould cavity.
    b. Open the mould halves as soon as the cavity is filled.
    c. Take out the moulded part from the runner system after moulding.
    d. Separate the part from the cavity after moulding.

9. Use of parison is associated with which one of the following plastic shaping processes?
    a. blow moulding
    b. injection moulding
    c. compression moulding
    d. pressure thermoforming

10. Which one of the following is not an advantage of plastics over metals?
    a. ease of manufacturing and possibilities of large variety of product geometries
    b. resistance to chemicals and corrosion
    c. high strength-to-weight ratio
    d. high density

11. Which one of the following is not an advantage of plastics over metals?
    a. ease of manufacturing and possibilities of large variety of product geometries
    b. resistance to chemicals and corrosion
    c. high strength-to-weight ratio
    d. high energy requirements for processing

12. The fundamental difference between the two basic types of plastics lies
    a. in their chemical behaviour when heated and cooled thereafter.
    b. in their machining characteristics.
    c. in the types of fumes they produce when welded.
    d. in the minimum thickness to which they can be cast.

13. Which one of the following is a thermoplastic material?
    a. bakelite
    b. melamine
    c. polyester
    d. polypropylene

14. Viscosity is a fluid property which
    a. indicates the amount of pressure required to squeeze it.
    b. relates the shear stress experienced during flow of the fluid to the rate of shear.

    c.   is related to its density at room temperature.

    d.   is found by its mass per unit volume.

15. For a polymer melt,

    a.   viscosity decreases with increase in shear rate (fluid flow rate).

    b.   viscosity increases with increase in shear rate (fluid flow rate).

    c.   viscosity does not change when heated up to a certain temperature.

    d.   viscosity decreases with applied pressure.

16. A property of polymer melt that makes its viscosity decrease with increase in shear rate (fluid flow rate) is called

    a.   pseudoplasticity.   c.   elasticity.

    b.   plasticity.   d.   pseudoelasticity.

17. Viscoelasticity is a property of a polymer melt, which can be illustrated by which one of the following phenomena in the plastic extrusion process?

    a.   die swell   c.   die opening

    b.   die squeeze   d.   die closing

18. The property of thermoplastics due to which hot plastic expands as it comes out of the die opening is called

    a.   pseudoplasticity.   c.   elasticity.

    b.   plasticity.   d.   viscoelasticity.

19. When a thermoplastic material is extruded using a circular die opening, die swell can be estimated by the *swell ratio*, given by

    a. D_x / D_o c. $D_x - D_o$

    b. $D_x + D_o$ d. D_o / D_x

where D_x = diameter of extruded cross-section, and D_o = diameter of the die opening.

20. The *die swell*, a phenomenon which occurs in extrusion of thermoplastic material,

    a.   can be reduced by increasing the time in which it remains in the channel, say by making the channel longer.

    b.   can be reduced by decreasing the time in which it remains in the channel, say by making the channel shorter.

    c.   cannot be reduced by any means.

    d.   cannot be increased beyond a certain limit by several means.

21. Various non-metallic materials are impregnated with thermosetting resin in a process called

    a.   blow moulding.   c.   lamination.

    b.   injection moulding.   d.   calendering.

22. Tanks or buckets of different sizes are generally made by a process called

    a.   lamination.   c.   slush moulding.

    b.   rotational moulding.   d.   calendering.

23. Welding of plastic materials can be done
    a. between two thermosetting plastics only.
    b. between two thermoplastic polymers only.
    c. if one of them is thermoplastic and the other is thermosetting plastic.
    d. whether they are thermosetting plastics or thermoplastic polymers.

24. Transfer moulding process is employed for shaping
    a. thermosetting plastics only.
    b. thermoplastic polymers only.
    c. thermosetting plastics as well as thermoplastic polymers.
    d. neither thermosetting plastics nor thermoplastic polymers.

25. Transfer moulding process is
    a. used for shaping thermoplastic polymers only.
    b. a variation of compression moulding process.
    c. a variation of extrusion process.
    d. a variation of slush moulding process.

26. The fundamental difference between the two basic types of plastics lies in their
    a. strength and hardness when heated.
    b. weight loss when dipped in weak acidic solution.
    c. chemical behaviour when heated and thereafter cooled.
    d. bending strength.

27. Bottles and other hollow shaped containers are mostly made out of plastics by
    a. compression moulding process.   c. injection moulding.
    b. blow moulding process.   d. transfer moulding.

28. Rotational moulding process is an alternative to
    a. compression moulding process.   c. injection moulding.
    b. blow moulding process.   d. transfer moulding.

29. Rotational moulding process uses
    a. air pressure inside a rotating mould.   c. rotating pieces of plastics inside a hot mould.
    b. gravity inside a rotating mould.   d. rotating steel balls inside a hot mould.

30. Which of the following processes is mostly used for manufacturing plastic footballs?
    a. compression moulding   c. injection moulding
    b. rotational moulding   d. transfer moulding

31. Continuous length of thermoplastic sheet is generally manufactured by which one of the following processes?
    a. compression moulding   c. transfer moulding
    b. injection moulding   d. calendering

32. Pages of Braille text for blind persons are generally manufactured by which one of the following processes?

    a. compression moulding
    c. thermoforming
    b. injection moulding
    d. calendering

33. The process widely used for encapsulation of electrical and electronic assemblies is

    a. compression moulding
    c. calendering
    b. injection moulding
    d. sush moulding

34. Plastic parts such as container caps, gaskets, seals, handles, dinnerware plates, electric plugs and sockets and washing machine agitators are mostly made by which one of the following processes?

    a. compression moulding
    c. calendering
    b. injection moulding
    d. slush moulding

35. Identify the product that is made using two or more of the plastic shaping processes described in the book.

    a. bucket
    c. water bottles
    b. housings
    d. knobs

36. Calendering is a process for producing quality plastic sheets. But the process has the limitation that

    a. it is expensive and the range of thickness of sheet that can be produced is small.
    b. it is expensive and the range of length of sheet that can be produced is small.
    c. it is expensive and range of width of sheet that can be produced is small.
    d. the range of thickness and width of sheet that can be produced is small.

Answers

1. a.	2. a.	3. a.	4. c.	5. b.	6. c.	7.c.	8.d.	9. a.	10. d
11.d	12. a	13. d	14. b	15.a	16. a	17. a	18. d	19. a	20. a
21. c	22. b	23. b	24. a	25. b	26. c	27. b	28. b	29. b	30. b
31. d	32. c	33. d	34. a	35. c	36. a				

Bibliography

METAL CASTING

Amstead, B. H., Ostwald, Myron L. Begeman, and Philip F. Ostwald, 1987. *Manufacturing Processes*. New York: John Wiley & Sons.

Beeley, P. R. 2001. *Foundry Technology*. England: Butterworths-Heinmann.

DeGarmo, E. P., J. Temple Black, Ronald A. Kohser, and Barney E. Klamecki. 2006. *Materials and Processes in Manufacturing* New Delhi: Prentice Hall of India.

Finn, R. A. 1987. *Fundamentals of Metal Casting*. Illinois: American Foundrymen's Society Des Plaines, Ill.

Groover, M. P. 2010. *Fundamentals of Modern Manufacturing*. New Delhi: Wiley.

Kalpakjian, S., and S. R. Schmid. 2002. *Manufacturing Engineering and Technology*. Delhi: Pearson Education.

Stefanescu, D. M., J. R. Davis, and J. D. Destefani. 1988. *Metals Handbook, Vol. 15 – Casting*. Ohio: American Society for Metals.

Niebel, B. W., A. B. Draper, and R. A. Wysk, 1989. *Modern Manufacturing Process Engineering*. New York: McGraw Hill.

Rao, P. N. 1998. *Manufacturing Technology*. New Delhi: Tata McGraw Hill.

Taylor, H. F., M. C. Flemmings, and J. Wulff. 1987. *Foundry Engineering*. Des Plaines, Ill: American Foundrymen's Society.

METAL FORMING

Amstead, B. H., Ostwald, Myron L. Begeman, and Philip F. Ostwald, 1987. *Manufacturing Processes*. New York: John Wiley & Sons.

Bralla, J. G. 1998. *Design for Manufacturability Handbook*. New York: McGraw Hill.

DeGarmo, E. P., J. Temple Black, Ronald A. Kohser, and Barney E. Klamecki. 2006. *Materials and Processes in Manufacturing* New Delhi: Prentice Hall of India.

Dixon, R. H. T., and A. Clayton. 1971. *Powder Metallurgy for Engineers*. Brighton: The Machinery Publishing.

Groover, M. P. 2010. *Fundamentals of Modern Manufacturing*. New Delhi: Wiley.

Kalpakjian, S., and S. R. Schmid. 2002. *Manufacturing Engineering and Technology*. Delhi: Pearson Education.

Lange, Kurt. 1995. *Handbook of Metal Forming*. Michigan: Society of Manufacturing Engineers.

American Society for Metals. 1984. `Powder Metallurgy'. *Metals Handbook*, 9th ed., Vol. 7. Ohio: ASM.

Schey, J. A. 2000. *Introduction to Manufacturing Processes*. New York: McGraw Hill.

Wick, C., J. T. Benedict, and R. F. Veilleux. 1984. *Tool and Manufacturing Engineers Handbook*, Vol. 2, Forming. Soc. Michigan: Manuf. Eng.

METAL JOINING

Bralla, J. G. 1998. *Design for Manufacturability Handbook*. New York: McGraw Hill.

Boothroyd, G., P. Dewhurst, and Winston Knight. 1994. *Product Design for Manufacture and Assembly*. NY: Marcel Dekker.

Cary, H. R., and S. C. Helzer. 2005. *Modern Welding Technology*. Columbus: Pearson.

DeGarmo, E. P., J. Temple Black, Ronald A. Kohser, and Barney E. Klamecki. 2006. *Materials and Processes in Manufacturing* New Delhi: Prentice Hall of India.

Groover, M. P. 2010. *Fundamentals of Modern Manufacturing*. New Delhi: Wiley.

Kalpakjian, S., and S. R. Schmid. 2002. *Manufacturing Engineering and Technology*. Delhi: Pearson Education.

Laughner, Vallory H., and Augustus D. Hargan. 1956. *Handbook of Fastening and Joining of Metal Parts*. New York: McGraw-Hill.

American Society for Metals. 1983. `Welding, Brazing, and Soldering'. *Metals Handbook*, 9th ed., Vol. 6. Ohio: ASM.

Speck, J. A. 1997. *Mechanical Fastening, Joining, and Assembly*. NY: Marcel Dekker.

Whitney, D. E. 2004. *Mechanical Assemblies: their design, manufacture, and role in product development*. New York: Oxford University Press.

Index

impression-die drop forging, 194, 196
    schematic of, 195–197
inclusions, 131, 134, 140, 180, 182, 428, 433,
    445, 447, 454
incomplete fusion in weld, 376, 428, 454
incremental forging, 195, 203
indirect extrusion, 10, 218, 222–224
induction brazing, 333
industrial stitching, 326
inertia friction welding, 432
infrared brazing, 334
in-gate, 60
    types of, 60
ingot, 93, 101, 102, 161, 172, 180, 183
Injection moulding, 300–301, 470–471, 481–482,
    484, 489
    applications of parts produced by, 470
    defects in parts produced by, 472–473
    equipment, 470–471
inorganic fluxes, 337
inorganic adhesives, 318
integral fasteners, 323, 327–328
Integrated plastic parts, 492
    stresses in, 492
interference fits, 326
    press fit, 326–327
    shrink and expansion, 327
internal cracks, 212
inverted die, 271–272
investment casting, 21, 23, 32, 36, 40, 68
    advantages of, 70
    applications of, 70
    disadvantages of, 70
    process involved in, 68
iron-powder coatings, 202
isothermal forging, 202

joining processes, 5, 8, 316–317, 329, 338–339
    adhesive bonding, 8, 317–322, 327
    brazing, 330–336
    mechanical fastening, 317, 320–323, 328–329
    soldering, 8, 317, 329–330, 335–338
    welding, 329–330, 334, 338–339, 344
joint strength, 318, 320–321, 329, 335, 488
joints, *See* also welding

lamellar tear, 457
Lamination of plastics, 484
    applications of parts produced by, 485
lap joint, 325, 331, 344, 409, 436
laps, 129, 180, 212
laser beam welding (LBW), 424, 426
LBW. *See* laser beam welding (LBW)
leftward welding, 361
linear friction welding, 432, 487
liquid penetrant inspection, 449
longitudinal crack, 455–456
loose piece pattern, 37, 41, 57
low pressure die casting, 24, 85
    process involved in, 85
low-current plasma arc welding, 393
lubricants, 179, 183, 186, 200, 202, 211, 296, 302
    for forging, 200, 202, 211
    for rolling, 179, 183, 186

machine moulding, 35–36, 43
machining allowance, 39–41
machining metal powder production technique,
    306
magnetic particle inspection, 131, 134, 449
magnetic pulse forming, 286
manual feeding of parts in presses, 274
manual presses, 267
manufacturing, 1–2, 4, 8, 152, 161, 178, 228, 460
    materials used in, 2, 4, 8
manufacturing process, 2, 4–5, 8, 10, 228, 310
    basic model of, 2
    classification of, 4–8
    selection of, 8
mass continuity equation, 149
match plate pattern, 37, 44
material removal processes, 5, 40
mechanical fasteners, 320, 328–329, 485
    non-threaded, 322–324, 328
    threaded, 322–324, 328
mechanical fastening, 5, 317, 320–323, 328–329
    advantages of, 328
    applications of, 329
    limitations of, 321
    methods of, 323–326
mechanical joining. *See* mechanical fastening